INTERNATIONAL HANDBOOK ON MIGRATION AND ECONOMIC DEVELOPMENT

International Handbook on Migration and Economic Development

Edited by

Robert E.B. Lucas

Professor of Economics, Boston University, MA, USA

Edward Elgar

Cheltenham, UK • Northampton, MA, USA

Published by
Edward Elgar Publishing Limited
The Lypiatts
15 Lansdown Road
Cheltenham
Glos GL50 2JA
UK

Edward Elgar Publishing, Inc.
William Pratt House
9 Dewey Court
Northampton
Massachusetts 01060
USA

A catalogue record for this book
is available from the British Library

Library of Congress Control Number: 2014947030

This book is available electronically in the ElgarOnline.com Economics Subject Collection, E-ISBN 978 1 78254 807 2

FSC www.fsc.org MIX Paper from responsible sources FSC® C013056

ISBN 978 1 78254 806 5

Typeset by Servis Filmsetting Ltd, Stockport, Cheshire
Printed and bound in Great Britain by T.J. International Ltd, Padstow

Contents

Contributors

Calogero Carletto, Senior Economist and Manager of the Living Standards Measurement Study, Development Research Group, World Bank, Washington, DC, USA.

Michael A. Clemens, Senior Fellow and leader of the Migration and Development Initiative, Center for Global Development, Washington, DC, USA.

Jonathan Crush, Chair in Global Migration and Development, Balsillie School of International Affairs, Waterloo, Ontario, Canada; Honorary Professor, University of Cape Town; Director, Southern African Migration Program.

Pınar Derin-Güre, Assistant Professor, Department of Economics, Middle East Technical University, Ankara, Turkey.

John Gibson, Professor, Department of Economics, Waikato Management School, University of Waikato, Hamilton, New Zealand.

Flore Gubert, Research Fellow, Institut de Recherche pour le Développement, DIAL, Paris, France; Affiliate Member, Paris School of Economics.

Ana María Ibáñez, Decana Facultad de Economía, Universidad de los Andes, Bogota, Colombia.

Olena Ivus, Assistant Professor, Queen's School of Business, Queen's University, Kingston, Ontario, Canada.

Florence Kondylis, Senior Economist, Development Impact Evaluation Initiative, Development Research Group, World Bank, Washington, DC, USA.

Jennica Larrison, Assistant Professor, School of Public and International Affairs, University of Baltimore, Baltimore, MD, USA.

Robert E.B. Lucas, Professor, Department of Economics, Boston University, Boston, MA, USA.

Robert A. Margo, Professor, Department of Economics, Boston University, Boston, MA, USA.

David McKenzie, Lead Economist, Finance and Private Sector Development Unit, Development Research Group, World Bank, Washington, DC, USA.

Prachi Mishra, Senior Economist, Monetary and Capital Markets Department, International Monetary Fund, Washington, DC, USA.

Valerie Mueller, Research Fellow, Development Strategy and Governance Division, International Food Policy Research Institute, Washington, DC, USA.

Alireza Naghavi, Assistant Professor, Department of Economics, University of Bologna, Bologna, Italy.

Çaglar Özden, Senior Economist, Trade and Integration Team, Development Research Group, World Bank, Washington, DC, USA.

Christopher R. Parsons, Research Officer, International Migration Institute, University of Oxford, Oxford, UK.

Jackline Wahba, Professor of Economics, University of Southampton, Southampton, UK; member of the Migration Advisory Committee.

L. Alan Winters, CB, Professor of Economics, Department of Economics and Migrating Out of Poverty Research Consortium, University of Sussex, Brighton, UK; formerly Chief Economist, Department for International Development in the UK Government, and Director of the Development Research Group of the World Bank.

1. Migration and economic development: an introduction and synopsis

Robert E.B. Lucas

Much of the early interest in the economics of migration in developing countries focused on internal movements, especially the transfers of population from rural to urban settings. More recently attention has shifted toward international migration instead. This increased focus on international migration among analysts has been mirrored at the political level, heightened by changing realities: by the rise in immigration into the 'more-developed' regions, where the migrant stock now exceeds 10 percent of the population, including in large parts of Europe that traditionally saw net emigration; by the dramatic rise in recorded remittances in the last decade, reaching over $500 billion globally, of which more than $400 billion are going to the developing countries; by the expanding 'brain drain' from lower- to higher-income countries; and by security concerns surrounding international terrorism since 2001.

Migration and economic development are mutually linked. Development may impact migration and vice versa, though the signs of causal links in both directions remain a matter of some dispute, as we shall see in the course of this volume. The various chapters chart the state of thinking on a number of key facets of the reciprocal links between migration and development, but also, in several instances, extend our frontiers of understanding with fresh evidence.

Empirical research into the migration–development nexus has been, and continues to be, both shaped and hampered by the availability of migration data. Aggregate data on immigration into most of the OECD countries have been reported for some time now, though with little detail on the composition of the migrant stocks; data on South–South migration are far more scant, as is information on some of the large population movements into high-income, non-OECD countries, including those of the Persian Gulf. Chapter 2 examines where data collection on population movements stands. Gero Carletto and co-authors describe the limitations and strengths of the main sources of data currently available, at both the micro and aggregate levels; the conceptual and definitional issues that arise in assembling migration data; and how the extant data may generally be used to address some of the key areas of policy concern. This account provides an important backdrop to the remaining chapters in the volume, each of which draws on portions of the data described.

Migration is sometimes depicted as a temporary phenomenon, a feature of adjustment to disequilibrium that will pass. It is not. The great migrations of mankind stretch over our entire history: the initial migration of *Homo sapiens* out of Africa perhaps 70 000 years ago certainly transformed our world; the exodus of Jews out of Egypt and the Barbarian invasions of the Roman Empire; the Arabic and Atlantic trade in slaves; the mass migrations from Europe to North America; the consequences of partitioning India; and more recently the huge internal movements within China, to name but a few. In his chapter, Bob Margo takes a look at the nature and consequences of these mass flows through the lens of the USA before World War I, a lens that offers a broad and intriguing perspective. The evidence that Bob amasses indicates, *inter alia*: the role that the Age of Mass Migration played in economic convergence between North America and Europe; that the USA was never a melting pot, even during the nineteenth century; and how the history of slavery laid the foundations for another great migration, of African Americans departing the South for the industrial North of the USA.

Whereas North America and Australasia have been important magnets attracting large numbers of migrants over the last couple of centuries, Europe has never seen itself as a key migrant destination. Indeed, Europe provided many of the emigrants to the new lands. But this pattern has shifted; some European states now have a larger fraction of foreign-born residents than does the USA. Africa's population is projected to rise rapidly while that of parts of Europe may contract. Combined with the proximity of the two continents and the growing gap between their income levels, increased migration to Europe might well be anticipated. Deaths of migrants attempting boat journeys to reach Europe from Africa are already common. In some of the European states that have transitioned to become destinations of net immigration, an interest has been spawned in co-development, promoting economic progress of the poorer parts of the world, or using development aid as a bargaining tool, in the belief that emigration pressures will thus be diminished. The next three chapters in this volume address related portions of this strategy.

Christopher Parsons and Alan Winters focus on the links between trade, aid and migration. The trade portion of their contribution considers three main aspects: the implications and limitations of the Heckscher–Ohlin–Samuelson theorem, leading to factor price equalization with trade and migration as perfect substitutes; the theoretical literature on migration as a source of information and contract enforcement, leading to trade expansion; and the empirical literature, largely in the context of gravity models, of migration as a determinant of bilateral trade flows. Chris and Alan also summarize the much smaller literature on the link from aid to migration. Throughout, an underlying theme in their analysis is whether observed links can be identified as causal and where the gaps lie in the extant analyses. In concluding, Chris and Alan place the trade–aid–migration nexus within the context of co-development policies of which they are quite critical.

In her chapter, Flore Gubert shows us why, offering a critical perspective on the realities of European attempts to influence migration through development of the countries of origin. Flore details both the history of co-development efforts and the more recent forms that these have taken among the major European Union partners. What emerges is a substantial gap between the narrative and the realities of these policies. Flore then continues to examine various initiatives to involve diaspora in the development of their home states, including attempts to stimulate remittances through formal channels, to redirect remittances toward productive investments, and to facilitate skill and knowledge transfers. Harnessing remittances for development has also become a focus for many of the high emigration states, though Flore exposes both the weaknesses and inappropriate intent of much of this effort. This chapter appears to be the first comprehensive review of these varied efforts. Flore is clearly skeptical of many of the realities of these policies but, nonetheless, concludes by distilling some of the necessary conditions for their success.

The presumption underlying the co-development strategies is that improving economic conditions in the lower-income countries will dissipate pressures to emigrate. In his chapter, Michael Clemens summarizes 45 years of discussion and evidence to the contrary. The counter-argument is that emigration initially rises with increments to income at home, eventually turning downward to generate what is sometimes called a migration hump or transition. Michael itemizes and evaluates six arguments that have been hypothesized to underlie such a pattern of migration. The prior evidence on whether a turning point exists is mixed, in the context of both aggregate and micro data. The results vary with the data sources analyzed, tending to reveal a parabolic form more often in the cross-section than over time, and Michael considers why this may be the case. Adopting the latest, aggregate, panel data set, Michael finds a clear and significant 'hump' in both the stocks and flows of international migrants, lending substantial support to some of the reservations expressed about co-development strategies both by Chris Parsons and Alan Winters and by Flore Gubert in their respective chapters.

Circular migration of less-skilled workers is often touted as one of the most effective migration patterns for relieving poverty in the countries of origin. Remittances from less-skilled workers tend to go to poorer households; the intent or requirement to return home may enhance these transfer levels; and the departure of less-skilled workers may improve the labor-market lot of those remaining at home. Among host states, permanent entry of less-skilled workers is rarely welcomed, though seasonal workers and other temporary labor schemes are quite common. Circular migration may thus be in the interest of both home and host states, though perhaps not in the interest of the migrants themselves. This last caveat often renders the temporary nature of migrant-worker programs difficult to enforce, and Milton Friedman's more general statement is often paraphrased as 'Nothing is so permanent as a temporary migration program.'

The next group of three chapters in this volume addresses different aspects of temporary worker programs and the migration of less-skilled labor. John Gibson and David McKenzie note that almost all OECD countries have some form of seasonal worker programs, but that several of these are being cut back or eliminated. Against this backdrop, John and David take a careful look at New Zealand's Recognised Seasonal Employer program launched in 2007. They conclude that the program has been a triple winner: the migrant workers certainly gain from the experience; there is no evidence that New Zealand workers are displaced and employers gain access to foreign workers who prove more productive than locals, a productivity gap that increases with return visits; third, evidence is amassed showing at least small spillover benefits to locals in the origin countries. In the context of ongoing and politically charged debates over temporary worker programs the evidence in this chapter offers important insights.

Jonathan Crush paints a fascinating picture of the shifting balances in South Africa's migration and labor markets as the country has transitioned from the apartheid era to rule by universal franchise. Before 1994, immigration into South Africa was tightly controlled and bimodal. Europeans were welcomed as settlers; limited numbers of Africans were permitted temporary entry as cheap labor for the mines and other sectors. Jonathan documents the complexities of the transition from this legacy to the new era. After more than a century of reliance on foreign labor in South Africa's mines, much of this movement has ended. Although the conditions under which miners served during the apartheid period were justifiably criticized, the loss of this avenue for work has proved problematic in some of the surrounding states. Meanwhile irregular immigration of low-skilled workers and of those seeking asylum (from Africa and beyond) has exploded and xenophobia has risen markedly in South Africa, where unemployment levels are deplorable. Jonathan's account also brings out the transition from encouraging European immigration to emigration of many of the highly skilled, and he is critical of the government's attempts to address this through manpower planning in immigration policy.

The effect of immigration on wages in the destination countries has been the subject of copious research. The effect of emigration on wages in the countries of origin has not. Yet, as Prachi Mishra points out in her chapter on the subject, emigrants form a much larger fraction of the population in many countries of origin than is typical of per capita immigration rates. Prachi goes on to review the various approaches that have been adopted in an effort to examine this emigrant impact on home wages, as well as the methodological and data issues inherent in such an effort. The hunt for a negative effect of immigration on wages of prior residents has certainly been protracted and not always rewarded. In contrast, Prachi's review of the more limited evidence on emigrants' effects on wages of those left at home is surprisingly uniform: emigration results in significant and substantial wage escalation at home. Prachi puts this in context for us by considering some of the distributional consequences of these effects as well as some of the net welfare impacts. This rather neglected topic appears important and one might hope that Prachi's chapter will spur and aid further investigation.

Meanwhile, the competition to attract the highly skilled intensifies, with new competitors entering the fray and opportunities to study abroad expanding. The term 'brain-drain' may have been coined by the Royal Society in post-World War II Britain. Certainly, the extent of 'brain-drain' from the developing regions is growing and remains a common cause of concern in the home countries. Yet, more recently, economists have turned their attention to several mechanisms through which emigration of the highly skilled may actually promote development at home, resulting in offsetting 'brain gain'. In addition to remittances transferred by the highly skilled diaspora, at least four mechanisms of potential brain gain have been discussed: induced education among those remaining at home; the transfer of technology to the home country; promotion of bilateral trade as a result of bilateral migration; and through the influences of returned emigrants.

Olena Ivus and Alireza Naghavi address that part of the brain-gain argument dealing with the role of migrants in transferring technology. Specifically, Olena and Alireza survey three sets of literature: the theoretical and empirical modeling, over the last decade and a half, on the international diffusion of technology and its contribution to growth; the investigations, usually as case studies, into technology transfers enabled by migrants; and third, studies of the influence of the diaspora on institutions at home, including the evolution of democracy, and the incidence of rent-seeking and expropriation. The first of these sets has been more concerned with investigating the magnitudes of technology transfers and their effects, typically through analysis of patent registrations, rather than investigating the mechanisms of transfer. Such means of transfer may include technology conveyed as a result of direct investments, either within the firm or through learning by others; it may simply involve reverse engineering; but it clearly may also involve the movements of scientists and engineers. In light of this, Olena and Alireza explore the potential for linking the literatures on the extent of technology transfers and on diaspora transfers – literatures that have not really been integrated. Drawing on prior work by Alireza (with Chiara Strozzi), this chapter demonstrates that emigration and innovation at home are positively correlated when the institutional structure at home offers significant protection to intellectual property rights. In other words, emigration, technology transfer and institutional development all interact in important ways: emigration promotes knowledge transfer while enabling the institutional development necessary to make such transfers effective.

In my own chapter, I present fresh evidence on the empirical links between bilateral migration and trade, with particular emphasis on the case of lower-income countries, which have been omitted from most of the prior analyses. Comparisons are drawn with findings from the extensive literature on this link, which is surveyed by Chris Parsons and Alan Winters in their chapter. In fact, there is little agreement among prior studies, except for a positive association between migration and trade. The fresh findings include positive emigrant and immigrant links with trade in all four pairings of lower-income and higher-income countries, including South–South trade. In contrast to prior findings, it is estimated that the elasticity of this association increases with the level of migration over substantial ranges. The elasticity is also shown to be highest for the highly educated (at least among OECD immigrants), higher for females than males and positive for refugees who have fled from one lower-income country to another. The links prove weaker where the trade partners have a common language or colonial heritage, suggesting a role for migrants in overcoming lack of familiarity and associated incomplete information. Reduction in such barriers promotes openness to trade with a gain in efficiency, but the two-way effects offset, such that the balance of trade for lower-income countries may actually deteriorate. Network effects of third-country nationals are also explored and extended to include mutual emigration to third countries, which is estimated to result in trade diversion.

Jackline Wahba's chapter addresses the economics of return migration, its causes and consequences. This is a topic on which the data are especially scant, yet Jackie manages to show that the extent of return migration is far from negligible, while outlining the methodological difficulties in defining and measuring return rates. Advances have been made on both theoretical and empirical fronts with respect to the determinants of return migration, and are reviewed in this chapter. In examining the influences of returned migrants on economic development in their home countries, Jackie first lays out the complexities and need to correct for double selection: selection in who migrates and selection in who returns. Nonetheless a burgeoning empirical literature exists, and Jackie summarizes the findings, looking at the contribution of return migration in reducing credit constraints, allowing for brain circulation and gains, and transmitting of norms to sending economies.

Whereas the brain drain is almost entirely to the high-income countries, especially to the USA, only a very select set of refugees manages to be resettled in these high-income countries. The vast majority of the 10.4 million refugees of concern to UNHCR at the beginning of 2013 not only originated from developing countries but received asylum in neighboring developing countries. While the numbers of armed conflicts in the world and of recognized refugees escaping these conflicts have both declined in recent years, the number of internally displaced persons has risen, again especially within the developing countries, as crossing borders has become increasingly difficult. Traditionally, economists have shied away from consideration of these elements of forced migration, perhaps in large part because the term 'forced' suggests compulsion with no room for choice. More recently, as Ana María Ibáñez shows in her chapter, this perception has begun to change. Specifically, Ana María discusses three main elements of choice with respect to displacement in the face of conflict and violence, summarizing the evidence with respect to each. First is the deliberate choice of armed groups to target civilian groups with the intent to cause displacement. Second are household decisions to move in an attempt to escape conflict or violence, decisions in which more traditional determinants of migration are shown to play a role alongside the violence itself, drawing upon both cross-country and micro-level evidence. Third are the decisions among the displaced to return to their homes. This is a nascent field for economists, though less so for other social sciences, and Ana María lays out some thoughts on future directions for research, including integrating economics with other disciplines.

Given the selectivity with respect to who becomes displaced and to where, Florence Kondylis and Valerie Mueller address the problem of identifying the longer-run consequences of displacement and return, in the context of both conflict and of natural disasters. Florence and Valerie note the dearth of evidence on this subject in the context of developing countries, where most of the incidents actually occur. After reviewing such evidence as does exist and laying out a conceptual framework to tackle the several methodological issues arising in the identification of displacement as a causal effect, Florence and Valerie go on to present fresh evidence on those displaced by the 1992–95 conflict in Bosnia-Herzegovina and by the 2011 floods in Pakistan. Their evidence with respect to education, labor-market outcomes and asset holdings points to effects on the displaced that may stretch not just for long periods but even over generations. Given these important impacts, Florence and Valerie close their chapter with a consideration of potential policy strategies to ameliorate these shocks.

The rise in international terrorism has brought security concerns to the forefront of border control and migrant screening for many countries. In the final chapter in this volume, Pınar Derin-Güre summarizes three main aspects of the literature on development–migration–terrorism links: the economic roots of terrorist acts; the macroeconomic effects of terrorist incidents on the target countries; and analyses exploring the direct connections between immigration and terrorism. The last set of these finds that, although the majority of international terrorist attacks are carried out by immigrants, countries that are more open to immigration have not been subjected to more incidents. Where incidents occur, the macroeconomic effects in terms of a number of indicators have been shown to be negative, at least in the short run, though more work may be called for in looking at the longer-term consequences. The focus of Pinar's contribution is, however, on the economic roots of terrorism. Despite a common perception that poverty exacerbates terrorist tendencies, the bulk of the prior evidence finds little or no such association. However, using a very rich, bilateral, panel data set on the countries of terrorists' origin and target countries, Pinar is able to demonstrate that rising incomes within the average country are associated with diminished terrorism stemming from there.

Taken together, the contributions in this volume summarize and extend the state of thinking and evidence on some of the less well-trodden paths linking international migration and development: the coherence of trade–aid–migration strategies of the wealthier nations, the direction of effect of development on migration, the implications of temporary migration schemes and movements of less-skilled workers, elements of potential brain gain distilled from the diaspora and returned migrants, and the economic roots and consequences of forced migration and of international terrorism. Much remains to be done both in this range of topics and others besides. As the data on international migration become steadily richer, such extensions will be rendered increasingly feasible. It is to be hoped that the reviews and thoughts on future work offered here may help in shaping those future directions.

2. Informing migration policies: a data primer

Calogero Carletto, Jennica Larrison and Çaglar Özden

I. INTRODUCTION

While establishing his theory of human migration, which forms the basis of much of modern research on migration, Ernst Georg Ravenstein (1885, 1889) relied on various data sources from over 20 countries in Europe and North America to back up his assertions with facts. One of his main conclusions was the importance of high-quality primary data, mainly from national sources, for demographic and geographic research. Since then, researchers in numerous fields such as demography, economics, sociology and political science have established various data collection methodologies and principles via censuses, administrative registers, nationally representative or special-purpose surveys to answer a wide range of academic and policy questions. On one hand, the progress has been quite impressive in terms of the variety and quality of data sources available. On the other hand, some of the basic challenges from the nineteenth century still haunt us with all their vigor.

This chapter has two purposes. First, it answers some fundamental questions on who international migrants are and how their numbers as well as various demographic, personal and human capital characteristics are captured via different data sources. The critical issues are the construction of proper sampling frames in censuses, registers, surveys and the design of questionnaires in the relevant surveys. These are among the challenges with which collectors and users of migration data continue to struggle from the days of Ravenstein to date. Second, the chapter discusses how these data sources on migration can be used to answer different policy questions in various areas, such as labor markets, education policies or economic welfare. The focus of the discussion will be on how some of the existing shortcomings in terms of availability, quality and policy relevance of migration data can be overcome via improvements in data collection methods.

II. DATA SOURCES AND CHALLENGES[1]

Sources of Data

The majority of migration data come from destination countries, as it is often easier to capture people where they currently are rather than where they left. Destination countries use a wide range of tools to count and analyze characteristics of migrants within their boundaries. Among these data sources are (i) censuses that are aimed at capturing all people within borders at a given point, (ii) various surveys, such as labor market or specialized and multi-topic surveys, that sample a smaller portion of the population but ask more detailed questions, (iii) population registers, common in certain countries, and (iv) various administrative data sources such as border statistics, employment and residency permits, as well as naturalization records. Such data sources are used in quantifying migration patterns, especially between country pairs, as well as in identifying demographic, economic, social and cultural characteristics of migrants within a country. In addition, the impact of migration on destination countries' labor markets or various other social and economic outcomes can be assessed using these data in conjunction with other relevant data sources.

'Easier' data collection in destination countries in no way means 'easy', as collecting information from migrants presents many challenges and shortcomings that prevent researchers from answering many important policy questions. Most of these are concerned with the impact of emigration on the families and communities that migrants have left behind in their home countries. These effects range from the poverty alleviation impact of remittances to the decline in health and education services when doctors and teachers emigrate. While censuses and administrative records in origin countries may provide clues on these issues, most relevant data come from surveys with special migration questions or modules. The main challenge is that questions about migrants need to be answered by a proxy, generally a family member, which introduces many imperfections, as we discuss below.

Censuses

Censuses survey an entire population at a single point in time and are generally conducted decennially, even though there are plenty of exceptions. Everyone needs to be counted and the staff of the relevant National Statistics Office uses their expertise to reach everyone with the same, short questionnaire on mainly demographic variables. The main goal of a census is not to collect data on the migrant population, but on the whole population; the data on migration are generally a 'by-product'.

An important distinction is between a '*de jure*' census, which aims to count all 'usually resident', and a '*de facto*' census, which targets all physically present at the time of census. *De facto* censuses in origin countries would generally, by definition, fail to count the emigrants abroad, while *de jure* censuses might capture some recent or temporary emigrants. Thus it is the censuses from destination countries that can be reliably used in migration research.

Universal coverage is the main advantage of a census, and 'census rounds' are generally conducted within ten-year periods from the middle of each decade. For example, the 2010 round censuses are conducted between 2005 and 2014. Censuses are expensive; resources and expertise of the national statistical agencies determine the quality of the data and the results. Many statistical agencies just publish cross-tabulations of the main variables of interest as they process the data according to a priority list. Migration data, unfortunately, are among the least crucial for many countries and are published with a significant lag. While census data provide important snapshots of migration over time, they have two key shortcomings. First, they include only basic variables – such as gender, age, place of birth/nationality and maybe education – and thus cannot be used to answer many policy questions. Second, they cannot be used to analyze recent and nuanced trends. However, almost every country conducts a census and the questions are relatively homogeneous.[2] This degree of standardization and geographical breadth means that census data have become the backbone of most of the available global databases on migration stocks, especially in bilateral corridors.[3] A key challenge arises when the census tries to capture undocumented migrants who might be reluctant to respond due to concerns that their data will be used for identification and subsequent deportation. As a result, migrant populations may be grossly undercounted in censuses, unless proper corrective procedures are implemented.

Population registers

Population registers are continuous reporting systems used to enumerate the resident population of a particular area, which typically and historically corresponds to a municipality, parish or police precinct. Popular in many parts of Europe – especially the Benelux, Scandinavian and Baltic countries – population registers record the names and addresses of the residents as well as their key demographic variables, such as births, deaths and changes in marital or residential status. A legal requirement typically exists to register and notify any alterations in status. As such, they may be used to record both internal and international migration, and provide detailed up-to-date demographic and socioeconomic information. This makes them a rich, and often fairly exhaustive, source of (migration) data, although the incentive to keep records updated varies across individuals and subgroups of the population. In- and outflows can be tracked with much greater frequency and depth. Although the extent of register data is also rather limited, the continuous updating of the information makes registers more appropriate for tracking migration and for nuanced research questions in comparison with census data.

Population registers, unfortunately, are not widely available outside Europe, and suffer from a higher degree of heterogeneity across countries in terms of registration criteria as well as data scope and quality. The Nordic countries typically implement impressively accurate registers, while the precision of those from Southern Europe is far worse (Redfern, 1989). Undocumented migrants are, by definition, not captured at all since they would not want to register with local authorities. Another shortcoming is that departures are significantly underreported since many people avoid deregistering in order to retain residency rights, and some of the benefits that come with it (OECD, 2009).

Administrative data

There are various sources of administrative data that may provide detailed information about international migration. Again, most of these sources come from destination countries, as they collect data on the migrants themselves. The most common are residency permits, which give migrants many rights and are implemented across a wide range of countries. Many destination countries regularly publish such data, both on the stock of migrants with permits, as well as the flow of new permits issued within a given time frame. Data may be disaggregated by different qualification criteria, such as family reunification, professional qualifications, humanitarian reasons and lotteries. One has to be careful in interpreting residency permit data since issuances need not equal the number of new immigrants. Permits might be based on issuance but taken up by migrants with an extended delay. Another possibility is that permits are issued to those already in the country as they change their legal status, without a real change in the number of migrants within the country. Most importantly, the legal criteria and rights of permits vary greatly. In some countries, residency permits lead to citizenship, while in others they are granted for limited stays. In cases where free mobility agreements between countries exist, such as in the European Union, migration might not lead to issue of new permits. Students who are issued long-term visas may or may not be included in the official statistics.

There are other potentially useable administrative data sources, such as border crossings, police records and social security data. There have been several innovative papers that use social security data from European countries to analyze return and circular migration (e.g., Borjas and Bratsberg, 1996), since all employed individuals can be tracked for extended time periods. Ultimately, the quality of the administrative data depends on the responsible national agency in charge of collection and dissemination, and comparability across sources varies by country. But the use of this kind of data is often limited by the fact that they are seldom made public by government officials.

Household surveys

The final and possibly most useful and comprehensive sources of information on migration are surveys that include, among others, Labor Force Surveys (LFS), Demographic and Health Surveys (DHS), Living Standards Measurement Study Surveys (LSMS), as well as a variety of purpose-specific surveys. Specialized surveys are also fielded in many countries, often to investigate specific aspects of migration. These micro-level surveys provide a rich source of data and are essential for identifying microeconomic linkages between migration and other facets of households' livelihoods and outcomes that other data sources fail to capture. They are also useful as they better capture undercounted migrants if proper sampling frames and techniques are employed. Finally, such surveys can be conducted in both destination and origin countries, and enable researchers to explore a wide range of issues. Most importantly, surveys are the most reliable data sources in origin countries.

There are several potential drawbacks of survey data, including the relative variance of the difficulties faced in implementing household surveys in terms of data collection and processing, and their comparatively small sample sizes. These limit their potential for assessing global trends and performing comparisons. Ethnic and other minorities, including migrants, might be underrepresented in the data and stratified sampling can only be meaningfully applied should other nationwide data with proper sampling, such as a census, become available. The variation in surveying practices across countries and their relatively small sample sizes imply that they fail to capture migrants from smaller corridors and are seldom used in the construction of databases of bilateral migration stocks. But surveys remain an indispensable tool for studying migration, its determinants and impacts. Where migration modules have been successfully integrated in household surveys using appropriate sampling techniques, they have often succeeded in capturing sufficiently large numbers of migrants for meaningful analyses. Depending on the resources devoted, use of surveys will and should increase in the future (Center for Global Development, 2009).

Data Challenges

As discussed above, countries use a range of statistical methods and tools – censuses, registers, administrative records and surveys – to document and profile their populations, including migrants. Each source has advantages and disadvantages with respect to coverage, detail of data collected, frequency and comparability across time and countries. Changes in the questionnaires and data collection methods are two key determinants of comparability over time or within a country. Some issues are more relevant for data collected in the country of destination; others present more of a challenge when collecting data on migrants at the origin. Below we discuss some of the more systematic challenges faced in data collection and analysis.

Definition of a migrant

How a migrant is defined has been a challenge, and Ravenstein (1885) devoted a long discussion to the issue. According to the United Nations Statistics Division (1998, p. 6), a migrant is 'any person that changes his or her country of usual residence'. The essence is movement from one geographic location to another, which is the most relevant criterion for economic analysis. In practice, however, migration in official statistics manifests itself in myriad guises and is anchored to different concepts and definitions, including the individual's country of birth, country of citizenship, purpose of visit or visa type, place of last permanent residence, duration of stay, and even ethnicity.

Place of birth and nationality are the two most commonly used definitions. Foreign-born applies to the first generation that crosses the national boundary. Nationality, on the other hand, might apply to dependants and offspring if the destination country's laws are relatively restrictive in granting citizenship to migrants and/or their children born there. Individuals may be classified as migrants or non-migrants, depending on the definition, even in different sources within a single country. Variation in countries' adoption of definitions has hampered cross-country comparability of migration data. Some destination countries grant citizenship to foreign-born people who are family members of citizens or who satisfy certain legal and residency requirements. These naturalized citizens continue to be recorded as migrants under the foreign-born definition, but not under the foreign citizen definition. Many countries (for example, the USA) grant automatic citizenship to people born within their territory regardless of the citizenship status of the parents. Yet others, such as Japan, require at least one parent to be a citizen, even if children were born within the country's borders. Because of these differences in citizenship and naturalization laws, the number of migrants will be substantially higher in the USA if the foreign-born criterion is used. In Japan, on the other hand, the number of migrants is higher under the foreign citizenship criterion.[4]

Most bilateral migration databases use the criterion under which census data are collected, which tends to be the country of birth. First, this is more appropriate in analyzing physical movements and handling the cases of former colonies and dependencies. Second, while nationality can change, place of birth cannot. Third, the possibility of holding multiple nationalities complicates matters further. Fourth, naturalization laws and rates vary enormously across destination countries. Differences in laws on citizenship criteria (for both migrants and their children born in the destination country) do not affect data based on place of birth. Finally, when migrants, especially refugees and asylum seekers, cannot be assigned to a specific nationality, they are often recorded under an aggregated umbrella heading, leading to ambiguity.

All of these issues plague censuses, population registers and administrative data, as well as surveys. Thus it is critical for collectors of data to ask specific questions and users to be aware of the differences. Ideally, both place of birth and citizenship status should be asked about. However, many undocumented migrants will refrain from participation in the survey for fear of identification when faced with citizenship questions, which will bias the data collected. If a choice needs to be made, place of birth is preferable.

Variation in census dates and missing censuses

Despite the attempts by multilateral institutions to achieve coordination, countries choose when to conduct a census or a survey. Even though the standard procedure is to conduct the censuses in the middle of the round, say in 2010, and every ten years, many exceptions exist to both norms. For example, the census dates in France were 1962, 1968, 1975, 1982, 1990, 1999 and 2006. Such large variation can lead to difficulties in comparison across countries, especially in global databases.

The more serious problem is that many countries fail to conduct a survey or a census at a given time or fail to include relevant questions to identify migrants. Censuses are both expensive and demanding in terms of human resources, which make them less attractive activities in poorer countries. Wars, civil conflict or simple public opposition might prevent data collection. There might be political opposition since surveys and censuses collect data on potentially controversial subjects such as ethnicity, language and religion. Even if collected, data might not be released in detail or in a timely manner. Or worse, the data might be manipulated for political reasons. And, depending on the country's capacity and political sensitivities, adding even a minimal set of questions on migration is often deemed impractical and undesirable, as it may have adverse consequences for the quality of the census data. Researchers must therefore judge the reliability of the data source, as would be the case in other areas, before using it.

Definition of a country

Even if a survey or a census asks country of birth or citizenship questions of the participants, the definitions of countries change over time. Many countries gained independence (Eritrea, Timor-Leste, South Sudan and many other countries in sub-Saharan Africa), dissolved into smaller states (the Soviet Union, Yugoslavia and Czechoslovakia) or unified (Yemen, Germany, Vietnam) since the Second World War. Shifting national borders creates other challenges. First, with partition, millions of migrants are artificially created without ever moving from their homes. Those born in Moscow, but residing in Kiev, would never have been classified as migrants under either of the two most commonly used definitions until 23 August 1991, but are classified as such in the following censuses. For instance, as Özden et al. (2011) show, the sudden jump in international migrants' numbers between 1990 and 2000 is mainly due to the break-up of the Soviet Union.

Changing borders pose problems when analyzing time-series data. One option is to use the countries in existence at that point in time. Migrants from Africa who came to the USA before the 1970s were recorded under different origin countries in different censuses as their birth countries gained independence. Other changes are more subtle. The definition of an 'Ethiopian' included Eritreans in the 1970 census but not in 2000. Thus there is an artificial decline in Ethiopian migrants, as some have been relabeled as Eritreans in later years. Researchers need to keep these border changes in mind when performing their analysis and make the necessary adjustments.

Collecting migrant data through proxy respondents

Collecting survey data on migrants in destination countries presents a number of challenges. These difficulties center on the absence of a proper sampling frame and the high cost of tracking down individuals who tend to form a small portion of the population or might be present without proper documentation and want to avoid detection. Nevertheless, most high-income destination countries have sophisticated national data collection mechanisms, especially for surveys for labor-force, expenditure/income or health-related issues, and can overcome these challenges in relatively satisfactory ways. Among the most prominent examples is the micro sample of the US Census and the American Community Survey, where a smaller sample of the American population fills out an extensive questionnaire that covers migration-related questions such as the year of migration, languages spoken at home and ethnicity. When these are used together with information on education, income, occupation and demographic characteristics, researchers can answer questions on labor market performance, poverty, cultural integration and social outcomes. Similarly, Demographic and Health Surveys, Labor Force Surveys or Income and Expenditure Surveys with proper sampling frames and detailed questions to identify migrants in the data are used extensively to analyze linkages between migration and the applicable issues.

The real challenge in survey design and data collection emerges in origin countries, especially among those that lack adequate statistical capacity. The absence of migrants from the household where data are collected only complicates matters further. Such survey data collection operations require reliance on proxy respondents, in most cases a family member, to answer the questions on behalf of the absent migrants. Various concerns arise from eliciting information through proxy respondents, including whether respondents remember or even know the answers. The information collected through proxies in the household or community of origin can be complemented and cross-checked with short interviews of the migrant themselves via other means, such as phone or online interviews. Alternatively, for certain types of migration, say seasonal or circular migration, proper timing of fieldwork may enable eliciting information at the point of origin directly from the migrant. Finally, interviews at the origin can be administered directly to returnee migrants, often using long recall periods.

Deciding how to identify migrants is the first step in ensuring that desired individuals are captured in an origin-country survey. In order to assess the impact of overall migration patterns, one should try to identify (1) all current household members with past experience with international migration over a given period – return migrants, (2) all former household members who are now living abroad – current migrants, and (3) all former household members with past international migration experience who now live in the source country but in a different household – non-member returnees. As mentioned, collecting information for each group presents different challenges, especially when combined with the necessity to use a proxy respondent (groups 2 and 3) or not (group 1).

The criterion of household membership, generally defined as all individuals who normally live and eat their meals together, affects whether migrants are captured in a survey. In the case of migration questions, additional restrictions are generally imposed to refine the concept, for example by asking about the number of months individuals have been absent over the previous 12 months. In most standard surveys, if the absence is more than 3 (or 6) months, the person will no longer be considered a household member and thus excluded from data collection past the basic household roster. However, many of these people maintain linkages – such as through remittances – and they should be considered in the survey, especially if the goal is to assess the impact of migration on those left behind. Another question is whether these groups should include all former household members (i.e. any individual who used to live in the household at any point in time) or only members of the nuclear family. Although the latter approach may result in an underestimation of the total number of international migrants, it may be preferable. This method has been applied to internal migration in a nearly nationally representative survey collected in China (de Brauw et al., 2002), and again in the Mexican National Rural Household Survey (Richter and Taylor, 2005).

An alternative method takes advantage of the fact that many household surveys already contain a fertility module, in which information on all children ever born from all female members of reproductive age is collected. A drawback is that it will miss all children of women no longer in the household or who have passed away. A similar approach is to list in a separate module all adult children of the head of the household and/or his/her spouse regardless of when they left, especially if the mother is absent or no longer alive. These methods were used in various Albania Living Standards Measurement Surveys (INSTAT, 2002, 2005; Carletto and Azzarri, 2007).

In all of these techniques, the critical issue is double-counting of migrants, especially those who can be claimed as members in other households' rosters. The problem of double-counting is even more acute if household rosters are further extended to include any former household member irrespective of their relationship to the household head. Constructing the list based on clearly defined familial relationships, such as for children or siblings, renders the identification and recall of potential migrants simpler and more accurate, and the sample more demographically representative.

Collecting information to assess the impact of migration

Data collection needs to be designed according to objectives. Since migration, by its very definition, is a selective process, any analysis needs to control for the determinants of migration and collect the necessary information for identification of both migrant (treatment) and non-migrant (control) individuals and their households. In addition, data on pre-migration conditions are needed. Assuming a migrant is identified based on departure within a year, the pre-migration timing corresponds to the prior year. For longer reference periods, ideally one would want to collect information for each single year as the factors affecting migration are likely to have changed over time (Bilsborrow et al., 1997).

In terms of impact of migration, one must first decide where the impact occurs – on the migrant while abroad or on return, on the household left behind or on the community. Second, the outcome of interest needs to be collected properly. For example, if the topic of interest is poverty, the survey must collect consumption or income data from the household. Another important issue is the identification strategy, as unobservable factors affecting migration decisions are also likely to be correlated with the outcome of interest. Ideally, one would rely on an experimental design in which the treatment is randomly assigned, and before and after information is collected. However, given the nature of migration, this is hardly ever the case.[5] Sasin and McKenzie (2007) discuss these issues extensively.

The information collected will depend on a number of factors, including the length of the questionnaire, the capacity and training of fieldworkers, but, most importantly, whether information is gathered directly from the migrant or through a proxy respondent. Use of a proxy might severely constrain the ability to ask questions in depth. However, a minimum set of questions can easily be asked about the emigrants, including their basic demographic characteristics, education level, occupation abroad, country (and location) of current residence, the year of first (and last) migration and remittance behavior. Other questions may be asked about legal status, marital status, the basic demographic composition of the household abroad, frequency and nature of contact with the household, and occupation prior to migrating. Further questions that relate to the specific objectives of the survey can also be added. An attempt could be made to collect more extensive information on past migration episodes, including timing and country of destination.

Finally, to ensure that household conditions prior to migration are recorded, it is useful to collect other selected information within the recall period. For example, one could collect information on occupations or assets in the household prior to, during and after the migration spell of any household member who had migration experience. Other information, often subjective, might also be worth collecting for individuals who may be return migrants, such as whether or not they plan to leave the household again; and the reasons for return. Some potential reasons for return, such as health of household members, can be corroborated in other parts of the survey. While the design of a questionnaire is important to ensuring that the 'right' information is gathered for a study, a survey is only as good as its sample and sampling frame.

Tracking migrants

Another approach to collecting more exhaustive information about emigrants would be to track them. This requires detailed contact information to reach the migrant. Such methods have been used to examine the impacts of internal migration on welfare in Tanzania via a health and development panel data set (Beegle et al., 2011), and in Ethiopia combining a rural household survey with a migrant tracking survey (de Brauw et al., 2013). Given the high mobility of migrants, the tracking survey would ideally occur within weeks of the survey at the sending destination. Internationally, tracking surveys of this type have been carried out in a few countries, including between Mexico and the USA, and between Albania and Greece. Alternatively, one can first carry out a survey in destination countries and, using a similar approach, track down the original household in the sending countries. An example is the aforementioned study between New Zealand and Tonga (McKenzie et al., 2006).

Tracking surveys can also be used as validation of information that was gathered in the original household through proxy respondents, as well as to measure differences in perceptions between migrants and household members left behind. While allowing for direct interviews with the migrants, tracking presents a number of problems, which might outweigh the benefits. It can be too costly and is characterized by a high level of attrition, particularly when the share of undocumented migration is high.

Sampling design

Within migration surveys, a traditional probability sample based on a multi-stage cluster design will not succeed in finding many migrants, whether this is done in origin or sending countries. A probability sample, by assigning a known non-zero probability of selection to each sampling unit, allows for making inferences to the whole population. The foundation of a proper sample is an updated sampling frame. However, this is the main stumbling block in the design of migration-focused surveys, in origin and destination countries. As mentioned earlier, migrants with certain characteristics or from certain origin countries might not be present in large enough numbers to be properly captured in the sample. Furthermore, certain types of migrants might be reluctant to participate for cultural and legal reasons. The Census Department in the USA, for example, uses various techniques to adjust for these biases. These include conducting preliminary surveys to determine the extent of undocumented migration in certain areas, and then adjusting their weight in the sample after taking their response likelihood into account. In other cases, using listing from NGOs working with migrants is often the only, even if incomplete, frame from which to draw a sample. Snowballing and other quasi-random techniques are often used, but the resulting samples are seldom representative of the migrant population as a whole.

In origin countries, most available frames do not contain any information on the exposure to past or current migration of the listed households, preventing *ex ante* stratification of the sample based on migration status. As discussed at the beginning of this chapter, neither the population census nor available administrative records provide adequate sampling frames for selecting emigrants in a given sending country. Nor, in most cases, do they provide information on previous migration experience to help to identify temporary migrants and returnees.

As such, migration is considered a rare event, defined as an infrequent statistical occurrence. In a normal clustered sample design typical of multitopic surveys, the expected number of households associated with emigration may be very low. However, several techniques have been proposed in the literature to better identify rare events, such as migration (Kish, 1965; Huang, 2005). Two such approaches deemed more appropriate in capturing data on migrants, particularly if used in combination, are disproportionate sampling and two-phase sampling. However, both sample designs require some prior knowledge of migration in the population.

Disproportionate sampling implies that primary sampling units (PSUs) with higher migration rates are identified and oversampled. Thus the PSUs known to have a low rate of emigration would be allocated less probability of selection than PSUs with high migration. Representativeness would be regained through weighting. One drawback to this method is that the migration rate might still be too low within each PSU to use simple random sampling or systematic sampling to select households within each PSU.

Alternatively, one can initially select PSUs using the standard method, and then, within each PSU, oversample households known to be migrant households relative to other households. This method is known as two-phase sampling. A random draw of households within a PSU is unlikely to be an efficient way to select a sufficiently large number of migrant households, even in high-migration areas. In this case, a listing operation to clearly identify households with migrants may be a more cost-effective way to select a more balanced sample of migrant and non-migrant households. Listing operations are generally not very expensive and, except in special circumstances, they add up to only about 10–15 percent of the total survey budget (Muñoz, 2007), and the benefits may greatly outweigh the costs.

Finally, one could combine the two methods by initially giving more weight to PSUs with higher migration levels and then oversampling migrant households within each selected PSU. Whichever approach is used, the primary goal is to ensure that a large enough number of migrant households is drawn. It is important to note that using any of these methods is predicated on having prior information about the prevalence of migration in the population at either the area or household level. While this may be the case if one is interested in sampling immigrants in a destination country, it is rarely the case for the study of emigration in a source country. For methods 1 and 3, one needs information on the relative prevalence of emigration by PSU, and for methods 2 and 3 one needs information about emigration within PSUs.

One further decision to make, assuming that migrants can be properly identified in the frame, is whether to select based on the proportion of households with migrants out of the total number of households or to select based on the proportion of migrants over the population in the reference area. Given that a significant amount of analysis on migration is performed at the household level, the first option may be preferable (Bilsborrow et al., 1997).[6]

For the specific purpose of using surveys to learn about emigrants in sending countries, the lack of a suitable sampling frame would still be an obstacle to implementing a disproportionate sampling design. One possible modification, but a departure from a full probability sample, would be to use alternative data sources to identify high-emigration areas in a country. These sources may include, for example, expert opinions, qualitative surveys or surveys in destination countries where, in addition to the immigrant's country of origin, the specific location of departure is asked. However, the last method is not recommended unless most emigration from the source country has a specific destination and all of these main destinations are covered.

Lacking a proper sampling frame, a less than perfect alternative would be to select all area sampling units (or clusters) at different stages with probability proportional to the estimated size (PPES) of the overall population (or the number of occupied dwelling units) and carry out a full listing operation only in the area sampling unit last selected. The method would be appropriate only in the unlikely event that the shares of migrants or migrant households were similar across area units, but finding a sufficient number of migrants in the selected units might still be a challenge.

Other non-probability sampling techniques may also be used to capture rare events; for example, multiplicity methods such as snowballing have been used in the migration literature. One use of snowballing is to gather information on undocumented migrants, using as a starting point, or 'seed', a list of members of a diaspora organization or a list of migrants assisted by an NGO in destination countries. The 'seed' household is used to identify additional migrant households of the same country of origin, and so on until the necessary number of observations is reached. However, using data from Senegal, Beauchemin and González-Ferrer (2011) found snowballing to present a number of selection biases, including overrepresentation of migrants with close ties to the sending country.

Finally, techniques such as random walks and aggregation point intercept methods can be used to identify rare events, such as migration. Random walks using selected households in a community may act as a starting point to identify migration occurrences. A Brazilian survey of Nikkei population used the aggregation point intercept method, which, together with snowballing, was compared with more traditional census-based random sampling (McKenzie and Mistiaen, 2009). In all cases, when using these non-probabilistic methods, it is crucial to collect ancillary information on the implementation of the sample to be able to identify the reference population in an attempt to make 'educated inference' to a larger population group. This is particularly important given McKenzie and Mistiaen's (2009) findings that non-probability methods, such as the aggregation point intercept, are unlikely to provide representative samples and tend to overestimate the migrant population. However, they also show that reweighing the intercept point estimates to account for visits by the same individual to multiple aggregation points may generate estimates rather close to the census-based method.

III. MIGRATION AND POLICY: DATA REQUIREMENTS AND LIMITATIONS

With an understanding of the issues involved in measuring the migration process, we now turn to the specific policy questions that are often pursued with regard to migration. While other chapters in this book cover some of these topics in more detail, our focus here is on examining the data requirements and identifying the data limitations analysts are likely to face when analyzing these issues.

Welfare Impact: Poverty and Income Distribution

The interactions of migration, poverty and income distribution are of primary interest to researchers and policy makers, and have been extensively studied in the past (e.g. Lipton, 1980; Stark et al., 1986; de Haan, 1999). Income differences are among the key determinants of migration between countries and, conversely, migration flows tend to change income levels and distributions in both origin and destination economies. Yet because migration is difficult to identify statistically, few studies have been able to convincingly demonstrate a causal relationship between migration and either poverty or inequality. There are several fundamental challenges.

First, income levels and migration influence each other. Low-income levels are among the main causes of migration. On the other hand, extreme poverty may hinder migration as very poor people lack financial and other resources. For example, in Nicaragua, Murrugarra and Herrera (2011) find that the socioeconomic level of a migrant affects his choice of destination, with poorer migrants choosing destinations that have lower transaction costs, and fewer potential gains. While income levels and poverty may influence migration decisions, migration also leads to poverty reduction and changes in the income distribution, especially in origin countries. In Guatemala, Adams (2005) finds that remittances reduce the degree, depth and severity of poverty in the country. In addition, numerous studies examine expenditure or consumption patterns of households with migrants abroad currently or previously (Taylor and Mora, 2006; Yang, 2008; Adams and Cuecuecha, 2010). As a result of data requirements and the difficulties involved in identifying migration, research on the dynamics of the relationship between migration and inequality or income growth remains relatively limited (McKenzie and Rapoport, 2007; de Brauw and Giles, 2008; Gibson et al., 2009; Lokshin et al., 2010).

The primary requirement to study migration, poverty and income distribution is an accurate measure of well-being: the preferred measure is consumption, which is an integral part of any multi-topic survey. Deaton and Grosh (2000) provide a detailed description of the issues one faces in measuring consumption, and Deaton and Zaidi (2002) discuss issues related to the computation of a consumption aggregate in household survey data in detail. In order to measure the causal relationship between migration and welfare, one would need to estimate what the migrant household's per capita consumption level would have been if the migrant had remained within the household. Panel data with information on pre- and post-migration can be most useful. However, panel data are seldom available and cross-sectional data sets must be relied on. Although the counterfactual is difficult (if not impossible) to ascertain in a cross-sectional study, one can attempt to learn about it by collecting information on pre-migration conditions, such as measures of asset holdings, that can be reconstructed using recall methods.

The endogenous relationship between migration decisions and income outcomes requires a proper identification strategy. Except where the migrants are chosen randomly, for example in the case of Pacific Islanders in New Zealand (McKenzie et al., 2006), the general approach is instrumental variables (IV) estimation. The challenge of finding valid instruments that influence migration decisions but not the outcomes of interest, especially economic outcomes such as income, is one of the most severe challenges faced by researchers. Household surveys or labor force surveys with migration indicators are the main data sources used for poverty and income distribution analysis. The instruments are also constructed with the data in these surveys. Among the most common variables used in the literature are current and historical social networks and diaspora linkages (Hanson and Woodruff, 2003; Hildebrandt and McKenzie, 2005; De, 2008). In cases where purpose-specific surveys are used or the researcher has the option to design the questionnaire, certain questions can be inserted that will lead to construction of appropriate variables to be used as instruments. For example, McKenzie and Mistiaen (2009) use the generation of the migrant when analyzing Japanese–Brazilian migration to Japan.

Different types of migration may have differing effects on poverty and inequality (see Germenji and Swinnen, 2005). Furthermore, measurements at the household level must take into account the migrant's absence (Barham and Boucher, 1998). If emigrants are not accounted for in poverty estimates, poverty for some original group of individuals can also be overestimated (Clemens and Pritchett, 2008).

Migration may also have general equilibrium effects on the within-community income distribution. When migration occurs, one expects local wages, either explicitly or implicitly, to rise for the types of workers most likely to migrate, leading to more complex effects on the income distribution than the direct effects on inequality or income. In a cross-section, one could use questions about wages found in the labor modules or labor force surveys to investigate whether communities with more migration have higher increases in wages than other communities, if information on wages in the previous period are also collected. Otherwise, panel data are necessary to investigate general equilibrium effects.

Welfare Impact: Health and Education

The relationship between migration and human capital has also been widely examined, particularly the effects of migration on education and health outcomes of the families left behind (Kanaiaupuni and Donato, 1999; Cox Edwards and Ureta, 2003; Mansuri, 2006; Acosta et al., 2007; Nobles, 2007; Amuedo-Dorantes and Pozo, 2009). These are among the main development benefits of migration in labor-sending lower-income countries. Migration may have positive effects on educational attainment of children in migrant families through the provision of remittances to alleviate credit constraints. Calero et al. (2008) find that remittances increase school enrollment and act to ensure education through financial shocks in Ecuador. However, parental migration may also have negative consequences if the child must now fill the role of the absent parent by working more at home, or if there is loss of parental involvement. In Mexico, McKenzie and Rapoport (2007) report a decline in school attendance and attainment for boys aged 12–18 and girls aged 16–18 with a parent abroad. Similarly, in China, de Brauw and Mu (2011) find that the status of underweight children aged 7–12 is positively correlated with parental migration.

Type of migration and migrants affect welfare outcomes. Macours and Vakis (2010) find that maternal seasonal migration positively affected early cognitive development in Nicaragua. Gibson et al. (2011) show that children who migrate with parents experience improvements in diet reflected in improved weight-for-age and height-for-age, while children who remain have worsened diets and declining weight-for-age and height-for-age.

In examining health outcomes, a household survey could be combined with anthropometric indicators to examine issues of nutritional status and food security as related to migration (see Antón, 2010; and Carletto et al., 2011). Similarly, for education outcomes, purpose-specific surveys as well as general household surveys with relevant questions can be used. Information specifically on remittance income is also needed.

Last, but not least, migrant selectivity is again a key concern. Health and education outcomes are closely related to income levels, which have an endogenous relationship with migration decisions, as discussed above. Furthermore, in many surveys, migrants state that they choose to migrate specifically to provide the resources for their children's education and family's health expenditures. Thus a natural endogenous relationship can emerge between migration decisions and health/education outcomes. Since the data come from similar household survey data, parallel IV approaches can be used, as discussed in the previous section on poverty and income.

Labor Market Impact

Migration for employment can have several effects on the economy beyond the direct change in location of some workers. In countries of origin, at the household level, migration may change the household labor composition as well as labor supply decisions of family members who stayed behind. At the macro level, departure of a group of workers, especially if they are concentrated in certain skill, occupation and age categories, will have implications for absolute and relative wage levels as well as other labor market outcomes. These same issues are relevant in destination countries. Labor market implications receive extensive attention in OECD countries, where there is significant public and political opposition to migration flows on the grounds that migrants take jobs away from natives.

Different data sources can be used, depending on the questions asked. Multi-topic surveys are well suited to studying the impact of emigration on wages in specific sectors, labor mobility across sectors, and whether or not skills acquired through migration foster upward mobility among individuals. Aside from migration variables and data collected for potential identification strategies, surveys should include employment status, wage rates, job types and human capital variables in the employment module. For people with migration experience, it is particularly useful to collect information on occupations prior to migration and at the destination, as well as the present occupation for return migrants (as examples, see Schaffner, 2000; for examples in practice see Carletto and Kilic, 2011; Mendola and Carletto, 2012). A survey that includes oversampling of migrants may be particularly useful for statistical power, especially as the number of job types increases.

There are numerous studies on the impact of emigration on local labor market outcomes in origin countries. In Albania, Miluka et al. (2010) find that international migration reduces overall labor inputs into farming. Similarly, in the Kayes area of Mali, Azam and Gubert (2006) report that individuals left behind by international migrants can exhibit shirking behavior in terms of working in agriculture. Within China, de Brauw et al. (2008) find that, as internal migration increased, overall agricultural labor inputs decreased, but the average share of agricultural labor inputs provided by women did not change. Migration can also affect child labor: on one hand, households with out-migrants may become wealthier, reducing the need for child labor; on the other hand, migration could lead to labor shortages on the farm, potentially increasing the need for child labor. Migration need not only affect the households that migrants leave; at the source, emigration can have general equilibrium effects on wages (Hanson, 2007; Mishra, 2007).

The macro impact of immigration in source and destination countries can be analyzed using aggregate data as well as labor force survey data. The big debate (Borjas, 1988, 1989, 1994 and Card, 2001, 2009) on how migration affects native workers is concerned deeply with properly identifying endogenous location choices. Migrant workers are attracted to geographic areas and sectors where there are strong labor demand and promising future prospects. On the other hand, arrival of migrants is likely to cause native workers to move to other sectors and areas, causing the effect to ripple through the overall economy. Various authors use different methods to control for these endogenous processes, obtaining quite different results along the way. For example, Card (2001) uses geographic local markets, while Borjas (2003) chooses education-age cohort cells as the unit of analysis. Among the more recent papers, Docquier et al. (forthcoming) use the bilateral migration database of Artuc et al. (forthcoming) to analyze the impact of immigration and emigration on labor market outcomes – both wages and employment levels – of native workers of different skill levels in OECD countries. The analytical framework is typically based on a general equilibrium model of labor markets and production where the substitution elasticities between different types of labor, especially between migrants and natives, play a critical role. Most of these studies rely on data aggregated from labor force surveys and construct their instruments from macro data. Özden and Wagner (2014) use the age-distribution data from origin countries interacted with historical migration patterns as instruments of current migration patterns in Malaysia. Borjas (2014) is an excellent survey of the issues, empirical methods and data requirements in research on labor market implications of migration.

An underexplored but very important issue with development implications is return migration. Migrants obtain skills and financial resources during their time away, which can prove useful on return (Mayr and Peri, 2008; Gibson and McKenzie, 2011). The benefits may especially be concentrated in the labor market outcomes of return migrants (Bijwaard et al., 2013). A multi-topic survey should cover several important issues in order to study the implications of return migration. In addition to identifying return migrants in the labor force, it is also important to ask whether these individuals plan to migrate again. Although plans are not the same as actual migration after the survey, individuals who answer negatively can be labeled as truly returned migrants. It is important to ask further about the activities of a returned migrant in order to establish that the individual is truly a return migrant committed to staying.

Governments may want to encourage return migration, as migrants come back with valuable human and social capital acquired abroad. If programs exist to encourage return migration, such as job training or rural development programs, then the questionnaire should explicitly ask about whether migrants took part in any such programs. However, one might also want to know about the likelihood of return for current out-migrants, which is difficult to determine without a survey in the destination country. One can add questions to the survey about the integration of the migrant in the destination country or area. Specifically, one can ask whether or not the spouse lives with the migrant, if the migrant has children who were born or live at the destination, how often the migrant returns home, and whether or not the migrant has investments at home. If children live with migrants away from home, in cases of international migration or countries where multiple languages are spoken, one should also ask whether or not children living at the destination speak the native language.

In addition, migration itself can be affected by changing opportunities at potential destinations. As the populations of developed countries age, many developed-country governments realize that migrants can help fill gaps in their labor market that native workers would not fill, particularly prime-age workers. As migrants usually keep close ties to the households and communities they leave, policies that encourage temporary migration followed by a return can benefit both the source and destination countries.

Brain Drain, Gain and Waste

One of the most intensely debated issues in the migration literature involves the departure of highly skilled workers from poorer countries to wealthier ones. Often referred to as 'brain drain', loss of human capital in low-income countries that already suffer from relative skill shortages can have important negative development and growth implications. The main concern is that the positive externalities generated by high-skilled workers will disappear with their migration. The issue takes on an even more emotional dimension since the education of these migrants is funded through limited public resources and their move to high-income OECD countries implies a subsidy from the poor to the rich. Despite the extensive and old analytical literature (Bhagwati, 1979; Bhagwati and Hanson, 2009), empirical analysis has been relatively lacking. The first breakthrough was the construction of the bilateral migration databases for OECD destinations based on census data (Docquier and Marfouk, 2004, 2006; Dumont and Lemaître, 2004). These databases focused on migrant workers in the labor force, aged 15–65 generally, and disaggregated them by three education levels – primary, secondary and tertiary – since this was the most uniformly available human capital variable that could be used as a proxy for human capital and skill levels. Initially for the OECD countries, these data sets highlighted, for the first time, the extent of global skilled migration patterns.

There had been several extensions, starting with the gender dimension (Docquier et al., 2009, and Dumont et al., 2007). A more important issue is the age of migration, which is a proxy for the location of training. The issue is whether a Jamaican doctor who migrated to the USA as a child with his family, and trained in the USA, can be considered a real 'loss' for Jamaica. Beine et al. (2007) construct the database for OECD countries and show that the initial 'brain-drain' levels decline considerably for many countries as large numbers of their migrants obtained their tertiary education at the destination and did not necessarily impose a fiscal and productivity loss on the birth countries.

The next extension was the addition of non-OECD destinations. OECD's DIOC-e database added over 30 destination countries to the original OECD-centric data set, again using census-style sources. Artuc et al. (forthcoming) increase the number of countries to 63 in 1990 and 100 in 2000. Their main innovation is to use a gravity-type estimation model to predict the data – by gender and skill level – for the missing destination countries. The result is a truly global overview of human capital mobility. They estimate that there were slightly over 110 million working-age migrants between the ages of 15 and 64, with around half in OECD countries, half female and a quarter tertiary educated. They establish striking patterns. For example, over 70 percent of all tertiary educated migrants in the world end up in just four countries – the USA, the UK, Canada and Australia. The constructed database enables researchers to perform many analyses, including the paper by Docquier et al. (forthcoming), which evaluates the impact of both immigration and emigration in OECD labor markets.

One of the most interesting ideas to emerge in this literature is the possibility of 'brain gain'. The main premise is that higher expected returns to human capital in destination countries will induce people to invest more in their human capital. If some of these people end up staying at home, the final human capital level in the origin country might actually increase due to improved skilled migration opportunities. The important issue is that this likelihood of migration can neither be too high – too many people would leave and nobody would stay at home – nor too low – people would not invest in their education. Using the above-mentioned bilateral skilled migration databases, Beine et al. (2008) show that the brain-gain effect can take place if the tertiary education level in the labor force is between 2 and 8 percent and the skilled migration level is not very high. The brain-gain effect has also been shown to exist using single-country survey data. For example, Batista et al. (2009) find significant brain gain in Cape Verde, specifically through increased education attainment of non-migrants. Similarly, using survey data in Moldova, Böhme (2012) demonstrates that migration positively affects parental aspirations for children's education at the lower end of the human capital spectrum. In their survey of the 'best and brightest' in Tonga and Papua New Guinea, Gibson and McKenzie (2011) show that students who contemplated migration took additional classes. Chand and Clemens (2008) found that ethnic Indians were more likely to invest in their education relative to native Fijians after the 1987 coup, which led to violence against the Indian community and increased their desire to migrate.

The last concept to emerge in this literature is 'brain waste'. The first type of brain waste occurs in an origin country if it overinvests in a specific type of human capital (e.g., engineers) and restricts labor movement. As a result, there will be high unemployment levels for those workers and the resources spent on them will be wasted. The source economy would theoretically benefit by allowing those individuals to emigrate and realize returns to their human capital elsewhere, as they might be expected to send remittances back to the source economy.

Second, brain waste may occur when highly skilled migrants cannot find employment commensurate with their skills in the destination country. This is sometimes exemplified by Eastern European physicists driving taxis in New York. This might arise for various reasons. Their qualifications might not be recognized, such as foreign doctors who cannot obtain licenses. They might not be trained in location-specific skills, such as lawyers trained in a legal tradition that is different from the US legal regime. Finally, migrants may have the bureaucratic qualifications (the diplomas), but lack the actual human capital since their education is below the standards demanded in the destination labor markets. Mattoo et al. (2008) show that highly skilled immigrants to the USA from Eastern Europe and Latin America tend not to be able to find employment for which they are trained, whereas immigrants from OECD countries and Asia are more likely to find such employment. Their analysis shows that the main reasons are the lower quality of education in the origin countries, as well as selection effects. Since it is easier for Latin American migrants to enter the USA illegally or through family reunification programs, their average human capital level might be lower than that of Asian migrants who are forced to enter through more demanding employment-based preferences.

In addition to census-based global bilateral databases, multi-topic surveys are well suited to study brain drain, brain gain, and brain waste from the source-country perspective. Through an education module, one can characterize the educational background of a country's (or region's) out-migrants relative to the remaining population (Glewwe, 2000). To study brain gain, one can attempt to relate past migration variables constructed from a migration history to school enrollment. If the survey includes a detailed employment module, brain waste can be studied from the source-country perspective by examining job types held by individuals in different educational and experience cohorts. A survey that oversamples migrant households could be particularly informative in studying either brain drain or brain gain, as the distribution of educational attainment among migrants would be measured with less error. On the other hand, for learning about the brain-drain issue from the perspective of specific occupations, a specialized survey targeted at individuals with specific types of training (e.g. nursing school) would be more informative.

Trade, Foreign Direct Investment and Migration

The main premise of this area of literature is that migration can facilitate integration between countries in other areas, mainly through trade and foreign direct investment (FDI) flows. Migrants possess knowledge of specific conditions, regulations and product features in both import and export markets. By using their knowledge, they can lower transactions costs, match parties in a relationship and increase economic integration. Migrants also are consumers of specific products from their home countries. Starting with Rauch (1999), an extensive literature mentioned these information and demand channels as key to the relationships between trade, migration and FDI flows.

The main analytical framework consists of gravity models and focuses on OECD countries due to data availability. Most papers analyze a single country and its multiple trading partners (such as Head and Ries, 1998; Dunlevy and Hutchinson, 2001; Girma and Yu, 2002; Blanes-Cristóbal, 2003; Hatzigeorgiou, 2010). The main exceptions are Felbermayr and Toubal (2008), who perform cross-section analysis, and Felbermayr and Jung (2009), who use panel data. Other papers focus on the trade and migration links between province/regions of a country and its trading partners (Wagner et al, 2002; Co et al., 2004; Bardhan and Guhathakurta, 2005; Herander and Saavedra, 2005; Dunlevy, 2006; Bandyopadhyay et al., 2008; Peri and Requena-Silvente, 2010).

The empirical analysis requires the matching of bilateral trade, migration and FDI data. Migration data are generally obtained from macro sources such as censuses, while trade and FDI data come from relevant customs and financial administrations. Single-country studies find a positive relationship, but are likely to suffer from omitted-variable biases as we cannot implement country fixed effects due to the nature of the data, an issue emphasized strongly in the literature on gravity models (Anderson, 1979). Felbermayr and Jung (2009) control for country-pair unobserved heterogeneity (and multilateral resistances) using a panel for 1990 and 2000, but they can cover only North–South trade. These authors find a significant and positive effect as well. In a more recent paper, Parsons (2012) uses the Özden et al. (2011) database of global bilateral migration for 1960–2000. The long-term panel structure of the data, combined with the fact that they cover all countries, enables Parsons (2012) to control for pairwise heterogeneity as well as to instrument properly for migration patterns by using historical stocks.

The parallel analysis can be extended to linkages between FDI and migration flows. Similar macro sources are used for bilateral migration and FDI data. Among the important examples, Kugler and Rapoport (2005) use a standard gravity model while Javorcik et al. (2010) use the US data with education levels to analyze the role of skilled migration. In addition, they use geographic variables and passport costs as instruments to control for potential endogeneity problems.

Forced Displacement

The study of forced displacement is often associated with people fleeing from conflict. This may include, but is not limited to, generalized violence, armed conflict or persecution. As defined by the 1951 Convention on Refugees, a refugee is 'a person who is outside his or her country of nationality or habitual residence; has a well-founded fear of being persecuted because of his or her race, religion, nationality, membership of a particular social group or political opinion; and is unable or unwilling to avail him- or herself of the protection of that country, or to return there, for fear of persecution' (UNHCR, 2007, p. 3). While many individuals fleeing persecution may seek assistance across international borders either in the form of asylum or through temporary assistance, others may fear being returned and choose to remain anonymous.

Accurately recording refugees in data is extraordinarily difficult. The level of accuracy often depends on the destination of the refugees, the size of the displacement, and whether the refugee chooses to integrate into the destination community. The United Nations High Commissioner for Refugees (UNHCR) maintains a statistical database of refugees across the world. The data are usually reported by local UNHCR offices and reflect host-country data. In the developing world, this information largely incorporates refugees in camps, but may not include those who have integrated into society. In 25 industrialized countries, the data are estimated based on individual-country recognition of the refugee population over a ten-year period.[7] Furthermore, in OECD countries, refugees are most often integrated into society and may be registered in the census.

Forced displacement is not limited to those fleeing conflict, but may also include individuals fleeing natural disasters or environmental change. Such migration may be international or domestic, and therefore, while forced, environmental migrants often do not fit the legal definition of a refugee. Individuals fleeing natural disasters, such as Haitians responding to the 2010 earthquake by fleeing to the Dominican Republic, may do so temporarily or on a longer-term basis. Documenting the temporary migration may be done through administrative data, such as information on border crossings, or through targeted surveys at the destination shortly after the natural disaster. Alternatively, longer-term migration may be captured in census data or through multi-topic surveys. Individuals forced to migrate due to environmental change are unlikely to be able to return. Researchers are devising a number of ways to link multiple types of data in order to assess and anticipate environmental migration. In Ghana, Van der Geest et al. (2010) link census data to vegetation data to examine the connections between internal migration and vegetation dynamics. Feng et al. (2010) examine the connection between crop yields and migration by merging crop data with census data. Others are modeling climate change patterns in an attempt to understand future migration trends (Barbieri et al., 2010; Hunter et al., 2011; McLeman, 2013).

Forced migration may also include displacement due to development policies or projects. These could include the introduction of conservation areas or biosphere projects, or large infrastructure projects, such as the construction of dams or deforestation. Similar to many environmental refugees, those displaced by development projects/policies remain largely within their own country, and do not meet the legal requirements to be considered refugees. Surveys specifically targeting those who may be affected by such policies would be most beneficial. Moreover, in designing surveys to answer questions about all types of forced migration, it is important to include questions regarding where individuals lived previously and why they moved.

IV. CONCLUSIONS

The study of migration and its importance as a driver and consequence of many socioeconomic processes has long been a key component in many countries' development debates. However, the availability of data has been a major constraint hampering the formulation of proper policies in both destination and origin countries. A number of data sources exist, including censuses, various administrative data and surveys, but their thematic and geographic coverage remains inadequate and inconsistent.

Collecting migration data poses a number of technical and logistical challenges requiring special methods and techniques to properly sample and interview migrants. Furthermore, because migration is a highly selective decision, assessing the true impact of migration on the outcomes of choice remains particularly difficult and demanding in terms of data. The objective of this chapter was to give readers of this volume a primer on the issues surrounding the collection of migration data and on the data requirements to address some important questions at the center of national and global policy debates.

Each of the different data sources reviewed has its own strengths and weaknesses, depending of its specific use, but improving the linkages across these different data sources and the various available databases is probably an aspect of the migration data agenda that deserves more attention and would result in substantial benefits to policy analysts. Ultimately, no single data source will be able to meet all data demands; thus countries need to think systemically about how the various sources are integrated and complement each other.

The issue of representativeness, or the lack thereof, of many migration studies also highlights the difficulties associated with drawing suitable samples of migrants at both the origin and destination. Several techniques were highlighted, but the lack of complete and updated sampling frames is bound to continue to hamper future efforts.

Migration is innate to human nature, and both internal and international flows will undoubtedly continue to be a natural part of the policy debates of most countries. Some processes, like increasing rural–urban migration, are inevitable and come with countries' development and households' evolution. Other emerging issues, like climate change, are bound to accelerate these processes. And others, like the aging of population in developed countries, are sure to generate additional demand for unskilled and skilled labor from sending countries. However, how migration is managed and its positive impact fully exploited will ultimately depend on the availability of accurate and timely data on the different facets of the phenomenon. From Ravenstein's day much has changed in terms of global migration patterns, and our knowledge has steadily increased. Yet some of the same data challenges remain to this day, and this requires a concerted effort among researchers and policy makers to resolve.

NOTES

1. Some of the sections in this chapter draw from Carletto and de Brauw (2008) and de Brauw and Carletto (2012).
2. The United Nations Department of Economic and Social Affairs Statistical Division (UNDESASD) reports that 202 countries have completed a census since 2005, with 26 more countries planning one.
3. Censuses may be used to calculate migration flows by asking questions pertaining to migrants' residence in previous years and the date of their arrival in the current location.
4. Further confounding interpretation of the underlying definitions is the fact that countries variously apply the foreign-born definition (Docquier and Marfouk, 2006).
5. An exception is work by McKenzie et al. (2006), who take advantage of the random allocation of New Zealand visas to Tongan residents.

6. For a worked example of a three-stage disproportionate sample of immigrants using a suitable sampling frame, see Bilsborrow et al. (1997, pp. 280–83).
7. See the UNHCR website (http://www.unhcr.org/4a01417d6.html) for a list of the 25 industrialized countries and a complete explanation of the database.

REFERENCES

Acosta, P., P. Fajnzylber and J.H. López (2007), 'Remittances and household behavior: evidence for Latin America', in P. Fajnzylber and J.H. López (eds), *Remittances and Development: Lessons from Latin America*, Washington, DC: The World Bank, pp. 133–70.

Adams, R.H. (2005), 'Remittances and poverty in Guatemala', World Bank Policy Research Working Paper No. 3418, Washington, DC: The World Bank.

Adams, R.H. and A. Cuecuecha (2010), 'Remittances, household expenditure and investment in Guatemala', *World Development*, **38**(11), 1626–41.

Amuedo-Dorantes, C. and S. Pozo (2009), 'New evidence on the role of remittances on health care expenditures by Mexican households', Discussion Paper No. 4617, Bonn, Germany: Institute for the Study of Labor (IZA).

Anderson, James E. (1979), 'A theoretical foundation for the gravity equation', *The American Economic Review*, **69**(1), 106–16.

Antón, J. (2010), 'The impact of remittances on nutritional status of children in Ecuador', *International Migration Review*, **44**(2), 269–99.

Artuc, Erhan, Frederic Docquier, Çaglar Özden and Christopher Parsons (forthcoming), 'A global assessment of human capital mobility', *World Development*.

Azam, J.P. and F. Gubert (2006), 'Migrants' remittances and the household in Africa: a review of the evidence', *Journal of African Economies*, **15**(2), 426–62.

Bandyopadhyay, Subhayu, Cletus C. Coughlin and Howard J. Wall (2008), 'Ethnic networks and US exports', *Review of International Economics*, **16**(1), 199–213.

Barbieri, A.F., E. Doningue, B.L. Queiroz, Ricardo M. Ruiz, José I. Rigotti, José A.M. Carvalho and Marco F. Resende (2010), 'Climate change and population migration in Brazil's Northeast: scenarios for 2025–2050', *Population Environment*, **31**, 344–70.

Bardhan, Ashok Deo and Subhrajit Guhathakurta (2005), 'Global links of subnational regions: coastal exports and international networks', *Contemporary Economic Policy*, **22**, 225–36.

Barham, B. and S. Boucher (1998), 'Migration, remittances, and inequality: estimating the net effects of migration on income distribution', *Journal of Development Economics*, **55**, 307–31.

Batista, C., A. Lacuesta and P. Vicente (2009), 'Micro evidence of the brain gain hypothesis: the case of Cape Verde', Banco de España Working Paper No. 0902, Madrid: Banco de España.

Beauchemin, C. and A. González-Ferrer (2011), 'Sampling international migrants with origin-based snowballing method: new evidence on biases and limitations', *Demographic Research*, **25**, 103–34.

Beegle, K., J. de Weerdt and S. Dercon (2011), 'Migration and economic mobility in Tanzania: evidence from a tracking survey', *Review of Economics and Statistics*, **93**(3), 1010–33.

Beine, M., F. Docquier and H. Rapoport (2007), 'Measuring international skilled migration: a new database controlling for age of entry', ULB Institutional Repository 2013/10411, Université Libre de Bruxelles.

Beine, M., F. Docquier and H. Rapoport (2008), 'Brain drain and human capital formation in developing countries: winners and losers', *Economic Journal*, **118**(528), 631–52.

Bhagwati, J. (1979), 'International migration of highly skilled: economics, ethics and taxes', *Third Word Quarterly*, **1**(3), 17–30.

Bhagwati, J. and G. Hanson (2009), *Skilled Immigration Today: Prospects, Problems, and Policies*, New York: Oxford University Press.
Bijwaard, Govert E., Christian Schluter and Jackline Wahba (2013), 'The impact of labor market dynamics on the return migration of immigrants', *The Review of Economics and Statistics*, online.
Bilsborrow, R., G. Hugo, A.S. Oberai and H. Zlotnick (1997), *International Migration Statistics: Guidelines for Improving Data Collection Systems*, Geneva: International Labour Organization.
Blanes-Cristóbal, José Vicente (2003), 'The link between immigration and trade in Spain', Seville, Universidad Pablo de Olavide, Paper presented at XXVIII Simposio de Análisis Económico, 11–13 December, Seville. http://www.revecap.com/vieea/autores/B/62.pdf.
Böhme, M. (2012), 'Migration and education aspirations – another channel of brain gain?', Kiel Working Paper No. 1811, Kiel: Kiel Institute for the World Economy.
Borjas, G.J. (1988), 'Self-selection and the earnings of immigrants', National Bureau of Economic Research, Inc. Retrieved from http://ideas.repec.org/p/nbr/nberwo/2248.html.
Borjas, G.J. (1989), 'Economic theory and international migration', *International Migration Review*, **23**(3), 457–85.
Borjas, G.J. (1994), 'The economics of immigration', *Journal of Economic Literature*, **32**(4), 1667–717.
Borjas, George J. (2003), 'The labor demand curve is downward sloping: reexamining the impact of immigration on the labor market', *Quarterly Journal of Economics*, **118**(4), 1335–74.
Borjas, G.J. (2014), *Immigration Economics*, Cambridge, MA: Harvard University Press.
Borjas, G.J. and B. Bratsberg (1996), 'Who leaves? The outmigration of the foreign-born', *The Review of Economics and Statistics*, **78**(1), 165–76.
Calero, C., A.S. Bedi and R. Sparrow (2008), 'Remittances, liquidity constraints and human capital investments in Ecuador', *World Development*, **37**(6), 1143–54.
Card, David (2001), 'Immigrant inflows, native outflows, and the local market impacts of higher immigration', *Journal of Labor Economics*, **19**(1), 22–64.
Card, David (2009), 'Immigration and inequality', *American Economic Review*, **99**(2), 1–21.
Carletto, C. and C. Azzarri (2007), 'Migration in Albania: trends, determinants and impact on poverty', Background Paper to the 2007 Albania Poverty Assessment, mimeo, Washington, DC: The World Bank.
Carletto, C., K. Covarrubias and J.A. Maluccio (2011), 'Migration and child growth in Guatemala', *Food Policy*, **36**(February), 16–27.
Carletto, C. and A. de Brauw (2008), 'Measuring migration using household surveys', Migration Operational Vehicle, Operational Note No. 2, Washington, DC: The World Bank.
Carletto, C. and T. Kilic (2011), 'Moving up the ladder? The impact of migration experience on occupational mobility in Albania', *Journal of Development Studies*, **47**(6), 846–69.
Center for Global Development (2009), 'Migrants count: five steps toward better migration data', Report of the Commission on International Migration Data, Washington, DC: Center for Global Development.
Chand, S. and M.A. Clemens (2008), 'Skilled emigration and skill creation: a quasi-experiment', International and Development Economics Working Papers idec08-05, International and Development Economics.
Clemens, M. and L. Pritchett (2008), 'Income per natural: measuring development for people rather than places', *Population and Development Review*, **34**(3), 395–434.
Co, Catherine Y., Patricia Euzent and Thomas Martin (2004), 'The export effect of immigration into the USA', *Applied Economics*, **36**, 573–83.
Cox Edwards, A. and M. Ureta (2003), 'International migration, remittances, and schooling: evidence from El Salvador', *Journal of Development Economics*, **72**(2), 429–61.
De, P.K. (2008) 'Identifying the impacts of international migration on women's contraceptive use in Mexico', mimeo, New York: New York University.

De Brauw, A. and C. Carletto (2012), 'Improving the measurement and policy relevance of migration information in multi-topic household surveys', mimeo. http://siteresources.worldbank.org/INTLSMS/Resources/3358986-1199367264546/Migration_Data_v14.pdf.
De Brauw, A. and J. Giles (2008), 'Migrant opportunity and the educational attainment of youth in rural China', Policy Research Working Paper Series 4526, The World Bank.
De Brauw, A., J. Huang, S. Rozelle, L. Zhang and Y. Zhang (2002), 'The evolution of China's rural labor markets during the reforms', *Journal of Comparative Economics*, **30**(2), 329–53.
De Brauw, A., Q. Li, C. Liu, S. Rozelle and L. Zhang (2008), 'Feminization of agriculture in China? Debunking myths surrounding women's participation in farming', *China Quarterly*, **194**, 327–34.
De Brauw, A. and R. Mu (2011), 'Migration and the overweight and underweight status of children in rural China', *Food Policy*, **36**(February), 16–27.
De Brauw, A., V. Mueller and T. Woldehanna (2013), 'Does internal migration improve overall well-being in Ethiopia?', Ethiopia Strategy Support Program II (No. 55). Retrieved from http://essp.ifpri.info/2013/06/20/does-internal-migration-improve-overall-well-being-in-ethiopia/.
De Haan, A. (1999), 'Livelihoods and poverty: the role of migration – a critical review of the migration literature', *Journal of Development Studies*, **36**(2), 1–47.
Deaton, A. and M. Grosh (2000), 'Consumption', in M. Grosh and P. Glewwe (eds), *Designing Household Survey Questionnaires for Developing Countries: Lessons from 15 years of the Living Standards Measurement Study Volume 1*, Washington, DC: The World Bank, pp. 91–134.
Deaton, A. and S. Zaidi (2002), *Guidelines for Constructing Consumption Aggregates for Welfare Analysis*, Washington, DC: The World Bank.
Docquier, F., B.L. Lowell and A. Marfouk (2009), 'A gendered assessment of highly skilled emigration', *Population and Development Review*, **35**(2), 297–321.
Docquier, F. and A. Marfouk (2004), 'Measuring the international mobility of skilled workers (1990–2000): release 1.0', Policy Research Working Paper Series 3381, Washington, DC: The World Bank.
Docquier, F. and A. Marfouk (2006), 'International migration by educational attainment (1990–2000)', in Ç. Özden and M. Schiff (eds), *International Migration, Remittances and the Brain Drain*, Basingstoke, UK: Palgrave-Macmillan, ch. 5.
Docquier, Frederic, Çaglar Özden and Giovanni Peri (forthcoming), 'The wage effects of immigration and emigration', *The Economic Journal.*
Dumont, J.C. and G. Lemaître (2004), 'Counting immigrants and expatriates in OECD countries: a new perspective', mimeo, Paris: OECD.
Dumont, J.C., J.P. Martin and G. Spielvogel (2007), 'Women on the move: the neglected gender dimension of the brain drain', Discussion Paper Series No. 2920, Institute for the Study of Labor.
Dunlevy, James A. (2006), 'The influence of corruption and language on the protrade effect of immigrants: evidence from American states', *Review of Economics and Statistics*, **88**(1), 182–6.
Dunlevy, James A. and William K. Hutchinson (2001), 'The pro-trade effects of immigration on American exports during the period 1870 to 1910', Vanderbilt University Working Paper 01-W25.
Felbermayr, Gabriel J. and Benjamin Jung (2009), 'The pro-trade effect of the brain drain: sorting out confounding factors', *Economics Letters*, **104**(2), 72–5.
Felbermayr, Gabriel and Farid Toubal (2008), 'Revisiting the trade–migration nexus: evidence from new OECD data', mimeo.
Feng, S.F, A.B. Krueger and M. Oppenheimer (2010), 'Linkages among climate change, crop yields and Mexico–US cross-border migration', *Proceedings of the National Academy of Sciences USA*, **107**(32), 14257–62.
Germenji, E. and J. Swinnen (2005), 'Human capital, market imperfections, poverty and

migration: evidence from Albania', Licos Discussion Papers, No. 175, Leuven: Centre for Institutions and Economic Performance.

Gibson, J. and D. McKenzie (2011), 'The microeconomic determinants of emigration and return migration of the best and brightest: evidence from the Pacific', *Journal of Development Economics*, **95**(1), 18–29.

Gibson, J., D. McKenzie and S. Stillman (2009), 'The impacts of international migration on remaining household members: omnibus results from a migration lottery program', World Bank Policy Research Working Paper No. 4956, Washington, DC: The World Bank.

Gibson, J., D. McKenzie and S. Stillman (2011), 'What happens to diet and child health when migration splits households? Evidence from a migration lottery program', *Food Policy*, **36**(February), 7–15.

Girma, Sourafel and Zhihao Yu (2002), 'The link between immigration and trade: evidence from the U.K.', *Weltwirtschaftliches Archiv*, **138**(1), 115–30.

Glewwe, Paul (2000), 'Human capital', in M. Grosh and P. Glewwe (eds), *Designing Household Survey Questionnaires for Developing Countries: Lessons from 15 Years of the Living Standards Measurement Study Volume 1*. Washington, DC: World Bank, pp. 143–76.

Hanson, G. (2007), 'Emigration, labor supply, and earnings in Mexico', in G. Borjas (ed.), *Mexican Immigration*, Chicago, IL: University of Chicago Press and the National Bureau of Economic Research, pp. 289–328.

Hanson, G.H. and C. Woodruff (2003), 'Emigration and educational attainment in Mexico', mimeo, San Diego, CA: University of California.

Hatzigeorgiou, Andreas (2010), 'Does immigration stimulate foreign trade? Evidence from Sweden', *Journal of Economic Integration*, **25**(2), 376–402.

Head, Keith and John Ries (1998), 'Immigration and trade creation: econometric evidence from Canada', *Canadian Journal of Economics*, 47–62.

Herander, Mark G. and Luz Saavedra (2005), 'Exports and the structure of immigrant-based networks: the role of geographic proximity', *Review of Economics and Statistics*, **87**(2), 323–35.

Hildebrandt, N. and D. McKenzie (2005), 'The effects of migration on child health in Mexico', *Economía*, Fall, 257–89.

Huang, W. (2005), *Methods to Extract Rare Events* (Degree of Doctor of Philosophy), Los Angeles, CA: University of California.

Hunter, L.M., W. Twine and A. Johnson (2011), 'Adult mortality and natural resource use in rural South Africa: evidence from the Agincourt Health and Demographic Surveillance Site', *Society of Natural Resources*, **24**, 256–75.

INSTAT (2002), Albania Living Standards Measurement Survey, www.worldbank.org/lsms.

INSTAT (2005), Albania Living Standards Measurement Survey, http://www.worldbank.org/lsms.

Javorcik, Beata, Çaglar Özden, Mariana Spatareanu and Cristina Neagu (2010), 'Migrant networks and foreign direct investment', *Journal of Development Economics*, **94**, 231–41.

Kanaiaupuni, S. and K. Donato (1999), 'Migradollars and mortality: the effects of migration on infant survival in Mexico', *Demography*, **36**(3), 339–53.

Kish, L. (1965), *Survey Sampling*, New York: John Wiley.

Kugler, Maurice and Hillel Rapoport (2005), 'Skilled emigration, business networks and foreign direct investment', CESifo Working Paper Series 1455, CESifo Group, Munich.

Lipton, M. (1980), 'Migration from rural areas of poor countries: the impact on rural productivity and income distribution', *World Development*, **8**, 1–24.

Lokshin, M., M. Bontch-Osmolovski and E. Glinskaya (2010), 'Work-related migration and poverty reduction in Nepal', *Review of Development Economics*, **14**(2), 323–32.

Macours, K. and R. Vakis (2010), 'Seasonal migration and early childhood development', *World Development*, **38**(6), 857–69.

Mansuri, G. (2006), 'Migration, school attainment and child labor: evidence from rural Pakistan', mimeo, Washington, DC: The World Bank.

Mattoo, A., I.C. Neagu and Ç. Özden (2008), 'Brain waste? Educated immigrants in the US labor market', *Journal of Development Economics*, **87**(2), 255–69.
Mayr, K. and G. Peri (2008), 'Return migration as channel of brain gain', CReAM Discussion Paper Series No. 0804, Centre for Research and Analysis of Migration (CReAM), Department of Economics, University College London.
McKenzie, D., J. Gibson and S. Stillman (2006), 'How important is selection? Experimental versus non-experimental measures of the income gains from migration', World Bank Policy Research Paper No. 3906, Washington, DC: The World Bank.
McKenzie, D. and J. Mistiaen (2009), 'Surveying migrant households: a comparison of census-based, snowball and intercept point surveys', *Journal of the Royal Statistical Society, Series A*, **172**(2), 339–60.
McKenzie, D. and H. Rapoport (2007), 'Network effects and the dynamics of migration and inequality: theory and evidence from Mexico', *Journal of Development Economics*, **84**(1), 1–24.
McLeman, Robert (2013), 'Developments in modelling of climate change-related migration', *Climatic Change*, **117**, 599–611.
Mendola, M. and C. Carletto (2012), 'International migration and gender differences in the home labour market: evidence from Albania', *Labour Economics*, **19**(6), 870–80.
Miluka, J., G. Carletto, B. Davis and A. Zezza (2010), 'The vanishing farms? The impact of international migration on family farming', *Journal of Development Studies*, **46**(1), 140–61.
Mishra, P. (2007), 'Emigration and wages in source countries: evidence from Mexico', *Journal of Development Economics*, **82**(1), 180–99.
Muñoz, J. (2007), 'Sampling: what you don't know can hurt you', presented at the Multi-topic Household Survey course, January, Washington, DC: World Bank.
Murrugarra, E. and C. Herrera (2011), 'Migration choices, inequality of opportunities, and poverty reduction in Nicaragua', in E. Murrugarra, J. Larrison and M. Sasin (eds), *Migration and Poverty: Toward Better Opportunities for the Poor*, Washington, DC: World Bank, pp. 101–24.
Nobles, J. (2007), 'Parental migration and child health in Mexico', Conference paper presented at the Population Association of America Meetings, New York, March 29–31.
OECD (2009), *International Migration Outlook*. Paris OECD.
Özden, Ç., C. Parsons, M. Schiff and T. Walmsley (2011), 'Where on earth is everybody? The evolution of global bilateral migration 1960–2000', *The World Bank Economic Review*, **25**(1), 12–56.
Özden, Çaglar and Mathis Wagner (2014), 'Immigrant versus natives? Displacement and job creation', World Bank Policy Research Working Paper 6900.
Parsons, Christopher R. (2012), 'Do migrants really foster trade? The trade–migration nexus, a panel approach 1960–2000', Policy Research Working Paper Series 6034, The World Bank.
Peri, Giovanni and Francisco Requena-Silvente (2010), 'The trade creation effect of immigrants: evidence from the remarkable case of Spain', *Canadian Journal of Economics*, **43**(4), 1433–59.
Rauch, James (1999), 'Networks versus markets in international trade', *Journal of International Economics*, **48**, 7–35.
Ravenstein, Ernst Georg (1885), 'The laws of migration', *Journal of the Statistical Society*, **46**, 167–235.
Ravenstein, Ernst Georg (1889), 'The laws of migration: second paper', *Journal of the Royal Statistical Society*, **52**, 241–305.
Redfern, P. (1989), 'Population registers: some administrative and statistical pros and cons', *Journal of the Royal Statistical Society*, Series A (153), 1–41.
Richter, S. and J.E. Taylor (2005), 'Policy reforms and the gender dynamics of rural Mexico-to-U.S. migration', Davis, CA: University of California at Davis.
Sasin, M. and D. McKenzie (2007), 'Migration, poverty and human capital', Migration Operational Vehicle Operation Note No. 1, Washington, DC: World Bank.
Schaffner, J.A. (2000), 'Employment', in M. Grosh and P. Glewwe (eds), *Designing Household Survey Questionnaires for Developing Countries: Lessons from 15 Years of*

the Living Standards Measurement Study Volume 1, Washington, DC: World Bank, pp. 217–50.
Stark, O.J., E. Taylor and S. Yitzhaki (1986), 'Remittances and inequality', *Economic Journal*, **101**, 1163–78.
Taylor, J.E. and J. Mora (2006), 'Does migration reshape expenditures in rural households? Evidence from Mexico', World Bank Policy Research Working Paper No. 3842.
United Nations High Commissioner for Refugees (2007), *Convention and Protocol Relating to the Status of Refugees*, Geneva: UNHCR.
United Nations Statistics Division (1998), *Recommendations on Statistics of International Migration Revision 1*, New York: United Nations.
Van der Geest, K., A. Vrieling and T. Dietz (2010), 'Migration and environment in Ghana: a cross-district analysis of human mobility and vegetation dynamics', *Environment and Urbanization*, **22**(1), 107–24.
Wagner, Don, Keith Head and John Ries (2002), 'Immigration and the trade of provinces', *Scottish Journal of Political Economy*, **49**(5), 507–25.
Yang, D. (2008), 'International migration, remittances and household investment: evidence from Philippine migrants' exchange rates shocks', *The Economic Journal*, **118**(April), 591–630.

3. The economic history of migration: the pre-World War One USA as lens

Robert A. Margo

1. INTRODUCTION

This is a chapter about the economic history of 'migration', a human activity that pre-dates recorded history by millennia. The subject is far too complex and vast for a shelf of books, let alone a single chapter. To make my task even marginally manageable I narrow the focus to the USA for the period before World War One.[1] This is (much) less narrow than it seems because most of the central issues – why people migrate, who migrates, voluntary versus forced (that is, slavery) population movement, migrant outcomes and policy regimes – have been the subject of long scholarly inquiry for the pre-World War One USA.

The chapter begins with a brief presentation of the standard economic theory of migration as posited by Sjaastad (1962). This is followed by a discussion of the early history of population movement to the USA just prior to the American Civil War, which includes the slave trade. The USA attracted Europeans from the start because the marginal product of labor was high and the rental price of land was low, relative to the principal sending countries of Europe. Slaves were brought to the New World for fundamentally the same reason, although the economic returns to migration obviously did not accrue to the slave. The population spread out from the eastern seaboard, where settlement initially occurred, across the landscape – the westward movement – a process that was facilitated in the nineteenth century by improvements in internal transportation. As I show, this movement, too, can be explained in terms of differences in the marginal product of labor – higher, generally, on the frontier regions of the western frontier than in settled areas of the east, prompting the westward direction of movement.

The so-called 'Age of Mass Migration' comes next, the discussion of which is framed around the important project by Timothy Hatton and Jeffrey G. Williamson (1994, 1998, 2005). In their project, Hatton and Williamson have collected a country-level panel data set documenting migrant flows from Europe that also includes average economic and other characteristics of sending and destination countries. Econometric analysis of these data provides the basis for a stylized description of population flows from the Old World to the New, which is helpful in explaining the timing of migration from particular countries. Immigration also had effects on factor prices, raising the ratio of wages to land rents in the sending countries but lowering the ratio in the sending countries, thereby promoting economic convergence.

A central question in the economic history of migration is how migrants fared in their new home. Social scientists have long framed this question in terms of 'assimilation' – if migrants fare worse than natives initially on arrival, do they eventually catch up? Cross-sectional evidence from the turn of the twentieth century suggests that the USA was, indeed, a 'melting pot' in this sense but it has long been known that cross-sectional evidence could be misleading because of return migration, which was very common (perhaps as many as one in four immigrants to the USA around the turn of the twentieth century eventually returned home). I summarize the results of the important ongoing project by Abramitzky et al. (2012; forthcoming), which follows immigrants over time using linked US census data. The linked data suggest that, on average, there was no assimilation; rather, what appears to be assimilation in the cross-section is that return migrants were 'negatively selected' – that is, the less successful returned home, while, on average, those who stayed permanently tended to do about as well as natives from the very start.

The final section touches briefly on two key issues of the twentieth century. The first is the imposition of quotas in the aftermath of World War One, which dramatically reduced the volume of migration to the USA for many decades until policy was liberalized in the mid-1960s. I also briefly examine the economics behind the 'Great Migration' of southern blacks from the region, linking a modern (and epic) voluntary movement to an initial regional imbalance that itself can be traced to the geographic consequences of an earlier forced migration – slavery – and the economic impact of the Civil War on the South. The chapter concludes with some brief discussion of post-1965 developments and a list of topics for further historical research.

2. THE ECONOMIC THEORY OF MIGRATION: A PRIMER ON THE SJAASTAD MODEL

Economic theory provides useful insights into why and when people move from one location to another.[2] Strictly speaking, the theory pertains to individuals, but, if the relevant factors are common to groups, 'mass' migration may ensue. That said, there are important interactions between individual and mass migration, for example, because the costs of migration are usually decreasing in the extent of previous migration or because large-scale migration can leave a significant footprint on factor prices – wages and land prices, in particular – in both the sending and receiving regions, promoting economic convergence across locations (see the discussion below).

The canonical paper in the economics of migration is Sjaastad (1962). In Sjaastad's model, migration is viewed as a kind of investment in human capital – the optimal matching of an individual and a location. Individuals choose to migrate if the benefits of doing so exceed the costs. These benefits and costs are both pecuniary – for example, higher incomes in the region of destination – and non-pecuniary – for example, the psychic costs of being physically distant from friends and relatives back home.

To make this somewhat more formal, I begin my exposition with a one-period version of the model. At the start of the period agents choose to remain in O or move to D, and then experience an economic outcome. Simplifying to the case of just two locations, if agent i remains in region O, let the outcome be $y_O + \varepsilon_{iO}$, whereas if she moves to region D, the outcome is $y_D + \varepsilon_{iD}$. In this setup, the ys can be viewed as average outcomes and the εs are random, idiosyncratic components such that $E(\varepsilon_{iO}) = E(\varepsilon_{iD}) = 0$. The cost of moving between the two locations is $C_D + \gamma_{iD}$, where C is the average cost and γ is the idiosyncratic component. It is optimal to move – 'invest' in migration – if the net economic benefits $NB(D,O)$ are positive:[3]

$$\text{Move from } O \text{ to } D \text{ if } NB(D,O) = y_D + \varepsilon_{iD} - (y_O + \varepsilon_{iO}) > C + \gamma_{iD}$$

Letting $M = 1$ if the individual moves and O if she stays, $\beta = \varepsilon_{iD} - \varepsilon_{iO} - \gamma_{iD}$ and $\Delta y = y_D - y_O$, the probability of migration can be rewritten:

$$P(M = 1) = P(\beta + (\Delta y - C) > 0)$$

Even in this simple form the model admits an embarrassing variety of behavior unless the covariance matrix of the idiosyncratic benefits and costs is (severely) restricted in particular ways. For example, even if $\Delta y - C$ is positive – on average, the net gains to migration are positive – an agent might not migrate because β might be sufficiently negative to offset the average net gains ($\Delta y - C$). Or, an agent might still migrate when the average net gains are negative ($\Delta y - C < 0$) because β is sufficiently positive.

The two possibilities just described may occur when the covariance of ε_D and ε_O is negative – that is, an agent whose idiosyncratic outcome component is positive in the region of origin ($\varepsilon_O > 0$) has a negative component in the region of destination ($\varepsilon_D < 0$). In these circumstances some high-'ability' individuals choose to stay in their region of origin, whereas those with low ability choose to migrate. In this case, migrants are said to be 'negatively selected'. Alternatively, imagine that agents with a high value of ε_O have below-average costs of migration – in this case, high-'ability' agents are more likely to migrate, or there is 'positive' selection. Lastly, imagine the case where $\varepsilon_D = \varepsilon_O$ and their covariances with respect to the idiosyncratic component of migration costs are zero. In this case, an individual will migrate as long as the average gains exceed their personal costs of migration. By definition, movers have lower costs than stayers, but there is no relationship between the idiosyncratic outcome components and idiosyncratic costs.

While complex in its predictions, the model makes two central points. First, movers must anticipate some type of personal economic gain net of the costs of moving. Other factors held constant, this is more likely if there are large differences on average in outcomes between the region of origin and the region of destination. Second, technological change that lowers the costs of migration for everyone will likely increase the rate of migration, especially for individuals whose personal gains to migration may be relatively low.

Although this simple, canonical form of the Sjaastad model is extremely useful in thinking about migration, there are caveats and extensions to keep in mind. The first caveat concerns general equilibrium effects. One type of general equilibrium effect concerns costs – there is considerable evidence that, on average, these costs are decreasing in the extent of prior migration because prior migrants establish networks or other types of assistance to ease the transition faced by new migrants in the region of destination. In addition, if the volume of migration flows is sufficiently large relative to the existing labor forces in the sending and receiving countries, there could be aggregate effects on wages and other factor prices, particularly factors in fixed supply, such as land. Specifically, wages will rise relative to the rental price of land in the region of origin but will decrease in the region of destination. The possibility that migration flows were historically large enough to create such general equilibrium effects motivates the important project by Hatton and Williamson later in the chapter.

Second, although usually cast in terms of economic outcomes, there is nothing inherently economic about the outcome '*y*' in the Sjaastad model. Indeed, some migrations could be explained overwhelmingly by individual or collective differences in consumption possibilities between locations – climate, culture, political institutions, the treatment of ethnic or other minorities – even if the economics *per se* are not favorable to moving.

Third, the single-period setting is very restrictive. In reality, migration is an economic action for which the payoffs are uncertain and these may not, in any event, occur for some time; the action can be delayed to just the 'right' period, or can be reversed (return migration). In the simplest multi-period extension with uncertainty there are now many *y*s (for each period) and many εs for each period; the current and past values of y_D, y_O, C and the εs are known at the start of each period, but ε_{iD} has yet to be realized, as have future values of the *y*s, C and εs. From a theoretical perspective, instead of choosing a single location once to maximize y net of migration costs, there is a now an intertemporal problem to solve in which the agent chooses an optimal sequence of locations. This could have, for example, the individual migrating in period zero to maximize the period over which returns could be realized, and staying in the region of destination for the rest of his life. Or the individual might choose to delay migration if current conditions do not seem so favorable – because in such a framework waiting may have option value. Or the agent might move at some point in the life cycle but then return to the region of origin at a later age. Historically, this last possibility of return migration was extremely common in the case of the USA – perhaps a quarter of those who migrated to the USA around the turn of the century eventually returned home – and failure to take it into account can fundamentally confound analyses of migrant outcomes (see the discussion later in the chapter).

Fourth, and very important, the Sjaastad model is written as is to account for *voluntary* migration. Historically, a significant fraction of the population movement to the New World represented the forced transportation of African slaves across the Atlantic. In such cases the various terms in the Sjaastad model need to be reinterpreted as benefits and costs accruing to whoever is compelling the migration – the slave owner – and to those facilitating the transactions – that is, individuals involved directly in the slave trade.

3. POPULATION FLOWS TO THE NEW WORLD, 1500–1860

In this section I sketch the history of population movement from Europe to the 'New World', chiefly that which later became the independent nation of the USA, from the early sixteenth century to just before the American Civil War. It is important to keep in mind that the modern concept of 'immigration' does not really apply to the portion of this period before the 1790s, at which juncture the USA became an independent nation free to set its own immigration policy. The modern notion of immigration presupposes that individuals move voluntarily between established nation states that, without exception, have policies regulating the official entry and exit of foreign nationals. Europeans who moved in, say, the early sixteenth century to the portion of North America that later became the USA were 'colonizing', not emigrating in the modern sense. For the most part, those who arrived somewhat later but before the American Revolution were moving from their domestic nation to one of its colonies. A significant portion of arrivals in North America consisted of African slaves, who were brought forcibly, not voluntarily.

Over the several centuries before 1500 Europeans slowly developed the technology of ocean transportation, eventually achieving the means to explore the oceans. In the case of the Americas, its 'discovery' by the Spanish late in the fifteenth century prompted (horrendous) exploitation of the native peoples in Latin America. In particular, the discovery of silver and gold fueled Spanish coffers at home and indirectly led to wage and price inflation in Europe. The other European nations skirmished with the Spanish and their bounty, hoping to find additional stores of precious metals elsewhere in the New World, but generally with little success. However, as Europeans were soon to realize, the New World offered riches far more extensive than gold and silver.

Eventually the British settled further up the Atlantic coast, first at Jamestown, Virginia and shortly after in Plymouth. Death rates were extremely high initially but the British persisted and a foothold was established. Meanwhile, the Dutch had colonized 'New Amsterdam' (approximately, modern New York City and its environs) in the 1620s, spreading into Long Island and the Hudson Valley. Late in the seventeenth century the British wrested control of New York from the Dutch and the area soon received English settlers. France concentrated its attention on Canada, the area around the Great Lakes, and portions of the Ohio and Mississippi valleys.

The New World had a high ratio of fertile land to labor, whereas the opposite was true in the Old World. Some Europeans who moved to the New World came with the expertise and capital to establish farms, but these could not be profitable without the labor to work the land. The requisite labor was typically youthful, but the cost of moving across the Atlantic was prohibitively high to finance the journey from savings. Hence was born the institution of 'indentured servitude' (Galenson, 1984; Grubb, 2011). An indentured servant agreed to work for a specific farmer in the New World for a period of time in exchange for transit, room and board, other consumption items (for example, clothing) and often training and so-called 'freedom dues' (a payment at the end of the indenture contract to give the servant an incentive not to run away). The intermediary between the servant and the farmer was a ship's captain, who transported servants from Europe and deposited them in the New World, where their contracts (with the captain) were sold to farmers.

For some time the market for indentures flourished. Highly competitive, the primary margin on which the market equilibrated was the length of indenture. Because the cost of passage was approximately the same for everyone, variation in the length of indenture primarily reflected variation across servants in their marginal product in the New World, or else the desirability (or opposite) of particular locations. Servants who were more productive – for example, those who had skills to begin with – had shorter periods of indenture, as did those going to the Caribbean, where mortality rates of Europeans were high.

By the late eighteenth century the market for indentures was in decline. The supply of servants was diminishing as the Industrial Revolution began to take hold in England and elsewhere in continental Europe, resulting in improved economic conditions in the sending region. The demand for servants also began to diminish, as the crop mix in Virginia and other southern colonies shifted towards crops for which African slave labor appeared to have a comparative advantage. Slave arrivals to the American colonies had to be bid away from the sugar plantations of the Caribbean, where slave labor was in high demand. Slave labor could be used (and was used) to produce many crops grown with free labor, but it was only in cotton, sugar, rice and tobacco where its use was sufficiently profitable for the labor to be imported to the USA.

Slavery was a dilemma for the USA, in which morality traded off with economics. Where slavery was profitable and economically viable, the morality gave way to the economics, but where slavery was either unprofitable or brought no special advantage over free labor, morality won the day (Fogel, 1989). Congress enacted legislation banning the slave trade in 1808, but this did nothing to stop the spread of slavery in the South, where the rate of natural increase was high (relative to other New World slave economies, especially the Caribbean). Slavery had been legal in the northern colonies during the British period and remained legal in some northern states into the early nineteenth century but, eventually, the existing population of slaves was emancipated and state legislatures abolished the institution in the North.

The era of true immigration to the USA in the modern sense, then, begins in the late eighteenth century. In 1790 the federal government passed the Act of March 26, 1790, which established the process of naturalization (citizenship) that, it is important to note, was limited to free whites. This was followed by further legislation in 1798 that gave the president authority to exclude any alien deemed 'undesirable' – that is, unworthy of entry into the USA. By these two acts the federal government asserted its fundamental authority over immigration policy, although afterwards states regularly (and to this day) attempted to enact their own restrictions. In 1819 the Steerage Act was passed, which required the reporting of official immigration statistics (the conventional historical time series dates from 1820).[4]

It is extremely important to recognize that the official US immigration statistics are just that. It is generally believed by economic historians that unofficial arrivals (many of these would have come overland from Canada) were substantial and thus the official statistics understate the true extent of the migration (McClelland and Zeckhauser, 1982). That said, it seems unlikely that correcting for the undercounting would vastly alter scholarly understanding of migration patterns, and thus most economic historians studying migration have relied to some extent on the official statistics (or on the US censuses, which from 1850 distinguish foreign from native born).

Figure 3.1 charts official immigration to the USA beginning in the 1820s. According to the official statistics, roughly 5 million immigrants arrived in the four decades before the Civil War.[5] In the 1830s the average number arriving per year was of the order of 55000, or roughly 4 per 1000 population. The number arriving jumped significantly in the late 1840s and early 1850s; many of these were fleeing political upheaval in Europe or famine in Ireland.[6] The peak year of antebellum immigration was 1854, when, according to the official statistics, 427833 arrived on

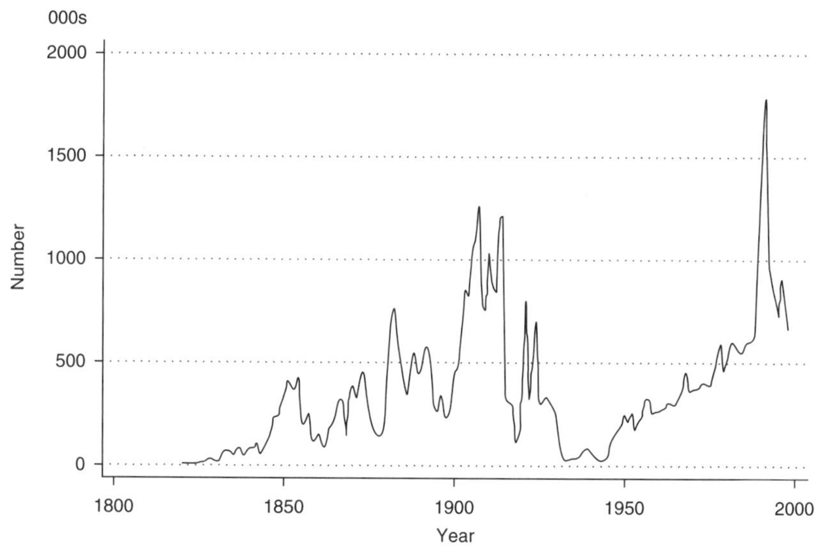

Source: Carter and Sutch (2006).

Figure 3.1 Official immigration to the USA, 1820–1998

America's shores. The pace then fell sharply in the five years leading up to the American Civil War; in 1860, just before the War began, the number arriving was 153 600.

For the typical immigrant, the USA was a welcoming environment in which to earn a living and accumulate wealth (Ferrie, 1994, 1997). On arrival many an immigrant took a job as an unskilled laborer, but fairly quickly a significant fraction of these regained the non-farm occupations that they had in Europe or else moved into farming. Upward mobility in this sense was more common in locations where economic growth was vibrant, and also seems to have been facilitated by literacy and internal migration (Ferrie, 1995, 1997).

Whether voluntary or forced, people arrived primarily on the eastern seaboard of North America. Particularly after the USA became a free nation and began acquiring land, through either purchase or conquest, there was a strong impetus for population to move away from the east coast. When the economy was primarily agricultural, as in the early nineteenth century, it was optimal for population to be spread relatively evenly and thinly across the landscape. Within agriculture a great deal of migration followed latitude, because of crop-specific investments in human capital. Thus, for example, planters who grew cotton in Georgia might move to Louisiana or to Texas, but were less likely to move to the upper South, where cotton could not be grown (Steckel, 1983).

The first great internal migration in US history, then, was from east to west. At the start of the nineteenth century, virtually the entire labor force (93 percent) was located in the Northeast and South Atlantic regions, mostly near the Atlantic Ocean. Population began to move west relatively early in the century, causing the eastern share of the labor force to decline steadily. On the eve of the Civil War, slightly less than half of the labor force was located in the Northeast and South Atlantic (Margo, 2000, table 5.1, p. 99).

The westward movement was not simply a migration of people, but also of capital. Midwestern land was naturally fertile, but needed to be improved to become productive in agriculture. These improvements were costly, accounting for a significant share of aggregate capital accumulation in the nineteenth century, especially before the Civil War (Gallman, 1986). After improvement, yields were high, but profitability depended on market access. Access improved dramatically with the 'transportation revolution' (Taylor, 1951). Initially the improvements came in water transportation – ports and related facilities on rivers and, especially, canals. These were followed by a more dramatic innovation – the development and diffusion of railroads. Improvements in internal transportation facilitated the westward movement of the labor force and capital, urbanization and also regional trade (Atack et al., 2010). The improved integration of product markets is evident in a sharp narrowing of regional differences in prices of goods like flour or wheat.

From an economic point of view the westward movement of population could be explained in terms of the Sjaastad model if the marginal product of labor were higher in the west than in the east. Initially, this seems like a puzzle because per capita incomes were lower in the Midwest than in the Northeast before the Civil War. However, there is a variety of reasons, some related to measurement issues, that can explain the income gradient.[7] Margo (1999, 2000) shows that real wages were higher in the Midwest than in the Northeast in the 1820s. As population moved internally across regions before the Civil War, the share of population by region and the region's real wage relative to the national average were negatively correlated, which is consistent with relative shifts in labor supply (that is, migration) dominating relative shifts in labor demand. The one exception was the South Atlantic region, which experienced a decrease in relative wages and in its share of the labor force, suggesting that the demand for labor was shifting away from this region.

Although the settlement of the west was largely incremental in the nineteenth century, in one important instance 'leapfrogging' – that is, bypassing large tracts of land – occurred. This was the California Gold Rush. The Rush began with the discovery of gold in January 1848 and was essentially over by the mid-1850s. The origins of California's settlement can be traced to the eighteenth century. The Spanish monarch Charles III sent the adventurer Jose de Galvez in order to encourage Spanish settlement into modern-day California. Galvez created the 'mission', a type of settlement-cum-fort whose purpose was to convert the indigenous population to Christianity, settle them into agriculture, and create a set of local economies interlinked with that of Spanish Mexico. The missions were unsuccessful in keeping California in Spanish hands. American fur traders arrived in Northern California around 1800, while Russia established a fort in 1812. Other Americans became Mexican citizens in exchange for land grants. Eventually conflicts between American settlers and the Spanish reached a boiling point in 1846, the start of the Mexican War. The War was over by February 1848 – ironically a treaty was signed two weeks after the discovery of gold – and in exchange for the end of hostilities, Mexico ceded California and the modern-day Southwest to the USA.

A model of the impact of the Gold Rush on the local labor market is presented in Margo (2000). The model is inspired by similar frameworks developed to analyze so-called 'Dutch disease' – that is, the impact of the discovery of a natural resource on a small, open economy. The model's predictions are straightforward. The discovery of gold increases the demand for labor in California, causing nominal wages to rise. Because, among other reasons, gold has value in exchange, the local cost of living will also rise, but under reasonable conditions real wages will rise in the short run. In response to the rise in real wages, labor will migrate to California. If the Gold Rush is a transitory shock – that is, the effect of local labor demand is gone once all of the gold is 'discovered' – labor will return home and wages will return to their pre-Gold Rush equilibrium. Using archival data, Margo (2000) provides nominal, price-deflator and real-wage indices (for three occupations, common labor, skilled artisans and clerks) for California from 1847 to 1860. The data largely confirm the model's predictions. Nominal wages increased sharply in the aftermath of the discovery, followed by prices, but the increase in wages was greater than in prices, so real wages rose. Labor migrated in, and nominal and real wages fell. When the Rush had ended by the mid-1850s, however, wages had not returned to their pre-Rush level, but were much higher – in real terms, about equal in California to the rest of the northern USA. Since there is good evidence that initially wages were much lower in California, the implication is that the Gold Rush, although transitory, left a permanent imprint on California's settlement. In fact, once settlers arrived in the Golden State it was clear that there were many reasons to stay there rather than return back east. In other words, the discovery of gold arguably speeded up the process of settlement of the far western portion of the USA.

4. THE AGE OF MASS MIGRATION: MIGRATION TO THE UNITED STATES AFTER THE AMERICAN CIVIL WAR

In the aftermath of the Civil War (1861–65) annual immigration to the USA increased significantly (see Figure 3.1).[8] The expansion can be explained in part by dramatic reductions in transatlantic transportation costs; in particular, the development of steamships capable of international travel after 1870 greatly lowered the costs of long-distance migration, and prospective migrants responded accordingly. Aggregate flows from Europe increased, and Latin America in particular attracted a far greater share of immigrants than had been the case earlier in the century. That said, the USA remained the favored destination – 69 percent of international migrants moved to the USA between 1871 and 1914 (computed from Cohn, 2013, table 23.1, p. 265).

Although the long-run trend in immigrant arrivals to the USA was strongly upward, annual and decadal variations were sizable. Some of these variations can be attributed to business cycles in the USA and Europe. When economic conditions were especially favorable in the USA relative to sending countries, more migrants came, *ceteris paribus*; when there was an economic downturn in the USA compared with elsewhere, migration flows slowed. Harvest failures (the Irish potato famine is an infamous example), political upheaval and similar shocks in the sending countries also affected the rate of outmigration.

More generally, the variation over time reflects the entry and exit of different countries of origin into the transatlantic labor market. Some European countries 'exported' people to the USA from the very beginning, while other countries, such as Italy, entered the market much later in the game. Mexico figured little in migration to the USA until well after World War Two, even though proximity obviously favored such migration compared with Europe. Moreover, the nineteenth-century experience suggests that there was a country life cycle to migration. Huge numbers of Italians left their native land for the New World in the late nineteenth and early twentieth centuries, but no longer do so.

The dramatic variation over time in migrant flows from specific countries of origin is at the heart of the important project on the economic history of international migration by Timothy Hatton and Jeffrey Williamson (1994, 1998, 2005). In conjunction with others, Hatton and Williamson collected a panel data set for European countries documenting total outflows, destination countries, and sending-country characteristics both in levels and relative to receiving countries (for example, the real wage in Belgium relative to the USA in 1850). Hatton and Williamson use the data to econometrically analyze the determinants of migration rates for 44 countries over the period 1860 to 1914 (Hatton and Williamson, 1998, p. 39; 2005, p. 65).

There are four key findings from Hatton and Williamson's analysis. First, the outmigration rate is a negative function of the sending country's real wage relative to the real wage of the destination country; other factors held constant, a country will export more people if its real wage is generally low, and relatively more to those countries whose real wages are high compared with the level in the sending country. Over the time period in question, real wages in the USA were not only far higher than in Europe; they were far higher in the USA than in other destinations (controlling for distance), so the fact that, once the decision was made to leave, most migrants went to the USA is unsurprising on purely economic grounds.[9]

Second, the rate of outmigration is a positive function of the rate of natural increase – countries in which the birth rate substantially exceeds the death rate generated more migrants. The implication is that migration was connected to the demographic transition – during the initial phase of such a transition, the rate of natural increase would rise (because of either a fall in the death rate or a rise in the birth rate). This transition began in many European countries in the second half of the nineteenth century, providing further impetus to the movement from the Old to the New World.

Third, migration responds positively to the stock of previous migrants – the greater the extent of past migration, the higher the current migration rate. The usual interpretation of this result is that previous migrants, by providing information and other resources, ease the transition of new migrants into the receiving economy. Fourth, the migration rate is serially correlated – that is, a higher migration rate in the recent past leads to a higher migration rate in the present.

From these patterns, Hatton and Williamson deduce a stylized life cycle of migration at the country level. As noted above, real wages in Europe were, on average, much lower than in the USA, but by itself this would not necessarily be enough of an incentive for people to move, as the Sjaastad model makes clear. A transitory phenomenon – a shock in the sending country or unusually favorable conditions in the USA – gets the migration process under way. As it begins, the process starts to feed back on itself, due to the serial correlation in migration and as the stock of former migrants builds up. If the country is undergoing a demographic transition at the same time – and, as noted, many European countries did so in the late nineteenth century – this too will propel further migration.

As migrants left Europe, their actions prompted economic convergence between the Old and New worlds. In any given year new migrants were but a tiny fraction of the aggregate labor force in the USA, but they were a quantitatively more significant part of labor force growth. Migrant departures from Europe, however, often represented a substantial fraction of the existing labor force. Migrant arrivals increased the aggregate supply of labor in the USA, while departures reduced aggregate labor supply in Europe. *Ceteris paribus*, the increase in labor supply in the USA would have reduced wages there; however, most economic historians believe these negative wage effects were fairly small, except perhaps in the late 1840s and early 1850s in the Northeast (where most immigrants at the time arrived) and in the early twentieth century (Williamson, 1974; Goldin, 1994; Hatton and Williamson, 1998; Carter and Sutch, 1999; Margo, 2000). In the Old World, we would predict that the labor supply shifts would reduce wages, and here the effects seem to have been much larger. By the nineteenth century aggregate capital flows were (fairly) elastic across countries, so one would not anticipate much of a medium- or long-run effect on interest rates. But land was (relatively) fixed in supply, and there is some evidence that the migration flows raised land rents in the

New World and lowered rents in the Old World (Hatton and Williamson, 1998).

As every economic historian knows, the Industrial Revolution began in England but by the second half of the nineteenth century industrialization was well under way elsewhere in Europe. As industrialization took hold, labor productivity and real wages in Europe increased. Thus, through a combination of the general equilibrium effects of international migration and modern economic growth, the incentives for outmigration were reduced. That said, it is almost certainly the case that, had migration not been largely cut off during World War One and then slowed appreciably afterwards by the imposition of quotas in the USA (see below), many more Europeans would have migrated during the first three decades or so of the twentieth century.

Hatton and Williamson's project analyzes migration at the macroeconomic level. As the Sjaastad model suggests, however, it is not likely that migrants would be a random sample of the population of their home countries. It is relatively straightforward to examine the characteristics of migrants to the USA because the various population censuses indicate place of birth (and some indicate year of arrival), allowing immigrants to be identified and their personal characteristics measured.

Before World War One, the foreign born in the USA were disproportionately males, mostly in prime working ages (15–44) and often single (although families and young couples also migrated in large numbers to the USA). Around the turn of the twentieth century the proportion of single males reached an historic peak; it is thought that, for many of these immigrants, the move to the USA was temporary, and the costs of returning home were relatively low due to steamship travel (Nugent, 1992).

Perhaps the most important characteristic, however, concerns skill. It is often casually assumed that migration is 'positively selected' – that is, skilled, educated workers are more likely to migrate long distances than the less skilled and less educated but, in fact, as the previous discussion of the Sjaastad model indicates, the economics are far more complex. Occupation data, albeit incomplete, suggest that in the early nineteenth century migrants to the USA were relatively skilled, but the mix shifted towards lower-skilled workers in the two decades before the Civil War. The skill mix appears to have been stable until late in the nineteenth century, when it again shifted even further towards the unskilled (Cohn, 2013).

A central question in the economic history of the USA, as well as the economic history of immigration, is how immigrants fared in the American labor market. There is a vast social science literature examining immigrant 'assimilation'. The basic idea is to compare outcomes for immigrants and the native born. Suppose, for example, that one finds, at a point in time, that recently arrived immigrants fare worse than the native born, but the longer an immigrant has been in the country, the narrower the gap in economic outcomes between foreign and native born. Such a pattern suggests the USA was a 'melting pot' – although immigrants typically started behind the native born, their economic outcomes eventually converged.

A serious problem, however, with examining assimilation at a point in time is the failure to distinguish among cohort, selection and true assimilation effects. Cohort effects refer to differences in the characteristics of new immigrants relative to previous arrivals. As noted above, immigrants who arrived in the USA around the turn of the twentieth century were less skilled than previous cohorts. Failure to control for cohort will tend to bias downward the assimilation effect (Hatton and Williamson, 1998).

Selection refers to unmeasured attributes of the migrant – recall the discussion of the Sjaastad model – and, most importantly, expected length of stay in the USA; and how unmeasured attributes and length of stay are correlated. Suppose, for example, that migrants who are less skilled in their unmeasured attributes are more likely to return to their home countries. This will bias upward the assimilation effect, even if it is measured from repeated cross-sections. The true assimilation effect, then, is the treatment effect of the US labor market conditional on remaining in the USA, controlling for the impact of unmeasured attributes on the probability of staying.

The recent and ongoing project by Ran Abramitzky, Leah Boustan and Katherine Eriksson (ABE, 2012; forthcoming) goes a long way towards resolving these issues. ABE begin with a sample of individuals from the 1900 US census of population. The next step is the important one – they link their sample to subsequent censuses. Thus they are able to observe what happens to migrants after they arrive and also observe how long they stay in the USA.

The base ABE sample consists of males who were 18–35 years of age in 1900. Immigrants in this sample are restricted to those who arrived between 1880 and 1900, excluding African Americans and native-born southern whites. For the large sending countries ABE draw a random sample of immigrants from the 5 percent IPUMS sample of the 1900 census, but for smaller sending countries they compile the full count of immigrants, based on the complete schedules archived at www.ancestry.com. Next, they search for individuals in the base sample in 1910 and 1920 using an iterative matching strategy developed by Ferrie (1996). Linkage to 1910 and 1920 from 1900 is done separately and the final data set is restricted to individuals found in all three censuses (1900, 1910 and 1920).

Because the pre-1940 US censuses did not collect information on income, ABE rely on occupational status instead. They construct their own measure using estimates of average earnings by occupation from a Bureau of Labor Statistics cost of living survey in 1900. This survey did not measure farm incomes, which is obviously a major problem for the turn-of-the-twentieth-century USA (the farm labor force was approximately 35 percent of the total), so ABE develop a protocol for assigning farm incomes based on contemporary data on farm revenues and costs.

ABE begin by comparing the mean occupation scores of native- and foreign-born men in the cross-section versus panel samples in 1920. They re-weight the panel to reflect the distribution of country of origins in the 1920 US population, finding that immigrants slightly out-earned natives. ABE infer selection effects indirectly by comparing occupational upgrading patterns in the repeated cross-section versus the panel; any difference between the two must be due to selective attrition from the cross-section, which, given the age restrictions, is mostly due to selective return migration. The main specification divides the foreign born into two cohorts – those arriving before 1890 and those arriving after. ABE see more assimilation in the cross-section than in the panel, implying that return migrants came from those whose outcomes in the USA were below average. The negative selection among return migrants is so large that in the panel data not only is there no evidence of assimilation on average, but there is no initial occupation–income gap in favor of the native born. That is, among immigrants who moved to the USA in the late nineteenth century and, essentially, stayed for their entire working lives, occupational status never differed on average with the native born.

ABE conduct a number of sensitivity analyses. For example, omitting county-of-origin fixed effects from the earnings regressions reveals that permanent migrants actually outperform natives. Their results are not sensitive substantively to a more finely articulated set of arrival cohorts or to using the IPUMS occupation scores.

Up to this point ABE's analysis has focused on the average immigrant. However, it could well be that there were differences in selectivity across countries. In fact, when they analyze the data by sending country, they do find heterogeneity in selectivity. For example, in the case of Norway, return migration was negatively selected, but it appears to have been positively selected in the case of Sweden. In the case of Norway, return migration was so heavy that the Norwegian government added a supplement on return migration in the 1910 census. ABE show that such return migrants held lower-paying jobs than Norwegians who remained in the USA, suggesting that the negative selection was present from the very beginning.

5. CLOSING THE DOOR

The rise of the nation state preceded modern economic growth, but industrialization hastened and solidified the process. As nation states emerged, a key policy issue was the distinction between insiders – 'citizens' – and outsiders – 'aliens'. With citizenship came privileges – access to nation-specific public goods, income transfers, voting in the case of democracies – as well as responsibilities and costs – paying taxes, military service. In the case of the USA, citizenship could be conferred by birth or by following a 'naturalization' process. Because modern economic growth was, and is, an uneven process, it creates incentives for migration, as the Sjaastad model makes clear. As national economies grow and change, however, the benefits and costs of placing restrictions on gaining access – whether for a brief period of time, such as a tourist, or for a longer period of time, as an immigrant – will vary. Interest groups emerge in the political debate over immigration policy because there may be general equilibrium consequences to immigration, as was observed earlier in the chapter.

It is sometimes believed that until the imposition of immigration quotas just after World War One, immigration to the USA was essentially 'free' – that is, there were no restrictions of consequence. This is incorrect in general, and, strictly speaking, incorrect even for the group – effectively, the white population of European ancestry – that was favored from the beginning. However, it is true that favored-group restrictions on immigration before the imposition of quotas were relatively mild. As it evolved over time, US immigration policy became increasingly – and extremely – complex. At its core the policy is a federal responsibility, but state and local governments can, and do, exercise some discretion by enacting legislation that discouraged (or attracted) specific immigrant groups.

As noted earlier, the first key piece of immigration legislation was passed in 1790. This legislation did not provide for restrictions on immigration *per se*, but limited naturalization to white immigrants. This restriction remained in place until 1870, when naturalization was made available to African aliens and persons of African descent. In the late nineteenth century, policies turned more restrictive. In 1882, the importation of Chinese laborers was banned for ten years, and Asian immigrants were excluded from the naturalization process. Another act passed in 1882 expanded the list of 'inadmissible' aliens to those thought likely to become a burden on the public purse, or the mentally disabled, and also for the first time imposed a head tax on immigrants. Legislation passed in 1887 restricted real-estate ownership in the USA to citizens and to those who had formally declared their intention to become naturalized.

The pace of legislation quickened after the turn of the twentieth century. The Naturalization Act of 1906 made knowledge of English a requirement. The Immigration Act of 1907 was the first to codify the legal distinction between immigrants and non-immigrants, expanded the list of excludable aliens, and raised the entry tax. At the outbreak of hostilities in World War One, foreign males flooded US shores to avoid military service in Europe, but soon the War caused migration to slow to a trickle. In 1917, while the War was still raging, Congress passed further restrictive legislation, barring illiterates from entry and placed further limitations on Asian immigrants.

Then, in the aftermath of World War One, Congress passed the first set of quantitative restrictions in the Quota Law of 1921. The most important provision of the law limited the number of immigrants from any particular nation to no more than 3 percent of those already living in the USA in 1910. This was followed by the National Origins Act of 1924, which radically transformed the entire system by setting quotas based on national origins and which remained the key law until 1952. In 1965, Congress passed the Immigration and Nationality Act, which eliminated quotas based on national origins but which set limits on overall numbers from the eastern and western hemispheres and a maximum (20 000) per year from any country. The law provided for entry preferences based on occupational skills, relatives of US citizens and permanent resident aliens.[10]

As can be seen in Figure 3.1, the effect of the 1920s restrictions was a dramatic falling-off of immigration numbers relative to the turn of the twentieth century, and these remained absolutely low until after the reforms of the 1960s, when the numbers increased. Why did the USA 'close the door' shortly after World War One? A recent paper by Claudia Goldin (1994) provides an insightful and detailed answer. Goldin begins her analysis by noting that immigration restrictions could have been passed as early as 1890 in the form of a literacy test, but the literacy test, as noted above, was not passed until 1917. In fact, the literacy test was less restrictive than it seems at first glance, because, as Goldin notes, literacy was on the rise in Europe at the time. The key point, however, is that a majority in Congress was in favor of the legislation but not enough to override a presidential veto. Presidents at the time were in favor overall of not imposing onerous restrictions because naturalized citizens were swelling the population of voters.

As Goldin shows, there were numerous votes to impose a literacy test before 1917, but none had majorities sufficient to override. Goldin examines econometrically the vote to override Wilson's veto of legislation passed in 1915, using city-level data. She shows that the vote to override was more likely if the city experienced weak wage growth from 1907 to 1915, which politicians could attribute to the negative effects of immigration on local wages. Eventually, as noted above, the votes to pass the literacy test were present in 1917; anti-immigrant sentiment in the wake of World War One did the rest.

At the turn of the twentieth century approximately 90 percent of African Americans lived in the South, where the per capita income was half of the national average. The South–non-South difference in per capita income strongly favored a redistribution of black (and white) labor from the South to the rest of the nation. Initially, the outmigration was slow, and tended to be selective – better-educated blacks were more likely to leave the South than their less-educated counterparts (Margo, 1990). However, when European immigration to the northern USA largely ceased with the onset of World War One, and then remained low after the imposition of quotas discussed above, northern employers sought a new labor supply – and found it in Southern blacks (Collins, 1997). Migration flows picked up in the 1920s, only to be slowed substantially during the Great Depression. The black migration resumed with World War Two. Eventually the migration slowed in the 1960s as wages and employment conditions in the South improved.

The vast majority of black migrants settled in cities. As new migrants arrived, distinct black neighborhoods emerged and residential segregation increased. For a time the migration paid large economic dividends in the form of higher real wages. However, many of the cities that received large influxes of black migration, especially in the industrial Midwest (for example, Detroit), experienced economic decline in the 1970s and beyond. In recent decades blacks have returned to the South, where economic growth has been more robust.

6. CONCLUDING REMARKS

The economic history of immigration is a complex and vast topic, perhaps as complex and vast as modern economic growth itself. In this brief chapter I have surveyed some of the major issues involved in the study of immigration's economic history, viewed through the lens of the American experience to the end of the 'long nineteenth century' (that is, World War One). This lens, while narrow, is useful because the central issues – why people move, what happens to them after they arrive at their destination, who moves, and how immigration is shaped by public policy – have been central to the economic history of the USA and hence the subject of much study.

The USA was a 'nation of immigrants' during its crucial growth phase of the nineteenth century because its economy offered, on average, a much higher real income than did the economies of Europe at the time. The American economy absorbed immigrants and, as more came, the population moved from east, where most had arrived, to the western frontier. Until somewhat later, immigration had relatively limited effects on factor prices in the New World, but helped to raise wages back in Europe, thereby promoting economic convergence.

By the early twentieth century the period of mostly unrestricted immigration to the USA was drawing to an end, and the USA closed the door in the early 1920s. For the next three decades or so, immigration to the USA remained low, but, driven in part by the displacement and refugees created by World War Two, among other factors, pressure began to build for a relaxation of policies. This relaxation began in the 1950s, culminating in a major change in policy in the mid-1960s, which 'opened the door' for larger legal immigrant flows, most of which have come from Asia rather than the traditional European sources. The USA also became a magnet for illegal immigrants, primarily from Latin America. These flows demonstrate that, at a very basic level, the economic forces that compelled millions of Europeans to move to the USA in centuries past have not fully played out, even as the source countries have changed dramatically.

ACKNOWLEDGMENT

Comments from the editor are gratefully acknowledged.

NOTES

1. My recounting of the history stops around World War One because shortly after this the USA imposed its first set of immigrant quotas ('closing the door'), which remained in effect until liberalized in the mid-1960s.
2. The leading modern scholar of the economics of immigration is George Borjas. The economic issues briefly touched on in this section receive much more thorough treatment in Borjas's research articles, of which there are far too many to list here. A convenient place to start is Borjas (1999).
3. If there are multiple-destination locations to choose from, the agent solves the problem arg max $\{NB\,(j,O)\}$ where j indexes all possible locations – that is, chooses the location with the maximum net benefits to migration.
4. A convenient compilation of official immigration statistics, along with an excellent overview of US immigration history, is Barde et al. (2006).
5. See Ferrie (1999) and Cohn (2009) for excellent, general accounts of antebellum immigration to the USA.

6. Between 1847 and 1854 average annual arrivals were approximately 335 000, or 14 per 1000 population; see Cohn (2013, table 23.2).
7. It is important to note that between 1860 and 1880 there was a dramatic increase in per capita incomes in the Midwest relative to the rest of the USA, consistent with the hypothesis that some of the pre-Civil War migration to the region was promoted by the possibility of long-term economic gains, which, in fact, were realized on average; see Margo (1999, 2000).
8. Between 1865 and 1873, average annual arrivals were approximately 328 000, or 8.4 per 1000 population. As noted in the text, there was significant variation in immigrant rates. For example, from 1881 to 1893, annual arrivals were approximately 525 000, or 8.9 per 1000 population; from 1894 to 1899, arrivals were 277 000 per year on average, or 3.9 per 1000 population; see Cohn (2013, table 23.2).
9. It is also worth noting that, during the peak of the Age of Mass Migration, most European migrants went to the northern USA, not the south. Again, this is not surprising on economic grounds because wages were far lower in the south than in the non-south *ca* 1900 (see Margo, 2004): a prospective migrant from Italy would not have realized much in the way of economic gains by moving to Alabama, as opposed to New York.
10. Because of the family reunification preference and also because the USA has at various points admitted refugees from the Caribbean (Cuba, Haiti) and Southeast Asia (Vietnam), the quotas have not been binding in a strict sense in recent decades, although they obviously still shape the volume of legal immigration; see Cohn (2013, p. 269). Although official immigration has increased substantially since the 1965 Act, as a percentage of the resident population, immigration rates in recent years have generally been below the rates observed during the Age of Mass Migration; see Barde et al. (2006, p. 524).

REFERENCES

Abramitzky, Ran, Leah Boustan and Katherine Eriksson (2012), 'Europe's tired, poor, huddled masses: self-selection and economic outcomes in the Age of Mass Migration', *American Economic Review*, **102** (5), 1832–56.

Abramitzky, Ran, Leah Boustan and Katherine Eriksson (forthcoming), 'A nation of immigrants: assimilation and economic outcomes in the Age of Mass Migration', *Journal of Political Economy*.

Atack, Jeremy, Fred Bateman, Michael Haines and Robert A. Margo (2010), 'Did railroads induce or follow economic growth? Urbanization and population growth in the American Midwest, 1850–1860', *Social Science History*, **34** (2), 171–97.

Barde, Robert, Susan B. Carter and Richard Sutch (2006), 'International migration', in Susan B. Carter, S.S. Gartner, Michael R. Haines, Alan L. Olmstead, Richard Sutch and Gavin Wright (eds), *Historical Statistics of the United States: Earliest Times to the Present – Millennial Edition, Volume 1: Population*, New York: Cambridge University Press, pp. 527–652.

Borjas, George (1999), 'The economic analysis of immigration', in Orley Ashenfelter and David Card (eds), *Handbook of Labor Economics, Volume 3A*, Amsterdam, The Netherlands: North-Holland, pp. 1697–760.

Carter, Susan B. and Richard Sutch (1999), 'Historical perspectives on the economic consequences of immigration into the United States', in C. Hischman, P. Kasinitz and J. DeWind (eds), *The Handbook of International Migration: The American Experience*, New York: Russell Sage Foundation, pp. 319–41.

Carter, Susan and Richard Sutch (2006), 'Table Ad1-2: U.S. Immigrants and Emigrants, 1820–1998', in Susan B. Carter, S. S. Gartner, Michael R. Haines, Alan L. Olmstead, Richard Sutch and Gavin Wright (eds), *Historical Statistics of the United States: Earliest*

Times to the Present – Millennial Edition, Volume 1: Population, New York: Cambridge University Press, pp. 541–2.
Cohn, Raymond L. (2009), *Mass Migration under Sail: European Immigration to the Antebellum United States*, New York: Cambridge University Press.
Cohn, Raymond L. (2013), 'The economic history of immigration', in Robert Whaples and Randall E. Parker (eds), *Routledge Handbook of Modern Economic History*, New York: Routledge, pp. 265–76.
Collins, William J. (1997), 'When the tide turned: immigration and the delay of the Great Black Migration', *Journal of Economic History*, **57** (3), 607–32.
Ferrie, Joseph P. (1994), 'The wealth accumulation of antebellum European immigrants to the U.S., 1840–1860', *Journal of Economic History*, **54** (1), 1–33.
Ferrie, Joseph P. (1995), 'Up and out or down and out? The occupational mobility of immigrant non-persisters in the nineteenth century U.S.', *Journal of Interdisciplinary History*, **26** (3), 33–55.
Ferrie, Joseph P. (1996), 'A new sample of Americans linked from the 1850 Public Use Micro Sample of the Federal Census of Population to the 1860 Federal Census Manuscript Schedules', *Historical Methods*, **29** (4), 141–56.
Ferrie, Joseph P. (1997), 'The entry into the US labor market of antebellum European immigrants, 1840–1860', *Explorations in Economic History*, **29** (3), 295–330.
Ferrie, Joseph P. (1999), *Yankees Now: Immigrants in the Antebellum United States, 1840–1860*, New York: Oxford University Press.
Fogel, Robert W. (1989), *Without Consent or Contract: The Rise and Fall of American Slavery*, New York: W.W. Norton.
Galenson, David (1984), *White Servitude in Colonial America: An Economic Analysis*, New York: Cambridge University Press.
Gallman, Robert E. (1986), 'The United States capital stock in the nineteenth century', in Stanley L. Engerman and Robert E. Gallman (eds), *Long-Term Factors in American Economic Growth*, Chicago, IL: University of Chicago Press, pp. 165–214.
Goldin, Claudia (1994), 'The political economy of immigration restriction in the United States, 1890 to 1921', in Claudia Goldin and Gary D. Libecap (eds), *The Regulated Economy: A Historical Approach to Political Economy*, Chicago, IL: University of Chicago Press, pp. 223–58.
Grubb, Farley (2011), *German Immigration and Servitude in America, 1790–1920*, New York: Routledge.
Hatton, Timothy and Jeffrey G. Williamson (eds) (1994), *Migration and the International Labor Market, 1850–1939*, New York and London: Routledge.
Hatton, Timothy and Jeffrey G. Williamson (1998), *The Age of Mass Migration: Causes and Consequences*, New York: Oxford University Press.
Hatton, Timothy and Jeffrey G. Williamson (2005), *Global Migration and the World Economy*, Cambridge, MA: MIT Press.
Margo, Robert A. (1990), *Race and Schooling in the South, 1880–1950: An Economic History*, Chicago, IL: University of Chicago Press.
Margo, Robert A. (1999), 'Regional wage gaps and the settlement of the Midwest', *Explorations in Economic History*, **36** (1), 128–43.
Margo, Robert A. (2000), *Wages and Labor Markets in the United States, 1820–1860*, Chicago, IL: University of Chicago Press.
Margo, Robert A. (2004), 'The North–South wage gap, before and after the Civil War', in David Eltis, Frank Lewis and Kenneth Sokoloff (eds), *Slavery in the Development of the Americas*, New York: Cambridge University Press, pp. 324–51.
McClelland, Peter and Richard Zeckhauser (1982), *Demographic Dimensions of the New Republic: American Inter-regional Migration, Vital Statistics, and Manumissions, 1800–1860*, New York: Cambridge University Press.
Nugent, Walter (1992), *Crossings: The Great Transatlantic Migrations, 1870–1914*, Bloomington, IN: Indiana University Press.
Sjaastad, Larry (1962), 'The costs and returns of human migration', *Journal of Political Economy*, **70** (5), 80–93.

Steckel, Richard (1983), 'The economic foundations of East–West migration', *Explorations in Economic History*, **20** (1), 14–36.
Taylor, George Rogers (1951), *The Transportation Revolution, 1815–1860*, New York: M.E. Sharpe.
Williamson, Jeffrey G. (1974), 'Migration to the New World: long-term influences and impact', *Explorations in Economic History*, **11** (3), 357–89.

4. International migration, trade and aid: a survey

Christopher R. Parsons and L. Alan Winters

International trade, foreign aid and international migration are all key facets of globalization, which are therefore probably interconnected. Among these three elements we can identify three separate dyads and therefore delineate six unidirectional pairwise links. Those between trade and aid do not belong in a book on migration, but one might expect this chapter to discuss the remaining four. In fact, we focus on the links running from migration to trade and from aid to migration. This choice is governed by the almost complete absence of literature of any note on the remaining two.

Simmering beneath the surface of these literatures is the issue of causation. Changes in all three phenomena are connected by the general equilibrium adjustment of the economy to shocks. Thus a trade shock may affect the returns to factors of production, which in turn change the incentives for migration, but equally, a migrant inflow will influence the baskets of goods produced and consumed, and thereby affect trade. Similarly, an aid flow may increase emigration by raising incomes in the recipient country, thereby allowing greater numbers of people to more easily afford the costs of migration; but additionally, a flow of migrants may affect average incomes (in either the sending or receiving country), which in turn may alter a donor's willingness to grant aid. Perhaps even more challenging, the three phenomena also share many determinants, including, for example, shared culture, geographical proximity or a common (colonial) history. Pinning down causation in this melee is bound to be difficult, and so the economics profession has devoted nearly all its effort to examining those links, which are both easier to identify and most pressing in terms of policy concerns.

There is probably no significant international migration flow around the world that fails to arouse some opposition, and so if one could show that migration led to an increase in something that was almost universally held to be a 'good thing' – for example, international trade – one could start to address that opposition. This, implicitly and sometimes explicitly, is the thrust of the majority of the studies linking migration and trade. A similar motive drives the migration and aid literature, since if aid were to be shown to reduce migration voluntarily, would that not represent an attractive outcome for (at least some) policy makers? In the same vein, trade liberalization is often touted for similar reasons, for example, that increases in income reduce emigration from developing countries. To our knowledge, however, the academic community has failed to produce convincing evidence that establishes a direct causal link from trade to migration.

This chapter first considers trade and migration. We start by identifying three seminal pieces of scholarship that have shaped the research agenda – one exploring the general equilibrium connections between them and suggesting that, at least under certain conditions, trade and migration might be substitutes, and two that address the ways in which migrants may directly reduce the costs and/or increase the benefits of international trade and so render them complements. From this base we discuss the methods and results of two decades of empirical research that has explored the connection with increasing sophistication. As hinted above, the major challenge is one of identification – proving causation – and we organize the literature around various approaches to meeting this challenge. It is a story of considerable variety and ingenuity, and while no single exercise addresses all statistical concerns concurrently, the very fact that so many different approaches seem to show migration bolstering levels of international trade is, in the end, fairly persuasive.[1]

Section 2 of the chapter examines the aid–migration connection. It begins by illustrating the extent of policy makers' yearning to hear that aid and trade liberalization will reduce the pressure for emigration from developing to developed countries. It suggests reasons why this is probably not true in principle and why, even if it were, the magnitude of any such effect would be likely to be vanishingly small. We then survey the main studies relating migration directly to aid flows, and show that overwhelmingly they conclude that, if anything, aid boosts migration. Finally, we briefly consider the history of the European policy of co-development that attempts to place aid in a coherent policy framework, with the aim of reducing the pressure of migration to Europe. *Prima facie*, it has not been a success.

1. INTERNATIONAL TRADE AND MIGRATION

Three Classic Papers

This section discusses three seminal pieces of scholarship that constitute the foundations of modern research on the link between international trade and migration. First, we introduce the classic statement of the connection between international trade and international migration from Robert Mundell (1957). He observes that, under precisely specified conditions, the neoclassical model of international trade, in which trade is determined by differences in countries' endowments of factors of production, implies that 'commodity-price equalization is sufficient to ensure factor price equalization and factor-price equalization is sufficient to ensure commodity-price equalization'. This implies that trade and migration are perfect substitutes.

The fundamental premise of the neoclassical theory of international trade is that the incentive to trade arises from differences in countries' relative costs of producing different goods, which, in turn, arise from differences in those countries' endowments of factors of production. These endowments are assumed to be immobile between countries but mobile between sectors. Free (and costless) trade in goods between countries ensures that goods prices are equalized across countries. Then, in its purest form, with two countries, two factors and two goods, as well as identical technologies between countries, neoclassical theory generates the remarkable prediction that free trade between two countries whose endowments are 'not too different' is sufficient to ensure that their factor prices are equalized – the so-called 'Factor Price Equalisation Theorem' of Paul Samuelson (1949). If, on the other hand, trade in goods were restricted, so that goods prices differed, differences in factor prices would persist, and if international migration were costless, factors would move. If this occurred until factor prices were equalized, goods prices would also be equal, since technology is the same across countries. According to this theory, only the ratio of the endowments of the two factors matters for the costs of goods production, so it does not tell us whether labour, capital or both would move between countries, which in turn implies that labour and capital mobility are also substitutes. But if we assume that there are frictions to capital movement (as there certainly were in 1957), trade and migration would be substitutes. Intuitively, this result is clear if one thinks of goods as bundles of their constituent factors, since then trade in goods and the migration of factors are two means to the same end.

No one, least of all Samuelson and Mundell, believes that the conditions assumed by the theory are valid in the real world. The casual evidence against them is simply overwhelming. Nonetheless, the basic insight is important and can be seen to operate, for example, in the way in which some agricultural production in developed countries depends on immigrant labour for its very existence – for example Martin (1997). Moreover, once we move beyond strict neoclassical theory, by allowing trade to be determined by things such as technology differences or tax structures, international migration can increase trade rather than reduce it. Markusen (1983) explores these cases in an interesting way: he shows that if something makes producing a particular good in a particular location attractive beyond factor endowments, location matters (unlike in the neoclassical model) and factor mobility will occur to take advantage of these specificities. Reasons why the equivalence of trade and migration may break down include: that the productivity of factors varies between countries, either in general or factor by factor; that not all countries can produce all goods because, for example, they lack a geographically specific input such as climate or, except in the very long run, good governance and strong institutions; that taxes and, say, labour market policies influence factor rewards; that imperfect competition in goods markets distorts the link between the costs and prices of goods, and that economies of scale allow larger economies to pay higher wages.[2]

It is worth noting that in the neoclassical model the effect of migration on trade is indirect, operating via general equilibrium. Immigration, say, increases the labour supply and sets off forces that tend toward reducing wages and the prices of labour-intensive goods. In turn, the returns to producing these latter goods increase, accompanied by an increase in their supply, which fuels an increase in exports or else a reduction in imports. In fact, subject to certain limits, the quantity responses entirely offset the price effects, so that prices and wages remain at their initial levels, which is the basis of the equivalence of free trade and free factor mobility.

By contrast, the second and third fundamental contributions analyse direct connections between migration and trade, with the former affecting the relative costs or benefits of the latter. The second is a series of theoretical works led by economists at Stanford University during the early 1990s. Milgrom et al. (1990) study the role of the *Lex Mercatoria* or the Merchant Law enforcement system that provided incentives for economic agents to trade honestly by 'coordinating the actions of people with limited knowledge and trust' (Benson, 1989, p. 648). Avner Greif further stressed, in a series of pioneering theoretical contributions, the trade-fostering roles of institutions in two historical contexts, specifically the Maghribi Traders' Coalition in the eleventh century (Greif, 1989, 1993), and the merchant guild during the Commercial Revolution of the eleventh to fourteenth century (Greif et al., 1994). In a nutshell, Greif's work argues that myriad social and political forces at various times in history culminated in the formation of institutions that helped to overcome the commitment issues that would otherwise have undermined trade relations. They did so by disseminating information on members' past trading behaviour and coordinating traders' responses in order to punish aberrant behaviour, both of which serve to improve compliance with commercial agreements. Greif explicitly distanced his work from the trade theory prevailing at the time, advocating the crucial role of (social) institutions in nurturing trade relationships as opposed to the traditional theoretical drivers of international trade such as 'endowments, technology, preferences and the nature of competition in international markets' (Greif, 1992, p. 128).

The third pivotal work was an outstanding piece of empirical scholarship, which laid the intellectual foundations for the now burgeoning literature that examines the mechanisms and interactions underpinning the trade–migration nexus. Gould (1994) motivates his seminal contribution by observing that immigrant labour is different from the domestic workforce: receiving countries do not simply benefit from a corresponding increase in labour or human capital, but additionally from the immigrants' links to their home countries. Gould proposes two key mechanisms by which migrants might bolster trade: an 'immigrant preference hypothesis' by which migrants increase the demand in their country of destination for goods produced in their country of origin, and a more important 'immigrant-link hypothesis', through which migrants lower the transaction costs of trade between the two countries by, for example, reducing communication costs through speaking the same language, lowering the costs of obtaining foreign market information through their knowledge of home markets, and reducing the costs of negotiating and enforcing contracts by drawing on their trusted networks at origin. The immigrant-link hypothesis therefore suggests that the ability of migrants to foster trade is a function of the existing foreign market information in the host country and 'the ability of immigrants to relay information and to integrate their communities into the host country' (ibid., p. 303). A corollary of this hypothesis is that migrants should exert more effect on bilateral trade in environments of weaker institutions where contract enforcement is more costly, that is, in and with developing countries. The empirical validity of this corollary is explored in Chapter 13 of this volume.

Gould argues that immigrants' preferences necessarily operate in the same direction as immigration, therefore fostering imports, while the immigrant-link effect can affect transaction costs for both imports and exports. He estimates separate regressions for exports and imports:

$$\ln X_{ij} = \alpha + \beta \ln Mig_{ji} + \vartheta' Z_{ij} + \varepsilon_{ij} \qquad \text{(4.1a – exports)}$$

$$\ln X_{ji} = \gamma + \rho \ln Mig_{ji} +' \phi' Z_{ij} + v_{ij} \qquad \text{(4.1b – imports)}$$

where $\ln X_{ij}$ and $\ln X_{ji}$ are the natural logarithms of, respectively, exports from *i* to *j* and exports from country *j* to *i*; that is, *i*'s imports from *j*, $\ln Mig_{ji}$ and $\ln Mig_{ij}$ are the natural logarithms of the bilateral migrant stock from *j* to *i* and from *i* to *j*, and ϑ and ϕ are vectors of coefficients for all remaining controls. For identification purposes, Gould compares the elasticities of imports and exports with respect to immigration, arguing that if immigrants affect only imports ($\rho > 0$ and $\beta = 0$), then the preference channel is the more relevant, while if they affect only exports ($\beta > 0$ and $\rho = 0$) the immigrant-link hypothesis is the most likely connection. Estimating a gravity model for the USA and 47 of its trading partners, Gould finds that both elasticities are strongly positive, from which he argues that both mechanisms are relevant. His inference is not entirely secure, however, because it is quite possible that the immigrant-link channel alone may account for this result.

Gould further examines various immigrant characteristics, namely their education levels and their duration of stay, and also the size of the immigrant community. These features, which according to the immigrant-link hypothesis should affect the degree to which immigrants foster trade, do not appear again in the literature for many years to follow. Interestingly in terms of skill level, Gould shows that, except in the equation for producer imports, the estimated parameter of the ratio of skilled to unskilled workers is always negative. He argues that this reflects offsetting forces: all immigrants lower transactions costs through their foreign market information, but educated ones are also more likely to create industries that are substitutes for traded goods; the positive effect on producer goods could arise if the educated migrants' firms used producer goods from their home nations. Gould estimates that the 'immigrant information effect' changes with the size of the immigrant community, finding that around 12000 immigrants are sufficient to exhaust 90 per cent of the effect for aggregate exports flows, while the corresponding figure for imports is around 371000. Finally, Gould's model includes terms for the duration of immigrants' stay and its square; the estimates suggest that, for imports, the immigrant effects increase bilateral trade at a decreasing rate over time, which might demonstrate the waning of preferences for goods produced in the home country, while for exports they start low and increase after about four years. This latter finding is consistent with the idea that immigrants need time to assimilate into the destination country in order to best use their foreign market information.

Aside from representing the first empirical paper in the literature, Gould's work distinguishes itself in a number of important respects. First, by distinguishing two main hypotheses he recognized that immigrant preferences might play an important role in fostering bilateral trade. Second, in contrast to many of the subsequent (and less convincing) papers that adopt rather *ad hoc* specifications, Gould builds on what was, at its time, widely viewed as the most sophisticated theoretical specification for aggregate trade equations: he extended the gravity model proposed by Bergstrand (1985) by modelling inter-country transaction costs such that they could decline via the foreign market information brought by immigrants. Third, Gould's empirical specification is very rich in terms of explanatory variables, which in turn allows him to investigate the immigrant-link hypothesis in a far more nuanced way – for example, the ways in which the information effect varies according to the characteristics of the immigrant population. Fourth, in distinguishing consumer and producer imports and exports, Gould also provided the conceptual framework for subsequent theoretical models (see below); in doing so he recognized that different types of goods may embody different characteristics that reflect the differing extents to which prices convey the full set of information necessary for commercial transactions.

Although Gould's study is a time-series analysis, which militates against easily comparing his results with those of other studies, its principal shortcomings pertain mostly to its identification strategies. Perhaps most obviously, Gould fails to include time dummies, so that macro trends that might be driving both trade and migration are not captured in the model. Other failings of this ilk include an inability to prove that migrant preferences supplement the 'immigrant-link' connection (because the latter can explain the positive effects on both exports and imports), a failure to establish formally that causality runs from migration to trade and finally, as Gould himself recognizes, that his specification might evoke omitted variable bias since 'another variable suggested by the analytical model but not included in the estimating equations here is the number of immigrants from the United States in the home countries' (ibid., p. 309). It is no exaggeration that these shortcomings have to a large extent motivated many of the subsequent papers in the literature.

The Subsequent Literature

The theoretical and empirical literatures were subsequently advanced by James Rauch, whose name today is often associated with the 'network/search view of trade'.[3] Relaxing the assumption in models of differentiated goods under monopolistic competition that buyers and sellers are automatically matched by some perfectly operating international market, Rauch (1996, 1999) argues that the heterogeneity in traded manufactures along 'the dimensions of both characteristics and quality' (Rauch, 1996, p. 1) means that prices no longer offer sufficient information to allow them to be sold on international organized exchanges. Rather, according to his partial equilibrium theory, buyers and sellers are matched through a costly search process that is a function of both the proximity of buyers and sellers and, crucially, of 'pre-existing ties'.

Drawing on the terminology of one of the most cited sociological works in history, 'The strength of weak ties' (Granovetter, 1973), Rauch argues that more distant and weaker ties (e.g. older ties or ties that involve less frequent social interactions) might actually be strongest in terms of yielding the 'best' outcome – in our case, greater volumes of trade – because there will be less overlap between the information that they have and that which you possess. Thus the exchange of differentiated goods is fostered by international networks as opposed to traditional markets, which is all the more important given that the majority of world trade comprises differentiated goods (Rauch, 1999). Rauch's key insight therefore follows directly from Gould (1994), who noted 'Because producer goods tend to be the least differentiated product (for instance, scrap metal) across countries, trade flows in these products may not benefit much from country-specific trade information' (p. 310). Rauch and Casella (2003) extend the analysis to a more formal general equilibrium matching model, in which group ties extend complete information about their domestic markets across international borders within groups, thereby fostering a more efficient international matching of pairs of producers.

Despite his earlier pessimism that 'It is doubtful that studies using data on bilateral trade flows such as Gould (1994) can be anything more than suggestive' (Rauch, 1996, p. 19), Rauch (1999) tests his theoretical conjecture by including in a gravity model of bilateral trade a dummy variable that takes the value of one if a trading dyad shares either a language or a colonial link. Since the coefficient on this variable is smaller for homogeneous than for differentiated goods, Rauch provides indirect support for the theory even in the absence of bilateral migration data. Rauch and Trindade (2002) go further, and, while abstracting from the preference channel, use bilateral data on Chinese ethnic networks to dig deeper into the immigrant-link hypothesis by distinguishing between the (foreign) market information effect and the trust and enforceability-of-contracts channel. Their key tool for identification is Rauch's (1999) classification of goods. Rauch distinguishes (i) 'homogenous goods', which comprise commodities that are sold on organized exchanges and thus can be traded efficiently because their prices are kept up to date so that traders can arbitrage between opportunities in the absence of additional information, and 'reference goods', which are priced without mention of a brand but not sold on organized exchanges, and (ii) 'differentiated goods', the prices for which fail to transmit full information relevant to international commerce. It is the latter in which co-ethnic networks can use their intra-network foreign market information to match buyers and sellers. Rauch and Trindade's identification strategy hinges on the supposition that the contract reinforcement mechanism should apply equally across all types of goods, while the foreign market information channel should apply only to differentiated goods; thus while the effect of Chinese ethnic networks on homogeneous goods can be taken as a 'baseline' impact through the mechanism of contract enforcement, the difference in the trade-creating effects between differentiated and homogenous goods can be taken as a measure of the market information channel. The authors' central hypothesis is borne out: ethnic Chinese networks affect trade in all types of goods but are found to exert additional effects on flows of differentiated products. Building on Gould's previous finding, Rauch and Trindade also find diminishing marginal returns to potential network size.

At the core of the theories of Greif, Gould and Rauch, therefore, is the crucial role of social capital that operates through the twin mechanisms of diffusing information and maintaining trust. A key difference, however, is that while Greif places more emphasis on networks providing information on agents' past behaviour, Gould and Rauch instead emphasize immigrant links and migrant networks providing information in the form of foreign market knowledge (to overcome issues of incomplete information).[4] The great contribution of Rauch's work is in providing a formal, tractable and ahistorical model, which includes the salient features of the models of both Greif and Gould and can be applied relatively easily to the data in various contexts. In this way, the role of migrant networks has been brought closer to the vanguard of the economics literature. In addition to the network/search theory of trade being able to provide a cogent explanation for the fact that bilateral distances do not exert a more negative impact on the volume of trade as transportation costs increase as a percentage of value,[5] the failure of networks to eliminate informal trade barriers entirely is a leading contender to explain the 'puzzle of the missing trade' (Trefler, 1995; Rauch and Trindade, 2002).

The literature to date focuses mainly on immigrants hosted by developed countries. This choice has largely been governed by the availability of trade and migration data and, in turn, the increasing complexity of studies generally reflects the gradual availability of richer data. What is perhaps most remarkable about the literature is the consistency with which a positive relationship between migration and trade has been found, albeit with a wide variation in magnitude, which presumably reflects differences in empirical specification. Genc et al. (2011), for example, in their meta-analysis of 45 immigrant-link studies, find that on average a 10 per cent rise in immigration is associated with a 1.5 per cent rise in bilateral trade, and that generally the elasticity on imports is greater than that on exports, as would be expected given that preferences additionally operate in this direction. The majority of the trade-migration literature, however, provides evidence of a strong correlation between the two facets of globalization. The remainder of this chapter seeks to guide the reader through the highlights and the main threads of the recent literature, and, in doing so, we maintain the same focus as the majority of the literature – that is, we try to identify the causal transmission mechanisms at play.

The ever-expanding literature examines the trade–migration nexus in a variety of geographical settings (see Table 4.1). The most frequent contributions study single countries and multiple trading partners: in, for example, Australia (White and Tadesse, 2007), Canada (Head and Ries, 1998), Denmark (White, 2007a), France (Briant et al., 2014), Greece (Piperakis et al., 2003), New Zealand (Law et al., 2013), Spain (Blanes, 2008), Sweden (Hatzigeorgiou, 2010a), Switzerland (Vézina, 2012), the USA (Dunlevy and Hutchinson, 1999, 2001; White, 2007b; White and Tadesse, 2008, 2010) and the UK (Girma and Yu, 2002). Another strand of the literature instead draws on data for national sub-divisions: American states (Bandyopadhyay et al., 2008; Bardhan and Guhathakurta, 2004; Co et al., 2004; Coughlin and Wall, 2011; Dunlevy, 2006; Herander and Saavedra, 2005; White and Tadesse, 2007), Canadian provinces (Wagner et al., 2002), Italian NUTS-3 regions (Bratti et al., 2014), Spanish provinces (Peri and Requena, 2010) or Italian, Portuguese and Spanish sub-regions (Artal-Tur et al., 2012). Yet another thread examines either groups of countries in a cross-sectional setting: Aleksynska and Peri (2014), Felbermayr et al. (2010), Felbermayr and Toubal (2012), Muller and Tai (2012) and Hatzigeorgiou (2010b), or groups of countries in a panel setting: Felbermayr and Jung (2009) and Sangita (2013). Still others study the links between internal migration and trade either in France (Combes et al., 2005) or in the USA (Millimet and Osang, 2007).

Specification

The gravity model is the work-horse of trade–migration research and this sub-section discusses some of the issues surrounding its specification. The most common objective in the literature is to distinguish ever more carefully between Gould's two effects, specifically to attempt to separate the transaction cost mechanism, which is unambiguously welfare improving, from the preference channel, otherwise termed 'nostalgia trade' (Vézina, 2012), 'transplanted home bias' (White, 2007b), or the 'taste channel' (Sangita, 2013). Initial contributions typically used aggregate trade and migration data, regressing both imports and exports on the bilateral stocks of immigrants (see Equations 4.1a and 4.1b), relying on the identification

Table 4.1 Methodological overview of immigrant-link literature

Paper	Time period	Data structure	Estimator	Standard errors	Geographic/time fixed effect sets
Gould (1994)	1970–86	USA + 47 national trading partners	Times series (non-linear least squares)	Unspecified	Partner country
Head and Ries (1998)	1980–92	Canada + 136 national trading partners	Tobit (Eaton–Tamura method)	Unspecified	Region, year
Dunlevy and Hutchinson (1999, 2001)	1870–1910 (5-year intervals)	USA + 17 national trading partners	Scaled OLS	Unspecified/robust	None
Girma and Yu (2002)	1981–93	UK + 48 national trading partners	OLS	Robust	Year (robustness with partner-time dummies)
Rauch and Trindade (2002)	1980, 1990	63 nations	Tobit (Eaton–Tamura method)	Robust	None
Wagner et al. (2002)	1992–95	5 Canadian regions + 160 national trading partners	Heckman selection model	Robust	Partner country
Piperakis et al. (2003)	1981–91	Greece + unspecified number of national trading partners	OLS	Robust	Year
Bardhan and Guhathakurta (2004)	1994–96	2 US coastal regions + 51 national trading partners	OLS	Robust	Year

Table 4.1 (continued)

Paper	Time period	Data structure	Estimator	Standard errors	Geographic/time fixed effect sets
Co et al. (2004)	1993	USA states + 28 national trading partners	Scaled OLS, Tobit	Robust	None
Combes et al. (2005)	1993	95 French départements	OLS (2SLS), also odds and 'frictions' specifications	Robust	Département (importer and exporter)
Herander and Saavedra (2005)	1993–96	US states + 36 national trading partners	Tobit (Eaton–Tamura method), censored least absolute deviation estimator	Unspecified	Region
Dunlevy (2006)	1990–92 (averaged, i.e. cross-section)	US states + 87 national trading partners	Tobit	Unspecified	State, partner country
Tadesse and White (2007)	2000	USA + 75 national trading partners	Tobit (Eaton–Tamura method)	Unspecified	None
White (2007a)	1980–2000	Denmark + 170 national trading partners	Tobit	Robust	Year
White (2007b)	1980–2001	USA + 73 national trading partners	OLS	Robust	Year
White and Tadesse (2007)	1989–2000	Australia + 101 national trading partners	Iterative feasible generalized least squares, Tobit,	Unspecified	None

			pooled corrected standard error		
Blanes (2008)	1995–2003	Spain + 83 national trading partners	OLS	Robust	Year
Bandyopadhyay et al. (2008)	1990, 2000	US states + 29 national trading partners	OLS, panel FE	Unspecified	Year, state, partner country, state–country
White and Tadesse (2008)	1997–2004	USA + 54 national trading partners	Random effects feasible generalized least squares	Robust	Year
Felbermayr and Jung (2009)	1990, 2000	OECD + all national trading partners	OLS, first-difference estimator	Robust	Importer–year, exporter–year
Felbermayr et al. (2010)	1980, 1990, 2000	World	OLS, PPML-DV	Cluster robust	Importer, exporter
Hatzigeorgiou (2010a)	2000	75 nation states	OLS, PPML	Cluster robust	Importer, exporter
Hatzigeorgiou (2010b)	2002–07	Sweden + 180 national trading partners	OLS, panel, tobit	Robust	Year, region
Peri and Requena (2010)	1993–2008	50 Spanish provinces + 77 national trading partners	OLS, panel IV, 2SLS, scaled OLS, PPML, tobit	Cluster robust	Province–year, country–year, province–country
White and Tadesse (2010)	1996–2001	USA + 59 national trading partners	Random effects generalized least squares	Unspecified	Year

Table 4.1 (continued)

Paper	Time period	Data structure	Estimator	Standard errors	Geographic/time fixed effect sets
Artal-Tur et al. (2012)	2002–10	103 Italian & 50 Spanish provinces and 20 Portuguese districts	OLS	Cluster robust	Province–country, country–year
Felbermayr and Toubal (2012)	2000	OECD + all national trading partners	OLS	Robust	Importer, exporter
Muller and Tai (2012)	2000	19 OECD countries + all potential worldwide national trading partners	Scaled OLS	Cluster robust	Importer–sector, exporter–sector, importer–exporter
Vézina (2012)	Average 1995–2009	Switzerland + 174 trading partners	OLS, 2SLS, PPML, Poisson-IV, negative binomial, Poisson-FE	Robust/clustered	Trading partner (Poisson FE model)
Aleksynska and Peri (2014)	2000	89 destinations + 233 origins	Scaled OLS, PPML, Tobit	Cluster robust	Importer, exporter (year for exact year of data collection)
Briant et al. (2014)	Average 1998–2000	94 French départments + 100 national trading partners	OLS, 2-step negative binomial model, 2SLS	Robust	Department, partner country

Law et al. (2013)	1981–2006	New Zealand + 190 national trading partners	Heckman selection model with correlated random effects	Unspecified	Year, partner country
Sangita (2013)	1990, 2000	OECD + 200 national trading partners	OLS, 2SLS	Unspecified	Importer, exporter
Bratti et al. (2014)	2002–09	20 Italian regions/107 Italian provinces + 210 national trading partners	Scaled OLS, 2SLS	Cluster robust	Region/province–year, partner country–year FE, region/province–country

Note: The papers listed include those that the authors considered as belonging to the core of the immigrant-link literature. Only sets of fixed effects are recorded; in other words, should a dummy variable be included, for example for a single specific region, this is not recorded. 'Scaled OLS' refers to OLS when one has been added to the dependent variable before taking its log.

strategy that the preference channel operates solely on imports while the information channel operates instead on both imports and exports.

As highlighted by Hatzigeorgiou (2010b), however, a more satisfactory approach involves regressing one-way trade on both immigrant and emigrant stocks, that is:

$$\ln X_{ij} = \alpha + \beta \ln Mig_{ji} + \rho \ln Mig_{ij} + \vartheta' Z_{ij} + \varepsilon_{ij} \tag{4.2}$$

This is because, as first elucidated by Ravenstein (1885), migrant flows often lead to migrant counter-flows. Should this be the case, immigrant and emigrant stocks will be positively correlated and, as recognized by Gould (see quote above) and demonstrated by the empirical results of Combes et al. (2005), a failure to include both immigrant and emigrant stocks will result in upwardly biased coefficient estimates on the former. Second, since the emphasis of the literature is on trying to isolate the immigrant-link hypothesis, the 'transaction channel' can be better identified should a flow of migrants against the direction of trade be found to foster that trade flow, since it is impossible for preferences to operate in that direction. In other words, if, in Equation (4.2), $\beta > 0$, that is, if immigrants from country j living in country i foster exports from i to j, this effect must manifest itself through the transaction cost channel. Isolating this effect is possible only if one controls for migration in both directions, however, since both immigrants and emigrants may establish both importing and exporting businesses.

While the complexities of the empirical models used in the migration literature mirror the advances made in the wider econometric literature, the control variables it uses are fairly standard, including the usual features such as measures of economic mass, distance, colonial ties, common language and regional trade agreements. Typically trade and migration enter these specifications in (log) levels, although, in order to try to reduce scale effects, a handful of papers implement either or both in terms of shares (e.g. Rauch and Trindade, 2002; Felbermayr et al., 2010; Felbermayr and Toubal, 2012).

The specification of the gravity model has evolved significantly since the *ad hoc* specifications of the early literature, in which additional covariates of interest were added somewhat haphazardly into the estimated regression in the absence of more formal theoretical justifications. Gould is a notable exception since he extended the gravity model of Bergstrand (1985) by endogenizing transaction costs with respect to the foreign market information provided by immigrants. In an important development, Combes et al. (2005), the representative consumer's utility function is defined over differentiated varieties. A weight is attached to all varieties imported from region *j*, which denotes the preferences that *i* consumers have for *j* varieties; that is, a bilateral affinity term is used to weight the importance attached by representative consumers in country *i* to country *j*'s products, which explicitly allows preferences to be included in the derivation of the model. Peri and Requena (2010) instead rely on the distorted gravity model of Chaney (2008) to examine how immigrants affect the intensive and extensive margins of trade. Finally, Sangita (2013) introduces a simple extension to the Anderson and van Wincoop (2003) gravity model, by explicitly splitting their 'trade frictions' into 'knowledge gaps' that migrants are purported to surmount, and transportation costs.

This increasing complexity has been accompanied by ever more stringent specifications in terms of the number of controls or, more precisely, the large number of fixed effects applied (in order to militate against omitted-variable bias). But there is still no consensus on a number of econometric issues. The first is how best to deal with the large number of zeros in bilateral trade data. The three most common approaches that feature in many of the earlier contributions in the literature are (1) to use a Tobit model, setting the censoring threshold to zero; (2) to add a small value, typically one, to all cells before taking the log and proceeding with OLS; or (3) to simply drop zero observations and use OLS, which necessarily results in selection bias, which Rauch (1999) shows has significant effects on results. More recently, in a highly influential piece of work, Santos Silva and Tenreryo (2006) argue that a pseudo-Poisson maximum likelihood estimator offers a satisfactory way of dealing with zeros.

One empirical issue that should be in no doubt, however, relates to clustering standard errors by the relevant observational unit (as opposed to simply using robust standard errors), because observations of bilateral trade across partners will generally not be independently distributed. Unfortunately, studies correctly clustering standard errors are still in the minority (see Table 4.1). The preceding arguments, namely the increasingly stringent empirical specifications, the inclusion or exclusion of zeros, the variety of estimators used and the fact that relatively few papers in the literature cluster standard errors correctly, mean that any comparisons of the point estimates from across the various studies remain somewhat confounded.

Identification – Product Types

The trade and migration literature seeks to address the extent to which a causal link can truly be established from migration to trade. To this end, papers typically aim to both (a) isolate the transaction cost mechanism by drawing upon richer more disaggregated data and (b) insulate their results from both omitted-variable bias and reverse causality that might otherwise confound their results.

Perhaps the most common method to isolate the transaction cost mechanism is to examine the pro-trade effect on different classifications of goods, since theory suggests that migrants should exert the greatest pro-trade effect on those most differentiated. While Gould examines consumer and producer goods (as do Herander and Saavedra, 2005 and Blanes, 2008), most authors instead follow Rauch's (1999) classification of goods (e.g. Briant et al., 2014; Hatzigeorgiou, 2010b; Vézina, 2012; Sangita, 2013). Similarly, Peri and Requena (2010) and Aleksynska and Peri (2014) apply the estimated elasticities from Broda and Weinstein (2006) to categorize the degree of product differentiation in various sectors. Other authors simply use manufactured goods, which are often considered to be the most differentiated type of goods (e.g. Dunlevy, 2006) or simply distinguish between manufactures and non-manufactures (e.g. White and Tadesse, 2010). Dunlevy and Hutchinson (1999, 2001), in their historical studies of the USA, instead distinguish between five product categories: crude foodstuffs, crude materials, processed foodstuffs, semi-manufactures and manufactures for consumption.

Most studies find that immigrants exert a stronger effect on differentiated as opposed to homogeneous goods, although exceptions exist. White (2007a), for example, fails to find the usual effect. This might be because he fails to include a full set of controls (i.e. fixed effects) to account for omitted-variable bias. Similarly, Felbermayr et al. (2010) do not find that immigrants generally matter more for differentiated products, but this does not worry them because it is 'not overly surprising since the theory-based gravity model signals that the estimated coefficients confound the elasticity of substitution with the trade cost elasticity of networks, so that comparing across categories of goods is not an ideal identification strategy' (p. 63). A further weakness in drawing on the now standard Rauch classification is that it has not changed over time, and thus, while we might expect that concurrent with rapidly expanding global trade would be an increase in the numbers and types of differentiated goods, authors typically estimate regressions with a fixed definition of what constitutes a differentiated good. Sangita (2013) takes a different tack, separating intermediate from final goods, arguing that the former should not be affected by any preference effects. Since, in the absence of taste effects, the pro-trade effect of migration is maintained, this lends further support for the existence of the transaction cost channel. Interestingly, Law et al. (2013) also examine the pro-trade effect of both immigrants and emigrants on tourism to New

Zealand, and find that this effect is substantially higher than that for trade in goods. They are unable to establish, however, whether the effect on tourism is due to information about New Zealand being transmitted from the diaspora to others around the world or whether it is due to increased numbers of visits by family and friends.

Identification – Geographical Proximity

In other contexts, authors have exploited geography to isolate the causal impact of migration on trade. Since search costs and thus the social interactions that are purported to govern the trade–migration nexus will probably depend on proximity (Rauch, 1999), Herander and Saavedra (2005) suggest that geographic distance within the USA between host-country agents and immigrants is crucial in terms of communicating host-country exporting opportunities. Bratti et al. (2014) thus argue that the proper geographical unit from which to assess the existence of interactions and knowledge flows between natives and immigrants is small areas (p. 5). Bratti et al. (2014) represent a great advance in the literature in this regard by using provincial data (i.e. NUTS-3 regions) on 107 Italian provinces with an average area of 2800 square kilometres, which additionally allow for the imposition of a full battery of fixed effects to further isolate their results from omitted-variable bias. Herander and Saavedra (2005) specifically highlight the role of geography as a key component of network structure, since they find that while in-state migrant populations exert the greatest state pro-export effect, out-of-state populations also foster such links. Conceptually, this avenue of research is similar to the work of Felbermayr et al. (2010), who document the fact that, having controlled for the general openness of states through the imposition of country fixed effects, those migrants born in neither the importing nor the exporting country can still foster international trade links. These they call indirect links, the presence of which, importantly, cannot be due to preference effects. Artal-Tur et al. (2012) perhaps go furthest in this regard, however, since they combine regional trade and migration data for Italy, Portugal and Spain. The results from these authors' most stringent specification highlight the importance of the role of geography since they find (for all three countries in their sample) that only immigrants within a trading province – as opposed to those from the same country residing in other parts of the Southern European countries – exert a pro-trade impact. This constitutes evidence against Herander and Saavedra (2005), but it is not clear if these results are robust to the inclusion of province–year fixed effects.

Identification – Firms

Combes et al. (2005) importantly distinguish between migrant networks (measured by intra-region worker stocks) and networks of firms (measured as the number of potential business connections of various business groups across regions), thus separating out the effects of social and business networks. They therefore introduce an additional mechanism through which networks can foster trade, that is, through business networks overcoming informational asymmetries via FDI. Compared to a situation of no networks, social networks are found to double trade, while business networks are estimated to boost trade by a factor of up to four. Related to this is the paper by Bardhan and Guhathakurta (2004), who similarly distinguish between international sociocultural networks (measured as the numbers of foreign born) and business networks (measured as the proportion of multinational exports or intra-firm exports as a fraction of total exports), and examine the impact of each on East and West Coast US exports to 53 nations worldwide. They find that business ties are important for both coasts, but that social networks are relevant only to the West coast. No convincing explanation is offered for this, although the authors argue somewhat loosely that the industrial and immigrant structures of the two coasts differ. It seems likely that the *ad hoc* gravity specification adopted, in tandem with the fact that only 53 countries of origin are included in estimation, might be driving these findings. Relatedly, Greaney (2005) examines network effects by comparing the trading patterns of foreign affiliates in the USA with those of domestic firms. Foreign affiliates are found to exert an unbelievably strong home bias; in particular, Japanese affiliates are found to trade more than 130 times more with Japan than elsewhere. Interestingly, affiliates are found to trade less with countries located further from their home countries, even when controlling for the distance between an affiliate and the destination country, which implies the existence of regional networks (and potentially cultural connections), based neither on trade costs nor on information. If the geographical patterns of FDI and migration are positively correlated (and presumably they are via country size as well as cultural and historical links), these results raise the possibility that studies that do not include FDI will give upwardly biased estimates of the pro-trade effects of migration.

These results naturally lead one to conjecture that migrants might exert the greatest effects on trade if they are employed by firms, although firms no doubt have access to alternative resources that would allow them to trade in the absence of foreign workers. This proposition is examined by Hiller (2013), who focuses on manufacturing firms that export to at least one destination; that is, she does not consider firms that switch to becoming exporters. By matching employer and employee data at the firm level, Hiller documents how Danish firms adjust their product portfolios in response to both regional immigration and foreign employment. She finds strong evidence that foreign employees foster Danish exports, while only weak evidence that the local presence of foreigners increases export sales. The introduction of firm-level data potentially introduces an additional source of endogeneity, however, since it is not clear whether firms export to a particular country because they have hired migrants or vice versa. Hiller (2013) tries to insulate her results from such reverse causality by introducing instruments into her regressions, namely the average number of immigrants from a given origin employed in other firms in the same industry, or the number of foreigners from country *j* who work elsewhere in the region of firm *i*. What remains unclear, however, is the extent to which foreigners working locally or in the sector are correlated with the 'local presence of foreigners', which she has already identified as having a (weak) positive effect, for example through employees migrating with their family who work outside of the firm. Hiller assumes that regional immigrant stocks are exogenous to the firm, but, given the preceding argument, this assumption may be invalid.

Muller and Tai (2012) instead match migrants by occupation to trade data across 18 manufacturing sectors, and employ a sectoral gravity model to try to pin down the causal impact of immigrants on bilateral trade. Since their results are robust to stringent specifications saturated with fixed effects, they provide further evidence that immigrants foster international bilateral trade flows through the transaction cost channel, but have no riposte to charges of reverse causality. Bastos and Silva (2012) match 'historically determined' emigration stocks from Portugal, with Portuguese firm-level export data, and find that larger stocks of Portuguese emigrants increase both the export participation and export intensity of Portuguese firms, and furthermore that export participation is most associated with those firms that existed before emigration occurred. In other words, Portuguese emigrants affect both the extensive and the intensive margins of trade. These authors argue that emigration from Portugal stemmed largely from a mass movement in the 1960s during the Estado Novo regime, which governed from 1933 to 1974. This implies that a large fraction of the stock in the year 2000 would comprise these older emigrants, which in turn would insulate their results from concerns of reverse causality. It is unknown to what extent Portuguese emigrant stocks in 2000 reflect the exodus from decades beforehand, however, and so, plausibly for any country that has received a fairly large number of Portuguese emigrants in recent years, the authors' conjecture seems unlikely to hold.

Several authors have examined the effect of immigrants on the margins of trade. Peri and Requena (2010) base their immigrant-link study on use of Spanish data on the distorted gravity model of Chaney (2008), which provides a theoretical foundation for examining how immigrants affect the margins of trade. According to the model, migrants lower the fixed costs of exporting such that less productive firms (those previously below the productivity threshold necessary to export) are now able to enter the export market. Using the number of transactions and the average value per transaction as proxies for the external and internal margins of trade, they find corroborative evidence for the underlying theory, since the largest part of trade creation is through the extensive margin, with little to no effect on the intensive margin. This result seems to be in contrast with Bastos and Silva's work (2012), but in the latter case, since they use data on emigrants, it is possible that emigrants foster the intensive margin through the preference channel. Similarly, Hiller (2013), defining the extensive margin as 'net churning' (Iacovone and Javorcik, 2010), that is, the difference between products created and destroyed within a firm, concludes that firms increase export sales through the extensive margin. Vézina (2012) reports the same finding in the context of Switzerland.

Identification – Migrant Characteristics

While detailed firm- and trade-level data allow for a closer identification of immigrant links, the majority of the literature relies on more aggregate data and typically examines migrants' occupation and education levels in order to ascertain which migrants underpin the trade–migration nexus. Highly skilled migrants and those in particular (business-orientated) occupations might well have access to greater amounts of foreign market information and thus be better placed to transmit and use that knowledge. As noted by Gould (1994), however, skilled individuals are also more likely to be able to establish businesses in the destination country to produce what might otherwise have been imported, and so the net effect of more highly skilled migrants on bilateral trade is unclear *a priori*. Since highly skilled migrants are often defined by their level of education, it also matters where migrants were educated. For example, if they have received their education in the receiving country, they will tend to assimilate faster but have fewer home ties than other migrants. Given these opposing forces and the level of aggregation of the data used to test these types of linkages, it is perhaps not surprising that the results are mixed.

Blanes (2008) concludes that only immigrants who have secondary education affect trade in the case of Spain, although his empirical specification is not as tight as other work, say on the role of education, in terms of avoiding omitted-variable bias. Felbermayr and Jung (2009) find that those with primary and tertiary levels of education foster North–South trade links more strongly than those with secondary education. Sangita (2013), using the same migration data, finds that the impact of immigrants on trade is monotonically increasing in migrants' education level, however. Similarly, Felbermayr and Toubal (2012) find in a cross-section of OECD countries in 2000 that the pro-trade effect of highly skilled migrants is more than double that of the overall effect of migrants. Finally, Muller and Tai (2012) find that, while immigrants of all education levels affect trade, those with tertiary education have roughly twice the effect of others.

Head and Ries (1998) find that immigrants who entered Canada under the 'Family' and 'Independent' visa classes exert the greatest pro-trade effect, while refugees have a negligible effect on trade. Interestingly, Head and Ries find that those entering Canada as 'Business Visitors' have no impact on trade, which they conclude might be due to their wishing to create businesses that cater to the Canadian market. Similarly, White and Tadesse (2010) find for the USA that refugees have a considerably smaller pro-trade effect than immigrants entering the labour market or for purposes of family reunification. This they sensibly argue is due to the fact that refugees have spent considerable amounts of time in a third-party country, which might have eroded their links to the home country in addition to altering their preferences. Parsons and Vézina (2014), on the other hand, find a significant long-term impact of refugees residing in the USA on US bilateral trade with Vietnam, in the case of the Vietnamese Boat People. It seems likely that trading links will be lower for countries that are generating refugees than for other countries, but the evidence of Parsons and Vézina (2014) suggests that if the status of such countries changes over time, the original refugee status may matter little in terms of long-run pro-trade effects.

Herander and Saavedra (2005), in their study of US states, define their ratio of skilled migrants as the number employed in the Labor Department's occupations 1–4 divided by those in categories 5–9. They consistently find that skilled workers strongly influence consumer-good exports (as opposed to total exports). Blanes (2008), in the case of Spain, finds that immigrants who are 'managers' foster both Spanish imports and exports, while employees are not found to exert any effect, albeit using an extremely simplified econometric specification. Similarly, Aleksynska and Peri (2014), while focusing on immigrants employed in the OECD in managerial positions, find that the pro-trade effect of these migrants is ten times larger than that of non-business network migrants. Moreover, when combined with migrants' education levels, they find that, above and beyond the effect of the total migrant stock, only the highly educated in management positions underpin the trade–migration nexus.

Mechanisms Governing the Trade–Migration Nexus

While the literature surveyed until now goes some way to elucidating which immigrants underpin the trade–migration nexus, and how, in this section we delve deeper into the underlying mechanisms through which migrants facilitate trade. To this end, the literature, drawing on Gould's and Rauch's insights, typically adopts indirect approaches in order to ascertain the underlying mechanisms by which migrants might reduce transaction costs.

An interesting starting point is Girma and Yu (2002), who distinguish the individual effects of migrants (i.e. personal contacts) from the non-individual effects (knowledge, for example, of home institutions that are not individual-specific but rather assumed known by the population). By interacting a commonwealth dummy with the immigrant stock variable, these authors find that, while the UK trades more with countries of the Commonwealth, immigrants exert no influence of exports to these countries, but that a 10 per cent rise in immigration from non-Commonwealth countries is associated with a 1.6 per cent rise in UK exports. Since the countries of the Commonwealth, which include the UK, share similar laws and institutions, the authors conclude that non-individual effects are the ones that drive the trade–migration nexus. Similarly, Blanes (2008), in the case of Spain, interacts a colonial dummy with the immigrant stock variable and finds that migrants from both former colonies and non-colonies affect trade, but that the effect is stronger for immigrants from non-colonies. While this is an important insight, the evidence of Combes et al. (2005), who find significant positive influences of internal migrants on internal trade, is clear that individual effects also play important roles, because internal migrants bring no incremental benefit to local non-individual knowledge. In a similar vein, Dunlevy (2006) finds no evidence in the case of US states that the information brought by immigrants is less useful when they come from a country with similar institutions, a result also found by Herander and Saavedra (2005).

As we noted above, immigrants might not simply foster trade because of their knowledge of home-market institutions, but (and perhaps more likely) might also substitute for them in weak institutional environments, where contract enforcement is problematic and issues of trust are important. Anderson and Marcouiller (2002) provide evidence that poor institutions located in the importer's country significantly deter trade. Berkowitz et al. (2006) further show that institutions on both sides of the trading relationship play key roles in determining the level of trade and, furthermore, that institutions matter more for more complex goods since they embody characteristics that are most difficult to include in contracts. As opposed to studying institutional similarity (as above), therefore, many studies in the literature instead address the issue of how migrants may substitute for weak institutions. Dunlevy (2006) examines US state-level trade with foreign countries, specifically examining the roles of information and trust. Trust is represented in these studies by including an interaction term between a measure of corruption and the immigrant stock, which is postulated to sidestep the weak institutions to provide an assured, stable and profitable environment for business negotiations at the export destination. Dunlevy finds that the pro-trade effect of migrants is stronger the higher the level of corruption in the destination country.

Briant et al. (2014) examine the complexity of French trade in tandem with the quality of institutions in partner countries. They conclude that immigrants matter for the importation of complex goods regardless of institutional quality at origin, while, conversely, for simple products, they affect imports only when institutions at origin are weak. On the export side, their results are weaker and show that immigrants affect exports only to countries with weak institutions (regardless of product complexity). Similarly, Muller and Tai (2012) find that migrants substitute for weak institutions at both origin and destination (although the former effect is more accurately identified), and that migrants matter more for trade when underdeveloped legal environments prevail. In a slightly different vein, Rotunno and Vézina (2012) provide evidence of a link between Chinese ethnic networks and tariff evasion with trade both to, and from, China, an effect that is more severe when their host countries are most corrupt. They argue that networks are ideally placed to engineer tariff evasion, since smuggling requires access to market information and high levels of trust. These conclusions resonate with the works of Greif, Gould and Rauch, and go some way to shedding further light on the mechanisms underlying the trade–migration nexus.

The other key channel by which migrants are purported to facilitate trade is through the diffusion of foreign market information. Dunlevy (2006) proxies immigrants' knowledge of market information by the use of a shared language variable, arguing that market information is more difficult to obtain across linguistic boundaries. Since Dunlevy finds that the pro-trade effect of migrants is weaker if the importing and exporting nations share a similar language, he takes this as evidence of the market diffusion aspect of the transaction cost channel since migrant networks are likely to contribute more where the host-country population has more difficulty obtaining information itself. Similarly, Law et al. (2013) find, in the case of New Zealand, that non-English-speaking immigrants and members of the New Zealand diaspora who reside in non-English-speaking countries have additional pro-trade effects on bilateral imports and exports. Wagner et al. (2002), taking advantage of the variation in the level of English and French spoken across Canadian provinces, construct a language variable that is the probability that a randomly chosen immigrant and a randomly chosen individual from a Canadian province are able to speak the same language. These authors find that speaking the same language has no statistically significant effect on bilateral trade, but these results are not directly comparable with those above, since Wagner et al. do not interact their language variable with their immigrant stock variable.

These results suggest that culture plays a key role in determining global trading patterns, which the trade–migration literature addresses by evoking notions of cultural proximity or cultural distance. A novel approach in this regard is Felbermayr and Toubal (2010), who use voting patterns from the Eurovision Song Contest to construct measures of cultural proximity. They conclude, for the highest degree of cultural proximity, that bilateral trade in differentiated goods is some 16 percentage points higher, and indeed argue that these types of effects are above and beyond any impact of immigration. No effect is found for homogeneous goods. It is not clear to what extent these results are driven by bilateral migration flows, however, since across all the specifications in the paper these are never explicitly modelled. White and Tadesse (2008) construct measures of 'cultural distance' using the World Values and European Values Surveys, since home–host country dissimilarity may 'engender opportunities for immigrants to exert pro-trade influences' (White and Tadesse (2008), p. 1079). They show that, while trade is inversely related to the cultural distance between trading partners, migrants partially offset this effect.

We may conclude that, in general, migrants exert the greatest effects on trade in differentiated products and immigrants have their largest effect by lowering fixed trade costs, that is, through the extensive margin. Migrants of all skill levels and occupations may influence trade, but these effects are likely to be strongest where migrants are more educated, employed in a firm and, most specifically, in a managerial position. To this end, migrants exploit both their personal contacts and their home-market information to transmit their knowledge across international (and national) borders, to establish trusting relationships, to substitute for weak institutional environments where contract enforcement is more costly and, not least, where cultural differences between trading partners are greatest.

Non-linear Effects

Up to now we have said little about how such effects change either over time or with changes in the extent of migration (i.e. non-linearities). Although both Gould and Rauch devoted space to discussing possible non-linearities in the effect of migration on trade, surprisingly few studies have taken this matter up. Typically, constant elasticity models are used that do not allow for the effect of migration on trade to change, although exceptions exist. Two key sources of such non-linearities are migrants' length of stay and the size of the immigrant community.

Wagner et al.'s (2002) random encounter model allows for diminishing returns to immigration and, like Gould, suggests that the pro-trade effect of immigrants tapers off more quickly for exports than for imports. Peri and Requena (2010) find support for a convex relationship across Spanish provinces between immigrant density and pro-trade effect, and conclude that a minimum threshold is needed for an immigrant network to operate. Finally, Law et al. (2013), when studying New Zealand, find diminishing returns of immigrants on exports but not on imports by including an immigrant quadratic term.

Herander and Saavedra (2005) introduce a variable to capture immigrants' length of stay and its square, and find that immigrants increase US state exports at a decreasing rate as stays extend. Collectively, these results might suggest that a fairly fixed set of opportunities exists on the transaction cost side that is largely exhausted once a particular threshold is reached, but that preference effects are more persistent. Herander and Saavedra (2005) also test whether previous immigration reduces the role of current immigrants in facilitating US state exports. To this end, they interact their state-level migrant stock variable with a measure of ancestor origin, defined as the number of US residents per state that report ancestors from a particular export destination. These authors find that the local state populations from high-ancestry countries increase bilateral exports by 1.1 per cent, as opposed to 1.6 per cent for those from low-ancestry countries. This indicates that, since the flow of information between the USA and low-ancestry countries is lower, the role of immigrant populations from these countries is higher.

Jansen and Piermartini (2009) specifically examine the effects of temporary migration in the USA on trade, using H1B visa admissions as a proxy for temporary migration, while additionally controlling for permanent migration as captured through the total stock of immigrants. They argue that, while permanent migrants are likely to have better host-country contacts, temporary migrants will tend to have more up-to-date home-country information that can be exploited to the benefit of trade. These authors find not only that temporary migration has a positive and statistically significant impact on trade, above and beyond permanent migration, but also that the effects of temporary migration are significantly larger. Establishing causality in the case of temporary migration is more difficult, however, since firms might well aim to hire workers of particular nationalities in order to take advantage of specific trading opportunities.

Negative Effects

While the overwhelming majority of results across all of the papers surveyed in this chapter uncover a positive relationship between trade and migration, it is important to note that in a limited number of cases authors have found negative results. Dunlevy and Hutchinson (1999), for example, in the case of immigrants from 'New Europe', find a strong negative effect on US imports. They argue that this result might hinge on the characteristics of this migrant group, which arrived predominantly after 1890, typically stayed for shorter periods and thus had less time to establish host-country contacts, and, perhaps most pertinently, possessed little capital with which to import native goods or indeed establish importing businesses. Moreover, the authors argue that some of these immigrants originated from small regions, such as the Azores, that might have exported little anyway. Girma and Yu (2002) also find a negative, trade-substituting, effect on UK imports for immigrants from Commonwealth countries.

These results all occur on the import side of the trade–migration relationship, which might imply that such effects operate through the preference channel. One plausible explanation offered by Diaz-Alejandro (1970), however, is that immigrants might establish import-substituting businesses in the country of destination. It is also not inconceivable that the presence of large numbers of immigrants whose preferences differ from the domestic population will increase the incentives of local nationally owned firms to produce substitute products. A second alternative to Rauch's (2001, p. 1200) network/search view of trade is that

> less desirable network members may choose to enter the anonymous international market where their characteristics are not known, harming non-members even though the existence of a transnational network still increases world output in the aggregate. Second, a transnational network can have an effect analogous to harmful trade diversion if it links the 'wrong' countries. Third, organization of international trade through networks may hinder its growth if transnational networks tend to be closed to new members.

Since the overwhelming methodology of migration–trade studies is the regression model, which estimates average effects across origin countries and migrant characteristics, we might conclude that negative effects exist, but that they are usually dwarfed by the positive, pro-trade, effects of immigrants. An interesting avenue for future research, therefore, might be to apply richer, more disaggregated data so as to identify exactly in which circumstances these negative effects arise.

Omitted Variables and Causality

Both trade and migration data typically suffer from measurement error. Such measurement issues are no doubt exacerbated among those studies that impute migration data, which they often do, relying on a stock–flow rule (examples include Head and Ries, 1998; White, 2007; Piperakis et al., 2003; White and Tadesse, 2007, 2010; Law et al., 2013). With regard to endogeneity, however, the trade–migration literature focuses not on these errors but on addressing concerns about omitted-variable bias and reverse causality.

It is beyond the scope of this chapter to provide a detailed account of the received wisdom on the specification of the gravity model – see, for example, Baldwin and Taglioni (2006) on the trade aspects of the question. As mentioned above, however, and as recognized in Gould's original study, arguably the most commonly omitted variable on the migration side is the failure to include migrants in both directions of a bilateral link. Since these variables are highly positively correlated – according to Özden et al. (2011) the correlation is 0.604 for all decades between 1960 and 2000, but has sharply decreased from 0.811 in 1960 to 0.334 in 2000 – if both sets of migrants matter, the absence of one will necessarily lead to overestimates of the effect on trade of the other. The most notable omitted variables in the general gravity model literature are the various combinations of fixed effects that can be used to account for various unobserved heterogeneities. Wagner et al. (2002, p. 513) note 'omitted variable bias may underlie the large elasticities estimated in cross-sectional studies'. More broadly, the seminal contribution of Anderson and Van Wincoop (2003) highlights the need to account for multilateral resistances to trade, and, as Feenstra (2004) notes, one convenient way of accounting for these price indices is through the imposition of country fixed effects (or country–time fixed effects in panel models). Their omission often comes at a high price. Felbermayr et al. (2010), for example, demonstrate that Rauch and Trindade's original results are 2–4 times larger than they should be when one accounts for multilateral resistance terms. Cheng and Wall (2005) also argue for the need to include origin–destination fixed effects in gravity models of trade, although given that this requires quite long panels of data, it is only the most recent studies that can do so.

Authors address the issue of reverse causality in a variety of ways. Gould argues that immigration is subject to binding quotas and occurs before the onset of trade, and hence that reverse causality is not relevant. Felbermayr and Jung (2009), however, argue that causality runs from migration to trade on the basis of a regression test for strict exogeneity (Wooldridge, 2002, p. 285). Without question, however, the most widely accepted approach to address reverse causality is to implement instrumental-variable regressions. Drawing on the seminal work of Altonji and Card (1991) and Card (2001), Peri and Requena (2010) and Bratti et al. (2014) instrument changes in immigrants at the sub-national level with an imputed inflow of immigrants calculated by applying the net growth of immigrants at the national level to historical sub-regional immigrant stocks.

> If immigrants tend to settle, at least initially, where other persons of the same nationality are already settled, then this constructed inflow of immigrants will be correlated to the actual one. On the other hand, as it is based on the distribution of immigrants across provinces as of 1993, the constructed flows are not affected by any province-specific demand shock during the considered period. (Peri and Requena, 2010, p. 1447)

This approach is not free from criticism, however: Chaflin and Levy (2012) have argued recently that the province-specific element of the instrument will reflect persistent sub-regional characteristics that may affect trade behaviour other than via migration, and thus lead to inconsistent estimates. These authors further argue that the exclusion restriction will be violated if the total outflow of emigrants from a particular origin country were correlated with conditions in particular receiving sub-regions, which would be the case if such immigrants tended to cluster strongly in those provinces. Combes et al. (2005) rather instrument 1993 migrant stocks in France with historical migrant stocks from 1978.

In an alternative approach, Vézina (2012) uses Swiss visa restrictions and migration to a neighbouring country (France) as instruments for Swiss immigration. Sangita (2013) proposes an instrument based on the variation in destination-country citizenship laws, that is, the number of years of residency required in order to obtain citizenship, arguing that such changes are exogenous to changes in trade, investment, business and political climate. While all of the above can be argued to be pretty much exogenous, it is not obvious that any of them passes the exclusion restriction since unobserved cultural and historical factors might be confounding meaningful interpretation.

Most recently, Parsons and Vézina (2014) draw on a unique natural experiment to identify causality running from migration to trade – which, as Felbermayr et al. (2012) note, is potentially the most convincing method for addressing endogeneity concerns – namely the exodus of the Vietnamese Boat People to the USA between 1975 and 1994. These authors note that the large influx of Vietnamese refugees entered the USA at this time during a complete trade embargo of Vietnam. Moreover, the first wave of refugees that entered the USA under the auspices of the Indochina Migration and Refugee Assistance Act 1975 was exogenously allocated across US states. Parsons and Vézina (2014) are thus able to insulate their results from fears of either simultaneity or endogenous location decisions of immigrants. After trade was opened up in 1995, Parsons and Vézina explain state-level trade flows by migration stocks in 1995, but are able to instrument the latter securely with the corresponding 1975 stocks. They find a robust positive causal link from migration and trade. This lends considerable credence to the positive impacts found in the majority of the literature, although the very particular circumstances of this case mean that one can never be entirely sure of its external validity – that is, its applicability to other cases.

2. AID AND MIGRATION

This section focuses on the literature on aid and migration, which has several parallels with that on trade and migration: there are multiple links – in each direction, direct, indirect, general equilibrium – as well as exogenous third factors such as former colonial links that affect both; the problem again is establishing causality, and the focus again is almost entirely on one direction – in this case the extent to which aid flows affect (actually reduce) migration flows from recipient to donor countries. The section comprises four elements. The remainder of this introduction shows how widespread is the view that trade and aid might be used to reduce immigration to developed countries. Subsequently, we discuss the general equilibrium route that operates via recipient countries' income levels. We then look at a number of studies that simply regress migration on aid flows before finally considering 'co-development', which is an essentially European construct that attempts to put an intellectual and policy framework around an anti-immigration stance.

The influence of international trade policy and overseas development aid on migration flows is an issue of some intrinsic interest, but its intellectual interest is dwarfed by its relevance to the policy debate over the last 20 years (and, we predict, the next 20). Governments in developed countries often justify aid to developing countries or the liberalization of their import barriers in terms of helping countries to develop – get richer – so

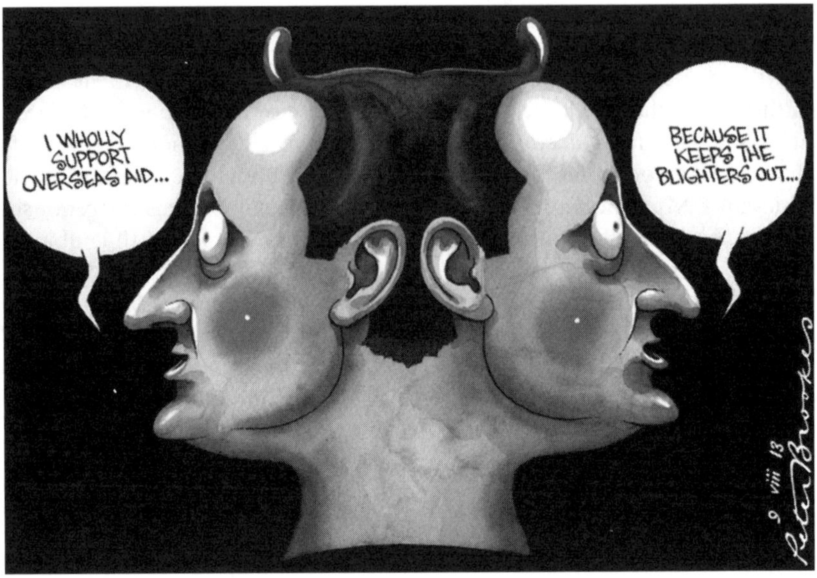

Source: Reproduced with kind permission of Peter Brookes, *The Times* and NewsSyndication.com.

Figure 4.1 The truth about overseas aid?

that their people will not 'come over here'. Figure 4.1, from *The Times*, puts this sentiment into the mouth of David Cameron, the British prime minister.

On aid, for example, the European Union's High Level Working Group on Asylum and Migration, established in 1999, was charged with assessing 'the effectiveness of aid and development strategies in the battle to limit economic migration' (see van Selm, 2004). As recently as 9 October 2013, the president of the European Commission, José Manuel Barroso, said, following the fatal sinking of a refugee boat off Lampedusa, Italy, 'We must also continue our political and development action to improve the living conditions in the countries of origin, working with them there, so that people do not have to flee their homes.'[6]

At a global level, Lucas (2005) estimates a regression of aid inflows per head on net out-migration, together with a few control variables, on a sample of 77 developing countries over 1995–2000. He shows a significantly positive relationship. At a bilateral level, aid and migration are likely to be connected via a common cause – colonial or other long-standing links between countries (Nyberg-Sørensen et al., 2002) – but, given that there are many donors, this cannot explain Lucas's aggregate relationship. Moreover, no positive correlation is observed between aid inflows and developing countries' net in-migration; hence Lucas argues that it is highly plausible to believe that Western countries' aid to developing countries is indeed partly geared towards stemming migration flows.

Similar claims are made for trade liberalization. Schiff (1994), for example, cites Germany's then foreign minister, Klaus Kinkel, as declaring in 1994 that in the context of concern about emigration from East and Central Europe, opening the West European markets to goods from the East was the highest priority of EC policy towards the region. When NAFTA was being negotiated and seemed under threat, US Attorney General Janet Reno is reported to have said: 'If NAFTA passes, my job guarding the border will be easier. If NAFTA fails, my job stopping the flow of illegal immigrants will become even more difficult', and Mexican President Carlos Salinas said 'We want NAFTA because we want to export goods, not people.'[7,8]

Do Trade and Aid Influence Migration?

The transmission mechanism implied in all these views about trade, aid and migration is indirect: trade liberalization and aid are expected to affect the determinants of migration, most obviously incomes in developing countries, under the assumption that higher incomes reduce emigration. In principle, this reasoning is correct, but trade policy and aid might also affect other determinants of migration and so encourage flows, for example the creation of networks or the immediate effect of higher incomes that might encourage emigration because greater numbers of individuals can finance migration costs. Hence the net effect in practice is wholly unclear.

In the very long run, income effects are probably the major determinant of international migration flows. Consider Korea, among the poorest of countries in the early 1960s. Around 2 million Koreans left for temporary employment overseas between 1960 and about 1990 (Park, 1994) and permanent exits ran to approximately 30 000 per year throughout the 1980s (Lee, 1997). By 1993–4, following what were then unprecedented rates of economic growth, permanent exits had fallen to 18 000 per annum, the stock of temporary workers abroad to just 20 000 and immigration was starting to grow – to perhaps 200 000 by 1996 (Lee, 1997). But in Korea, GDP per head (in constant prices) had grown relative to 1960 by 73 per cent in 1970, 191 per cent in 1980, 498 per cent in 1990 and 883 per cent in 2000 (GDP per capita in constant local currency prices, WDI Online, 10 January 2014).

Aid and the openness of export markets clearly contributed to Korean growth, but the growth miracle consisted of far more than these changes alone. Moreover, current policy towards migration has horizons much shorter than four decades, and so Korea is not the 'killer fact' that links aid to declining emigration. A quick back-of-the-envelope calculation shows that the effects of aid as a policy instrument for tackling migration must be very small. A thoughtful account of the effectiveness of aid on economic growth – Clemens et al. (2012, p. 591) – suggests that 'a one percentage-point increase in aid/gross domestic product (GDP) (at mean aid levels) [is] typically . . . followed within several years by . . . a 0.1–0.2 percentage-point increase in growth of real GDP per capita'. That is, *ceteris paribus*, an increase in aid of this magnitude takes five years or more to add 1 per cent to a developing country's income per capita.

A typical income gap between developed- and developing-country GDP per head (measured in PPP) is, say, 2700 per cent of the latter's income (this is the gap between Mozambique and Portugal in 2011). A 1 per cent increase in Mozambique's GDP will not influence the incentives for migration – and at 1 per cent of GDP (approximately $14.2 billion for Mozambique in 2012) it would cost $142 million a year. Even if aid were much more effective than Clemens et al.'s calculations suggest, and even given the much stronger growth effects likely to emanate from increased trade (see, e.g., Winters and Masters, 2013), the qualitative story would not be much changed within several decades. Even should one argue that migration does not respond to simple income gaps but to more subtle differences in welfare and opportunity, these are still massive gaps between rich and poor countries, and it is hard to believe that aid will address them in anything other than the very long run.

Use of a second envelope might allow one to compare the aid- or trade-induced gain in income with the overall relationship between national migration and national income, as sometimes represented by the so-called migration hump. The migration hump is far from uncontentious (see Lucas, 2005, ch. 2, for example), and is discussed in detail by Michael Clemens in Chapter 5 below. To the extent that it exists, however, at incomes below about $7500 per head, further increases in income appear to encourage migration – probably by directly or indirectly relaxing financing constraints – and even once over the hump, the migration-reducing impact of income growth will initially be small.

The links between development and migration are surveyed by Nyberg-Sørensen et al. (2002) and de Haas (2007); both works conclude, for several reasons, that the hope that development will stem the tide of migrants from low- and lower-middle-income countries is a vain one. Much of the rest of this book discusses the determinants of migration, which might be affected by trade or aid. Readers who feel that they know the magnitude of these impacts can construct their own estimates of the indirect effects of aid and trade on migration. Here we focus on the literature that makes these links explicitly. The early discussions essentially unpacked the aid–migration relationship into its indirect links, but, more recently, economists have estimated reduced-form relationships running directly from aid to emigration (from developing countries). Such direct estimates of the effects of trade on migration are very scarce, and while several authors explore whether trade and migration are substitutes or complements, explicitly recognizing that causation may run from trade to migration, none has been able convincingly to separate that link from the opposite one discussed above.[9]

Aid

An early, thoughtful and partly quantitative discussion of aid and migration is Morrison (1982). He observes the likelihood of considerable heterogeneity between cases, but argues that there is little to suggest that realistic improvements in development will curtail migration to the USA, even over decades. He reports some suggestive evidence that 'good jobs' are a way of accumulating the money required to finance emigration from the Dominican Republic, and that the 'social, commercial and political ties' engendered by aid also contribute to increases in migration flows, initially by reducing costs and/or information deficits. He identifies aid-financed employment programmes as the most likely to ease migration pressures, but concedes that, 'Given the relative magnitude of foreign assistance, it cannot be expected that migration "push" factors will be arrested' (ibid., p. 15). Rhoda (1983) makes somewhat similar points about the improbability of stemming rural to urban migration by means of rural development programmes.

Faini and Venturini (1993) take up the same issues a decade later, but from a more macroeconomic perspective. Citing Stanton Russell and Teitelbaum (1992), they argue that income growth may fail to curtail emigration because it relaxes credit constraints and that, given that the latter are more frequently binding in the poorest countries, we should expect to see a migration hump. They then offer a simple regression exercise on four European countries that supports this expectation. Although they are careful not to over-claim the results from their exercise, this paper has been heavily cited in favour of the view that trade liberalization and aid are not suitable instruments for controlling migration.

An important innovation in this area of research is to conduct the analysis at the level at which migration decisions are made, that is, at the individual or household level. Angelucci (2004) studies the Mexican conditional cash transfer programme Progresa (now continued as Oportunidades), which is targeted at poor rural households. The programme includes an unconditional nutrition support grant and some (larger) schooling subsidies that are conditional on attendance in the last four years of primary school and the first three years of secondary school. Angelucci categorizes the nutrition and primary education grants as unconditional, the latter on the grounds that almost all families would continue their children's education to the end of primary school anyway, while considering the secondary schooling grant as genuinely conditional. As discussed above, unconditional transfers may discourage migration by increasing its opportunity cost (making staying put more attractive), or encourage it by relaxing credit constraints on financing migration. The latter effect would be stronger for international than for internal migration because it is costlier. The conditional secondary education grants also increase income and relax credit constraints, but additionally incentivize behaviour that requires families to remain in Mexico. Progresa is additionally attractive from a research perspective since, in 1998 and 1999, the years examined, eligibility for Progresa grants varied across space, grant levels showed considerable heterogeneity across eligible households and grants were large for poor families (e.g. for secondary-school attendance grants rose to around two-thirds of the wage that a teenager might otherwise earn).

While Angelucci's results are not very well determined statistically, they are strong enough to suggest some very interesting forms of behaviour. The programme, for example, is associated with an increase in average international migration but not average domestic migration. This effect is evident largely for households that previously did not have any migrants. Moreover, migration occurred after the transfer of small sums, suggesting that the grants were used to underpin borrowing to finance migration. Households receiving large grants for secondary schooling, on the other hand, showed reduced international migration with Progresa, suggesting that the conditions mattered; moreover, migration was not enhanced, as one might have expected, once schooling was finished and the condition no longer applied. In other words, the effect appeared permanent. Since around one-third of Mexican international migration comprises individuals aged between 13 and 19, such effects could influence overall migration.

The obvious import of these results is that 'aid' targeted at households can affect migration outcomes. The bulk of the aid and migration literature operates at an aggregate level, though, which is clearly different. For at least some developing countries, however, conditional cash transfers are supported by donors either directly (they pay for the programme) or indirectly (they support other activities so that government money can be devoted to the conditional cash transfer). Angelucci's results therefore suggest that, while some transfers tend toward encouraging emigration, that is not necessarily the case if conditions are drawn up with sufficient subtlety.

An influential cross-country study that relates migration directly to aid flows is Berthélemy et al. (2009). They postulate a two-equation model in which the stock of migrants from developing country *i*, in developed country *j*, is potentially influenced by bilateral aid flows, because aid increases the amount of contact between residents of the two countries, by *i*'s total aid receipts, as these might relax a budget or liquidity constraint, and by *j*'s policies towards migration in general. They estimate a gravity model explaining migration as a function of each partner's GDP and population, bilateral trade flows and a series of control variables capturing the cultural and political proximity of the bilateral relationship (e.g. a previous colonial link or having a common language). To these they add the bilateral aid flow, *i*'s total aid inflow and a measure of *j*'s openness to immigrants. Berthélemy et al. recognize the possible endogeneity of bilateral aid. To this end, the authors estimate a second equation modelling aid as a function of *i*'s GDP per head, population and institutional development – the usual variables used to explain aid flows – *j*'s total aid expenditure, *i*'s and *j*'s bilateral trade and historical links. This equation seeks to explain the amount of aid, given that an aid flow exists, but not the selectivity process, whereby donors choose the recipients of their aid, which they assert is unimportant.

The results obtained from estimating this model on a cross-section of 22 OECD migrant-recipient countries and 187 sending countries, suggest strongly that both bilateral aid and *i*'s total aid receipts have significantly positive impacts on migrant stocks. A 10 per cent increase in bilateral aid is associated with (perhaps causes) an approximately 3 per cent increase in the bilateral migrant stock, while a 10 per cent increase in total aid is associated with approximately a 1.5 per cent increase in the migrant stock. The migration policy effect is also significant, with more liberal policies inducing greater migration. Berthélemy et al. investigate the migration hump by allowing for the effects of GDP per head on migration to be non-linear and add to it by recognizing that their model also allows an indirect effect whereby, as developing countries get richer, their aid flows decline, thus reducing migration. The turning point of the combined effect is around US$7300 in terms of 2000 PPP prices, which they argue is approximately the same level as other scholars have found in terms of nominal US dollars.

An interesting disaggregation is between skilled workers (with secondary and tertiary education) and unskilled workers. The latter are more responsive to total aid and less responsive to bilateral aid than the former. This reinforces Berthélemy et al.'s preferred interpretation of their results – namely that total aid operates on the budget/liquidity constraint (which we expect to be far tighter for poorer/less skilled workers), while bilateral aid operates at least partly on the basis of making connections (which are typically more important for skilled workers).

A potential problem that Berthélemy et al. recognize in their specification is that their dependent variable is the migration stock – the number of people in country *j* born in country *i* – which is determined over many years, whereas their aid variables refer to averages over five or ten years. For example, in their migration data (from Parsons et al., 2007) the country that provided the most emigrants in 2000 is the UK, almost certainly due to the length of time over which Britons have been emigrating for reasons quite unrelated to inflows of foreign aid. Two further problems, according to Azam and Berlinschi (2009), are the control variables that Berthélemy et al. choose to include and their failure to allow adequately for the endogeneity of aid. Almost unremarked, Azam and Berlinschi switch from a stock to a flow measure of migration and focus on aggregate rather than bilateral immigration. They seek to explain aggregate inflows of migrants from low- and lower-middle-income countries to 22 OECD countries from 1995 to 2003. Their control variables in the migration flow equation are GDP per head, social expenditures and unemployment in *j*, the stock of native-born people from the sending countries in *j* and a set of fixed effects capturing time-invariant characteristics of receiving countries. With no correction for endogeneity, they replicate Berthélemy et al.'s positive effect of aid on migration (albeit not significant in this exercise). However, when they instrument aid flows, they instead find large negative effects, that is, that aid discourages immigration.

This, of course, is exactly the result that popular debate and the politicians hope for, but, unfortunately for them, Azam and Berlinschi's results are not convincing. Their instruments for aid, which, recall, ought to explain aid flows, while not having any direct effect on migration, are the recipient country's public expenditure on order and security and the percentage of right-wing members in the parliament, each of which they show has a positive effect on aid flows. The difficulty is the ease with which one can imagine that countries with strong right-wing parliamentary representation and high law-and-order spending make unattractive destinations for migrants, and so have lower immigration *ceteris paribus* than other countries. In Azam and Berlinschi's estimates, this direct negative effect is falsely attributed to aid. Thus, while Azam and Berlinschi offer an interesting discussion of migration and the effectiveness of aid (the issue on which their work aims to contribute), their paper does not overturn the widespread finding that aid to low- and lower-middle-income countries is more likely to encourage emigration.

Another off-shoot of Berthélemy et al. (2009) is Moullan (2013), who analyses the medical brain drain and health-related overseas aid flows. Moullan analyses a panel comprising eight years (1998–2005), 17 destination countries and 192 source countries, using a model that relates the annual outflow of physicians from sending countries (strictly the pseudo-flow derived by differencing stock data) to receipts of health aid over the three preceding years, together with some controls. The relationship between the two appears to be positive in a simple OLS regression, but when he allows for the endogeneity of aid by applying the generalized method of moments (GMM), it turns out to be significantly negative. In fact, in the long run, the effect is large. A doubling of health aid reduces the outflow of physicians by 71 per cent. Interestingly, Moullan finds that aid in the form of technical assistance is more effective than financial aid in stemming outflows. He speculates that this is because financial aid is vulnerable to both fungibility and predatory or inefficient bureaucracies, which reduce the net amounts getting through to health services. It may also arise if the medical brain drain reflects physicians' frustration with their inability to get good training or to provide good health services at home, as well as their low rewards, as is often claimed (Kangasniemi et al., 2007). One might also question the ability of GMM to really neutralize endogeneity (see, e.g., Clemens et al., 2012), but in fact Moullan's result is perfectly consistent with the general results of Berthélemy et al. Physicians are much less subject to budget or liquidity constraints than are less skilled workers, and the links from health aid to physicians' welfare in the absence of migration are much more direct and easily internalized than those between official assistance in general and the overall workforce.

Co-development

We assess the evidence as showing fairly strongly that aid flows to low- and lower-middle-income countries will tend to encourage rather than discourage emigration. Nonetheless, as we noted above, and as Figure 4.1 captures so crisply, politicians persist in believing or wishing the opposite were true.[10] The most evident manifestation of that desire is the European policy of co-development, a tortured combination of development and migration policies – which aspires to reconcile the interests of developing countries in terms of leveraging migration for development – and the overwhelming desire of European policy makers to curtail inflows of immigrants, especially illegal immigrants and asylum seekers, but also, in truth, legal labour migrants.[11] The torture reflects the near impossibility of reconciling these interests, the divisions among European bureaucrats about development policy and the sensitivity of discussing migration without being (or appearing to be) racist, or at least condescending, about developing-country residents.

The essence of the term 'co-development' in the migration context is captured in the Conclusion of the European Council Meeting in Tampere in 1999, which stated the EU's need for

> a comprehensive approach to migration addressing political, human rights and development issues in countries and regions of origin and transit. This requires combating poverty, improving living standards and job opportunities, preventing conflicts and consolidating democratic states and ensuring respect for human rights . . . Partnership with third countries concerned will also be a key element for the success of such a policy, with a view to promoting co-development. (European Council, 1999, para. 11, quoted by van Selm, 2004, p. 10)

Van Selm (2004) gives a fascinating account of the evolution of the European policy positions around co-development since 1998. There was always more to it than just incentivizing developing countries to introduce policies to reduce emigration in return for flows of foreign assistance, but this aspect was never far from the surface. In principle, other elements could include policies to encourage remittance flows and other diaspora contributions to development, return programmes, repatriation agreements for asylum seekers, more active policies to discourage illegal migrants from setting off for Europe, 'ethical' recruitment whereby Europe did not poach skilled workers (notably medical staff) and easier visa formalities for those workers who were permitted to migrate (Weil, 2002). But as Weil shows, actual policy fell a long way short of such aspirations.

The initial European statements were pretty direct about curtailing migration flows. For example, an Austrian Strategy Paper for the Presidency in 1998 states that EU migration policy 'must obviously cover . . . Reduction of migratory pressure in the main countries of origin' (van Selm, 2004, p. 5). However, over time the rhetoric became a little more conciliatory and policies became a little more developing-country-oriented, although at the cost of becoming much vaguer – see, for example, Reslow (2010) on the 'Global Approach to Migration' and the 'Policy Plan on Legal Migration', both of 2005. This was partly in response to complaints from developing countries (for example, there was considerable friction with Morocco; see Reslow, 2010), and partly because of the resistance of the development agencies of the European Commission and national administrations to having aid monies devoted to curtailing legitimate migration, especially that of asylum seekers who might be fleeing human rights abuses.

The difference between co-development and the more general discussion above is that the former supplements the hope that development will curtail migration flows, with the explicit orientation of aid flows towards policies that will have that effect. During the 2000s, the volume of aid increased quite substantially and significantly faster than most elements of government expenditure. Home Affairs and Justice Ministries hoped to use some of that resource for migration policies, while development specialists resisted – often citing the requirements that for the OECD to count a flow as aid (and the OECD's Development Assistance Committee is the official arbiter of what does so count), it must be focused on the recipient's development needs.

Despite the objections by aid agencies, however, aid has been geared to reducing migration in quite significant amounts, as Adepoju et al. (2010) report.[12] For example, the EU had 'to provide substantial assistance to ensure the long-term sustainability of control efforts' in Morocco. The EU–Mali migration control agreement signed in 2006 promised €426 million in aid over 2008–13. Spain 'offered Gambia and Guinea €5 million each in direct development aid in exchange for signing global migration agreements involving re-admission, migration control and labour migration'. Finally, in 2003 the UK and Spain suggested punitive cuts in aid flows against countries that failed to 'actively collaborate in the fight against illegal migration', although other members blocked the policy.

Because of the difficulties of devising a counter-factual, it is impossible to evaluate the effectiveness of co-development. Certainly we know of no attempts to do so. Adepoju et al. report that, in 2001, 500 immigrants volunteered to return to Mali from France in return for US$3600 each to start a business, and that after two years 80 per cent of them were still in business. What we do not know, of course, is how many of them were intending to return anyway.

It is easy to see where the idea of co-development comes from – the application of an instrument concerning developing countries (aid) to an objective concerning developed countries (that they stop their people from coming to Europe). It is gradually evolving towards a more constructive and cooperative form, but only slowly, and it is difficult at present to see it as either elegant or successful. Developing countries are generally not willing participants, and the bulk of the expenditure is fairly obviously devoted to developed-, not developing-country objectives and should not be considered as aid. Flows of resources may thus buy a reduction in migration, but only by spending on what are basically coercive measures;

the reductions do not arise because aid, properly conceived, reduces migration.

CONCLUSION

We have reviewed the literature on some of the connections between international trade, international migration and international aid. It is a flawed and frustrating literature, but this is because the subject is complex and resistant to many of the recent advances in economic methodology based on microeconomic data. The difficulties do not reflect a lack of interest – indeed there is now quite a large and active literature – and that is because migration is becoming one of the most sensitive and contentious policy issues to confront economists. This in turn means that the profession cannot turn its back on the question in a fit of methodological purity, but instead must do the best job it can in difficult circumstances.

The fundamental challenge is identifying causation – a necessary step if one is to make useful contributions to policy. General equilibrium theory implies that everything potentially depends on everything else, but the elegant neoclassical theory of international trade says more – namely that international migration and international trade are perfect substitutes, such that you need only one of them to achieve exactly the outcome that you would get with the other. Thus empirical work, which observes outcomes and seeks to infer causes, faces a Sisyphean task. Fortunately, however, the assumptions of the neoclassical model are manifestly not true and we can identify many ways in which trade and migration are linked either indirectly or directly. The literature essentially tries to quantify these links and to insulate itself as best it can against the possibility that other causal channels are in play.

Nearly all the extant empirical results suggest that migration and trade are positively related, and considerable ingenuity has gone into trying to identify the relevant causal channels. Migrants may affect trade directly by demanding products from their home countries and/or facilitating trade with other countries via their information about or networks in those countries. Different elements of trade are potentially affected by these different links to different extents, and different sorts of migrants may deliver them in different mixes. By exploiting these differences, economists have started to map out the details of the direct (i.e. non-general equilibrium) links between the two. Thus empiricists have sought identification by examining differences in the sensitivity of trade to migration across product types, geographical distance, firm versus personal networks and migrant characteristics. One persistent result is that migrants have a stronger pro-trade effect when other pro-trade features – such as sound institutions, the rule of law, common language or shared cultural background – are weak or missing.

Turning to aid and migration, we observe the strength and ubiquity of the wish that aid flows from rich to poor countries might curtail the flow of people in the opposite direction. Little of the evidence lends weight to this hope, and indeed most seems to suggest that aid increases migration – probably either because it raises incomes and hence relaxes constraints on financing emigration, or because it results in more frequent interactions and network formation between donor and recipient countries. Nevertheless, European policy makers have sought to leverage aid to reduce migration through policies of so-called co-development, which, *inter alia*, use donor finance to fund or incentivize policies that operate on emigration directly. We note that this has been neither elegant nor successful.

Clearly the literature is primarily devoted to quantifying the effect of international migration on international trade and the effect of international aid on international migration. We argue that this is because these links are both easier to isolate and identify, while also being of greater policy relevance. While there is a small literature on the link from trade to migration, it fails to convince. This is a strong candidate for future research, however. Future research on all links is likely to be facilitated by richer data, especially more detailed microeconomic data on migrants, which includes their histories and their activities. Such data are unlikely to be collected for other purposes, however, so it will require a concerted effort by academics and funders of research to generate them, which, given the topicality of migration, we deem extremely worthwhile.

NOTES

1. Of course another explanation for consistency is publication bias, but the fact that we identify a number of published studies where migration is said to reduce trade should alleviate that concern somewhat.
2. In addition there are some more technical factors that might cause the equivalence to break down – for example, there may be more factors than goods, or technology may be such that the same goods prices are consistent with different factor prices (the case of so-called factor intensity reversals).
3. Gould mentioned 'networks' but once in his paper, while Rauch uses the term 18 times in Rauch (1996) and 17 times in Rauch (1999).
4. Felbermayr et al. (2012) build on this interpretation by distinguishing networks, further militating against asymmetric information.
5. Rauch's solution based on his model of differentiated goods is that low-transportation-cost goods are traded through networks, while, conversely, high-transportation-cost

commodities are sold on international organized exchanges, in which case product homogeneity results in correct price signals being transmitted.
6. http://europa.eu/rapid/press-release_SPEECH-13-792_en.htm.
7. *Migration News*, February 2000, **7**(2), http://migration.ucdavis.edu/mn/more.php?id=2025_0_2_0).
8. According to Morrison (1982), however, Salinas was echoing a previous president, Lopez Portillo, in 1978.
9. Faini et al. (1999) contains several chapters on the substitute/complement question, and Del Río and Thorwarth (2009) offer an interesting discussion of NAFTA and illegal Mexican–US migration.
10. Or maybe they just pretend to wish that. In the field of international trade policy, Jagdish Bhagwati (1988) has coined the phrase 'porous protection' to cover precisely those cases where policy makers pursue ostensibly vigorous anti-import policies while understanding that they will have little actual effect.
11. Chapter 6 below by Flore Gubert discusses the history and nature of co-development in more detail.
12. Not all financial support for migration control policies in developing countries was billed as aid, but we do not make a distinction here.

REFERENCES

Adepoju, A., Van Noorloos, F. and Zoomers, A. (2010). Europe's migration agreements with migrant-sending countries in the global South: a critical review, *International Migration*, **48**(3), 42–75.

Aleksynska, M. and Peri, G. (2014). Isolating the network effect of immigrants on trade, *The World Economy*, **37**(3), 434–55.

Altonji, J.G. and Card, D. (1991). The effects of immigration on the labor market outcomes of less-skilled natives. In John Abowd and Richard Freeman (eds), *Immigration, Trade and the Labor Market*. Chicago, IL: University of Chicago Press, pp. 201–34.

Anderson, J.E. and Marcouiller, D. (2002). Insecurity and the pattern of trade: an empirical investigation, *The Review of Economics and Statistics*, **84**(2), 342–52.

Anderson, J.E. and van Wincoop, E. (2003). Gravity with gravitas: a solution to the border puzzle, *American Economic Review*, **93**(1), 170–92.

Angelucci, M. (2004). Aid and migration: an analysis of the impact of Progresa on the timing and size of labour migration. IZA Discussion Papers 1187, Institute for the Study of Labor (IZA).

Artal-Tur, A., Pallardo-Lopez, V.J. and Requena-Silvante, F. (2012). The trade-enhancing effect of immigration networks: new evidence on the role of geographic proximity, *Economics Letters*, **116**, 554–7.

Azam, J. and Berlinschi, R. (2009). L'aide contre l'immigration, *Revue d'économie du développement*, **23**(4), 81–108.

Baldwin, R. and Taglioni, D. (2006). Gravity for dummies and dummies for gravity equations. National Bureau of Economic Research Working Paper Series No. 12516.

Bandyopadhyay, S., Coughlin, C.C. and Wall, H.J. (2008). Ethnic networks and U.S. exports, *Review of International Economics*, **16**(1), 199–213.

Bardhan, A.D. and Guhathakurta, S. (2004). Global linkages of sub-national regions: coastal exports and international networks, *Contemporary Economic Policy*, **22**(2), 225–36.

Bastos, P. and Silva, J. (2012). Networks, firms, and trade, *Journal of International Economics*, **87**(2), 352–64.

Benson, B.L. (1989). The spontaneous evolution of commercial law, *Southern Economic Journal*, **55**(3), 644–61.

Bergstrand, J.H. (1985). The gravity equation in international trade: some microeconomic foundations and empirical evidence, *The Review of Economics and* Statistics, **67**(3), 474–81.

Berkowitz, D., Moenius, J. and Pistor, K. (2006). Trade, law, and product complexity, *The Review of Economics and Statistics*, **88**(2), 363–73.
Berthélemy, J., Beuran, M. and Maurel, M. (2009). Aid and migration: substitutes or complements?, *World Development*, **37**(10), 1589–99.
Bhagwati, J. (1988). *Protectionism*. Cambridge, MA: MIT Press.
Blanes, J.V. (2008). Characteristics of immigrants and bilateral trade, *Revista de Economia Aplicada*, **16**(48), 133–59.
Bratti, M., Benedictis, L. and Santoni, G. (2014 forthcoming). On the pro-trade effects of immigrants, *Review of World Economics*.
Briant, A., Combes, P. and Lafourcade, M. (2014). Product complexity, quality of institutions and the protrade effect of immigrants, *The World Economy*, **37**(1), 63–85.
Broda, C. and Weinstein, D.E. (2006). Globalization and the gains from variety, *The Quarterly Journal of Economics*, **121**(2), 541–85.
Card, David (2001). Immigrant inflows, native outflows, and the local labor market impacts of higher immigration, *Journal of Labor Economics*, **19**(1), 22–64.
Chaflin, A. and Levy, M. (2012). The effect of Mexican immigration on the wages and employment of U.S. Natives: evidence from the size of Mexican birth cohorts. Working Paper, University of California at Berkeley.
Chaney, T. (2008). Distorted gravity: the intensive and extensive margins of international trade, *American Economic Review*, **98**(4), 1707–21.
Cheng, I.-H. and Wall, H.J. (2005). Controlling for heterogeneity in gravity models of trade and integration. Working Papers, Federal Reserve Bank of St Louis, No. 1999-010.
Clemens, M.A., Radelet, S., Bhavnani, R.R. and Bazzi, S. (2012). Counting chickens when they hatch: timing and the effects of aid on growth, *The Economic Journal*, **122**(561), 590–617.
Co, C.Y., Euzent, P. and Martin, T. (2004). The export effect of immigration into the USA, *Applied Economics*, **36**(6), 573–83.
Combes, P., Lafourcade, M. and Mayer, T. (2005). The trade-creating effects of business and social networks: evidence from France, *Journal of International Economics*, **66**(1), 1–29.
Coughlin, C.C. and Wall, H.J. (2011). Ethnic networks and trade: intensive versus extensive margins, *Economics Letters*, **113**(1), 73–5.
De Haas, H. (2007). Turning the tide? Why development will not stop migration, *Development and Change*, **38**(5), 819–41.
Del Río, A.M. and Thorwarth, S. (2009). Tomatoes or tomato pickers? Free trade and migration between Mexico and the United States, *Journal of Applied Economics*, **12**(1), 109–34.
Diaz-Alejandro, C.F. (1970). *Essays on the Economic History of the Argentine Republic*. New Haven, CT and London: Yale University Press.
Dunlevy, J. (2006). The influence of corruption and language on the pro-trade effect of immigrants: evidence from the American States, *Review of Economics and Statistics*, **88**(1), 182–6.
Dunlevy, J. and Hutchinson, W. (1999). The impact of immigration on American import trade in the late nineteenth and twentieth centuries, *Journal of Economic History*, **59**(4), 1043–62.
Dunlevy, J. and Hutchinson, W. (2001). The pro-trade effects of immigration on American exports during the period 1870 to 1910. Vanderbilt University Working Paper 01-W25.
European Council (1999). *Presidency Conclusions, Tampere European Council*. Brussels: Council of Ministers.
Faini, R. and Venturini, A. (1993). Trade, aid and migrations: some basic policy issues, *European Economic Review*, **37**(2), 435–42.
Faini, R., Zimmerman, K.F. and de Melo, J. (1999). *Migration: The Controversies and the Evidence*. Cambridge: Cambridge University Press.
Feenstra, R. (2004). *Advanced International Trade: Theory and Evidence*. Princeton, NJ: Princeton University Press.
Felbermayr, G.J. and Jung, B. (2009). The pro-trade effect of the brain drain: sorting out confounding factors, *Economics Letters*, **104**(2), 72–5.

Felbermayr, G.J., Jung, B. and Toubal, F. (2010). Ethnic network, information and international trade: revisiting the evidence, *Annales d'Economie et de Statistique*, **97/98**, 41–70.
Felbermayr, Gabriel J. and Toubal, Farid (2010). Cultural proximity and trade, *European Economic Review*, **54**(2), 279–93.
Felbermayr, G.J. and Toubal, F. (2012). Revisiting the trade–migration nexus: evidence from new OECD data, *World Development*, **40**(5), 928–37.
Felbermayr, Gabriel, Grossmann, Volker and Kohler, Wilhelm (2012). Migration, international trade and capital formation: cause or effect? IZA Discussion Papers 6975, Institute for the Study of Labor (IZA).
Genc, M., Gheasi, M., Nijkamp, P. and Poot, J. (2011). The impact of immigration on international trade: a meta-analysis. IZA Discussion Paper 6145.
Girma, S. and Yu, Z. (2002). The link between immigration and trade: evidence from the UK, *Review of World Economics*, **138**(1), 115–30.
Gould, D.M. (1994). Immigrant links to the home country: empirical implications for U.S. bilateral trade flows, *The Review of Economics and Statistics*, **76**, 302–16.
Granovetter, M.S. (1973). The strength of weak ties. *The American Journal of Sociology*, **78**(6), 1360–80.
Greaney, T.M. (2005). Measuring network effects on trade: are Japanese affiliates distinctive?, *Journal of the Japanese and International Economies*, **19**(2), 194–214.
Greif, A. (1989). Reputation and coalitions in medieval trade: evidence on the Maghribi traders, *Journal of Economic History*, **XLIX**, 857–82.
Greif, A. (1992). Institutions and international trade: lessons from the commercial revolution, *American Economic Review*, **82**(2), 128–33.
Greif, A. (1993). Contract enforceability and economic institutions in early trade: the Maghribi traders' coalition, *American Economic Review*, **83**(3), 525–48.
Greif, A., Milgrom, P. and Weingast, B. (1994). Coordination, commitment and enforcement: the case of the Merchant Guild, *Journal of Political Economy*, **102**, 912–50.
Hatzigeorgiou, A. (2010a). Does immigration stimulate foreign trade? Evidence from Sweden, *Journal of Economic Integration*, **25**(2), 376–402.
Hatzigeorgiou, A. (2010b). Migration as trade facilitation: assessing the links between international trade and migration, *The B.E. Journal of Economic Analysis & Policy*, **10**(1), 1–35.
Head, K. and Ries, J. (1998). Immigration and trade creation: econometric evidence from Canada. *Canadian Journal of Economics*, 47–62.
Herander, M.G. and Saavedra, L.A. (2005). Exports and the structure of immigrant-based networks: the role of geographic proximity, *The Review of Economics and Statistics*, **87**(2), 323–35.
Hiller, S. (2013). Does immigrant employment matter for export sales? Evidence from Denmark, *Review of World Economics* (*Weltwirtschaftliches Archiv*), **149**(2), 369–94.
Iacovone, L. and Javorcik, B.S. (2010). Multi-product exporters: product churning, uncertainty and export discoveries, *Economic Journal*, **120**(544), 481–99.
Jansen, M. and Piermartini, R. (2009). Temporary migration and bilateral trade flows, *The World Economy*, **32**(5), 735–53.
Kangasniemi, M., Winters, L.A. and Commander, S. (2007). Is the medical brain drain beneficial? Evidence from overseas doctors in the UK, *Social Science & Medicine*, **65**(5), 915–23.
Law, D., Genç, M. and Bryant, J. (2013). Trade, diaspora and migration to New Zealand, *The World Economy*, 582–606.
Lee, H.K. (1997). The employment of foreign workers in Korea: issues and policy suggestions, *International Sociology*, **12**(3), 353–71.
Lucas, R.E. (2005). *International Migration and Economic Development: Lessons from Low-income Countries*. Cheltenham, UK and Northampton, MA, USA: Edward Elgar Publishing.
Markusen, J.R. (1983). Factor movements and commodity trade as complements, *Journal of International Economics*, **14**(3–4), 341–56.
Martin, P. (1997). Economic instruments to affect countries of origin. In Rainer Munz and

Myron Weiner (eds), *Migrants, Refugees, and Foreign Policy: US and German Policies towards Countries of Origin*. Oxford: Berghahn Books, pp. 231–70.
Milgrom, P.R., North, D.C. and Weingast, B.R. (1990). The role of institutions in the revival of trade: the law merchant, private judges, and the champagne fairs. *Economics & Politics*, **2**(1), 1–23.
Millimet, D.L. and Osang, T. (2007). Do state borders matter for U.S. intranational trade? The role of history and internal migration, *Canadian Journal of Economics*, **40**(1), 93–126.
Morrison, T.K. (1982). The relationship of US aid, trade and investment to migration pressures in major sending countries. *International Migration Review*, 4–26.
Moullan, Y. (2013). Can foreign health assistance reduce the medical brain drain? *Journal of Development Studies*, **10**(49), 1436–52, doi: 10.1080/00220388.2013.794261.
Muller, T. and Tai, S.H.T. (2012). The role of migration networks in international trade: a sectoral approach. Conference paper, 5th International Conference on Migration and Development, Paris.
Mundell, R. (1957). International trade and factor mobility, *American Economic Review*, **47**, 321–35.
Nyberg-Sørensen, N., Hear, N.V. and Engberg-Pedersen, P. (2002). The migration–development nexus: evidence and policy options: state-of-the-art overview, *International Migration*, **40**(5), 3–47.
Özden, Ç., Parsons, C.R., Schiff, M. and Walmsley, T.L. (2011). Where on earth is everybody? The evolution of global bilateral migration, 1960–2000, *World Bank Economic Review*, 25(1), 12–56.
Park, Y.-B. (1994). The turning point in international migration and economic development in Korea, *Asian and Pacific Migration Journal*, **3**(1), 149–75.
Parsons, C.R., Skeldon, R., Walmsley, T. and Winters, L.A. (2007). Quantifying international migration: a database of bilateral migrant stocks. In Ç. Özden and M. Schiff (eds), *International Migration and Economic Development*. New York: Palgrave Macmillan, pp. 17–58.
Parsons, C.R. and Vézina, P.L. (2014). Migrant networks and trade: the Vietnamese Boat People as a natural experiment. Conference paper, 8th Empirical Investigations in Trade and Investment (EITI) Conference in Phuket, Thailand (20–22 March).
Peri, G. and Requena, F. (2010). The trade creation effect of immigrants: evidence from the remarkable case of Spain, *Canadian Journal of Economics*, **43**(4), 1433–59.
Piperakis, A.S., Milner, C. and Wright, P.W. (2003). Immigration, trade costs and trade: gravity evidence for Greece. *Journal of Economic Integration*, **18**(4), 1–13.
Rauch, J. (1996). Trade and search: social capital, Sogo Shosha, and spillovers. National Bureau of Economic Research Working Paper 5618.
Rauch, J. (1999). Networks versus markets in international trade, *Journal of International Economics*, **48**(June), 7–35.
Rauch, James E. (2001). Business and social networks in international trade, *Journal of Economic Literature*, **39**(4), 1177–203.
Rauch, J. and Casella, A. (2003). Overcoming informational barriers to international resource allocation: prices and ties, *Economic Journal*, **113**(January), 21–42.
Rauch, J. and Trindade, V. (2002). Ethnic Chinese networks in international trade, *Review of Economics and Statistics*, **84**, 116–30.
Ravenstein, E.G. (1885). The laws of migration, *Journal of the Statistical Society*, **48**(2), 167–235.
Reslow, N. (2010). Migration and development? An assessment of recent EU initiatives, *Journal of Contemporary European Research*, **6**(1), 3–21.
Rhoda, R. (1983). Rural development and urban migration: can we keep them down on the farm?, *International Migration Review*, 34–64.
Rotunno, L. and Vézina, P. (2012). Chinese networks and tariff evasion, *The World Economy*, **35**(12), 1772–94.
Samuelson, P.A. (1949). International factor-price equalisation once again, *The Economic Journal*, **59**(234), 181–97.

Sangita, S. (2013). The effect of diasporic business networks on international trade flows, *Review of International Economics*, **21**(2), 266–80.
Santos Silva, J.M.C. and Tenreyro, S. (2006). The log of gravity, *Review of Economics and Statistics*, **88**(4), 641–58.
Schiff, M.W. (1994). How trade, aid, and remittances affect international migration. World Bank Policy Research Working Paper No. 1376.
Stanton Russell, S.S. and Teitelbaum, M.S. (1992). *International Migration and International Trade* (Vol. 160). Washington, DC: World Bank-free PDF.
Tadesse, B. and White, R. (2007). Cultural distance as a determinant of bilateral trade flows: do immigrants counter the effect of cultural differences? *Applied Economics Letters*, **17**(2), 147–52.
Trefler, D. (1995). The case of the missing trade and other mysteries, *American Economic Review*, **85**(5), 1029–46.
Van Selm, J. (2004). The EU as global player in the refugee protection regime. Academy for Migration Studies in Denmark (AMID) Working Paper Series, 35.
Vézina, P.L. (2012). How migrant networks facilitate trade: evidence from Swiss exports, *Swiss Journal of Economics and Statistics*, **148**(III), 449–76.
Wagner, D., Head, K.C. and Ries, J.C. (2002), Immigration and the trade of provinces, *Scottish Journal of Political Economy*, **49**, 507–25.
Weil, P. (2002). Towards a coherent policy of co-development, *International Migration*, **40**(3), 41–55.
White, R. (2007a). An examination of the Danish immigrant–trade link, *International Migration*, **45**(5), 61–86.
White, R. (2007b). Immigrant–trade links, transplanted home bias and network effects, *Applied Economics*, **39**(7), 839–52.
White, R. and Tadesse, B. (2007). Immigration policy, cultural pluralism and trade: evidence from the white Australia policy, *Pacific Economic Review*, **12**(4), 489–509.
White, R. and Tadesse, B. (2008). Cultural distance and the US immigrant–trade link, *The World Economy*, **31**(8), 1078–96.
White, R. and Tadesse, B. (2010). The effects of refugee and non-refugee immigrants on US trade with their home countries, *The Journal of International Trade & Economic Development*, **19**(2), 289–317.
Winters, L.A. and Masters, A. (2013). Openness and growth: still an open question? *Journal of International Development*, **25**(8), 1061–70.
Wooldridge, J.M. (2002). *Econometric Analysis of Cross Section and Panel Data*. Cambridge, MA: MIT Press.

5. The discourse and practice of co-development in Europe

Flore Gubert[1]

INTRODUCTION

Over the last 15 years or so, the relations between migration and development, and the influence they have on each other, have captured the attention of an increasing number of researchers and policy makers. In a context of globalization and growing mobility, the former have devoted much work to assessing the developmental impact of migration for the countries of origin. Part of their motivation has come from the spectacular increase in remittance flows to developing countries, which are estimated to have totaled $401 billion in 2012.[2] Overall, their conclusions suggest that the impact of international migration strongly varies from one country to another, depending on a number of factors among which are the number of migrants, their characteristics, the type of migration, the conditions of stay in host countries as well as the quality of institutions in sending countries. However, it is generally acknowledged that remittances, at least in the short term, improve the living standards of thousands of households, particularly in Africa, and that they are often better at combating transitory poverty than the external financial flows associated with development assistance because they are more precisely targeted. Migrants' collective contributions through hometown associations have also been recognized as significantly improving the provision of public goods in the localities of origin. Last but not least, other less tangible contributions have been put forward, such as the transfer of know-how and competencies, or the diffusion of ideas, values and behaviors towards migrant-sending countries.

Among European policy makers, the idea that migration is a force that can contribute to development has also gained ground. At the EU level, this is attested by the many communications that have been issued in this area for the last ten years or so, and the motivation displayed by policy makers for engaging in the migration and development area.[3] However, there is a huge gap between EU discourse and EU concrete action towards the goal of making migration work for development. Indeed, if migration were considered as having positive effects on development, and if development were a priority for the EU, one obvious policy option would be to open borders or, at least, to set more generous quotas for the legal entry of immigrants. Another policy option would be to allow migrants to earn more and therefore to remit more, or to make return or circular migration more likely by offering legal status to migrants or easing the availability of re-entry visas. What the EU and its member states have chosen instead is to concentrate on trying to restrain labor migration and to combat irregular migration. And when development enters into the story, it is generally because decision makers see it as a cure for migration much more than as a result from it. In other words, while endorsing and contributing to the mainstream discourse linking migration to development, the EU has continued to erect barriers preventing migration and thus limiting its developmental potential.

Admittedly, things have changed a little in the last few years. As underlined by Collyer (2011), the most obvious example of widespread practical changes has been in relation to remittances, with many initiatives taken here and there to lower the cost of transferring funds from destination to origin countries and to increase legal options for sending money.[4] Moreover, incoherencies at the national and supranational levels have not inhibited civil-society actors from collaborating with a view to designing and experimenting programs aimed at reinforcing the development impact of migration. In the meantime, the content as well as the form of migration and development discussions have been slowly changing.

In order to highlight and better appreciate these evolutions, this chapter first presents a historical overview of European policy experience in the field of migration and development. The discussion mainly focuses on the emergence of the so-called co-development approach which was first adopted in France before being emulated by other European countries. As will be made clear, different interpretations have been given of the term. Initially identified with policies to control migration flows and with the promotion of returns, the concept of co-development has progressively evolved to encompass any measure aimed at promoting and supporting migrants as agents for development. However, the experiences of France, the Netherlands, Spain and Italy with co-development policies shed light on the diverse understanding and application of the concept.[5] The chapter then provides concrete examples of state and non-state initiatives in the migration and development field, and highlights good practices, challenges and lessons learned. It ends with some concluding remarks on the way forward.

I. CO-DEVELOPMENT POLICIES IN EUROPE: A HISTORICAL PERSPECTIVE

Since the economic recession that followed the oil crisis of 1973, national governments in Europe have mostly seen migration as a phenomenon to be controlled. As a result, European co-development policies have always had the double agenda of curbing migration and encouraging returns while promoting development. However, the failure of return migration policies in the 1970s and 1980s, together with the growing appreciation of the scale of migrants' remittances and transnational practices, have resulted in more optimistic views regarding migration and how it affects development. Therefore policies have been recently implemented in several European member states in order to increase the potential developmental impact of migration, and even if there are some remaining incoherencies and ambiguities as to the objectives pursued, there are now many projects under way in the field of migration and development involving a variety of state and non-state actors.

I.1 The Early Phases of Europe's Co-development Approach (1970s–1980s): Voluntary Return Programs

The interest in the complex relationship between migration and development in Europe dates from the early 1970s. After the oil crisis of 1973, which resulted in a massive economic downturn and increasing unemployment, several Western European governments implemented more restrictive immigration policies. Guest-worker recruitments were put to an end and borders were closed for low-skilled migrants. In the meantime, various countries, including France, Germany and the Netherlands, started experimenting with development aid programs aimed at encouraging migrants, especially unemployed ones, to return to their origin countries. Most assisted voluntary return (AVR) programs, on paper at least, were aimed at mixing different objectives: first, the effective and 'sustainable' return of legal and/or illegal immigrants; second, the increase in source-country development; and third, the reduction of the push factors of migration from those countries. To this end, some of them included various combinations of four types of assistance: financial support for return travel expenses; one-off grants; start-up grants or loans for micro-enterprises; and vocational training (Koser, 2001).[6]

In France, two successive programs were launched in 1977 and 1984 respectively in the context of the first massive industry restructuring plans following the economic recession, particularly in the automobile industry (Linares, 2009). The first program, called '*Aide au retour*', granted financial support of up to 10000 French francs (€1500) to legal migrants willing to return home. Better known as the '*Million Stoléru*' after the name of its initiator, this program failed to achieve its objective of 100000 repatriations per year. At the time it was abrogated, in November 1981, only 94984 persons had taken up the offer, most of whom were Spanish or Portuguese guest workers near retirement age (not the targeted African immigrants) who had already decided to return to their home countries (Observatoire permanent de la coopération française, 1998, p. 119). The second scheme, called 'Aide publique à la réinsertion' (APR), concerned legal foreign workers from all countries (except EC citizens) at risk of losing their jobs or unemployed for less than three months. Eligible migrants could benefit from a lump sum of 20000 French francs (€3049) to facilitate their reintegration into their country of origin. Their travel expenses were borne by the state and they were entitled to unemployment benefit. As for the '*Aide au retour*', the efficiency of this scheme proved to be limited. According to the figures provided by the French Office des Migrations Internationales (OMI), which was in charge of implementing the program, only 30936 workers took advantage of the offer before 1991 (although when one considers all family members, 70481 persons were affected in total). This figure boiled down to 3237 for the 1991–99 period and to 113 for the 2000–05 period (Secrétariat Général du Comité interministériel de contrôle de l'immigration, 2007). Other return or reintegration programs followed in subsequent years: in 1991, a return scheme targeting illegal resident migrants or failed asylum seekers (the so-called 'Invités à quitter la France', or IQF) was launched ('Aide au Retour Volontaire', ARV), followed, one year later, by a similar scheme targeting migrants in a difficult financial situation or in distress ('Aide au Retour Humanitaire', ARH) (see Figure 5.1a).

In Germany, several return programs were set up in the 1970s for guest workers and asylum seekers or refugees. Concerning the latter, the Ministry for Family, Youth and Health gave the International Organization for Migration (IOM) the authority to implement the Reintegration and Emigration Program for Asylum-Seekers in Germany (REAG) in 1979, complemented by the Government Assisted Repatriation Program (GARP) in 1989 (Schibel, 2004). Both were humanitarian programs assisting with financial and operational support the voluntary return and migration to third countries. Eligible candidates were (and have been since then) asylum seekers, rejected asylum seekers and recognized refugees as well as war and civil-war refugees, victims of forced prostitution or trafficking and other foreigners.[7] More than half a million people have been assisted to return home voluntarily or emigrate to a third country since the start of the programs, which are still running (see Figure 5.1b). With regard to

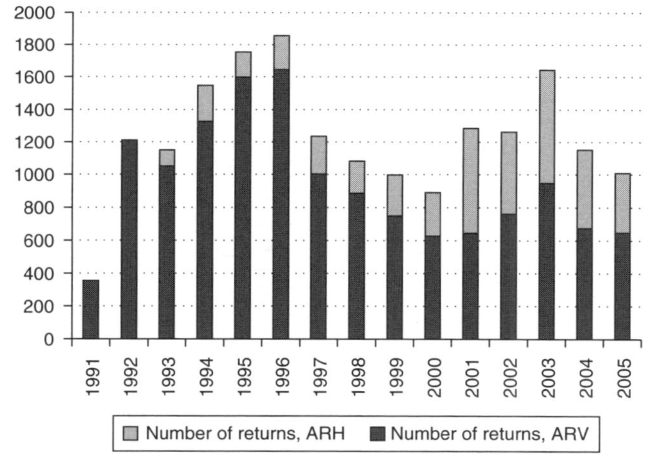

Source: Secrétariat Général du Comité interministériel de contrôle de l'immigration (2007).

Figure 5.1a Number of returns through the French ARV and ARH programs (1991–2005)

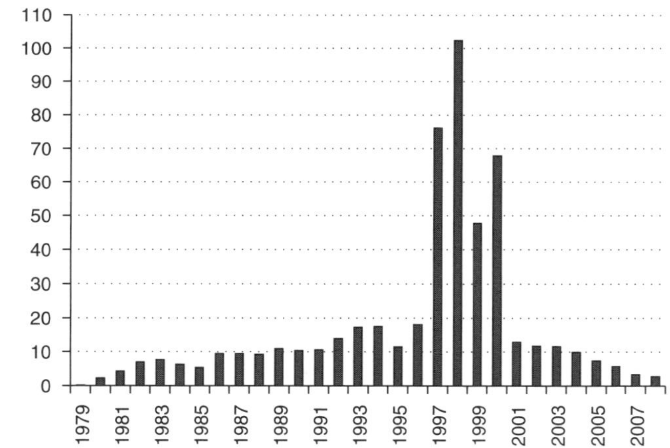

Note: The huge increase observed in years 1997 to 2000 is due to the very high number of Bosnian and Kosovar refugees who left Germany immediately after the end of the Yugoslav wars.

Source: Schneider and Kreienbrink (2010).

Figure 5.1b Number of returns through German REAG or REAG/GARP (1979–2008) (in 000s)

guest workers, the first repatriation support programs were implemented by German state governments (*Länder*) from 1975 onwards, but it was not until 1983, with the entry into force of the Act to Promote the Preparedness of Foreign Workers to Return that the federal government authorized two such programs: one consisting in the immediate reimbursement of social security contributions and the other consisting of return aid amounting to DM10 500 per adult and DM1500 per child. Although both programs were available to non-EC migrants willing to depart from Germany, the second was limited to those migrants who had become unemployed or forced to work reduced hours. Beneficiaries of both programs were prohibited from returning to Germany to work. Between 1975 and 1984, the social security program approved 120 000 applicants, including 93 000 Turks, while the return-aid program approved 16 920 applicants, including 14 459 Turks. The federal government did not renew them after June 1984, claiming that it was job creation in the countries of origin that should form the basis for a return policy (Plewa, 2012).

In the Netherlands, the Reintegration of Emigrant Manpower and Promotion of Local Opportunities for Development (REMPLOD) scheme was introduced in 1974 and was targeted at guest workers from Turkey, Tunisia and Morocco, who were encouraged to return home and start entrepreneurial ventures in their country of origin with support from the Dutch government. This scheme is generally put forward not only as one of the oldest voluntary return programs in Europe, but also as the first one to explicitly point out economic development in migrants' countries of origin as one of its goals (Aumüller, 2004). For the Dutch Ministry for Development Cooperation indeed, the idea was that, thanks to REMPLOD funding, returnees would establish new businesses and, by so doing, create the structural conditions needed for rural development. However, the results of the scheme actually fell short of those expected by policy makers, especially given its costs, so that it was put to an end in the mid-1980s.

In sum, the success of the early repatriation support programs implemented through the 1970s and 1980s has been only moderate. Even if none of these programs has been assessed in a comprehensive manner, a few conclusions can be drawn about the reasons for their failure to reach their goals. First, the financial incentive provided to returning migrants has always been rather low, especially when compared with the average amount of funds remitted each year by resident migrants or with unemployment assistance. Second, in most schemes, re-entry into the immigration country for work purposes was disallowed after the payment of the financial grant. The beneficiaries of the programs were thus predominantly immigrants who would have returned anyway and did not care about exchanging their work or residence permits for money. Additional constraints explain the disappointing results of the programs, in which the financial sponsorship of return was coupled with a professional traineeship and/or a start-up grant. First, the lack of employment or entrepreneurial opportunities in the countries of origin deterred many migrants from applying, and resulted in a high failure rate among returnees' projects. Second, many targeted migrants were coming from the weakest segment of the migrant population, namely the unemployed or the poorly integrated, who often lacked entrepreneurial skills and ended up creating businesses that proved unsustainable in the long run. Third, the offered training programs were often too short and inadequately tailored to employment prospects in the home countries. Last but not least, neither the migrants nor the sending countries ever believed in the stated development intentions of most reintegration programs, which were seen as nothing but a means of making return policies acceptable.

I.2 The 'More Development for Less Migration' Approach (1990s)[8]

Despite the lack of success of most repatriation schemes, national governments in Europe persisted in considering migration as a phenomenon to be extensively controlled and in paying little attention to its development potential. A sharp distinction between development policy and migration policy was thus maintained. The early 1990s saw the conclusion of many bilateral readmission agreements by EU countries with third countries, in order to facilitate expulsion and control immigration.[9] In the meantime, return migration policies, while sometimes redesigned, continued. However, given the low development potential of return migration, policy makers put an increased emphasis on development aid as an instrument to reduce migration.[10] Generally referred to as the 'root-causes' or as the 'more development for less migration' approach, this policy orientation focused on identifying and tackling the causes of economically motivated migration so as to reduce emigration flows, or, in other words, to promote 'stay-at-home development'. It resulted in attempts to expand economic opportunities and improve social services and community infrastructure in specific migration-prone areas in order to absorb and sustain the return of migrants to those regions.[11]

In France, this orientation translated into a program known as 'Programme Développement Local Migration' (PDLM), consisting of linking individual repatriation support with aid for local development in three countries, namely Senegal, Mali and Mauritania. Sponsored by the Ministry of Cooperation, the Ministry of Labor and Social Affairs, and the Office des Migrations Internationales, this program was first tried between 1993 and 1995 in three regions located near the Senegal River (Bakel in Senegal, Kayes in Mali and Guidimakha in Mauritania), before being implemented on a broader scale from 1995 onwards. The program had two components: the first one was aimed at helping migrants wishing to set up small-scale enterprises by allocating them a maximum grant of €3600, conducting feasibility studies and providing assistance with planning and marketing. Technical and managerial support of each project was also provided for one year. The grant was not allocated systematically and was conditional on the quality of the project proposed. It was available both to regularized and non-regularized migrants who had spent at least two years in France. The second component was aimed at supporting various local development projects designed to make the region more attractive and reduce migration flows (support to some particular production sectors and to marketing organizations, upgrating of some farm roads etc.). To this end, a €2.6 million budget was invested over a period of five years. Although the scheme represented interesting opportunities for migrants, the number of projects has been rather limited. In addition to the 20 projects supported in its pilot phase, the program contributed to the creation of 100 projects per year between 1996 and 2000 in Mali, mainly concerned with transport and commerce, and a total of 60 projects in Senegal (Kaba and Force, 2002; Raunet, 2005). This came as no surprise for its promoters, as the focus of the program was on the quality of returns rather than on their quantity. Nevertheless, the figures were below expectations. In fact, the lack of success of the program was mainly due to the context in which it was created. At the same time, the French Office for the Protection of Refugees and Stateless Persons (OFPRA) was being reformed in order to toughen asylum policy, and more restrictive measures towards immigration were being adopted (Gubert, 2008). Many migrants thus perceived it as a way to humanize returns and not to promote development. Moreover, many development practitioners in both Mali and Senegal had concerns about the strong priority given to migration-prone areas at the expense of other regions in the allocation of development aid. Lastly, the program was strongly criticized for not taking into account the role of Malian and Senegalese migrants' associations located in France in favor of local development initiatives. Indeed, while the focus at the state level was on the development potential of return migration, several studies documenting the emergence of African immigrants' associations in France and their role in the provision of public goods in the localities or origin were being published (see, e.g., Quiminal, 1991; Lavigne Delville, 1991; Institut Panos, 1993; Daum, 1995, 1998; Blion and Verrière, 1998). According to these studies, there were, at the beginning of the 1990s, no fewer than 143 Malian migrants' associations registered in France, and about 400 such associations formed by migrants originating from the Senegal River Valley (Mali, Senegal and Mauritania), with the majority of them initiating and funding projects for the development of village infrastructures in their countries of origin. Despite their positive development-related accomplishments and growing recognition by both international solidarity organizations and French local authorities,[12] these associations were completely ignored by the state actors in charge of development planning policy and strategy. More generally, the criticisms leveled at France's PDLM or at similar programs in other European countries were much less of the contents of the scheme and its limited scope than the claim that unwanted migration can be stemmed through development. Thanks to a growing body of empirical literature (see, e.g., Martin and Taylor, 1996), more and more voices were raised at the time to push the idea that development stimulates migration rather than reduces it, at least in the short and medium run. However, it is now generally acknowledged that, with PDLM, France took its first step towards a development-oriented migration policy and towards what has been since then referred to as 'co-development' (De Haas, 2006; Möhl, 2010). In 1997, a national symposium on international cooperation and solidarity initiated by non-governmental organizations (NGOs) was held with the support of the French Ministry of Foreign Affairs and the State Secretariat for Cooperation. It highlighted migrants' positive role in development cooperation and called for closer governmental engagement with migrant associations without any return obligation. Following this symposium, a co-development working group was created. It resulted in the publication of the influential *Rapport de bilan et d'orientation sur la politique de co-développement liée aux flux migratoires*' (*Final Report on the Co-development Policy Related to Migration Flows* – Naïr, 1997). Based on the recognition that migrants were important actors in the development of their countries of origin, and that their contribution in development should be valued and encouraged, this report encouraged original proposals aimed at providing support to their projects, reinforcing the action of international solidarity organizations and 'organizing' mobility in order to allow for the legal possibility of residing temporarily in France for employment purposes. The report also recommended that the support to migrant engagements in their country of origin be no longer accompanied by return obligation ('Codevelopment policy should not be aimed at encouraging migrants to return if they do not want to. On the contrary, their legal presence in France is what enables them to contribute in an efficient way to the development of their country ' (p. 3)). In the meantime, however, the report was very cautious about the possibility of relaxing France's migration policy and did not depart from the 'more development for less migration' approach ('Codevelopment should not be aimed at promoting new immigration flows, as it does not advocate liberalizing immigration. Its main focus is on facilitating migrants' integration in France while encouraging solidarity efforts towards origin countries, in order to create the social conditions that will allow the potential migrants to stay at home' (p. 3)).

As highlighted by Magoni (2004), Sami Naïr's report was a historic milestone as it officially and for the first time acknowledged the role of migrants in the development of their countries of origin. It also gained international attention as it was the first report referring to the political concept of co-development and framing the term theoretically as well as postulating objectives and concrete measures.[13] Following the example of France, several European countries will start to implement their own co-development policy. In the meantime, co-development will slowly make its way into the European Union's (EU) official policy process. However, different interpretations will be made of the concept. Depending on the country and the period in question, the term will refer to different areas of work, ranging from the exchange of development aid for migratory control to the promotion of remittances, or of development projects initiated by migrant associations (Möhl, 2010).

I.3 The Various Approaches to Co-development (2000s)

Even if the first attempts to set up a common European asylum and immigration policy and a 'comprehensive approach' to migration through 'partnership with third countries' can be traced back to the end of the 1990s,[14] concrete policy initiatives aimed at enhancing synergies between migration management and development cooperation were tried almost exclusively at the level of individual member states until the mid-2000s. However, overall interest of Europe's main immigration countries in co-development has been fairly weak, with only France, Spain and to some extent the Netherlands and Italy engaging in a more visible policy effort.

France's co-development approach

Considered as the 'European cradle of codevelopment policy' (Nijenhuis and Broekhuis, 2010), France usually serves as the reference framework even if migration and development policies have been implemented elsewhere in Europe, and sometimes earlier than in France. What actually makes France special as compared to other European countries is the stated policy priority given to this issue, as illustrated by the nomination of a Deputy Ambassador for co-development in 2002, and by the creation, in May 2007, of a ministry dedicated to designing and implementing co-development policy.[15] However, as in any other European member state, policy discourses and practices in the migration and development field in France have remained quite ambiguous as to the objectives pursued. Despite several political changes over the last 15 years and co-development being transferred from one ministry or state department to another, the agenda has always been strongly determined by migration issues.[16]

The ambiguities of the French co-development approach were apparent right from the start. After the publication of Naïr's report, in 1998, the government set up the 'Mission Interministerielle au co-développement et aux migrations internationales' (MICOMI), an interministerial committee with representatives of the Ministry of Foreign Affairs, the Ministry of Interior and the Ministry of Social Affairs. Its task was to give a concrete meaning to the policy concept of co-development and, to this end, to propose measures towards a partnership approach with countries of emigration with a view to promoting co-development while better controlling migration flows. Created in the aftermath of the regularization program of 1997–98, however, MICOMI's first assignment consisted in implementing a scheme, called the Contrat de Réinsertion dans le Pays d'origine (CRPO), which was specifically designed to encourage illegal migrants from Mali, Morocco and Senegal who were not eligible for amnesties to return home voluntarily. This emphasis on return altered the credibility of co-development and led to the dismantling of MICOMI (Lacroix, 2009). At about the same time, however, tangible progress in engaging with and learning from the migrants was made. The recognition of the positive role of the migrants and their associations in the development of their origin countries allowed them to gain representation in the advisory councils of French development policy, namely the Haut Conseil de la Coopération Internationale (HCCI) and the Comité interministériel de la Coopération Internationale et du Développement (CICID) (Möhl, 2010). To give more voice and power to migrants' interests, a national platform called the Forum des Organisations de Solidarité Internationale Issues des Migrations (FORIM), federating between 600 and 700 associations, was created in 2002, with the assigned task of representing them in the different interest groups and structures involved in policy making. Progress was also made from 2000 onwards in designing new tools of cooperation with third countries. One such new tool was the program implemented through the bilateral co-development convention signed with Mali in December 2000. This convention materialized in 2002 with the launch of a three-year (2003–05) program of €2.6 million funded by the French Ministry of Foreign Affairs within the framework of the 'Fond de Solidarité Prioritaire'.[17] Supervised by the newly appointed Deputy Ambassador for co-development, its aim was fourfold: (1) supporting local development through the co-funding of development projects initiated by diaspora organizations; (2) assisting in personal enterprises of migrants wishing to return to Mali or willing to invest from France; (3) mobilizing the Malian scientific diaspora through brain circulation; and (4) improving the integration of young persons with a migratory background.[18] Similar bilateral programs followed with Senegal,[19] Morocco (€3.8 million) and the Comoros (€2.5 million). The co-development agenda was thus much broader than in previous schemes and not solely intended to encourage the reintegration of migrants in their countries of origin. In addition, thanks to their increasing visibility, migrant organizations began to establish their own networks in order to promote diaspora engagement in the countries of origin. As highlighted by Möhl (2010), a decentralization process was thus initiated, with responsibilities and powers progressively transferred from national state agencies to civil-society networks and migrant associations, often working at the local level. All those efforts, undertaken with a view to distancing co-development policies from policies to fight undocumented migration and stimulate return migration were partly wiped out by the adoption of the Immigration and Integration Law of 2006 and the creation, one year later, of the Ministry of Immigration, Integration, National Identity and Codevelopment, whose mission rested on three pillars: selective immigration; mandatory integration for long-term residents; and co-development (Chou and Baygert, 2007). In line with the two first objectives, a renewable three-year 'Skills and Talents Permit' ('Carte compétences et talents'), designed to facilitate the entry of new migrants whose talents would be an asset for France, was introduced and the rules for family reunification were redefined in a restrictive way. The 'Reception and Integration Contract' ('Contrat d'Accueil et d'Intégration') was also created for those migrants willing to settle in France. Regarding the third objective, new co-development tools were designed (tax breaks for migrants' productive savings, co-development prizes awarded to migrants or diaspora organizations etc.). But the real shift came with the way in which the partnership with third countries was redefined. This shift was materialized by the signature of bilateral agreements on concerted management of migration flows ('Accords de gestion concertée des flux migratoires') between France and its main partners.[20] With those agreements, the commitment of countries of migrants' departure and transit to combat illegal migration became a precondition for privileged access to legal migration and to more easily benefit from development aid, which made it clear that the focus of the Ministry was much more on migration management than on development cooperation. The analysis of the budget devoted to the French Ministry of Immigration brings further support to this assertion. At the time the Ministry was operating, between 2008 and

2010, and despite the stated political priority given to co-development, the budget allocated to it represented only about 5 percent of the total budget of the Ministry (Table 5.1), and less than 1 percent of French ODA (Table 5.2). It was also insignificant compared to the funds channeled by migrants. The Malian diaspora remitted about €200 million in 2005, while the co-development program signed between France and Mali provided €2.6 million over the 2003–05 period (Nijenhuis and Broekhuis, 2010).

Therefore, at a time when co-development was given more visibility, the discrepancies between stated objectives and actual means, and the strategy consisting in using aid as leverage for increased migration controls 'at source', did nothing but further discredit the policy concept of co-development.

The Netherlands' co-development approach[21]

Just as in any other European immigrant-receiving country, Dutch immigration and immigrant integration policies have become more restrictive and demanding since the 1990s. The Aliens Act of 2000 in particular made the Dutch policy on asylum seekers stricter and the conditions for family reunification and marital migration less lenient. It also emphasized remigration to stimulate and, if necessary, force undocumented aliens and rejected asylum seekers to return to their countries of origin (Snel et al., 2003). In the meantime, migrant groups have been increasingly forced to meet requirements for integration through the implementation of a system of compulsory introduction programs for newcomers since 1998. This is also expressed in the attempts of the Dutch government to establish 'umbrella entities', such as the Surinaams Inspraak Orgaan (SIO) (the Surinamese consultation body) and the Samenwerkingsverband van Marokkanen in Nederland (SMN), its Moroccan equivalent, to represent all migrant organizations in encounters with the Dutch government (Nijenhuis and Zoomer, 2012).

Parallel to this tendency towards more restrictive policies, the Netherlands has also undergone a shift in migration and development thinking, as illustrated by the publication of two Development and Migration Policy Memoranda in 2004 and 2008, respectively (Nijenhuis and Broekhuis, 2010). However, a close look at the proposed measures and stated objectives reveals that migration management policies, via circular and return migration programs, continue to dominate. The conclusions of the 2004 document, for example, acknowledge that there is considerable room to improve the coherence between migration and development policies, in particular through (1) improving the capacity building in the field of migration management and protection in the region; and (2) encouraging effective return of illegal migrants deemed necessary for the integrity of

Table 5.1 *Respective budgets allocated to 'Co-development' and 'Immigration, asylum and integration' programs in the French budget, 2008–2013 (in million euros)*

	2008		2009		2010		2011		2012		2013	
		%		%		%		%		%		%
Immigration, asylum and integration	609.6	95.5	513.8	95.4	560.4	94.1	561.4	94.9	631.9	95.8	670.9	97.3
Immigration and asylum	414.2	64.9	436	81.0	480.6	80.7	488.6	82.6	560.3	84.9	604.7	87.7
Integration/access to citizenship	195.3	30.6	77.8	14.5	79.8	13.4	72.8	12.3	71.6	10.9	66.2	9.6
Co-development	29.0	4.5	24.5	4.6	35.1	5.9	29.9	5.1	28.0	4.2	18.5	2.7
Total	638.6	100.0	538.3	100.0	595.4	100.0	591.3	100.0	659.9	100.0	689.4	100.0

Note: Between 2008 and 2010, the budgets allocated to 'Immigration, asylum and integration' and to 'Co-development' formed the total budget of the Ministry of Immigration, Integration, National Identity and Solidarity Development. In 2011 and 2012, they became part of the budget of the Ministry of Interior. In 2013, the budget allocated to 'Immigration, asylum and integration' remained in the hands of the Ministry of Interior, but the 'Co-development' budget was merged with that allocated to 'Solidarity with developing countries' and became part of the budget of the Ministry of Foreign Affairs.

Source: République Française, Projet de loi de finance, Exercices 2008, 2009, 2010, 2011, 2012, 2013 (http://www.performance-publique.budget.gouv.fr/ressources-documentaires/lois-projets-de-lois-et-documents-annexes-par-annee/, accessed on January 21, 2014).

Table 5.2 French official development assistance, 2008–2013 (in million euros)

	2008		2009		2010		2011		2012		2013	
		%		%		%		%		%		%
Financial and economic aid for development	972.2	31.6	1041.5	33.0	1186.8	35.5	1170.1	35.1	1191.9	35.8	1161.9	37.2
Solidarity with developing countries	2072.0	67.4	2086.8	66.2	2119.9	63.4	2134.0	64.0	2113.3	63.4	1945.2	62.2
Co-development	29.5	1.0	24.3	0.8	34.8	1.0	30	0.9	28	0.8	18.5	0.6
Total	3073.7	100.0	3152.6	100.0	3341.5	100.0	3334.1	100.0	3333.2	100.0	3125.6	100.0

Source: République Française, Rapports annuels de performances, Annexe au projet de loi de règlement des comptes et rapport de gestion, Aide publique au développement (years 2008, 2009, 2010, 2011, 2012, 2013).

and public support for the asylum system and migration policy in general, assisted voluntary return and circular migration (De Haas, 2006). While the contributions to development by migrants and their organizations are recognized, no concrete measures to involve them in development cooperation are proposed.

Nevertheless, the Dutch government indirectly supports migrant and development organizations by providing funds to co-financing agencies (i.e. development non-governmental NGOs such as Oxfam Novib or Cordaid) that perform co-development activities. One example is the Linkis initiative instigated by the Directorate for International Cooperation (DGIS) of the Ministry of Foreign Affairs and implemented by the National Commission for International Cooperation and Sustainable Development (NCDO) and five co-financing agencies (Oxfam Novib, Cordaid, ICCO, Hivos and Plan Nederland). In order to improve the involvement of Netherlands-based individuals and (migrant and non-migrant) organizations in development cooperation, the Linkis online facility was launched in 2004 to inform and advise groups of citizens on concrete opportunities to submit proposals for small-scale projects in developing countries (with co-funding of up to €50 000) with the participating development agencies. In addition to the Linkis framework, Dutch co-financing agencies and other development NGOs also have policies that are specifically targeted towards migrants and migrant organizations. Oxfam Novib, for example, has initiated several activities aimed at strengthening the involvement of diaspora organizations and their members in development cooperation, such as: (1) the strategic financing of small and large development projects of diaspora organizations; (2) capacity building in project management, fund-raising, lobbying and so on; (3) supporting alliance building with other NGOs; (4) linking and learning/exchange visits; and (5) organizing expert meetings and conferences (De Haas, 2006).

Thus, while the Dutch development agenda seems somehow subordinate to the migration agenda at the official policy level, development NGOs and diaspora organizations have managed to engage in fruitful alliances supported by co-financing government funds for development cooperation (De Haas, 2006). More recently, Dutch municipalities with large groups of immigrants have also shown a growing interest in establishing contacts with municipalities in main origin countries. In 2009, there were about 40 municipal twinnings from the Netherlands with immigrant-sending countries such as Turkey, Suriname and Morocco, and this number has been increasing since then (Hoetjes, 2009; Van Ewijk and Baud, 2009).

Spain and Italy's co-development approach

The Spanish and Italian experiences in the field of co-development are often discussed jointly because they share a number of similarities. In terms of their migration history, both Spain and Italy have moved from being predominantly emigration countries to countries that have attracted large-scale immigration from Northern Africa (Morocco, Tunisia), Western Africa (Senegal), Eastern Europe (Romania, Ukraine, Albania) and, in the case of Spain, Latin America (Ecuador, Dominican Republic). Their migrant communities are thus less established as well as relatively less organized, which may partly explain why co-development policies in those two countries are still at the draft stage. By contrast to France, a traditionally centralized state, co-development initiatives in Spain and Italy have taken place much more at the level of the municipalities and regions than at the state level, and largely overlap with decentralized development practices (Chaloff and Piperno, 2004; Grillo and Riccio, 2004; Terrón, 2004; Nijenhuis and Broekhuis, 2010). In Spain, co-development initiatives exist in Catalonia, the Community of Madrid, the Basque country, Valencia, Andalusia, Murcia, and Aragon, but not in other regions. In Madrid's Master Plan 2005–08, for example, the term co-development is explicitly referred to as a strategic measure, treating both migrant organizations and migrants as 'partners' in the cooperation projects with Madrid. Co-development is also included in the 2004–07 and 2008–11 Master Plans for the Valencian Development Cooperation, with measures including awareness raising in the countries of origin about the migrants' developmental potential; supporting the possibility of repatriation; recruiting active participants from the migrant residents in Valencia to promote development projects in their home countries; and establishing co-development agencies with town councils in towns with high proportions of migrants (Boni and Lacomba, 2011). In Catalonia, the Fons Català de Cooperació al Desenvolupament has started to work along the lines of co-development since 1996 (Fauser, 2007). As emphasized by Acebillo-Baqué and Østergaard-Nielsen (2011), co-development at the level of local governments in Spain has often been grounded in concerns with migrant integration. Being directly confronted with large inflows of immigrants, municipalities and regions have tried to support developmental projects initiated by migrants or their organizations while promoting their successful incorporation. The expansion of the municipalities and regions' international cooperation with emigration countries has also been a way to increase the legitimacy of their international activities. The same holds true in Italy, where a broad range of pilot schemes in the area of co-development has been attempted at the regional level since the 1990s, in such regions as the Veneto, Lombardy, Piedmont, Emilia Romagna and

Tuscany. Their main areas of action include workforce training, selection and recruitment projects; mandatory and voluntary return; projects to create employment and reduce migratory pressure; and projects for the optimal use of remittances (Chaloff and Piperno, 2004).

In Spain, but not in Italy, co-development also entered the national policy debate, but later on and with a different meaning.[22] The term *codesarrollo* first appeared in the Programa Global de Regulacion de la Extranjeria e Immigracion 2001–2004 (better known as Plan GRECO), during the second legislature of the Partido Popular from 2000 to 2004. Issued by the Ministry of Interior and the Ministry of Foreign Affairs and Cooperation, the program included five action plans in the field of co-development that much resembled those implemented within France's PDLM (Möhl, 2010): training programs for returnees, assisted return programs, micro-credit funding for productive activities; technical assistance in source countries as well as channeling remittances into productive investments. The program was criticized for being highly centralized, disregarding the engagement of the civil society and migrants in particular, and having a strong return component. In addition, the political will to address *codesarrollo* did not translate into a specific budgetary commitment, so that the suggested measures were not implemented in practice (Terrón, 2004). With the Socialist Labor Party coming into power, in March 2004, new policy strategies focused on the integration of immigrants residing in Spain were initiated. In the meantime, *codesarrollo* shifted to the field of development cooperation instead of immigration, and, as a consequence, the former elements of migration management and control of the Plan GRECO were replaced by development-oriented instruments. Since then, *codesarrollo* has been defined as a strategy aimed at facilitating the engagement of diaspora associations with the development of their countries of origin. However, it has remained a concept that is much more discussed at the regional level than at the national one.

In short, the meaning and application of co-development as a policy concept, as well as the importance attributed to it, have been rather different in France, the Netherlands, Spain and Italy. However, and as highlighted by Royo (2010), it seems rather clear that the use of the same term to refer to actions as different as return policies, the control of flows and of borders, remittances or transnational relations has been one of the principal problems of co-development. It undermined trust and, to quote Jonathan Chaloff, did not form a 'workable policy approach' (Chaloff, 2005). And even if efforts have been made in recent years to clarify and circumscribe the concept in such a way as to limit it to any action or practice linking migrant communities with the development of their countries of origin, the damage has been done. This probably explains why, in both national and European policy discourses, the notion of 'migration and development' is now preferred over the concept of co-development.

As suggested by the above discussion, incoherencies at the official policy levels did not prevent development agencies, regional and municipal governments, as well as NGOs, from partnering with and learning from migrants or migrant organizations. This co-development 'from below', as opposed to 'from above', has led to an increasing number of (sometimes innovative) programs and actions aimed at enhancing the contribution of migrants and diasporas in development processes, reviewed in the next section.

II. CONCRETE EXAMPLES OF STATE AND NON-STATE DIASPORA INITIATIVES IN EUROPE

As suggested by Carling (2008), there are several ways of classifying diaspora-related policy measures. One criterion may be whether they target emigrants explicitly or not. Special bank accounts for emigrants, remittance bonds or specific training sessions, for example, belong to the first category, while any measure aimed at improving the investment climate in countries or regions of out-migration belong to the second. Another criterion may be their scope. Some, such as those targeting remittances only, are narrowly scoped, while others, such as bilateral labor migration treaties or dual citizenship legislation, have a much wider scope. In what follows, we focus mainly on diaspora-related policy programs or measures initiated by European state and non-state actors that explicitly target migrants or migrant organizations and whose scope is to enhance the developmental impact of remittances, be they individual or collective, financial or non-financial. This focus on remittances is driven by the considerable attention that they have attracted since the early 2000s, and all the efforts undertaken since then to increase their volume and promote their productive use.

Our review deals mainly with programs or measures that are quite small scale and/or still in the experimental phase, and since their impact has not been properly assessed, it is unfortunately hazardous to say that they achieved their purpose. Nevertheless, we make an effort as much as possible to highlight good practices, challenges and lessons learned.[23]

II.1 Stimulating Transfers through Formal Channels

Among the measures that have been implemented to stimulate formal remittance methods, some consist in information campaigns about existing remittance transfer mechanisms and transfer fees so as to improve the efficiency of the remittance market. Examples of such measures are the websites comparing remittance services offered by banks and money transfer organizations, including the costs charged for various destinations that have been created in several European countries: Envoidargent.com in France, finansportalen.no in Norway; mandasoldiacasa.it in Italy; sendmoneyhome.org in the UK (which changed its name to fxcompared.com); geldtransfair.de in Germany; GeldNaarHuis.nl in the Netherlands; and so on. A few of them (the French, the Italian and the Norwegian ones) have been certified by the World Bank, which has its own website that covers 220 'country corridors' worldwide from 32 remittance-sending countries to 89 receiving countries (remittanceprices.worldbank.org). By making the information on transfer fees publicly available, the envisioned consequences are increased competition among providers, reduced transfer costs, better-informed remittance senders and higher use of formal remittance channels.[24] To our knowledge, no evaluation of these remittance service comparison websites has been carried out, except for the 'Geld Naar Huis' website, and the conclusions are rather mixed (Siegel et al., 2010, p.3). As stated in the report,

> The website has experienced limited usage by members of its target audience, and its lacking visibility has resulted in meager impacts on migrants' understanding of the Dutch remittance market and operators functioning within it . . . The website has not had a significant impact on the behavior of remittance transfer operators, especially as engagement with banks and money transfer operators (MTOs) has been limited at best.

The report ends with some suggestions for improvements that include ensuring more up-to-date and accurate information and providing users with more information on financial news and services linked to remittances. Related to this, a randomized experiment was recently designed to measure the impact of providing financial literacy training to migrants in New Zealand and Australia, two countries that launched a remittance cost comparison website for sending money to the Pacific Islands, and, in the case of New Zealand, where regulatory reform led to the introduction of new remitting methods (Gibson et al., 2014). Among other things, the training taught migrants the different elements that make up the cost of sending remittances and how to compare costs across methods. As suggested by the results, the training appears to increase financial knowledge and information-seeking behavior, and reduce the risk of switching to more expensive remittance products. But no impact is found on the frequency or the level of remittances. Some one-off measures have also attempted to remove the obstacles that deter migrants from opening bank accounts. The German National Development Agency (GIZ), for example, tried to help banks become more accessible to migrants by organizing a conference in 2009 that brought together Serbian banks and several Serbian migrant organizations from Germany to discuss reasons behind migrants' reluctance to use formal remittances channels (Agunias and Newland, 2012). However, it is unlikely that this kind of measure will really make a difference since there are many additional obstacles that prevent migrants from opening bank accounts or using formal channels against which destination countries cannot take direct action. The local branches of commercial banks based in destination countries, for example, often require identification documents that migrants (at least the unauthorized ones) cannot provide. In addition, some migrants may have had a negative experience with banks in their home country and thus distrust the system. Another huge challenge that makes informal channels much more preferable to (non-mobile) banks is the so-called 'last mile' of remittance transactions, which refers to access to a contact point at which remittance recipients can withdraw the cash sent. Banks in origin countries generally have a limited payout presence in rural and/or remote areas. And even if innovative mobile-phone-based money transfer services have successfully entered the remittance market and much improved the number of remittance payout locations, they sometimes find it hard to compete with informal systems that have proven effective for several years. In the case of Mali, for example, despite the strong increase in the number of remittance payout locations (with, respectively, 315 and 1792 contact points for Western Union[25] and Orange mobile banking[26]), informal channels still have an estimated 59 percent of the market share in France (AfDB, 2008). Informal transfers include hand-carried cash transfers, in-kind transfers, or transfers sent through the 'fax system' (even if a fax machine is hardly used). This last method relies on strong networks that connect Malian migrants in France with people in Mali, generally traders. When a migrant wants to remit, he gives a sum of money to a person in charge of centralizing the funds, who often resides in the same *foyer* and originates from the same village. This person then contacts the agent (the trader) closest to the recipient and requests him to pay the amount (generally minus a commission) in exchange for a promise to be paid later. In the meantime, the migrant calls the recipient in the village to inform him of the availability of the funds or the goods. The trader gets paid later, either in cash or in goods.

The fact that some migrants sometimes prefer to send goods is also rarely analyzed and taken into account. As suggested by personal interviews with migrants, the choice of sending goods instead of money is much more driven by their desire to control remittance use than by their wish to pay lower fees. This explains part of the success of the recently created website niokobok.com, which makes it possible for members of the Senegalese diaspora to buy food and other daily consumer goods online for their origin households in Senegal. As suggested by some of the comments dropped by users of the website, having better control on remittance use is what made them choose this channel:[27]

> This website is such a good idea! Otherwise how can you be certain that the money you send is used for the house? (Comment posted by M. on August 15, 2013, our translation)
>
> I love it. It is of very simple use, and when the family is far away, one is always worried about how the money is spent. Now I am sure that they will eat. Congratulations! (Comment posted by J.T. on May 7, 2013, our translation)

As additional evidence, the level of control that migrants have over remittance use as a factor influencing remittance behavior has been recently confirmed by three recent academic papers (Batista and Narciso, 2013; Batista et al., 2013; Ashraf et al., 2013). They all provide evidence that the greater the control over remittance use, the higher the remittances. This suggests that enhancing the control exerted by migrants on remittance use could also be a way to stimulate remittances.

II.2 Stimulating Investment of Remittances[28]

Most European migrant-receiving countries have attempted to facilitate the establishment of businesses by entrepreneurial migrants in their countries of origin. One of the first NGOs to embark on this issue is the Dutch NGO IntEnt (which stands for INTernational ENTrepreneurship). It was created in 1996 in response to a growing number of successful migrant entrepreneurs operating in the Netherlands and wishing to start a business in their country of origin, but who faced difficult access to information, financial facilities and specialized services (De Haas, 2006). Initially exclusively funded by the Dutch government, the program has benefited from additional sources of funding from HIVOS, a Dutch co-financing agency and the European Union. Up to 2000, business development services were provided to individuals originating from countries from which sizable populations in the Netherlands emigrated (Morocco, Suriname, Ghana and Turkey). Since then, IntEnt has expanded its activities with services to migrants from Cape Verde, Sierra Leone, Afghanistan, the Netherlands Antilles (Curaçao) and Ethiopia. By 2009, more than 1500 potential entrepreneurs had requested information from IntEnt, and 350 companies had started up (IntEnt, 2009, cited by Kleush and Schuster, 2012). The program, which is tailored to the specific needs of migrant entrepreneurs, is divided into three phases: (1) sourcing and selection in the starting country (e.g. informational meetings, intake interviews and general workshop sessions); (2) preparation for entrepreneurship (e.g. support for writing business plans, country information workshops, market research, evaluation of business plans); (3) implementation of the entrepreneurship in the program country (e.g. start-up coaching, financial support, and post start-up support for a maximum of 1.5 years).[29] Migrants are urged to finance a major part of their businesses, but can get additional resources through grants of up to €50 000 from the Friends and Family Fund (FFF). To get funded, friends and family of the entrepreneur should provide a guarantee for half of the investment to the FFF; the entrepreneur's financial plan should be approved; and the entrepreneur should accept guidance during the first year after start-up of their business (Agunias and Newland, 2012).

Quite similar programs have been implemented since then, in the Netherlands[30] as well as in other European countries. The Business Ideas for Morocco program, for example, was created in 2009 with the Kompass Zentrum für Existenzgründung (Kompass Center for Business Start-ups) based in Frankfurt and the German Chamber of Commerce and Industry (CCI) in Morocco to enable Moroccans who have completed their education in Germany to acquire the skills they need to set up a new company in their home country. As with IntEnt, the program is divided into three phases. First, participants take part in introductory seminars in Germany: they develop their business idea and clarify issues such as the level of competition in Morocco and finding the right location. This is then followed by individual coaching sessions. An entrepreneur from Morocco also attends the seminars, passing on experience to the budding entrepreneurs. During the third stage, the participant receives advice and support in Morocco. By 2011, more than 150 Moroccans had benefited from the program and created a business. An analogous program aimed at young graduates originating from the Maghreb and Mashriq countries, notably Tunisia, Morocco, Algeria, and Lebanon, has existed in France since 2011. Called the Programme d'Aide à la Création d'Entreprises Innovantes en Méditerranée (PACEIM; Aid Program for the Creation of Innovative Businesses in the Mediterranean), it is administered by the Institute of Research for Development, a French research organization that addresses international development issues.[31] Laureates can be funded through grants of up to €35 000. The 2011 and 2012 editions of the program involved respectively 30 and 28 entrepreneurs. Since 2006, France has also had an agreement with Senegal to support diaspora initiatives by Senegalese living in France through the Programme d'appui aux initiatives de solidarité pour le développement (PAISD; Support

Program for Initiatives Encouraging Development). Among other objectives, the PAISD supports migrants who wish to invest at home by providing advice, expertise to start a small business, training and a follow-up over 12 months.[32] By June 2009, 36 months after its effective start date, the program had supported 221 projects of business creation in sectors as diverse as agriculture, trade, tourism, ICT, transport and services.[33] The volume of funds invested by entrepreneurs at the time amounted to more than 2 billion CFA francs (about €3 million). Interestingly enough, returnees only made up about half of the participating entrepreneurs, with the other half being individuals residing abroad and investing at distance.

Again, the success of all above-mentioned programs (whose list is far from exhaustive) is hard to assess since no rigorous evaluation has been carried out so far. Follow-up reports, where they exist, highlight the number of newly created businesses and the number of jobs that have been generated, but they usually do not provide any information on failure rate, the average lifetime of businesses and so on. In a communication given at a conference in New York in 2006, a staff member of the Dutch NGO IntEnt listed some of the lessons learned during the pilot phase of the project: (1) enterprise promotion programs take time and most migrant entrepreneurs tend to underestimate the problems they have to overcome to be successful as businessmen in their country of origin; (2) the program reaches relatively small numbers but the investments made are significant and sustainable; and (3) negative economic and political developments in the country of origin have a direct and long-lasting effect on the willingness of the entrepreneurs to implement their plans. At a seminar organized as part of the French Programme Migrations et Initiatives Economiques in 2004, it was revealed that many projects face difficulties due to various problems such as lack of experience, vagueness and the often naïve character of business plans, the heterogeneous character and lack of quality of counterpart organizations, high costs and the difficult access to poorly developed local credit markets (De Haas, 2006).

It is very likely that most of these observations apply equally to all the schemes that have been designed in recent years to stimulate the productive use of remittances. And among the reasons given for their limited appeal, poor local conditions and unfavorable business investment climate certainly are the most salient. However, two other factors may further hamper investment efforts. One relates to the distance management of the businesses created by migrant entrepreneurs. The latter often complain that their businesses are poorly managed by unqualified staff, friends or family members, leading to financial losses and business collapse. Certainly, the progress of information and communication technologies (ICT), together with cheaper airfares and the possibility of opening and managing online bank accounts, have enabled migrant entrepreneurs to oversee their business in person, but allowing dual citizenships for members of the diaspora would be additional progress. The second factor relates to the insurance role of migrants, which has been much documented in the literature.[34] By serving as insurance for their families, migrants make up for the lack, or inadequacy, of local insurance markets. They also allow families to engage in activities that entail more risks but are potentially more profitable. In this perspective, remittances are not just another source of capital. The share of remittances earmarked for this specific purpose being generally high, that for investment in productive projects can be nothing else but low. Therefore, as long as migrants have the fundamental duty to support their families, any measure aimed at attracting remittances towards productive investment will only have mixed results. This may partly explain why the initiatives by French authorities to stimulate immigrant savings in order to channel them into productive investment in countries of origin failed. In 2006 and 2007 respectively, two financial products especially designed for immigrants, the so-called Compte épargne co-développement (CEC; (co-development savings accounts) and the *Livret d'épargne pour le Codéveloppement* (LEC); co-development savings passbook) were created. With a CEC, depositors could benefit from a tax exemption equal to 40 percent of their savings, up to €20 000. In return, fund withdrawals were only permitted to finance development projects in the origin country.[35] In other words, to qualify for tax relief, savings had to be spent on activities contributing to development. If not, depositors had to pay a penalty equal to the tax exemption with added interest. None of the products raised the interest of the migrants, and both were suppressed in 2009.

II.3 Providing Outreach and Support to Migrant Organizations

Diaspora-led or migrant organizations are not a new phenomenon, but their number has been increasing in recent years, as well as overall interest in their transnational activities. This has resulted in several policy initiatives aimed at maximizing their contribution to development through capacity building, matching funds or both. Most diaspora-led organizations, generally referred to as hometown associations (HTAs), are organizations spontaneously formed by migrants coming from the same community of origin and wishing to maintain ties with and materially support those left behind. They generally start as informal, small and underfunded organizations, with volunteer staff whose time and resources are limited. And even if they mature over time, and turn into formal associations, their leaders often lack the appropriate organizational and technical skills and capacities. In addition, most diaspora members do not have the necessary networks to access opportunities available in the country of settlement. To address this problem, a few NGOs and other development actors have set up capacity-building programs specially designed for migrant organizations. One of the pioneers in this field is the Dutch development NGO Oxfam Novib.[36] Since 2002, with a dedicated budget of €300 000 per year, it has organized and funded courses on topics such as 'Project Cycle Management and Planning', 'Proposal Development', 'Fundraising', 'Financial Literacy' and 'Peace Building'. It has also organized meetings and conferences to enable migrant organizations to learn from each other's experiences (De Bruyn and Huyse, 2008). The overall objectives include developing capacities and skills to improve development and enabling migrant organizations to scale up their projects and organizational capacities; alliance building; and empowering migrants to speak for themselves. Oxfam Novib's Capacity Building Program was evaluated in 2008, after six years of activity. As suggested by the evaluators, the program has succeeded in strengthening the position of migrant organizations in the debate on development cooperation and in enhancing their organizational capacities. In addition, the combination of funding opportunities through the Linkis system (see above) with tailored assistance and capacity-building measures has allowed some of them to upscale their projects. But the project proposals of a number of organizations still lack the quality required for funding (De Bruyn and Huyse, 2008).

Two other interesting examples are the project moveGLOBAL in Germany and the initiative Bistandsskolen in Norway. The project moveGLOBAL has been implemented by the Berliner Entwicklungspolitischer Ratschlag e.V. (BER), a network organization of initiatives and organizations active in development cooperation in Berlin since 2009 (Kleush and Schuster, 2012). Its main goals are threefold: (1) to qualify and link diaspora organizations; (2) to make them visible as development actors and to encourage them to position themselves in public discourse; and (3) to enhance their contribution to development through long-term support. The second scheme, Bistandsskolen (Development school), is a series of weekend courses on the basics of professional development cooperation: 'Introduction to Development Cooperation'; 'The Project Cycle'; 'Financial Management'; 'Measuring Results'; and so on (Horst et al., 2010). The target group includes migrant organizations and small Norwegian voluntary organizations. The main goal is to enable participants to develop good projects in collaboration with partners in the South, to apply for funds and subsequently report to NORAD, the Norwegian Agency for Development Cooperation, and to successfully implement their projects. Again, these projects are too recent to claim that they achieved their purpose.

Interestingly enough, to further build the capacity of diaspora groups and increase their visibility, a supranational initiative has recently emerged at the instigation of the African Diaspora Policy Centre (ADPC) in the Netherlands, the African Foundation for Development (AFFORD) in the UK, the Forum des Organisations de Solidarité internationale issues des Migrations (FORIM) in France, the Coordination Générale des Migrants pour le Développement (CGMD) in Belgium and the International Centre for Migration Policy Development (ICMPD) in Belgium to promote the contribution of the African diaspora in Europe. As part of its objectives, the initiative aims at (1) creating a European platform of African diaspora organizations working on development issues in Africa; (2) improving coordination, communication and cooperation of development activities undertaken by African migrant organizations through the development of tools and mechanisms to share information knowledge and expertise; and (3) enhancing the capacities of diaspora organizations to meaningfully participate in the development cooperation process in Africa. Several concrete activities are planned and will start as soon as the project is finalized.[37]

In addition to capacity-building programs, most countries have funding schemes. What varies from country to country is the ways in which those funding schemes are arranged. In France, the main funding scheme, called PRA-OSIM, is managed by FORIM, a forum of migrant organizations representing about 700 associations working in Africa, Asia and the Caribbean, in conjunction with the Ministry of Foreign Affairs. PRA-OSIM provides technical assistance and co-financing so as to enable OSIM to play a role among international cooperation actors and enhance and leverage their development practices. The projects concerned with co-financing are ones that (1) are local development projects carried out by International Migrant Solidarity Organizations (OSIM); (2) have co-financing capped at €15 000 (in all cases, the grant cannot represent more than 70 percent of the total budget); (3) are aimed towards a country of the Priority Solidarity Zone[38] (excluding Haiti, Mali, Senegal and the Comoros, which are supported by other systems); (4) have a total budget not exceeding €120 000; and (5) have an implementation period of a maximum of one year. Since its inception in 2003, the total amount of funds released under PRA-OSIM for projects has been €861 479. A total of 159 requests for co-financing have been made and 66 projects have been co-funded.[39] France also has co-development programs with Mali,[40] Senegal,[41] the Comoros[42] and Haiti that contain similar schemes to support migrant organizations. Whatever the country of origin, additional funding can be provided by French municipalities and regions. Some localities have a dedicated budget for financing decentralized cooperation activities with third countries to which migrant organizations and development NGOs can apply. The same holds true in Italy, where development cooperation and its related funding is highly decentralized. In the case of Milan, for example, the municipality launched in 2007 a three-year program on co-development for co-funding projects developed by diaspora organizations towards their countries of origin. Two sets of proposals have been realized between 2007 and 2010, with an overall budget of over €2 million. Organizations were expected to provide 30 percent of the funding (10 percent in cash, 10 percent through labor, and 10 percent through overhead costs). Neither the net contribution of migrant organizations to development, nor the impact of co-development programs providing matching funds, have been properly assessed.[43] The advocates of such programs generally claim that they constitute a new form of development cooperation that is better than the traditional one, given the central place it confers on immigrants in the development process. Donors generally have very high expectations regarding the contribution of migrant organizations. First, the latter are credited with possessing valuable knowledge about culture, language, society, history, religion and politics, so that they are in a good position to identify local needs in their country of origin and may for that reason enable more culturally appropriate, equitable, targeted and sustainable projects to emerge. Their resources also include networks in both destination and origin countries so that they can act as bridge-builders between NGOs, government bodies and other stakeholders in the country they reside in, and regional and local authorities, civil-society actors and potential beneficiaries of development projects in their country of origin. This bridging function might help to legitimize external engagement locally, as members of migrant organizations may be viewed as representing locals. Last, as underlined by Horst and her co-authors (2010), migrant organizations have a level of commitment and personal motivation that is unmatched by other actors, since the direct beneficiaries of their projects are members of their family or friends. This may translate into greater sustainability of efforts and the continuation of projects even after external funding runs out. However, there have been criticisms of this optimistic vision. Skeptics first argue that migrants should not always be considered as on a par with local actors, as living abroad for many years may have altered their habits and viewpoints (Horst et al., 2010). The assumed sustainability of their interventions is also challenged by the instability of their organizations and the fact that second and third generations are generally found to be less interested in contributing to the development of their parents' or grandparents' regions of origin. Last, migrants are often viewed with ambivalence in their societies of origin and there may be a lack of trust between migrant organizations and local actors.

Migrants may reinforce social and political fragmentations, may intervene with a 'Western dominance' and be dominated by male, elite leaders. They may, in short, face some of the same problems that plague established development players (Judge and De Plaen, 2011). This is very likely if migrant organizations and their members are taught how to 'do' development. As highlighted by De Haas (2006), there is a delicate balance to be found between strengthening and patronizing migrant organizations. Sustaining capacity building, for example, is likely to succeed only if it is based on a true willingness and openness to mutual learning among both diaspora organizations and development actors.

II.4 Facilitating Skill and Knowledge Transfers

Several international programs have tried to promote the transfer of knowledge, competencies and technologies through short-term consultation stays with a three- to six-month maximum duration by experts in their countries of origin. The best-known such program is the Transfer of Knowledge through Expatriate Nationals (TOKTEN) program instituted by UNDP. Launched in Turkey in 1977, it has expanded since then and now covers about 35 developing countries, with many successful outcomes in countries such as China, Poland, Palestine, Turkey and Vietnam. TOKTEN allows professionals, including top scientists, engineers, doctors, economists, environmentalists and business executives, to return to their countries for short periods of time to share the expertise they have gained abroad in research, academic, public or private institutions. Transfer of knowledge occurs at a low cost because TOKTEN consultants volunteer their services, forgoing the normally high fees of international experts. The objectives of the program are to reduce the impact of brain drain; transfer the latest know-how and cutting-edge technology through national professionals working in the developed world; pass on to the private sector knowledge of the latest technical know-how, business and management practices with the assistance of expatriate consultants; and promote institutional capacity-building through technical expertise and policy advice. Over its first 20 years of operation, some 5000 people have taken part in projects.

In the same vein, the IOM has developed three programs respectively entitled Return of Qualified Afghans (RQA), Migration for Development in Africa (MIDA), and Temporary Return of Qualified Nationals (TRQN).[44] The RQA program began in December 2001, after the fall from power of the Taliban government, with the aim of encouraging the return of qualified Afghan nationals abroad who were motivated to contribute their skills for the benefit of the reconstruction process on a short- or long-term basis. Between 2002 and 2012, 1307 Afghan experts returned to Afghanistan with IOM's assistance.[45] Similar to RQA, MIDA is a program that aims to develop synergies between the profiles of African migrants and the demand from countries by facilitating the transfer of vital skills and resources of the African diaspora to their countries of origin. MIDA is focused on facilitating temporary movement and does not entail the permanent return of migrants. It operates in 11 African countries (Benin, Burundi, the Democratic Republic of Congo, Ethiopia, Ghana, Guinea, Kenya, Rwanda, Senegal, Tanzania and Uganda). As mentioned on the IOM website, MIDA is a generic strategy, but various configurations are possible, with specific MIDA projects designed according to country, region and/or sector of activity: the MIDA Great Lakes program, for example, allows professionals who reside in Belgium to return to their home countries (Burundi, the Democratic Republic of the Congo and Rwanda) and offer technical short-term assistance and expertise in technical fields including agriculture, banking, engineering, economics, environmental protection and social and educational sciences. Another example is the MIDA Ghana Health project, which was implemented from 2005 until 2012 with funding from the Dutch Embassy in Accra. It enabled Ghanaian and other African health professionals residing in the Netherlands and some European countries to contribute to the health sector of Ghana by returning for up to three months to provide health services including clinical and surgical procedures in various hospitals and clinics. Last, the TRQN program began in April 2006 with the aim of contributing to the reconstruction and development of a number of former war countries, namely Afghanistan, Bosnia-Herzegovina, Ethiopia, Georgia, Sierra Leone and Sudan. This is done by temporarily placing in each country of origin higher-educated persons who originate from that country but live in the Netherlands. The focus of the program is on the transfer of knowledge in positions where expertise is lacking locally. The TRQN program is demand-driven and based on the identified and expressed priorities in the country of origin.

As well as those international programs, many diaspora-related professional and expert networks started to develop in the 1990s (French Ministry of Foreign Affairs, 2012). As an illustration, several African professional diaspora organizations engaged in human resources for health and health sector development have emerged in Europe, among which are the Swiss-based Afro-European Medical and Research Network (AERN) and the London-based charity and diaspora organization, Sierra Leone Diaspora Network. Many other self-organized networks of expatriates working for the scientific and technological development of their home countries, the so-called 'scientific and technological (S&T) diasporas', have emerged.[46] However, most of them did so independently of any formal, direct ties with specific government-sponsored programs and the question of whether governments should encourage the development of S&T diasporas or devote the equivalent amount of energy to other forms of action is still an open one. The experience of the USA with India, China and their diasporas suggests that S&T diasporas can be very strong and increasingly valued and used by their countries of origin without much support from the host country, but these are probably special cases given the high level of S&T development in China and India (Barré et al., 2003).

Despite the lack of support policy for diaspora-related professional and expert networks in European countries, a few lessons can be drawn from existing international programs aimed at facilitating skill and knowledge transfers.[47] First, for those programs to be sustainable and efficient, a proper identification of the specific needs of origin countries is necessary to make sure that 'the right persons are placed in the right spot'. Creating databases with detailed information on skills, qualifications, experience and employment patterns in expatriate communities could be helpful for this matching stage. Second, programs need to give appropriate incentives for diaspora members to get involved. They should also make sure that there are enough resources in hosting institutions (computer facilities, Internet access etc.) so that diaspora members can do their work efficiently. Preparatory courses may also be useful, especially when migrants have lost track of the local context in their country of origin. Last, the sustainability and success of the programs depends heavily on whether governments in the countries of origin have committed themselves to support their implementation.

III. CONCLUSION

The issue of migration and development has raised considerable interest in Europe in recent years, and has been the focus of many discussions both at the national and supranational levels. In-depth analyses of the content of those discussions and the concomitant so-called co-development policies put into place reveal several ambiguities as to the objectives pursued. The most salient ambiguity has been in the key motivation of European member states to engage in the migration and development area. In most cases, development objectives have been clearly subordinated to domestic migration management objectives, raising suspicion among development practitioners and migrant communities, and resulting in their weak adherence to the proclaimed 'new approach'. The increasing recognition of the importance of migrants' transnational practices, however, has called for greater policy coherence and better policies. From an operational viewpoint, this has translated into a huge variety of innovative practices and more cooperative links between government bodies, civil society, multilateral agencies, the private sector and migrant organizations and their members. Some of those initiatives are still in their experimental phase. It is thus premature to say that they really make a difference. However, based on the outcomes of some of the concrete actions undertaken in the past few years, it is possible to list some of the necessary basic conditions for success. One is to disconnect assistance to migrants or their organizations from return obligations. Most assisted return programs have indeed failed or recorded disappointing results for the simple reason that migrants are strongly reluctant to return home. Conditions in the home country are generally not attractive enough, so that return by the migrants is considered much too risky an enterprise, and the financial support provided to them is negligible when compared to the amount of remittances that they are able to send to their family of origin annually. Another condition for success, which is discussed in depth in De Haas (2006), is for development actors not to impose their views on how migrants or their organizations should intervene in their country of origin. Most migrant organizations have spontaneously emerged and learned by themselves how to contribute positively to the development of the home country. This calls for a willingness and openness to mutual learning among diaspora organizations and development actors. A third condition for success is a good knowledge and understanding of the real intentions of migrants and their organizations when they decide to 'do something' for their country, community or family of origin. Some migrant organizations have been found to focus their interventions at the level of blood relations, for example, or to reinforce social and political fragmentation in the communities of origin so that providing assistance to them raises a number of ethical issues. Moreover, some interventions have been designed without fully measuring the type and intensity of the constraints encountered by the migrants. Policy interventions aimed at facilitating and reducing the costs of remittances, for example, lack a clear understanding of the reasons why migrants prefer to use informal channels or to send remittances in kind rather than in cash. The same holds true for projects trying to channel remittances into productive investments. These projects will have only mixed results as long as the migrants have the fundamental duty to support their families.

More generally, the importance of the debates in the migration and development area tends to overshadow the essential, namely the causes of underdevelopment. Despite their financial capability, migrants and their organizations are far too small to bring definitive solutions to the structural weaknesses of most origin countries, characterized by low productivity, poor infrastructure, lack of efficient institutions, corruption and so on. Expectations with regard to their contribution to development should thus not be too high.

NOTES

1. I warmly thank Jean-Pierre Garson and Gilles Spielvogel for their comments on a previous draft. The views expressed in this chapter are entirely my own.
2. Retrieved from http://go.worldbank.org/RR8SDPEHO0 (accessed on February 11, 2014).
3. In its 2005 Communication to the Council and the Parliament, for example, the EC stated that *'countries and international organisations increasingly perceive migration as a phenomenon whose positive impacts in development terms can be substantial, provided that appropriate policies are in place'* (European Commission, 2005, p. 2). More recently, in its contribution for the 2013 UN High-level Dialogue on International Migration and Development, the EC reiterated its position by stating that '*Migration is increasingly coming into sharp focus on the global agenda and is recognised as a powerful vehicle for boosting development in both countries of origin and destination*' (European Commission, 2013, p. 2).
4. The marked enthusiasm of policy makers for such measures is partly due to the fact that they are much less politically controversial than any attempt to ease restrictions on immigration.
5. For an in-depth discussion on the various interpretations of the concept of co-development, readers should refer to Möhl (2010), especially to the introduction by Enric Royo.
6. The OECD 2008 *International Migration Outlook* contains a full chapter on return migration that analyzes the scope and different types of return migration, and provides an overview of AVR programs in OECD countries.
7. http://www.iom.int/germany/en/projects_avr.htm (accessed on January 14, 2014).
8. This expression is borrowed from a paper by Ferruccio Pastore (2003).
9. An inventory of the agreements linked to readmission is provided by the Return Migration and Development Platform (RDP) of the European University Institute (see http://rsc.eui.eu/RDP/research/analyses/ra/). As clearly shown by the RDP data set, the majority of bilateral readmission agreements that entered into force in the 1990s were signed with Central and Eastern European countries (Coleman, 2009). The objective of European members states was to avoid the expected increase in unauthorized entry and residence resulting from the lifting of visa requirements for nationals of a number of Central and Eastern European countries.
10. Extending trade liberalization and increasing foreign direct investment were also perceived at that time as means to promote economic growth and, hence, to contribute, over the long term, to greater control over migration flows. For a detailed discussion, see OECD (2000).
11. At the EU level, this policy orientation translated into the establishment in 1998 of the High Level Working Group (HLWG) on Asylum and Migration. Its objective was to define a migration prevention strategy through Action Plans promoting cooperation between sending countries regarding foreign policy, development and trade.
12. Several municipalities, including Montreuil, Evry and Saint-Denis, and regions (Ile de France, Nord-Pas de Calais) had strong links with some migrant associations composed mostly of Malian migrants originating from the Kayes area, in the Western part of Mali, long before co-development entered the national policy debate.
13. The 'paternity' of the concept of co-development actually belongs to Michel Rocard

when he was Secretary of the Unified Socialist Party (Parti Socialiste Unifié, PSU). At that time, the objective was to improve the effectiveness of official development assistance (ODA) by focusing on aid in recipient countries granted to sectors with an important export potential towards donor countries. Migration issues were thus not considered.

14. Co-development was first mentioned in an official EU document in the 1999 Tampere Council Conclusions, which are generally considered as the basis for the development of a common European asylum and immigration policy, and which officially established the EU as a common Area of Freedom, Security and Justice. 'The European Union needs a comprehensive approach to migration addressing political, human rights and development issues in countries and regions of origin and transit. This requires combating poverty, improving living conditions and job opportunities, preventing conflicts and consolidating democratic states and ensuring respect for human rights, in particular rights of minorities, women and children. To that end, the Union as well as Member States are invited to contribute, within their respective competence under the Treaties, to a greater coherence of internal and external policies of the Union. Partnership with third countries concerned will also be a key element for the success of such a policy, with a view to promoting co-development' (Tampere European Council, Presidency Conclusions, Point 11).
15. The Ministry of Immigration, Integration, National Identity and Codevelopment was created after the presidential elections of 2007. It was renamed the Ministry of Immigration, Integration, National Identity and Solidarity Development one year later, before being suppressed in November 2010.
16. The recent period is particularly illustrative of the evolving institutional architecture in which co-development policy has been carried out. Between 2008 and 2010, the state budget allocated to 'co-development' was part of the Ministry of Immigration, Integration, National Identity and Solidarity Development (MIINISD). In 2011 and 2012, it was transferred from the MIINISD to the Ministry of Interior. In 2013, it was merged with the budget allocated to 'Solidarity with developing countries' and was transferred from the Ministry of Interior to the Ministry of Foreign Affairs.
17. This first program was followed by a second three-year (2006–09) program of €2.5 million.
18. Cf. http://www.pseau.org/outils/ouvrages/codev_plaquette.pdf (accessed on January 22, 2014).
19. A first program of €2.5 million was implemented between 2005 and 2008, and a second one of €9 million, known as Programme d'Appui aux Initiatives de Solidarité pour le Développement (PAISD), between 2009 and 2011.
20. The first agreements were signed in 2007 with Benin, the Congo and Gabon. Since then, new agreements have been signed with Cape Verde, Mauritius, Senegal and Tunisia (in 2008), Burkina Faso, Cameroon, Montenegro, Serbia and Macedonia (in 2009), and Lebanon (in 2010). See Panizzon (2011).
21. This section borrows heavily from De Haas (2006), Nijenhuis and Broekhuis (2010) and Nijenhuis and Zoomer (2012).
22. This section heavily borrows from Terrón (2004) and Möhl (2010).
23. For a more comprehensive overview of the state of the art in policies and programs aimed at enhancing the resources, both human and financial, that migrants contribute to development, refer to Agunias and Newland (2012). Another useful reference is Horst et al. (2010), which focuses on diaspora-focused initiatives in five European countries: Finland, Germany, Italy, the Netherlands and Norway.
24. For further reading on existing options to reduce remittance cost, see Bourenane et al. (2011).
25. This figure is taken from Devriendt (2008).
26. Retrieved from http://www.orangemali.com/omoney/distribution.php?p=distribution (accessed on January 30, 2014).
27. Retrieved from http://www.niokobok.com/avis-boutique-1.html (accessed on January 30, 2014).

28. OECD (2005) has a whole chapter on the menu of policy options that origin countries may wish to follow in order to provide support to migrants seeking to create or invest in businesses (see Bobeva, 2005).
29. Retrieved from http://www.value-chains.org/dyn/bds/bds2search.details2?p_phase_id=336&p_lang=en&p_ phase_type_id=3 (accessed on January 30, 2014).
30. In the Netherlands, the SEVA network foundation was created in 2003. SEVA provides loans and (start-up) grants to promising enterprises initiated by members of diaspora communities with substantial own contribution in the investment. In case of a (start-up) grant the own contribution must be at least 50 percent of the investment costs. SEVA also provides technical assistance to the implementation of business plans in the countries of origin, as well as training to migrants in the Netherlands who are looking for assistance in process of formulating their business plans. For this purpose, the SEVA Business School was created (retrieved from http://www.seva-group.org/activiteiten/, accessed on January 30, 2014).
31. Cf. http://www.ird.fr/les-partenariats/valorisation-et-transfert-de-technologie/accompagner-la-creation-d-entreprises/paceim.
32. PAISD came in the wake of another program, the Programme Migrations et Initiatives Economiques (PMIE), established in 2001, which provides technical and financial support to migrants seeking to create or invest in businesses in France or their countries of origin.
33. Retrieved from http://www.codev.gouv.sn/?Actions-realisees (accessed on January 30, 2014). As suggested by the front page of the website, a total of 485 entrepreneurs have participated in the program since its start.
34. See in particular, for Africa, Lucas and Stark (1985) on Botswana; Hoddinott (1992, 1994) on Kenya; Gubert (2002) and Azam and Gubert (2005) on Mali; for Asia, Yang and Choi (2007) on the Philippines; and for Latin American and the Caribbean, Amuedo-Dorantes and Pozo (2006, 2011) on Mexico; Clarke and Wallsten (2003) on Jamaica and Halliday (2006) on El Salvador.
35. In the UK, the idea of introducing a remittance tax relief for international development has been strongly advocated by Gibril Faal, the chairman of the African Foundation for Development (AFFORD) and the founder of RemitAid.
36. Van Heelsum (2004) (cited by De Bruyn and Huyse, 2008) estimates the number of migrant organizations in the Netherlands at 4000, representing 16 ethnic communities. However, only a small proportion of these focuses on development cooperation. In another study focused on sub-Saharan migrants (Kuster et al., 2006, cited by De Bruyn and Huyse, 2008), there are 67 such organizations, among which are 14 Somalian, 9 Sudanese, 7 Ghanaian, 6 Ethiopian, 5 Burundian and 5 Congolese.
37. Retrieved from http://www.diaspora-centre.org/home/projects/eadpd/ (accessed on January 31, 2014).
38. The list includes Algeria, Benin, Burkina Faso, Burundi, Cambodia, Cameroon, Congo, Côte d'Ivoire, Djibouti, Gabon, Ghana, Guinea, Lao, Madagascar, Morocco, Mauritania, Niger, Nigeria, the Central African Republic, the Democratic Republic of the Congo, Rwanda, Somalia, Suriname, Chad, Togo, Tunisia and Vietnam.
39. Retrieved from http://www.euroresources.org/guide/funding_programmes_open_to_national_applicants/ fr_8_support_programme_for_migrant_solidarity_organisations_pra_osim.html (accessed on January 31, 2014).
40. See http://www.codeveloppementmali.org/.
41. See http://www.codev.gouv.sn/.
42. See http://www.codevcomores.org/v3/spip.php?page=accueil.
43. One exception is the paper by Chauvet et al. (2013), which is one of the first to quantitatively assess the impact of hometown associations on development, using original data on Malian hometown associations based in France on the one hand, and panel data on public goods in all Malian localities on the other hand. The results suggest that Malian HTAs have significantly contributed to improve the provision of schools, health centers and water amenities over the 1987–2009 period.

44. The description of the three programs has been retrieved from the IOM website, http://diaspora.iom.int/migration-and-development (accessed on February 27, 2014).
45. Retrieved from http://www.iom.int/jahia/webdav/shared/shared/mainsite/activities/countries/docs/ afghanistan/IOM-Afghanistan-RQA-Factsheet-January-2012.pdf (accessed on February 27, 2014).
46. A book written by French researchers provides an in-depth discussion on these S&T diasporas (Barré et al., 2003). The electronic version, in French, is available at http://books.openedition.org/irdeditions/2591.
47. This discussion draws heavily upon Agunias and Newland (2012, pp. 177–86).

REFERENCES

Acebillo-Baqué, M. and Østergaard-Nielsen, E. (2011), Local dynamics of codevelopment and migrant incorporation in three Catalan cities. Paper presented at the International RC21 conference on 'The struggle to belong. Dealing with diversity in 21st century urban settings', Amsterdam, July 7–9.

AfDB (2008), *Les transferts des fonds des migrants, un enjeu de développement*. Rapport (retrieved from http://www.afdb.org/fileadmin/uploads/afdb/Documents/Publications/70000012_ FR_Transfert%20des%20fonds%20FR.PDF).

Agunias, D.R. and Newland, K. (2012), *Developing a Road Map for Engaging Diasporas in Development. A Handbook for Policymakers and Practitioners in Home and Host Countries*, Geneva and Washington, DC: International Organization for Migration and Migration Policy Institute.

Amuedo-Dorantes, C. and Pozo, S. (2006), 'Remittances as insurance: evidence from Mexican immigrants', *Journal of Population Economics*, **19**(2), 227–54.

Amuedo-Dorantes, C. and Pozo, S. (2011), 'Remittances and income smoothing', *American Economic Review*, **101**(3), 582–7.

Ashraf, N., Aycinena, D., Martínez, C. and Yang, D. (2013), 'Savings in transnational households: a field experiment among migrants from El Salvador', mimeo, University of Michigan.

Aumüller, J. (2004), *Migration and Development Aid Policy – Practical Models of Implication*, in Berliner Institut für Vergleichende Sozialforschung (Hg.), International Intervention, Transition and the Governance of Migration, Band 1, Berlin 2004.

Azam, J.P. and Gubert, F. (2005), 'Those in Kayes', *Revue économique*, **56**(6), 1331–58.

Barré, R., Hernandez, V., Meyer, J.-B. and Vinck, D. (eds) (2003), *Diasporas scientifiques: Comment les pays en développement peuvent-ils tirer parti de leurs chercheurs et de leurs ingénieurs expatriés?* Montpellier: IRD Éditions.

Batista, C. and Narciso, G. (2013), 'Migrant remittances and information flows: evidence from a field experiment', CReAM Discussion Paper No. 31/13.

Batista, C., Silverman, D. and Yang, D. (2013), 'Directed giving: evidence from an inter-household transfer experiment', Novafrica Working Paper No. 1302. Available at SSRN: http://ssrn.com/abstract=2384586 or http://dx.doi.org/10.2139/ssrn.2384586.

Blion, R. and Verrière, V. (1998), 'Epargne des migrants et outils financiers adaptés', *Migrations/Etudes*, Synthèse des travaux sur l'immigration et la présence étrangère en France no. 82.

Bobeva, D. (2005), 'Turning remittances into investments', in OECD, *Migration, Remittances and Development*, Paris: OECD Publishing, pp. 297–313.

Boni, A. and Lacomba, J. (2011), 'The new co-development agenda: official and non-official initiatives between Morocco and Spain', in T.D. Truong and D. Gasper (eds), *Transnational Migration and Human Security*, Berlin and Heidelberg: Springer, pp. 91–103.

Bourenane, N., Bourjij, S. and Lhériau, L. (2011), *Reducing the costs of migrants' remittances and optimising their impact on development: Financial products and tools for North Africa and the franc zone*, AfDB Report (retrieved from http://www.afdb.org/fileadmin/

uploads/afdb/Documents/ Publications/Reducing%20the%20Cost%20of%20Migrant%20 Remittances%20to%20Optimize%20their%20Impact%20on%20Development.pdf).
Carling, J. (2008), 'Policy options for increasing the benefits of migration', Centre on Migration, Policy and Society, University of Oxford, Working Paper 8.
Clarke, G. and Wallsten, S. (2003), 'Do remittances act like insurance? Evidence from a natural disaster in Jamaica', Development Research Group, The World Bank.
Chaloff, J. (2005), 'Co-development: a myth or a workable policy approach?', Rome, Centro Studi di Politica Internazionale.
Chaloff, J. and Piperno, F. (2004), 'International migration and relations with third countries: Italy', in Jan Niessen and Yongmi Schibel (eds), *International Migration and Relations with Third Countries: European and US Approaches*, Migration Policy Group.
Chauvet, L., Gubert, F., Mesplé-Somps, S. and Mercier, M. (2013), 'Migrants' home town associations and local development in Mali', DIAL Working Paper 2013-11.
Chou, M.H. and Baygert, N. (2007), 'The 2006 French Immigration and Integration Law: Europeanisation or Nicolas Sarkozy's presidential keystone?', ESRC Centre on Migration, Policy and Society, Working Paper No. 45, University of Oxford.
Coleman, N. (2009), *European Readmission Policy: Third Country Interests and Refugee Rights* (Vol. 16), Leiden: Brill.
Collyer, M. (2011), 'The development challenges and the European Union'. Background Paper EU–US Immigration Systems 2011/08, Robert Schuman Centre for Advanced Studies, San Domenico di Fiesole: European Institute for Migration.
Daum, C. (1995), *Les migrants, partenaires de la coopération internationale: le cas des Maliens de France* (No. 107), Paris: OECD Publishing.
Daum, C. (1998), *Les associations de Maliens en France: migrations, développement et citoyenneté*, Paris: KARTHALA Editions.
De Bruyn, T. and Huyse, H. (2008), *Evaluation of Oxfam Novib's Capacity Building Progamme for Diaspora Organisations*, Amsterdam: Oxfam Novib.
De Haas, H. (2006), *Engaging Diasporas: how governments and development agencies can support diaspora involvement in the development of origin countries [electronic resource]*, International Migration Institute, University of Oxford.
Devriendt, A. (2008), 'Les Maliens de Montreuil, des "Quêteurs de Passerelles"', Mémoire de Master 1 de Géographie, parcours 'Pays émergents et en développement', Université Paris 1 Panthéon-Sorbonne.
European Commission (2005), Communication from the Commission to the Council, the European Parliament, the European Economic and Social Committee and the Committee of the Regions, *Migration and Development: Some Concrete Orientations*, Brussels, Office for Official Publications of the European Communities.
European Commission (2013), Communication from the Commission to the European Parliament, the Council, the European Economic and Social Committee and the Committee of the Regions, *Maximising the Development Impact of Migration*, Brussels, Office for Official Publications of the European Communities.
Fauser, M. (2007), 'The local politics of transnational cooperation on development(s) and migration in Spain', COMCAD Working Paper 24.
French Ministry of Foreign Affairs (2012), 'Harnessing the skills of migrants and diasporas to foster development: policy options', Report 2012, OECD and French Ministry of Foreign Affairs.
Gibson, J., McKenzie, D. and Zia, B. (2014), 'The impact of financial literacy training for migrants', *World Bank Economic Review*, **28**(1), 130–61.
Grillo, R. and Riccio, B. (2004), 'Translocal development: Italy–Senegal', *Population, Space and Place*, **10**(2), 99–111.
Gubert, F. (2002), 'Do migrants insure those who stay behind? Evidence from the Kayes area (Western Mali)', *Oxford Development Studies*, **30**(3), 267–87.
Gubert, F. (2008), '(In)Cohérences des politiques migratoires et de co-développement françaises. Illustrations maliennes', *Politique africaine*, **109**, 42–55.
Halliday, T. (2006), 'Migration, risk, and liquidity constraints in El Salvador', *Economic Development and Cultural Change*, **54**(4), 893–925.

Hoddinott, J. (1992), 'Modelling remittance flows in Kenya', *Journal of African Economies*, **1**(2), 206–32.
Hoddinott, J. (1994), 'A model of migration and remittances applied to western Kenya', *Oxford Economic Papers*, **46**(3), 459–76.
Hoetjes, B. (2009), 'Trends and issues in municipal twinnings from the Netherlands', *Habitat International*, **33**(2), 157–64.
Horst, C., Ezzati, R., Guglielmo, M., Mezzett, P., Pirkkalainen, P., Saggiomo, V., Sinatti, G. and Warnecke, A. (2010), *Participation of Diasporas in Peacebuilding and Development. A Handbook for Practitioners and Policymakers*, Oslo: Peace Research Institute Oslo (PRIO).
Institut Panos (ed.) (1993), *Quand les immigrés du Sahel construisent leur pays*, Paris: Editions L'Harmattan. IntEnt (2009), *Annual Report 2009*.
Judge, R. and De Plaen, R. (2011), '"Courting the Diaspora": emerging roles of diaspora groups in the international development industry', INTRAC Policy Briefing Paper 27.
Kaba, O. and Force, E. (2002), 'Pratiques et politiques d'aide au retour au niveau européen. Analyse de la situation française', pS-Eau, Fonds Européen pour les réfugies, AGEF.
Kleush, M. and Schuster, N. (2012), *European Good Practice Examples of Migration and Development Initiatives with a Particular Focus on Diaspora Engagement*, Vienna: Vienna Institute for International Dialogue and Cooperation.
Koser, K. (2001), 'The return and reintegration of rejected asylum seekers and irregular migrants: an analysis of government assisted return programmes in selected European countries' (No. 4), International Organization for Migration.
Kuster, J., Plug, R., Schapendonk, J. and Van Naerssen, T. (2006), *Een inventarisatie von Afrikaanse migrantorganizaties in Nederland betrokken bij ontwikkelingssamenwerking*, Radboud University, Nijmegen.
Lacroix, T. (2009), *Migration, Développement, Codéveloppement: quels acteurs pour quels discours?*, Rapport de synthèse du programme IDEM, Institut Panos.
Lavigne Delville, P. (1991), *La Rizière et la Valise: Irrigation. Migration et Stratégies paysannes dans la Vallée du fleuve Sénégal*, Paris: Éditions Syros-Alternatives.
Linares, A. (2009), *Pourquoi les aides au retour et à la réinsertion de l'Etat français n'incitent pas les immigrés à rentrer dans leur pays d'origine? L'exemple des Maliens*, Recueil Alexandries, Collections Synthèses.
Lucas, R.E. and Stark, O. (1985), 'Motivations to remit: evidence from Botswana', *The Journal of Political Economy*, 901–18.
Magoni, R. (2004), '*International migration and relations with third countries: France*', in Jan Niessen and Yongmi Schibel (eds), *International Migration and Relations with Third Countries: European and US Approaches*, Migration Policy Group.
Martin, P. and Edward Taylor, J. (1996), 'The anatomy of a migration hump', in J. Edward Taylor (ed.), *Development Strategy, Employment and Migration: Insights from Models*, Paris: OECD Development Centre, pp. 43–62.
Möhl, S. (2010), 'The same but different? Codevelopment policies in France, Germany, Spain and the institutions of the European Union from a comparative perspective', Documentos Cidob migraciones20.
Naïr, S. (1997), *Rapport de bilan et d'orientation sur la politique de codéveloppement liée aux flux migratoires*, Paris: Ministère des affaires étrangères.
Nijenhuis, G. and Broekhuis, A. (2010), 'Institutionalising transnational migrants' activities: the impact of co-development programmes', *International Development Planning Review*, **32**(3), 245–65.
Nijenhuis, G. and Zoomer, A. (2012), 'Transnational activities of immigrant organizations in the Netherlands: Do Ghanaian, Moroccan and Surinamese diaspora organizations enhance development?', Paper prepared for the 2nd meeting of the Transnational Organizations Network, Princeton, May 11–12.
Observatoire permanent de la coopération française (1998), *Rapport 1998: l'APD 98 et la réforme de la coopération, le développement rural, l'immigration, la coopération et le développement, la santé*, Karthala éditions.
OECD (2000), *Globalisation, Migration and Development*, Paris: OECD Publishing. doi: 10.1787/9789264180413-en.

OECD (2005), *Migration, Remittances and Development*, Paris: OECD Publishing.

OECD (2008), *International Migration Outlook 2008*, Paris: OECD.

Panizzon, M. (2011), 'France's Codevelopment Program: financial and fiscal incentives to promote diaspora entrepreneurship and transfers', in D. Ratha and S. Plaza (eds), *Diaspora for Development in Africa*, Washington, DC: World Bank, pp. 183–229.

Plewa, P. (2012), 'The effects of voluntary return programmes on migration flows in the context of the 1973/74 and 2008/09 economic crises', *Comparative Population Studies: Zeitschrift für Bevölkerungswissenschaft*, **37**(1–2).

Pastore, F. (2003), '"More development for less migration" or "better migration for more development"? Shifting priorities in the European debate', *Migration Europa*, Periodical analysis bulletin on migration policies in Europe, Special issue, CeSPI.

Quiminal, C. (1991), *Gens d'ici, gens d'ailleurs*, Paris: Editions C. Bourgois.

Raunet, M. (2005), 'Mobiliser les migrants pour le développement socio-économique du Mali et du Sénégal', in OCDE (ed.), *Migration, transferts de fonds et développement*, Paris: OCDE, pp. 337–68.

Royo, E. (2010), 'Does codevelopment exist?', in S. Möhl (ed.), *The Same but Different? Codevelopment Policies in France, Germany, Spain and the Institutions of the European Union from a Comparative Perspective*, Documentos Cidob migraciones 20.

Schibel, Y. (2004), 'International migration and relations with Third countries: Germany', in Jan Niessen and Yongmi Schibel (eds), *International Migration and Relations with Third Countries: European and US Approaches*, Migration Policy Group.

Schneider, J. and Kreienbrink, A. (2010), 'Return assistance in Germany: programmes and strategies fostering assisted return to and reintegration in third countries', German European Migration Network Contact Point, Working Paper 31.

Secrétariat Général du Comité interministériel de contrôle de l'immigration (2007), *Les orientations de la politique de l'immigration. Rapport au parlement 2006*, Paris: La Documentation française (retrieved from http://lesrapports.ladocumentationfrancaise.fr/BRP/074000232/0000.pdf).

Siegel, M., Fransen, S., and Vanore, M. (2010), *Website Evaluation 'Geld Naar Huis': User-Friendliness, Effectiveness, and Financial Sustainability*, Maastricht Graduate School of Governance, Maastricht University.

Snel, E., Boom, J. and Engbersen, G. (2003), *Migration and Migration Policies in the Netherlands*, Dutch SOPEMI 2003 Report for the Continuous Reporting System on Migration (SOPEMI) of the OECD.

Terrón, A. (2004), 'International migration and relations with third countries: Spain', in Jan Niessen and Yongmi Schibel (eds), *International Migration and Relations with Third Countries: European and US Approaches*, Migration Policy Group.

Van Ewijk, E. and Baud, I. (2009), 'Partnerships between Dutch municipalities and municipalities in countries of migration to the Netherlands, knowledge exchange and mutuality', *Habitat International*, **33**(2), 218–26.

Van Heelsum, E. (2004), *Migrantenorganizaties in Nederland*, Utrecht: FORUM.

Yang, D. and Choi, H. (2007), 'Are remittances insurance? Evidence from rainfall shocks in the Philippines', *World Bank Economic Review*, **21**(2), 219–48.

6. Does development reduce migration?

Michael A. Clemens

1. INTRODUCTION

Will economic development in poor countries cause less migration, or more? This simple question has tremendous relevance to the future of migration policy as the world develops, and to development assistance policy as many donor countries seek ways to deter migration. It has spawned 45 years of theoretical and empirical research, in economics as well as in sociology, demography and geography.

This chapter reviews what economists know and what they do not know about the effect of development on international migration. I begin by summarizing the conventional wisdom, in the policy worlds of aid and trade diplomacy, that economic development swiftly creates conditions that deter emigration. I then summarize the basic facts about the observed association between economic development and emigration, in the best and most recent data we have. These show a clear and pronounced inverted-U relationship, across countries, between economic development and both stocks and flows of emigrants. This inverted-U relationship goes by many names, but here I refer to it by the earliest name: the 'mobility transition'.

I proceed to sketch six classes of theory that the literature has offered to explain the mobility transition. I then summarize the macro- and micro-level quantitative evidence we have testing the existence and shape of the mobility transition in different settings. I conclude by suggesting five questions that require further research, all of which relate to sorting out the mechanisms that produce the transition.

2. CONVENTIONAL WISDOM IN POLICY CIRCLES

Two generations have passed since Isaac (1947: 98) suggested that developed countries could substitute for migration with overseas aid and trade policy, reducing migration via 'the establishment of new industries in under-capitalized, densely populated countries'. The International Labor Organization (1976) formally recommended that 'multilateral and bilateral cooperation' should encourage 'appropriate intensified capital movements and transfers of technical knowledge . . . designed to avoid the need for workers to migrate'. A decade later the ILO (1984) again recommended 'bilateral and multilateral agreements' to 'create more employment opportunities . . . in countries of emigration so as to reduce the need to migrate'. Böhning and Schloeter-Paredes (1994) review some of this history.

The idea that development assistance can reduce migration has continued to captivate leaders in aid and diplomacy circles. In the USA, the development effects of aid and trade diplomacy have been explicitly marketed as a migration deterrent. The US Commission for the Study of International Migration and Cooperative Economic Development (CSIMCED, 1990: xiv) recommended a range of aid and trade policies for the Western hemisphere to the George H.W. Bush administration, because '[d]evelopment . . . is the only way to diminish migratory pressures over time'. As he signed side agreements to the North American Free Trade Agreement, US president Bill Clinton predicted that 'as the benefits of economic growth are spread in Mexico . . . there will be less illegal immigration because more Mexicans will be able to support their children by staying home' (White House, 1993). Mexican president Carlos Salinas agreed that 'higher wages in Mexico . . . will mean fewer migrants to the United States and Canada' (State Dept., 1993).

Similar beliefs have driven aid and diplomacy discussions in Europe. Unveiling a massive aid package for Africa, European Commission president José Manuel Barroso stated that 'the problem of immigration, the dramatic consequences of which we are witnessing, can only be addressed effectively in the long term through an ambitious and coordinated Development cooperation to fight its root causes' (European Commission, 2005). The European Commission (2008) recommends that EU migration policy should 'shift from a primarily security-centered approach focused on reducing migratory pressures' and should 'focus much more on . . . improving the . . . socio-economic situation in low-income and middle-income countries, and in regions characterized by high emigration pressures'. France built its 'co-development' policy, the basis for aid agreements with numerous African countries starting in 2006, on the idea that 'development should contribute, in the shorter or longer term, to reducing emigration pressures in Third World countries' (Khoudour-Castéras, 2009: 3).

This policy consensus is not without nuance. Many policy makers – especially those in migration policy circles – acknowledge that the shorter-term relationship between development and migration may not be simple. The US Commission above (CSIMCED, 1990: xiv) found that 'while job-creating economic growth is the ultimate solution to reducing these migratory pressures, the economic development process itself tends in the short term to stimulate migration by raising expectations and enhancing people's ability to migrate'. This idea is widely accepted among migration researchers and policy makers (Martin and Taylor, 1996; Lucas, 2005: 49), and finds expression in the qualifiers 'over time' and 'longer term' that appear in many policy claims that development must eventually reduce migration.

That said, such statements rarely define the length of the 'short term', and are often made in the context of ongoing crises of high migration flows under pressure for short-term action. This leaves them open to interpretation as suggesting that, at least after a few years, development policies will indeed serve to reduce migration. In short, aid and diplomacy discussions are dominated by the idea that the relationship between development and 'migratory pressure' must be negative, though they often allow that the relationship may be ambiguous in some settings and for an unspecified period. Few such statements have an empirical basis to posit any part of this pattern – the dominant negative relationship between development and migration, the possibility of a temporary positive relationship, or the duration of 'temporary'.

3. THE MOBILITY TRANSITION IN RECENT DATA

Data on international migration flows are generally poor. Migration data easily available for research stand at a level of coverage and accuracy attained several decades ago by data on international trade flows (Migration Data Commission, 2009). Recent years, however, have seen tremendous advances. Though most countries lack effective means to measure permanent emigration at the border, researchers have had success in measuring emigration by counting the foreign-born in laborious compilations of censuses, surveys and population registers of destination countries – then inferring emigration from the origin (Parsons et al., 2005; Dumont and Lemaître, 2005; Docquier and Marfouk, 2007).

Recently a team based at the World Bank created a set of five global migration matrices spanning the last half of the twentieth century (Özden et al., 2011). Built using over 1000 censuses and population registers, the five matrices count the number of people born in each country on earth residing in each other country, once per decade from 1960 to 2000. Summing across all countries of destination allows unprecedentedly accurate estimation of total emigrant stocks for each country at each point in time, as well as decade-by-decade net emigration flows. The United Nations Population Division has recently created similar matrices, using

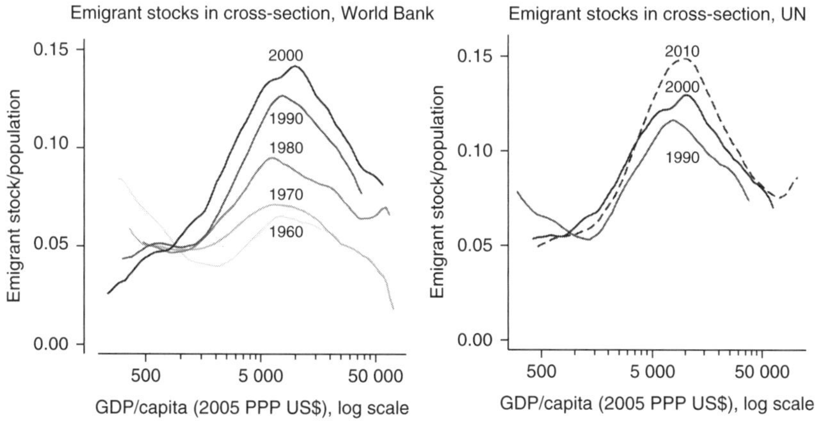

Notes: Lines show Nadaraya–Watson kernel-weighted local mean, Epanechnikov kernel, bandwidth 0.5 natural log points. Emigrant stocks are the number of people born in each country residing outside that country, divided by national population. Observations are country-years. In World Bank data, N is 106 for 1960, 140 for 1970, 140 for 1980, 164 for 1990 and 164 for 2000. Macau and Brunei omitted. In UN data, N is 155 in 1990–2010.

Figure 6.1 Cross-section nonparametric regressions of emigrant stocks on real income per capita, 1960–2010

similar methods, for the years 1990, 2000 and 2010. These data allow us for the first time to inquire whether richer countries exhibit broadly lower or higher rates of emigration, whether measured as emigrant stocks or net medium-term emigration flows.

There is a marked inverted-U relationship between emigrant stocks and real income per capita throughout the late twentieth century, and the inverted-U became more pronounced as years passed. Figure 6.1 shows nonparametric cross-country regressions of emigrant stock on income per capita at purchasing power parity (PPP). Here, each country's emigrant stock is measured as the total number of people born in that country residing outside it, divided by that country's population. The left-hand side of the figure shows the five timepoints in the World Bank data (1960–2000); the right-hand side shows the three timepoints in the UN data (1990–2010).

In all years, there is no hint of a negative relationship between income and emigrant stock between PPP income per capita of roughly \$600 (that of today's Niger or Ethiopia) and about \$7500 (today's Albania or Colombia). In this range of income, in fact, the relationship is positive. The rise in emigrant stocks associated with higher income levels in this range is statistically significant at the 5 percent level (see Appendix). The magnitude of the positive relationship is substantial. Early in the second half of the twentieth century, richer countries in this range on average had emigrant stocks about three percentage points larger than the poorest countries. By the end of the century, this difference grew to nine percentage points, and seems to have continued growing since then.

At higher levels of income the pattern reverses. For countries with per capita incomes above roughly PPP$7000–8000, there is a clear negative relationship in all years. This negative relationship, likewise, is statistically significant at the 5 percent level. All countries in this range of income are defined by the World Bank as 'upper-middle-income countries' or 'high-income countries'. The richest countries on earth on average had emigrant stocks about three to five percentage points lower than the middle-income countries with the greatest emigrant stocks.

We see similar patterns for net emigration flows. Figure 6.2 shows nonparametric cross-country regressions of the decade-by-decade net emigration flows from each country on the level of PPP income per capita. Net emigration flow rates are measured as the difference between emigration stocks at the end of the decade and stocks at the beginning of the decade, divided by population at the beginning of the decade. The flow rates are per decade, not per annum. Income per capita is likewise measured at

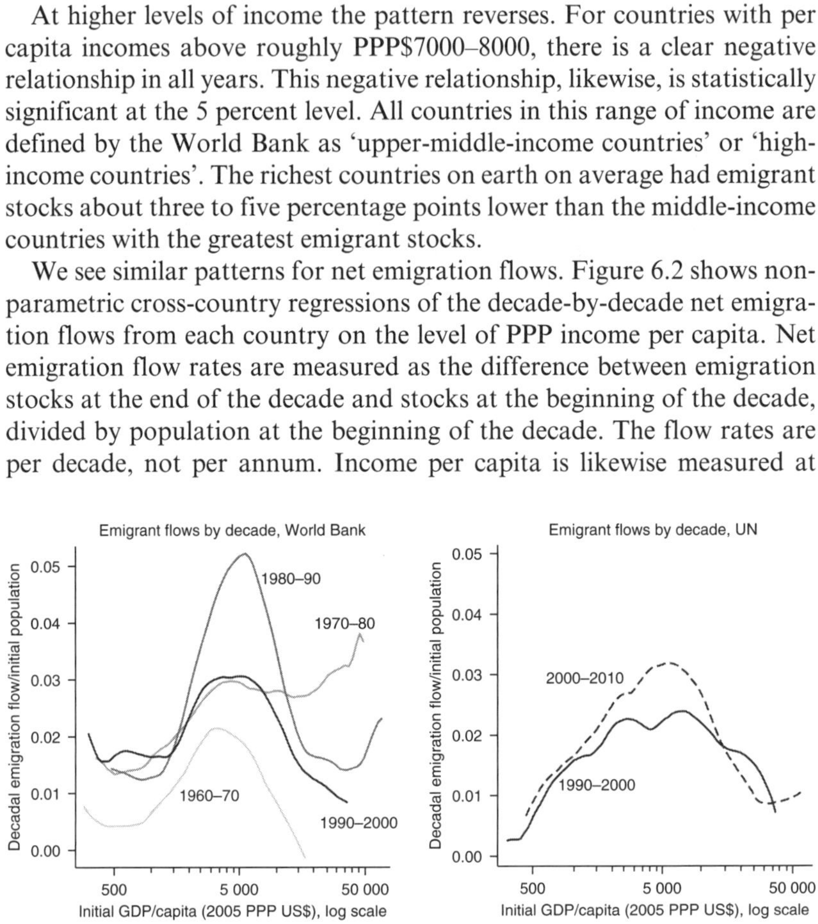

Note: Lines are Nadaraya–Watson kernel-weighted local mean, Epanechnikov kernel, bandwidth 0.5 natural log points. Emigrant flow is the decadal change in the number people born in each country who reside outside it, divided by decade-initial national population. The flow rate is thus per decade, not per annum. 'Initial' GDP/capita means in the first year of each decade. Observations are country-decades. In World Bank data, N is 106 for 1960–70, 140 for 1970–80, 140 for 1980–90, 164 for 1990–2000. Macau and Brunei omitted. In UN data, N is 155 for both periods.

Figure 6.2 Nonparametric regressions of decadal emigrant flows on initial real income per capita, 1960–2010

the beginning of each decade. Again, the World Bank data for four flow periods are on the left (1960–70, 1970–80, 1980–90, 1990–2000), and the UN data for two flow periods on the right (1990–2000, 2000–10).

In all of these decades there is no sign of a negative relationship between income and net emigration flows below an income per capita of roughly PPP$5000–6000 (today's Jordan or Jamaica). For countries with higher incomes there is a marked negative association between rising incomes and net emigration flows. Almost all such countries, again, are defined as 'upper-middle-income' or 'high-income' by the World Bank. The positive relationship at low income levels is statistically significant in all four decades; the negative relationship at higher income levels is statistically significant in all decades except 1970–80 (see Appendix). The rise and fall are substantial in magnitude: countries at the turning point have net emigration rates two or three percentage points higher than the world's poorest countries – measured in percentage of the population per decade. The world's richest countries exhibit emigration rates two or three percentage points lower than countries at the turning point, in all decades except 1970–80.

In short, the best available data show an unmistakable inverted-U pattern across countries in the relationship between overall economic development and emigration. The data offer no sign that, among low-income or lower-middle-income countries, rising incomes are associated with smaller emigrant stocks or lower net emigration rates. To the contrary, typical countries in this group show a positive, significant association between average incomes and emigration. The relationship changes markedly somewhere around PPP$6000–8000. Among countries above this level of income – upper-middle-income countries or richer – higher incomes are associated with reduced emigration. But even the very richest countries do not systematically exhibit lower emigration rates than the poorest countries.

These data do not necessarily demonstrate a transition path that any given country must take, for the same reason that mortality rates in an observed population do not determine the life expectancy of any given child. But if the observed inverted U does approximate a transition path even roughly, how long might such a transition take? Figures 6.1 and 6.2 suggest a rough timescale – under the strong assumption that these cross-sectional snapshots of stocks and flows are informative about the path that given groups of countries followed. We can approximate the transition time as the time for a given country to reach income per capita of PPP$7000. At a healthy real per capita growth rate of 2 percent per year, it would take 133 years for a country starting from $500 per capita (today's Niger or Burundi) and 63 years for a country starting from $2000 per capita (today's Cambodia or Zambia). At a strong growth rate of 3 percent per year, these durations would be 89 years and 42 years, respectively. These are optimistic growth scenarios, given that during 1960–2000 the average country experienced real growth in per capita income of 1.8 percent per year (Barro and Sala-i-Martin, 2003: 4). And most poor countries grew more slowly. If the path followed by given groups of developing countries over time resembles these cross-sectional relationships, then the migration transition is a process of generations. For some it may take on the order of a century. This duration has implications for macro-empirics on the mobility transition, to which I shall return below.

4. THEORIES OF A MOBILITY TRANSITION

Why would the migration–development relationship trace out an inverted U? Intuition and the simplest models of economic migration suggest something quite different: higher earnings in origin countries should be accompanied by monotonic declines in the propensity to emigrate. The founding economic theories of migration – sometimes collectively called the 'neoclassical' model – posit migration as a costly move from worse economic circumstances to better ones (Ravenstein, 1885; Isaac, 1947: 23; Lewis, 1954). Migration is, then, a form of investment in human capital (Schultz, 1961; Sjaastad, 1962; Schultz, 1972: 4). Higher reservation earnings strictly reduce the incentive to make such an investment. Even as these models have evolved to include risk (Todaro, 1969; Harris and Todaro, 1970) and income distribution (Roy, 1951; Borjas, 1987), they still predict that rising average incomes at the origin will tend to strictly reduce migration.

In the 1970s, a series of researchers began to sketch a different class of theories about the relationship between rising average incomes and emigration. These theories predict an initial period, starting from low levels of income, during which rising incomes are accompanied by rising rates of emigration. Only after some turning point are further increases in income accompanied by falling rates of emigration. This inverted-U relationship has been called the 'mobility transition' (Zelinsky, 1971), 'migration curve' (Akerman, 1976), 'migration transition' (Gould, 1979), 'migration hump' (Martin, 1993), and 'emigration lifecycle' (Hatton and Williamson, 1994).

All theories of the mobility transition posit other forces, accompanying economic growth, that exert a separate, upward pressure on emigration. At low levels of income, this upward pressure tends to dominate the emigration-deterrent effect of a rising reservation wage. For this reason there is no necessary conflict between the 'neoclassical' model and the 'mobility transition' model. In the language of calculus, the partial derivative of emigration with respect to income can be negative – all else equal – while the total derivative is either positive or negative – because all else is not equal. In the language of economics, observed mobility transitions do not refute the neoclassical model for the same reason that the existence of inferior goods (in the presence of substitutes) does not refute the basic theory of consumer demand (in the absence of substitutes).

Different scholars have stressed different theories for a mobility transition. Many of these are reviewed by Massey (1999), Lucas (2005: 50–51), Hatton and Williamson (2005a: 64, 252), and Williamson (2014). Here I briefly but comprehensively survey these theories.

4.1 Demographic Transition

Rising incomes can be associated with demographic changes that favor emigration. At early stages of economic development, rising incomes generally cause child mortality to fall (Pritchett and Summers, 1996) well before fertility consequently falls (Lee, 2003). During this demographic transition, then, a rising population and youth bulge can accompany continued economic growth. If wages are downwardly rigid, this can mean rising unemployment and thus emigration pressure – compounded because younger workers are much more likely to migrate internationally than their older counterparts. This exerts upward pressure on emigration even as average incomes at home rise. As the demographic transition ends, emigration falls with further economic growth. Easterlin (1961) first suggested this explanation for concurrent rises in incomes and emigration, which was developed by Tomaske (1971). It is discussed as a theory of the mobility transition by Zelinsky (1971), Hatton and Williamson (1994) and Lucas (2005: 50).

4.2 Credit Constraints

Rising incomes can help potential migrants finance the costs of international mobility. Credit markets in developing countries are incomplete and highly distorted. While international migration often raises workers' incomes by hundreds of percent (Clemens et al., 2008), these benefits occur well into the future. Prior to migration, potential migrants must finance costly prerequisites that can include overseas search, insurance, transportation, education, visa fees, passports (McKenzie, 2007) and smuggling (Salt and Stein, 1997).

So first, as development of the origin country proceeds, more and more households may be able to finance these costs simply because growth brings them disposable income (Vanderkamp, 1971; Faini and Venturini,

1994; Hatton and Williamson, 1994; Ghatak and Levine, 1994). Second, and compounding this effect, previous migrants often help finance the costs of migration by their family and friends (Gould, 1980: 293; Hatton and Williamson, 1994). Third, development at the origin brings deeper financial markets, which can be used to finance borrowing for migration. Fourth, credit constraints could produce a mobility transition by another channel. If migrants use overseas work to finance profitable investments in the origin country, development at the origin can raise the returns to those investments. For example, a credit-constrained worker wishing to take advantage of home-country growth by opening a business may migrate to earn startup capital (Lucas, 2005: 51).

4.3 Information Asymmetry

Once a few workers have migrated, they can accelerate migration even as origin-country incomes rise by providing information to potential migrants (Greenwood, 1969; Massey, 1988). Prior migrants can provide information about job search, earning potential, cost of living, marriage partners, legal formalities and extralegal channels of movement. This can lead to an S-shaped diffusion process of cumulative migration stocks, equivalent to an inverted-U timepath of migration flows coincident with economic growth.

Epstein (2008) builds a formal model of how information asymmetries across borders can generate migrant herding and a mobility transition, even as growth is occurring at the origin. Previous migrants can also reduce potential migrants' need for information, such as by offering in-kind insurance against risk – offering food and housing during unemployment (Martin and Taylor, 1996). These mechanisms for the mobility transition are discussed less formally by Gould (1980: 293) and Baines (1994).

4.4 Structural Change and Worker Dislocation

Economic development can be associated with structural change that alters the costs and benefits of emigration. In the development process new sectors rise and old sectors – particularly agriculture – decline. This can encourage geographic mobility as the opportunity cost of departing declining sectors falls, changing the relative costs and benefits of both domestic and international migration. 'The onset of modernization . . . brings with it a great shaking loose of migrants from the countryside' (Zelinsky, 1971: 236). The process of development 'displaces many people from traditional livelihoods and past ways of life . . . Most become internal migrants, . . . [b]ut some always migrate internationally, seeking wider opportunities in more dynamic economies abroad' (Massey, 1988: 384).

Moreover, these changes can encourage specifically international labor mobility when they occur in the context of liberalizing trade, through either lower policy barriers or lower transportation costs. Venables (1999) reviews how this can occur in various workhorse theories of international trade. For example, while in basic trade theory the liberalization of goods trade tends to equalize the price of the most intensively used factor between home and foreign, with sector-specific factors the prices of less-intensively used factors may not equalize. A simple case is that liberalization of agriculture trade between two countries (specific factor: land) can create pressure for labor mobility from the agriculture importer to the exporter – if the exporter's initial endowment of labor is relatively low.

Faini and Venturini (1993) and Martin and Taylor (1996) discuss various other mechanisms in this family as theories of the mobility transition. For instance, if infrastructure in the migrant-origin country is extremely poor, this reduces their productivity at home. If trade is liberalized between the migrant-origin and migrant-destination country, firms in the destination country might be able to outcompete firms at the origin by employing migrants made more productive by superior infrastructure. Similar country-specific differentials in worker productivity could arise through economies of scale in production, or barriers to technology diffusion such as intellectual property law. These too would create migration pressure even as trade raises economic growth at the origin.

4.5 Inequality

Economic development can be associated with changes in the distribution of income that affect the demand for migration. Because rising incomes are never uniformly distributed, 'development is apt to be characterized by a growing gap between expectations and achievements – that is, by an increased awareness of insufficiency and a decreased tolerance of both poverty and privilege' (Heilbroner, 1963: 26). As average incomes rise, a group's reference level of satisfactory income can rise faster than the incomes of some members of the group. Thus rising average incomes can be accompanied by rising numbers of the relatively deprived, who might seek to join a different reference frame by moving. And even if potential migrants care about their absolute rather than relative gains, the Roy model as elaborated by Borjas (1987) can still yield a mobility transition via inequality dynamics: changing inequality as development proceeds at the origin can mean that the gains from migration accruing to workers at different points in the income distribution can shift over time – raising and lowering migration rates.

The economic theory behind these forces is extensively elaborated (Stark, 1984; Stark et al., 1986; Stark and Yitzhaki, 1988; Stark et al., 1988; Stark and Taylor, 1991; Stark, 2006). A broad prediction of these models is that emigration is positively associated with inequality in the country of origin. There is substantial evidence of patterns in the level of inequality at different stages of development (e.g. Thornton, 2001; Frazer, 2006), corroborating Kuznets' (1955) hypothesis that early stages of development tend to cause rising inequality – though the evidence on falling inequality at later stages of development is weaker (Piketty, 2014). The effect of growth trajectories on inequality is not settled, but any effect at all could shape the mobility transition.

Feedback effects could further heighten or reduce the effect of inequality on emigration. Migration could raise or lower inequality at the origin, depending on where in the income distribution migrants come from, how much return migration occurs, and how much migrants earn (Massey, 1988). This mechanism is discussed as a theory of the mobility transition by Martin and Taylor (1996). Gould (1980: 295) appears to be the first to discuss links between emigration and inequality.

4.6 Immigration Barriers Abroad

All the preceding theories generate a mobility transition due to changes in the demand for migration. A mobility transition can also be shaped by changes in the supply of legal migration opportunities (Hatton and Williamson, 2005a: 240–41; Hatton and Williamson, 2011). All important migrant-destination countries have visa classes that are more easily available to high-income workers than low-income workers. These include 'points'-based settler visas, skilled-employment-based work visas, temporary business visas, student visas and investor visas.

Many non-visa policies likewise constitute *de facto* migration barriers (Czaika and de Haas, 2013). These too can impose constraints on migration from poorer countries that can decrease as they develop. For instance, many of the poorest African countries lack internationally accredited nursing and medical schools, making it difficult for health professionals from there to obtain licenses to work abroad – even if they can get a visa on other grounds. To the extent that international accreditation of training facilities tends to expand with economic development, this too could contribute to a mobility transition.

In this short review, it may seem fragmentary to offer six classes of theory. It reflects a fragmentary literature, despite longstanding aspirations of synthesis. 'Indeed, we have no theory of migration as of yet!' (Lucas, 1978: 101). 'At present, there is no single, coherent theory of international migration, only a fragmented set of theories that have developed largely in isolation from one another' (Massey et al., 1993: 432). Many years later, these assessments remain valid.

5. EMPIRICAL TESTS OF THE INCOME ELASTICITY OF MIGRATION

Researchers have studied the quantitative empirical link between income and migration over four decades. Much of this work analyzes 'macro' data – aggregate flows out of some broad geographic area such as a nation, province or state. Some more recent work analyzes 'micro' data – propensity to migrate across individuals, households or villages.

This section points out a few strong patterns that describe the empirical literature as a whole. I identify these patterns with the knowledge that this literature defies concise summary. The studies use a wide variety of locations, time periods, indicators of 'development', indicators of 'migration', estimation methods and functional forms. Many issues thus remain unsettled, as I shall discuss in the section to follow.

5.1 Macro Studies

The macro literature begins with Vanderkamp's (1971) first regressions of aggregate area-to-area migration flows on average incomes at the origin. He studies interprovincial migration flows within Canada, in repeated cross-sections 1947–66. Lucas (1975) is the first to investigate the question at the international level, studying the 1973 cross-sectional association between origin-country income per capita and the flow of nontemporary labor certification applications to the USA from 103 countries. More than a dozen studies have followed.

A coarse summary of this literature is that cross-sectional studies generally find either a positive or inverted-U relationship between income and emigration from developing countries, while time-series studies do not find a consistent relationship between income and emigration. I shall detail these descriptions and then propose an explanation for the broad disagreement: the duration of the mobility transition is much longer than the data used in most time-series studies.

Macro studies in cross-section generally find a positive linear or inverted-U relationship between emigration and income across large numbers of developing countries. That is, studies that test only a linear income term generally find a positive coefficient, and studies that also include a squared income term find that the linear term is positive and the squared term negative. I include in this group pooled panels without fixed effects, in which between-group variance in income is typically much larger than within-group variance. Some of these find a positive relationship between emigration and linear income per capita at the origin and do not test for a nonlinear effect (Vanderkamp, 1971; Bertoli and Fernández-Huertas Moraga, 2012a [without fixed effects]; Ortega and Peri, 2013 [without fixed effects]), while others include a squared income term and find an inverted-U relationship (Adams and Page, 2003; Letouzé et al., 2009; de Haas, 2010; Djajic et al., 2013 [for low-skill majority of migrants]). Lucas (2006) finds that African countries above PPP$2000 per capita income have higher emigration rates to the OECD than those below this line, though this pattern does not hold for intra-African migration.

The emigration–development association remains positive among developing countries in cross-section in studies that proxy for 'development' with an indicator other than income per capita. They find a positive linear relationship between emigration and measures of industrialization in output and the labor force (Greenwood and McDowell, 1991), the inverse of a poverty measure (Hatton and Williamson, 2005b), and the Human Development Index (Czaika and da Haas, 2012). Two studies find a positive linear relationship between emigration rates and foreign aid receipts, in sub-Saharan Africa (Belloc, 2014) and across developing countries in general (Berthélemy et al., 2009).

This consensus finding of the cross-sectional studies accommodates the three studies that do not find a positive relationship, because each of the three is incommensurable with the preceding studies. First, Lucas (1975) finds a negative linear relationship between nontemporary employment visa certification applications to the USA and income per capita of the origin country, but this result is not commensurable with those above because (1) this visa covers only 7 percent of 1973 US permanent visa applications, most of which were related to family reunification, and (2) it reflects visa applications rather than movement. Second, Karemera et al. (2000) find a negative linear relationship between migration to the USA and origin-country income per capita (though the same relationship is positive for migration to Canada). But neither is this result commensurable with the above findings; it obtains only when controlling for several origin-country traits that are related to the level of development – including unemployment, inflation, a civil liberties index, financial ratings and region fixed effects. It is thus unclear how to interpret the coefficient on income. Third, Belot and Ederveen (2012) regress bilateral migration flows on origin-country income and find a negative linear relationship. But the sample comprises exclusively migration flows between high-income OECD countries. This setting, too, is thus incommensurable with that of the above studies. In high-income OECD countries many of the theoretical mechanisms for the mobility transition – such as the demographic transition and credit constraints – would be much less important.

The pattern is quite different in time-series macro studies, which begin with Wilkinson (1970). Time-series studies do not consistently find a positive (or negative) relationship between emigration and the level of income. Here I use 'time-series' to refer to macro studies that discard between-group variation in the level of initial income – either by controlling for country fixed effects, controlling for lagged emigration, or regressing on changes in income rather than levels of income. Some of the same studies that find a positive linear relationship between emigration and income in pooled data across all countries, dominated by between-group variance in income, find a negative relationship when country fixed effects are added (Bertoli and Fernández-Huertas Moraga, 2012a; Ortega and Peri, 2013).

But the findings of other time-series studies are mixed. There is no relationship between linear origin-country income per capita and migration in Mayda's (2010) study of migration from all countries to the OECD, in Naudé's (2010) study of emigration from sub-Saharan Africa, or in Hanson and McIntosh's (2012) study of migration to the USA, UK, Canada and Spain – all of which include origin-country fixed effects. Again with fixed effects, Vogler and Rotte (2000) find an inverted-U relationship between origin-country incomes and migration to Germany from 86 Asian and African countries, and Telli (2014) offers similar findings for migration to the UK, while Clark et al. (2004, 2007) find a negative linear relationship for migration to the USA. Hatton and Williamson (2003) find a negative relationship between income growth and emigration from 21 African countries, but do not test the *level*. Faini and Venturini (1993, 2010) find an inverted-U relationship between time-series emigration from Southern Europe and incomes at the origin, while Hatton and Williamson (2011) find an inverted-U relationship between time and migration rates from all countries to the USA, controlling for origin-country fixed effects and for lagged migration. Carlos (2002) finds a negative linear relationship between income per capita in the Philippines and emigration from the Philippines alone to 26 destination countries, including destination fixed effects. In pre-1914 data, Wilkinson (1970) finds a typically negative relationship between annual emigration rates from Europe and origin-country incomes, but Hatton and Williamson (1994) find a positive, insignificant linear relationship between emigration and origin-country real wages, while finding an inverted-U relationship with time.

Why do the time-series studies show such a wide range of inconsistent findings, while the cross-section studies consistently find a positive linear or inverted-U relationship? One explanation is that the time-series dimension of most of these studies is much shorter than a plausible timescale for the mobility transition. Most of the time-series studies have a time dimension in the range of 15–25 years. If indeed the typical duration of the mobility transition is on the order of two centuries, as estimated earlier – a century to reach the peak, another to fall – each observation of a country over time captures only a small slice of the transition. Such a slice, even if the overall transition follows an inverted U, can be locally close to linear and either rising or falling monotonically.

Figure 6.3 illustrates this explanation, showing first a single hypothetical data set in cross-section and then the same data in time-series. Each line segment between two dots represents one country. In that idealized situation, a cross-section or pooled regression would show an inverted-U relationship. A linear regression would show a positive relationship if the richest countries on the right-hand side were omitted. This is what is found in the cross-section or pooled studies. But the same data set in time-series would yield no clear pattern in the coefficient – it would be roughly zero, somewhat positive, or somewhat negative. The time-series studies broadly corroborate this pattern.

Another potential reason for the markedly different pattern in time-series studies is that many of them use high-frequency data – often annual (e.g. Wilkinson, 1970; Clark et al., 2007; Mayda, 2010; Ortega and Peri, 2013). When between-group variance in incomes is largely or completely controlled away – that is, when the effects of very long-term changes in income are controlled away – the income–migration relationship is more sensitive to annual fluctuations. If a country while under observation experiences one crisis that provokes a sudden fall in income and a sudden spike in emigration, this will tend to generate a negative relationship between emigration and income even if both shortly return to pre-crisis levels. It is theoretically plausible that, for a poor country, 50 years of positive growth can increase migration in the long run (through the mobility transition) but one year of negative growth can increase migration in the short run (as workers temporarily flee the crisis). The balance between these two effects shifts when we move from cross-section to time-series data. Observing countries over time series that are short relative to the transition duration tends to wipe out the longer effect, leaving evidence only of the shorter effect.

The literature to date offers limited evidence on the six theoretical mechanisms discussed earlier. Many of these studies test the income–emigration relationship only incidentally to some other purpose,

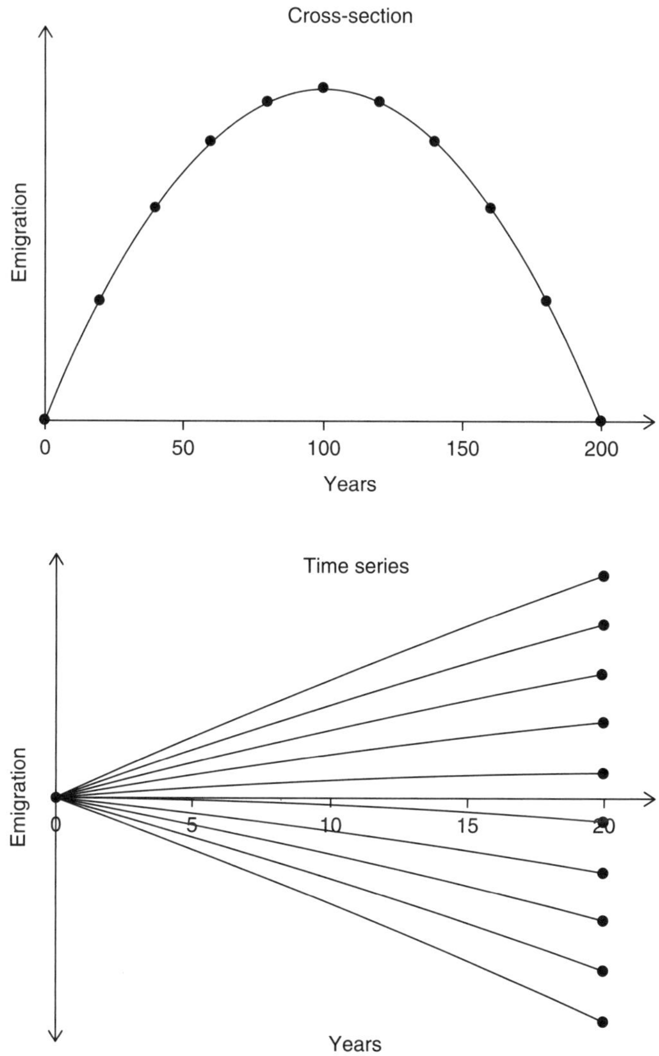

Note: The two parts of the figure show the same, hypothetical, data in two ways. The upper part shows a hypothetical transition in emigration stocks or flows over many years, in a cross-section of ten curve segments. The lower part shows the same ten curve segments in time series. Imagine a regression of emigration on time, or on anything generally rising over time, such as income per capita. In cross-section, the regression would yield an inverse U over 200 years. In time series, the same data over 20 years would yield no relationship. Any curvature would be difficult to detect.

Figure 6.3 Why a long-term migration transition can be difficult to detect in time-series data

without setting out to characterize the mobility transition. Some studies finding a positive emigration–income relationship interpret it strictly as evidence of credit constraints (e.g. Vanderkamp, 1971; Djajic et al., 2013). Carlos (2002: 93) interprets her negative relationship between average earnings in the Philippines and emigration rates as a sign that Filipino migrants are not credit-constrained, and are able to finance their moves via family, informal credit institutions or their overseas employers. Other studies fit this pattern as well: Lucas (2006) finds that richer African countries have higher emigration rates to the OECD, but not higher emigration rates to nearby African countries, consistent with an important role for credit and information constraints in shaping emigration rates. Belot and Ederveen (2012) find no sign of a mobility transition in bilateral flows among the richest countries, also consistent with an important role for credit constraints in shaping the transition in poor countries.

A handful of macro studies set out to test different mechanisms for the mobility transition against each other. Hatton and Williamson (1994) find that, in pre-1913 European emigration, the inverted-U 'emigration lifecycle' was shaped by structural transformation and demographic change at the origin and by networks of previous migrants at the destination (helping migrants reduce credit constraints and information asymmetry). Hatton and Williamson (2003: 483) find that 'exactly the same forces' shaped emigration rates from Africa in the late twentieth century, and predict that 'there is a good chance that by 2025 Africa will record far greater mass migrations than did nineteenth-century Europe'. Hatton and Williamson (2005b: 35) find that three of the biggest forces shaping the migration transition worldwide since 1850 are 'poverty constraints on the move in poor sending countries; the size of the young adult share in sending and receiving country populations; and the size of the foreign-born migrant stock from the sending countries currently residing in the receiving countries'. But the precise relative contributions of each of these forces to the mobility transition, or their importance relative to that of immigration barriers abroad or inequality shifts at home, is difficult to judge in existing work.

Separately, a substantial literature tests the effects underlying some of the posited mechanisms for a mobility transition, without directly testing them against other possible mechanisms for the transition. For example, various recent studies test the effects of migrant networks and visa policy on migration flows (subsections 4.2, 4.3 and 2.6 above), but do not assess the ability of these effects to explain the mobility transition (e.g. Mayda, 2010; Bertoli and Fernández-Huertas Moraga, 2012b; Ortega and Peri, 2013).

5.2 Micro Studies

A somewhat smaller literature explores the relationship between economic resources and emigration rates at the micro level – where the unit of analysis is workers, households or villages. The micro literature begins with Lucas (1985). Of the 24 studies I am aware of, the large majority (17) study cross-sectional data rather than panels, and 10 of the 24 study data from Mexico. The measure of economic resources varies greatly across studies. It includes both stocks (land holdings, land access, education, public infrastructure) and flows (income, consumption, expenditure, cash transfers), and is measured by some studies in absolute terms, by others in relative terms. This heterogeneity makes the studies difficult to compare systematically, though some very broad patterns emerge.

Most of these studies find evidence of a positive relationship between micro-level migration and some measure of wealth or income, in settings where credit constraints are plausibly important. Bilsborrow et al. (1987) find an inverted-U relationship between land assets and rural–urban migration in Ecuador. Stark and Taylor (1989, 1991) find a positive linear relationship between household wealth and migration from a small region of Mexico to the USA, and Stark and Taylor (1991) find an inverted-U relationship between nonremittance income and migration. Various studies find inverted-U relationships between emigration and landholdings in El Salvador (Halliday, 2006), nondurable household consumption in Mexico (McKenzie and Rapoport, 2007), household consumption in India (Czaika, 2012), and land holdings and rice income in Indonesia (Bazzi, 2013). Beauchemin and Schoumaker (2005: 1129) find that in Burkina Faso, 'contrary to policy expectations, most components of rural development either have no effect on migration or rather tend to encourage migration to cities'. Chort (2012) finds that household expenditures are positively associated with emigration in a panel of Mexican households. Both Azuara (2009) and Angelucci (2014) find that conditional cash transfers in Mexico caused higher migration rates from poor rural communities, contradicting earlier work by Steckov et al. (2005).

In a few micro studies the findings are less clear-cut, but nevertheless often show patterns compatible with the importance of credit and information barriers. Lucas (1985) finds a negative relationship between cattle assets and rural–urban migration in Botswana, but no relationship between cattle assets and longer-haul migration to South Africa. The greater travel cost and information barriers associated with long-distance migration are a plausible reason for this pattern. Orrenius and Zavodny (2005) find that unauthorized migration from Mexico is positively associated with agricultural GDP per capita in Mexico for migration trips longer than three years, but negatively associated for shorter trips. McKenzie and Rapoport (2010) find a positive association between human capital stocks and emigration in Mexican households, but only in areas of low migration prevalence – where credit and information barriers are plausibly highest. Kennan and Walker (2011) find a negative association between income and intra-US migration in a long panel, but credit constraints are less likely to bind within a rich country. In two studies using nineteenth-century micro data, Abramitzky et al. (2013) find that household wealth has a negative linear association with emigration from Norway – interpreting this as evidence that credit and information constraints had been reduced by prior migration of many Norwegians; while Groote and Tassenaar (2000) find that the absence of hunger tended to encourage emigration from an impoverished portion of the rural Netherlands.

Finally, two of the micro studies investigate the association between exclusively relative economic resources and migration, finding that lower migration rates are associated with greater relative access to land in Nepal (Bhandari, 2004) and higher relative wages in Mexico (Quinn, 2006). But these studies control for absolute measures of assets (e.g. toilet facilities in Bhandari, 2004; household education in Quinn, 2006), so these relative findings are compatible with the existence of (for example) a mobility transition due to credit constraints in absolute terms.

Few of these studies seek to explicitly test different mechanisms for a micro-level mobility transition against each other. Many interpret their findings as evidence of the degree to which households are credit-constrained (e.g. McKenzie and Rapoport, 2007; Abramitzky et al., 2013), but other mechanisms for a mobility transition are less studied. Amuedo-Dorantes and Mundra (2007) find that stronger social networks among Mexican migrants are associated with higher earnings in the USA, but do not explicitly test this as a mechanism for the transition.

5.3 Inequality and Migration

A number of macro and micro studies investigate the effect of inequality on emigration – and vice versa. I briefly summarize these because they are relevant to the theoretical channel by which shifts in inequality could shape the mobility transition. But most of these do not explicitly test the degree to which changes in inequality could explain the mobility transition relative to other explanations.

The literature begins with Gould (1980: 295), who is the first to empirically estimate the emigration–inequality link in historical macro data. In other macro work, Adams and Page (2003) find a positive association between the origin-country Gini coefficient and emigration, and Czaika and de Haas (2013) likewise find a positive relationship between origin-country indices of relative deprivation and bilateral migration stocks. There is an inverted-U relationship between the relative Gini coefficient at the origin (relative to the destination) and migration in Hatton and Williamson (2005b), Clark et al. (2007), and Mayda (2010).

The micro studies begin with Stark and Taylor (1989, 1991), who find a positive association between purely relative deprivation and emigration from a small part of rural Mexico, just as Bhandari (2004) and Quinn (2006) find in other settings. Reversing the direction of causation, McKenzie and Rapoport (2007) find that migration tends to reduce inequality in Mexico. Quinn (2006) finds the opposite, though the results are difficult to compare since the two studies use different surveys with different sampling methods, different measures of migration and different measures of inequality.

6. WHAT WE DO NOT KNOW ABOUT THE MOBILITY TRANSITION

Much remains to be done. The theoretical literature on the mobility transition is somewhat well developed, though parts could benefit from clearer formulation through formalization. The empirical literature has made progress in detecting the existence of a mobility transition, in macro- and micro-level data, but less progress in definitively sorting out the relative importance of the six classes of mechanisms theoretically capable of generating a transition.

Many important questions lie at this frontier of sorting out the mechanisms of the transition. Here I discuss five. All relate to understanding the mechanisms that create the transition.

1. *Will the same relationship continue in the future?* To the extent that the drivers of the mobility transition change, the transition could have a very different shape in the future than in the past. For example, the relationship between demographic change and economic growth is likely to be different in coming decades than in the late twentieth century, and even quite poor countries could proceed through a demographic transition as shifting Preston curves alter past relationships between economic growth and child survival. This could reshape the inverted-U (Lucas, 2005: 50–51). A recent literature has shown interest in using the mobility transition to predict, at least in sign and in rough magnitudes, future changes in migration for Mexico (Chiquiar and Salcedo, 2013), Morocco (de Haas, 2007a), and the

world (Hatton and Williamson, 2011). These predictions will be more accurate to the extent that we understand the relative contributions of the six theories of the mobility transition, and how those differ among settings.

2. *Is the mobility transition shaped primarily by supply or by demand?* Most theories of the mobility transition express interest in understanding the determinants of 'migration pressure' or the willingness of workers in developing countries to supply their labor to other countries. But in nearly all empirical work we observe realized migration flows, not willingness to supply labor. Migration flows are determined by the intersection of labor supply with overseas jobs and overseas demand for foreign labor. That demand can be influenced by many natural forces characteristic to the destination country – demographic change at the destination, language, geography. Demand for overseas labor is also heavily regulated by a worldwide thicket of visas, quotas, licensing restrictions, interdiction ships and physical barriers. These barriers, as discussed above, can also shape the mobility transition. One approach to isolating the effects of labor supply determinants from labor demand determinants is to explore the relationship between economic development and expressed interest or intent to migrate, either in micro data (Van Dalen et al., 2005; Arnold et al., 2011) or at the national level (Pelham and Torres, 2008). But this is suboptimal for various reasons. People's interests and intentions are shaped by what they perceive as realistic, which in turn can be shaped on overseas restrictions on demand for foreign labor. Expressed intent is not, then, a pure measure of labor supply. Another problem is that expressed interest in migrating can be quite different from actual migration behavior (Chort, 2012; Beam et al., 2013). Creative empirical strategies are needed to identify supply effects and demand effects on the shape of the mobility transition.
3. *Is there a micro–macro conundrum?* We lack a unified theory that can explain the shape and characteristics of the mobility transition at both the micro and macro scales, accounting for changes in both absolute income and relative income. Observe the following pattern in data from the Gallup World Poll, which asks adults in most countries if they would like to emigrate ('ideally, if you had the opportunity'): 'In countries that are at the bottom quartile in GDP worldwide, desired migration rates are about twice as high as they are in countries in the top quartile in GDP. However, for countries at every level of GDP, it is generally those individuals who are richer rather than poorer (by the standards of their own countries) who are more likely to say they wish to migrate' (Pelham and Torres, 2008). It is no doubt possible to

construct a single model that coherently displays all of these features – predicting that desired labor supply to overseas work falls when richer respondents are among richer people, but rises when respondents among poorer people get richer. Such a synthesis, coherently explaining all of these features at all scales, has not been carried out. It would generate a rich set of empirically testable predictions.

4. *What determines the relative importance of different mechanisms in different settings?* I have discussed the fact that few empirical studies have set out to test different mechanisms for the transition against each other. A handful of studies do this at the macro level and none at the micro level. None is set up to comprehensively test the relative contributions of all six mechanisms in a single empirical setting. Much less is any set up to assess why the relative contributions of different mechanisms would differ across different empirical settings.
5. *What are welfare-optimal policy responses to the mobility transition?* To state a fact bluntly, much of the research interest in the mobility transition has been spurred by a broad policy interest in finding ways to deter poor people from turning up at airports and beaches in rich countries. '[M]any of the policy statements about migration suggest that investing in development is a means to reduce migration' (Bakewell, 2008: 1350). There is no empirical economic basis for this view, after decades of testing, at least on a timescale that is meaningful to most politicians. The weight of our current evidence is that this view is generally false. This leaves a hole in policy makers' toolkit for encouraging welfare-optimal outcomes at the interface between migration and development. What could fill the hole? Martin and Straubhaar (2002: 18) review some of the alternatives, and conclude: 'The best practices to manage migration lie primarily in two areas: maximizing the amount and payoff from remittances and encouraging nationals abroad to return and assist in the development of their areas of origin.' Other policies designed to accommodate greater flows as development proceeds are discussed by Pritchett (2006) for low-skill workers and Clemens (2009) for high-skill workers. Much more and more creative policy development is needed, supported by the best evidence.

7. SUMMARY

Forty-five years of research have made progress in understanding the mobility transition. We have six classes of theory that can explain aspects of the transition, none of which is mutually exclusive. We have recently compiled data showing a clear bivariate inverted-U pattern for emigration stocks and flows in cross-section, across the full range of observed GDP per capita.

We have a range of macro studies showing strong evidence of a tendency for emigration stocks and flows to be higher among developing countries that are progressively richer in cross-section, though many of these do not test for the decline in the right half of the inverted U. There is no evidence that emigration rates tend to fall as countries get richer, until they are above an income per capital PPP$7000–8000. We also have a growing number of micro studies, from several countries, showing that among poor households the richer ones in absolute terms display a greater tendency to migrate to faraway rich countries.

We have more mixed results from macro studies in time series, but this appears to have an explanation. The cross-section evidence suggests that most of the data sets used in time-series studies do not cover a sufficient length of time to describe the shape of the transition. Very little of the micro evidence is in time series, as household panels that track international migration were very rare until recently.

All of this suggests that today's typical poor countries are unlikely to exhibit lower emigration rates as they develop: (1) until they reach income levels in the upper range of middle-income countries, and (2) unless they follow patterns of demographic and structural transition markedly different from developing countries in the past. If anything, they are likely to exhibit somewhat higher rates of emigration as they develop.

We do not know enough about the mechanisms that create this observed pattern. Theories of the transition are well developed, though they could benefit from more formalization and unification in a single framework that can explain patterns observed at both the macro and micro levels. And we know much too little about the relative importance of the six classes of theoretical mechanism that have been identified, what makes their relative importance change in different settings, and how they might alter the shape of the mobility transition in the future. Empirical work would move forward fruitfully with research designs set up to test the full range of mechanisms against each other.

But we do know enough to begin to advise policy makers more confidently on the broad outlines of the mobility transition. Twenty-six years ago, Massey (1988: 384) wrote,

> A realistic appraisal of the relationship between migration and economic development, therefore, suggests that policies to promote additional economic growth in sending nations will not reduce immigration to the United States in the short run; indeed, they may increase it . . . If it is in the interest of the United States to promote rapid economic development in Mexico, then it is also in its interest to accept relatively large numbers of Mexican immigrants.

But policy makers in the aid and development world have not been guided by such research. Twenty years on, de Haas (2007b: 837) laments the continuing prevalence of unsupported ideas:

> In the poorest countries, especially (such as the sub-Saharan African countries which are the target of much international aid), any take-off development is likely to lead to accelerating take-off emigration for the coming decades, which is the opposite of what 'development instead of migration' policies implicitly or explicitly aim to achieve.

In short, there is enough evidence now for researchers to be confident that the mobility transition exists, and for policy makers to move beyond 'development instead of migration policies'. Further research progress will help us better characterize the transition, especially the mechanisms that blend to create it. 'This might make it easier to avoid the assumption that mobility is normal for the wealthy, international elite, but a symptom of failure among the poor' (Bakewell, 2008: 1356).

ACKNOWLEDGMENTS

JEL codes F22, J61, O15. I thank Nabil Hashmi for excellent research assistance. I received generous support from the John D. and Catherine T. MacArthur Foundation, the William and Flora Hewlett Foundation, and GoodVentures. I received helpful ideas from Samuel Bazzi, Timothy Hatton, Robert E. B. Lucas, Lant Pritchett, Hillel Rapoport, and Jeffrey Williamson. Any errors are mine alone. Nothing herein necessarily represents the views of the Center for Global Development, its board, or its funders.

REFERENCES

Abramitzky, R., L.P. Boustan and K. Eriksson (2013), 'Have the poor always been less likely to migrate? Evidence from inheritance practices during the Age of Mass Migration', *Journal of Development Economics*, **102**(1), 2–14.

Adams Jr, R.H. and J. Page (2003), 'International migration, remittances, and poverty in developing countries', World Bank Policy Research Working Paper, 3179.

Akerman, Sune (1976), 'Theories and methods of migration research', in Harald Runblom and Hans Norman (eds), *From Sweden to America: A History of the Migration*, Minneapolis, MN: University of Minnesota Press, pp. 19–75.

Amuedo-Dorantes, C. and K. Mundra (2007), 'Social networks and their impact on the earnings of Mexican migrants', *Demography*, **44**(4), 849–63.

Angelucci, M. (2014), 'Migration and financial constraints: evidence from Mexico', *Review of Economics and Statistics*, forthcoming.

Arnold, Alex, Paul Hamilton and Jimmy Moore (2011), 'Who seeks to exit? Security,

connections, and happiness as predictors of migration intentions in the Americas', AmericasBarometer Insights, No. 64, Vanderbilt University.
Azuara, O. (2009), 'Does poverty alleviation increase migration? Evidence from Mexico', Munich Personal RePEc Archive (MPRA), Paper 17599.
Baines, D. (1994), 'European emigration, 1815–1930: looking at the emigration decision again', *Economic History Review*, **47**(3), 525–44.
Bakewell, O. (2008), '"Keeping them in their place": the ambivalent relationship between development and migration in Africa', *Third World Quarterly*, **29**(7), 1341–58.
Barro, Robert J. and Xavier Sala-i-Martin (2003), *Economic Growth*, 2nd edn, Cambridge, MA: MIT Press.
Bazzi, Samuel (2013), 'Wealth heterogeneity, income shocks, and international migration: theory and evidence from Indonesia', Working Paper, Boston University Dept. of Economics.
Beam, E., D. McKenzie and D. Yang (2013), 'Unilateral facilitation does not raise international labor migration from the Philippines' (No. 1319). Centre for Research and Analysis of Migration (CReAM), Department of Economics, University College London.
Beauchemin, C. and B. Schoumaker (2005), 'Migration to cities in Burkina Faso: does the level of development in sending areas matter?', *World Development*, **33**(7), 1129–52.
Belloc, F. (2014), 'International economic assistance and migration: the case of sub-Saharan countries', *International Migration*, forthcoming.
Belot, M. and S. Ederveen (2012), 'Cultural barriers in migration between OECD countries', *Journal of Population Economics*, **25**(3), 1077–105.
Berthélemy, J.C., M. Beuran and M. Maurel (2009), 'Aid and migration: substitutes or complements?', *World Development*, **37**(10), 1589–99.
Bertoli, S. and J. Fernández-Huertas Moraga (2012a), 'Multilateral resistance to migration', *Journal of Development Economics*, **102**(1), 79–100.
Bertoli, S. and J.F.H. Moraga (2012b), 'Visa policies, networks and the cliff at the border', Discussion Paper 7094, Bonn: IZA.
Bhandari, P. (2004), 'Relative deprivation and migration in an agricultural setting of Nepal', *Population and Environment*, **25**(5), 475–99.
Bilsborrow, R.E., T.M. McDevitt, S. Kossoudji and R. Fuller (1987), 'The impact of origin community characteristics on rural–urban out-migration in a developing country', *Demography*, **24**(2), 191–210.
Böhning, W.R. and M.-L. Schloeter-Paredes (1994), 'Introduction', in W.R. Böhning and M.-L. Schloeter-Paredes (eds), *Aid in Place of Migration?* Geneva: International Labour Office, pp. 1–12.
Borjas, George J. (1987), 'Self-selection and the earnings of immigrants', *American Economic Review*, **77**(4), 531–53.
Carlos, R.D. (2002), 'On the determinants of international migration in the Philippines: an empirical analysis', *International Migration Review*, **36**(1), 81–102.
Chiquiar, Daniel and Alejandrina Salcedo (2013), *Mexican Migration to the United States: Underlying Economic Factors and Possible Scenarios for Future Flows*, Washington, DC: Wilson Center and Migration Policy Institute.
Chort, I. (2012), 'New insights into the selection process of Mexican migrants. What can we learn from discrepancies between intentions to migrate and actual moves to the US?', Working Paper 2012-18, Paris School of Economics.
Clark, X., T.J. Hatton and J.G. Williamson (2004), 'What explains emigration out of Latin America?' *World Development*, **32**(11), 1871–90.
Clark, X., T.J. Hatton and J.G. Williamson (2007), 'Explaining US immigration, 1971–1998', *Review of Economics and Statistics*, **89**(2), 359–73.
Clemens, M.A. (2009), 'Skill flow: a fundamental reconsideration of skilled-worker mobility and development' (No. HDRP-2009-08). Human Development Report Office (HDRO), United Nations Development Programme (UNDP).
Clemens, M., C. Montenegro and L. Pritchett (2008), 'The place premium: wage differences for identical workers across the US border', World Bank Policy Research Working Paper (4671).

CSIMCED (1990), *Unauthorized Migration: An economic development response. Report of the Commission for the Study of International Migration and Cooperative Economic Development*. Washington, DC: The Commission.
Czaika, M. (2012), 'Internal versus international migration and the role of multiple deprivation: some evidence from India', *Asian Population Studies*, **8**(2), 125–49.
Czaika, M. and H. de Haas (2012), 'The role of internal and international relative deprivation in global migration', *Oxford Development Studies*, **40**(4), 423–42.
Czaika, Mathias and Hein de Haas (2013), 'The effectiveness of immigration policies', *Population and Development Review*, **39**(3), 487–508.
de Haas, Hein (2007a), 'Morocco's migration experience: a transitional perspective', *International Migration*, **54**(4), 39–70.
de Haas, Hein (2007b), 'Turning the tide? Why development will not stop migration', *Development and Change*, **38**(5), 819–41.
de Haas, H. (2010), 'Migration transitions: a theoretical and empirical inquiry into the developmental drivers of international migration', International Migration Institute, Working Paper 24.
Djajic, S., M.G. Kirdar and A. Vinogradova (2013), 'Source-country earnings and emigration', Working Paper, The Graduate Institute Geneva.
Docquier, Frédéric and Abdeslam Marfouk (2007), 'Brain drain in developing countries', *World Bank Economic Review*, **21**(2), 193–218.
Dumont, Jean-Christophe and Georges Lemaître (2005), 'Counting immigrants and expatriates in OECD countries', *OECD Economic Studies*, **3**(1), 49–83.
Easterlin, R.A. (1961), 'Influences in European overseas emigration before World War I', *Economic Development and Cultural Change*, **9**(3), 331–51.
Epstein, Gil S. (2008), 'Herd and network effects in migration decision-making', *Journal of Ethnic and Migration Studies*, **34**(4), 567–83.
European Commission (2005), 'EU Commission adopts new European Union Strategy for Africa', EC05-332EN, Brussels, 12 October.
European Commission (2008), 'Strengthening the global approach to migration: increasing coordination, coherence, and synergies', COM(2008) 611/3, Brussels, 17 June.
Faini, R. and A. Venturini (1993), 'Trade, aid and migrations: some basic policy issues', *European Economic Review*, **37**(2), 435–42.
Faini, R. and A. Venturini (1994), 'Migration and growth: the experience of Southern Europe', CEPR Discussion Papers No. 964.
Faini, Riccardo and Alessandra Venturini (2010), 'Development and migration: lessons from Southern Europe', in Gil S. Epstein and Ira N. Gang (eds), *Migration and Culture*, Frontiers of Economics and Globalization, Volume 8, Emerald Group Publishing Limited, pp. 105–36.
Feenstra, Robert C., Robert Inklaar and Marcel P. Timmer (2013), *The Next Generation of the Penn World Table*, Groningen: University of Groningen.
Frazer, Garth (2006), 'Inequality and development across and within countries', *World Development*, **34**(9), 1459–81.
Ghatak, S. and P. Levine (1994), 'A note on migration with borrowing constraints', *Scandinavian Journal of Development Alternatives*, **13**(4), 19–26.
Gould, J.D. (1979), 'European inter-continental emigration 1815–1914: patterns and causes', *Journal of European Economic History*, **8**(3), 593–679.
Gould, J.D. (1980), 'European inter-continental emigration: the role of "diffusion" and "feedback"', *Journal of European Economic History*, **9**(2), 267–315.
Greenwood, Michael J. (1969), 'An analysis of the determinants of geographic labor mobility in the United States', *Review of Economics and Statistics*, **51**(2), 189–94.
Greenwood, M.J. and J.M. McDowell (1991), 'Differential economic opportunity, transferability of skills, and immigration to the United States and Canada', *Review of Economics and Statistics*, **73**(4), 612–23.

Groote, P. and V. Tassenaar (2000), 'Hunger and migration in a rural-traditional area in the nineteenth century', *Journal of Population Economics*, **13**(3), 465–83.
Halliday, T. (2006), 'Migration, risk, and liquidity constraints in El Salvador', *Economic Development and Cultural Change*, **54**(4), 893–925.
Hanson, G.H. and C. McIntosh (2012), 'Birth rates and border crossings: Latin American migration to the US, Canada, Spain and the UK', *Economic Journal*, **122**(561), 707–26.
Harris, John R. and Michael P. Todaro (1970), 'Migration, unemployment and development: a two-sector analysis', *American Economic Review*, **60**(1), 126–42.
Hatton, Timothy J. and Jeffrey G. Williamson (1994), 'What drove the mass migrations from Europe in the late nineteenth century?', *Population and Development Review*, **20**(3), 533–59.
Hatton, T.J. and J.G. Williamson (2003), 'Demographic and economic pressure on emigration out of Africa', *Scandinavian Journal of Economics*, **105**(3), 465–86.
Hatton, Timothy J. and Jeffrey G. Williamson (2005a), *Global Migration and the World Economy: Two Centuries of Policy and Performance*, Cambridge, MA: MIT Press.
Hatton, T.J. and J.G. Williamson (2005b), 'What fundamentals drive world migration?', in G. Borjas and J. Crisp (eds), *Poverty, International Migration and Asylum*, Helsinki: UNU WIDER, pp. 15–38.
Hatton, T.J. and J.G. Williamson (2011), 'Are third world emigration forces abating?', *World Development*, **39**(1), 20–32.
Heilbroner, R.L. (1963), *The Great Ascent: The Struggle for Economic Development in our Time*, New York: Harper & Row.
International Labor Organization (1976), 'ILO World Employment Conference and international migration of workers', *International Migration Review*, **10**(3), 389–93.
International Labor Organization (1984), 'Employment Policy (Supplementary Provisions) Recommendation, 1984 (No. 169)', Geneva: ILO.
Isaac, Julius (1947), *Economics of Migration*, London: Kegan Paul.
Karemera, D., V.I. Oguledo and B. Davis (2000), 'A gravity model analysis of international migration to North America', *Applied Economics*, **32**(13), 1745–55.
Kennan, J. and J.R. Walker (2011), 'The effect of expected income on individual migration decisions', *Econometrica*, **79**(1), 211–51.
Khoudour-Castéras, David (2009), 'Neither migration nor development: the contradictions of French co-development policy', Paper presented at 'Migration: A World in Motion: A Multinational Conference on Migration and Migration Policy', University of Maryland, 18–20 February, 2010, Paris: CEPII.
Kuznets, S. (1955), 'Economic growth and income inequality', *American Economic Review*, **45**(1), 1–28.
Lee, Ronald (2003), 'The demographic transition: three centuries of fundamental change', *Journal of Economic Perspectives*, **17**(4), 167–90.
Letouzé, Emmanuel, Mark Purser, Francisco Rodríguez and Matthew Cummins (2009), 'Revisiting the migration-development nexus: a gravity model approach', MPRA Paper 19227, University Library of Munich, Germany.
Lewis, W. Arthur (1954), 'Economic development with unlimited supplies of labour', *The Manchester School*, **22**(2), 139–91.
Lucas, R.E. (1975), 'The supply-of-immigrants function and taxation of immigrant's incomes: An econometric analysis', *Journal of Development Economics*, **2**(3), 289–308.
Lucas, Robert E.B. (1978), 'Internal migration in developing countries: a review of theory, evidence, methodology and research priorities: Michael P. Todaro', *Journal of Development Economics*, **5**(1), 101–3.
Lucas, R.E. (1985), 'Migration amongst the Batswana', *Economic Journal*, **95**(378), 358–82.
Lucas, Robert E.B. (2005), *International Migration and Economic Development: Lessons from Low-Income Countries*, Cheltenham, UK and Northampton, MA, USA: Edward Elgar.
Lucas, R.E. (2006), 'Migration and economic development in Africa: a review of evidence', *Journal of African Economies*, **15**(suppl 2), 337–95.
Martin, Philip L. (1993), *Trade and Migration: NAFTA and Agriculture*, Policy Analyses in International Economics 38, Washington, DC: Institute for International Economics.

Martin, Philip L. and Thomas Straubhaar (2002), 'Best practices to reduce migration pressures', *International Migration*, **40**(3), 5–23.
Martin, Philip L. and J. Edward Taylor (1996), 'The anatomy of a migration hump', in J. Edward Taylor (ed.), *Development Strategy, Employment, and Migration: Insights from Models*, Paris: Organization for Economic Cooperation and Development, pp. 43–62.
Massey, Douglas S. (1988), 'Economic development and international migration in comparative perspective', *Population and Development Review*, **14**(3), 383–413.
Massey, Douglas S. (1999), 'Why does immigration occur? A theoretical synthesis', in Charles Hirschman, Josh DeWind and Philip Kasinitz (eds), *The Handbook of International Migration: The American Experience*, New York: Russell Sage Foundation, pp. 34–52.
Massey, D.S., J. Arango, G. Hugo, A. Kouaouci, A. Pellegrino and J.E. Taylor (1993), 'Theories of international migration: a review and appraisal', *Population and Development Review*, **19**(3), 431–66.
Mayda, A.M. (2010), 'International migration: a panel data analysis of the determinants of bilateral flows', *Journal of Population Economics*, **23**(4), 1249–74.
McKenzie, D. (2007), 'Paper walls are easier to tear down: passport costs and legal barriers to emigration', *World Development*, **35**(11), 2026–39.
McKenzie, D. and H. Rapoport (2007), 'Network effects and the dynamics of migration and inequality: theory and evidence from Mexico', *Journal of Development Economics*, **84**(1), 1–24.
McKenzie, D. and H. Rapoport (2010), 'Self-selection patterns in Mexico–US migration: the role of migration networks', *Review of Economics and Statistics*, **92**(4), 811–21.
Migration Data Commission (2009), *Migrants Count: Five Steps Toward Better Migration Data*, Report of the Commission on International Migration Data for Development Research and Policy, Washington, DC: Center for Global Development.
Naudé, W. (2010), 'The determinants of migration from Sub-Saharan African countries', *Journal of African Economies*, **19**(3), 330–56.
Orrenius, P.M. and M. Zavodny (2005), 'Self-selection among undocumented immigrants from Mexico', *Journal of Development Economics*, **78**(1), 215–40.
Ortega, F. and G. Peri (2013), 'The effect of income and immigration policies on international migration', *Migration Studies*, **1**(1), 47–74.
Özden, Çaglar, Christopher R. Parsons, Maurice Schiff and Terrie L. Walmsley (2011), 'Where on earth is everybody? The evolution of global bilateral migration 1960–2000', *World Bank Economic Review*, **25**(1), 12–56.
Parsons, C.R., R. Skeldon, T.L. Walmsley and L.A. Winters (2005), 'Quantifying the international bilateral movements of migrants', Working Paper T1. Development Research Centre on Migration, Globalisation and Poverty at Sussex University.
Pelham, Brett and Gerver Torres (2008), 'A country's richest citizens report greatest desire to migrate', *Gallup World*, 30 July.
Piketty, Thomas (2014), *Capital in the Twenty-First Century*, Cambridge, MA: Harvard University Press.
Pritchett, Lant (2006), *Let Their People Come: Breaking the Gridlock on Global Labor Mobility*, Washington, DC: Center for Global Development.
Pritchett, Lant and Lawrence H. Summers (1996), 'Wealthier is healthier', *Journal of Human Resources*, **31**(4), 841–68.
Quinn, M.A. (2006), 'Relative deprivation, wage differentials and Mexican migration', *Review of Development Economics*, **10**(1), 135–53.
Ravenstein, E.G. (1885), 'The laws of migration', *Journal of the Statistical Society of London*, **48**(2), 167–235.
Roy, A.D. (1951), 'Some thoughts on the distribution of earnings', *Oxford Economic Papers*, New Series, **3**(2), 135–46.
Salt, J. and J. Stein (1997), 'Migration as a business: the case of trafficking', *International Migration*, **35**(4), 467–94.
Schultz, T.W. (1961), 'Investment in human capital', *American Economic Review*, **51**(1), 1–17.
Schultz, T.W. (1972), 'Human capital: policy issues and research opportunities', in

T.W. Schultz (ed.), *Economic Research: Retrospect and Prospect Vol. 6: Human Resources*, Cambridge, MA: National Bureau of Economic Research, pp. 1–84.
Sjaastad, L.A. (1962), 'The costs and returns of human migration', *Journal of Political Economy*, **70**(5), 80–93.
Stark, O. (1984), 'Rural-to-urban migration in LDCs: a relative deprivation approach', *Economic Development and Cultural Change*, **32**(3), 475–86.
Stark, O. (2006), 'Inequality and migration: a behavioral link', *Economics Letters*, **91**(1), 146–52.
Stark, O. and J.E. Taylor (1989), 'Relative deprivation and international migration', *Demography*, **26**(1), 1–14.
Stark, O. and J.E. Taylor (1991), 'Migration incentives, migration types: the role of relative deprivation', *Economic Journal*, **101**(408), 1163–78.
Stark, O. and S. Yitzhaki (1988), 'Labour migration as a response to relative deprivation', *Journal of Population Economics*, **1**(1), 57–70.
Stark, O., J.E. Taylor and S. Yitzhaki (1986), 'Remittances and inequality', *Economic Journal*, **96**(383), 722–40.
Stark, O., J E. Taylor and S. Yitzhaki (1988), 'Migration, remittances and inequality: a sensitivity analysis using the extended Gini index', *Journal of Development Economics*, **28**(3), 309–22.
State Dept. (1993), 'Opening remarks at the U.S. Binational Commission Mtg. Office of the Spokesman', as delivered by US Secretary of State Warren Christopher, 21 June.
Steckov, G., P. Winters, M. Stampini and B. Davis (2005), 'Do conditional cash transfers influence migration? A study using experimental data from the Mexican PROGRESA program', *Demography*, **42**(4), 769–90.
Telli, Henry (2014), 'Less poverty, more emigration: understanding migrant flows from developing countries', *Migration & Development*, forthcoming.
Thornton, John (2001), 'The Kuznets inverted-U hypothesis: panel data evidence from 96 countries', *Applied Economics Letters*, **8**(1), 15–16.
Todaro, Michael P. (1969), 'A model of labor migration and urban unemployment in less developed countries', *American Economic Review*, **59**(1), 138–48.
Tomaske, John A. (1971), 'The determinants of intercountry differences in European emigration: 1881–1900', *Journal of Economic History*, **31**(4), 840–53.
Van Dalen, H.P., G. Groenewold and J.J. Schoorl (2005). 'Out of Africa: what drives the pressure to emigrate?', *Journal of Population Economics*, **18**(4), 741–78.
Vanderkamp, J. (1971), 'Migration flows, their determinants and the effects of return migration', *Journal of Political Economy*, **79**(5), 1012–31.
Venables, A. (1999), 'Trade liberalisation and factor mobility: an overview', in Riccardo Faini, Jaime deMelo and Klaus Zimmermann (eds), *Migration: The Controversies and the Evidence*, Cambridge: Cambridge University Press, pp. 23–47.
Vogler, M. and R. Rotte (2000), 'The effects of development on migration: theoretical issues and new empirical evidence', *Journal of Population Economics*, **13**(3), 485–508.
White House (1993), 'Remarks by President Clinton, President Bush, President Carter, President Ford, and Vice President Gore in signing of NAFTA side agreements', Office of the Press Secretary, 14 September.
Wilkinson, M. (1970), 'European migration to the United States: an econometric analysis of aggregate labor supply and demand', *Review of Economics and Statistics*, **52**(3), 272–9.
Williamson, Jeffrey G. (2014), 'World migration in historical perspective: four big issues', in Barry Chiswick and Paul Miller (eds), *Handbook of the Economics of International Migration*, Vol. 1A, Amsterdam: North Holland.
Zelinsky, Wilbur (1971), 'The hypothesis of the mobility transition', *Geographical Review*, **61**(2), 219–49.

APPENDIX: DATA SOURCES AND FULL NONPARAMETRIC REGRESSIONS

The 'World Bank' stock of emigrants from each country in each year of the set 1960, 1970, 1980, 1990 and 2000 is taken from the World Bank Global Bilateral Migration database (Özden et al., 2011), accessed Dec. 27, 2013. The 'UN' stock of emigrants in each year of the set 1990, 2000 and 2010 is taken from United Nations, Department of Economic and Social Affairs (2013), Trends in International Migrant Stock: Migrants by Destination and Origin (United Nations database, POP/DB/MIG/Stock/Rev.2013).

Total emigrant stock is defined as the number of people born in a country residing in a different country. The emigrant stock rate is the total emigrant stock in a year divided by national population in the same year. The emigrant flow rate is the change in the emigrant stock over a decade, divided by national population at the start of the decade. For these calculations, the 'World Bank' numbers use the national population given in the Penn World Table (below); the 'UN' numbers use: United Nations, Department of Economic and Social Affairs, Population Division (2013), World Population Prospects: The 2012 Revision, DVD Edition.

Real GDP per capita is in 2005 PPP US$ and is taken from the Penn World Table version 8.0, as expenditure-based real GDP, 'to compare relative living standards across countries and over time', (Feenstra et al., 2013) divided by total population. Accessed Dec. 27, 2013.

Figures 6A.1 and 6A.3 show the full data underlying the kernel-weighted local average curves for each cross-sectional nonparametric regression of emigrant stock on real income per capita in Figure 6.1, plus the associated 95 percent confidence interval. Figures 6A.2 and 6A.4 show the same information for the flow regressions in Figure 6.2. Countries are identified by their three-letter codes as in ISO 3166-1 alpha-3.

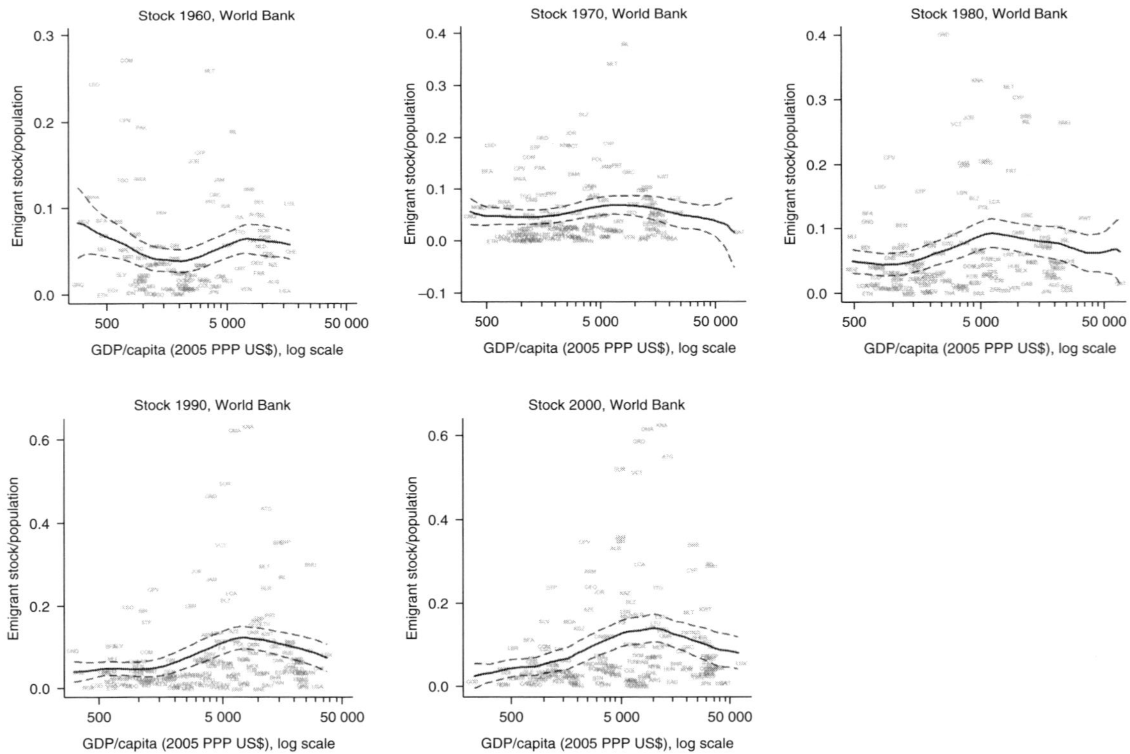

Note: Solid lines are Nadaraya–Watson local mean with dashed lines showing 95 per cent confidence interval, Epanechnikov kernel, bandwidth 0.5 natural log points. Observations are country-years; *N* is 106 for 1960, 140 for 1970, 140 for 1980, 164 for 1990 and 164 for 2000. Macau and Brunei omitted.

Figure 6A.1 Nonparametric regressions of emigrant stocks on real income per capita, cross-sections by decade: World Bank data

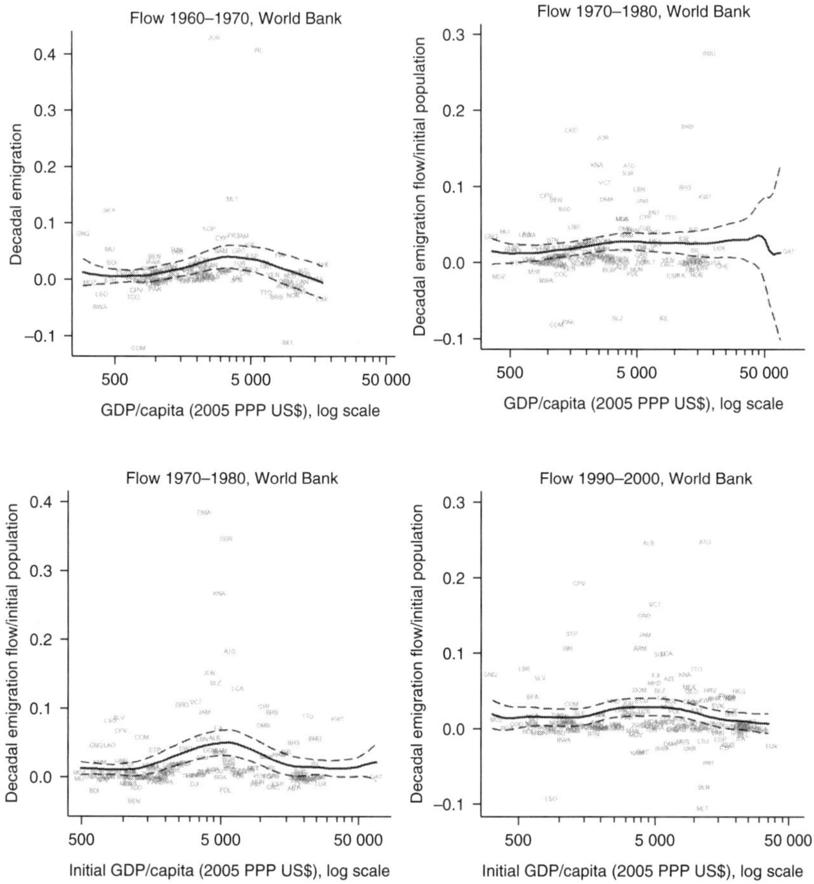

Note: Solid lines are Nadaraya–Watson local mean with dashed lines showing 95 per cent confidence interval, Epanechnikov kernel, bandwidth 0.5 natural log points. Observations are country-decades; *N* is 106 for 1960–70, 140 for 1970–80, 140 for 1980–90 and 164 for 1990–2000. Macau and Brunei omitted.

Figure 6A.2 Nonparametric regressions of emigrant flows on decade-initial real income per capita: World Bank data

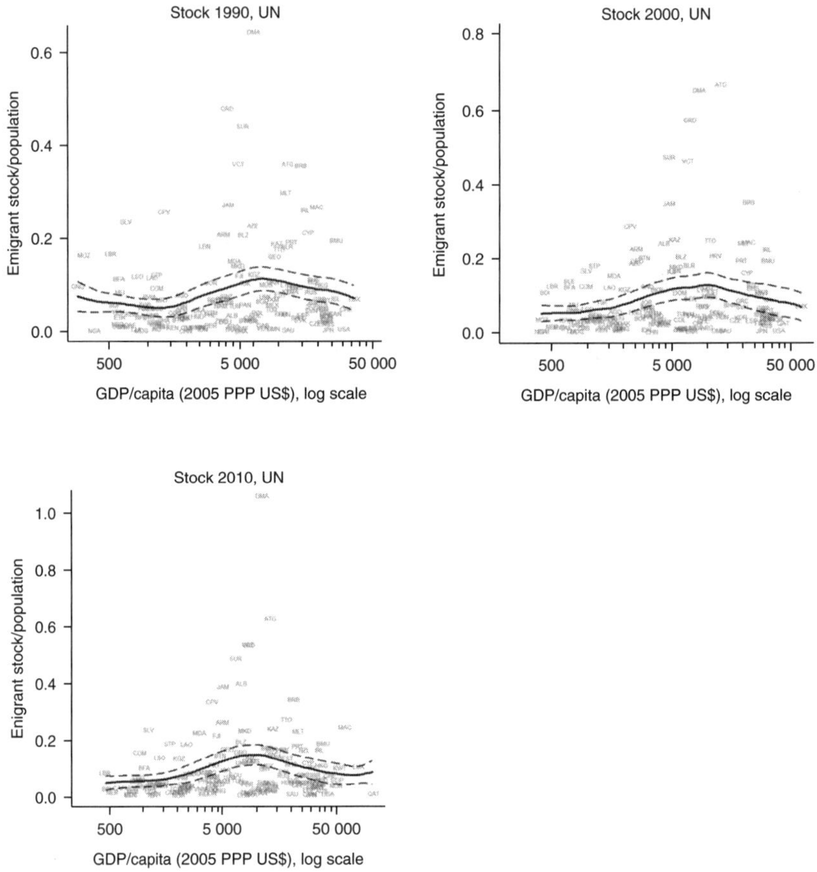

Note: Solid lines are Nadaraya–Watson local mean with dashed lines showing 95 per cent confidence interval, Epanechnikov kernel, bandwidth 0.5 natural log points. Observations are country-decades; N is 155 in all periods.

Figure 6A.3 Nonparametric regressions of emigrant stocks on real income per capita, cross-sections by decade: United Nations data

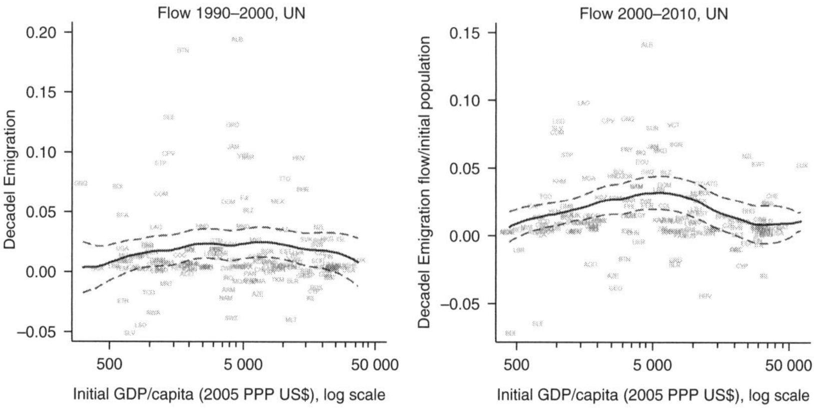

Note: Solid lines are Nadaraya–Watson local mean with dashed lines showing 95 per cent confidence interval, Epanechnikov kernel, bandwidth 0.5 natural log points. Observations are country-decades; *N* is 155 in all periods.

Figure 6A.4 Nonparametric regressions of emigrant flows on decade-initial real income per capita: United Nations data

7. Development through seasonal worker programs: the case of New Zealand's RSE program

John Gibson and David McKenzie

1. INTRODUCTION

Almost all OECD countries have temporary worker migration programs, with seasonal workers usually the largest single category, averaging over 500000 workers a year over the 2006–11 period (OECD, 2013). Seasonal worker programs have historically been one of the few opportunities for low-skilled workers from poor countries to benefit from the higher incomes to be earned abroad, and have been seen as a more politically palatable way of doing this than permanent migration (Luthria, 2008).

However, recently there have been divergent policy movements across countries in the willingness to use seasonal worker programs. The UK ended its Seasonal Agricultural Workers Scheme at the end of December 2013, when EU transitional arrangements for Bulgarians and Romanians ended; and the number of workers entering Germany under its seasonal worker program has likewise fallen as workers now come under the EU free circulation regime. In contrast, Italy and Korea have recently eased entry conditions for seasonal workers (OECD, 2013). Meanwhile, Canada's Seasonal Agricultural Workers Program (SAWP), which began in 1966, and the US H2-A temporary agricultural worker program, have seen reasonably steady numbers of workers entering over the last five years.[1]

A more recent policy direction has been to view these seasonal worker programs as a part of an explicit international development policy, and design such programs with this goal in mind, in addition to the traditional goal of meeting domestic agricultural needs. The subject of this chapter, New Zealand's Recognised Seasonal Employer (RSE) program, is of interest as one of the first and most prominent of these programs. The RSE was designed to meet the labor needs of New Zealand employers while also encouraging economic development in the Pacific Islands, which were designated as the main source area for workers. The policy was developed taking account of lessons from previous seasonal worker programs elsewhere and is viewed as a possible model for other countries. For example, the ILO good practices database states:

> The comprehensive approach of the RSE scheme towards filling labour shortages in the horticulture and viticulture industries in New Zealand and the system of checks to ensure that the migration process is orderly, fair, and circular could service as a model for other destination countries.[2]

Australia has subsequently launched its own seasonal agricultural worker program, which also has an objective of aiding development in the Pacific (Gibson and McKenzie, 2011).

Examination of the details of how the RSE operates should therefore be of interest for development as well as immigration policy makers. Moreover, it is of additional interest from a research perspective, because the policy's launch was accompanied by a systematic program of prospective research designed to carefully measure the impact of the program on local employers and native workers (NZDoL, 2010), as well as its impact on development outcomes in the sending countries (Gibson and McKenzie, forthcoming). Although a relatively new program, the RSE has also been the main subject for at least two doctoral dissertations (e.g. Bedford, 2013) and several other graduate research projects. The openness of employers, officials, source communities and workers to being researched is notable, since seasonal and other guest-worker programs are potentially controversial issues in some countries. This openness may be one reason why the RSE has been largely free of alarmist claims and other misleading publicity that immigration programs sometimes attract.

We begin by detailing the background context to the launch of the RSE program, and the details of how the policy operates in practice, including the role of development policy facilitation measures, the recruitment process, and program features designed to minimize the dual risks of workers overstaying or being exploited. Next we discuss the evolution of the program in terms of worker numbers, and the degree to which workers return for multiple seasons. This is followed by analysis and new evidence of the impacts of the program on New Zealand employers and New Zealand workers, and of the impacts on development outcomes for Pacific Islanders participating in the program. We conclude with lessons from the RSE for both development and immigration policy.

2. THE RECOGNISED SEASONAL EMPLOYER SCHEME

2.1 Origins

New Zealand's horticultural industry has grown from NZ$200 million in export sales in 1991 to NZ$2.23 billion in 2011, making it the sixth-largest export industry in New Zealand.[3] New Zealand's wine industry has seen even more rapid export growth, growing from NZ$300 million in export sales in 2004 to almost NZ$1.2 billion in 2012.[4] Collectively it is estimated that the horticultural and viticulture industries need at least 50 000 workers a year at peak times to pick and pack fruit, prune, and prepare orchards and vines for the next season (Ramasamy et al., 2008).

Historically these employers had relied on a range of students, local casual workers, people entering New Zealand as working holidaymakers, and migrant workers coming through a range of other temporary work schemes to help carry out these tasks. But the rapid growth in these industries, coupled with low levels of unemployment in New Zealand, meant that by the mid-2000s employers were increasingly having trouble obtaining sufficient numbers of workers at peak times. Moreover, on top of concerns about the number of workers, employers were also concerned about worker quality, with high levels of worker turnover resulting in few opportunities for sustained training of workers and poor-quality work reducing the value of crops harvested. Ramasamy et al. (2008) report that the horticultural industry estimated that the shortage and poor quality of labor was annually costing NZ$180–300 million in lost output and NZ$140–230 million in lost value added.

In response, in 2004 the New Zealand government introduced temporary policies to allow employers to recruit labor on seasonal work permits during the 2005–06 season while working to develop a more comprehensive policy response. Some employers brought in temporary workers on employer approval-in-principle (AIP) schemes whereby foreign workers could be offered work provided they could show they could not meet this need with the local labor force. Approximately 2000 workers came through such categories in the 2005–06 financial year, including 60 workers from Samoa, 7 from Tonga and 11 from Vanuatu (Gregory, 2006).

During the same period, there was growing pressure from Pacific Island governments to allow more movement of unskilled and low-skilled migrants from these countries to New Zealand and Australia. The New Zealand government undertook an inter-agency consultation (involving the Department of Labour, Ministry of Foreign Affairs and Trade, and New Zealand Agency for International Development), leading to a 2006 cabinet policy paper. A major World Bank (2006) report on mobility in the Pacific noted how the small and remote countries in the region facing growing youth populations would struggle to provide sufficient jobs, and highlighted the potential gains from more labor mobility.

The World Bank initiated a small pilot of 45 workers under the AIP process to test recruitment of workers from Vanuatu, a country with very little previous migration to New Zealand (Luthria and Malaulau, 2013).

They were hired by Seasonal Solutions, a cooperative in Central Otago. This enabled demonstration that recruitment was possible, and helped cement ties that led to Vanuatu ultimately being the largest participant in the scheme.

A Horticulture and Viticulture Seasonal Working Group, styled as a partnership between industry, government and other organizations such as labor unions, was formed to develop a medium- to long-term strategy for the industry, and from this the details of the Recognised Seasonal Employer (RSE) were formed.

2.2 The RSE Policy and Recruitment

The RSE was announced on October 25, 2006, and officially launched on April 30, 2007. It initially imposed an annual cap of 5000 seasonal workers, who could come to New Zealand for a maximum of seven months per 11-month period to work in horticulture and viticulture.[5] A specific objective of the program was to encourage economic development in the Pacific, with Winston Peters, New Zealand's Minister of Foreign Affairs, stating at the announcement that 'First and foremost it will help alleviate poverty directly by providing jobs for rural and outer island workers who often lack income-generating work. The earnings they send home will support families, help pay for education and health, and sometimes provide capital for those wanting to start a small business.'[6]

In order to mitigate displacement of New Zealand workers, and encourage employers using the program to recruit from the Pacific, there is a multi-tier approach to recruitment. A 'New Zealanders first' principle requires that employers first lodge their vacancies with the Ministry of Social Development (which provides welfare benefits and job search services) before attempting to recruit offshore. Then preference is given to recruiting workers from the Pacific Forum countries (except Fiji, which was made ineligible to participate after a coup). Employers are able to recruit from outside the Forum Island countries only if they can show that (i) reasonable attempts to recruit from these countries have not been successful; or (ii) the employer has pre-established relationships with workers of other countries, or can otherwise provide reasonable grounds why it is not feasible to recruit from the Pacific countries.

On top of this, bilateral inter-agency understandings were negotiated between New Zealand and five Pacific states: Kiribati, Samoa, Tonga, Tuvalu and Vanuatu.[7] These five countries were referred to as the 'kick-start' countries, and received facilitation efforts from NZAID and other agencies to launch the scheme and recruit in these countries. These inter-agency agreements covered how workers were to be recruited, the provision of pre-departure orientation material, visa processing and compliance with regulations.

Employers wishing to recruit workers under the RSE first have to register and get approved as a recognized seasonal employer. This requires demonstrating that they are financially viable, can pay workers at least the minimum wage for 30 hours per week, that they can provide accommodation and pastoral care to workers, that they have a dispute resolution process for workers, and that they have in the past met all relevant immigration and employment laws. They then need to apply for an Agreement to Recruit (ATR) from the Ministry of Labour, which specifies the number of workers required, the types of position, the length of time the positions are open for, the employment agreement that workers will be offered, and the countries the employer intends to recruit workers from. Employers are required to pay half the return airfare for the workers, and ensure that return tickets are purchased when the workers are recruited. If they pay the full cost of the airfare, they can recover up to half from deductions from worker wages.

Under the 'pastoral care' requirement in the RSE, employers must provide arrangements to help workers arrive, settle in and have access to adequate facilities while in New Zealand. This includes arranging transport to and from the port of arrival and departure, providing access to suitable accommodation (which workers pay for), arranging transportation to and from the worksite, providing safety equipment when needed, providing access to banking facilities and opportunities for recreation and religious observance and so on.

The provision of pastoral care and the adherence to other general labor market conditions is monitored by labor inspectors who are employed by the same government agency that handles all immigration matters. This unified approach to employment demand, visa processing and workplace monitoring may have helped with the relatively smooth implementation of the RSE. In contrast, in many countries these functions are each undertaken by separate agencies, and may even come from different levels of government in federal settings, allowing scope for bureaucratic competition to slow down implementation of a seasonal work program.

An employer with an ATR can then recruit seasonal workers. However, the problem then arises of how a farmer in New Zealand can match with an appropriate worker in the Pacific Islands, at least in the early years of the program when the possibility of using repeat workers to recruit others was unavailable. The 'kick-start' facilitation process aimed in part to facilitate this process. Moreover, the Pacific Island governments were interested in ensuring the benefits of participating in the program were spread throughout their countries, and that the workers they sent developed a good reputation for the country as a source of seasonal workers. The inter-agency agreements therefore spelled out how workers could be recruited in each country.

The first method of recruitment, which was particularly important in the first year of the program, was for employers to recruit from a 'work-ready pool' of workers who were pre-screened and selected by the labor ministry in the kick-start state. For example, in Tonga, more than 5000 Tongans registered for the work-ready pool within the first three months of the program (Gibson et al., 2008). District and town officers, together with church and community leaders, pre-select and screen candidates. The Ministry of Labour in Tonga provides guidelines, along with an indication of the number of candidates to nominate, specifying that the number that can be nominated will be distributed fairly in proportion to population size. These individuals are then checked to ensure that there are no court orders to prevent the individuals from leaving, and form the pool from which recruiters can select. Employers can then indicate the number of workers needed, any specialist skills or attributes (such as height), and if they would prefer nominees all from a single district in order to establish a community linkage, or to select nominees across different districts, and the Ministry then provides a shortlist from which they can make their selection.

The second method of recruitment is for RSEs to use an agent, who is responsible for screening and selecting the workers. This process has been used most extensively in Vanuatu (and subsequently in the Solomon Islands), where the government licenses agents for this purpose, and requires that they are only allowed to charge the employers, not the workers, for this service (McKenzie et al., 2008). The agents then use community contacts and village councils to help pre-screen workers. Employers have been reluctant to pay agents at times, given that free government-facilitated recruitment has been available in most countries, and also given their option of direct recruiting (Luthria and Malaulau, 2013).

The third method of recruitment is directly by employers. Clearly when a potential employer has no existing links to an overseas recruiting area, this is a difficult option. However, once employers have participated in the RSE scheme for several years and started to develop contacts in particular countries or regions, this option becomes more attractive as they can rely on past workers to help identify and screen promising new workers for subsequent seasons, in addition to re-hiring those who have previously worked for them.

Recruitment policy matters for both the efficiency of the program and for its distributional impact. If recruitment is costly and burdensome, this increases the costs to employers of participating, and reduces the overall demand for workers. But as well as how many get recruited, the policy can play an important role in terms of who is recruited. In Tonga, the Labour Ministry ensured that all villages in the country had workers in the scheme, and emphasis was put on selecting individuals from low-income families in financial need (Gibson et al., 2008). The result is that RSE participants from Tonga in the first year tended to be poorer, more rural, and with less schooling than non-participants. In contrast, in Vanuatu, the workers selected for the RSE tended to be wealthier and more urban than both the non-successful applicants and those who did not apply. This likely reflects a combination of both the recruitment approach, with a greater role for direct recruiting and agents, and less emphasis on choosing poorer individuals, as well as the fact that international migration was relatively new for most households in Vanuatu and poorer households lacked knowledge and/or financing to participate.

Some employers may need workers only for a peak harvest time, and not for long enough to meet the requirements of the program or needs of the workers. Several possibilities exist. First, employers can join together to submit joint applications to recruit, so that, for example, a worker may then be employed by one farmer to pick apples for two months, then a second employer may hire them for three months to work on their kiwifruit orchard. Second, in several cases, grower cooperatives such as Seasonal Solutions have registered as an RSE, and the workers can then be placed by the cooperative in several farms over the recruitment period.

2.3 Key Program Features Designed to Reduce Potential Negative Impacts

Two of the biggest policy concerns raised about temporary worker programs is the risk that workers overstay, and the risk that workers are exploited or abused. There can be a tension between these two concerns, since some measures designed to reduce the risk of workers overstaying (e.g. limiting their ability to claim asylum or restricting them from switching employers) may increase the risk that employers will exploit them. We discuss features of the RSE program that are designed to address these issues.

Several features of the RSE are designed to reduce the risk of workers overstaying by changing the incentives of both employers and workers for doing so. Perhaps the most important is that workers are limited as to the time they can stay in any given year, but are free to return in subsequent years. Since the work itself is seasonal, this induces a natural return in the off season, with employers then able to request the same workers back the subsequent year if they wish (and workers can also apply to other employers in subsequent years). Second, by having employers cover half the airfare and guarantee at least a minimum remuneration, workers can quickly recoup the costs of travel and do not need to overstay in order to repay debt incurred to participate.[8] Third, employers are required to pay the costs associated with removal of workers from New Zealand if they overstay (up to a maximum of NZ$3000), giving them incentives to select workers that they do not think will overstay or be complicit in overstaying.

An additional interesting feature in reducing overstaying is the role of reputation and competition for places on the program. This occurs both at the source-country level, and at the village level within countries. Since employers have a range of potential countries to recruit from, the Pacific kick-start states are acutely aware of the need to build a reputation for reliable, dependable workers. This is made explicit in the Inter-Agency Understandings; for example, the 2009 IAU for Vanuatu states, 'The New Zealand Government has zero tolerance for overstaying under the RSE Policy . . . RSEs are unlikely to seek to recruit further workers from Vanuatu if they experience negative consequences for non-compliance relating to Vanuatu workers.' This then translates into consequences for selection within countries. For example, in Samoa the prime minister announced that as punishment for any shameful behavior by RSE workers while in New Zealand, the worker's whole village would be banned from taking part in the program for two to four years (Duggan, 2013). The consequence is social pressure not to jeopardize the future possibilities for others by overstaying and thereby creating a negative reputation for one's community.

The result has been very low overstay rates, as seen in Table 7.1. Overstay rates have averaged under 1 percent for the first six seasons. NZDoL (2010) attributes overstaying in the first two years largely to a couple of isolated cases in which workers had disputes with employers about insufficient work being available.

A common concern in temporary worker programs in which a worker's employment status is tied to a particular employer is that this leads to a disparity of power between the employer and the worker, with the possibility that workers are then exploited or sent home by the employer if they complain too much (Maclellan, 2008). The RSE tries to mitigate this risk in several ways. It mandates that employers provide 'pastoral care' to workers, including accommodation, transportation, recreational and religious opportunities, and so on. RSE workers are subject to the same employment and workplace legislation as native workers, including minimum wage laws and work safety laws, and are eligible to join unions. Labor inspectors investigate complaints and issues raised by

Table 7.1 RSE overstay rates by financial year

Financial year	Overstay rate (%)
2007/08	0.47
2008/09	0.62
2009/10	1.25
2010/11	1.02
2011/12	1.03
2012/13	0.70
Overall first six years	0.86

Source: Data provided by New Zealand Ministry of Business, Innovation and Employment. Cases not resolved in one fiscal year are carried over to the next fiscal year, so these rates are upper bounds for the number of stayers.

workers. In addition, Samoa and Tonga have liaison officers drawn from their diaspora in New Zealand who can address issues around migrant worker welfare (Luthria and Malaulau, 2013). These efforts appear to have prevented any of the horror stories sometimes heard with captive guest workers in some other countries. Nevertheless, Maclellan (2008) notes a couple of concerns with the initial year of the program: first, some complaints about the quality of housing conditions; and second, a concern that a few workers who were sent home for alcohol-related incidents were subject to a different standard than local workers would have been.

2.4 RSE Numbers and the Cap

The RSE initially imposed an annual limit of 5000 visas, which was to be reviewed based on the capacity of the New Zealand labor market. This was raised to 8000 in 2009. The annual limit is measured from July 1 to June 30, based on the New Zealand government financial year. It is a cap, not a quota, with actual numbers depending on employer demand up to this cap. Table 7.2 reports the overall numbers, and numbers by main source country, over the first six years of the program. In total, 39 079 worker arrivals have been recorded over the first six years, with 28 849 coming from the five kick-start countries (73.8 percent), and a further 1887 coming from the Solomon Islands – a Pacific Forum state that was not one of the initial five kick-start states, but which entered into an Inter-Agency Understanding in 2010. The main three remaining countries for recruiting are Indonesia, Malaysia and Thailand, based largely on prior linkages some employers had to these regions.

Vanuatu has supplied the most workers to the RSE, which is some-

Table 7.2 RSE worker arrivals by financial year (July to June)

Financial year	Total	Kick-start states					Solomons	Other countries
		Tonga	Samoa	Vanuatu	Kiribati	Tuvalu		
2007/08	4486	805	647	1698	69	99	238	930
2008/09	6821	1355	1228	2342	38	49	311	1498
2009/10	6216	1142	1021	2137	48	54	256	1558
2010/11	7091	1411	1219	2352	149	51	252	1657
2011/12	7009	1398	1162	2412	142	88	407	1400
2012/13	7456	1573	1137	2829	138	56	423	1300

Source: New Zealand Department of Labour, http://www.dol.govt.nz/initiatives/strategy/rse/information.asp.

what unexpected given that Tonga and Samoa both had initially much stronger ties to New Zealand through existing migrant networks, and through permanent migration programs. The positive experience of Seasonal Solutions, a large cooperative, in hiring ni-Vanuatu during the initial pilot of 45 workers seems to have been important here. A common theme in discussions with officials from several countries is that an employer-driven scheme like the RSE can see a supplying country quickly gain momentum if workers from that country establish a good reputation. For example, when exploring how the Solomon Islands became the fourth-largest supplier, despite the initial absence of any facilitation measures and a limited diaspora in New Zealand, officials in Honiara repeatedly stressed that the good performance of the initial group caused employers to recruit more from this country. It also may have helped that the largest single RSE, with a labor demand of approximately 1000 workers, was one of the first employers of Solomon Islanders (as part of a mixed workforce of other Pacific Islanders) and is one of the few RSEs with sufficient scale to have large increases in demand for labor from a supplying country.

Another lesson from the data in Table 7.2 concerns the importance of geography and costs. Despite the kick-start efforts, the numbers of workers coming from the more remote countries of Kiribati and Tuvalu have been relatively small. Bedford et al. (2010) discuss the case of Tuvalu, and note a number of factors for low recruitment, including the larger geographic distance and small population size, and a lack of proactive actions by the government of this country. For Kiribati, the constraining distances are not only for international travel (which is recognized by allowing a longer worker period in New Zealand), but also for domestic travel in order to be recruited, given that the Gilbert Islands region of Kiribati is several thousand kilometers from the capital city. The increase in workers from Kiribati since 2010 reflects deliberate efforts by the New Zealand authorities, under the Strengthening Pacific Partnerships program, to target recruitment, with workers particularly going into pack houses. While this ongoing and special set of facilitation measures was successful in the short run, if employers faced the burden of these extra costs it is likely that they would look for workers from nearer Pacific countries.

The cap of 8000 workers was binding in the 2012/13 season. In this year 8175 RSE visas were approved, but the actual number of arrivals was 7456 since employers at times find themselves needing fewer workers than they apply for. Marquet (2013) reports some requests from the horticulture and viniculture industries for this cap to be raised, but that currently there is no plan to do so. However, the cap does not seem to be vastly lower than employer demand, with recruitment occurring throughout the year and the available permits not all being exhausted within a few days, as occurs with programs like the US H1-B worker program.

3. CIRCULARITY AND WORKER RETURN

Circularity is one of the key features of the RSE policy. By allowing workers the opportunity to return to work in subsequent seasons, the policy gives incentives for workers to go home at the end of each season, and provides the potential for employers to benefit in subsequent seasons from the training they have given to workers in the current season.

Merwood (2012) uses administrative data to investigate the rate of return migration over the first four seasons of the RSE. Table 7.3 summarizes these data. Each year of the first three years saw approximately half the workers return to work in the next season, most for the same employer. For example, 52.2 percent of workers from the first year (2007/08) returned to work in the RSE in 2008/09, and 86.1 percent of these did so by returning to work for the same employer. Some workers who did not return immediately did so in a subsequent season, so that 60 percent of those who had participated in the first season also returned for at least one of the subsequent three years. Just under one quarter (23 percent) of the workers from the first season participated in every one of the first four seasons.

Table 7.4 provides a more recent update, looking at the RSE workers working in the 2012/13 season, which is the sixth year of the RSE. Overall, 31 percent of the migrants working in this season were in their first year of the program, 22 percent in their second year, 16 percent in their third, and 31 percent in their fourth season or above. The three main Pacific nations

Table 7.3 Repeat migration in the RSE

Financial year	Percent of RSE workers who returned in the next year	Percent of return workers going back to the same employer	Percent of workers in this season who have worked in any previous RSE season
2007/08	52.2	86.1	0
2008/09	44.6	88.2	34.8
2009/10	52.3	86.6	59.5
2010/11	n.a.	n.a.	62.1

Source: Merwood (2012).

Table 7.4 Seasonal composition of RSE workers in 2012/13 season

Nationality	Number of RSE workers 2012/13	Percentage of workers by number of seasons worked			
		1st season	2nd season	3rd season	4th season (or above)
Vanuatu	2829	34	25	13	27
Tonga	1573	31	20	17	32
Samoa	1137	28	22	19	32
Thailand	565	12	21	24	44
Solomon Islands	423	42	23	13	22
Indonesia	303	19	12	15	54
Malaysia	273	49	14	11	26
Kiribati	138	27	29	26	19
Others	215	32	16	11	41
Total	7456	31	22	16	31

Source: Ministry of Business, Innovation and Employment (2013). Analysis by Paul Merwood.

participating in the program all have worker breakdowns similar to these overall averages.

Table 7.5 uses data from surveys of Tongan and Vanuatu RSE workers conducted by the authors at the end of the second season of the RSE to summarize the self-reported reasons for individuals not returning for a second season. Approximately two-thirds in each country say they would like to migrate again, but were not selected for a second year. Few migrants say they have reached a target level of savings, or that injury or

Table 7.5 Reasons for not returning for a second RSE season

	Percentage of one-season migrants who say this is an important reason for not returning for another season	
	Tonga	Vanuatu
Dissatisfied with how much they earned the first time	42.7	50.0
Missed their family too much while away	66.0	23.1
Would like to go again, but haven't yet been selected	64.1	65.4
Earned enough the first time to reach their target	0.0	24.0
Personal sickness, injury, or family emergency	4.9	8.0
Prefer to try and work in Australia's program	23.3	48.0
It was too cold in New Zealand	0.0	64.0
Other	4.9	7.7
Number of respondents	103	26

Source: Survey Responses of Single Season Migrants, from surveys described in Gibson and McKenzie (forthcoming).

sickness is preventing them from going. The launch of Australia's seasonal work program had led some to consider working there instead, given the higher pay rates available in Australia. The ni-Vanuatu workers expressing dissatisfaction with earnings the first time attributed this in part to the deductions from their wages being higher than they had anticipated – both because of income tax (something they were not used to) and the cost of airfares and accommodation. The Tongan workers expressing dissatisfaction with earnings mainly attributed this to the fact that there were fewer hours of work than they had anticipated.

Among those workers who returned for a second season, Tongans said they would like to work in New Zealand for a median of two more seasons, while ni-Vanuatu would like to work for a median of four more seasons.

4. IMPACTS ON NEW ZEALAND EMPLOYERS AND THE LOCAL WORKFORCE IN NEW ZEALAND

An evaluation of the first two years of the RSE program in New Zealand was undertaken by a New Zealand consulting firm specializing in program evaluations of public sector programs (NZDoL, 2010). It used a mixed-methods approach to evaluate the impacts of the program, but largely used qualitative interviews with employers, government officials and workers.

In terms of worker displacement, the evaluation suggests that there was some displacement of New Zealand workers in the kiwifruit industry in one region of New Zealand in the first season, due to a large employer overestimating the number of RSE workers they would require – although it is unclear what the evidence for this displacement is. In the second year the report concludes that displacement of New Zealand workers does not appear to have been an issue because employers were better able to judge demand.

In practice, the extent of displacement is complicated to estimate rigorously. In theory the RSE can influence the employment of locals through a large number of channels. Clemens (2013) describes some of these channels in the case of US agricultural migrant labor. The obvious direct effect that is foremost in the public mind is that migrant workers do work that might otherwise be done by local labor. However, in practice it is not always clear how willing native workers are to do the same work. The qualitative evaluation reports that local workers were less likely to want to do physically demanding 'front-end' work, or to want to work night shifts; and preferred 'back-end' or inside work like (daytime) pack-house work, truck driving, and fork-lifting. Moreover, employers had difficulties retaining New Zealand workers when temperatures began to drop.

Moreover, apart from this direct effect, seasonal labor can have a number of indirect impacts on the employment opportunities for local workers. To the extent that the RSE makes farmers more productive (which we examine next), it can lead to farms expanding scale and/or being more likely to survive, both of which increase the total number of jobs available in agriculture. This is especially likely to raise employment in jobs that are complementary to immigrant labor. There can also be impacts throughout the supply chain – for example, better-quality grapes can expand the demand for New Zealand wine, creating more employment in the New Zealand wine industry.

Ideally one would like to compare the employment of New Zealand workers relative to a counterfactual of no RSE. Business cycle and annual changes in growing conditions mean that simply comparing their employment before the RSE to that after will not give the causal impact of the program. A difference-in-differences approach in which workers likely to work in agriculture pre-RSE had their changes in employment compared to those of workers of similar skill levels likely to work in other industries would at least account for business cycle conditions, but would still not account for industry-specific shocks such as better or worse growing conditions. In larger countries one might be able to look at regional variation in the uptake of the seasonal worker program using instruments (such as historic networks interacted with production shocks in sending countries) to obtain variation in the use of the program, but such an approach is unlikely to work in a small country like New Zealand.

As such, it may not be possible to obtain rigorous estimates of the impact of the RSE on worker displacement. But the demand pressures that lead to the scheme being introduced suggest that any impacts are unlikely to be that large. Employers reported difficulties hiring local workers before the implementation of the RSE, and also reported high worker turnover. It seems likely that some of the displacement effect occurred for working holiday-makers (typically young tourists who would work for several weeks to earn money before leaving to holiday in other areas of New Zealand), rather than local workers. Indeed, one reason suggested for the much slower growth of Australia's seasonal worker program is that policy biases favoring employment of working holiday-makers have stunted the demand for Pacific workers (Hay and Howes, 2012), suggesting a degree of substitutability between these two labor sources. In contrast, the supply of local workers may be more inelastic, and in fact there continue to be reports of growers struggling to find local workers, with Murdoch (2013) reporting that only 178 clients of the New Zealand Work and Income Service took jobs in seasonal work in the last year.

Indeed, employers identify a more stable and predictable workforce with lower worker turnover as one of the main benefits to them in the first year of the program, with higher productivity gains in the second year as returnee workers were able to operate at a higher quality level immediately (NZDoL, 2010). This reduces training costs to employers, ensures that they have workers at the optimal times to harvest fruit, and, by reducing uncertainty, potentially gives them more confidence to invest. In interviews employers stressed the importance of being able to get fruit off the vines and packed quickly at the optimal harvest time, otherwise it would not be saleable. One employer in these interviews with the evaluation team said that their fruit was graded and packed according to quality standards; these standards were met only 70 percent of the time in 2007/08, increasing to 90 percent in 2008/09 as they benefited from the second season of RSE workers. In employer surveys, 95 percent of RSEs agree that participation in the program has resulted in better quality and more productive workers, and employers rate Pacific workers as more dependable, productive and enthusiastic than all other categories of seasonal workers (Department of Labour, 2012).

To measure the impact of the RSE on employers, one would ideally like

Table 7.6 Gross earnings of full-season workers at one citrus orchard by years of experience in the RSE

Year of RSE experience	Number of workers	Mean earnings per worker in 2010/11	Productivity premium over 1st year workers	Median earnings per worker in 2010/11	Productivity premium over 1st year workers
First	24	14408		14318	
Second	17	15726	9.1	15916	11.2
Third	10	16262	12.9	16258	13.5
Fourth	10	17050	18.3	16880	17.9

Source: Data provided by citrus RSE.

to measure changes in employer production and earnings (to account for quality improvements) relative to these same changes for a comparable control group of employers who do not participate in the RSE. We set out to try to collect data from farmers in New Zealand, but were unable to collect detailed production data from many farmers. However, in a couple of cases we were able to collect data that at least provide some case-study evidence on the relative productivity of new and return RSE workers, and of RSE workers versus other workers. We present this evidence for the first time here.

Table 7.6 uses data from a citrus orchard in 2011 to compare the productivity of first-, second-, third- and fourth-year RSE workers. Since workers are paid piece rates, earnings are a reasonable approximation to productivity. Considering only workers who worked for the full season, we see that workers in their second year earned approximately 10 percent more than workers in their first year of the RSE, with this premium increasing to 13 percent for two years of prior experience, and 18 percent for three years of prior experience.

Table 7.7 presents similar data from an apple orchard that employed a mix of RSE workers, New Zealand contract labor, casual labor and backpackers. Again the RSE workers are more productive in their second and third years than in their first, with the productivity premium similar in magnitude (for the change in the mean) to that in the citrus orchard. The RSE workers are 50–60 percent more productive than backpackers and New Zealand casual labor, and 11–18 percent more productive than other New Zealand contract workers, even those returning for multiple seasons.

It is unclear how much of the higher productivity of return RSE workers can be attributed to gains to experience versus selection effects of which workers are invited back for another season. Worker productiv-

Table 7.7 Weekly earnings of RSE and local apple workers at one orchard during 2011 season

	Number of workers	Mean weekly earnings per worker in 2011	Productivity premium over 1st year workers	Median earnings per worker in 2010/11	Productivity premium over 1st year workers
RSE workers					
First year	46	679		641	
Second year	25	733	8.0	773	20.6
Third year	12	771	13.5	774	20.7
New Zealand workers					
First year	32	608		622	
Second year	15	621	2.1	617	−0.8
Third year	7	657	8.1	637	2.4
Backpackers	21	511		519	
New Zealand casual labor	36	475		469	

ity and earnings are greatly affected by weather factors, which determine how good the crop is from one year to the next. As such, even if workers are more productive in their second or third season, they may earn less than they did in their first year if drought or other weather factors reduce the amount of fruit available to pick. We therefore use microdata on workers in an apple orchard to explore this issue. We compare the earnings in 2010 of workers who worked in 2009 for the first time and then returned for 2010 to the earnings in 2010 of workers who worked in 2010 for the first time, but returned for 2011. Assuming the selection process of whether to return for a second year is unchanged, the 9.6 percent higher wages of those in their second year reflects a productivity premium, and suggests that there is not strong positive selection in who returns taking place at this orchard.

One may be concerned that differences in earnings also reflect differences in tasks or in bargaining arrangements, and so may not be a true measure of productivity. Table 7.8 therefore provides the one example where we were able to obtain data on physical productivity. Here all workers were picking bins of mandarins during the same seven-day period in 2011. We see that the RSE workers are vastly more productive: they picked an average of 54 percent more fruit per day than New Zealand contract labor, and 82 percent more than backpackers and working holiday-makers.

In general, this new evidence supports the notion that RSE workers are significantly more productive than local labor or working holiday-makers, and suggests that the returns to experience for RSE workers are

Table 7.8 Physical productivity of labour at peak of mandarin harvest of 2011

	RSE Pacific workers	New Zealand contract labor	Backpackers (including working holiday-makers)
Average number of pickers per day	60	21	17
Average kilograms picked per person per day	759	494	416
Average wage earned per person per day ($)	125.36	84.93	98.48
Average wage paid per kilogram harvested (cents)	17	17	24

Source: Data provided by citrus RSE.

approximately 8–10 percent for the first year, and continue to increase for the next two seasons.

5. DEVELOPMENT IMPACTS OF THE RSE

Despite the prevalence of seasonal worker programs throughout the OECD, there is strikingly little evidence on the impacts of participating in these programs for the migrants, their families, and their home countries. An innovative feature of the RSE was that the launch of the program was accompanied by the launch of a prospective impact evaluation designed to measure these impacts (Gibson and McKenzie, forthcoming).

Between October 2007 and April 2008 we conducted baseline surveys of households and communities in Tonga and Vanuatu before workers left to work in New Zealand. To construct a baseline, we worked with officials to identify households with RSE workers, households with members of the RSE work-ready pool who had not yet been selected, and then randomly selected households in the same villages which had no applicants to the program. In Tonga our sample had near national coverage given the wide geographic participation in the program, with the baseline survey covering 448 households containing 2335 individuals in 46 villages. Vanuatu was a more challenging country to survey in, with the combination of rugged geography and high transportation costs making it infeasible to survey in all islands: we therefore limited the evaluation to three islands from which we believed there was a high chance of workers coming. Ultimately our baseline survey covered 456 households containing 2173 individuals in 48 villages or communities.

We then re-interviewed these same households 6, 12 and 24 months later. The surveys collected detailed data on household income, expenditure, labor supply, subjective well-being and the migration experience. Attrition was extremely low in Tonga, with every follow-up including at least 98 percent of the baseline households. Attrition was higher in Vanuatu, averaging 15–16 percent in each of the first two follow-ups, and 24 percent in the last follow-up. Bounding approaches are used to show robustness of our main results to this attrition.

To measure the impact of participating in the RSE on households, we use propensity-score matching to identify a group of households with RSE migrants and a group of households without RSE migrants that are similar in terms of a rich set of baseline characteristics. In particular, we are able to include a large number of characteristics that communities and employers are likely to have paid attention to when selecting workers, as well as characteristics of the household that may have determined the deci-

Table 7.9 Development impacts of the RSE in Tonga and Vanuatu

	Tonga	Vanuatu
Increase in per capita income	34–38%	35–43%
Increase in per capita expenditure	9–10%	28%
Increase in savings	122%	181%
Increase in subjective standard of living	0.45 s.d.	0.43–0.50 s.d.
Percentage point increase in dwelling improvements	10–11	7–8
Percentage point increase in bank account use	10–14	17–18

Notes: s.d. denotes standard deviation.

Source: Gibson and McKenzie (forthcoming).

sion of whether to apply: this includes demographic variables, the health, education and labor market experience of male workers, household networks in New Zealand, household wealth, geographic location and past income over the last two years. Using this information, we pre-screen the sample to identify comparable households.

We then employ two approaches to measuring the impacts of the RSE. The first is difference-in-differences estimation on this propensity-score screened sample, and the second is panel-data estimation with fixed effects. Both give similar results in most cases, and they allow us to control for unobserved time-invariant characteristics of RSE households that may differ from those in households that did not participate in the RSE. Table 7.9 summarizes some of the main impacts. Over a two-year period, households participating in the RSE are typically earning 35 percent more income. Some of this goes to an increase in income, while household savings and durable asset ownership increase. Subjective standard of living increases by approximately the same amount (in terms of standard deviations) as the increase in income.

The median after-tax income earned in New Zealand reported by the seasonal migrants in our surveys is approximately NZ$12000. This is in line with administrative data reported by Merwood (2012), and is several multiples of mean household income per capita of RSE households at baseline of NZ$1400 in Tonga and NZ$2500 in Vanuatu. One might then wonder why households did not experience even larger increases in per capita incomes. In Gibson and McKenzie (forthcoming) we note several reasons why the per capita gain in income to participating households is much less than would be suggested by just comparing incomes earned in New Zealand with those in the Pacific.

A first reason is that workers face costs in New Zealand, both from living expenses (including rent and health insurance) and from repaying their share of the airfare. From the NZ$12 000 in income, the average worker remitted or brought back with them an average of NZ$5500. Second, when we consider per capita income, this gain in income has to be shared among the family, most of whom are not RSE workers. This requires dividing the amount by 5.7 in Tonga and 4.7 in Vanuatu. Third, we are looking at average impacts over two years, so since just over half the households sent a worker in one year only, the per capita per year effect for these households has to be divided by two. Finally, households also lose any wage income and contribution to agricultural production the household member would have contributed while in New Zealand. Our evaluation strategy allows us to capture all these effects, and thereby measure the net gain to households from participating in the program.

These gains in income per participating worker can be scaled up by the number of participating workers to give a first-order approximation of the total development impact of the RSE over the first two years. We estimate an impact of $NZ5.3 million in Tonga and $NZ9.7 million in Vanuatu. This amount is equivalent to 42–47 percent of total annual bilateral aid from New Zealand to these countries, and is equivalent to almost 50 percent of annual export earnings for Tonga and 25 percent of annual export earnings for Vanuatu.

Samoan workers earned an average of NZ$11 720 in the first year and NZ$10 790 in the second year, which is slightly less than the Tongan and ni-Vanuatu workers, but not that much different (Merwood, 2012). Although our evaluation did not cover Samoa (except for a one-off survey), it seems reasonable, based on the data available and our experience with the program, to believe that the development impacts would have been similar, or just slightly less, per worker than in Tonga and Vanuatu, so that the overall impact over the first two years would also have been of the order of NZ$5 million.

In contrast, Kiribati and Tuvalu had a much smaller number of workers participating in the program. Moreover, those that participated earned less – only averaging NZ$6400 in the first season and NZ$10 390 in the second season (Merwood, 2012). In the first season i-Kiribati workers employed by one employer experienced difficulties obtaining sufficient work (NZDoL, 2010). Bedford et al. (2010) discuss the Tuvalu case, and note that there were also problems with some workers getting sufficient work in the first year, which, coupled with the high costs of participating in the scheme (workers had to cover the cost of getting from Tuvalu to Fiji, and then half the transport cost from Fiji to New Zealand, along with visa, food, accommodation and other such costs), meant that many workers returned with very little money or were even in debt after the first year. One lesson from this was the need for workers to work on contracts longer than three or four months to ensure they make enough. The RSE policy recognizes the higher costs for these two countries, allowing workers from these countries to work a maximum of nine months in an 11-month period (compared to a maximum of seven for all other countries), but few workers have been hired for this long. Table 7.2 shows some small growth in RSE participation from Kiribati in seasons 4 through 6 due to the ongoing facilitation measures, but that Tuvalu continues to average only 50 to 60 workers each season.

While the largest benefits of participating in such a program accrue to the migrant workers and their families, there is often a hope among policy makers that there may also be broader benefits to other households in the sending countries. There are several channels through which this can occur. The most direct impact is through migrants contributing directly to community projects. As an example, NZDoL (2010) notes that the local government in the Lolihor area of North Ambrym, Vanuatu, requires all workers to contribute approximately NZ$200 per season towards a community fund that then supports projects run by local women such as small business initiatives and crop production, as well as going towards a scholarship fund for local children. In our surveys of communities in Tonga, we found communities saying that they had funded the local village water supply, street lighting, a school scholarship fund and community halls out of contributions from seasonal workers. Based on our impact estimates, the average migrant contributes approximately 5 to 10 percent of the net gain in income per migrant to such endeavors.

The more difficult channel to measure is impacts on local development through multiplier and general equilibrium effects. For example, if migrants and their families spend the increase in income on local production, this raises incomes for the sellers of these products, but can also increase prices if supply is limited. Migrants leaving may open up jobs for the unemployed, or push up wages for other workers who have fewer individuals to compete with. However, our sense in the case of the Pacific Islands is that to date these impacts have been small. Many workers come from rural backgrounds, where their main occupations would have been subsistence farming, and there is not a strong wage labor market. Moreover, much of the spending appears to have gone on imported durable goods and renovations, potentially having limited multiplier effects.

6. CONCLUSIONS

Temporary or circular migration programs have been touted as a way for less-skilled workers to benefit from the higher incomes to be earned abroad as part of a 'triple win', whereby migrants, the sending country and the receiving country all benefit (e.g. UN, 2004; GCIM, 2005; World Bank, 2006). New Zealand's Recognised Seasonal Employer program appears to have largely lived up to this promise. Migrants from the main participating countries have experienced large gains in income and well-being, and employers in New Zealand have gained access to a more productive and stable workforce. Overstay rates have been low, and although the evidence base is not as strong as one would like, there does not appear to have been large displacements of New Zealand workers. There also appear to be positive, albeit limited, spillover benefits for others in the sending communities in the form of public-goods contributions.

These results make this seasonal migration program one of the most effective development interventions for which rigorous evaluations are available. As discussed, the RSE has been carefully designed with a number of important features mitigating some of the risks and concerns often associated with temporary worker programs. These design features offer important lessons for other countries. However, while the program is very much employer-led, there has been important investment by both the New Zealand and Pacific governments in setting up this program. Although there are many willing foreign workers, and a number of New Zealand employers desiring to hire them, it is likely to be difficult for many matches between them to be made without initial assistance. Then, with time and experience, employers can select return workers and use them to assist in finding new workers, reducing the need for such assistance as the program develops.

A final lesson from the RSE experience has been the importance of good monitoring and evaluation from the very start of the project and an openness by participants to being researched. Measuring the impacts of the program and process evaluation have been important for identifying changes that can make the policy work even more effectively for workers and employers, as well as for helping to cement support for the program among policy-makers. Moreover, given the relative lack of information about the impacts of migration policies, such analysis has an important research contribution as well. We look forward to seeing the launch of more such programs, and hope that rigorous evaluation will also be a feature of their launches.

ACKNOWLEDGMENTS

We thank Charlotte and Richard Bedford for their interviews of RSE employers which we use in this chapter, Paul Merwood and Anne Masoe for providing new statistics on RSE returnees and overstaying, and Halahingano Rohorua for interviews of village and government officials in the Pacific Islands. We thank Manjula Luthria, the New Zealand Department of Labour, Tonga Department of Labour, Vanuatu Department of Labour, MFAT, and other members of the RSE Interagency Governance Committee for their collaboration in the initial years of this research.

NOTES

1. The Canadian SAWP had 28 231 workers in 2008 and 29 025 in 2012 (http://www.hrsdc.gc.ca/eng/jobs/foreign_workers/lmo_statistics/annual2012.shtml), while the US H2-A had 64 404 visas in 2008 and 65 345 in 2012 (http://travel.state.gov/visa/statistics/graphs/graphs_4399.html).
2. http://www.ilo.org/dyn/migpractice/migmain.showPractice?p_lang=en&p_practice_id=48 (accessed August 11, 2010).
3. http://www.hortnz.co.nz/Overview/About-Us/Industry-statistics.htm (accessed October 18, 2013). NZ$1 = US$0.85 (October, 2013).
4. http://www.nzwine.com/assets/sm/upload/da/9i/te/eu/NZW_Annual_Report_2013_web.pdf (accessed October 18, 2013).
5. Given their greater travel costs, citizens of Kiribati and Tuvalu are allowed to stay for a maximum of nine months per 11-month period, instead of seven.
6. Quoted in 'Seasonal work policy benefits Pacific, says Peters', *Islands Business*, October 26, 2006. http://www.islandsbusiness.com/news/index_dynamic/containerNameToReplace=MiddleMiddle/focusModuleID=130/focusContentID=6691/tableName=mediaRelease/overideSkinName=newsArticle-full.tpl (accessed August 11, 2010).
7. These can be found at http://www.dol.govt.nz/initiatives/strategy/rse/understanding.asp (accessed October 18, 2013).
8. The minimum remuneration is the greater of 240 hours at the 'per hour' rate regardless of the actual availability of work, and payment for an average of 30 hours per week at the 'per hour' rate for the period worked.

REFERENCES

Bedford, Charlotte (2013) *Picking Winners?: New Zealand's Recognized Seasonal Employer (RSE) Policy and its Impacts on Employers, Pacific Workers and their Island-based Communities*, PhD thesis, School of Social Sciences, University of Adelaide.

Bedford, Charlotte, Richard Bedford and Elsie Ho (2010) 'Engaging with New Zealand's Recognised Seasonal Employer Work Policy: the case of Tuvalu', *Asian and Pacific Migration Journal*, **19**(3): 421–45.

Clemens, Michael (2013) *International Harvest: A Case Study of How Foreign Workers Help American Farms Grow Crops – and the Economy*, Partnership for a New American Economy, and Center for Global Development, Washington, DC.

Department of Labour (2012) 'RSE Monitoring: key findings from the 2011 Employer Survey', New Zealand Department of Labour, http://www.dol.govt.nz/publications/research/rse-employer-survey2011/survey-report.pdf.
Duggan, Kat (2013) 'Samoa ban won't hurt RSE scheme', *Marlborough Express*, 26 September, http://www.stuff.co.nz/marlborough-express/news/9211593/Samoa-ban-won-t-hurt-RSE-scheme (accessed October 21, 2013).
Gibson, John and David McKenzie (2011) 'Australia's Pacific Seasonal Worker Pilot Scheme (PSWPS): development impacts in the first two years', *Asia Pacific Viewpoint*, **52**(3): 361–70.
Gibson, John and David McKenzie (forthcoming) 'The development impact of a best practice seasonal worker policy', *Review of Economics and Statistics*.
Gibson, John, David McKenzie and Halahingano Rohorua (2008) 'How pro-poor is the selection of seasonal migrant workers from Tonga under New Zealand's Recognized Seasonal Employer (RSE) program?' *Pacific Economic Bulletin*, **23**(3): 187–204.
Global Commission on International Migration (GCIM) (2005) *Migration in an Interconnected World: New Directions for Action*, The Global Commission on International Migration, www.gcim.org.
Gregory, Angela (2006) 'Pacific solution considered to labour market shortages', http://www.nzherald.co.nz/nz/news/article.cfm?c_id=1&objectid=10388069 (accessed October 18, 2013).
Hay, Danielle and Stephen Howes (2012) 'Australia's Pacific Seasonal Worker Pilot Scheme: why has take-up been so low?', Discussion Paper 17, Development Policy Centre, Australian National University.
Luthria, Manjula (2008) 'Seasonal migration for development? Evaluating New Zealand's RSE program: overview', *Pacific Economic Bulletin*, **23**(3): 165–70.
Luthria, Manjula and Mai Malaulau (2013) 'Bilateral labor agreements in the Pacific: a development-friendly case study', in Sebastian Sáez (ed.), *Let Workers Move: Using Bilateral Labor Agreements to Increase Trade in Services*, Washington, DC: World Bank, pp. 129–48.
Maclellan, Nic (2008) 'Workers for all seasons? Issues from New Zealand's Recognised Seasonal Employer (RSE) program', Swinburne Institute for Social Research Working Paper.
Marquet, Sarah (2013) 'Views differ on cap for RSE scheme', *Otago Daily Times*, July 27.
McKenzie, David, Pilar Garcia Martinez and L. Alan Winters (2008) 'Who is coming from Vanuatu to New Zealand under the new Recognised Seasonal Employer (RSE) program?', *Pacific Economic Bulletin*, **23**(3): 205–28.
Merwood, Paul (2012) 'Return migration and earnings of workers in New Zealand's Recognised Seasonal Employer Scheme', New Zealand Department of Labour, http://www.tonganz.net/home/wp-content/uploads/2013/05/IMSED12_Return-Migration-and-Earnings-of-Workers-in-NZs-RSE-Scheme.pdf (accessed October 18, 2013).
Murdoch, Helen (2013) 'Pickers in demand', *Nelson Mail*, 11 April, http://www.stuff.co.nz/nelson-mail/communities/8536384/Pickers-in-demand (accessed November 18, 2013).
New Zealand Department of Labour [NZDoL] (2010) *Final Evaluation Report of the Recognised Seasonal Employer Policy (2007–2009)*. Department of Labour, Wellington. http://dol.govt.nz/publications/research/rse-evaluation-final-report/rse-final-evaluation.pdf (accessed October 18, 2013).
OECD (2013) *International Migration Outlook 2013*, Paris: OECD.
Ramasamy, Sankar, Vasantha Krishnan, Richard Bedford and Charlotte Bedford (2008) 'The Recognised Seasonal Employer policy: seeking the elusive triple wins for development through international migration', *Pacific Economic Bulletin*, **23**(3): 171–86.
United Nations (UN) (2004) *World Economic and Social Survey*, New York: United Nations.
World Bank (2006) *At Home and Away: Expanding Job Opportunities for Pacific Islanders through Labour Mobility*, Washington, DC: World Bank.

8. Southern hub: the globalization of migration to South Africa

Jonathan Crush

1. INTRODUCTION

During the long apartheid night, migration to South Africa took two main forms, both tightly regulated and controlled by the state and fundamentally racist in design and execution. Whites, primarily from Europe, were given financial and other incentives to immigrate and settle in South Africa (Peberdy, 2009; Klotz, 2013). Blacks from other African countries were recruited on temporary work contracts to serve the labour needs of South African mining and commercial agriculture (Crush et al., 1992). They were prohibited from bringing their families and settling in South Africa and were sent home when their contracts expired. The collapse of apartheid undermined the fundamental rationale of both of these forms of controlled migration. Immigration from Europe quickly dwindled to almost nothing as the new government dissociated itself from the racist immigration policies of the apartheid era. The bigger challenge was what to do about the other migration pillar of the apartheid system – the entrenched migrant labour system that had delivered cheap contract workers from neighbouring countries for most of the twentieth century (Crush and James, 1996). This rights-abusing and highly exploitative system may have seemed inimical to the post-apartheid dispensation, but has proved more durable, primarily because the ANC government was unwilling or unable to abolish by fiat a mode of labour mobilization that the country's corporate sector continued to defend as indispensable to the economy.

Changes to inherited immigration and migration policies are not the only factors driving the reconfiguration of migration since the end of apartheid. The opening of South Africa to the forces of globalization led to a major, ongoing surge in the volume of people moving temporarily in and out of the country (Figure 8.1). Legal entries through South Africa's land border posts and airports rose dramatically from fewer than 1 million in 1990 to nearly 10 million in 2008. The numbers declined during the global economic crisis of 2008 but have since resumed their upward trajectory. These entrants (totalling 134 million over the entire period)

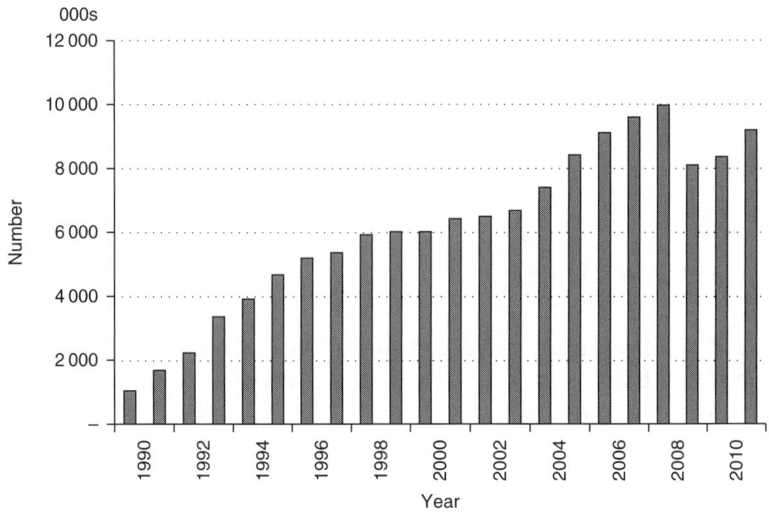

Figure 8.1 Legal entries to South Africa, 1990–2011

include tourists, visitors, migrant workers, immigrants, students, medical travellers, shoppers, informal traders, investors, conference delegates, diplomats, asylum-seekers – in fact, everyone with a passport who enters for a fixed and predetermined period of time (now usually 90 days). It does not include returns by members of the extensive South African diaspora who still hold South African citizenship. Among the entrants are those who give one purpose for entry (for example 'holiday') and then engage in other activities (such as working in the formal or informal economy). In these statistics are also to be found the bulk of South Africa's irregular migrants (or 'illegal foreigners', in official terminology). Despite South Africa's long and porous borders, and many informal border-crossing points, ease of entry tends to channel all but the desperate through official ports. Most irregular migrants enter legally and then overstay, primarily to work, and rates of unemployment among migrants are extremely low.

At the heart of post-apartheid South Africa's approach to migration are four main propositions: first, immigration is a zero-sum game and every job occupied by a non-South African means one fewer job for a South African. Second, the role of government is to ensure that South Africa's future skills needs are met by increasing the local production of skills, not acquiring them from abroad. Third, the importation of skills is fundamentally undesirable but might be necessary in the short term. However, safeguards must be put in place to ensure that no one stays a moment longer than they are needed. And fourth, given South Africa's extremely high unemployment rate and super-abundance of poorly educated and unskilled working-age adults, there is no need for any employer to hire a non-South African except in the most specialized and skilled positions.

These propositions, laid out here in rather bald fashion, are consistent with the perceptions and preferences of most South Africans. A 2010 Southern African Migration Program (SAMP) survey, for example, found that 60 per cent of South Africans believe that migrants take jobs from South Africans (Crush et al., 2013). Only 34 per cent felt that migrants bring skills needed by South Africa and just one quarter said that migrants created jobs for South Africans. From the mid-1990s to the present day, the World Values Survey (WVS) has consistently found South Africans to be more hostile to immigration than the citizens of any other country (Facchini et al., 2013). The latest WVS found that 30 per cent wanted a total ban on immigration and another 48 per cent wanted to place strict limits on entry for those who wanted to come and work. Only 16 per cent agreed that migrants should be let in if jobs were available for them (the lowest proportion in the world). A mere 6 per cent (again the lowest global figure) felt that anyone who wanted to come and work should be allowed to do so. Coupled with these highly restrictionist views, only 54 per cent in the SAMP survey felt that temporary migrants legally in the country should enjoy police protection and only 38 per cent that they should enjoy legal protection (the figures for irregular migrants were even lower at 22 per cent and 18 per cent respectively). As many as 62 per cent favoured a policy of deporting all migrants who were not contributing to the South African economy and 27 per cent wanted to see all migrants, irrespective of their legal status, deported from the country.

To advocate for a more open post-apartheid migration policy that no one really believes in has proved to be a major and ongoing challenge for independent researchers, think-tanks and the private sector, who argue that immigration and migration are not necessarily inimical to South Africa's economic interests (Stern and Szalontai, 2006; Johnson et al., 2010; Segatti and Landau, 2011; Klotz, 2012). What has emerged from the lack of official and popular appetite for immigration is a temporary migration framework for skills import enabled by the heavily bureaucratic 2002 Immigration Act, which puts a brake on the use of migration to meet the country's growing skills gap (Dodson and Crush, 2004; Crush and Dodson, 2007). Other features of the post-apartheid migration regime include the entrenchment of the apartheid-era migrant labour system in certain sectors (notably mining and commercial agriculture); a free-for-all at the lower end of the labour market where employers hire irregular migrants with impunity and migrants are disciplined (by the state and citizens) for coming and accepting the jobs; and a massive, but corrupt and ultimately ineffectual, campaign of mass deportations that bears an uncomfortable resemblance to the policing of influx controls and the pass laws under apartheid (Vigneswaran et al., 2010; Sutton and Vigneswaran, 2011; Steinberg, 2012; Vigneswaran, 2012).

Against this backdrop, the present chapter seeks to document the fate of the two main apartheid migration pillars since 1990. It then examines the attempt to fashion a temporary skills-based migration system to meet South Africa's chronic skills shortage. As the chapter shows, this system has been a mixed success and appears to be in the process of being reworked in a more restrictive direction. One of the reasons for this is the widespread perception that South Africa is being 'overrun' by the outside world. Certainly, there appears to be no shortage of jobs and other economic opportunities for enterprising migrants who (often with the active and tacit assistance of employers) find other means, both legal and irregular, to access the lower tiers of the labour market. The chapter also examines the way in which South Africa has become a new destination for asylum-seekers and refugees from other African countries, and how the refugee protection system has become embroiled in 'mixed migration' flows of refugees and economic migrants. Finally, the chapter looks at the Zimbabwean case and how temporary migration from that country is transitioning spontaneously into more permanent settlement in South Africa.

2. SOUTH AFRICA'S MIGRANTS

Accurate figures on the numbers of migrants in South Africa are hard to obtain partly because of the phenomenon of irregular migration and partly because of inadequate data collection systems. The difficulties are apparent in the widely varying figures for South Africa's migrant stock (residents born outside the country) provided by three different sources: (a) the Sussex University Global Migrant Origin Database (GMOD) (Version 4); (b) the 2001 South African Census and (c) the World Bank (Table 8.1). The GMOD and the Census come up with virtually identical totals for 2001, yet widely varying country-of-origin figures (compare, for example, Angola, DRC, Lesotho). The World Bank Migrant Stocks database is supposedly an update of the GMOD, yet provides data for only six source countries. The 2010 Bank update simply multiplies all the 2005 figures by 68 per cent, which improbably assumes an identical proportional increase from all countries.

According to the South African Census, the number of foreign-born people in the country increased from 814450 in 1996 to 1025087 in 2001

Table 8.1 Variable estimates of migrant stock in South Africa

Country of Origin	2001 South Africa Census	GMOD (Version 4)	World Bank, 2005	World Bank, 2010
Angola	11 806	152 057	0	0
Botswana	17 819	2 989	24 849	41 846
DRC	4 541	149 462	0	0
Lesotho	114 941	8 246	208 226	350 657
Madagascar	220	316	0	0
Malawi	25 090	26 568	10 662	17 955
Mauritius	3 500	32 149	0	0
Mozambique	269 669	150 369	269 918	454 548
Namibia	46 225	4 215	0	0
Seychelles	257	3 144	0	0
Swaziland	34 471	2 007	80 593	135 720
Tanzania	3 923	52 554	0	0
Zambia	23 550	44 809	0	0
Zimbabwe	131 887	59 109	510 084	858 993
TOTAL	687 899	687 994	1 104 331	1 859 819

Sources: Statistics South Africa Census 2001,
GMOD v4 at http://www.migrationdrc.org/research/typesofmigration/global_migrant_origin_database.html;
World Bank 2005 at http://siteresources.worldbank.org/INTPROSPECTS/Resources/334934-1110315015165/T1EstimatesMigrantStocks.xls,
World Bank 2010 at http://siteresources.worldbank.org/INTPROSPECTS/Resources/334934-1110315015165/T1.Estimates_of_Migrant_Stocks_2010.xls.

to 2 151 644 in 2011. A declining proportion (22 per cent in 2001) were born in Europe, a legacy of apartheid-era immigration to the country. The Census also shows the importance of the Southern African Development Community (SADC) sub-region as source of African migrants (over 90 per cent in 2001). Complete data on country of origin are not yet available for the 2011 Census. A recent study of Gauteng Province (where 10 per cent of the population are foreign-born) found that 82 per cent of the migrant stock were from other SADC countries, 7 per cent were from the rest of Africa, 5 per cent were from Europe and 5 per cent were from Asia (Peberdy, 2013: 9). The fundamental question, though, is what explains the overall increase in the foreign-born population of South Africa by over 1 million during the last decade. As the next two sections will show, the post-apartheid period has witnessed a decline in both of the forms of migration that typified the apartheid era, though for different reasons. This suggests that the continued growth in South Africa's migrant population is attributable to new, post-apartheid forms of migration to the country.

2.1 The End of Immigration

Immigration for permanent residence in South Africa began to decline in the 1980s and continued after the collapse of apartheid (Figure 8.2). The primary reason for the decline in the 1980s was political and economic turbulence in South Africa as international and domestic opposition to apartheid intensified. The continued decline after 1994 was a post-apartheid immigration policy that discouraged permanent immigration from all areas, not just Europe. Between 1990 and 2000, the annual number of immigrants dropped from 14 500 to just over 3000 and the number of African immigrants fell by half from 1600 to only 800 (see Table 8.4). Fears that South Africa would 'poach' skills from the rest of Africa were unfounded, although the proportion of African immigrants increased from 11 per cent in 1990 to 27 per cent in 2000.

There was a slight increase in immigration immediately after 2000, as the government responded to arguments in the 1999 White Paper on International Migration that the country was in the midst of a serious skills crisis (Figure 8.2). However, this policy was largely abandoned in favour of an exclusive focus on temporary migration once the 2002 Immigration Act came into force. The Department of Home Affairs and Statistics South Africa did not release immigration figures for several years, probably because there was very little to report. In 2012, publication of immigration data was finally resumed (SSA, 2013) and showed that a mere 1283 permanent residence permits were issued that year (of which only 441 were for employment purposes). South Africa has thus virtually abandoned permanent immigration as a policy option. In this respect, it turned its back on its

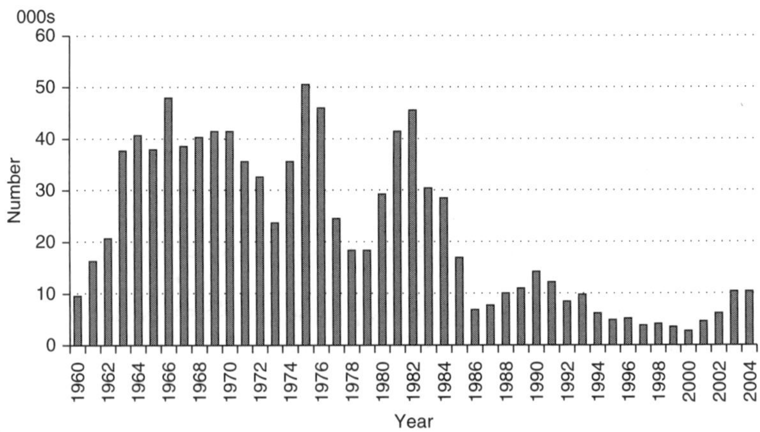

Figure 8.2 Immigration to South Africa, 1960–2004

apartheid past, broke with the immigration incentive system that countries in the North use to compete in the global hunt for talent, and adopted the same policy as most other African countries after independence.

2.2 End of Empire

In the early 1990s, the South African mining houses toyed with the idea of moving away from contract migrancy and stabilizing their migrant workforce in family housing (Crush and James, 1996). However, they soon cried poor and shelved most of these plans. Certainly it was a time of crisis for an industry used to easy profit. Gold production fell from 600 tonnes in 1990 to 200 tonnes in 2008, and South Africa's share of global production from 25 per cent to 8 per cent. Accompanying mine closures, downsizing and restructuring was a dramatic shrinkage of South Africa's sub-continental labour recruiting empire. In 1987, 477 000 migrant workers were employed on the mines. The numbers dropped precipitously throughout the 1990s to 207 000 in 2001 (Figure 8.3).

After 2000, the mine workforce temporarily expanded again as profitability was restored with higher prices for gold and other metals. However, rather than drawing in more workers from outside the country (as they had done for decades during previous periods of expansion), the mines increased their South African complement. The number of South African miners increased from 99 000 in 1999 to 187 000 in 2008, while the

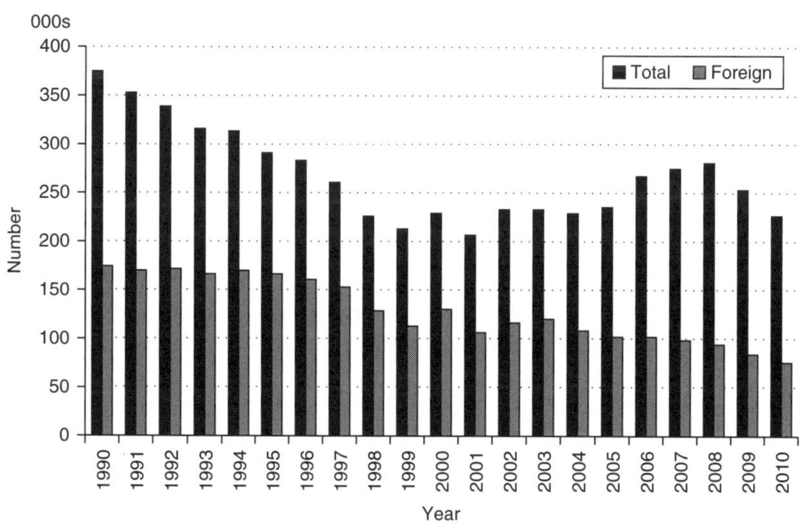

Figure 8.3 Migrant workers on South African mines, 1990–2010

non-South African complement remained relatively steady as there was little or no recruiting outside the country. After 2008, the numbers began to fall again, with further retrenchments. In the case of both Lesotho and Mozambique, the number of migrant miners fell from nearly 60 000 in 2000 to 35 000 in 2010. Swaziland's share fell from 9000 to 5000 and Botswana's from 6500 to 2000. The proportion of foreign workers in the mine workforce also fell, from nearly 60 per cent in 2000 to 24 per cent in 2008.

For the last two decades, migrant miners who remained on the mines have held on desperately to their jobs, and the mine workforce, long seen as a young man's domain, began to age: by the turn of the century, the average miner was in his mid-40s. Mine retrenchments have led to major changes in the rural areas from which most migrants come (Molefe, 2009; Mensah and Naidoo, 2011; Naidoo et al., 2011). Miners with jobs continued to earn, remit and invest in the accumulation of livestock and property. Those without them became increasingly disaffected and alienated. The sons of both, who might once have counted on the mines for employment, were shut out of the mine labour market, adding further to the large pools of unemployed youth in the region. One result has been growing inequality in the source areas between households with and without access to mine wages. Another has been a restructuring of patterns of out-migration from traditional mine source regions and countries. In Lesotho, for example, households with retrenched miners and unemployed sons have begun sending their daughters out to work in the country's textile factories or as migrants to South Africa (Crush et al., 2010).

In the 1990s, during protracted debates over a post-apartheid immigration policy, the South African mining industry mounted a strong lobbying campaign to maintain its unfettered access to foreign labour and to contest plans to treat migrant miners like all other migrants by having them apply for individual work permits. The result of this campaign was the last-minute incorporation in the 2002 Immigration Act (see below) of a new 'corporate work permit'. These permits allow a 'corporate entity' (which ranges from a whole mining group to an individual farmer) to temporarily employ a predetermined and approved number of workers for a period requested by the applicant.

The corporate permit system was designed to give the state more control over the influx of foreign contract workers to the country. Before the permit is issued, for example, the Department of Home Affairs is supposed to refer the application to the Departments of Labour and Trade and Industry, who approve the number of foreign workers who can be employed by the entity. In practice, the new system has added layers of bureaucracy while simultaneously allowing approved companies to import groups of workers, rather as they have always done. The Department of Home Affairs has released no data at all on how many corporate permits have been issued and how many foreign workers are employed under corporate permits. A crucial condition of the issue of a corporate permit, however, is that the employer guarantees that 'all foreign workers will leave South Africa on completion of their duties'. The government has made no secret of the fact that it does not think the mines should be employing anyone from outside the country with so many South Africans unemployed. The policy lever – in the form of the corporate permit system – certainly exists to control the numbers, but it is not clear whether it has used this leverage or whether the mines themselves, for reasons of economy, are abandoning the remnants of their regional labour empire.

The other major sector of the South African economy to latch on to the corporate permit system is commercial agriculture. Over the years, this sector has enjoyed a fraught relationship with the law. Without the benefit of a centralized recruiting system, farmers relied on a host of dubious and often clandestine channels to hire workers from outside the country. Unprotected by labour law or labour unions, they endured many years of intense exploitation and abuse. The response of commercial farmers after the end of apartheid was that South Africans would not work for them and the seasonal employment of foreign migrants was essential to their survival. Both the Department of Labour and the Department of Home Affairs had no idea what to do and, as a result, commercial farms (particularly in the border areas with Lesotho, Mozambique and Zimbabwe) were allowed to hire irregular migrants without a great deal of interference (Mather, 2000; Johnston, 2007; Rutherford, 2010; Ulicki and Crush, 2010). While farms themselves were rarely raided for undocumented migrants, workers still had to get to and from the farms, and were constantly harassed by local police. From that standpoint, the coming of the corporate permit system was a godsend for both farmers and migrants. Many farmers obtained corporate permits, and their foreign workers, hired under the permits, had legal standing in South Africa and were protected from arbitrary arrest and deportation (Rutherford, 2011). There is no evidence that this led to any dramatic improvement in working conditions on the farms, however (Bolt, 2012; Hall et al., 2013). For all but a core of permanent workers, farmwork continues to be a job of last resort for migrants or a stepping-stone to get to the cities and the hope of better-paid employment.

3. SOUTH AFRICA'S TEMPORARY SKILLED MIGRATION POLICY

In the early 1990s, the number of temporary residence permits issued to skilled workers initially increased (from 4000 in 1991 to 19 500 in 1996). However, the policy imperative to accelerate the employment of black South Africans and reduce dependence on outsiders (who were widely perceived as taking jobs from South Africans in a situation of high unemployment) soon affected access to temporary work permits. The number of permits quickly fell back to 6600 in 2000. As protracted debates over a new immigration policy dragged on, private sector employers and researchers forcefully argued that South Africa was experiencing a skills crisis (caused in part by an accelerating 'brain drain' to Europe, North America and Australasia). This eventually led to a shift in official thinking and the passage of the first post-apartheid immigration legislation. The Immigration Act No. 13 of 2002 (which came fully into force in 2004) sought to imitate broader international trends in Europe and North America by introducing a system of temporary migration for skilled workers. The Act put in place a four-part temporary residence (TRP) system: (a) quota work permits; (b) general work permits; (c) exceptional skills work permits and (d) intra-company transfer work permits.

Critical assessments of the 'scarce skills' quota system regard it as a failure (Johnson et al., 2010; Pokroy, 2012). The first list was not published until 2005, and subsequent lists are virtual duplicates of the first. The lists make no mention of sectors and occupations with well-documented shortages (Erasmus and Breier, 2009). The 2009 list, for example, has no quota for doctors, yet provides quotas for 200 astronomers, 200 space scientists, 500 agricultural economists and 300 research pharmacologists. The compilation and contents of the list also reflect a lack of inter-departmental coordination (Daniels, 2007). In 2005 and 2006 combined, only 1633 permits were issued. In 2007, 3600 of the available 35 200 were filled by four major corporations: Anglo American (1400), Mittal Steel (1200), Lafarge Cement (600) and the Gautrain Consortium (400) (de Lange, 2007). In 2008, 36 350 quota permits were available but only 1133 were filled (Johnson et al., 2010: 16).

The issue of other types of TRP was somewhat more successful, the numbers nearly doubling from 11 781 in 2003 to 21 848 in 2008. Over this six-year period, a total of 79 626 temporary work permits was issued. The next glimpse we have of the policy at work is in 2011, when 106 173 TPRs were issued, of which 20 673 were work permits (Table 8.2) (SSA, 2013). In 2012, the number of work permits increased to 33 253. Critics argue that this policy has hardly made a dent in South Africa's overall skills

Table 8.2 Temporary residence permits issued, 2012

	No.	%	No.	%
Visitors	36135	34.0	44828	31.7
Relatives	28468	26.8	37612	26.6
Work	20673	19.5	33253	23.5
Study	16928	15.9	20087	14.2
Medical	1399	1.3	1870	1.3
Business	1346	1.3	1585	1.1
Waiver	–	–	1068	0.8
Retired persons	732	0.7	980	0.7
Treaty	212	0.2	206	0.1
Exchange	100	0.1	61	0.0
Corporate	180	0.1	–	–
Total	106173	100.0	141550	100.0

Source: SSA (2012, 2013).

shortage (Johnson et al., 2010: 14). Companies and immigration lawyers complain about the long processing time and the backlog of unprocessed applications. Johnson et al. (2010) argue that government's commitment to skilled migration is confusing, ambiguous and inadequate. Others concur that the policy is not working well (Ellis and Segatti, 2011; Rasool et al., 2012). Recent amendments to the Immigration Act have tightened up on in-country renewals, prohibited someone from changing jobs and restricted intra-company transfer permits to a period of two years, suggesting that government remains fundamentally ambiguous about the value of skills import (Pokroy, 2013). In early 2014, the Department of Home Affairs tabled further amendments that would abolish both the quota permit and the exceptional skills permit and replace them with a single critical skills permit accompanied by an annual critical skills list.

The TRP data provide a window into the geography of contemporary skills migration to South Africa (Table 8.3). Around 83 per cent of the movement in 2011–12 classifies as South–South with almost half emanating from Asia (primarily China and India). A third of the permits were issued to migrants from other SADC countries, and 13 per cent to those from other parts of Africa. In terms of individual countries, unsurprisingly, migrants from Zimbabwe were most numerous (at 26 per cent of all permits issued) (Figure 8.4). The only other African country with more than 1 per cent of permits issued is Nigeria, which is consistent with the growing importance of South Africa as a destination for Nigerians (Singh and Sausi, 2010; Olatuyi et al., 2013). However, over 30 per cent

Table 8.3 Source regions of temporary work permit holders, 2011–12

	2011	2012	2011–12	%
North–South				
Europe	2229	3397	5626	10.4
North America	425	558	983	1.8
Australasia	79	183	262	0.5
South–South				
Asia	8735	13197	21932	49.7
Southern Africa	6329	10948	17277	32.0
West Africa	1282	2033	3315	6.1
East & Central Africa	961	2011	2972	5.5
North Africa	193	365	558	1.0
Middle East	142	209	351	0.6
Central & South America	275	352	627	1.2
Total	20650	33253	53903	

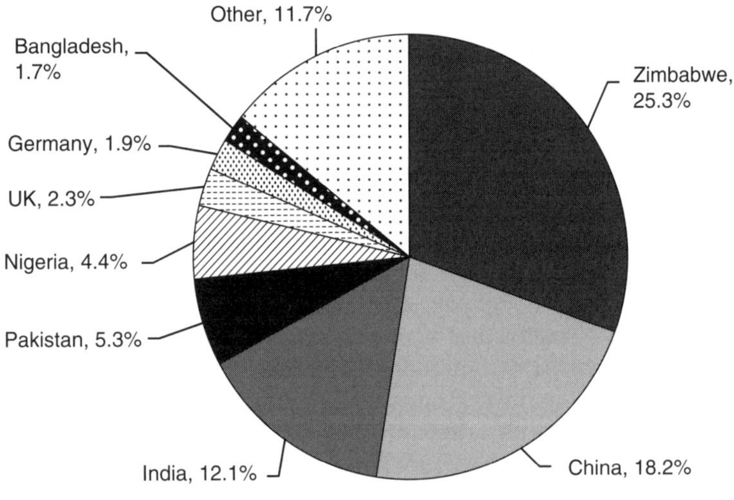

Figure 8.4 Country origins of South Africa temporary work permit holders, 2011–12

of permits were acquired by migrants from other countries in the South outside Africa. The most important of these were China (18 per cent), India (12 per cent), Pakistan (6 per cent) and Bangladesh (2 per cent). In other words, South Africa is emerging as a destination for South–South migrants from Asia. The country's historical connections with the Indian sub-continent may well be facilitating that movement, although South African private hospitals have also recently begun recruiting nurses from India. The relatively large number of permits given to migrants from China is consistent with the growing Chinese presence in Africa more generally (Harrison et al., 2012).

4. THE RISE OF THE REFUGEE

Another major shift in post-apartheid temporary migration has been the integration of South Africa into the global refugee regime. The movement of forced migrants to South Africa certainly pre-dates the end of apartheid. One of the ironic legacies of the apartheid state's destabilization and proxy wars in the Southern African region in the 1970s and 1980s was that South Africa itself became a destination for refugees from countries such as Angola and Mozambique (Crush and Chikanda, 2014). By the end of the civil war in Mozambique, for example, over 300 000 Mozambicans had fled to South Africa. The apartheid state did not subscribe to either the UN or OAU Refugee Conventions, although the refugees were allowed to stay if they remained in the border areas and away from the large urban centres. One of the first actions of the first democratic government in 1994 was to ratify the Conventions and to develop new refugee protection legislation (the 2008 Refugees Act). By that stage, the war in Mozambique had ended and few Mozambicans qualified for protection. Those who did not voluntarily return to Mozambique were allowed to stay, but their status was increasingly precarious, particularly for those who had moved to the cities (Polzer Ngwato, 2012). Many were caught up in the police dragnet and deported as 'illegal aliens'. The conundrum was eventually resolved, after lengthy bureaucratic delays, by offering the former refugees permanent residence status in South Africa. A total of 130 000 Mozambicans applied for permanent residence, of whom approximately 111 000 were successful.

The logical implications of the ratification of the UN Conventions and the new Refugees Act of 1998 appeared to catch the government by surprise. South Africa immediately became a desirable and accessible place of refuge within the African continent at exactly the same time as the countries of Europe and North America were slamming their doors on asylum-seekers (Handmaker et al., 2008). As a result, asylum-seekers from many of Africa's crisis states began to make their way to South Africa and claim asylum. Somalis, Ethiopians, Rwandans, Angolans and Congolese, in particular, appeared in increasing numbers. The number of successful refugee claimants living in South Africa increased steadily, from 15 063 in 2000 to 65 210 in 2012 (Figure 8.5).

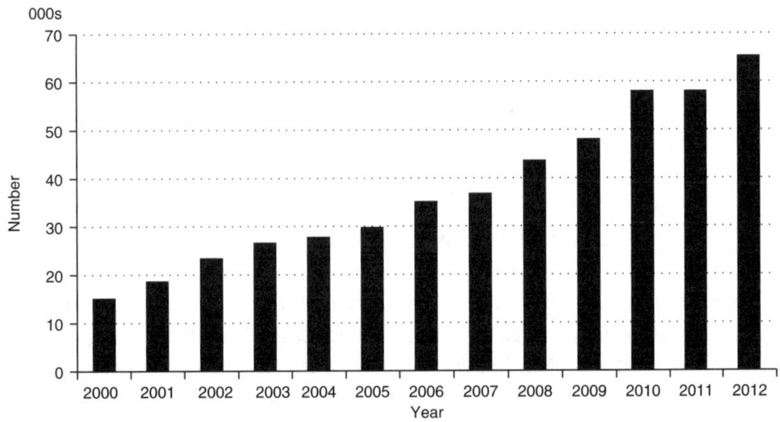

Figure 8.5 Number of refugees in South Africa at year end, 2000–2012

While the majority of asylum-seekers came from Africa's crisis states, migrants from a number of other African countries also began to arrive and claim asylum. Non-African asylum-seekers appeared from countries such as India, Pakistan, Bangladesh and China. On arrival, anyone could claim asylum and be issued with an asylum-seeker's permit. The relatively progressive nature of the 1998 Refugees Act (which human rights lawyers had a prominent role in drafting) meant that asylum-seekers were not corralled in camps, enjoyed freedom of movement within the country and were permitted to engage in economic activity to support themselves while their claims were adjudicated (Handmaker et al., 2008). The number of asylum-seekers rose dramatically after 2000. From the start, the administration of the 1998 Refugees Act was plagued by problems and irregularities. The Department of Home Affairs did not have, and did not develop, the capacity and expertise to properly adjudicate individual claims for protection. As a default, certain countries were classified as 'refugee-generating' and most claimants from those countries were afforded refugee status. Once a country was re-classified as 'non refugee-generating', claims by asylum-seekers from those countries were usually rejected, regardless of the individual merits of the case. Rates of acceptance of claims for asylum were thus highly correlated with country of origin of the claimant. For example, in 2012, the refugee rolls were dominated by Somalis (17864), Congolese (13386), Angolans (5805), Ethiopians (5538) and Burundians (2359). In general, the poor capacity to process claims has led to a growing backlog and ill-founded decisions (Amit, 2012). The numbers of asylum-seeker permit holders continued to grow while the numbers given refugee status increased at a snail's pace.

Between 2001 and 2012, for example, 960 733 claims for asylum were lodged, of which only 33 583 were accepted.

Surveys by SAMP of South African attitudes towards refugees show that they are lukewarm about South Africa's obligation to offer refugee protection and, furthermore, believe that the vast majority of refugee claimants are 'bogus' (Crush et al., 2013). The South African government increasingly agreed that the refugee protection system was being abused by 'economic migrants' to enter and stay in the country. Certainly, migrants from a wide variety of countries in Africa and outside it have lodged applications for asylum over the years but it is hard to say how many of these claimants are not actually in need of protection. The result of this perception is very real, however. As Amit (2012) argues, the fundamental rights protection mandate of the asylum system has been supplanted, leading to significant rights violations for 'bona fide asylum-seekers' as the government focuses its efforts on combatting perceived abuse of the system rather than offering a safe haven to the bona fide asylum-seekers the system was designed to protect. Despite the challenges and difficulties, distinctive communities of refuge now exist in many South African cities (e.g. Steinberg, 2005; Gebre et al., 2011; Shaffer, 2012; Naidu and Nzuza, 2013).

5. MIGRATING NEIGHBOURS

The decline of permanent immigration and contract mine migration, and the rise of temporary skills migration and forced migration constitute the four major migration developments of South Africa's last two decades. A fifth development, irregular or undocumented migration, is harder to assess since there are no reliable statistics, a great deal of official and media myth-making, and only isolated qualitative case studies of particular communities on which to rely (e.g. Muanamoha, 2008; Bloch, 2010; Morreira, 2010; Muanamoha et al., 2010; Vidal, 2010; Griffin, 2013). This section argues that the net effect of these five migration streams is a far more heterogeneous migrant population in South Africa than at any time in the past. In the case of one country, Zimbabwe, a distinctive pattern of 'mixed migration' has developed that merits a separate analysis and discussion (Crush and Tevera, 2010).

Quite apart from migrants from East and West Africa and Asia, migration streams from South Africa's neighbours have also become far more varied. For example, a 2006 SAMP survey of migrant-sending households in five Southern African countries shows that migration is becoming more feminized, is participated in by a wage range of individuals (of varying age, marital status, education and economic status) and involves a much broader range of activity when in South Africa (Pendleton et al., 2006). The occupational profile of migrants is clear evidence of a migrant population in transition (Table 8.4). The survey found that 12 per cent

Table 8.4 Occupations of SADC migrants in South Africa, 2006

Occupation	Country of origin					
	Botswana %	Lesotho %	Mozambique %	Swaziland %	Zimbabwe %	Total %
Skilled						
Professional worker	1.6	2.9	1.7	3.5	14.7	4.8
Health worker	0.6	0.3	0.3	0.5	10.6	2.3
Employer/manager	0.0	0.0	0.0	0.4	1.3	0.3
Teacher	0.0	0.1	0.1	0.8	7.0	1.5
Farmer	1.1	0.3	0.1	0.4	0.7	0.5
Businessman/woman	0.6	1.2	4.0	1.1	4.2	2.2
Office manager	0.3	0.2	0.0	0.8	3.5	0.9
Sub-total	4.2	5.1	6.2	7.5	42.0	12.5
Semi-Skilled						
Office worker	1.1	0.3	0.4	1.7	4.6	1.5
Manual worker	0.8	6.2	8.0	6.1	4.9	5.6
Foreman	0.6	0.1	0.5	0.7	0.5	0.5
Police/military	0.2	0.0	0.1	0.2	0.4	0.1
Security personnel	0.0	0.2	0.5	1.9	0.1	0.6
Mineworker	87.2	68.4	30.5	62.3	3.0	49.5
Sub-total	89.7	75.0	40.0	72.9	13.5	57.8
Low-Skilled						
Farm worker	0.2	2.0	2.2	0.5	1.2	1.3
Service worker	1.1	1.1	1.2	2.5	9.9	3.1
Domestic worker	1.7	9.0	0.9	1.6	1.9	3.2
Unskilled manual	0.5	1.5	9.5	7.8	2.1	4.7
Informal producer	0.2	2.8	0.8	0.4	4.8	1.8
Trader/hawker/vendor	0.0	2.0	6.0	0.7	14.7	4.6
Sub-total	3.7	18.4	20.6	13.5	34.6	18.7
Other	0.8	0.0	16.9	4.3	2.9	11.0
N	633	1076	987	1132	857	4685

Source: SAMP.

of migrants were working in skilled jobs and professions, which certainly challenges the common perception that all migrants from African countries are impoverished and uneducated. More numerous were semi-skilled (58 per cent) and low-skilled (19 per cent) occupations. The majority of the semi-skilled workers were mineworkers (49 per cent of the total number of all migrants and over 80 per cent of the semi-skilled). These individuals would have legal residence and work status in South Africa through the corporate permit system, though a small number (mostly from Lesotho) may have been illegal miners. We can also assume that most, if not all, of the skilled workers had work permits. A further 6 per cent were informal economy producers, traders and vendors. Theirs is a twilight status since they are in the country legally and generally only spend very short periods there. Assuming that the rest of the semi-skilled and low-skilled migrants do not have work permits, this would mean that around 20 per cent might be irregular migrants.

The occupational profile of migrants from four of the five countries (excepting Zimbabwe) is quite similar. Skilled migrants made up less than 10 per cent of the total from each country and mineworkers constituted over two-thirds of the migrants from Botswana, Lesotho and Swaziland, and a third of those from Mozambique. Adjusting for informal sector workers, this means that the guesstimate for working irregular migrants would be Zimbabwe (26 per cent), Swaziland (25 per cent), Mozambique (23 per cent), Lesotho (20 per cent) and Botswana (6 per cent). The majority probably entered the country legally (on 90-day visitor's permits) and are employed without work permits. In the case of female domestic workers from Lesotho, they do not even have to go home to renew their permits. Minibus taxi drivers offer a 'paid service' by taking passports to the Lesotho border, where, for an additional consideration, they are stamped with another 90-day permit by border officials.

The survey confirms the temporary nature of virtually all migration from these five countries (Table 8.5). As many as 36 per cent return to their home country at least once a month, another 13 per cent return once every three months, 19 per cent make it home once a year and only 11 per cent go home less often. Mozambican migrants return home less often than migrants in the other countries (43 per cent once a year); Lesotho migrants come home the most often (56 per cent monthly). These differences can generally be accounted for by the variable constraints of distance and cost. A migrant mineworker from Lesotho on the Free State gold mines may only be an hour or two away from home by minibus taxi. His co-worker from Mozambique would take the best part of a day just to reach the Mozambican border and then might have to travel by bus for another day before reaching his home in rural central Mozambique. Given the

Table 8.5 Frequency of return to home country, 2006

	Botswana %	Lesotho %	Mozambique %	Swaziland %	Zimbabwe %	Total %
Twice or more per month	4.7	1.5	2.2	7.5	16.5	6.2
Once a month	38.5	55.6	2.4	35.9	14.5	30.1
More than twice in 3 months	8.4	9.2	1.2	16.6	7.8	9.0
Once in 3 months	14.6	15.2	5.1	16.5	10.8	12.5
Once every 6 months	5.5	8.1	17.5	8.9	6.8	9.7
Once a year	13.5	8.2	42.5	10.2	19.0	18.5
At end of the contract	8.1	0.2	2.3	1.4	3.9	2.6
Other	6.7	2.2	26.9	3.0	20.7	11.4

relentless work schedule on the mines, return for annual leave is all that is realistically possible.

The vast majority of migrants from all five countries send cash remittances and goods back home (Crush and Pendleton, 2009). In every country, remittances are the main source of income for migrant-sending households. The figures are highest in the case of Lesotho (95 per cent of households receive cash and 20 per cent goods), followed by Zimbabwe (84 per cent and 68 per cent), Mozambique (77 per cent and 65 per cent), Botswana (76 per cent and 53 per cent) and Swaziland (65 per cent and 17 per cent). The importance of goods remittances to households in Mozambique and Zimbabwe is noteworthy. The average cash remittances received by migrant-sending households also varied: Botswana (ZAR 10412 p.a.), Lesotho (ZAR 9094 p.a.), Swaziland (ZAR 6297), Mozambique (ZAR 2607 p.a.) and Zimbabwe (ZAR 2760 p.a.) (Table 8.6). In terms of frequency of remitting, about 80 per cent of migrants send cash remittances at least once every three months; Botswana (62 per cent), Lesotho (77 per cent) and Swaziland (71 per cent) have the highest percentages who remit once a month (Table 8.6).

Considerable attention is given in the remittance literature to the methods that migrants use to remit and the expense involved in remitting, through both formal and informal channels. The main policy recommendation is that migrants will benefit from formalization and that governments and institutions at both ends should lower the transaction costs of remitting. In the case of Southern Africa, most migrants are relatively satisfied with the methods they use. Unsurprisingly, personal transfer of cash and goods is easily the most important channel (used by 47 per cent of

Table 8.6 Frequency of cash remitting

	Botswana %	Lesotho %	Mozambique %	Swaziland %	Zimbabwe %	Total %
Twice or more per month	4.7	1.2	2.7	3.0	12.8	4.6
Once a month	61.8	76.6	20.0	71.4	48.2	58.3
More than twice in 3 months	6.5	8.9	5.9	10.1	9.0	8.4
Once in 3 months	9.9	6.4	23.1	8.9	16.4	12.2
Once every 6 months	2.6	1.6	13.6	2.9	4.4	4.6
Once a year	7.6	5.0	13.9	3.3	2.7	6.0
At end of the contract	0.0	0.2	0.8	0.0	0.3	0.2
Other	4.7	0.0	12.3	0.2	3.8	3.5
Don't know	2.2	0.2	7.7	0.3	2.4	2.2
Total	100.0	100.0	100.0	100.0	100.0	100.0

migrants). It is hard to see how transaction costs of personal transactions can be reduced unless the reason for return home is only to transfer remittances, in which case transportation costs make this a very costly means of remitting. Also common is sending remittances with a friend or co-worker (used by 26 per cent) or through the post office (7 per cent). In the case of Zimbawe, an informal door-to-door courier service (*mayalisha*) has grown up to deliver remittances to people's homes (Thebe, 2011). Within the region itself, migrants do not generally see that there is a problem in need of a solution. This does not mean, of course, that, if cost-effective financial services were available, migrants would not use them.

A central question in debates about the developmental value of remittances is how households actually spend this income. The relative importance of types of expenditures may be seen by looking at the percentage of households incurring an expense in the previous month. Looking at household averages for all countries, food and groceries are by far the most important (93 per cent of households purchased food), followed by transportation (44 per cent), fuel (44 per cent), utilities (38 per cent), education (31 per cent) and medical expenses (30 per cent). Certain categories of expenses are more important in certain countries. Education (primarily school fees) is important in Zimbabwe (57 per cent) and Mozambique (44 per cent); medical expenses are important in Zimbabwe (40 per cent), Swaziland (39 per cent) and Mozambique (31 per cent); savings are important in Zimbabwe (36 per cent) and Botswana (28 per cent); housing is a major category only in Zimbabwe (46 per cent); clothing is a major category in Lesotho (73 per cent) and Zimbabwe (54 per cent); while farming expenses are important only in Swaziland (39 per cent).

Across the five countries, the most common expenditure items for remittance money are food (90 per cent of households), school fees (52 per cent), clothing (52 per cent) and fares (transportation) (34 per cent). The rank order changes a little for different countries but the items remain generally the same. Certain categories of remittance contributions are more important in certain countries. In Swaziland, farming items (seed, fertilizers, tractors) are important and seed is also important in Lesotho and Mozambique. In Botswana, remittance money is used for cattle purchase (21 per cent). Although of less importance, remittance money helps with many other expenditure items such as building materials and funerals.

Further dramatic proof of the importance of remittances to household food security and other basic needs is provided by a tabulation of the types of goods that migrants send home. There is little evidence of luxury goods being remitted. Instead, clothing (41 per cent of households) and food (29 per cent) are clearly the items most frequently brought or sent. Mozambique migrants bring more building materials than migrants in other countries (e.g. roofing 16 per cent and cement 9 per cent) and Zimbabwe migrants are the only ones who remit a significant percentage of goods for sale (14 per cent). The survey showed very little evidence of reinvestment of income (remittance and otherwise) in entrepreneurial or other income-generating activity. Finally, many migrant-sending households do not have savings. In Lesotho, Mozambique and Swaziland, about half or more of the households have none. Botswana (58 per cent) and Zimbabwe (53 per cent) have the largest percentages of savers.

6. MIXED MIGRATION FROM ZIMBABWE

Over the last two decades, the political and economic crisis in Zimbabwe has transformed the country from a migrant-receiving to a major global migrant-sending country (Crush and Tevera, 2010). The numbers of Zimbabweans crossing legally into South Africa began to increase after 1990 (Figure 8.6). In response, South Africa imposed tough visa restrictions in 1996, which had an immediate depressing effect on legal cross-border movements. One unintended effect of the new visa regime was that it pushed migrants who failed to meet the strict conditions into clandestine channels. A mini-cross-border smuggling industry quickly grew up. However, the trans-Limpopo River crossing between Zimbabwe and

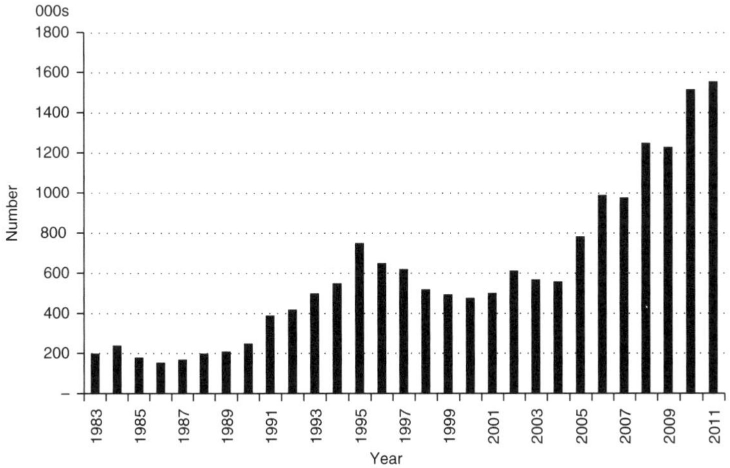

Figure 8.6 Legal cross-border movement from Zimbabwe to South Africa, 1983–2011

South Africa was extremely hazardous. In 2005, South Africa abolished its visa requirements. Smuggling declined as people now found it much easier to cross through legal border posts and acquire a 90-day visitor's permit while they looked for work in South Africa. The numbers of Zimbabweans crossing into South Africa immediately began to increase again, as the Zimbabwean crisis intensified. In 2004, just under 600 000 people entered South Africa legally from Zimbabwe. By 2011, the figure was nearly 1.6 million.

The profile of Zimbabwean migration to South Africa differs significantly from other SADC countries, where younger male migrants continue to dominate migration streams. The rapid expansion of migration after 2000 was reflected in the 2006 SAMP survey in Zimbabwe (Pendleton et al., 2006). Nearly three-quarters of the migrants had been migrating to South Africa for less than 5 years. Another 21 per cent had been migrating for 6–10 years. Only 10 per cent had been migrating to South Africa since before 1995. Ongoing feminization of migration increased the proportion of female migrants to 44 per cent of the total. Migrants were also staying in South Africa for longer periods: fully half were going for 6 months or more. Not only were migrants employed in a wider variety of skilled, semi-skilled and low-skilled jobs (see Table 8.4); there was considerable inter-sector mobility. Other studies showed considerable de-skilling of migrants once they moved to South Africa towards low-skilled jobs in farmwork, the service industry, informal trade and security, and away from more skilled jobs like teaching, the trades, financial services and administrative/clerical work (Bloch, 2006; Mosala, 2008).

A new cohort of socially and economically marginalized people began to enter South Africa after 2000. The most visible, and troubling, case concerned disabled Zimbabweans who made their way to South Africa because there was no longer a viable social support system in Zimbabwe. By early 2005, several hundred blind Zimbabweans were living in cramped and squalid conditions in inner-city Johannesburg, surviving on handouts and begging on the streets. Most lived in constant fear of arrest and deportation back to Zimbabwe. The Central Methodist Church in downtown Johannesburg became the only shelter that they and other destitute Zimbabweans could find. In 2004 and 2005, Zimbabweans began arriving at the church to seek accommodation, basic provisions and financial assistance. By mid-2008, the church housed over 4000 refugees and migrants, including unaccompanied child migrants and orphans (Kuljian, 2013). General unaccompanied child migration to South Africa also increased, leading to considerable abuse and exploitation (Crush and Tawodzera, 2013).

One of the most striking findings of a 2010 SAMP survey of recent (post-2005) Zimbabwean migrants in Johannesburg and Cape Town was how many did not come straight there from Zimbabwe (Crush et al., 2012). At least 30 per cent had been in other SADC countries before coming to South Africa, including Botswana (19 per cent), Mozambique (5 per cent), Zambia (3 per cent) and Namibia (2 per cent). Once inside South Africa, Zimbabweans often started out in other towns and provinces before moving to Cape Town or Johannesburg. Fully 42 per cent had started out living in another province before moving to Gauteng or the Western Cape. The proportion of female migrants in the post-2005 group was 44 per cent, and the proportion of young, unmarried migrants aged 15–24 rose dramatically from 15 per cent in 2005 to 31 per cent in 2010. Most of the new migrants were school-leavers and (unlike their predecessors) a third had never had a job in Zimbabwe. Half of the migrants had been unemployed before leaving Zimbabwe, while only 18 per cent were unemployed in South Africa.

The primary South African response to the post-2000 influx of Zimbabweans was a mass arrest and deportations campaign. Tens of thousands of Zimbabweans were being rounded up and deported every year with a minimum of due process. Most came straight back again, while others responded to this campaign by turning to the only option they had for avoiding deportation: the refugee protection system. Zimbabwean applications for asylum rose from zero in 2000 to nearly 20000 in 2006 and then to almost 150000 in 2009 (Figure 8.7). At the time of the 2010

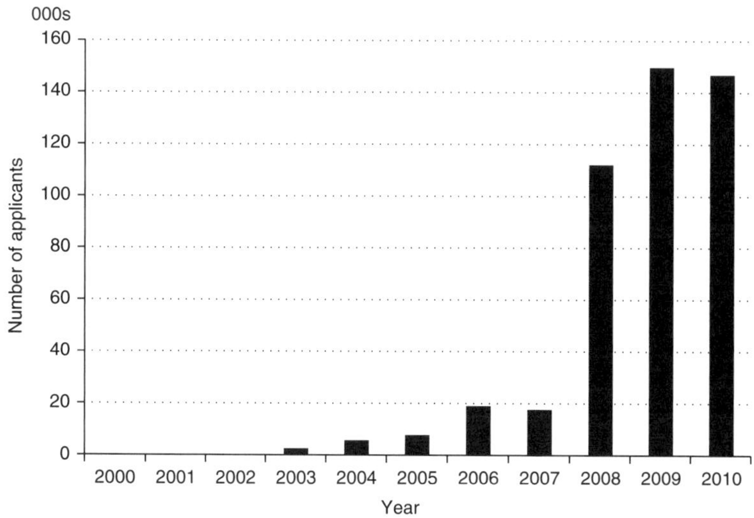

Figure 8.7 Asylum applications by Zimbabweans in South Africa, 2000–2010

SAMP survey, 52 per cent of interviewees were holding asylum permits. Another 28 per cent had official documentation to be in the country (including work permits), 2.5 per cent were permanent residents, leaving just 17 per cent in irregular status. Asked about their main reason for coming to South Africa, few respondents mentioned the search for asylum or indeed a political motivation of any kind. A total of only 4 per cent of the respondents said they needed to seek political asylum in South Africa.

Migration from Zimbabwe since the 1990s has been characterized by circulation in which the vast majority of migrants spend only short periods in South Africa, returning home frequently and showing very little inclination to remain in South Africa for any length of time (see Table 8.5). However, fewer than 1 per cent of the post-2005 migrants return once a month and only 9 per cent return once every few months. As many as 46 per cent had not been back to Zimbabwe since coming to South Africa. South Africa is seen by many as a longer-term destination rather than a temporary place to earn quick money. A number of studies have shown that fundamental change in the present economic and political environment is one of the most important preconditions for return migration to Zimbabwe. However, a change in these conditions does not automatically mean that Zimbabweans will move back to the country in large numbers. The majority of post-2005 migrants in South Africa are in no hurry to return to Zimbabwe. As many as 46 per cent of the respondents said that they wanted to remain in South Africa 'for a few years'. Another 13 per cent said they wished to remain 'indefinitely' and another 8 per cent want to remain 'permanently'. In other words, two-thirds of the migrants view a long-term stay in South Africa as desirable.

Migrants adopt various strategies to narrow the gap between their desire to remain in South Africa and the likelihood of doing so. The first, and most risky of all, is to live and work in South Africa 'under the radar'. Before the temporary suspension of deportations in 2009, this meant constant vigilance, avoidance of places where the police commonly target people for deportation, and having a few hundred rand in the pocket to pay the bribe demanded by arresting officers. Second, some migrants try to legitimize their stay by acquiring legal residence permits. Only 2.5 per cent of recent migrants had managed to acquire permanent residence permits in South Africa, which would be the ultimate goal for someone wishing for an extended stay. The third strategy, as noted above, is to apply for asylum and obtain an asylum-seeker's permit. In 2010, the sheer pressure on the refugee determination system from the deluge of applications forced the South African government into implementing an 'immigration amnesty' for Zimbabweans. By the time the so-called Zimbabwe Dispensation Project ended in mid-2011, a total of 275 000 Zimbabweans had applied for four-year residence permits in South Africa (Amit, 2011). The government deliberately set the figure at four years since five years' residence qualifies someone for permanent residence. The struggle for permanent settlement will therefore resume in 2015. In the meantime, Zimbabweans continue to come and deportations have resumed.

7. CONCLUSION

South Africa came relatively late to the 'age of migration', the new world of globalized population migration. As a result, it was ill prepared to comprehend, much less manage, post-apartheid migration to the country. Both of the forms of migration that characterized the apartheid years – white immigration from Europe and black contract migration from neighbouring states – were tightly regulated and could be manipulated almost at will. The new era of globalization, with its greatly increased population mobility across international boundaries and complex interplay of permanent and temporary forms of migration, did not easily respond to the blunt policy instruments that were inherited by South Africa's first democratically elected government. For nearly a decade, the new South African state tried to use those instruments under the mistaken impression that it could seal South Africa off from the world, keep South African territory for new South Africans through mass deportations, and run a modern economy that was bleeding skills without resort to importing new ones. The 2002 Immigration Act signified, at least in theory, an attempt to come to grips with a new globalized reality and to use migration as a tool for economic growth and development.

A defining characteristic of the new globalized migration regime is the global hunt for talent. Countries in the North have reformulated their immigration systems to increase their attractiveness to the world's skilled. South Africa became a fertile recruiting ground and the country entered a sustained period of skills loss through emigration in the early 1990s. It has scarcely let up since. Instead of adopting a racially inclusive immigration policy, the new South Africa eschewed immigration completely and made it more and more difficult for anyone to immigrate and settle permanently. Partly this was because of the association of immigration with the racist past, partly it was because South Africa wanted to claim the moral high ground and not 'poach' skills from developing countries, and partly it was because of the imperatives of a newly inclusive nation-building project that simplistically equated in-migration with the denial of citizens' rights.

In the competitive search for the 'best and brightest', rapid-response temporary migration has become the new norm in many countries (including permanent immigration countries of long standing such as Canada and Australia). The crafters of South Africa's Immigration Act were, somewhat reluctantly, persuaded that the country should follow suit. Even today, there are many in government (and most of the general population) who oppose this policy. Some mechanisms, such as the quota system, have been a farce. Others, such as the exceptional skills permit, are reportedly on their way out. Even the general work permit and intra-company transfer permit are constantly bedevilled by bureaucratic overkill and a desire to let people in for as short a time as possible. What seems clear is that the profile of those skilled migrants who do jump over the hurdles is changing in a way that is consistent with global movements and trends. It is not surprising that Zimbabwe has become the major source of skills for South Africa. What is more unexpected is that the next four source countries in order of importance are now China, India, Pakistan and Nigeria.

Another defining feature of the new globalized migration regime is the rapid growth of temporary migration and temporary work schemes for semi-skilled and low-skilled in many parts of the world. While temporary migration and circulation are now touted as a 'triple-win' option in global policy circles, South Africa has long been host to a temporary work system that is among the worst and most exploitative ever seen in the modern world. If a racist immigration policy was seen as unpalatable and unreformable, then there is no logical reason why the same should not have been true of the mine labour system. Yet, as this chapter has shown, that system has survived. Admittedly, the harsh cost realities of low-grade mining in South Africa led to a major downsizing and decline in the significance of the industry to the economy. But the arguments and lobbying of the private sector were such that an exemption was built into the Immigration Act, in the form of the corporate work system, which allowed the mines and commercial farms to continue to operate a downsized regional migrant labour system. The internalization of the mine workforce over the last decade (drawing less labour from outside the country and relying instead on internal migrants) is a cost and efficiency decision in an era when the two advantages of non-South African labour (willingness to accept lower wages and lower levels of militancy) are less important. Current trends seem to indicate that the state's long quest (which precedes the end of apartheid) to get the mines to employ only South Africans seems, finally, to be working. With the exception of Botswana (with its own relatively vibrant mining-based economy), the unintended consequence is that retrenched foreign miners are being replaced by other household members crossing into South Africa to look for work in other sectors.

A fourth characteristic of the contemporary migration regime is the globalization of forced migration. Most refuges in search of protection asylum tend to move to nearby safe havens. But for those with the means, determination and contacts to search for permanent refuge, destinations further afield can be more desirable. Since it ratified the UN and OAU Conventions and was persuaded (by the UNHCR and human rights groups) to embed permanent rather than temporary protection in its domestic legislation, South Africa has become one of those desirable destinations. The system was also designed to allow anyone landing on South African soil the right to apply for asylum and stay in the country until their case was heard. The attractions of this system for non-forced migrants are obvious. Despite the fact that refugee status is rarely granted to migrants outside a select group of African crisis states, claimants from across the global South still arrive in considerable numbers and lodge asylum claims. The system is so overburdened (particularly when Zimbabwean migrants followed suit as a response to mass deportations) that even an asylum-seeker who has little chance of being accepted can prolong their stay well beyond the 90 days allowed by a visitor's permit.

The final feature of the global regime relevant to this chapter is the erection of ever-tighter controls on entry by recipient states (in the name of security) and ever-more ingenious ways of circumventing those controls by people-traffickers and human smugglers. There is no evidence that trafficking and smuggling occur on a large scale to South Africa. The country's

4000 km long border with its neighbours is extremely porous and US-style border fortification would require a massive investment and probably not make much of a difference anyway. Coplan (2002) has argued that the main function of the border posts between South Africa and its neighbours is to line the pockets of border guards and officials. While this argument about the 'business of the border' may overstate the case, it is undoubtedly the fact that many border posts become instantly more porous with the payment of the appropriate bribe. To give just one example: the brother of a Zimbabwean colleague was recently arrested in Johannesburg and driven to the Beit Bridge border post between South Africa and Zimbabwe in a Home Affairs van for deportation. On arrival, the van was waved through the border and then stopped several hundred metres up the road. The driver then asked the deportees who wanted to return to Johannesburg. Those who could pay the 'fare' stayed on board. Those who couldn't were left by the side of the road. The van then turned round and went back through the border, again without being stopped. Many such scams exist. But for those with passports who want to work in South Africa, the easiest way is to enter South Africa as perfectly legal 'visitors', along with the millions of others who cross the borders every day to shop, to buy and sell, to visit friends and relatives, to visit a South African hospital. Once in the country, they have 90 days to find work, free of official harassment.

South Africa's response to the phenomenon of regular entry and irregular work is consistent with that of many other sovereign states. Despite a nominal commitment to increased regional integration and freer movement, the South African state regularly engages in bouts of territorial cleansing. Since 1990, nearly 2 million individuals from neighbouring countries (especially Mozambique and Zimbabwe) have been deported with a minimum of due process. This cost-intensive and draconian operation is widely regarded as a failure by experts and a minor inconvenience by migrants, most of whom simply turn round and come back. The major beneficiaries are the police and Home Affairs officials who supplement their income through extortion and bribes. When citizens perceive that this ineffectual campaign is not working, they take the law into their own hands and attempt to violently remove migrants from their communities and country in regular paroxysms of xenophobic violence.

ACKNOWLEDGEMENTS

I wish to acknowledge the research support of the International Development Research Centre (IDRC) and the following for their assistance: Abel Chikanda, Mariella Salamone and Bronwen Dachs.

REFERENCES

Amit, R. (2011). 'The Zimbabwean documentation process: lessons learned', Research Report for African Centre for Migration and Society, Wits University, Johannesburg.

Amit, R. (2012). 'No way in: barriers to access, service and administrative justice at South Africa's refugee reception offices', Research Report for African Centre for Migration and Society, Wits University, Johannesburg.

Bloch, A. (2006). 'Emigration from Zimbabwe: migrant perspectives', *Social Policy & Administration*, **40**(1), 67–87.

Bloch, A. (2010). 'The right to rights? Undocumented migrants from Zimbabwe living in South Africa', *Sociology*, **44**, 2233–50.

Bolt, M. (2012). 'Rooting production: life and labour on the settler farms of the Zimbabwean–South African border', PhD Thesis, London School of Economics and Political Science (LSE), London.

Coplan, D. (2002). 'The border within: the future of the Lesotho–South Africa international boundary', Migration Policy Series No. 26, Southern African Migration Programme (SAMP), Cape Town.

Crush, J. and A. Chikanda (2014). 'Forced migration in Southern Africa', in E. Fiddian-Qasmiyeh, G. Loescher, K. Long and N. Sigona (eds), *Handbook of Refugee and Forced Migration*, Oxford: Oxford University Press.

Crush, J. and B. Dodson (2007). 'Another lost decade: the failures of South Africa's post-apartheid migration policy', *Tijdschrift voor Economische en Sociale Geografie*, **98**(4), 436–54.

Crush, J. and W. James (eds) (1996). *Crossing Boundaries: Mine Migrancy in a Democratic South Africa*, Cape Town and Ottawa: Idasa and IDRC.

Crush, J. and W. Pendleton (2009). 'Remitting for survival: rethinking the development potential of remittances in Southern Africa', *Global Development Studies*, **5**(3–4), 53–84.

Crush, J. and G. Tawodzera (2013). 'The perilous trek: Zimbabwean child migrants and access to education in South Africa', in L. Bartlett and A. Ghaffar-Kucher (eds), *Refugees, Immigrants, Education in the Global South: Lives in Motion*, New York: Routledge, pp. 54–69.

Crush, J. and D. Tevera (eds) (2010). *Zimbabwe's Exodus: Crisis, Migration, Survival*, Cape Town and Ottawa: SAMP and IDRC.

Crush, J., A. Chikanda and G. Tawodzera (2012). 'The third wave: mixed migration from Zimbabwe to South Africa', Migration Policy Series No 59, Southern African Migration Programme (SAMP), Cape Town.

Crush, J., A. Jeeves and D. Yudelman (1992). *South Africa's Labour Empire: A History of Black Migrancy to the Gold Mines*, Boulder, CO and Cape Town, South Africa: Westview Press and David Philip.

Crush, J., S. Ramachandran and W. Pendleton (2013). 'Soft targets: xenophobia, public violence and changing attitudes to migrants in South Africa after May 2008', Migration Series No. 64, Southern African Migration Programme (SAMP), Cape Town.

Crush, J., B. Dodson, J. Gay and C. Leduka (2010). 'Migration, remittances and gender-responsive local development: the case of Lesotho', Report for UN-INSTAW and UNDP, Santa Domingo, Dominican Republic.

Daniels, R. (2007). 'Skills shortages in South Africa: a literature review', Working Paper 07/121, Development Policy Research Unit, School of Economics, University of Cape Town.

De Lange, D. (2007). 'State to tackle scare skills quotas', *IOL News*, 15 November.

Dodson, B. and J. Crush (2004). 'A report on gender discrimination in South Africa's 2002 Immigration Act: masculinizing the migrant', *Feminist Review*, **77**, 96–119.

Ellis, S. and A. Segatti (2011). 'The role of skilled labour', in A. Segatti and L. Landau (ed.), *Contemporary Migration to South Africa: A Regional Development Issue*, Washington, DC: World Bank, pp. 67–80.

Erasmus, J. and M. Breier (2009). *Skills Shortages in South Africa: Case Studies of Key Professions*, Pretoria: HSRC.
Facchini, G., A. Mayda and M. Mendola (2013). 'What drives individual attitudes towards immigration in South Africa?', *Review of International Economics*, **21**(2), 326–41.
Gebre, L., P. Maharaj and N. Pillay (2011). 'The experiences of immigrants in South Africa: a case study of Ethiopians in Durban, South Africa', *Urban Forum*, **22**, 23–35.
Griffin, L. (2013). 'Unravelling rights: "Illegal" migrant domestic workers in South Africa', *South African Review of Sociology*, **42**(2), 83–101.
Hall, R., P. Wisborg, S. Shirinda and P. Zamvhiya (2013). 'Farm workers and farm dwellers in Limpopo Province, South Africa', *Journal of Agrarian Change*, **13**(1), 47–70.
Handmaker, J., L. de la Hunt and J. Klaaren (eds) (2008). *Advancing Refugee Protection in South Africa*, New York: Berghahn Books.
Harrison, P., K. Moyo and Y. Yang (2012). 'Strategy and tactics: Chinese immigrants and diasporic spaces in Johannesburg, South Africa', *Journal of Southern African Studies*, **38**(4), 899–925.
Johnson, S., A. Altbeker and A. Bernstein (2010). 'Skills, growth and borders: managing migration in South Africa's national interest', Research Report No. 17, Centre for Development and Enterprise, Johannesburg.
Johnston, D. (2007). 'Who needs immigrant farm workers? A South African case study', *Journal of Agrarian Change*, **7**(4), 494–525, http://onlinelibrary.wiley.com/doi/10.1111/joac.2007.7.issue-4/issuetoc.
Klotz, A. (2012). 'South Africa as an immigration state', *Politikon: South African Journal of Political Studies*, **39**(2), 189–208.
Klotz, A. (2013). *Migration and National Identity in South Africa, 1860–1910*, Cambridge: Cambridge University Press.
Kuljian, C. (2013). *Sanctuary: How An Inner-City Church Spilled Onto A Sidewalk*, Johannesburg: Jacana.
Mather, C. (2000). 'Foreign migrants in export agriculture: Mozambican labour in the Mpumalanga lowveld, South Africa', *Tijdschrift voor Economische en Sociale Geografie*, **91**(4), 426–36.
Mensah, S. and V. Naidoo (2011). 'Migration shocks: integrating Lesotho's retrenched migrant miners', *International Migration Review*, **45**(4), 1017–42.
Molefe, N. (2009). 'Socio-economic impacts of mine retrenchments on household livelihoods in Lesotho', MA Thesis, University of Witwatersrand, Johannesburg.
Morreira, S. (2010). 'Seeking solidarity: Zimbabwean undocumented migrants in Cape Town', *Journal of Southern African Studies*, **36**(2), 433–48.
Mosala, S. (2008). 'The work experience of Zimbabwean migrants in South Africa', Issue Paper No. 33, ILO Sub-Regional Office for Southern Africa, Harare.
Muanamoha, R. (2008). 'The dynamics of undocumented Mozambican labour migration to South Africa', PhD Thesis, University of Kwazulu Natal, Durban.
Muanamoha, R., B. Maharaj and E. Preston-Whyte (2010). 'Social networks and undocumented Mozambican migration to South Africa', *Geoforum*, **41**(6), 885–96.
Naidoo, K., R. Matsie and A. Ochse (2011). '"Resting", AIDS-affliction and marital constraints: engendered livelihood issues in the aftermath of Lesotho mineworker retrenchments', *Development Southern Africa*, **28**(5), 681–9.
Naidu, M. and N. Nzuza (2013). 'Food and maintaining identity for migrants: Sierra Leone migrants in Durban', *Journal of Sociology and Social Anthropology*, **4**(3), 193–200.
Olatuyi, A., Y. Awoyinka and A. Abiodun (2013). *Nigerian Diasporas in the South*, Brussels: ACP Migration Observatory.
Peberdy, S. (2009). *Selecting Immigrants: National Identity and South Africa's Immigration Policies 1910–2008*, Johannesburg: Wits University Press.
Peberdy, S. (2013). 'Gauteng: a province of migrants', Data Brief No, 5, Gauteng City Regional Observatory, Johannesburg.
Pendleton, W., J. Crush, E. Campbell, T. Green, H. Simelane, D. Tevera and F. de Vletter

(2006). 'Migration, remittances and development in Southern Africa', Migration Series No. 44, Southern African Migration Programme (SAMP), Cape Town.
Pokroy, J. (2012). 'Quota work permit confusion', available at http://www.hrfuture.net/legal/quota-work-permit-confusion.php (accessed 15 December 2013).
Pokroy, J. (2013). 'Home Affairs tightens things up', available at http://www.hrfuture.net/legal/home-affairs-tightens-things-up.php (accessed 15 December 2013).
Polzer Ngwato, T. (2012). 'Negotiating belonging: the integration of Mozambican refugees in South Africa', PhD Thesis, London School of Economics and Political Science (LSE), London.
Rasool, F., C. Botha and C. Bisschoff (2012). 'The effectiveness of South Africa's immigration policy for addressing skills shortages', *Managing Global Transitions*, **10**(4), 399–418.
Rutherford, B. (2010). 'Zimbabweans on the farms of northern South Africa', in J. Crush and D. Tevera (eds), *Zimbabwe's Exodus: Crisis, Migration, Survival*, Ottawa and Cape Town: IDRC and SAMP, pp. 244–68.
Rutherford, B. (2011). 'The uneasy ties of working and belonging: the changing situation for undocumented Zimbabwean migrants in northern South Africa', *Ethnic and Racial Studies*, **34**(8), 1303–19.
Segatti, A. and L. Landau (eds) (2011). *Contemporary Migration to South Africa: A Regional Development Issue*, Washington, DC: World Bank.
Shaffer, M. (2012). '"This is South Africa, not Somalia": negotiating gender relations in Johannesburg's "Little Mogadishu"', PhD Thesis, Ohio State University, Columbus, OH.
Singh, A. and K. Sausi (2010). 'Voluntary associations and remittances among Nigerian migrants living in central Durban', *Journal of Sociology and Social Anthropology*, **1**(1–2), 59–70.
SSA (2012). *Documented Immigrants in South Africa, 2011*, Pretoria: Statistics South Africa.
SSA (2013). *Documented Immigrants in South Africa, 2012*, Pretoria: Statistics South Africa.
Steinberg, J. (2005). 'A mixed reception: Mozambican and Congolese refugees in South Africa', Monograph Series No. 117, Institute for Security Studies, Pretoria.
Steinberg, J. (2012). 'Security and disappointment: policing, freedom and xenophobia in South Africa', *British Journal of Criminology*, **52**(2), 345–60.
Stern, M. and G. Szalontai (2006). 'Immigration policy in South Africa: does it make economic sense?', *Development Southern Africa*, **23**(1), 123–45.
Sutton, R. and D. Vigneswaran (2011). 'A Kafkaesque state: deportation and detention in South Africa', *Citizenship Studies*, **15**(5), 627–42.
Thebe, V. (2011). 'From South Africa with love: the *mayalisha* system and households' quest for livelihood reconstruction in south-western Zimbabwe', *Journal of Modern African Studies*, **49**, 647–70.
Ulicki, T. and J. Crush (2010). 'Poverty, gender and migrancy: Lesotho's migrant farmworkers in South Africa', in J. Crush and B. Frayne (eds), *Surviving on the Move: Migration, Poverty and Development in Southern Africa*, Midrand and Cape Town: DBSA and SAMP, pp. 164–82.
Vidal, D. (2010). 'Living in, out of, and between two cities: migrants from Maputo in Johannesburg', *Urban Forum*, **21**, 55–68.
Vigneswaran, D. (2012). 'Taking out the trash? A garbage can model of immigration policing', in L. Landau (ed.), *Exorcising the Demons Within: Xenophobia, Violence and Statecraft in Contemporary South Africa*, Johannesburg: Wits University Press, pp. 150–71.
Vigneswaran, D., T. Araia, C. Hoag and X. Tshabalala (2010). 'Criminality or monopoly? Informal immigration enforcement in South Africa', *Journal of Southern African Studies*, **36**(2), 465–82.

9. Emigration and wages in source countries: a survey of the empirical literature*

Prachi Mishra

I. INTRODUCTION

A vast theoretical and empirical literature has considered the labor-market impact of immigration. In contrast, the literature on the labor-market impact of emigration or the outflow of workers was almost exclusively theoretical for a long time until the early 2000s.[1] The absence of an empirical literature on the labor-market impact of emigration is surprising because the shares of labor force leaving many individual source countries is considerably higher than the proportionate changes in the labor force of many receiving countries due to immigration.

To cite a few examples, during 1970–2000, the labor forces in Mexico, El Salvador and Jamaica were reduced by more than 10 percent due to emigration to the USA. For several source countries, the reduction in the labor force due to emigration to the USA was in the range of 7–27 percent. There are countries like Turkey and Algeria where the labor force has been reduced by about 10 percent due to emigration to Western Europe over the same period. Elsewhere, there is anecdotal evidence of sizable flows to the gulf countries from African and Asian countries for which no systematic data exist (Sources: US Census, OECD Migration Statistics, World Development Indicators). In comparison, immigrants constituted about 12 percent of the US labor force in 2000 (Davis and Weinstein, 2002). Immigration is indeed considered to be a very important issue and has attracted a great deal of attention in the literature. Given the parity in magnitudes, the sparse literature on the effect of emigration on national wages is striking. In fact until recently there was no econometric study on the topic.

More importantly, the percentage reduction in the labor force is much greater in the higher schooling categories of the labor force. As Table 9.1 shows, the highly educated labor force in Guyana and Jamaica has been

* Nothing contained in this chapter should be reported as representing the views of the IMF, its executive board, member governments, or any other entity mentioned herein. The views in this chapter belong solely to the author.

Table 9.1 Percentage of labor force that has migrated to the OECD (by schooling)

	Primary	Secondary	Tertiary
Antigua and Barbuda	9	64	67
Bahamas, The	3	10	61
Barbados	18	28	63
Belize	7	58	65
Dominica	19	67	64
Dominican Republic	6	33	22
Grenada	25	71	85
Guyana	18	43	89
Haiti	3	30	84
Jamaica	16	35	85
St Kitts and Nevis	32	42	78
St Lucia	12	21	71
St Vincent and the Grenadines	18	33	85
Suriname	39	74	48
Trinidad and Tobago	8	22	79
Average	15	42	70

Source: Docquier and Marfouk (2004).

reduced by more than 80 percent as a result of emigration to the OECD. These numbers are based on the censuses of destination countries, and some of these migrants may have acquired their education in the OECD. Even adjusting for this, these numbers are striking.

Starting in the early 2000s, there has been an emerging literature on the effects of emigration on wages in source countries. This chapter provides an overview of this strand of literature and is organized as follows. Section II discusses the methodological issues that have been encountered in this literature on emigration and wages. Section III provides a summary of the existing evidence, and Section IV discusses some welfare implications of the wage effects from emigration. Section V concludes with some policy implications.

II. METHODOLOGICAL ISSUES

The literature on emigration has encountered several measurement and estimation issues that have long precluded systematic studies of emigration. Some of the key issues are presented below.

II.1 Measurement of the Emigrant Supply Shock – Who is an Emigrant?

One of the most difficult issues encountered in the literature is to quantify the magnitude of emigration because source countries, in general, do not record information on those who leave. Emigration is usually measured by obtaining information on the migrants from the censuses in the recipient countries (see, e.g., Mishra, 2007a; Docquier and Marfouk, 2004; Carrington and Detragiache, 1998). For example, Docquier and Marfouk (2004) estimate emigration rates to the OECD for a number of source countries. Emigrants to most OECD countries are defined by country of birth. For example, an emigrant from source country *j* residing in the USA is defined as a person whom the US Census counts as born in country *j*. The migrants include naturalized citizens, temporary and permanent residents as well as unauthorized migrants. Migrants to the USA also include asylum seekers who sought refuge from political turmoil, oppression and total totalitarian governments (e.g. in the case of Haiti). The exceptions are Germany, Greece, Italy, Japan and Korea, where an emigrant is defined by citizenship.

Emigration rate to the OECD is defined as the fraction of the labor force having migrated to OECD countries. It is expressed as

$$m_t^j = \frac{M_t^j}{M_t^j + N_t^j} \tag{9.1}$$

where M_t^j is the number of migrants from country *j* counted in the receiving countries' censuses at time *t*, and N_t^j is the labor force in source country *j* at time *t*.

Similarly, emigration rate from country *j* in schooling category *S* is defined as

$$m_{t,s}^j = \frac{M_{t,s}^j}{M_{t,s}^j + N_{t,s}^j} \tag{9.2}$$

where $M_{t,s}^j$ is the number of migrants from source country *j* with schooling *S* who are recorded in the OECD Censuses at time *t*, and $N_{t,s}^j$ is the labor force in source country *j* with schooling *S*.

Mishra (2007a) estimates emigration rates from Mexico to the USA using data on migrants from the US Census. The measure of the emigrant supply shock for the schooling group *i*, experience group *j*, and time *t* is denoted by $m_{ijt} \equiv \frac{M_{ijt}}{N_{ijt}}$, where M_{ijt} is the number of Mexican emigrants in the USA in cell (i, j, t) and N_{ijt} is the national workforce in Mexico in cell (i, j, t). Using emigrant share as a measure of the emigrant supply shock follows the framework in immigration literature that uses the immigrant share of the native population as a measure of the immigrant supply shock (e.g. Borjas, 2003, 1994; Friedberg, 2001; Altonji and Card, 1991 for representative studies). An emigrant from Mexico to the USA is defined as a person whom the US Census records as being born in Mexico. Hence, by this definition, an emigrant is a Mexican-born person in the USA who may be a naturalized citizen or a non-citizen. Using the census data, it is not possible to distinguish between legal and illegal immigrants in the USA. There is also evidence of an undercount of the illegal migrants in the census data, and hence also of emigration from Mexico (Costanzo et al., 2001).

II.2 Where did the Emigrant Acquire Schooling?

Identify schooling of emigrants using US Census

The problem is aggravated when measuring emigration rates at a disaggregated level, for example by schooling categories. Typically, the emigration rates by schooling do not take into account where the migrant acquired his/her schooling. The figures are based on the assumption that the migrants recorded in the OECD Censuses got their schooling in the source countries. Alternatively, for those who got their schooling in the OECD, the counterfactual assumption is that had they stayed behind, they would have got the same level of schooling. For migrants who got their schooling in destination countries, it is not straightforward to estimate the emigration shocks by schooling groups in the Caribbean.

There are two possibilities:

1. Had they stayed behind, they could have got more schooling. The possibility to migrate and get a job as unskilled workers reduces their incentive to go to school. In this case, the emigration shocks would be underestimated in the high-schooling groups, and overestimated in the low-schooling groups.
2. Had they stayed behind, they could have got less schooling, since the opportunities, institutional structure and laws related to schooling are better in the OECD countries. In this case, the emigration shocks would be overestimated in the high-skill groups and underestimated in the low-schooling categories.

The Censuses in the recipient countries do not record information on where did the migrants get their schooling. Hence, given the data, it is not possible to conclude the direction of the bias. However, it is possible to try to adjust for this bias in the case of migrants to the USA. There is strong evidence in the case of migrants from developing countries that those who migrate in their late teens or later are significantly less likely to have got their schooling in the USA (e.g. Grogger and Trejo, 2002; Gonzalez, 2003; Chiquiar and Hanson, 2005; Clark and Jaeger, 2002).

The US Census provides information for the foreign-born on the years spent in the USA. Using this information, it is possible to calculate their age at migration. Restricting the sample of migrants from, say, the Caribbean to those who emigrated as adults, it is less likely that these migrants would have acquired their schooling in the USA. Chiquiar and Hanson (2005), Mishra (2007a, 2007b) use this logic to adjust for the bias.

The unadjusted as well as adjusted emigration rates from the Caribbean countries to the USA in the tertiary education category (for cut-off ages of 16, 18, 21 and 25) are shown in Table 9.2. Given that a typical student in the Caribbean enters university at the age of 18 after 13 years of schooling, 18 years seems to be a reasonable cut-off to exclude emigrants who are likely to have had less than 13 years of schooling in the Caribbean. The magnitude of the adjusted emigration rates in the tertiary schooling category decreases in columns [2]–[5] (compared to column [1]). In both cases (adjusted and unadjusted), Guyana, Haiti and Jamaica have the highest tertiary emigration rates in the region. The highly educated labor force in the Caribbean has been reduced by one-third due to emigration to the USA, even after excluding all migrants who emigrated at less than 25 years. On the upper bound, it is reduced by 56 percent, when we exclude all migrants who emigrated at less than 16 years.

Note that the estimates of the emigration rates in the tertiary schooling categories, by restricting the age at migration at 25 years, are likely to be underestimates because (i) those who migrated at less than 25 years of age could have got part or all of their secondary (9–12 years of schooling) and tertiary education (defined as more than 12 years) in the Caribbean or (ii) for those who got their schooling in the USA, the possible counterfactual is that they could have had the same or more years of schooling had they not migrated.

Alternative sources of data on immigrants

Another option is to use sources other than the censuses to identify the emigrants. An alternative source of data on immigrants is the New Immigrant Survey (NIS). The NIS is a public-use database on new legal immigrants to the USA. The age at entry into the USA in the US Census is based on the question: 'When did you come to live in the United States?' According to Rosenzweig (2005), the question can be subjective since it is not clear whether the respondents answered the question when they got a permanent visa (not a student visa), or when they first came. Moreover,

Table 9.2 Percentage of labor force that has migrated to the USA in the tertiary education category

	[1]	[2]	[3]	[4]	[5]	[6]
	Not restricting age at immigration	Age at immigration greater than or equal to				*New Immigrant Survey*
		16 years	18 years	21 years	25 years	
Antigua-Barbuda	56	49	47	47	35	41
Bahamas	58	51	45	19	13	48
Barbados	46	39	36	31	24	30
Belize	62	55	51	32	23	46
Dominica	49	46	43	35	28	41
Dominican Republic	18	15	13	11	8	18
Grenada	75	72	70	43	33	50
Guyana	80	77	75	66	59	53
Haiti	79	75	73	67	59	58
Jamaica	78	72	70	63	56	51
St Kitts-Nevis	65	59	57	47	37	44
St Lucia	53	48	46	16	11	36
St Vincent & Grens.	71	66	63	29	19	48
Trinidad & Tobago	68	63	60	54	45	49
Average	61	56	54	40	32	44

Note: Tertiary: >12 years of schooling

Source: US Census (2000); Docquier and Marfouk (2005); NIS (2003), and author's calculations.

if a person emigrated at 25 or more years, it is not guaranteed that the person acquired schooling in the home country.

The NIS improves on the US Census in this respect and asks a direct question about the years of completed schooling in the USA. For tertiary-educated immigrants born in the Dominican Republic, Haiti and Jamaica respectively, 97, 73 and 65 percent did not acquire schooling in the USA. Column [6] in Table 9.2 shows the adjusted estimates for emigration rates in the tertiary education category using the NIS data. The magnitudes of emigration rates are smaller compared to Column [1]; nonetheless, even the adjusted rates are extremely high. The tertiary educated labor force in the Caribbean has reduced by more than 40 percent due to emigration to the USA. As in Column [1], Guyana, Haiti, Jamaica and Grenada have the highest tertiary emigration rates followed by St Vincent and Grenadines, Trinidad and Tobago, and St Kitts and Nevis.

Source-country data on emigration

There have been very few attempts in the literature to use data from source countries to identify the emigrants. For example, Mishra (2007b) uses administrative enrollment data from some key institutions for higher education in the Caribbean in order to gauge the number of tertiary educated immigrants counted in the US Census. These institutions include the University of West Indies (UWI, which includes three campuses in Barbados, Jamaica and Trinidad and Tobago), University of Technology, Jamaica, and University of Guyana. The data from the UWI include (i) on-campus student registration at one of the three campuses, and (ii) registration in affiliated institutions and distance education programs. The statistics on the UWI are prepared by the Office of Planning and Institutional Research at the MONA Campus in Jamaica. The data on all these institutions have been available since 1991.

Based on the US Census data, on average, close to 11 000 Caribbean migrants with some tertiary education leave for the USA in any given year. Making the NIS adjustment, this translates to about 8000 emigrants every year. As a benchmark, close to 30 000 students are registered in the three principal institutions of higher learning: UWI, University of Technology Jamaica, and the University of Guyana. These figures suggest that the number of emigrants counted in the US Census as emigrating in any particular year from the Caribbean is only about a third or lower compared to the total number of students enrolled in the key institutions. Therefore the count of high-skilled emigrants in the US Census who have come to the USA since 1991 does not seem to be overestimated in comparison with the administrative enrollment data. Yet, with a significant potential of measurement errors, using micro data from source countries to identify the emigration shock more accurately (in aggregate and by skill) remains a promising area for future research.

II.3 Identification of the Effect of Emigration on Wages

Apart from the measurement issues in emigration shocks, another important issue is the identification strategy to estimate the impact on source-country wages. The immigration literature struggled for a long time to find any significant impact of immigration on wages of US natives. The general approach in this literature had been to use variation in immigrant shares across different US cities (Borjas, 1994, 2001; Friedberg and Hunt, 1995). These papers generally found an insignificant impact of immigration on US wages. There could be several concerns related to identification of the true effect of immigration on wages of natives when using cross-city variation. First, immigrants are mobile across cities (Borjas, 2001), implying that the nation as a whole might be the preferable unit of analysis. The key innovation in Borjas (2003) is to use national-level data and use experience as an additional source of variation (in addition to schooling and time). Given the identification challenge, the emigration literature has used both regional- and national-level data (e.g. Hanson, 2007 uses regional variation, whereas Aydemir and Borjas, 2007 and Mishra, 2007a use the national-level approach).

II.4 Selection Bias in Estimating the Effect of Emigration

Another potential source of bias in the estimated effect of emigration on wages is due to self-selection, which would render the emigrants as a non-random sample from the population. Selection bias may arise because wages in the source country are observed only for the workers who decide not to migrate. If the 'lowest-ability' individuals are most likely to migrate from every skill group, then the positive correlation between emigration and wages might not be due to the favorable impact of emigration on wages. Instead it could be due to the 'lowest-ability' individuals leaving and raising the average wage in that skill group. Very few studies in the emigration literature have tried to address this potential bias from selection.

II.5 Endogeneity of Emigration and Wages

Finally, another potential concern in identifying the true effects of emigration on source-country wages is the issue of endogeneity. It is possible that the emigrant supply shock may be correlated with the unobserved component of source country wages. Consider the case of Mexico. There is some evidence that migration from Mexico to the USA tends to increase when wages decline in Mexico (Hanson and Spilimbergo, 1999; Hanson et al., 2001). If wage falls precede emigration, the estimated coefficient on emigration would clearly be an underestimate of the impact of emigration on wages. Even though this concern is commonly known, existing studies on emigration have not used any exogenous variation or a natural experiment – as, for example, in Card (1990), which studied the effects of the Mariel Boatlift on the Miami labor market, a natural experiment.

II.6 Labor Demand Shocks as Determinant of Wages

The literature on emigration and wages aims to isolate the impact of emigration, controlling for other covariates that affect wages. One of the confounding factors in this regard is labor demand shocks that are correlated with emigration and drive up wages. Two standard sources of labor demand shocks are technological changes and capital flows. Productivity-enhancing technological change as well as capital flows would increase wages and thus discourage emigration. Emigration would thus be negatively correlated with the unobserved component of wages, implying that the positive estimates that appear from the studies discussed below would actually be biased downwards. Alternatively, consider technology shocks, which are positively correlated with emigration. Here the impact of emigration on wages would be overestimated and raise more serious concerns because of the direction of the bias. An example of this scenario could be positively correlated labor demand shocks in the US and Mexican labor markets that raise labor demand and wages in Mexico but also attract Mexican migrants to the USA. To address this concern, studies typically control for average wages in the destination countries (see, e.g., Mishra, 2007a).

III. OVERVIEW OF THE EVIDENCE

The empirical evidence in the literature on emigration can be broadly divided into four categories: (i) case studies; (ii) simulation exercises; (iii) studies using regional variation; and finally (iv) national-level studies. This section discusses the evidence in each of these categories.

III.1 Case Studies on Emigration and Wages

There are a few case studies on the effects of emigration on wages by the International Labor Organization (Stalker, 1994). These case studies provide very useful background information on emigration. However, they do not use rigorous identification strategies to address the issue of whether the observed change in wages is caused by an outflow of workers or is due to other factors. Mahmood (1991) also addresses the issue of emigration and wages in the context of Pakistan. Based on the predictions of the 3-good, 3-factor Heckscher–Ohlin model, the paper proposes that the rise in real wages in Pakistan in the mid-1970s could be due to emigration.

III.2 Simulation Exercises on Effects of Emigration on Wages

Another methodology that has been applied to estimate the effects of emigration on wages has been based on using simulation models. O'Rourke and Williamson (1999) and Boyer et al. (1994) analyze the impact of emigration from Europe in the nineteenth century, simulating shocks in calibrated general equilibrium models, and conclude that emigration significantly increased real wages in Ireland and Sweden. The results from such studies are, however, specific to the model and its parameterization.

More recently, Budnik (2012) developed a partial equilibrium search and matching model with migration flows for Poland following the EU enlargement. Between 2003 and 2007, the fraction of Polish permanent residents staying abroad increased from 3 percent to 9 percent. She simulates the model to assess the effect of emigration on Polish wages; and calculates the deviation of the predicted wage rate from the actual as well from a counterfactual scenario that assumes emigration rate stabilized at the 2002 level. The implied half-elasticity (log wage to emigration rate) from Budnik (2012) equals 0.13, and is lower than the estimate in Mishra (2007a) or in Aydemir and Borjas (2007). The increase in the emigration rate explains about 8 percent of the increase in wages between 2003 and 2007 in Budnik (2012).

III.3 Econometric Studies Using Region-level Variation

In general, studies using regional variation either focus on specific cities or address the question of how different regions are affected relative to one another. Hanson et al. (2002), Hanson (2004) and Hanson (2007) comprise econometric studies on labor market effects of emigration where the source of variation used is across regions. Hanson et al. (2002) examine the impact of illegal migration measured by the number of person-hours the US Border Patrol spent policing the border from 1987 to 1997 on the wages in the border cities of the USA and Mexico. Hanson (2004) addresses the question of how globalization after NAFTA (North American Free Trade Agreement) affected the regional wage structure in

Mexico, including a measure of regional opportunities to migrate to the USA.

Similarly, Hanson (2007) examines how emigration has affected regional labor supply and regional earnings in Mexico. Mexico has a long history of sending migrants to the USA. Since the early 1900s, emigration rates have varied widely across Mexican regions, with individuals from west-central states having the highest propensity to migrate. The paper exploits regional persistence in emigration behavior by classifying states as either high migration or low migration to the USA, as measured by state emigration rates in the 1950s. Evidence in Hanson (2007) shows that, controlling for observable factors, wages in high-migration states rose relative to low-migration states by as much as 6–9 percent. This implies an elasticity of wages with respect to the labor supply of 0.7–0.8. It can be seen below that this elasticity is higher than those estimated based on national-level studies. This is expected since it captures both the direct effects of emigration on the labor supply and any indirect effects of historical emigration patterns on current regional wage growth.

More recently, Dustmann et al. (2012) used region-level variation to estimate the effect of emigration on wages in Poland, a large European country. One unique feature of this study is that, rather than identifying emigrants based on census data and survey information from the destination countries, the authors use detailed information on all emigrants measured in the source country. Specifically, when a household member is not present, another member of the household is asked about the person's whereabouts. Using within-region variation, the authors find that emigration has a positive effect on the wages of those who do not migrate. Similar to the case of Mexico, the effect is strongest in the middle of the income distribution. The results in Dustmann et al. (2012) are supported by an instrumental-variables strategy using variations in economic conditions in the main destination countries. Their estimates suggest that a 1 percent increase in the size of the emigrant labor force increases wages by between 0.01 and 0.02 percent in Poland. This compares with Mishra's (2007a) partial elasticity of 0.033 (evaluated at 10 percent emigrant share, and the coefficient estimate of 0.33).[2]

Similarly, looking at a specific sector, Lucas (1987) examines the effect of temporary labor emigration to South Africa's mines on wages in tea and tobacco plantations in five African countries. He finds that, in both Malawi and Mozambique, emigration to South Africa's mines has increased wage costs for the local estate and plantation operators.

The potential problems associated with using variation across regions have been discussed extensively in the context of immigration (Borjas et al., 1997). Applying the same logic, non-emigrants may respond by moving labor into or capital away from high-emigration regions. Such neutralizing flows of labor or capital within the country would underestimate the impact on wages. Just as in case of immigration, the labor market impact may be measurable only at the national level. Moreover, regional-level studies analyze how emigration has a differential effect across regions – in other words, how earnings in states/regions that experienced higher emigration were affected relative to those that sent fewer migrants – and does not address the question of how emigration affects source-country wages for the nation as a whole. This brings us to the discussion of national-level studies on emigration and wages.

III.4 National-level Studies

Mishra (2007a) is the first econometric study of the effect of emigration on national wages in a source country that examines empirically the effect of Mexican emigration to the USA on wages in Mexico using data from the Mexican and the US censuses from 1970 to 2000. The questions addressed in the paper are: how does emigration affect real wages in Mexico? What is the direction and magnitude of the impact? What are the implications of emigration for (i) wage inequality across schooling groups and (ii) national income distribution between labor and the other factors in Mexico?

The identification strategy to estimate the impact of emigration on Mexican wages follows Borjas (2003) in that she utilizes variation across schooling and experience groups in the labor force, and over time. Emigration is assumed to be exogenous in the baseline specification. However, she also addresses concerns about endogeneity and self-selection biases in the estimates.

Mishra (2007a) finds a strong and positive impact of the outflow of workers on wages in Mexico. A 10 percent decrease in the number of Mexican workers due to emigration in a skill group (defined by schooling and experience) increases the average wage in that skill group by about 4 percent. The estimates suggest that the outflow of Mexican workers to the USA between 1970 and 2000 has increased the wage of an average Mexican worker by about 8 percent.

The impact on wages, moreover, differs dramatically across schooling groups, with the greatest increase in wages being for the higher-wage earners (those with 12–15 years of schooling). Hence the estimates in this paper suggest that emigration could serve as one possible explanation for the increasing wage inequality in Mexico. However, emigration as a channel to explain the increasing wage inequality in developing countries has received little attention in the literature.[3]

In the context of national-level studies, Mexico offers an ideal case to study because almost all emigration from Mexico is to the USA. More than 95 percent of the international migrants from Mexico go to the USA (Woodruff and Zenteno, 2001). This gives an excellent opportunity to use the US data sources to study the effect on a source country's labor market.[4] Further, the outflow of workers is sizable in proportion to the Mexican labor force. In 2000, Mexican emigrants constituted about 16 percent of the labor force, or approximately one out of seven Mexican workers migrate to the USA. The rate of outflow is particularly striking in the higher schooling categories. Mexican emigrants in the USA with 12–15 years of schooling constituted a little less than half of the corresponding labor force in Mexico.[5] Hence, there is evidence of some brain drain from Mexico.[6] There are several countries that lose high proportions of their educated labor force because of migration. Hence the estimated impact on wages of highly educated workers in Mexico would only serve as a lower bound of the effect in many other source countries.

Since Mishra (2007a) provides a generic framework for looking at the issue of the effect of emigration on wages, I discuss the methods in Mishra (2007a) briefly here. Following Borjas (2003), the regression equation in Mishra (2007a) is specified as

$$w_{ijt} = \delta m_{ijt} + s_i + v_j + \pi_t + s_i^* \pi_t + v_j^* \pi_t + s_i^* v_j + \varepsilon_{ijt} \qquad (9.3)$$

where w_{ijt} is the mean value of monthly earnings (in logs) for workers in Mexico with education level i, experience j and observed in year t. s_i, v_j and π_t are vectors of fixed effects indicating the group's schooling, work experience and time respectively, which control for differences in wages across schooling, experience groups and over time. The interaction terms $(s_i{}^*\pi_t)$ and $(v_j{}^*\pi_t)$ are introduced to control for the possibility that the returns to schooling and experience could change over time. The interaction terms $(s_i{}^* v_j)$ control for the possibility that the experience profile for wages could differ across schooling groups. Further, the last several decades have been a period of turmoil for Mexico, with four currency crises since 1970 for which adequate controls are needed in equation (9.5).[7]

The regressions are weighted by the number of workers in Mexico in cell (i, j, t). The parameter δ gives the percentage change in wages due to a 1 percent change in the number of Mexican workers due to emigration. δ is identified by within-skill-group changes in emigrant shares over time.

III.5 Self-selection and Endogeneity Issues

Mishra (2007a) addresses the issue of self-selection of emigrants from the population of Mexico. To address this concern, she estimates the impact of emigration on the wages of a sub-sample of Mexican workers from low-migration states of Mexico. The sample selection problem can be expected to be less severe in this sub-sample because it has 'all' the workers and not just the ones who decide not to migrate. As a validation, she finds that emigration has a strong and positive effect on the wages in low-migration states as well. The fact that the impact of emigrant supply shocks gets transmitted to the country as a whole is striking, and provides evidence that the results are not likely to be driven by sample selection but rather through supply effects that are transmitted throughout the integrated Mexican labor market.

In order to address the other concern of endogeneity, Mishra (2007a) applies the idea from the sociology literature that 'social capital formation' (based on social connections to the US migrants) is an important factor explaining USA–Mexico migration. This allows use of an instrumental-variables strategy with historical migration rates (as a proxy for networks) as an instrument for current migration rates. The strong and positive impact of emigration on Mexican wages is reinforced after addressing the potential bias owing to endogeneity.

Mishra (2007a) was followed by a new strand of literature looking at the effect of emigration on wages in various source countries. Aydemir and Borjas (2007) use data from the Canadian, Mexican and US censuses, and find that labor supply shifts are associated with opposite-signed change in wages for migrants in receiving and in sending countries. For Mexico, they confirm the finding in Mishra (2007a) of a positive correlation between log monthly earnings of Mexican workers in a particular skill group and the emigration rate of that group. The estimated wage elasticity in Aydemir and Borjas (2007) is 0.56, indicating that a 10 percent emigrant-induced reduction in labor supply increases monthly earnings by 5.6 percent. Further, as in Mishra (2007a), Aydemir and Borjas (2007) also find that emigration is associated with increased wage inequality in Mexico, with a reduction in relative wages of workers at the bottom of the skill distribution.

Bouton et al. (2011) estimate the effect of emigration from Moldova on Moldovan wages. Moldova's emigrant population comprises 30 percent of its labor force. In the baseline specification, the authors estimate an individual-level wage regression including the emigrant share as an explanatory variable. They find that a 10 percent increase in Moldova's emigration rate is associated with a 3.2 percent increase in wages. Their estimates are similar to those of Mishra (2007a). One interesting finding in the study is that the effect differs significantly across sectors. For example, they find that the wage elasticity in construction and service sectors is double that in agriculture and industry. The authors argue that the differences across sectors could be explained by recent changes in labor demand in each sector. For example, the lack of job creation in the agricultural sector and the expansion of the construction and service sectors could be driving the results.

Borjas (2008) uses the national-level approach to analyze the effect of both labor inflows into and outflows from Puerto Rico. His preferred estimates suggest that a 10 percent migration-induced reduction in the number of workers increases the wages of Puerto Rican workers left behind by 2.1 percent, whereas a 10 percent immigration-induced increase in supply reduces wages by 4 percent. The Puerto Rican case is unique in that it allows estimation of wage responses to both immigration and emigration in the same market at the same time. The estimates of labor inflows are similar to those in Borjas (2003), whereas that of outflows is broadly similar to Mishra (2007a) and Aydemir and Borjas (2007). The paper also estimates the effect of 'net migration rates' (calculated as the difference between in-migration and out-migration rates), and finds that the wage elasticity associated with a 10 percent migration-induced net shift in supply is −0.30.

Finally, Gagnon (2011) applied the national-level approach to study the effect of emigration on wages in Honduras. Honduras is a good example to study as Hurricane Mitch in 1998 constituted an exogenous shock, which was followed by a wave of emigration. By 2006, more than 11 percent of households in Honduras had at least one migrant abroad. As a proportion of the country's population, emigrants comprised 5.8 percent, lower than that in Mexico. Using the same empirical specification as in Mishra (2007a) with schooling-experience-time as the unit of analysis, the study finds that a 10 percent labor supply shift due to emigration yields a 2 percent increase in wages in Honduras. However, using individual-level data, and instrumenting for the emigration rate by US wages, they find much bigger estimates: a 10 percent increase in emigration is associated with a 10 percent increase in wages. These estimates are significantly higher than those in any other study on emigration, which raises the question of the validity of the instruments, which is not established rigorously in the paper.

Overall, the national-level studies provide robust evidence that emigration raises wages in source countries. Importantly, the effect is statistically and economically significant. Table 9.3 provides a summary of the estimates from the national-level studies. The baseline estimates in these studies range from 2 percent to 5.5 percent increase in wages owing to a 10 percent emigrant supply shock. An interesting area for further research would be to explore the wage effects of emigration using cross-country data on wages and emigrant supply shocks, and to determine what country characteristics drive differences in estimates across countries.

Table 9.3 Effect of 10 percent emigrant supply shock on source countries

Country	Estimate (%)	Source
Mexico	4.4	Mishra (2007a)
Mexico	5.6	Aydemir and Borjas (2007)
Moldova	3.2	Bouton et al. (2011)
Puerto Rico	2.1	Borjas (2008)
Honduras	2.0	Gagnon (2011)

IV. WELFARE IMPLICATIONS

There are at least two key quantifiable implications of the estimated impact of emigration on real wages. First, the variation across schooling groups has implications for wage inequality within the source countries. Second, the estimated elasticity can be used to compute simple welfare measures based on a standard partial equilibrium model of labor demand and labor supply.

IV.1 Emigration and Wage Inequality

The estimates of the effect of emigration on wages can be used to calculate the wage impact in different schooling groups. For example, Mishra (2007a) looks closely at the estimated increase in wages due to emigration between 1990 and 2000 because the Mexican Census data show increasing wage inequality during this period. As shown in Figure 9.1, between 1990 and 2000 the relative wages of high-school graduates increased by 11 percent, of those with some college education by 21 percent and of college graduates by 8 percent (relative to high-school dropouts). Using the estimated coefficients, the outflow of workers between 1990 and 2000 increased the relative wages of high-school graduates by 4 percent and those with some college education by 3 percent (relative to high-school dropouts). Thus the estimated impact of emigration accounts for approximately 37 percent of the increase in relative wages of high-school graduates and 14 percent of the increase in relative wages of those with some college education. The greater impact of emigration on wages of workers with 12–15 years of schooling is driven by the highest emigration rates of this group, and the fact that the labor demand elasticity is assumed constant across schooling groups. Further, emigration does not explain the increase in relative wages of college graduates.

The magnitude of the positive effect of emigration on the wages of high-

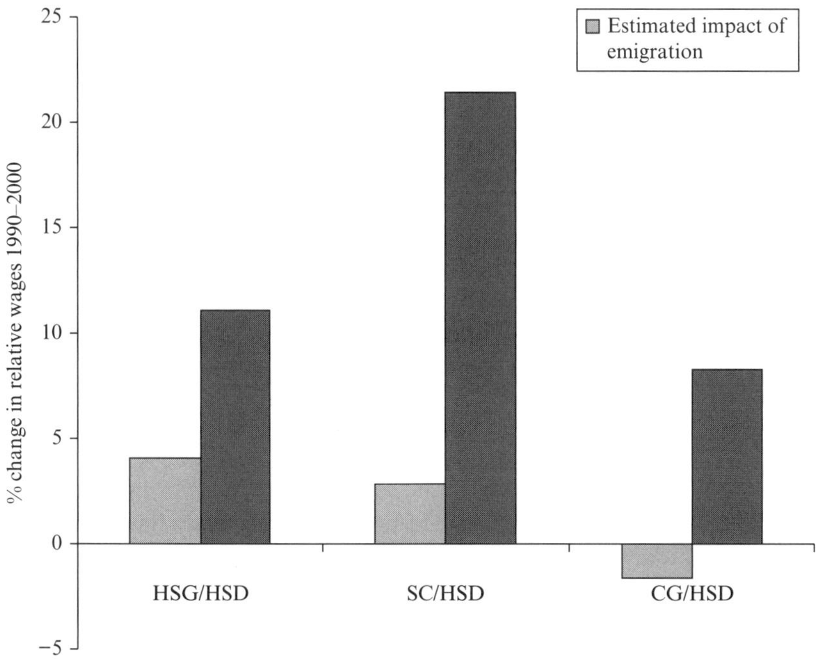

Notes: The figures are for males, in the labor force, who are not enrolled in school, and have work experience of 1–40 years, and report positive monthly earnings. HSD = high-school dropouts; HSG = high-school graduates; SC = those with some college schooling; CG = college graduates. Relative wages are measured as the ratio of real monthly earnings in schooling category *s* (*s* = HSG, SC, CG) to the real monthly earnings of HSD. Monthly earnings are deflated by the CPI from the IMF.

Figure 9.1 Emigration and increase in wage inequality in Mexico: 1990–2000

school dropouts is higher than that on the wages of college graduates; hence emigration leads to a decrease in the relative wage of college graduates. Since emigration does not explain the entire rise in wage inequality, Mishra (2007a) argues that it should be treated as a complementary explanation for the rising wage inequality in Mexico. The estimates in the case of Mexico suggest that it could be an important factor. Yet emigration as a channel to explain increasing wage inequality in developing countries has received little attention in the literature (Robbins, 2002). An interesting area for future research would be to explore the distributional effects of emigration on source countries, and to correlate them with country characteristics.

IV.2 Welfare Implications

The estimated impact of emigration on wages can be used to compute simple welfare measures based on the standard model of labor demand and supply. The simple economic model of labor demand and supply is an important starting point to quantify the welfare implications. It has been used in the literature before in the context of immigration and capital flows (Borjas, 1995; MacDougall, 1960). The aim of the simple model is to quantify the welfare effects due to movement of labor, everything else remaining unchanged.[8]

Welfare is measured by GDP accruing to those who have stayed behind (TSB) in Mexico. Consider a single numeraire good and its production function given as

$$Q = F(K, L) \tag{9.4}$$

Where K is the fixed factor assumed to be internationally immobile, L is the labor employed in production and Q is the gross domestic product. Figure 9.2 shows the simple model of labor demand and supply.

The pre-emigration equilibrium wage is w_0. A large emigration flow

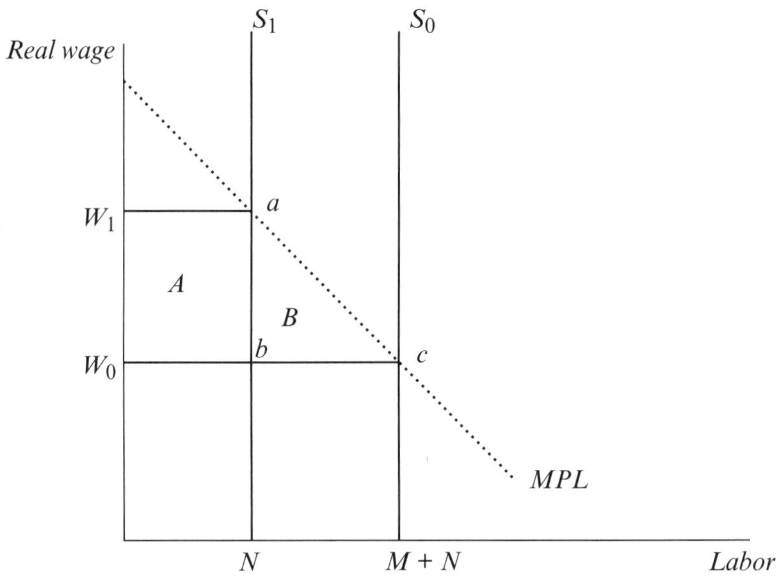

Figure 9.2 Emigration and wages in a simple labor demand supply framework

of a magnitude M of workers reduces the labor force from $(N + M)$ to N. Wage rate as a result increases from w_0 to w_1. The workers who have stayed behind gain an area equal to w_0w_1ab (rectangle region A), owners of the fixed factors in the economy lose an area equal to w_0w_1ac (rectangle region A + triangle region B) and the country as a whole loses the triangle abc (region B). The triangle abc (region B) can be termed the '*emigration loss*'. The emigration loss arises because the cost of employing the infra-marginal workers who migrate is less than the value of their marginal product. The surplus on these workers is therefore lost due to emigration, which imposes a cost on those who stayed behind.

As a fraction of the post-emigration GDP:

$$\text{Emigration loss (triangle } B \text{ in Figure 9.2)} = (1/2)sem^2 \qquad (9.5)$$

Gain to workers who have stayed behind (rectangle A in Figure 9.2) = $\boldsymbol{sem}$ (9.6)

Loss to the owners of fixed factors (A $+B$ in Figure 9.2) $= \frac{1}{2}sem^2 + sem$ (9.7)

where $e = e_{LL}\big|_{L=N} = \frac{\Delta w}{\Delta L}\frac{N}{w}$, $s = \frac{wN}{wN + rK}$, $m = \frac{M}{N}$, s is the share of labor in GDP, e is the percentage change in wages due to a 1 percent change in the labor force, where the elasticity is measured at the post-emigration labor force and m is the ratio of emigrants to the workforce in the home country.[9] The emigration loss and distributive impact as a result of flow of workers between 1970 and 2000 can be estimated using equations (9.5)–(9.7).

In Mishra (2007a), the estimated change in wages of a typical worker in Mexico due to flow of emigrants between 1970 and 2000 (e^*m) is around 8 percent. The assumed share of labor income in GDP (s) is 0.7 (Borjas, 1995, 2003; Hall and Jones, 1999). The emigrant share of the Mexican workforce (m) estimated from the 2000 Mexican and US censuses is about 16 percent. The estimated emigration loss to Mexico is about 0.5 percent of Mexico's GDP in 2000. The economic loss from emigration in a $580 billion economy is about $3 billion per year. The estimated welfare loss is lower than the official worker remittances to Mexico, which were about 1 percent of GDP in 2000 (IMF).[10] The emigration loss would also be easily outweighed by the big gains of the migrants themselves. The emigration loss, however, is higher in percentage terms than the estimate of immigration surplus of 0.1 percent of GDP for the US economy in Borjas (1995). Borjas (1995) simulates the partial equilibrium model using outside information on labor demand elasticity, while Mishra (2007a) is based on estimated elasticity from Mexican data.

Table 9.4 Emigration loss and remittances

	Emigration loss e=0.3	Emigration loss e=0.4	Remittances (as % of GDP) average 1980–2002
Antigua and Barbuda	1.5	2.0	3.0
Barbados	1.1	1.5	2.3
Belize	0.9	1.2	4.7
Dominica	1.7	2.3	8.4
Dominican Republic	0.2	0.2	5.3
Grenada	3.0	4.0	11.0
Guyana	1.9	2.5	1.9
Haiti	0.1	0.2	10.1
Jamaica	1.3	1.7	7.4
St Kitts and Nevis	2.6	3.4	6.9
St Lucia	0.6	0.7	4.0
St Vincent and the Grenadines	1.4	1.9	7.2
Suriname	2.4	3.1	0.5
Trinidad and Tobago	0.7	0.9	0.3
Average	1.4	1.8	5.2

Note: e denotes the elasticity of factor price of labor (i.e., percentage change in wages resulting from a 1 percent change in the size of the labor force). See text for details on calculation of emigration loss.

Source: Author's calculations.

Though aggregate losses are somewhat small, there is a significant distributional impact. The gain to the workers who have stayed behind is about 5.9 percent of GDP and the loss to the owners of the fixed factors is about 6.4 percent of GDP, the difference being the estimated aggregate economic loss to Mexico. Thus the estimated distributive impact is about 12–13 times the aggregate economic loss to Mexico.

Mishra (2007b) also estimates the emigration losses for several Caribbean countries. Table 9.4 shows the estimates of emigration loss to individual Caribbean countries as a percentage of GDP. Since elasticities and the share of labor in GDP are assumed to be the same for all countries, the differences in emigration losses come only from differences in the emigration rates across countries. On average, official remittances outweigh the emigration loss for the region. Even under the assumption of high elasticity, except for Guyana, Suriname and Trinidad and Tobago, official remittances outweigh emigration loss in all countries. Also, since the wage differentials between the Caribbean and OECD countries are large, the emigration loss would be easily outweighed by the gains of the migrants

Table 9.5 Emigration loss due to high-skilled migration

	Emigration loss $e=0.3$	Emigration loss $e=0.4$	Remittances (as % of GDP) average 1980–2002
Antigua and Barbuda	2.0	2.7	3.0
Barbados	1.8	2.4	2.3
Belize	1.9	2.6	4.7
Dominica	1.9	2.5	8.4
Dominican Republic	0.2	0.3	5.3
Grenada	3.3	4.3	11.0
Guyana	3.6	4.7	1.9
Haiti	3.1	4.2	10.1
Jamaica	3.3	4.3	7.4
St Kitts and Nevis	2.8	3.7	6.9
St Lucia	2.3	3.0	4.0
St Vincent and the Grenadines	3.2	4.3	7.2
Suriname	1.0	1.4	0.5
Trinidad and Tobago	2.8	3.8	0.3
Average	2.4	3.2	5.2

Note: e denotes the elasticity of factor price of labor (i.e., percentage change in wages resulting from a 1 percent change in the size of the labor force). See text for details on calculation of emigration loss.

Source: Author's calculations.

themselves. However, redistributive impact of emigration is significant. On average, the gain to the workers who have stayed behind is 6 percent of GDP and the loss to the owners of the other factors is about 8 percent of GDP. Even for Trinidad and Tobago, where the emigration losses are relatively small (in relation to remittances), a sizable redistribution exists in favor of the workers.

Further, *ceteris paribus*, the emigration loss due to emigration of skilled labor is significant. The estimates in Table 9.5 show that the emigration loss as a fraction of GDP due to movement of high-skilled workers (everything else remaining unchanged) is much larger. The aggregate emigration rate combines the emigration rates of the high- as well as the low-skilled. As lower-skill groups have smaller emigration rates, their inclusion results in a smaller measure of emigration rates. If instead, only the high-skilled workers are considered, the emigration rates are considerably higher. Consequently the emigration loss is also larger. Still, remittances outweigh or almost equal the emigration loss due to high-skilled migration for the region as a whole and for most of the countries (except Guyana, Suriname, and Trinidad and Tobago).

V. CONCLUSIONS AND POLICY IMPLICATIONS

This survey summarizes the empirical literature on the effect of emigration on wages in a source country. Overall, the literature finds substantial evidence that there is a strong and positive relationship between emigration and wages in source countries. The impact of emigration on wages has important implications also for wage inequality across schooling groups and for national income distribution between labor and other factors. The measured welfare impact on those who have stayed behind in the sending country is based on the very simple static partial equilibrium framework.

Importantly, there may be other counteracting forces, such as the impact on human capital formation (see, e.g., Beine et al., 2008), positive external effects through networks and diaspora, remittances and so on that may outweigh this loss and result in a net benefit to the source country. Also, if source countries have some market power in the world market, emigration may also affect the terms of trade of Mexico. Quantifying how these additional channels through emigration can affect the welfare of source-country workers who have stayed behind is a subject for further research.

Even if countries incur a net loss due to emigration, as predicted by a static partial equilibrium model, a border tax might not be the most reasonable policy response. Appealing to the pioneering work of Bhagwati in the 1970s and 1980s on policy responses to emigration, an argument could be made for a border tax on migrants (similar to a Tobin tax). The tax was proposed by Bhagwati (1976), with the prior that developing countries lose due to migration. It is in principle also an extension of the idea of progressive income taxation – the improvement of the well-being of migrants to be taxed for the benefit of those left behind. The main reasons why the border tax is not reasonable are the problems in implementing such a tax. Taxes can also have distortionary effects. Since the absolute number of migrants from, say, the Caribbean countries is not very large, the per capita tax rate will have to be onerous to raise a sizable revenue. In fact, the USA is the only country that taxes individuals on the basis of citizenship rather than place of residence.

Retaining workers, particularly the high-skilled, without the possibility of taxes would be facilitated by reorienting education. The high rates of emigration from many regions, particularly Africa and the Caribbean, are due not only to the 'pull factor', that is, higher wages abroad, but also the limited opportunities for highly, but similarly, educated people at home (the 'push factor'). One approach to creating the right incentives is to reorient the higher education system towards providing skills in demand within the region, in particular the services sector, which dominates these economies. Such reorientation could include, for example, the establishment of hotel management institutes or specialized banking and finance institutes. It is particularly important for those regions to consider the possibilities for reorienting education, where a major portion of the cost of education of their citizens is covered by education subsidies. Governments might reap higher returns by investing in education infrastructure that leads to more retention of the high-skilled.

Since the international experience has been that it is difficult to prevent emigration, the real policy challenge is how countries can maximize the benefits from their population living and working overseas. Remittances should be the most immediate focus, as they can affect growth through investment, both physical and human. Evidence from micro-level studies suggests that remittances lead to greater human and physical capital investment (see Edwards and Ureta's 2003 study of El Salvador, Hanson and Woodruff's 2003 and Woodruff and Zenteno's 2001 studies of Mexico, and Lucas's 1987 study of Africa). Countries need to recognize the importance of remittances and improve recording of the data.

NOTES

1. See Borjas (1994, 1995) and Friedberg and Hunt (1995) for surveys of the empirical literature. The theoretical literature on international movement of factors includes, for example, Bhagwati and Hamada (1974), Rivera-Batiz (1989) and Quibria (1989).
2. Note that the explanatory variable in Mishra (2007a) is the ratio of emigrants to residents.
$$\beta = \frac{\partial \ln w}{\partial\left(\frac{M}{N}\right)} = \frac{\partial \ln w}{\partial \ln M} * \frac{\partial \ln M}{\partial\left(\frac{M}{N}\right)} \rightarrow \frac{\partial \ln w}{\partial \ln M} = \beta * \frac{M}{N}.$$
3. Robbins (2002) and Zhu and Trefler (2005) provide evidence for increasing wage inequality in developing countries.
4. Chiquiar and Hanson (2005) also merge US and Mexican Census data for 1990 to examine who migrates from Mexico to the USA. They find evidence of intermediate/positive self-selection in terms of observable skills, which is consistent with the findings in this chapter.
5. Source: author's calculations from Mexican and US censuses. The figures are for individuals in the age group 16–65 years, and are a part of the labor force. Individuals in the labor force are those who are defined by the censuses as being at work or seeking work in a particular reference week.
6. See Commander et al. (2002) for a survey of the literature on brain drain. The term brain drain is used to denote migration of high-skilled workers. I do not quantify any 'drain' effect in the chapter due, for example, to negative human capital externalities. Hence the term 'brain migration' could be used as an alternative.
7. Following the 1980s crises, there was a series of trade and investment reforms in

Mexico, including GATT membership in 1985, investment reforms in the 1980s and the implementation of the North American Free Trade Agreement (NAFTA) in 1994. These shocks are likely to be correlated with emigration from Mexico. The impact of the economy-wide shocks would be captured through the period fixed effects. The shocks, which have differential impact on schooling and age groups, would be captured through the interaction of the period fixed effects with schooling and experience respectively.

8. Davis and Weinstein (2002) simulate the welfare impact due to inflow of both labor and capital into the USA.
9. The expressions in (9.11)–(9.13) are analogous to Borjas's (1995) study of immigration.
10. It is, however, important to note that the official remittance figures are under-reported since they exclude large amounts of unrecorded remittances.

REFERENCES

Altonji, J. and D. Card (1991). 'The effects of immigration on the labor market outcomes of less-skilled natives', in J. Abowd and R. Freeman (eds), *Immigration, Trade, and the Labor Market*. Chicago, IL: University of Chicago Press, pp. 201–34.

Aydemir, Abdurrahman and George J. Borjas (2007). 'Cross-country variation in the impact of international migration: Canada, Mexico, and the United States', *Journal of the European Economic Association*, **5**(4), 663–708.

Beine, Michel, Frederic Docquier and Hillel Rapoport (2008). 'Brain drain and human capital formation in developing countries: winners and losers', *The Economic Journal*, **118**(April), 631–52.

Bhagwati, J. (1976). *The Brain Drain and Taxation. Theory and Empirical Analysis*, Amsterdam: North Holland.

Bhagwati, J.N. and K. Hamada (1974). 'The brain drain, international integration of markets for professionals and unemployment: a theoretical analysis', *Journal of Development Economics*, **1**(1), 19–42.

Borjas, G.J. (1994). 'The economics of immigration', *Journal of Economic Literature*, **32**(4), 1667–717.

Borjas, G.J. (1995). 'The economic benefits of immigration', *Journal of Economic Perspectives*, **9**(2), 3–22.

Borjas, George (2001). 'Does immigration grease the wheels of the labor market?', *Brookings Papers on Economic Activity*, **1**, 69–119.

Borjas, G.J. (2003). 'The labor demand curve is downward sloping: reexamining the impact of immigration on the labor market', *Quarterly Journal of Economics*, **118**(4), 1335–74.

Borjas, George (2008). 'Labor outflows and labor inflows in Puerto Rico', *Journal of Human Capital*, **2**(1), 32–68.

Borjas, George J., Richard B. Freeman and Lawrence F. Katz (1997). 'How much do immigration and trade affect labor market outcomes?' *Brookings Papers on Economic Activity*, **1**, 1–67.

Bouton, L., P. Saumik and E.R. Tiongson (2011). 'The impact of emigration on source country wages: evidence from Republic of Moldova', World Bank Policy Research Working Paper No. WPS 5764.

Boyer, G.R., T.J. Hatton and K. O'Rourke (1994). Impact of emigration on real wages in Ireland, 1850–1914. In Timothy J. Hatton and Jeffrey G. Williamson (eds), *Migration and the International Labor Market, 1850–1939*, London and New York: Routledge, pp. 221–39.

Budnik, Katarzyna B. (2012). 'Impact of emigration on wages: a search equilibrium analysis for Poland', mimeo, National Bank of Poland, May.

Card, David (1990). 'The impact of the Mariel boatlift on the Miami labor market', *Industrial and Labor Relations Review*, **43**(2), 245–57.
Carrington, W.J. and Enrica Detragiache (1998). 'How big is the brain drain?', IMF Working Paper 98/102, Washington: International Monetary Fund.
Chiquiar, D. and Gordon H. Hanson (2005). 'International migration, self-selection, and the distribution of wages: evidence from Mexico and the United States', *Journal of Political Economy*, **113**(2), 239–81.
Clark, M. and David A. Jaeger (2002). 'Natives, the foreign born, and high school equivalents: new evidence on returns to the GED', Working Paper No. 462, Princeton University Industrial Relations Section.
Commander, S., M. Kangasniemi and L.A. Winters (2002). 'The brain drain: curse or boon? A survey of the literature'. Mimeo.
Costanzo, J., C. Davis, C. Irazi, D. Goodkind and R. Ramirez (2001). 'Evaluating components of international migration: the residual foreign born population', US Bureau of the Census, Division Working Paper No. 61.
Davis, D.R. and D.E. Weinstein (2002). 'Technological superiority and losses from migration', NBER Working Paper No. 8971.
Docquier, F. and Abdeslam Marfouk (2004). 'Measuring the international mobility of skilled workers', World Bank Policy Research Working Paper No. 3381.
Docquier, F. and Abdeslam Marfouk (2005). 'International migration by educational attainment (1990–2000)', Dataset Release 1.1, Washington, DC: World Bank.
Dustmann, Christian, Tommaso Frattini and Anna Rosso (2012). 'The effect of emigration from Poland on Polish wages', CReAM Discussion Paper Series 1229, Centre for Research and Analysis of Migration (CReAM), Department of Economics, University College London.
Edwards, Alejandra Cox and Manuelita Ureta (2003). 'International migration, remittances, and schooling: evidence from El Salvador', *Journal of Development Economics*, **72**(2), 429–61.
Friedberg, R.M. (2001). 'The impact of mass migration on the Israeli labor market', *Quarterly Journal of Economics*, **116**(4), 1373–408.
Friedberg, R.M. and J. Hunt (1995). 'The impact of immigrants on host country wages, employment and growth', *Journal of Economic Perspectives*, **9**(2), 23–44.
Gagnon, Jason (2011). 'Stay with US? The impact of emigration on wages in Honduras', OECD Development Centre Working Paper No. 300.
Gonzalez, Arturo (2003). 'The education and wages of immigrant children: the impact of age at arrival', *Economics of Education Review*, **22**(2), 203–12.
Grogger, J. and S.J. Trejo (2002). *Falling Behind or Moving Up? The Intergenerational Progress of Mexican Americans*. San Francisco: Public Institute of California.
Hall, R. and C.I. Jones (1999). 'Why do some countries produce so much more output per worker than others?', *Quarterly Journal of Economics*, **114**(1), 83–116.
Hanson, Gordon (2004). 'What has happened to wages in Mexico since NAFTA?', in Toni Estevade-Ordal, Dani Rodrik, Alan Taylor and Andres Velasco (eds), *FTAA and Beyond: Prospects for Integration in the Americas*. Cambridge, MA: Harvard University Press, pp. 505–38.
Hanson, Gordon (2007). 'Emigration, labor supply and earnings in Mexico', in George J. Borjas (ed.), *Mexican Immigration*. Chicago, IL: University of Chicago Press (for NBER), pp. 289–328.
Hanson, G.H. and A. Spilimbergo (1999). 'Illegal immigration, border enforcement and relative wages: evidence from apprehensions at the U.S.–Mexico border', *American Economic Review*, **89**, 1337–57.
Hanson, G.H. and Christopher Woodruff (2003). 'Emigration and educational attainment in Mexico', mimeo, University of California at San Diego.
Hanson, G.H., R. Robertson and A. Spilimbergo (2002). 'Does border enforcement protect U.S. workers from illegal immigration?', *The Review of Economics and Statistics*, **84**(1), 74–92.
Hanson, G.H., K.F. Scheve, M.J. Slaughter and A. Spilimbergo (2001). 'Immigration and the US economy: labor market impact, illegal entry and policy choices', in T. Boeri,

G.H. Hanson and B. McCormick (eds), *Immigration Policy and the Welfare System*. Oxford: Oxford University Press, pt 2.
Lucas, R.E. (1987). 'Emigration to South Africa's mines', *American Economic Review*, **77**, 313–30.
MacDougall, G.D.A. (1960). 'The benefits and costs of private investment from abroad', *Economic Record*, **36**, 13–35.
Mahmood, Z. (1991). 'Emigration and wages in an open economy: some evidence from Pakistan', *Pakistan Development Review*, **30**, 243–62.
Mishra, Prachi (2007a). 'Emigration and wages in source countries: evidence from Mexico', *Journal of Development Economics*, **82**, 180–99.
Mishra, Prachi (2007b). 'Emigration and brain-drain: evidence from the Caribbean', *The B.E. Journals in Economic Analysis & Policy*, **7**(1), Article 24.
New Immigrant Survey (2003). http://nis.princeton.edu/.
O'Rourke, K.H. and J.G. Williamson (1999). 'Mass migrations: impacts on labor markets, home and abroad' in *Globalization and History: The Evolution of a Nineteenth Century Atlantic Economy*. Cambridge, MA: MIT Press, pp. 145–66.
Quibria, M.G. (1989). 'International migration and real wages: is there any neo-classical ambiguity?', *Journal of Development Economics*, **31**(1), 177–83.
Rivera-Batiz, F.L. (1989). 'The impact of international migration on real wages: another look', *Journal of Development Economics*, **31**(1), 185–92.
Robbins, D. (2002). 'The impact of trade liberalization upon inequality in developing countries: a review of theory and evidence'. Mimeo.
Rosenzweig, M. (2005). 'International migration and global development', Northeastern Universities Development Conference Keynote Speech, Brown University, September (www.econ.brown.edu/econ/neudc05/dinner.pdf).
Stalker, P. (1994). *The Work of Strangers: A Survey of International Labor Migration*. Geneva: ILO.
US Census (2000). Integrated Public Use Microdata Series: Version 5.0 (machine-readable database). Minneapolis: University of Minnesota.
Woodruff, C. and R. Zenteno (2001). 'Remittances and micro enterprises in Mexico', IR/PS Working Paper.
Zhu, S. and D. Trefler (2005). 'Trade and wages in developing countries: catch up as a catalyst', *Journal of International Economics*, **65**, 21–48.

10. Migration, technology diffusion and institutional development at the origin

Olena Ivus and Alireza Naghavi

1. INTRODUCTION

International migration has reached an unprecedented pace and scale in recent years. As of 2010, 216 million people resided outside their country of origin compared to 156 million in 1992 (World Bank, 2011). Studies have shown that skilled workers are among the most likely classes to emigrate (Docquier and Marfouk, 2006; Docquier et al., 2007). Between 1990 and 2000, the share of high-skilled workers in the overall migrant population increased from 18.9 percent to 25.8 percent. Foreign-born workers with post-secondary education represented 34.6 percent of the OECD immigration population in 2000, when the share of world labor force with post-secondary education was just 11 percent. The destination patterns of these high-skilled migrants are quite pronounced. The countries enjoying the highest-skilled immigration are the USA (hosting 50 percent of total OECD high skilled immigrants worldwide), Canada (13.4 percent) and Australia (7.5 percent). In some small countries (e.g. Guyana, Jamaica and Haiti), immigrants make up 80 percent of the skilled labour force.

As a result of these trends, international migration of innovators has taken on greater priority for many countries. At one end we find developed countries, with their promise of economic stability, opportunity and entrenched democratic institutions. These countries compete to attract talent from abroad and, accordingly, many have shifted their immigration policy to a merit-based focus, including Canada, Australia and the UK. The USA is not far behind, with the US Senate passing a bill providing for talent-based immigration system in June of 2013.[1]

At the other end are the developing countries from which skilled migrants depart. For these countries, emigration is perceived as an alarming loss of human capital or 'brain drain', and a trend to be stifled through restrictive policies. However, as will be discussed below, obstructing mobility to prevent brain drain has proven ineffective. Such restrictions prevent a country from reaping gains from migration that could arise, for example, when high-skilled expatriates transfer knowledge attained abroad to their home countries. Bhagwati (2003) argues that source countries' policies should focus on organizing diaspora networks, and that this strategy is much more likely to succeed today than a retention policy. In fact, most attempts to control and manage skilled emigration by prohibition and taxation have failed (Lowell, 2001).

The literature on skilled migration has focused largely on the effects of migration on host and source countries. The pre-1990s literature was primarily concerned with the brain-drain phenomenon and identified various mechanisms through which skilled emigration could be detrimental to country welfare and growth (e.g. Berry and Soligo, 1969; Bhagwati and Hamada, 1974; Miyagiwa, 1991). More recent literature considered the possible benefits to source countries from the migration of skilled workers. This strand of literature argues that skilled emigration need not harm emerging and developing economies, and may even contribute to their development. Remittance transfers are the most direct way by which migrants can contribute to their home country's economy (Özden and Schiff, 2005). This literature has also examined the factors that turned source countries' brain drain into 'brain gain' (e.g. Stark et al., 1997; Vidal, 1998; Kapur et al., 2005; Docquier and Rapoport, 2012; Gibson and McKenzie, 2012). These studies show that brain gain can take several forms. For instance, the mere prospect of migration provides an incentive for human capital formation among potential immigrants (Mountford, 1997; Fan and Stark, 2007; Beine et al., 2001, 2008). *Ex post*, source countries benefit from any return of migrants who have acquired skills abroad (Mayr and Peri, 2009; Dustmann et al., 2011), and even the skilled migrants who do not return communicate foreign knowledge to their home countries through migrants' diaspora networks and close-knit, ethnic scientific communities (Saxenian, 1999, 2002; Saxenian et al., 2002; Kerr, 2008; Agrawal et al., 2011; Devan and Tewari, 2001).

Diaspora networks can increase source countries' access to foreign-produced knowledge without skilled emigrants returning home. Instead, skilled emigrants speed up the flow of knowledge between source and host countries. The influence of diaspora networks and return migration is particularly strong in China and India. Saxenian (1999) is one of the first studies to highlight the role of diaspora and ethnic professional networks in mutual aid, trust building and knowledge circulation. The author analyzed 11 443 high-tech start-up companies in Silicon Valley during the 1980–98 period and found that 25 percent of these companies had ethnic Chinese and Indian immigrants as senior executives. In addition, 40 percent of the companies in Taiwan's science-based industrial park in Hschinchu were started and managed by migrant returnees. Saxenian's study highlights the role of international, ethnic professional networks in the repatriation of skilled workers. The typical role of immigrant associations in mutual aid and trust building was extended internationally to facilitate access to capital, marketing skills and markets for Taiwanese start-ups. Saxenian (2002) and Saxenian et al. (2002, p. 25) provide evidence on Silicon Valley's ethnic networks and report that 82 percent of Chinese and Indian immigrant scientists and engineers 'share information about technology with colleagues in their native countries (and 28% do so on a regular basis)'.

Devan and Tewari (2001) also encourage developing countries to mobilize their diaspora brain resources, leverage expatriate talent and encourage emigrants to play an active role in the economic development of their home countries. This recommendation is supported by the apparent success of China and India in taking advantage of their brain banks abroad.

Against that background, we note that today's knowledge economy is fast-paced, fiercely competitive and worldwide in reach. To succeed in this environment where so many fail, participating firms are driven to seek out the brightest minds from talent pools across the world. The location of talent defines the geography of innovation, and so determines a country's prospect for development and growth. What role do economic planners and policy makers have in this recruitment race? What can governments do to give homegrown firms a competitive edge internationally, while also serving the general interests of the domestic economy?

As discussed above, the government response is nearly always to pass immigration reforms. This response serves as a frontal assault on the problem, and definitely creates the appearance of proactive, effective governance. However, there are other, more subtle ways to derive maximum benefits from skilled migration and contribute to the development of knowledge-based economy. Taking a lead role in the growth and strengthening of diaspora networks of expatriate talent is one such opportunity. Institutional reforms might also have a significant impact on the mobility of skilled workers and the diffusion of knowledge. Indeed, with skilled migration and innovative capacity taking on greater importance for many governments, the relationship between the two and their effect on growth has received a great deal of attention from researchers and policy makers. Given that innovators are the producers of intellectual property, home-country institutions that protect the latter have a central role to play in knowledge circulation and the maximization of brain gains from innovator migration. Home-country institutions are also likely to impact these countries' success in connecting to global innovation networks, which will in turn determine their ability to catch up with other innovative economies.

A phenomenon little explored in economic literature is the effect of international migration itself on home-country institutions. The first question that arises is whether or not international migration results in the depletion of active voice that promotes better institutions in the home country. Recent studies surveyed in the next section argue that institutional norms such as democratic values may in fact be transferred to the home country. The mobility of institutional norms through migration can in turn be linked with the mobility of knowledge and technology. Under what circumstances can migration play the same role as trade, introduced in Eaton and Kortum (2002) in the worldwide diffusion of technology? A primary attempt to disclose this mechanism is Naghavi and Strozzi (2011), which shows that gains from international emigration can be realized only if intellectual property rights institutions are sufficient to put the newly acquired knowledge to use in the form of patents in the source countries. Nevertheless, the interplay of international migration, home-country institutions and technology diffusion remains a vast unexplored field. We hope that this chapter can serve to emphasize the importance of this relationship and encourage further theoretical and empirical research to explain the facts regarding the trends and the correlations that connect its elements.

2. EMIGRATION AS AN ENGINE FOR INSTITUTIONAL DEVELOPMENT

As discussed above, the literature has traditionally focused on the economic consequences of migration for sending and receiving countries. The political impact of migration in terms of institutional development has received less attention in the literature. The quality of home-country institutions can also be endogenously determined as a function of migrants shaping development. Migration can affect institutions at home in several ways. First, emigration creates 'exit' and 'voice' alternatives, as described in Hirschman (1970). Briefly, in this context, exit is emigration to a country with relatively better institutions, while voice is remaining at home and protesting against unproductive activities and weak institutions. Exit obviously curtails the individual exiter's lobbying at home, and the direct effect of exit on institutions is similar to that of brain drain, in that it reduces the existing voice in the country. This effect is especially strong among skilled migrants, as typically additional education is associated with greater propensity for political activity. The alternative is to stay at home, organize opposition to the status quo, and seek improvements in home institutions.

When a country's emigrants are from the more educated segment of the society, emigration may generate a second indirect effect on institutional development at home. Skilled workers living abroad may acquire political influence in their host country, and gain experience with the various modern political and democratic institutions offered by developed host countries. Some of these migrants ultimately revisit their lobbying efforts there with fresh vigor, and with clear conceptions of the alternative institutions and systems for which to lobby.

So what is the net effect of migration on institutional development? Spilimbergo (2009) uses a novel empirical methodology to study the relationship between the quality of institutions in the country where emigrants study and the migrants' country of origin. The variables of interest are (i) the number of students abroad as a share of total population in the sending country (lagged five years to capture the effect of foreign education), (ii) the average level of democracy in the host country (to capture the type of political institution foreign students are exposed to) and (iii) the interaction of the two (to see whether the marginal effect of foreign education depends on the level of democracy in the host country). The paper demonstrates that foreign-trained individuals who acquire their education in democratic countries promote democratic values in their home countries. The author refers to this phenomenon as the 'transfer of norms'. Two micro studies, Batista and Vicente (2011) and Mahmoud et al. (2011), support this claim for Cape Verde and Moldova respectively.

Docquier et al. (2011) introduce support for a competing hypothesis introduced in Beine et al. (2001, 2008); namely that it is incentives for education caused by migration prospects rather than transfer of norms that is responsible for institutional development in the home country. They reach this conclusion by showing that both total emigration rate and human capital have a positive and significant effect on democracy and economic freedom in the home country. Their results suggest that the impact of skilled migration is ambiguous for institutional development in the home country because skilled migration in principle increases total emigration while reducing average human capital at the same time. The explanation provided for this is that the impact of emigration on home-country institutions is present only when the skilled remain in their country of origin.

Follow-up studies have used similar strategies to determine whether the concept of transfer of norms concept applies to other types of institutions. In the spirit of Spilimbergo (2009), Beine and Sekkat (2013) conduct a direct test of the exit versus voice argument by focusing on the quality of 'market-friendly' institutions, as measured by Kaufmann et al. (1999). More specifically, they construct four variables: total migration rate; skilled migration rate; and the weighted average of the levels of governance quality across countries of destination based on total and skilled migration. Institutions studied in this paper are (i) voice and accountability, (ii) control of corruption, (iii) government effectiveness and (iv) regulatory quality. Three interesting findings emerge. First, for both types of migration the coefficients are significant and negative for voice and accountability. This suggests that the 'exit' channel discussed above is present, where migration reduces active voice in the country. Second, the coefficient of the transfer of norms (the interaction) related to voice and accountability is positive and significant for both types of migration. This confirms the feedback effect of values and norms from diasporas to the natives in the original country. Third, the magnitude of the above-mentioned effects is larger under skilled relative to total migration. This completes the validation of the hypothesis that the level of education of emigrants matters – that is, foreign education training is what contributes more to an enhancement of domestic institutions.

2.1 Rent-seeking

Mariani (2007) develops a theoretical framework to show how skilled migration improves institutions in the home country by limiting rent-seeking and shifting the economy towards more entrepreneurial activities. The underlying assumption in this model is that only productive skills are mobile; therefore migration reduces the relative expected returns from rent-seeking, generating a reallocation of the remaining skilled workers from wasteful to productive activities.

We present a simplified version of the model here to emphasize the point regarding the mechanism at play. In the model, a nation is composed of homogeneous workers who can either carry out productive activities using their human capital to earn h or choose to engage in rent-seeking. Rent-seeking here is modeled as a meeting between the two types of agents, after which the rent-seeker extorts a fraction q of the worker's income, earning a total of qh. The proportion of rent-seekers and productive workers is identified by p and $1 - p$, respectively. For the sake of simplicity we assume that the number of rent-seekers exceeds the number of entrepreneurs (that is, $p > 1/2$). This leaves an income of $(1 - q)h$ to workers after extortion takes place, whereas the rent-seekers earn $qh(1 - p)/p$ where $(1 - p)/p$ represents the probability that a rent-seeker meets and is matched with a productive worker.

Introducing migration gives workers in the productive sector a chance to migrate to a country with better institutions, where wages (and intellectual property) are better protected. This creates a lower loss of their income that occurs due to rent-seeking, $f < q$. This gives the probability to migrate m or to stay at home, $1 - m$. Expected earnings of production workers and rent-seekers respectively become

$$v_S(p, m) = [(1 - m)(1 - q)] + m(1 - f)h$$

$$v_R(p, m) = \frac{(1 - m)(1 - p)}{p} qh$$

It is easy to see that a positive probability of migration, m, raises expected income of the skilled due to higher prospective net wages and reduces that of rent-seekers because they have a lower probability of meeting a 'prey'. Finally, endogenizing the proportion of rent-seekers *vis-à-vis* productive workers, p, the equilibrium value can be found by equating the income of the two segments of the society. This yields $p^e(m) = \frac{(1-m)q}{1-mf}$, which is decreasing in m. Lower expected rents therefore discourage predatory activities in the country of origin, or in other words result in an endogenous improvement in home-country institutions.

2.2 Expropriation

Docquier and Rapoport (2003) tackle the issue of home-country institutions by dividing the society into a minority and a majority (ethnic) group and looking at the extent of expropriation by the group in power. The factor in play here is a discriminatory tax levied on the educated segment of the minority and redistributed among the majority. Migration provides a form of protection for the minority group by reducing discriminatory policies such as biased redistribution against the latter. In their framework, the government maximizes the welfare of a privileged majority. The population in turn decides whether to invest in education to improve their productivity in the first period and whether to emigrate in the second.

Agents are given a minimal level of human capital normalized to 1, and are heterogeneous in their learning ability, z. All agents earn 1 in the first period. In the second period those who forgo education continue to earn 1, while those who undergo education earn $1 + z$. Income in each scenario can be presented as

$$v_{00} = 1 + \frac{1}{1 + r}$$

$$v_{10} = 1 - e + \frac{1 + z(1 - t)}{1 + r}$$

$$v_{11} = 1 - e + \frac{1 + z - m}{1 + r},$$

where e is the cost of education, m is the cost of migration, t is the tax rate and r is the interest rate (measuring discount rate on future earnings). The first binary subscript indicates education and the second depicts migration. The setting creates a continuum of agents sorted according to their capabilities with two thresholds z_1 and z_2, which represent the indifferent agent with respect to education and migration, respectively. Agents in the minority with ability $z < z_1$ do not invest in education, those with $z_1 < z < z_2$ invest in education but stay home, and the highest-skilled segment ($z > z_2$) also migrate.

An increase in the tax rate, t, increases the size of the population in the first and the third zone, whereas those in the middle who are subject to taxes gradually disappear. This captures the role of discrimination in deterring investment in education while inducing the more educated to emigrate. The gains are more tax revenue from the educated who remain at home on the intensive margin, and the losses are the shrinking size of that group in the extensive margin. The government, which optimally sets the tax rate on the educated minority (or the extent of discrimination), must assure that enough agents choose to go through education, while limiting emigration. As migration costs decrease, optimal discriminatory taxes must be reduced to compensate and encourage the educated minority to stay in their home country. Once again, migration is shown to improve the quality of institutions by reducing discriminatory behavior by a non-democratic government in power.[2]

3. INTERNATIONAL MIGRATION AND TECHNOLOGY DIFFUSION

Knowledge circulation and technology diffusion are critical for countries' growth and performance in the modern-day knowledge economy (Romer, 1990; Aghion and Howitt, 1992). This is especially true for those developing countries where domestic innovative capacity is lacking and diffusion of foreign technologies is an important source of innovation. To access foreign technologies, countries largely rely on trade in goods and services, foreign direct investment and technology licensing – the most significant channels of technology transfer. Growing evidence also suggests that cross-border movement of inventors, researchers, scientists, engineers, entrepreneurs and the like facilitate knowledge exchange and diffusion of innovative ideas. With increased mobility of high-skilled workers, international migration could become another major channel through which innovative ideas and technologies diffuse worldwide, and carry with it important implications for the world distribution of prosperity and welfare.

The link between international migration, knowledge circulation and technology adoption has yet to be firmly established. Most of our insight comes from two separate strands of the literature. The first concerns the innovation impact of high-skilled migration. Although limited, this literature points to high-skilled migration providing an important contribution to innovation in major host countries, and the potential for increased innovative capacities in sending countries. These effects are possible when migration facilitates the exchange of knowledge and ideas across countries through return migration, diaspora networks, ethnic communities and so on. The second strand of the literature concerns knowledge creation, international technology diffusion and productivity growth. For the purposes of this discussion, the most relevant contributions are those of Eaton and Kortum (1999), Lucas (2009) and Comin et al. (2012), which underscore the role of individuals' knowledge, human interactions and geographical distance in the technology adoption process. In what follows, we highlight the key insights provided by each strand of the literature and then briefly outline potential connections between the two.

The literature on the innovation impact of high-skilled migration is still in its infancy. What we know to this point suggests that high-skilled immigrants are making major host countries more innovative. A commonly cited fact is that high-skilled immigrants account for a large share of US innovation activity. As examples, immigrants started 25 percent of US public-venture-backed companies between 1990 and 2005, most of which are concentrated in sectors with the highest innovation rates, such as high-technology manufacturing, information and life sciences (Anderson and Platzer, 2006). Immigrants also represented 26 percent of US-based Nobel Prize winners between 1990 and 2000 (Peri, 2007). By comparison, foreign-born individuals comprised 12 percent of the US population in 2000 (Hunt and Gauthier-Loiselle, 2010). Among college graduates in the USA, immigrants patent about twice as much as their native counterparts (Hunt and Gauthier-Loiselle, 2010). Immigrant non-US citizens accounted for 24 percent of international patent applications filed from the USA in 2006 (Wadhwa et al., 2007). The trends in Canada and Europe are similar. At least 35 percent of all Canada Research Chairs – arguably the most efficacious research talent – are foreign-born, when the share of the country's foreign-born was 20 percent in 2000 (Downie, 2010). A positive relationship between high-skilled immigrant and patenting activity has also been found across Canadian provinces (Partridge and Furtan, 2008) and regions in Europe (Ozgen, 2013).

There is also evidence to suggest that high-skilled migration could contribute to innovative capacities of sending countries, although the evidence is more limited. These gains can be realized as migrants who have acquired skills and innovative ideas abroad return to their home countries (Mayr and Peri, 2009; Dustmann et al., 2011). Sending countries can also gain from high-skilled migration as emigrants circulate knowledge acquired abroad back to their home countries through cross-border diaspora networks and close-knit, ethnic scientific communities. In Agrawal et al. (2011), the emigration of inventors weakens local knowledge networks but creates diaspora knowledge networks that improve remaining innovators' access to foreign knowledge. The authors find that the diaspora effect on knowledge flows – also referred to as the 'brain-bank' effect – is particularly strong in India and is most valuable for the highest-value inventions. Kerr (2008) explores whether ethnic scientific and entrepreneurial communities in the USA facilitate technology transfer to foreign countries of the same ethnicity. The findings suggest that the ethnicity channel plays an important role in foreign technology transfer and is particularly strong in high-tech industries and Chinese communities. Saxenian (2005) also shows that highly skilled diasporas from China and India contributed significantly to the transfer of knowledge and technology from host countries to the Chinese and Indian economies.

The underlying premise of the above literature is that cross-country exchange of knowledge is facilitated by the movement of people across international borders. Related is the literature on knowledge creation and international technology diffusion, which emphasizes the role of individuals' decisions and human interactions in the process. Insightful contributions in this area are provided by Eaton and Kortum (1999), Lucas (2009) and Comin et al. (2012), which we briefly review below.

In Eaton and Kortum (1999), countries simultaneously contribute to and benefit from each other's inventions, and this interdependence in innovative activity across countries contributes to productivity growth. A central measure of the innovation–growth linkage is the rate at which technologies generated abroad are eventually adopted in a given country. Countries that are quicker to adopt foreign technologies have higher productivity ranking in the steady state.

Eaton and Kortum (1999) assume that the diffusion of new technologies across countries is governed by inventors' patenting decisions. An inventor will seek patent protection in a given country if the likelihood of the invention being used in that country is high enough that the expected value of patent protection exceeds the costs of obtaining the patent in that country. Data on international patent applications are used to quantify the direction and magnitude of international technology diffusion. These data contain information on residence of inventor and country of application, allowing researchers to trace the source and uses of innovative ideas (that is, observe where an idea originates and where it is eventually used) to measure the extent to which countries utilize ideas conceived in other countries.

Eaton and Kortum (1999) fit the model to data on productivity levels, research employment and patenting from five countries (the USA, Japan, Germany, the UK and France) in the late 1980s. The authors find that technology diffusion is extensive: relative to the adoption of domestically generated ideas, countries generally adopt from one-half to three-quarters of ideas generated abroad. The adoption of foreign ideas contributes considerably to each country's growth. In fact, the USA is the only country in which domestic innovation is a primary driver of growth.

In Lucas (2009), it is individuals who acquire and generate knowledge, and in so doing shape the knowledge of an economy. As individuals interact, each contributes to and benefits from the ideas and knowledge of people around them. Human interactions thus facilitate knowledge exchange and so further contribute to the intellectual activity of an economy and the overall growth of knowledge.

To relate an individual's knowledge to the knowledge of an economy, Lucas (2009) builds on the Kortum (1997) and Eaton and Kortum (1999) model in which the distribution of knowledge over individuals (that is, the technology frontier) describes the state of knowledge of an economy. Since an individual's contribution to the economy's knowledge varies over their lifespan (e.g. knowledge is lost when the individual dies), Lucas (2009) incorporates a cohort structure with overlapping generations into the model. The focus of the paper is on modelling a technology of knowledge creation and learning, with individual behavior taken as given. One could further develop the framework to incorporate a wide range of individual allocative decisions (e.g. occupational choice and migration) that are expected to influence knowledge circulation and technology diffusion within countries or across international borders.

Comin et al. (2012) study how technology diffuses across countries and over time, and propose the theory of human interactions to account for the observed pattern of technology diffusion. The empirical analysis utilizes Comin and Hobijn (2004, 2010) Cross-Country Historical Adoption of Technology (CHAT) data on the adoption of 20 major technologies in 161 countries over the last 140 years. The focus is on the existence of cross-country interactions in technology adoption and the role of geographical distance in the transmission of technological knowledge. The key variable is the spatial distance from other countries' technology (SDT) measure. It is constructed as the interaction between distance and technology adoption:

$$\sum_{\forall k \neq c} d_{ck} x^j_{kt}$$

where d_{ck} is the distance between countries c and k and x^j_{kt} is the adoption of technology j in country k at time t. In other words, the SDT measure is the scalar product of the vector of distances to the other countries and the vector of adoption levels in these other countries. Using this measure, the authors find negative spatial effect, suggesting that adoption of technology is slower in countries that are further away from the adoption leaders. Not surprisingly, however, the effect of geography diminishes over time as technology diffuses.

The theory proffered in Comin et al. (2012) builds on the insight of Eaton and Kortum (1999) and Lucas (2009). The underlying premise is that technology is diffused across countries through human interactions. Individuals meet randomly and, as they interact, share ideas and learn from each other about newly adopted technologies. If only one of the two agents who meet has adopted the new technology, the other agent also adopts that technology. The speed and spatial scope of technology adoption depends on (i) the frequency of interactions and (ii) the probability that two agents from different locations meet. Interactions are more frequent for newer technologies and so these technologies diffuse faster. The probability of interactions falls with distance. Individuals in close proximity interact the most, which is why a large portion of technological knowledge is localized.

Perhaps surprisingly, the two strands of literature discussed above have been pursued in isolation from one another. Bringing together these areas may prove useful in strengthening the link between international migration of high-skilled workers and cross-country knowledge circulation and technology diffusion. One could, for example, build on the insights provided by a theory of human interactions to model migration and incorporate it into Eaton and Kortum's (1999) theory of innovation and technology diffusion. Such a theory would assume that adopting a technology requires new knowledge, which comes from interactions between adopters and non-adopters. Migration reduces social distance and helps overcome 'man-made' barriers to cross-border interactions. In so doing, it increases the potential for interaction of agents from different countries and the international sharing of ideas. Migrant-innovators arrive in host countries with a plethora of know-how and skills. This knowledge is supplemented with ideas and expertise acquired while abroad. Diffusion of technology could occur both in the host country where the innovator lives and works, and in the source country through diaspora networks and other means. In these ways, migration is expected to stimulate the diffusion of technology from the location of invention to the location of adoption.

Empirical migration studies have provided important, but limited, insights. One obvious shortcoming is that the studies focused on only a few countries over short time periods. To a large extent, this deficiency is attributable to the lack of data on migration flows. The World Intellectual Property Organization (WIPO) has acknowledged and addressed this concern directly, by committing to 'develop[ing] an informed research agenda on intellectual property, migration, and associated knowledge flows, providing the basis for future studies on this topic' (WIPO, 2011). As part of this commitment, WIPO collected and recently released data on migrant inventors (Miguelez and Fink, 2013). The data set has four principal advantages over its predecessors. First, it focuses on inventors – a specific class of high-skilled workers who create knowledge, as distinct from other tertiary educated workers. Second, it is derived from the residence and nationality information disclosed by inventors themselves in their patent applications, which is more precise than, for example, inferring migration history from the cultural origin of inventors' names. Third, this data set is based on patent applications filed under the Patent Cooperation Treaty (PCT). This is important because PCT operates worldwide in nearly all countries, and implements a uniform application procedure and process – allowing for easier cross-country comparisons. Finally, the data cover many countries and years (241 countries/territories for every year from 1978 to 2012).

To gain a better understanding of the link between inventor migration and international knowledge circulation, we relate inventor emigration rates from Miguelez and Fink's (2013) data to the degree of international collaboration on PCT applications. The rate of inventor emigration is defined for each country of origin i as follows: $D_i/(R_i + D_i)$, where D_i is the number of country i's inventors residing abroad and R_{it} is the number of inventors residing in i (i's nationals and immigrants). This rate is calculated over the 2001–11 period. The degree of international collaboration is calculated for the year 2011 as follows: F_i/T_i, where F_i is the number of i's inventors in foreign-owned PCT applications (submitted by foreign firms for patenting in i) and T_i is the number of i's inventors in all PCT applications. The data for this measure are taken from Section A.6.2. of the WIPO World Intellectual Property Indicators (WIPO, 2012).

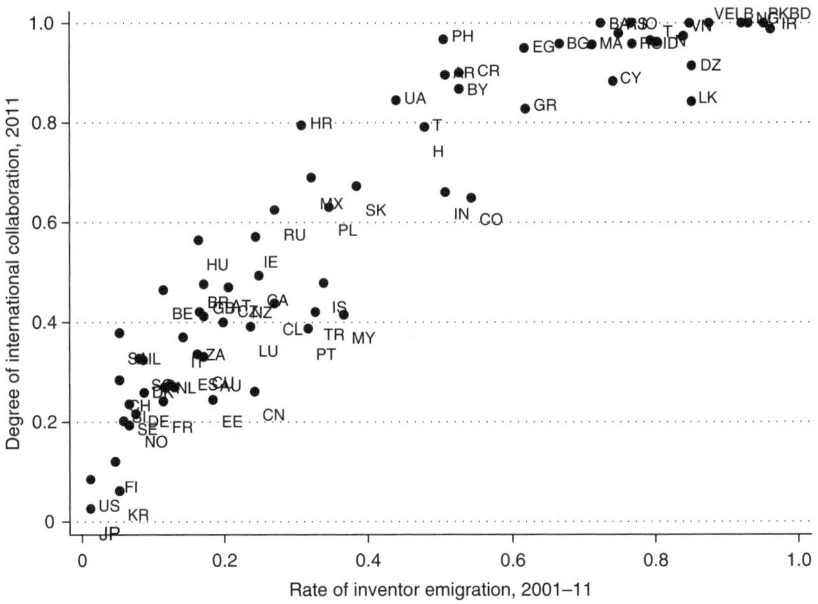

AR	Argentina	FR	France
AT	Austria	GB	UK
AU	Australia	GR	Greece
BA	Bosnia-Herzegovina	HR	Croatia
BD	Bangladesh	HU	Hungary
BE	Belgium	ID	Indonesia
BG	Bulgaria	IE	Ireland
BR	Brazil	IL	Israel
BY	Belarus	IN	India
CA	Canada	IR	Iran
CH	Switzerland	IS	Iceland
CL	Chile	IT	Italy
CN	China	JO	Jordan
CO	Colombia	JP	Japan
CR	Costa Rica	KR	Republic of Korea
CU	Cuba	LB	Lebanon
CY	Cyprus	LK	Sri Lanka
CZ	Czech Republic	LU	Luxembourg
DE	Germany	MA	Morocco
DK	Denmark	MX	Mexico
DZ	Algeria	MY	Malaysia
EE	Estonia	NG	Nigeria
EG	Egypt	NL	Netherlands
ES	Spain	NO	Norway
FI	Finland	NZ	New Zealand

Figure 10.1 Inventor collaboration and emigration by countries of inventors

PH	Philippines	RO	Romania
PK	Pakistan	RS	Serbia
PL	Poland	RU	Russian Federation
PT	Portugal	SA	Saudi Arabia
SE	Sweden	TR	Turkey
SG	Singapore	UA	Ukraine
SI	Slovenia	US	USA
SK	Slovakia	VE	Venezuela
TH	Thailand	VN	Viet Nam
TN	Tunisia	ZA	South Africa

Figure 10.1 (continued)

Figure 10.1 plots the data for 70 countries with highest number of inventors in all PCT applications.

It is apparent that the two variables are positively related: cross-border collaboration on PCT applications is high in countries with high inventor emigration rates. In India, for example, the inventor emigration rate was 51 percent over the period of 2001–11, with as many as 44 864 inventors residing abroad and 43 784 inventors residing in India over this period. Around 66 percent of Indian inventors (6631 out of the total of 10 019) were included in foreign PCT applications in 2011. In China, by contrast, the rate of inventor emigration and the share of inventors in foreign-owned PCT applications were 24 percent and 26 percent respectively. A positive association between inventor emigration rates and the degree of international collaboration could be the result of inventor migration promoting knowledge circulation and technology diffusion through diaspora knowledge networks. While further analysis is needed to reach definitive conclusions, the exhibited pattern nonetheless suggests that inventor migration facilitates international diffusion of innovative ideas and technologies.

4. CAN BETTER HOME COUNTRY INSTITUTIONS TRANSFORM BRAIN DRAIN TO BRAIN GAIN?

Naghavi and Strozzi (2011) turn around the question regarding the role of migration on the development of home-country institutions and ask whether the latter can influence the impact of migration on the home economy. As the focus of this paper is on innovation, the institution they consider is the legal infrastructure to protect intellectual property rights (IPRs). They show that, although emigration from a developing country may cause brain drain, it also generates brain gain through diaspora knowledge networks, the extent of which depends on the IPR institutions in the country of origin. In a sense they investigate the role of IPRs in the country of origin on promoting technology diffusion through migration.

Similar to the framework of Docquier and Rapoport (2003) discussed in Section 2.2, they built a model of agents with heterogeneous abilities, who decide to attain an education and migrate to a country with better wage opportunities. However, they divide the economy into two sectors: production and innovation. The least skilled, up to a threshold level z_1, work in the production sector, whereas workers with abilities above that threshold choose to put their skills to work in the innovation sector. Those with the highest skills above a higher threshold, z_2, can also afford to pay migration costs and emigrate. Obviously the skills that leave the economy cause an immediate brain drain on the extensive margin. However, Naghavi and Strozzi (2011) introduce a potential channel through which superior knowledge acquired abroad can flow back to the country of origin. This increases the skills of the remaining workers in the innovation sector in the intensive margin.

The protection of IPRs is presented as an increase in the probability that an inventor can exercise monopoly power in the market for his invention and, in turn, the value of skills. A higher probability of obtaining a patent also increases returns from skills, attracting workers into the innovation sector. At the lower end of skills, more workers invest in education, generating a shift of workers from production to innovation activities. At the higher end, enhanced returns to skills at home make potential migrants think twice before leaving their home country. New skills learned abroad and sent back by emigrants can be diffused over a larger innovation sector (the middle zone between z_1 and z_2), increasing potential gains from migration. A net brain gain is the outcome of migration if the magnitude of this skill upgrading is large enough to outweigh the direct negative effects of an outflow of skills in innovation.

The results show that diaspora networks may generate positive knowledge flows, but only to the extent that there is enough absorptive capacity in the home country. IPR protection creates the conditions for an innovation sector, in terms of either industrial development or foreign direct investment, employing workers in skilled occupations that can benefit from diasporas. They show that the strength of IPR institutions is a moderating factor to enable gains from diaspora networks. The results obtained by stronger IPRs are in line with an alternative explanation for brain gain, namely human capital incentives (Beine et al., 2001) and return migration (Mayr and Peri, 2009). IPRs function as an intermediary channel to exploit gains from migration by encouraging investment in education and thereby human capital formation in the sending country. Better IPR protection also encourages workers who have obtained better skills to return to the innovation sector of their home country. Notwithstanding the channel in play, one can conclude that skilled migration generates technology fusion when institutional development in the home country is sufficiently evolved to allow the absorption of knowledge flows through human capital development, return migration or intellectual diaspora networks.

The impact of emigration to OECD in the presence of IPRs on patenting activities by residents in the country of origin is empirically tested in Naghavi and Strozzi (2011) on a sample of 35 emerging and developing countries with data ranging from 1995 to 2006. The results of the paper find a direct negative and significant effect of emigration on innovation activities performed in the home economy, suggesting that the depletion of skill can initially result in brain drain. However, a positive interaction between emigration and IPR protection confirms a positive correlation between emigration and innovation when IPRs are sufficiently strong.

As an example, two countries with the weakest IPR regimes were Bangladesh and Iran (with an index lower than 2 out of 5), while in the same year Hungary and Bulgaria are the two countries with the highest degree of IPR protection (with an index higher than 4.5). In the same year, China and India had an index of 4.08 and 3.76 respectively. The findings show that the emerging and developing countries that had an IPR protection index greater than 3.6 can exploit the beneficial effects of migration on innovation and experience technological progress. With data taken from 2006, this implies that an increase in the number of emigrants by 10 percent in China leads to an increase in the number of patents there by 1.3 percent. The same increase in Iran leads to a decrease in the number of patents there by 4.6 percent (Naghavi and Strozzi, 2012). This reinforces the role of IPR institutions in the home country in determining whether international migration can result in brain drain or brain gain.

Interestingly, the authors also conduct an analysis in the spirit of Spilimbergo (2009) to see whether the intensity of knowledge transferred back to the countries of origin depends on the level of development in the host countries. To do so, emigration is weighed according to GDP per capita in the host countries to account for differences in potential technology diffusion between country pairs according to where emigrants land. More specifically, the emigration index lies at 0 if all emigrants are in countries with the lowest potential for learning better technologies, and at 1 if all emigrants go to the most advanced countries. The above results are confirmed: emigrating to countries with better potential for technology diffusion is more likely to instigate innovation in the home country when the quality of IPR institutions is adequate. The conclusion confirms the opportunity provided by emigration for emerging and developing countries and suggests that the greatest benefits can best be realized under a strong and well-developed regulatory environment.

5. CONCLUSION

This chapter has aimed to reveal the interplay of international migration, home-country institutions and technology diffusion. We first looked at the theoretical link between migration and home-country institutions. In short, migration can affect home-country institutions in many ways and it is not trivial that brain drain can result in their deterioration.

We saw that skilled migrants can influence the actions of the remaining population in the home country and ultimately the authorities. The emigration of politically active agents to jurisdictions with better protection naturally curtails lobbying efforts at home. However, better norms and institutions can be adopted and transferred to strengthen institutions in the home country. Emigrants can, for instance, engage in economic and political activities to reform institutions in their home country. The phenomenon can be thought of as a political-economy process in which migrants' lobbying efforts and potential migration push domestic reforms of institutions.

We also argued that for diaspora networks to improve source countries' access to foreign-produced knowledge, it is not required that skilled emigrants return to their home countries or make direct financial contributions to their home economies. Instead, skilled emigrants can speed up the flow of knowledge between source and host countries. First, by living and working abroad, skilled emigrants increase access to foreign-country markets and allow source countries to tap into foreign knowledge, which can then flow back to source countries as emigrants share their expertise with residents of their home countries. Migrant inventors, researchers, scientists, engineers, entrepreneurs and the like are thus not permanently lost to source countries; they have the potential to provide an invaluable contribution to knowledge and development of their home economics.

International migration also has an important role in technology diffusion, which has been mostly ignored in economic literature. Turning our attention away from trade and foreign direct investment and towards migration, we considered how the mobility of inventors can indeed result in the diffusion of new technologies. Although further research remains to be conducted in this area, stylized facts clearly signal a correlation between the physical diffusion of human capital and that of intellectual property.

Finally, we refer to the work of Naghavi and Strozzi (2011), which brings all the three above-mentioned elements together to see how (exogenously) stronger home-country institutions enable a country to absorb potential gains from international migration. Although South–North migration results in skill upgrading of migrants, for this knowledge to be exploited in a sending country, institutions need to be sufficiently strong. Although this work looks solely at the IPR institutions, it would be worth looking at the effect of other political and economic institutions in force. Nonetheless, this chapter once again confirms the link between our three variables of interest and highlights the need for further research to explore the links and potential causalities among them. We also expect that this survey will provide the information and motivation needed to empower policy makers, economic planners, intergovernmental organizations and non-governmental organizations in their respective efforts to manage the impacts of high-skill worker migration for the benefit of all.

NOTES

1. Senate bill S.744, entitled 'Border Security, Economic Opportunity, and Immigration Modernization Act of 2013'.
2. Testaverde (2013) takes a different approach, in which democracy is defined as a redistribution system. A rich ruling elite tries to maintain power by giving concessions to the poor, who can revolt or migrate. Migration increases wages, making the level of redistribution required by the poor lower. Democracy therefore becomes relatively less costly for the elite. In addition, less numerous poor increases payoff of a successful revolution, making them less willing to accept concessions. Migration therefore fosters a democratic redistribution system.

REFERENCES

Aghion, P. and Howitt, P. (1992). A model of growth through creative destruction, *Econometrica*, **60**(2), 323–51.

Agrawal, A., Kapur, D. and McHale, J. (2011). Brain drain or brain bank? The impact of skilled emigration on poor-country innovation, *Journal of Urban Economics*, **69**(1), 43–55.

Anderson, S. and Platzer, M.D. (2006). American made: The impact of immigrant entrepreneurs and professionals on US competitiveness. National Venture Capital Association.

Batista, C. and Vicente, P.C. (2011). Do migrants improve governance at home? Evidence from a voting experiment, *World Bank Economic Review*, **25**(1), 77–104.

Beine, M. and Sekkat, K. (2013). Skilled migration and the transfer of institutional norms, *IZA Journal of Migration*, **2**, 9.

Beine, M., Docquier, F. and Rapoport, H. (2001). Brain drain and economic growth: Theory and evidence, *Journal of Development Economics*, **64**, 275–89.

Beine, M., Docquier, F. and Rapoport, H. (2008). Brain drain and human capital formation in developing countries: winners and losers, *Economic Journal*, **118**, 631–52.

Berry, R. and Soligo, R. (1969). Some welfare aspects of international migration, *Journal of Political Economy*, **77**(5), 778–94.

Bhagwati, J. (2003). Borders beyond control, *Foreign Affairs*, **82**(1), 98–104.

Bhagwati, J. and Hamada, K. (1974). The brain drain, international integration of markets for professionals and unemployment: a theoretical analysis, *Journal of Development Economics*, **1**(1), 19–42.

Comin, D. and Hobijn, B. (2004). Cross-country technology adoption: making the theories face the facts, *Journal of Monetary Economics*, **51**, 39–83.

Comin, D. and Hobijn, B. (2010). An exploration of technology diffusion, *American Economic Review*, **100**(5), 2031–59.

Comin, D.A., Dmitriev, M. and Rossi-Hansberg, E. (2012). The spatial diffusion of technology (No. w18534). National Bureau of Economic Research.

Devan, J. and Tewari, P.S. (2001). Speakout: when the best brains go abroad, *IEEE Spectrum*, **38**(10), 16–18.

Docquier, F. and Marfouk, A. (2006). International migration by education attainment, 1990–2000. In Ç. Özden and M. Schiff (eds), *International Migration, Remittances and the Brain Drain*, New York: Palgrave Macmillan, pp. 151–99.

Docquier, F. and Rapoport, H. (2003). Ethnic discrimination and the migration of skilled labor, *Journal of Development Economics*, **70**, 159–72.

Docquier, F. and Rapoport, H. (2012). Globalization, brain drain, and development, *Journal of Economic Literature*, **50**(3), 681–730.

Docquier, F., Lowell, B.L. and Marfouk, A. (2007). A gendered assessment of the brain drain, IZA Discussion Paper 3235.

Docquier, F., Lodigiani, E., Rapoport, H. and Schiff, M. (2011). Emigration and democracy, IZA Discussion Paper 5496.

Downie, M. (2010). Immigrants as innovators boosting Canada's global competitiveness. Conference Board of Canada.

Dustmann, C., Fadlon, I. and Weiss, Y. (2011). Return migration, human capital accumulation and the brain drain, *Journal of Development Economics*, **95**(1), 58–67.

Eaton, J. and Kortum, S. (1999). International technology diffusion: theory and measurement, *International Economic Review*, **40**(3), 537–70.

Eaton, J. and Kortum, S. (2002). Technology, geography, and trade, *Econometrica*, **70**(5), 1741–79.

Fan, C.S. and Stark, O. (2007). International migration and 'educated unemployment', *Journal of Development Economics*, **83**(1), 76–87.

Gibson, J. and McKenzie, D. (2012). The economic consequences of 'brain drain' of the best and brightest: microeconomic evidence from five countries, *The Economic Journal*, **122**(560), 339–75.

Hirschman, A.O. (1970). *Exit, Voice, and Loyalty: Responses to Decline in Firms, Organizations, and States*, Cambridge, MA: Harvard University Press.

Hunt, J. and Gauthier-Loiselle, M. (2010). How much does immigration boost innovation? *American Economic Journal: Macroeconomics*, 31–56.

Kapur, D., McHale, J. and McHale, J.F. (2005). *Give us Your Best and Brightest: The Global Hunt for Talent and its Impact on the Developing World*. Washington, DC: Brookings Institution Press.

Kaufmann, D., Kraay, A. and Zoido-Lopaton, P. (1999). Governance matters, World Bank Policy Research Working Papers 2196.

Kerr, W.R. (2008). Ethnic scientific communities and international technology diffusion, *The Review of Economics and Statistics*, **90**(3), 518–37.

Kortum, S. (1997). Research, patenting, and technological change, *Econometrica*, **65**, 1389–419.

Lowell, L.B. (2001). Policy responses to the international mobility of skilled labour, International Migration Paper 45, Geneva: International Labour Office.

Lucas, R.E. (2009). Ideas and growth, *Economica*, **76**, 1–19.

Mahmoud, T.O., Rapoport, H., Steinmayr, A. and Trebesch, C. (2011). Do migrants remit political change? Westward migration and the decay of the Communist Party in Moldova. Mimeo.

Mariani, F. (2007). Migration as an antidote to rent-seeking, *Journal of Development Economics*, **84**(2), 609–30.

Mayr, K. and Peri, G. (2009). Return migration as a channel of brain gain, *B.E. Journal of Economic Analysis & Policy*, **9**(1), Article 49.
Miguelez, E. and Fink, C. (2013). Measuring the international mobility of inventors: a new database, WIPO Economics & Statistics Series Working Paper No. 8, WIPO.
Miyagiwa, K. (1991). Scale economies in education and the brain drain problem, *International Economic Review*, **32**(3), 743–59.
Mountford, A. (1997). Can a brain drain be good for growth in the source economy? *Journal of Development Economics*, **53**(2), 287–303.
Naghavi, A. and Strozzi, C. (2011). Intellectual property rights, migration, and diaspora, IZA Discussion Paper 5864.
Naghavi, A. and Strozzi, C. (2012). Sparking off the magic of diasporas, Vox column, November 18, http://www.voxeu.org/article/sparking-magic-diasporas.
Özden, C. and Schiff, M. (2005). *International Migration, Remittances, and the Brain Drain*. New York: Palgrave Macmillan.
Ozgen, C. (2013). Immigration and innovation in European regions, *The Quarterly Journal of Economics*, **128**(1), 249–85.
Partridge, J. and Furtan, H. (2008). Increasing Canada's international competitiveness: is there a link between skilled immigrants and innovation? American Agricultural Economics Association Annual Meeting, Orlando, FL, Proceedings, pp. 27–9.
Peri, G. (2007). Higher education, innovation and growth. In G. Brunello, P. Garibaldi and E. Wasmer (eds), *Education and Training in Europe*. Oxford: Oxford University Press, pp. 56–70.
Romer, P.M. (1990). Endogenous technological change, *Journal of Political Economy*, **98**, S71–S102.
Saxenian, A.L. (1999). *Silicon Valley's New Immigrant Entrepreneurs*. San Francisco, CA: Public Policy Institute of California.
Saxenian, A. (2002). Silicon Valley's new immigrant high-growth entrepreneurs, *Economic Development Quarterly*, **16**(1), 20–31.
Saxenian, A.L. (2005). From brain drain to brain circulation: transnational communities and regional upgrading in India and China, *Studies in Comparative International Development*, **40**(2), 35–61.
Saxenian, A., Motoyama, Y. and Quan, X. (2002). Local and global networks of immigrant professionals in Silicon Valley. Public Policy Institute of California.
Spilimbergo A. (2009). Foreign education and democracy, *American Economic Review*, **99**(1), 528–43.
Stark, O., Helmenstein, C. and Prskawetz, A. (1997). A brain gain with a brain drain, *Economics Letters*, **55**, 227–34.
Testaverde, M. (2013). Emigration, redistribution and political institutions in origin countries. Mimeo, University of Southampton.
Vidal, J.P. (1998). The effect of emigration on human capital formation, *Journal of Population Economics*, **11**(4), 589–600.
Wadhwa, V., Saxenian, A., Rissing, B. and Gereffi, G. (2007). America's new immigrant entrepreneurs: Part I. Duke Science, Technology & Innovation Paper, (23).
WIPO (2011). Intellectual property (IP) and brain drain. The World Intellectual Property Organization, Committee on Development and Intellectual Property (CDIP), Seventh Session, March 3.
WIPO (2012). World intellectual property indicators. WIPO Economics & Statistics Series, WIPO.
The World Bank (2011). *Migration and Remittances Factbook*, 2nd edn. Washington, DC: World Bank.

11. The migration–trade link in developing economies: a summary and extension of evidence

*Robert E.B. Lucas**

Gravity models of migration and of trade have much in common, and the last two decades have witnessed an integration of these two strands of literature. Since the appearance of the seminal paper by Gould (1994), a substantial empirical literature has emerged documenting significant positive associations between bilateral international trade and migration, typically within a gravity model framework, usually with the presumption that migration causes trade expansion. For the developing countries this potential link may be of considerable importance. The notion that openness to trade is the *sine qua non* of economic development has been largely abandoned since the 1980s. Nonetheless, reductions in trade barriers and improvements to the trade balance often remain critical for lower-income states. Yet only a small portion of the extensive empirical literature on the migration–trade link focuses on the context of developing regions. The aim of the present chapter is then twofold: first to present some fresh evidence on the migration–trade link with particular reference to developing countries, using data on bilateral trade and migration among 192 countries from 1960 to 2000; and second to summarize some of the prior literature tangential to these results. The chapter in this volume by Christopher Parsons and L. Alan Winters (Chapter 4) offers a more complete synthesis of this genre of literature.

1. MODELS AND ISSUES IN ESTIMATION

Three explanations are common for the enhancement by migrants of bilateral trade between the migrants' origin and host countries.

* I am grateful to Sam Bazzi, Chris Parsons, Çaglar Özden and the members of the KNOWMAD seminar group at the World Bank for helpful comments and suggestions on a preliminary version of this chapter.

1. The preference effect refers to emigrants retaining a taste for items from the old country. This may be enlarged by a consumption spill-over effect, in which natives of the host country learn to prefer goods from their immigrants' lands.
2. An information bridging effect: emigrants may well have a better grasp of trading opportunities and the norms of conducting business in their home country than do non-nationals. They may also possess more contacts able to realize potential trade deals.
3. A contract enforcement effect: in many parts of the world, and in some sectors in particular, contracts are sealed with a handshake rather than via legal documents. Members of a diaspora may possess friends and family at home who are able to enforce such informal deals, if only through social embargoes and pressure.[1]

The preference effect postulates that migrants from country *i* to country *j* may increase exports from *i* to *j*. The remaining two effects both suggest that migrants from country *i* to country *j* may enhance exports from *j* to *i* as well as from *i* to *j*. Since essentially every country undergoes simultaneous immigration and emigration, openness to trade in both directions should ensue. Openness is not synonymous with freer trade; however, to the extent that migrants mitigate trade costs, such as those associated with distance, efficiency gain results. Typically these mitigating effects are presumed to be associated with the information-bridging and contract-enforcement effects derived from migrants, but not from their preference effect on trade.[2]

Together the three effects indicate augmenting the standard gravity model of bilateral trade[3] along the following lines:

$$\mathrm{L}X_{ijt} = \phi_0 + \phi_1\,\mathrm{L}Y_{it} + \phi_2\,\mathrm{L}Y_{jt} + \phi_3\,\mathrm{L}D_{ij} + \phi_4\,F_{ij} + \phi_5\,\mathrm{L}N_{ijt} + \phi_6\,\mathrm{L}N_{jit} + \Phi'\,\mathbf{V}_{ijt} + \varepsilon_{ijt} \tag{11.1}$$

where: $\mathrm{L}X_{ijt}$ = the natural logarithm of exports, in current prices, from country *i* to *j* at time *t*

$\mathrm{L}Y_{it}$, $\mathrm{L}Y_{jt}$ = the natural logarithm of GDP, in current prices, in *i* and *j* at time *t*

$\mathrm{L}D_{ij}$ = the natural logarithm of distance between *i* and *j*

F_{ij} = a dummy variable for whether *i* and *j* have a common border

$\mathrm{L}N_{ijt}$ = the natural logarithm of the stock of migrants from *i* in *j* at time *t*

$\mathrm{L}N_{jit}$ = the natural logarithm of the stock of migrants from *j* in *i* at time *t*

$\mathbf{V}_{ijt}$ = a vector of control variables.

Along somewhat similar lines, a bilateral migration, gravity model may be specified as[4]

$$LN_{ijt} = \lambda_0 + \lambda_1\, LW_{it} + \lambda_2\, LW_{jt} + \lambda_3\, LP_{it} + \lambda_4\, LP_{jt} + \lambda_5\, LD_{ij} + \lambda_6\, F_{ij} + \mathbf{\Lambda}' \mathbf{U}_{ijt} + \xi_{ijt} \quad (11.2)$$

where: LW_{it}, LW_{jt} = real income per capita, or real wage, in countries i and j at time t
LP_{it}, LP_{jt} = the natural logarithm of population in i and j
$\mathbf{U}_{ijt}$ = a vector of augmenting control variables.

Together these present a recursive system in which trade is commonly presumed not to affect migration.[5] Although this exclusion restriction rules out reverse causality, correlation may remain between the migration and disturbance terms in (11.1). In particular, considerable overlap exists between terms commonly included in vectors **V** and **U**, the control or augmenting variables in the trade and migration equations respectively; omission of elements of **V** that are common to both **V** and **U** can then result in biased estimates of (11.1).

An alternative is to replace any observed or unobserved elements in **V** that are fixed with respect to the country of origin, the host country, or their dyad, by inclusion of corresponding fixed effects.[6] Any time dimension to the data also raises concerns about use of current price measurement of variables, which is common in estimating trade gravity models in part because of the lack of good trade deflators. Perhaps as a result, virtually all estimates that are based on panel data also include time fixed effects.[7]

Over the last two decades, at least 43 papers have appeared examining bilateral exports (or imports, or both), for a specific OECD country (or its sub-national states) in relation to that nation's immigrant stocks from a subset of partner countries (N_{jt}). It is apparent that estimation in such contexts requires some simplification of equation (11.1), resulting in a typical specification of the form

$$LX_{jt} = \phi_j + \phi_\tau + \phi_2\, LY_{jt} + \phi_5\, LN_{jt} + \Phi'\, \mathbf{V}_{jt} + \varepsilon_{jt} \quad (11.3)$$

where LX_{jt} is the logarithm of exports either to or from partner j; ϕ_j and ϕ_τ are fixed effects for the countries of immigrant origin and time periods respectively. The inclusion of any fixed effects representing the countries of origin necessitates omission of the distance and common-border variables from (11.1);[8] time fixed effects require omission of the OECD host's income levels. On the other hand, the omission of emigrant stock from the OECD country in its trading partners is typically forced by lack of data.

Naturally, contributions to this literature have included variations on this basic model. Some have included partner fixed effects; others have relied entirely on a vector of controls instead, particularly when only cross-section data are available.[9] The treatments of both zero migration and zero trade have also differed. Simply omitting observations on zero introduces the potential for selection bias from censoring. A number of alternatives have therefore been considered to address the fact that the logarithm of zero (trade or migration) is not defined, and a few notes on these are presented in the Appendix to this chapter. The treatment of zero-migration outcomes has typically either used a scaling approach, adding one to the number of migrants, or inserted a dummy for zero migration, though a few studies simply omit such instances. A couple of analysts also extend the term $\varphi_5 LN_{jt}$ in (11.3) to permit the elasticity of trade to vary with the level of immigration, while others introduce various interactions in one of three generic forms:

$$\gamma_1 \, LN_{jt} + \gamma_2 \, G_{jt} \qquad (11.4\text{i})$$

$$\gamma_1 \, LN_{jt} + \gamma_2 \, G_{jt} {*} \, LN_{jt} \qquad (11.4\text{ii})$$

$$\gamma_1 \log(N_{jt} * G_{jt}) + \gamma_2 \log(N_{jt} *(1 - G_{jt})) \qquad (11.4\text{iii})$$

where G_{jt} represents the fraction of immigrants from j possessing some characteristic and log indicates a natural logarithm. Both these latter extensions will be discussed in some detail in the following section. Meanwhile it will be useful to note that the alternative specifications in (11.4) have somewhat different implications.[10]

In comparison, the fresh evidence presented in this chapter adopts a basic specification:

$$LX_{ijt} = \theta_{ij} + \theta_t + \Theta_1'\mathbf{N}_{ijt} + \Theta_2'\mathbf{N}_{jit} + \Theta_3' LN_{ijt} {*} \mathbf{G}_{ijt} + \Theta_4' LN_{jit} {*} \mathbf{G}_{jit} + \theta_1 LP_{it} + \theta_2 LP_{jt} + \theta_3 LY_{it} + \theta_4 LY_{jt} + \Theta_5'\mathbf{V}_{ijt} + \varepsilon_{ijt} \qquad (11.5)$$

This includes fixed effects for each country dyad (θ_{ij}) and time period (θ_t).[11] The vector $\mathbf{N}_{ijt}$ is composed of five terms: LN_{ijt}, LN_{ijt}^2, LN_{ijt}^3, LN_{ijt}^4 and Z_{ijt}, where Z_{ijt} is a dummy variable for zero bilateral emigration from i to j (in which event LN_{ijt} is set to zero). $\mathbf{N}_{jit}$ encompasses the counterpart five terms. The logarithms of migration in both directions are also interacted with a vector of terms ($\mathbf{G}_{ijt}$ and $\mathbf{G}_{jit}$) that comprise the following elements:

A common language spoken in the two countries

The two countries either had a colonial link at some stage or had a common colonizer

If the two countries are signatories of a mutual trade agreement
Fraction of the migrants that are refugees
Fraction of the migrants that is female.

The first two of these elements are time invariant and hence encompassed in the dyad fixed effects; the remaining three are, however, incorporated into the vector of controls ($\mathbf{V}_{ijt}$) so as not to compromise the interaction terms. The interaction terms in (11.5) thus nest both (11.4i) and (11.4ii). $\mathbf{V}_{ijt}$ also includes the incidence of war in both i and j at time t. Other terms are as previously defined.

Estimation of (11.5) draws on cross-country, bilateral trade and migration data between 36864 dyads of 192 countries from 1960 to 2000. Annual data are available for all time-varying terms in (11.5), with the exception of migrant stocks, which are available at the turn of each decade. For years between the decennial points, the migrant stocks are therefore interpolated linearly here to be commensurate with the trade data. Tests on the restriction that all migration terms in (11.5) differ between the decades and in the intervening years fail to reject these restrictions. In other words, interpolating the migration data between census years to preserve continuity appears to have little bearing on the results. Equation (11.5) is estimated separately for each of four country-dyad groups. Each of the four groups is defined by whether the country of export (and hence of emigrant origin and of immigrant residence) is a developing or higher-income country and whether the bilateral partner is a developing or higher-income country. For present purposes, developing (or lower-income) countries are defined as those with a GDP per capita, at the time, below US$4035 in 2000 prices; higher-income countries are those above this cut-off. This corresponds to developing countries including all Low and Lower-Middle Income countries on the current World Bank definitions; the Upper-Middle and High Income countries are in our higher-income group.[12] Table 11.1 presents the patterns of export flows and of migrant stocks between these sets of countries as of 2000.

2. EXISTING AND FRESH EVIDENCE ON THE BILATERAL MIGRATION–TRADE LINK REFERRING TO DEVELOPING REGIONS

Rather than attempting to summarize the existing evidence separately from any fresh results, I present the two here in tandem, distinguishing particular elements within these results.

Table 11.1 Bilateral exports and migrant stocks as of 2000

	Total bilateral exports of goods (million US$) Importing countries			
	Low-income	Lower-middle	Upper-middle	High-income
Exporting countries				
Low-income	565	2708	2448	13584
Lower-middle	8453	47451	65661	524980
Upper-middle	6139	81154	130498	675679
High-income	18103	362742	599644	3511102
	Migrant stocks Host countries			
	Low-income	Lower-middle	Upper-middle	High-income
Home countries				
Low-income	2488611	8578473	2026359	3224232
Lower-middle	3258727	9111873	12480349	27201890
Upper-middle	492704	7371815	12069357	39007523
High-income	345442	1624417	3365820	26923264

2.1 Migrant Elasticities of Trade by Level of Development

Given the reliance on personal deals in doing business in many developing countries, one might presume that both the contract-enforcement and information-bridging opportunities afforded by migrants would assume particular importance. Yet the vast bulk of prior evidence refers exclusively to OECD countries' trade and there is little emphasis on the development status of their trading partners. The prior literature on this issue is consequently sparse, but falls into four types:

1. Single OECD country analyses that distinguish between developing and developed partners.
2. OECD studies adopting development-related surrogates.
3. Applications to single developing countries.
4. Cross-country studies that distinguish developing regions.

Studies under the first heading have appeared for three OECD countries: the USA, New Zealand and Spain. The two US analyses reach opposing results.[13] Co et al. (2004) find that exports by US states exhibit an elasticity with respect to immigrant stock that is greater in the case of high-income partner countries than for lower-income partners, though the absolute difference is slight and probably insignificant statistically. In contrast, White (2007a) estimates that immigrants from high- and middle-income countries have no significant effect on either US national exports or imports; on the other hand, immigrants from low-income countries have positive effects on both US exports and imports, and especially on the latter. Qian (2008) supports White's position, finding that New Zealand's imports have by far the greatest elasticity with respect to immigrants from lower-middle-income countries, while exports respond most to immigrants from the low-income countries (see also Law et al., 2009). In the analysis of exports from the provinces of Spain by Peri and Requena-Silvente (2010), immigrants from Africa have the biggest effect overall on highly, moderately and less differentiated goods, though immigrants from the Middle East have an even larger association in the specific case of moderately differentiated goods.

Developing countries are commonly characterized as having weak institutions, which result in a lack of transparency and laxity in the rule of law. Accordingly, Dunlevy (2006) shows that US state exports are particularly enhanced by immigrants if the migrants come from countries in which transparency of institutions is weak, a finding supported by Briant et al. (2009) for the case of French regions using an index of rule of law in the partner countries.[14]

In contrast to the plethora of studies of immigrant effects on trade of the OECD countries, only two papers have appeared examining the parallel case for developing countries. Unfortunately, neither study offers convincing evidence of whether immigrants in developing countries have comparable effects on trade as in the case of their OECD counterparts.[15]

With the advent of several bilateral migration matrices, four recent papers examine the role of migration in cross-country trade patterns among multiple countries, distinguishing developing regions in the process. Two of these focus exclusively on migration to the OECD countries. Felbermayr and Jung (2009) adopt the migrant stock matrices, for 1990 and 2000, compiled by Docquier and Marfouk (2004) to examine OECD immigration from, and trade with, the 'south', where the south is defined as countries with a GDP per capita below the sample eightieth percentile (which actually includes some eurozone countries). In the context of a gravity model, with country and time fixed effects as well as some dyad controls, the authors estimate an elasticity of 0.22 on immigrants from the south on the geometric mean of OECD imports and exports exchanged with their countries of origin. Bettin and Turco (2012) merge the Docquier–Marfouk data with the bilateral migrant stock matrix for 2005 prepared by Ratha and Shaw (2007). Again the focus is the effect of emigration from developing countries (here defined to include several OECD countries: the Czech Republic, Hungary, Mexico, Poland, Slovenia, South Korea and Turkey) to the remaining 21 OECD countries. Bettin and Turco estimate the elasticity of OECD exports to the 'developing' countries at 0.11 with respect to the stock of emigrants from the developing countries, but that for developing-country exports to the OECD at a value not significantly different from zero.

Two multiple-country studies are able to take a broader look at developing countries. White and Tadesse (2013) use the Ratha–Shaw 2005 matrix, which allows them to look, in the cross-section, at the influence on African trade of African emigration, from 43 nations to 110 host countries. Pooling the cross-sectional data and including a vector of various controls for the host and home countries as well as the dyad, the average emigrant elasticity is estimated at 0.132 for African imports and 0.259 for African exports. However, White and Tadesse go on to emphasize that these averages hide a good deal of variation with respect to both the African states of origin and the host countries.[16] Parsons (2012) appears to be the first to use the Global Bilateral Migration Database (GBMD), also used in the fresh evidence in the present chapter, to examine the migration–trade link.[17] Parsons adopts the bilateral trade data from Feenstra et al. (2005), which are based on the UN Comtrade, resulting in trade between 68 countries and 178 partners. In repeated cross-sections on the pooled data, Parsons finds results in line with those from prior studies; however, on introducing dyad fixed effects in the panel data the associations between bilateral trade and migration prove indistinguishable from zero. Parsons then partitions his data into four groups defined by the intersections of North and South[18] and finds that migrants positively affect only exports from North to South.[19]

The evidence on any migrant–trade link for the developing countries is thus fairly limited, particularly with respect to South–South links, and the findings are certainly mixed. Against this background, Figure 11.1 depicts the patterns emerging from the polynomial estimates on migration levels obtained here by scaled least squares estimates of (11.5), as reported in Table 11A.1 of the Appendix. These refer to elasticities of bilateral trade with respect to male, non-refugee migrants, when no common language, colonial link or regional trade agreement exists. Each of these refers to exports, but note that, given the symmetry in these estimates, the elasticity of higher-income countries' exports with respect to immigrants from lower-income countries is also the elasticity of lower-income countries' imports with respect to their emigrants to the higher-income countries, for example. At the sample mean levels of migration for all four of the respective country groups, the elasticities of exports with respect to both

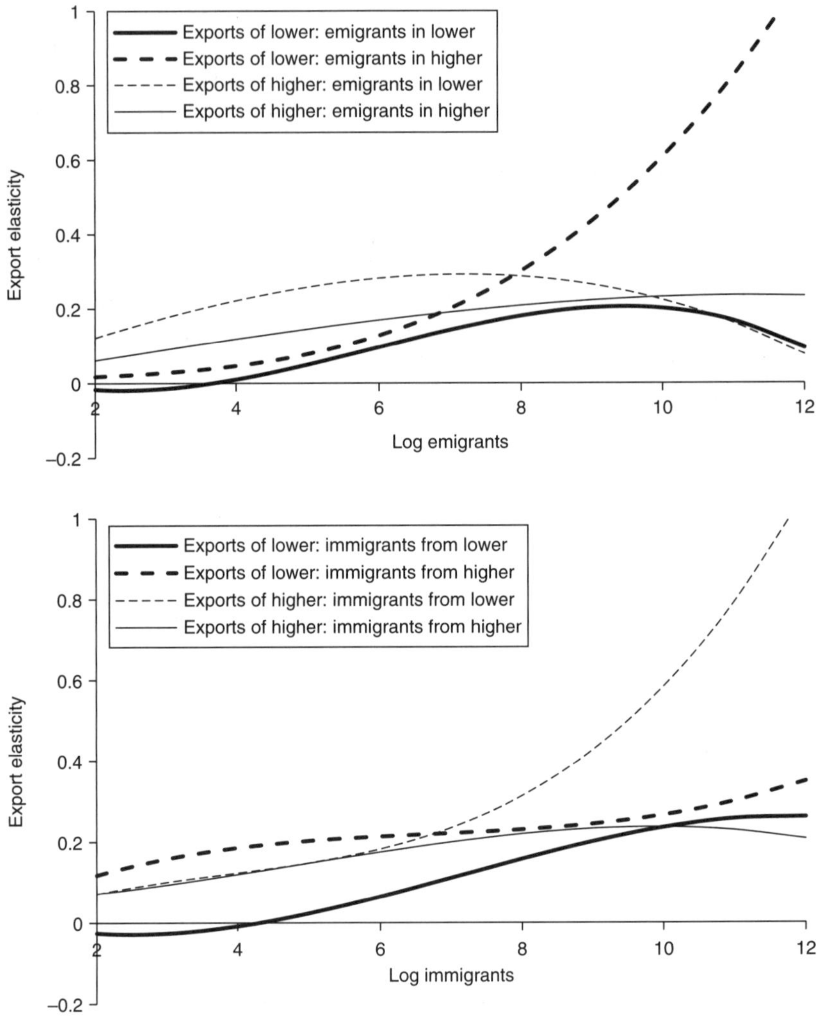

Figure 11.1 Migrant elasticities of home countries' exports

emigrants and immigrants prove significantly greater than zero with more than 99 percent confidence. At low levels of movement, migration from the higher- to lower-income countries has the largest impact on their bilateral trade in both directions. However, at higher levels of movement the reverse holds: emigration from lower- to higher-income countries has the largest effect on bilateral trade in both directions.

Summing up, much of the prior evidence on migration links with developing-country trade has been severely limited by data availability. Almost all of the evidence is confined to distinguishing developing-country immigrants in the OECD states, and some of these analyses have adopted rather liberal definitions of developing countries. Although not unanimous, most of this evidence points to larger bilateral trade elasticities of migrants from lower-income countries than of immigrants from higher-income nations, though hardly any prior evidence exists on South–South migrant–trade links. The complementary fresh evidence indicates that emigration from developing to higher-income countries has a particularly strong association with bilateral trade in both directions at higher levels of migration. Nonetheless, South–South migration in both directions is also significantly associated with greater bilateral trade flows among these lower-income states.

2.2 On the Constancy of Migrant Elasticities of Trade

A couple of prior papers delve into the presumption of a constant elasticity of trade with respect to immigration. Bryant et al. (2005) add a term in the squared logarithm of the number of immigrants in New Zealand; Gould (1994) for the USA and Wagner et al. (2002) for Canadian provinces adopt more complex functions, the latter requiring iterative estimation. All three find declining export and import elasticities as the levels of immigration increase.[20]

The squared, cubic and quartic terms in the logarithms of emigrants and immigrants prove, jointly, significantly different from zero, with high levels of confidence, in all four estimates in Table 11A.1. A presumption of a constant elasticity is almost ubiquitous in the prior literature, but may not be warranted.

A glance at Figure 11.1 establishes that, in contrast to the few prior findings addressing the issue, the elasticities of trade with respect to migration do not all decline with the level of migration: the patterns are somewhat mixed. However, the elasticities of export actually rise monotonically and with greater than 99 percent confidence, in seven of the eight cases illustrated, over a range of the logarithm of bilateral migration increasing from 4 through 10, an increase in the migrant stock from about 50 to 20000. The only exception is for the elasticity of exports with respect to emigrants from the higher- to lower-income countries, where the rise is smaller and statistically weaker. Indeed, most of the elasticity profiles continue to rise even beyond 20000 migrants. This is clearly particularly true with respect to trade in both directions as emigration from the lower- to higher-income countries rises.

2.3 Immigrants and Emigrants

Seven existing studies have managed to look at both immigrants and emigrants simultaneously, though two of these exclude any developing countries completely. Some, but not all, find positive associations of trade with both immigrants and emigrants.[21] More typically, data on emigrants are not available. However, if all measures on emigrants are omitted from the results in Table 11A.1, any change in the immigrant profiles depicted in Figure 11.1 is negligible, so perhaps prior studies that have omitted emigrants may still be representative. On the other hand, a joint test on whether the terms including emigrant stocks are all zero in Table 11A.1 is resoundingly rejected, as is a comparable test on the immigrant vector. Both immigrants and emigrants are indeed significantly associated with trade. Moreover, the trade elasticities in Figure 11.1 prove almost entirely positive over the entire range of migrant levels for both emigrants and immigrants for all four bilateral groups.

2.4 On Refugees and Gender of Migrants

As of 2000, the percentages of emigrants that were refugees and that were female are as shown in Table 11.2.

Not only are refugees a high fraction of migrants from one lower-income country in another lower-income country, but this movement between lower-income countries actually represents almost two-thirds of the world's refugees at the time. Despite this concentration, the only context in which the role of refugees in the migrant–trade link has been examined has been in two high-income countries. Head and Ries (1998) examine Canadian immigrants by class of admission, adopting a specification of type (11.4ii); White and Tadesse (2010) look at the numbers of US refugee and non-refugee immigrants, adopting approach (11.4iii).

Table 11.2 Percentage of migrants by refugee status and gender, 2000

	As percentage of emigrants in	
	lower-income	higher-income
Emigrants from	Refugees	
Lower-income	27.03	5.46
Higher-income	0.30	1.37
	Female	
Lower-income	47.54	48.59
Higher-income	55.33	50.46

Table 11.3 Marginal trade effects of refugee composition and gender of migrants

	Marginal effect on log exports of			
	Lower-income		Higher-income	
	Emigrants in/immigrants from			
	Lower	Higher	Lower	Higher
Fraction of refugees among				
Emigrants	−0.103	−0.150	−0.162	−0.159
	(58.91)	(55.69)	(16.41)	(8.16)
Immigrants	0.045	−0.091	−0.040	−0.206
	(11.35)	(5.37)	(3.74)	(13.78)
Fraction of females among				
Emigrants	0.084	0.173	−0.230	0.193
	(24.29)	(93.84)	(71.91)	(28.42)
Immigrants	−0.066	−0.042	−0.002	−0.041
	(259.77)	(128.43)	(1.36)	(18.16)

Note: F-statistics in parentheses.

Both conclude that refugees have no significant effect on trade with their country of origin, whereas other immigrants do. Perhaps this is to be expected, given refugees' presumed association with their original country.

If refugees have no significant effect on bilateral trade, this would have particularly important implications for some of the developing countries where refugee flows are far greater than for any high-income countries. Towards examining this issue, the specification in Table 11A.1 adopts a format that nests approaches (11.4i) and (11.4ii). Table 11.3 presents estimates of the resulting marginal effect of increasing the fraction of refugees among migrants, evaluated at the sample means of the log migrant stock.

Across the board, the higher the fraction of migrants that are refugees, the lower is the proportional increase in exports. Among immigrants, the same effect holds, with the exception of refugees from lower-income countries in lower-income countries (the dominant case), wherein a higher fraction of refugees is actually associated with an increase in the country of asylum's exports.[22] Does this imply that refugees do nothing to expand trade? To investigate this, turn to formula (11.4iii), in which the logarithms of refugee and non-refugee migrant stocks are included separately, each to the fourth power. Figure 11.2 depicts the resulting profiles for lower-income country exports. All three profiles (with respect to refugees fleeing to other lower-income countries and to higher-income countries,

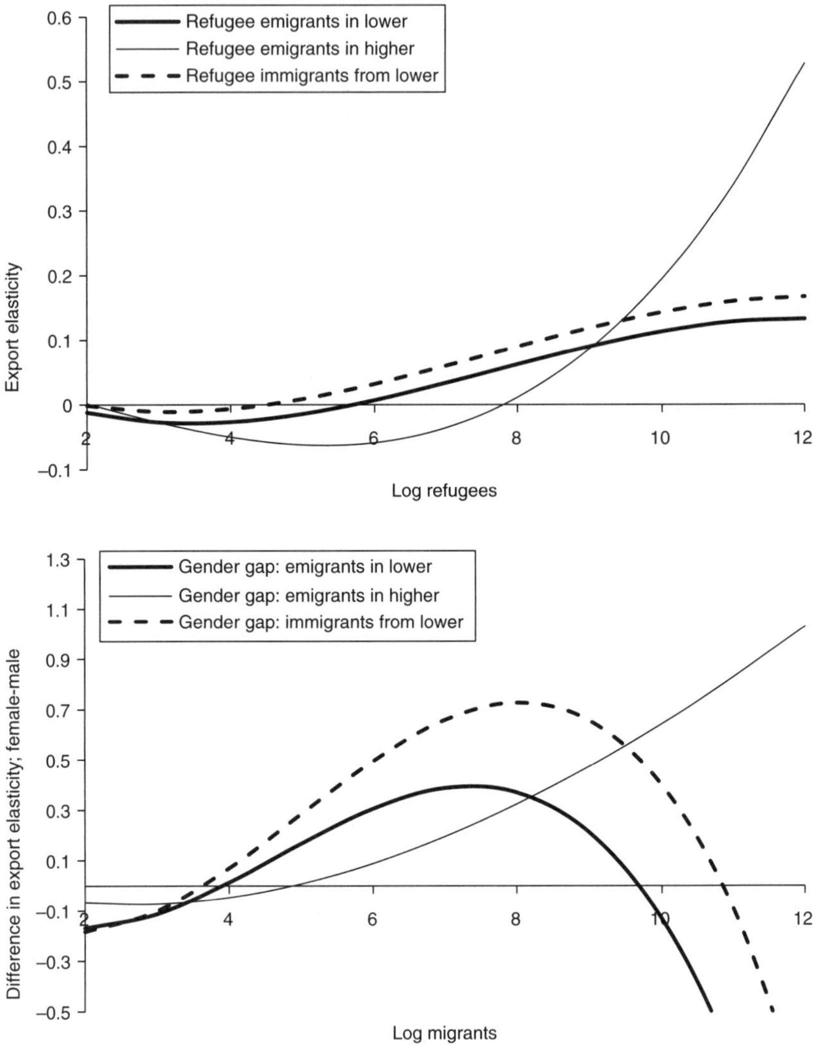

Figure 11.2 Elasticities of lower-income countries' exports: refugees and gender gap

as well as people from other lower-income countries taking refuge in the exporting country) rise with the stocks of refugees, becoming significantly positive at higher levels. Again the elasticity of lower-income countries' exports is particularly high with respect to refugees in the higher-income countries, though less so than for emigrants more generally over this corridor. Moreover, the profile (not shown in Figure 11.2) of imports by the lower-income countries from the higher-income countries proves very similar to that for exports over this same set of dyads. Although a higher fraction of refugees among migrants is associated with less bilateral trade, trade rises with the number of refugees given the number of non-refugee migrants.[23]

It is less apparent what to expect with respect to the role of migrants' gender; whether females or males are better placed to enforce contracts or to bridge information gaps; whether men or women are more likely to possess a preference for home goods or to pass that preference along to others. There appear to be no precedents in the literature, perhaps in part because the variation in the fraction of females among migrants across different corridors is generally small.[24] Table 11.3 again presents the results from the estimates of (11.5) evaluated at the mean of log migration. The higher the fraction of emigrants that is female from the lower-income states, the greater are bilateral exports, though the reverse is true with respect to the fraction of immigrants that is female.[25] The lower panel in Figure 11.2 shows estimates of the elasticity of exports with respect to number of female migrants minus that for males if specification (11.4iii) is adopted instead. Clearly, over most of the range of migration levels, the elasticity with respect to female migration proves larger than with respect to movement of men.[26] Note that since these results are obtained using dyad fixed effects, any differences in the role of females does not simply reflect differences in openness to trade being associated with differences in the stigma attached to women migrating in particular contexts. Certainly, given the significance of the estimated effects, this neglected topic would seem to warrant closer attention.

2.5 Dyad Links: Common Language, Colonial Heritage and Regional Trade Agreements

It is commonplace to augment gravity models of trade with indications of links between the trading partners, such as whether they speak a common language, share some form of colonial history or are signatories to a regional trade agreement. A number of contributions from the subset of these bilateral trade models that include migrant stocks also include dummy variables for such links within the vector of controls $\mathbf{V}_{ijt}$. The notion is that such links render trade simpler, given the ease of communication and familiarity with the setting.[27] By extension, this should leave migrants less essential in providing such bridges. Yet only a few studies have examined an interaction between the log of immigrants and whether the country of origin has a common language or colonial link with an

Table 11.4 Differences in migrant elasticities of exports under a common language, colonial link and regional trade agreement

	Difference in elasticity of exports by			
	Lower-income		Higher-income	
	Of emigrants in/immigrants from			
	Lower	Higher	Lower	Higher
Common language *				
Log(emigrants)	−0.021	−0.029	0.000	−0.053
	(6.22)	(6.94)	(0.01)	(7.30)
Log(immigrants)	−0.033	−0.021	−0.037	−0.008
	(9.90)	(3.74)	(8.76)	(1.13)
Colonial link *				
Log(emigrants)	−0.025	−0.038	−0.003	0.025
	(7.10)	(7.71)	(0.44)	(2.53)
Log(immigrants)	−0.027	−0.007	−0.018	−0.034
	(7.57)	(1.01)	(3.54)	(3.46)
Regional trade agreement *				
Log(emigrants)	0.004	0.043	0.018	0.028
	(0.94)	(4.17)	(1.72)	(4.45)
Log(immigrants)	0.056	0.002	0.056	0.054
	(14.10)	(0.18)	(5.27)	(8.66)

Note: t-statistics for a zero null hypothesis in parentheses.

OECD host. Dunlevy (2006), for example, finds a lower immigrant elasticity of US bilateral exports if immigrants are from either English- or Spanish-speaking countries; other results are more mixed, and none seems to differentiate with respect to levels of development involved.[28]

Table 11.4 reproduces the estimates from the Appendix for the interaction terms between the logarithms of migrants and whether a common language, colonial link or regional trade agreement exists.[29] Almost all of the migrant elasticities of developing countries' exports are significantly diminished where either a common language is spoken or a colonial link exists; the only exception is with respect to immigrants from higher-income countries, where the difference is indistinguishable from zero. The patterns with respect to higher-income countries' exports are a little more mixed, though imports by the lower-income from the higher-income countries are less elastic with respect to lower-income emigrants where either a common language or colonial link exists. These results thus tend to support the hypothesis that migrants play a less significant role in bridging trade gaps where familiarity is less of an issue. However, none of the differences is very large.[30]

Regional trade agreements are most common among the high-income countries, though some also exist among the developing countries; agreements involving both higher-income and developing countries are scant. Where two countries are part of a regional trade agreement, the elasticity of exports with respect to migration is estimated to be larger than where no agreement exists, though this positive association is statistically significant for migration in both directions only between higher-income partners. Quite why a positive association emerges is unclear. Many trade agreements also include clauses easing labor movement too.[31] One possibility is that freer migration and freer trade are then introduced simultaneously, resulting in a positive association. In future work it would be of interest to distinguish cases where effective labor mobility is a part of the regional trade agreement.

2.6 Education Levels of Migrants

Do highly skilled emigrants from the developing regions stimulate bilateral trade with high-income partners by more than do their less-well-trained counterparts? Do the lesser-skilled migrants offer a preference effect but prove ineffective in information bridging and contract enforcement? A small subset of existing analyses has begun to disaggregate immigrants' effects on trade by education or skill level of the migrants, offering potentially important insights into such questions and hence into any brain-gain calculus. To date, such studies seem confined to the contexts of Canadian, US and Spanish immigration, with rather mixed approaches and answers.

Head and Ries (1998) distinguish Canadian immigrants by category of visa, adopting a specification of type (11.4ii); those designated 'Independent' visa recipients tend to be the most highly skilled and have the largest, positive impact on both import and export elasticities. Herander and Saavedra (2005) instead define skill by the fraction of US immigrants in a skilled occupation, again applying this to specification (11.4i).[32] This follows a similar approach to that of Gould (1994), who finds the fraction deemed skilled among US immigrants from each country to be very weakly negatively associated with both exports and imports to that country. In sharp contrast, Herander and Saavedra find a positive association, at least with exports from various US states. In their cross-sectional analysis, Jansen and Piermartini (2009) explore both approaches to measuring skill, either by occupation or on the basis of receiving an H1B visa to enter the USA (reserved for those with special skills). Exploring both (11.4i) and (11.4ii) as specifications, Jansen and Piermartini find that neither measure of the fraction of US immigrants that is skilled has any clear positive effect on bilateral trade.[33] Blanes (2008) distinguishes four levels of education among immigrants in Spain: no education, primary, secondary and tertiary and estimates a form of type (11.4iii). In his results, the number of migrants with no or primary education has no effect on either imports or exports; more migrants with secondary education are significantly associated with both larger imports and exports, and more tertiary-educated migrants have a weak positive association with exports to their home country but not with imports from home.[34]

The international data on education of migrants remain very limited; nonetheless, the foregoing can be extended in a couple of directions. Two data sources on bilateral migration by education and gender are merged here for this purpose: one reports the immigrant stocks in most of the OECD countries as of 1990 and 2000 (see Docquier and Marfouk, 2004); the other extends the 2000 data to cover 32 OECD member countries and 68 non-members.[35] Despite the latter extension, insufficient observations are available to examine bilateral migration into the lower-income countries by education.[36] The present analysis is therefore confined to looking at emigrants in the higher-income countries from the lower-income countries. Four specifications are reported in Table 11.5, adopting each of the three alternatives presented in (11.4), plus a hybrid including both of the first two options. Otherwise, the specification is kept as in (11.5), again with dyad and year fixed effects. Table 11.5 displays only the relevant coefficients for education, estimated on 3600 observations for 2518 dyads.

No matter which specification is used, the association between trade in both directions and tertiary-educated migrants proves largest;[37] moreover, these effects are significantly larger than the estimated association with secondary-educated migrants (though there is less than 99 percent confidence in this difference for imports in the first specification). In each of the first three specifications, the association between bilateral exports and secondary-educated migration also tends to be larger than an association with primary-educated migrants (the omitted category), though this latter difference is statistically weaker for exports than imports. The last specification says that, given the number of emigrants without a tertiary education, the more tertiary-educated migrants, the greater is bilateral trade in both directions, but the converse does not hold, suggesting that lower-skilled emigrants have no significant effect on trade in either direction.

A viable interpretation is that the bridging roles played by migrants from the lower-income countries to their higher-income trade partners increase with the level of education of the migrants. To the extent that this represents an efficiency gain in trade, it potentially offers an important

Table 11.5 Logarithm of bilateral exports and imports of lower-income countries with respect to education of emigrants

	Exports	Imports	Exports	Imports	Exports	Imports	Exports	Imports
Fraction emigrants with secondary	0.607	0.965			0.087	0.938		
education	(1.97)	(3.52)			(0.17)	(2.12)		
Fraction emigrants with tertiary	1.643	1.650			0.718	0.779		
education	(5.30)	(6.01)			(1.36)	(1.67)		
Fraction secondary * Log(emigrants)			0.102	0.107	0.096	−0.013		
			(1.96)	(2.32)	(1.15)	(0.17)		
Fraction tertiary * Log(emigrants)			0.262	0.262	0.174	0.163		
			(5.57)	(6.27)	(2.17)	(2.29)		
Log(primary emigrants)							0.021	−0.011
							(0.81)	(0.46)
Log(secondary emigrants)							−0.011	0.101
							(0.15)	(1.53)
Log(tertiary emigrants)							0.315	0.278
							(5.19)	(5.15)

Note: t-statistics for a zero null hypothesis in parentheses.

mitigating factor in any costs incurred with emigration of the highly skilled.

In subsequent work, as more complete data become available, it may be important to examine this trade link with migrant skill level including both immigrants and emigrants, and to look at bilateral exchange between lower-income states in relation to migrants' skill levels, neither of which the present data permit.

2.7 Exports, Imports and the Balance of Trade

Within the extensive literature on the OECD countries, attention has been directed toward whether the elasticity of exports or imports with respect to immigration proves larger. In part, this reflects efforts to distinguish the preference effect of migrants on trade, which is commonly assumed confined to imports. The evidence proves mixed. In their survey, Genç et al. (2011, abstract) note that 'The migrant elasticity of imports is larger than that of exports in about half the countries considered.'

Despite this attention to the relative effects on exports versus imports, the net effect on the balance of trade has been largely neglected. For the low-income countries in particular, this balance has been a chronic concern.[38] Note, though, that which elasticity is bigger, exports or imports, only gives the balance of trade effect if trade is initially balanced. Consider, instead, the marginal effects of migration on the balance of trade. These may be derived for each country and year by multiplying the respective migrant elasticities of trade, evaluated at the observed migration level, by the ratio of observed exports or imports to the stock of migrants. Table 11.6 sets out the resultant means for the marginal effect of emigration on both the sum of bilateral exports and imports (openness

Table 11.6 Marginal effects of emigration on openness to trade and balance of trade

	Emigrants from			
	Lower-income in		Higher-income in	
	Lower	Higher	Lower	Higher
∂(exports + imports)/∂ emigrants	0.0056	0.0916	0.4526	0.8210
	(2.08)	(50.10)	(41.25)	(56.38)
∂(exports – imports)/∂ emigrants	0.0003	−0.0370	0.0234	−0.0806
	(0.28)	(27.86)	(4.39)	(8.60)

Note: t-statistics for a zero null hypothesis in parentheses.

to trade) and the difference between exports and imports (the balance of merchandise trade effect). For each of the four country-dyad groups the marginal effect on openness to trade is positive. The absolute magnitude of the effect is smallest and statistically weakest for emigration from one lower-income country to another, though this margin is added to a much smaller base of trade than for the other groups.

This migration between lower-income countries is estimated to have no significant effect on the bilateral balance of trade between these countries. On the other hand, emigration on the margin from lower-income to higher-income states results in a worsening of the balance of trade for the lower-income countries on average; in other words, this movement is estimated to do more to stimulate imports from the higher-income partner than to promote exports to that partner. In contrast, emigration from the average higher-income country to a developing country serves to improve the balance of trade for the wealthier country. Stated otherwise, immigration into the average lower-income country from a wealthier state does more to promote exports to the developing country than to help the latter's export performance, deteriorating the balance of trade for the lower-income partner.

Whereas migration is thus estimated to expand trade of the lower-income countries, potentially lowering trade barriers in the process, migration does not serve to improve the balance of trade but rather the opposite.

2.8 An Extension: Two Third-Party Effects

Rauch and Trindade (2002) introduce the notion that the presence of common, third-country ethnic networks in two trading partners may also serve to enhance bilateral trade between these partners. At least five variants on measuring such networks have now appeared in the literature:

$$\eta \textstyle\sum_k \log[(N_{kit} * N_{kjt})/(P_{it} * P_{jt})] \qquad (11.6\text{i})$$

$$\eta \textstyle\sum_k \log(N_{kit} * N_{kjt}) \qquad (11.6\text{ii})$$

$$\eta \textstyle\sum_k [(N_{kit} * N_{kjt})/(P_{it} * P_{jt})] \qquad (11.6\text{iii})$$

$$\textstyle\sum_k [\eta_k (N_{kit} * N_{kjt})/(P_{it} * P_{jt})] \qquad (11.6\text{iv})$$

$$\textstyle\sum_k [\eta_k \log(N_{kit} * N_{kjt})] \qquad (11.6\text{v})$$

where N_{kit} (N_{kjt}) is the number of persons from country k in country i (j) at time t; P_{it} and P_{jt} are the populations of i and j, as before, and

$k \neq i$, $k \neq j$. Rauch and Trindade consider only a single third country, China, adopting both (11.6i) and (11.6ii), noting that 'The first is the probability that, if we select an individual at random from each country, both will be ethnic Chinese. The second is the number of potential international connections between the ethnic Chinese populations of the trading partners.'[39] Rauche and Trindade estimate a large positive value for η on the ethnic Chinese network, distinguishing between direct effects (in which one of the trading partners is China itself) and indirect effects; though no other migration terms are included in their analysis. Felbermayr et al. (2010) introduce the linear variants (11.6iii) and (11.6iv), denoting the former, which constrains $\eta_k = \eta$ for all k, the average network effect. Felbermayr and his co-authors apply both form (11.6iii) and (11.6iv) to a cross-section of the bilateral volume of trade and migration amongst 63 countries in 2000, inserting dummies for each country. The average (indirect) network coefficient, η, proves significantly positive; the direct network effect also proves positive, but only once the indirect migrant networks are included. In other words, exclusion of these third-country migrant networks biases downward estimates of the link between bilateral trade and migration between these partners according to these results. Estimation of the heterogeneous network model, (11.6iv), in Felbermayr et al. points to a wide spread in values for η_k.[40] Parsons (2012) also explores heterogeneity in the indirect network effect but for 178 third-party countries and adopting the logarithmic form (11.6v). Inserting these indirect network terms into an equation that also includes the direct emigration and immigration terms from (11.1), ϕ_5 LN_{ijt} and ϕ_6 LN_{jit}, Parsons finds not only a very wide spread of effects, from positive to negative, but that these effects are quite sensitive to inclusion of dyad fixed effects.

None of the prior studies of third-country networks distinguishes between effects on lower-income versus higher-income countries' trade. Moreover, while the effects of third-country immigrants in the bilateral trading pair have received some attention, the effects of emigration from the trading pair to third countries have been universally neglected. Does emigration to one country result in less trade with others – an effect that might be dubbed trade diversion? Diversion may, for instance, occur because of supply constraints in producing exports, dilution of information flows, or competition in contract enforcement.

Following Parsons (2012), the third-party potential effects are here inserted into the basic equation (11.5) rather than representing the direct effects as in Rauch and Trindade, given the significant polynomial form estimated for our direct effects. Specifically, the additional terms may be written:

Table 11.7 Third-party effects

	Bilateral exports of			
	Lower-income to		Higher-income to	
	Lower-income	Higher-income	Lower-income	Higher-income
Average indirect network	0.508 (41.86)	0.744 (53.70)	0.859 (61.40)	0.840 (50.33)
Log emigrants elsewhere				
From origin in lower-income third countries	−0.042 (36.69)		−0.002 (1.19)	
From origin in higher-income third countries		−0.007 (2.49)		−0.013 (2.70)
From partner in lower-income third countries	−0.028 (24.23)		−0.048 (26.89)	
From partner in higher-income third countries		−0.043 (14.02)		0.053 (10.67)

Note: t-statistics for a zero null hypothesis in parentheses.

$$\eta \textstyle\sum_k \log(N_{kit}{}^* N_{kjt})/1000 + \alpha \log(\textstyle\sum_\kappa N_{i\kappa t}) + \beta \log(\textstyle\sum_\kappa N_{j\kappa t}) \qquad (11.7)$$

where k indexes all countries $k \neq i$ and $k \neq j$; $k\kappa$ indexes all lower-income (higher-income) countries within k when examining exports to lower-income (higher-income) countries.[41] Estimates of the additional terms are reported in Table 11.7.

The results in Table 11.7 indicate that the presence of third-country nationals, in common in both the home and partner country, is strongly positively associated with bilateral trade between the home and partner countries, no matter whether these trading countries are lower- or higher-income states.

Moreover, with respect to exports from the developing countries both to other lower-income states as well as to richer countries, having more emigrants in third countries, both from the home and trade partner, is associated with diminished bilateral trade. In other words, this supports the notion of trade diversion occurring through emigration elsewhere.

In contrast to some prior results, inclusion of these additional terms hardly alters the profiles with respect to direct migration shown in Figure 11.1. Together with the extent to which bilateral trade is diverted by migration elsewhere but enhanced by third-country migrant networks, this raises the issue of the net trade-creating effects of migrants. Given the positive signs on third-country immigrant networks, the question of net direction of effect arises only with respect to emigrants. One way to examine this is to consider the marginal effect of an additional emigrant on total exports, which can be derived from the expanded estimates of (11.5) as

$$\frac{\partial X_i}{\partial N_{ij}} = \frac{X_{ij}}{N_{ij}} \sum_{\chi=1}^{4} \chi \delta_\chi L N_{ij}^{\chi-1} + \alpha \frac{\sum_{\kappa} X_{i\kappa}}{\sum_{\kappa} N_{i\kappa}} \tag{11.8}$$

where δ_χ, $\chi = 1,4$, are the coefficients on the polynomial emigrant terms from vector Θ_1 in (11.5). The first term on the right of (11.8) represents the direct effect of a marginal emigrant upon exports; the second term adds in the indirect consequence of this emigration upon bilateral exports to other countries.

Figure 11.3 displays the resulting net marginal effects of emigration on exports.[42] The marginal effect on exports from lower-income to other lower-income partners is small, but is adding to a very low base. Each of the four marginal effects initially rises with the level of bilateral migration and at least by a level of 175 migrants ($LN_{ij} \approx 5.2$) there is greater than 99 percent confidence that all four marginal effects are positive. Thus significant trade-diverting, indirect effects are estimated as a result of emigration to third countries, but these effects are dominated by the trade-creating direct effects of bilateral emigration.

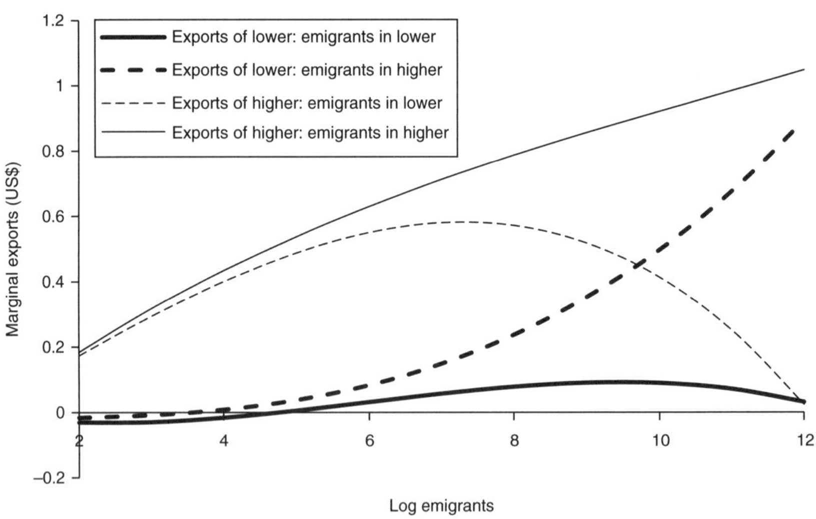

Figure 11.3 Marginal exports with respect to emigrants: direct and indirect effects combined

3. LESSONS TO BE DRAWN

The purpose of this chapter has been to look at the nature of the migrant–trade link, with particular reference to the developing countries. The extant literature on this topic is both sparse and riddled with contradictory results. Inevitably the fresh evidence presented here therefore disagrees with at least portions of this literature. Accordingly, any conclusions should be drawn guardedly.

Nonetheless, some patterns begin to emerge. Although the prior evidence is not unanimous, it seems fair to say that the elasticity of bilateral trade in both directions is particularly high with respect to migration from the developing to the industrialized countries. This makes sense to the extent that migrants play a role in information bridging and contract enforcement, both of which are likely to be especially important for lower-income countries. Given such roles, the migrant–trade link also proves significant across South–South corridors (though again not all observers agree). In a related vein, networks of third-country nationals also prove significantly related to bilateral trade, which holds for South–South and South–North pairings of trade as well as North–North. Our findings, that the migrant–trade link is less where trade partners have a common language or colonial heritage, may also support the notion that migrants are more critical where familiarity with the trade partner is less (though, once more, not all prior studies support this result).

The bulk of prior evidence is confined to looking at the link between immigrants and trade of OECD countries. Yet the results presented here indicate that both emigrants and immigrants are significantly associated with expanded trade for both lower- and higher-income countries. Only a couple of these earlier OECD studies examine whether the elasticity of trade varies with the level of immigration, and these uniformly find a declining association. In stark contrast, the fresh results here find a significant rise in the trade elasticities of both emigrants and immigrants for most cases. The facts that emigrants as well as immigrants can positively affect trade and that this responsiveness may rise with the levels of migration could have important implications for any consideration of the net benefits from migration in both directions.

The composition of migration clearly matters too. Refugee flows are a particularly important part of migration among the low-income countries, especially within Africa. The only previous evidence refers to refugees given asylum in Canada and the USA, concluding that refugees do nothing to expand trade with their countries of origin. The evidence presented here agrees that the larger the fraction of migrants who are refugees, the lower the impact on trade. However, at least in the context of refugees from and in the lower-income countries, who are the vast majority of refugees, trade with their home country is greater, the larger the number of refugees. This suggests some degree of continued ties with the country from which refugees have fled, though there may be complex issues of timing of flight that remain to be investigated. The availability of annual data on bilateral refugee stocks should permit more dynamic investigations of these links in future work.

The role of gender of migrants has been utterly neglected in prior work. Here it is shown that, over substantial ranges of migration levels, the elasticity of developing countries' exports is greater for female than for male emigrants and immigrants. There has been a growing trend of women from lower-income countries migrating alone. Whether the higher elasticity of exports with respect to female migration reflects this growing tendency or reflects, instead, a greater trade impact where couples migrate jointly remains to be disentangled. It is not clear that the data yet exist to separate these possibilities on a systematic basis.

The data on education levels of international migrants remain very limited and the literature on the influence of skill composition on trade remains accordingly thin with overtly conflicting findings, ranging from negative effects of the highly skilled, to no differences by skill level, to more positive effects at higher education levels. Our own evidence pertains only to immigration into the OECD states from lower-income countries. The results are quite unequivocal: it is only the movement of tertiary-educated adults from the lower-income countries into the OECD members that is associated with expanded trade in both directions. To the extent that this holds up as more data become available, it would have important implications. First, on average it seems that the less-educated developing-country emigrants could not be anticipated to help stimulate their home-country trade. Second, to the extent that trade expansion is beneficial to the home country, this adds a potentially important component to brain-gain as opposed to brain-drain. Third, apart from developing countries that are close to industrialized partners, few lower-income countries send large numbers of low-skill migrants to OECD states, so it is the influence of the tertiary-educated that is likely to dominate. Fourth, this may well reinforce the importance of information transmission by migrants, at which the highly educated may be more adept.

The evidence thus points to positive associations between bilateral migration and trade for the developing countries, and perhaps particularly so if the migrants are highly educated and female. Whether such associations are causal might be disputed; few studies have explored the use of instrumental variables, which is unsurprising given the difficulties of picking instruments that are correlated with migration but not with trade with the same partner. Meanwhile, the fairly universal contention that the association is recursive, combined with dyad fixed effects, perhaps reinforces a sense of causality. This is perhaps further buttressed by the demonstration in Artal-Tur et al. (2012) that the migrant–trade link is strongest for in-province immigrants in Italy, Spain and Portugal, weaker for immigrants in adjacent provinces and non-existent for other immigrants. Few micro-level studies have yet appeared, but in related fashion Hiller (2013) finds that Danish firms that employ foreign workers export more to these workers' home countries and that immigrants in the region have only a much smaller impact.

Several indications emerge from our results to suggest that migration plays an important role in breaking down information barriers to trade. The strong associations with highly educated migrants, the lesser role of migrants where common languages are spoken or a colonial heritage exists, all speak to such a role. In turn, overcoming information barriers in promoting openness to trade should represent an efficiency gain for both partners. On the other hand, it seems that developing countries probably should not hope for improvements to their trade balance as a result of migrant flows: the positive associations exist for both exports and imports and the two offset each other.

Much remains to be done in future work. Perhaps the largest lacuna in our present understanding is with respect to the education levels of migrants outside of corridors leading into the OECD countries. The dynamics of some of these processes certainly merit close attention, as does the modeling and alternative estimation of zero bilateral migration and trade. Much of the work at this point addresses averages; reasons for departures from these averages must remain of considerable interest. The present discussion has not touched on merchandise trade in different categories of goods, which has preoccupied substantial portions of the literature but has hardly been touched on in the context of developing countries. Meanwhile investigation of links between migration and trade in services remains in its infancy. And certainly more could be done to disaggregate the average effects observed for third-party networks. The current constraints on these varied extensions are both methodological and imposed by lack of migration data, though both aspects continue to make progress.

NOTES

1. See Greif (1993, 2012) and Rauch (2001). Gaston and Nelson (2013) offer an excellent survey in their section 4.3. White and Tadesse (2011) also offer a useful account in chapter 1 and add the potential for migrant remittances to expand spending and hence trade, plus any stimulus by the diaspora to direct investments in their state of origin, resulting in additional imports and exports by the multinational. A related literature presents estimates of gravity models of foreign direct investments, though this topic is beyond the scope of the present chapter. An example is provided in de Mello-Sampayo (2009).
2. Reductions in information and contract enforcement barriers to trade are tantamount to the lowering of protectionist policy barriers, and indeed the efficacy of the migrant-induced barrier reductions are occasionally depicted numerically as tariff-equivalent reductions (Anderson and van Wincoop, 2003).
3. For surveys of gravity trade models see Anderson and van Wincoop (2004), and Bergstrand and Egger (2011).
4. Among applications to international migration, see Borjas (1987), Karemera et al. (2000), Clark et al. (2007), Lewer and Van Den Berg (2008), Letouzé et al. (2009), Ortega and Peri (2009), Mayda (2010), Beine et al. (2011), Grogger and Hanson (2011) and Lucas (forthcoming).
5. However, to the extent that trade affects real incomes it may also have an effect on migration. In addition, some limited migration may be entailed in the execution of trade deals (see Peng and Ilinitch, 1998).
6. There seems some agreement that such fixed effects also provide a viable alternative to the far more complex, multilateral-resistance, iterative approach in Anderson and van Wincoop (2003). In panel data, country-by-year fixed effects are typically recommended to correct for such multilateral resistance. See Feenstra (2004), and Baldwin and Taglioni (2006). Stouffer (1940) discusses a related concept, intervening opportunities, in migration. Indeed, in their recent empirical work on Spanish immigration, Bertoli and Fernandez-Huertas Moraga (2013) apply the term multilateral resistance to migration and explore its importance. Head et al. (2010) develop a 'tetrad' approach, taking the ratio of ratios of trade among four countries to eliminate both exporter and importer fixed effects, taking advantage of the multiplicative form of the gravity model.
7. Gould (1994), Head and Ries (1998), White (2007a, 2007b) and Hatzigeorgiou (2010a) also add a Koyck lag structure. Mundra (2005) develops a semi-parametric, dynamic panel estimator and applies it to a gravity trade equation incorporating migration. See also Ghatak and Piperakis (2007), Faustino and Leitão (2008), Partridge and Furtan (2008) for other dynamic explorations. Behrens et al. (2012) add an examination of the potential for spatial correlation in errors.
8. Adoption of random effects estimation permits retention of country-specific terms but provides inconsistent estimates if the fixed terms are correlated with the disturbances. Bryant et al. (2005) and Law et al. (2009) adopt, instead, correlated random effects, which permit retention of such variables as distance and the common-border dummy while avoiding assumption of lack of correlation with the disturbance term. See Mundlak (1978).
9. Examples of cases forgoing partner fixed effects include Piperakis et al. (2003) on Greece, Bruder (2004) on Germany, Co et al. (2004) on the USA, and Blanes (2008) on Spain.
10. In particular, the elasticity of trade with respect to the extent of migration depends on G_{jt} in (11.4ii) and (11.4iii) but not in (11.4i), and the marginal effect on the logarithm of trade with respect to G_{jt} depends upon the extent of migration, LN_{jt}, in (11.4ii) and on G_{jt} itself in (11.4iii).
11. To include country-by-year fixed effects to further represent multilateral-resistance terms would require insertion of 15744 additional dummy variables, which is almost infeasible. Note that if it were feasible to insert such fixed effects, the terms in popula-

tion and GDP in (11.5) would need to be excluded. Interestingly, however, Parsons, who uses portions of these same data, finds that inclusion of such additional fixed effects has little effect on his estimates, noting that 'there seems to be little bias resulting from failing to account properly for multilateral resistance' (Parsons, 2012, p. 19).

12. The data are for GDP per capita (in constant 2000 US$), drawn from the World Development Indicators at the World Bank. This measure is available over a wider range of observations than are measures in purchasing power parity. Nonetheless, data are unavailable for about 16 percent of country time periods included in the estimation sample. In most cases the missing observations are for earlier years, in which case these early observations are here assigned to the income-level category in which GDP per capita is first observed. For 15, mostly very small, countries, no data on GDP per capita in constant prices are available, in which case these economies are assigned their current status (4 low-income, 7 high-income and 4 upper-middle). See the Appendix for more detail on sources and measurement of other variables.
13. The opposing results may well stem, in part, from the fact that the set of developing countries available to Co and her co-authors is not very representative; the data incorporate only 18 non-OECD countries, and 13 of these are in the Latin-America-Caribbean region.
14. Data on transparency and rule of law are available only for a small portion of the sample considered in the current chapter, and consequently these measures are not investigated here. Several papers focus, instead, on the cultural gap separating the partners from the OECD state. See Girma and Yu (2002) on the UK, White and Tadesse (2007b) on Australia, and White and Tadesse (2008) on the USA. Since a wide cultural gap can prevail between high-income countries, these papers are more tangential to the present, development, focus.
15. Hong and Santhapparaj (2006) examine, from 1998 to 2004, the effect on Malaysia's trade of skilled immigration into Malaysia from eight ASEAN countries and the eight non-ASEAN countries that represent Malaysia's most active trading partners. Their results prove extremely sensitive to alternative specifications, ranging from strong positive associations to no short-run effect at all, rendering interpretation difficult. Canavire Bacarreza and Ehrlich (2006) find a positive elasticity relating Bolivian bilateral exports, imports and intra-industry trade to both Bolivia's stocks of immigrants and of their emigrants, albeit treating immigration and emigration separately (which is necessitated by the lack of a unified sample). However, these positive associations may be biased, reflecting omission of either any vector of partner-country characteristics or fixed effects.
16. The authors re-estimate the gravity trade equations in two variants, both including fixed effects for the home and host countries: in one variant the emigrant stocks are interacted with dummies for each host; in the other variant they are interacted with dummies for the African country of origin. In both forms the elasticities still generally prove positive but of widely differing magnitudes. Moreover, White and Tadesse point out that the level and dispersal of emigrant stock differs substantially across the African nations, as does the level of their exports; these are combined with the differences in estimated elasticities, and the authors thus compile and note the very large differences in the linear, per emigrant effect on exports depending on the migrants' country of origin.
17. http://data.worldbank.org/data-catalog/global-bilateral-migration-database.
18. Here North is defined as the OECD countries minus the Czech Republic, Hungary, Korea, Mexico, Poland, the Slovak Republic and Turkey.
19. Felbermayr et al. (2012) also adopt the GBMD but combine this with the IMF Direction of Trade Statistics, also used in the present context, and find positive migrant–trade associations on the pooled data in first-difference form, though developing regions are not distinguished within this latter study. See also Hatzigeorgiou (2010b), who includes but does not distinguish some developing countries, using the bilateral migrant matrix from Parsons et al. (2007), a precursor to the GBMD.

20. Of the 47 partner countries in the analysis for the USA by Gould (1994), more than half were high-income at the time and only three were low-income. This is not the case, however, for either Wagner et al. (2002), which encompassed some 160 Canadian trade partners, or for Bryant et al. (2005), which included 179 partners of New Zealand.
21. Helliwell (1999), in his study of trade between Canadian provinces and US states, finds that emigrants affect exports from the locale whereas immigrants do not. Bruder (2004) looks at Germany's trade with Spain, Portugal, Greece, Italy and Turkey, finding that emigrants from Germany have no effect on bilateral trade with these partners, and immigrants affect only German exports, not imports. Murat and Pistoresi (2009) consider a wider set of 51 countries, using Italian registry data on Italians abroad; whereas Italian emigrants boost trade, Italian immigrants have only a weak effect on Italian exports and even a negative effect on imports. Tai (2009) finds that the stocks of both emigrants and immigrants affect Swiss imports and exports positively. Law et al. (2009) manage to assemble estimates of New Zealand's diaspora in 205 countries in 2000: immigrants have positive effects on both exports and imports; the diaspora has a positive effect on whether merchandise exports occur but not the amount of exports, while the opposite is found for imports. Hatzigeorgiou (2010b) finds that trade is positively affected by both emigrant and immigrant stocks in a single-time-period, cross-country analysis of patterns among 75 countries (13 of which are low-income). With more complete panel data, Parsons (2012) finds that both emigrants and immigrants positively affect bilateral trade when dyad fixed effects are omitted, but including these fixed effects wipes out both positive associations.
22. This is not a consequence of having included both the refugee fraction and its interaction with the logarithm of migrant stock; if either is inserted separately, exactly the same pattern emerges.
23. Note that wars at home, which generate these refugees, serve to diminish significantly the exports of lower-income countries, though the incidence of wars in partners has no significant impact.
24. A notable exception is with respect to migration to the Persian Gulf states. I am grateful to Çaglar Özden for a discussion on this point.
25. In this context the results are driven largely by the interaction terms denoted $\gamma_3 G_{ijt} * LN_{ijt}$ in (11.4). If these are omitted, the terms $\gamma_2 G_{ijt}$ prove insignificantly different from zero for the fraction of emigrants that is female in each case.
26. At least by a level of about 400 migrants (log migrant stock = 6) for each gender, this gap is statistically significant at greater than a 99 percent confidence level for the three cases depicted in Figure 11.2. More generally, the estimated gap is positive both for emigrants and immigrants for all four dyad groups where migration levels reach 3000 for each gender (log migrant stock = 8).
27. The signs of estimates reported in the prior literature are not all consistent with such a hypothesis. Note, however, that inclusion of such terms also necessitates exclusion of dyad (or partner) fixed effects, which may bias the estimates. Among this class of estimates, see Dunlevy and Hutchinson (1999) for an historical study of the USA; Blanes (2005) on Spain; Herander and Saavedra (2005) on trade by US states; Faustino and Leitão (2008) on Portugal; Jansen and Piermartini (2009) on the USA; and Artal-Tur et al. (2012) on Portugal and Spain.
28. On a common language interaction, see also Bryant et al. (2005), Qian (2008) and Law et al. (2009) on New Zealand and Peri and Requena-Silvente (2010) on Spain. Blanes (2008) actually finds a positive interaction between having a colonial link and the log of immigrants in examining Spanish exports and imports.
29. Common language and a colonial link are time-invariant within our sample; regional trade agreements are not. Data on possession of a common legal structure are available only for a small portion of our sample and are consequently not deployed.
30. Colonial links are defined to include two countries having shared a specific colonial power. As a result, colonial links are common even between low-income countries.
31. See the examples catalogued in Handjiski et al. (2010).

32. See, however, Mattoo et al. (2008) on the prevalence of highly educated US immigrants in low-skill occupations.
33. Interestingly, Jansen and Piermartini (2009) also distinguish permanent residents from those on temporary visas and find that temporary migrants actually have a slightly stronger effect on trade with the countries of origin; whether this would hold up if it were possible to introduce fixed effects for the countries of origin remains to be explored. Note, also, that in the US context a substantial portion of permanent residents has previously been on temporary stay visas, raising issues about the dynamics of effects.
34. Blanes also finds that more migrants in managerial positions in Spain are positively associated with greater trade in both directions.
35. This is the DIOC-E version 3 database prepared by the OECD. See the description at http://www.oecd.org/migration/48431754.pdf.
36. This is true also of the more recently available matrices for 1990 and 2000, discussed in Artuc et al. (2013), if only actual observations are included (as opposed to projected values).
37. Evaluated at the sample mean for the logarithm of emigrants, the third specification presents results quite close to the first specification.
38. During 1960–2000, the deficit on the merchandise trade balance amounted to more than 21 percent of GDP for the average low-income country.
39. Rauch and Trindade (2002, p. 119). Whereas Rauch and Trindade deploy data on the number of persons of Chinese ethnic origin, the subsequent papers by Felbermayr et al. (2010) and Parsons (2012) both use migrant stocks. Parsons notes that adopting country fixed effects (by time) in cross-section (panel) contexts, (11.6i) and (11.6ii) become identical since the population terms are collinear with the fixed effects.
40. The ranking of values for tariff-equivalent network effects of these η_k terms is rather curious, the five largest being for Morocco, Ghana, Denmark, Israel and Iceland. China proves among the lowest. Felbermayr and his co-authors also repeat Rauch and Trindade's estimates for a Chinese network alone and find that inclusion of a set of country dummies substantially lowers, but does not eliminate, the associated estimate of η.
41. Since (11.5) already incorporates the logarithms of populations in both i and j, (11.6ii) rather than (11.6i) is adopted here. In the very few instances in which no emigrants elsewhere are reported these terms are set to zero. A dummy variable is also included to represent these cases.
42. These are evaluated at the sample means for X_{ij}/N_{ij} and $\sum_{\kappa} X_{i\kappa}/\sum_{\kappa} N_{i\kappa}$. If the cross-terms on emigrants elsewhere, such as emigrants from lower-income countries in higher-income third countries, are inserted into the specifications in (11.7), the estimates reported in Table 11.7 are little changed, though calculation of the derivative in (11.8) is clearly more complex, requiring cross-equation testing.

REFERENCES

Anderson, J.E. and E. van Wincoop (2003), 'Gravity with gravitas: a solution to the border puzzle', *American Economic Review*, **93**(1), 170–92.

Anderson, J.E. and E. van Wincoop (2004), 'Trade costs', *Journal of Economic Literature*, **42**(3), 691–751.

Artal-Tur, A., V.J. Pallardo-Lopez and F. Requena-Silvente (2012), 'The trade-enhancing effect of immigration networks: new evidence on the role of geographic proximity', *Economics Letters*, **116**(3), 554–7.

Artuc, E., F. Docquier, Ç. Özden and C. Parsons (2013), 'A global assessment of human capital mobility: the role of non-OECD destinations', http://perso.uclouvain.be/frederic.docquier/oxlight.htm (accessed 11 November 2013).

Baldwin, R. and D. Taglioni (2006), 'Gravity for dummies and dummies for gravity equations', NBER Working Paper No. 12516, National Bureau of Economic Research, Cambridge, MA.

Behrens, K., C. Ertur and W. Koch (2012), '"Dual" gravity: using spatial econometrics to control for multilateral resistance', *Journal of Applied Econometrics*, **27**(5), 773–94.

Beine, M., F. Docquier and Ç. Özden (2011), 'Diasporas', *Journal of Development Economics*, **95**(1), 30–41.

Bergstrand, Jeffrey H. and Peter Egger (2011), 'Gravity equations and economic frictions in the world economy', in Daniel M. Bernhofen, Rod Falvey, David Greenaway and Udo Krieckemeier (eds), *Palgrave Handbook of International Trade*, New York: Palgrave-Macmillan, pp. 532–70.

Bertoli, S. and J. Fernandez-Huertas Moraga (2013), 'Multilateral resistance to migration', *Journal of Development Economics*, **102**, 79–100.

Bettin, G. and A.L. Turco (2012), 'A cross-country view on south-north migration and trade: dissecting the channels', *Emerging Markets Finance and Trade*, **48**(4), 4–29.

Blanes, J.V. (2005), 'Does immigration help to explain intra-industry trade? Evidence for Spain', *Weltwirtschaftliches Archiv*, **141**(2), 244–70.

Blanes, J.V. (2008), 'Characteristics of immigrants and bilateral trade', *Revista de Economia Aplicada*, **16**(3), 133–59.

Borjas, G.J. (1987), 'Self-selection and the earnings of immigrants', *American Economic Review*, **77**(4), 531–53.

Briant, A., P.-P. Combes and M. Lafourcade (2009), 'Product complexity, quality of institutions and the pro-trade effect of immigrants', CEPR Discussion Paper No. 7192, London: Centre for Economic Policy Research.

Bruder, J. (2004), 'Are trade and migration substitutes or complements? The case of Germany, 1970–1998', unpublished paper, Department of Economics, University of Rostock. http://www.etsg.org/ETSG2004/Papers/Bruder.pdf (accessed 2 February 2013).

Bryant, J., M. Genç and D. Law (2005), 'Trade and migration to New Zealand', paper presented at the 45th Congress of the Regional Science Association in Amsterdam. http://www-sre.wu-wien.ac.at/ersa/ersaconfs/ersa05/papers/192.pdf (accessed 31 January 2013).

Canavire Bacarreza, G.J. and L. Ehrlich (2006), 'The impact of migration on foreign trade: a developing country approach', *Latin American Journal of Economic Development*, **6**, 125–46.

Clark, X., T.J. Hatton and J.G. Williamson (2007), 'Explaining US immigration, 1971–1998', *Review of Economics and Statistics*, **89**(2), 359–73.

Co, C., P. Euzent and T. Martin (2004), 'The export effect of immigration into the USA', *Applied Economics*, **36**(6), 573–83.

Coughlin, C.C. and H.J. Wall (2011), 'Ethnic networks and trade: intensive versus extensive margins', *Economics Letters*, **113**(1), 73–5.

de Mello-Sampayo, F. (2009), 'Competing-destinations gravity model: an application to the geographic distribution of FDI', *Applied Economics*, **41**(16–18), 2237–53.

Docquier, F. and A. Marfouk (2004), 'Measuring the international mobility of skilled workers (1990–2000): release 1.0', Policy Research Working Paper Series no. 3381, World Bank, Washington, DC.

Dunlevy, J.A. (2006), 'The influence of corruption and language on the protrade effect of immigrants: evidence from the American states', *Review of Economics and Statistics*, **88**(1), 182–6.

Dunlevy, J.A. and W.K. Hutchinson (1999), 'The impact of immigration on American import trade in the late nineteenth and early twentieth centuries', *Journal of Economic History*, **59**(4), 1043–62.

Eaton, J. and A. Tamura (1994), 'Bilateralism and regionalism in Japanese and U.S. trade and direct foreign investment patterns', *Journal of the Japanese and International Economies*, **8**(4), 478–510.

Eichengreen, B. and D.A. Irwin (1995), 'Trade blocs, currency blocs and reorientation of world trade in the 1930s', *Journal of International Economics*, **38**(1–2), 1–24.

Faustino, H.C. and N.C. Leitão (2008), 'Immigration and trade in Portugal: a static and dynamic panel data analysis', Department of Economics Working Paper No. 31/2008, Lisbon: Instituto Superior de Economia e Gestão.

Feenstra, Robert C. (2004), *Advanced International Trade: Theory and Evidence*, Princeton, NJ: Princeton University Press.

Feenstra, R.C., R.E. Lipsey, H. Deng, A.C. Ma and H. Mo (2005), 'World trade flows: 1962–2000', NBER Working Paper No. 11040, National Bureau of Economic Research, Cambridge, MA.

Felbermayr, G.J., V. Grossmann and W. Kohler (2012), 'Migration, international trade and capital formation: cause or effect?' IZA Discussion Paper No. 6975, Bonn. First draft of a chapter forthcoming in Barry R. Chiswick and Paul W. Miller (eds), *Handbook on the Economics of International Migration*, Amsterdam: Elsevier Science.

Felbermayr, G.J. and B. Jung (2009), 'The pro-trade effect of the brain drain: sorting out confounding factors', *Economics Letters*, **104**(2), 72–5.

Felbermayr, G.J., B. Jung and F. Toubal (2010), 'Ethnic networks, information, and international trade: revisiting the evidence', *Annales d'Économie et de Statistique*, **97–8**, 41–70.

Gaston, N. and D.R. Nelson (2013), 'Bridging trade theory and labour econometrics: the effects of international migration', *Journal of Economic Surveys*, **27**(1), 98–139.

Genç, M., M. Gheasi, P. Nijkamp and J. Poot (2011), 'The impact of immigration on international trade: a meta-analysis', IZA Discussion Paper No. 6145, Bonn: Institute for the Study of Labor.

Ghatak, S. and A.S. Piperakis (2007), 'The impact of Eastern European immigration to UK trade', Kingston University Economic Discussion Paper No. 2007-03, London: Kingston University.

Girma, S. and Z. Yu (2002), 'The link between immigration and trade: evidence from the United Kingdom', *Weltwirtschaftliches Archiv*, **138**(1), 115–30.

Gould, D.M. (1994), 'Immigrant links to the home country: empirical implications for U.S. bilateral trade flows', *Review of Economics and Statistics*, **76**(2), 302–16.

Greif, A. (1993), 'Contract enforceability and economic institutions in early trade: the Maghribi traders'coalition', *American Economic Review*, **83**(3), 525–48.

Greif, A. (2012), 'The Maghribi traders: a reappraisal?', *Economic History Review*, **65**(2), 445–69.

Grogger, J. and G.H. Hanson (2011), 'Income maximization and the selection and sorting of international migrants', *Journal of Development Economics*, **95**(1), 42–57.

Handjiski, B., R.E.B. Lucas, P. Martin and S. Sarisoy Guerin (2010), 'Enhancing regional trade integration in Southeast Europe', World Bank Working Paper No. 185, World Bank, Washington, DC.

Hatzigeorgiou, A. (2010a), 'Does immigration stimulate foreign trade? Evidence from Sweden', *Journal of Economic Integration*, **25**(2), 376–402.

Hatzigeorgiou, A. (2010b), 'Migration as trade facilitation: assessing the links between international trade and migration', *B.E. Journal of Economic Analysis and Policy: Topics in Economic Analysis and Policy*, **10**(1), 1–33.

Head, K., T. Mayer and J. Ries (2010), 'The erosion of colonial trade linkages after independence', *Journal of International Economics*, **81**(1), 1–14.

Head, K. and J. Ries (1998), 'Immigration and trade creation: econometric evidence from Canada', *Canadian Journal of Economics*, **31**(1), 47–62.

Helliwell, J.F. (1999), 'National borders, trade and migration', NBER Working Paper No. 6027, Cambridge, MA: National Bureau of Economic Research.

Helpman, E., M. Melitz and Y. Rubinstein (2008), 'Estimating trade flows: trading partners and trading volumes', *Quarterly Journal of Economics*, **123**(2), 441–87.

Herander, M.G. and L.A. Saavedra (2005), 'Exports and the structure of immigrant-based networks: the role of geographic proximity', *Review of Economics and Statistics*, **87**(2), 323–35.

Hiller, S. (2013), 'Does immigrant employment matter for export sales? Evidence from Denmark', *Weltwirtschaftliches Archiv*, **149**(2), 369–94.

Hong, T.C. and A.S. Santhapparaj (2006), 'Skilled labor immigration and external trade in Malaysia; a pooled data analysis', *Perspectives on Global Development and Technology*, **5**(4), 351–66.
Jansen, M. and R. Piermartini (2009), 'Temporary migration and bilateral trade flows', *World Economy*, **32**(5), 735–53.
Karemera, D., V.I. Oguledo and B. Davis (2000), 'A gravity model analysis of international migration to North America', *Applied Economics*, **32**(13), 1745–55.
Law, D., M. Genç and J. Bryant (2009), 'Trade, diaspora and migration to New Zealand', NZIER Working Paper No. 2009/4, New Zealand Institute of Economic Research, University of Otago.
Letouzé, E., M. Purser, F. Rodríguez and M. Cummins (2009), 'Revisiting the migration–development nexus: a gravity model approach', Human Development Research Paper No. 2009/44, New York: United Nations Development Program. http://hdr.undp.org/en/reports/global/hdr2009/papers/HDRP_2009_44.pdf (accessed 12 April 2013).
Lewer, J.J. and H. Van Den Berg (2008), 'A gravity model of immigration', *Economics Letters*, **99**(1), 164–7.
Lucas, Robert E.B. (forthcoming), 'African migration', in Barry R. Chiswick and Paul W. Miller (eds), *Handbook on the Economics of International Migration*, Amsterdam: Elsevier Science.
Martin, W. and C.S. Pham (2008), 'Estimating the gravity model when zero trade flows are frequent', Economics Series 2008_03, Faculty of Business and Law, Deakin University.
Mattoo, A., I.C. Neagu and Ç. Özden (2008), 'Brain waste? Educated immigrants in the US labor market', *Journal of Development Economics*, **87**(2), 255–69.
Mayda, A.M. (2010), 'International migration: a panel data analysis of the determinants of bilateral flows', *Journal of Population Economics*, **23**(4), 1249–74.
Mundlak, Y. (1978), 'On the pooling of time series and cross-section data', *Econometrica*, **46**(1), 69–85.
Mundra, K. (2005), 'Immigration and international trade: a semiparametric empirical investigation', *Journal of International Trade and Economic Development*, **14**(1), 65–91.
Murat, M. and B. Pistoresi (2009), 'Migrant networks: empirical implications for the Italian bilateral trade', *International Economic Journal*, **23**(3), 371–90.
Ortega, F. and G. Peri (2009), 'The causes and effects of international migrations: evidence from OECD countries 1980–2005', NBER Working Paper No. 14833, Cambridge, MA: National Bureau of Economic Research.
Özden, Ç., C.R. Parsons, M. Schiff and T.L. Walmsley (2011), 'Where on earth is everybody? The evolution of international bilateral migration stocks 1960–2000', *World Bank Economic Review*, **25**(1), 12–56.
Parsons, C.R. (2012), 'Do migrants really foster trade? The trade–migration nexus, a panel approach 1960–2000', Policy Research Working Paper No. 6034, Trade and Integration Team, Development Research Group, World Bank, Washington, DC.
Parsons, C.R., R. Skeldon, T.L. Walmsley and A.L. Winters (2007), 'Quantifying the international bilateral movements of migrants', in Çaglar Özden and Maurice Schiff (eds), *International Migration, Economic Development and Policy*, New York: Palgrave Macmillan, pp. 17–58.
Partridge, J. and H. Furtan (2008), 'Immigration wave effects on Canada's trade flows', *Journal of Canadian Public Policy*, **34**(2), 193–214.
Peng, M.W. and A.Y. Ilinitch (1998), 'Export intermediary firms: a note on export development research', *Journal of International Business Studies*, **29**(3), 609–20.
Peri, G. and F. Requena-Silvente (2010), 'The trade creation effect of immigrants: evidence from the remarkable case of Spain', *Canadian Journal of Economics*, **43**(4), 1433–59.
Piperakis, A.S., C. Milner and P.W. Wright (2003), 'Immigration, trade costs, and trade: gravity evidence for Greece', *Journal of Economic Integration*, **18**(4), 750–62.
Qian, M. (2008), 'The economic relationship between trade and immigration in New Zealand', Integration of Immigrants Programme Working Paper No. 1, Albany, NY: Massey University and University of Waikato.

Ratha, D. and W. Shaw (2007), 'South–south migration and remittances', World Bank Working Paper No. 102, World Bank, Washington, DC.
Rauch, J.E. (2001), 'Business and social networks in international trade', *Journal of Economic Literature*, **39**(4), 1177–203.
Rauch, J.E. and V. Trindade (2002), 'Ethnic Chinese networks in international trade', *Review of Economics and Statistics*, **84**(1), 116–30.
Santos Silva, J.M.C. and S. Tenreyro (2006), 'The log of gravity', *Review of Economics and Statistics*, **88**(4), 641–58.
Santos Silva, J.M.C. and S. Tenreyro (2011), 'Further simulation evidence on the performance of the Poisson pseudo-maximum likelihood estimator', *Economics Letters*, **112**(2), 220–22.
Stouffer, S.A. (1940), 'Intervening opportunities: a theory relating mobility and distance', *American Sociological Review*, **5**(6), 845–67.
Tai, S. (2009), 'Market structure and the link between migration and trade', *Weltwirtschaftliches Archiv*, **145**(2), 225–49.
Wagner, D., K. Head and J. Ries (2002), 'Immigration and the trade of provinces', *Scottish Journal of Political Economy*, **49**(5), 507–25.
Wang, Z.K. and L.A. Winters (1991), 'The trading potential of Eastern Europe', CEPR Discussion Paper No. 610, London: Centre for Economic Policy Research.
Wang, Z.K. and L.A. Winters (1992), 'The trading potential of Eastern Europe', *Journal of Economic Integration*, **7**(2), 113–36.
White, R. (2007a), 'Immigrant–trade links, transplanted home bias and network effects', *Applied Economics*, **39**(7–9), 839–52.
White, R. (2007b), 'An examination of the Danish immigrant–trade link', *International Migration*, **45**(5), 61–86.
White, R. and B. Tadesse (2007), 'Immigration policy, cultural pluralism and trade: evidence from the white Australia policy', *Pacific Economic Review*, **12**(4), 489–509.
White, R. and B. Tadesse (2008), 'Cultural distance and the US immigrant–trade link', *World Economy*, **31**(8), 1078–96.
White, R. and B. Tadesse (2010), 'The effects of refugee and non-refugee immigrants on US trade with their home countries', *Journal of International Trade and Economic Development*, **19**(2), 289–317.
White, Roger and Bedassa Tadesse (2011), *International Migration and Economic Integration: Understanding the Immigrant-Trade*, Cheltenham, UK and Northampton, MA, USA: Edward Elgar Publishing.
White, R. and B. Tadesse (2013), 'Do African immigrants enhance their home nation's trade with their hosts?', *Journal of Developing Areas*, **47**(2), 199–228.

APPENDIX

Notes on the Data

The annual, bilateral trade data are from the IMF Direction of Trade Statistics Database, encompassing 208 countries from 1960 through 2000. Following Head et al. (2010, Appendix A.1), exports from country *i* to *j* are here measured by whichever is the larger of exports reported by *i* going to *j* or 90 percent of imports reported by *j* entering from *i*, assuming a 10 percent gap between f.o.b. and c.i.f. valuation. The migration data are provided by the Global Bilateral Migration Database, which reports the stock of persons born in country *i* and residing in country *j* at the turn of each decade from 1960 through 2000.[1] For years between the decennial points, these migrant stocks are interpolated linearly to be commensurate with the trade data. *F*-tests on the restriction that all migration terms in Table 11A.1 differ between the decades and in the intervening years fail to reject these restrictions in all four cases. Data on nominal GDP for each country are drawn from the World Bank's World Development Indicators. Almost all of the missing data are for GDP. No GDP data at all are available for 12 of the smaller and newly formed countries among the original 208 in the sample. For 93 other countries GDP data are missing for some years, such as in the case of the new countries of the former Soviet Union and of Yugoslavia, resulting in a loss of about 22 percent of the remaining sample. Whether states speak a common language or share a colonial link are taken from the CEPII Gravity Data Set.[2] Common language is defined to equal 1 if at least 9 percent of the populations in both countries speak the same language as their mother tongue or as a second language. The colonial link dummy equals one if the two countries ever had a direct colonial link or if they shared a common colonizer after 1945. Observations on gender of migrant stocks are from the Global Bilateral Migration Database and those on refugees from the UNHCR Online Statistical Database. The time-varying data on regional trade agreements between dyads of countries are from a data set prepared by Keith Head and his colleagues.[3] A war is defined to occur if there are at least 1000 battle-related deaths in a given year.[4] After subtracting cases in which data are missing, the sample has 1 141 798 observations on 36 864 dyads of 192 countries. Of these 192 countries, 28 were low-income in 2000, 55 lower-middle-income, 52 upper-middle-income and 57 high-income.

The estimates of equation (11.5), based on these data, are presented in Table 11A.1. These estimates include both dyad and time fixed effects, which are not shown. *T*-statistics for a zero null hypothesis are displayed in parentheses.

Table 11A.1 Fixed-effects estimates of bilateral exports equation

	Exports from			
	Low to low	Low to high	High to low	High to high
Log(emigrants)	0.0781	−0.0001	−0.0044	0.0028
	(11.22)	(0.01)	(0.37)	(0.20)
Log(emigrants)^2	−0.0440	0.0064	0.0336	0.0144
	(16.27)	(1.93)	(6.02)	(2.78)
Log(emigrants)^3	0.0076	−0.0012	−0.0005	0.0001
	(21.53)	(2.75)	(0.57)	(0.22)
Log(emigrants)^4	−0.0003	0.0002	−0.0001	0.0000
	(21.76)	(11.07)	(1.67)	(0.89)
Zero emigrants	0.0153	0.0244	−0.0084	0.0456
dummy	(3.04)	(3.63)	(1.11)	(3.85)
Log(immigrants)	0.0498	−0.0193	−0.0410	0.0500
	(7.15)	(1.64)	(4.64)	(3.55)
Log(immigrants)^2	−0.0334	0.0454	0.0410	0.0009
	(12.32)	(8.29)	(12.21)	(0.17)
Log(immigrants)^3	0.0053	−0.0041	−0.0052	0.0018
	(15.06)	(4.79)	(11.70)	(2.66)
Log(immigrants)^4	−0.0002	0.0002	0.0003	−0.0001
	(12.67)	(3.51)	(17.72)	(3.20)
Zero immigrants	−0.0113	−0.0371	0.0181	0.0317
dummy	(2.23)	(5.01)	(2.64)	(2.68)
Fraction emigrants	−0.0421	0.1205	−0.0612	0.2475
refugees	(1.94)	(3.63)	(0.91)	(2.33)
Fract refugees	−0.0167	−0.0696	−0.0319	−0.0882
*log(emig)	(4.98)	(11.70)	(2.10)	(4.79)
Fract immigrants	0.0015	0.2625	0.1670	0.3245
refugees	(0.07)	(3.99)	(4.93)	(3.05)
Fract refugees	0.0120	−0.1116	−0.0532	−0.1153
*log(immig)	(3.57)	(7.49)	(8.75)	(6.26)
Fraction emigrants	−0.0854	−0.0822	0.1046	−0.0630
female	(6.17)	(5.22)	(4.81)	(2.36)
Fract female	0.0465	0.0657	−0.1057	0.0555
*log(emig)	(7.98)	(11.71)	(9.59)	(5.73)
Fract immigrants	−0.1547	0.1045	−0.0550	−0.1400
female	(11.19)	(4.91)	(3.42)	(5.24)
Fract female	0.1178	−0.1281	0.0087	0.0639
*log(immig)	(20.23)	(11.86)	(1.52)	(6.59)
Common	−0.0206	−0.0288	0.0001	−0.0526
lang*log(emig)	(6.22)	(6.94)	(0.01)	(7.30)
Common	−0.0327	−0.0206	−0.0372	−0.0081
lang*log(immig)	(9.90)	(3.74)	(8.76)	(1.13)

Table 11A.1 (continued)

	Exports from			
	Low to low	Low to high	High to low	High to high
Colonial link*log(emig)	−0.0250	−0.0381	−0.0030	0.0250
	(7.10)	(7.71)	(0.44)	(2.53)
Colonial link*log(immig)	−0.0267	−0.0066	−0.0179	−0.0342
	(7.57)	(1.01)	(3.54)	(3.46)
Regional trade agreement	−0.2537	0.0918	−0.0226	0.3615
	(10.58)	(1.62)	(0.39)	(9.07)
RTA*log(emigrants)	0.0038	0.0429	0.0178	0.0275
	(0.94)	(4.17)	(1.72)	(4.45)
RTA*log(immigrants)	0.0559	0.0018	0.0557	0.0536
	(14.10)	(0.18)	(5.27)	(8.66)
Log(population) home	0.0394	−0.0211	−0.0620	−0.0682
	(4.74)	(1.68)	(8.57)	(5.85)
Log(population) partner	0.0943	−0.0687	0.0443	0.2860
	(11.35)	(9.70)	(3.45)	(24.52)
Log(GDP) home	0.0442	0.0760	0.0575	0.0726
	(37.95)	(43.62)	(35.28)	(28.63)
Log(GDP) partner	0.0322	0.0476	0.0541	0.0709
	(27.62)	(29.88)	(30.40)	(27.94)
War at home	−0.0113	−0.0519	−0.0130	0.0279
	(4.63)	(14.18)	(2.15)	(2.98)
War in partner	−0.0033	0.0243	−0.0283	0.0275
	(1.35)	(4.10)	(7.57)	(2.94)
Number of observations	279 284	284 576	284 576	293 362
R-squared	0.095	0.166	0.204	0.230

Notes on the Treatment of Zero Bilateral Trade

For simplicity, the estimates in Table 11A.1 are obtained by 'scaled' least squares, which replaces LX_{ijt} with $\log(1 + X_{ijt})$.[5] Eaton and Tamura (1994) pioneer an alternative in which an additive intercept, α, is introduced to the exponential form of the gravity equation; on taking logs, the dependent variable in the trade equation becomes $\log(\alpha + X_{ijt})$ and α is estimated along with other parameters by maximum likelihood applied to the nonlinear equation. Santos Silva and Tenreyro (2006) advocate use of a pseudo-maximum-likelihood Poisson estimator.[6] Helpman et al. (2008) offer a theoretical model leading to a two-part estimate, on the intensive and extensive trade margins, instead. Each of these has been applied to equations such as (11.3) though the scaled approach is the most common.[7]

Trade between each dyad of countries falls into three categories: trade is positive in each year; occasionally zero; or always zero. For reasons discussed in the text, it is highly desirable to include the dyad fixed effects. To do so, applying a Poisson estimator, excludes the last category of dyads where trade is never observed. Applying a logit or probit in a two-part approach with fixed effects drops both the first and third category. An Eaton–Tamura estimator is not simple to apply with a very large number of fixed effects, as in our fresh evidence, given the general lack of a fixed-effects, nonlinear estimator. Besides simplicity and comparison with the majority of estimates, the scaling approach adopted in the fresh evidence presented here has the advantage of incorporating cases in which exports are either always zero or always positive within the dyad.

Space limitations preclude a full exploration of other estimation techniques within this chapter. However, Figure 11A.1 compares select results on the migrant trade elasticity profiles for three alternative approaches to estimation: the intensive margin components of a two-part estimator; Poisson estimates; and the scaled estimates from the body of the text. Comparable estimates using the Eaton–Tamura estimator proved intractable given the large number of dyad fixed effects. Although the magnitudes of elasticity estimates differ somewhat in Figure 11A.1, no doubt in part because of the differences in samples entailed, the broad patterns are not dramatically dissimilar at least for these cases. Nonetheless, further work on the differences in these alternative estimators is clearly warranted.

Appendix Notes

1. For an account of the construction of the GBMD, see Özden et al. (2011).
2. http://www.cepii.fr/anglaisgraph/bdd/gravity.htm.
3. See supplemental material for papers co-authored by Keith Head at http://strategy.sauder.ubc.ca/head/sup/.
4. Data are from the Uppsala Conflict Data Program at http://www.ucdp.uu.se.
5. See Wang and Winters (1991, 1992), Eichengreen and Irwin (1995). A Tobit estimator is sometimes preferred to estimate such cases. However, Tobit with random effects is currently available but not with fixed effects.
6. See also Martin and Pham (2008), Santos Silva and Tenreyro (2011).
7. Within the literature on migration–trade links, examples of applying the Eaton–Tamura approach include Head and Ries (1998), Herander and Saavedra (2005), Jansen and Piermartini (2009); Briant et al. (2009) apply the Poisson quasi-maximum likelihood; Law et al. (2009) and Coughlin and Wall (2011) distinguish the intensive and extensive margins in a two-part estimation.

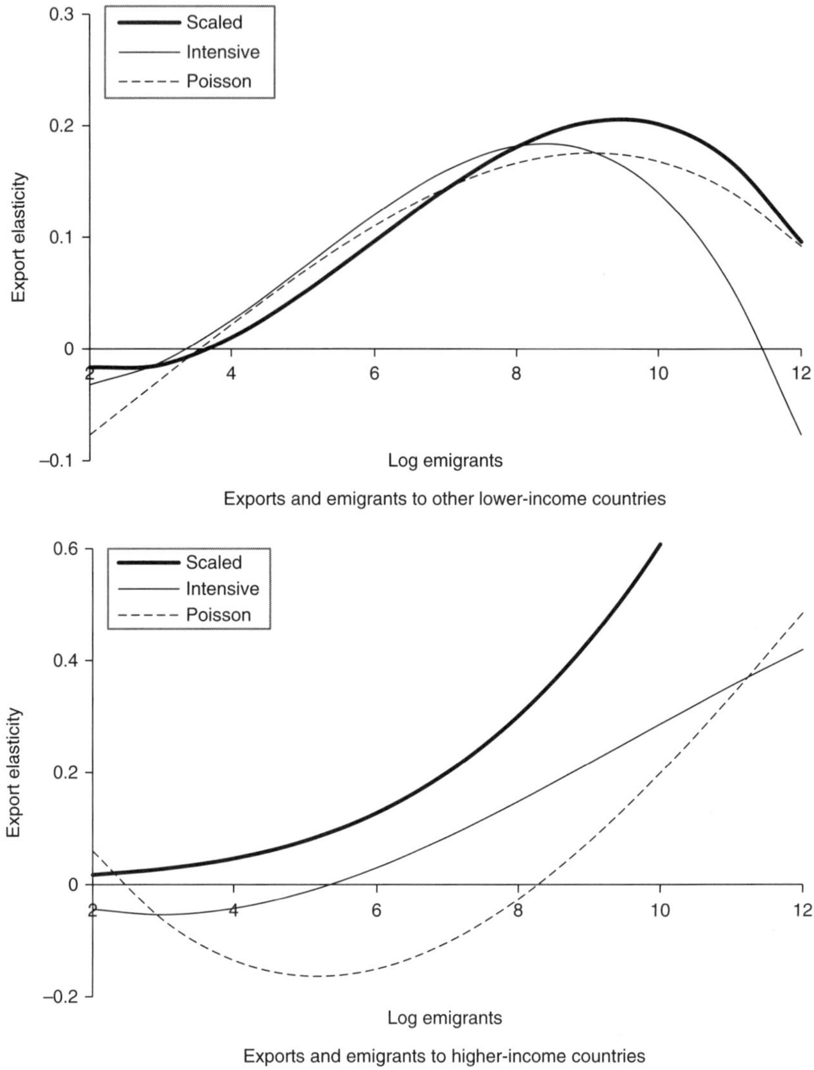

Figure 11A.1 Emigrant elasticities of lower-income countries' exports: alternative estimators

12. Return migration and economic development

*Jackline Wahba**

1. INTRODUCTION

Many people think of international migration as a one-way move. In reality, many immigrants move overseas only temporarily. This raises a set of important questions: who chooses to return and why? Who leaves faster? Do the successful or the unsuccessful immigrants return to their home countries? In this chapter we focus on return migration and review the economics literature on the determinants and impact of return migration on the economic development of the country of origin.

There is increasing evidence that international migration is characterized by frequent return migration. Return migration usually refers to temporary overseas migration, where migrants return to their country of origin by their own choice. Return migration is not only true of those who enter on a temporary visa (such as workers on work permits and seasonal agreements and students), but also of those on permanent visas.

Return migration is common, albeit our knowledge of its extent is hampered by lack of data. According to the OECD (2008), 20 per cent to 50 per cent of immigrants leave within five years after their arrival, either to return home or to move on to a third country. For European host countries, out-migration rates are considerable. For the UK, Dustmann and Weiss (2007) estimate out-migration rates of 40 per cent for men and 55 per cent for women after five years, using data from the 1990s. For the Netherlands, Bijwaard (2010) finds an out-migration rate of around 29 per cent after five years for the 1997 entry cohort, but with some groups of immigrants like labour immigrants and students exhibiting almost 45 per cent out-migration rate. For Norway, Bratsberg et al. (2007) estimate an average out-migration rate of around 50 per cent after five years of residence for those entering between 1967 and 2003. For Denmark, Jensen and Pedersen (2007) estimate an out-migration rate of 55 per cent after five years for the cohort of immigrants entering in 1983.

Out-migration rates among the traditional permanent immigration countries such as the USA, Canada and New Zealand are also far from negligible. For example, nearly one-third of the immigrants to the USA between 1908 and 1957 have returned home, according to Jasso and Rosenzweig (1982). Similarly, Warren and Peck (1980) estimate that around one-third of people who immigrated legally to the USA left in the 1960s. For Canada, Aydemir and Robinson (2008) find that 24 per cent of male migrants entering in 1996 left after five years of residence. For New Zealand, Shorland (2006) estimates that 23 per cent of the 1998 cohort left by 2003.

Although host countries can potentially observe out-migration, whether those exiting return to their home country or move on to another destination is rarely known. Nekby (2006), based on administrative data, finds that for Sweden during the 1990s, onward migration constituted approximately 28 per cent of total out-migration; this share has risen from 12 per cent in 1991 to 32 per cent in 2000. Obviously, we can not generalize the patterns of onward and return migration based just on Sweden; however, these figures provide an indication that the majority of out-migration is return migration. Another important dimension of out-migration is that it can be temporary. Bijwaard (2010), using population register data for the Netherlands, finds that 29 per cent of immigrants who arrived between 1997 and 2003 left the country. Yet about 6–14 per cent of the migrants that have left the Netherlands returned within the time frame. Although these figures give an under-representation of the circularity of migration because the study observes immigrants over a six-year period at most, repeat migration is common.[1] Thus it is clear that not only is return migration common; it is far from being one-dimensional.

Looking at the issue from a source-country perspective, Barrett and Goggin (2010) find that in 2006, 15 per cent of the Irish native workforce had lived outside Ireland for a period of at least one year. Ambrosini et al. (2011) also underscore that return migration is not a marginal phenomenon for Eastern European countries, as between 30 and 60 per cent of the total emigrants from Eastern Europe in the decade 1990–2000 returned to their home country within that same decade. Evidence on return rate from developing origin countries vary. For example, the last Moroccan Population Census in 2004 shows 165416 return Moroccans during the five years preceding the Census, which represents only about a 5 per cent return rate among Moroccans abroad. On the other hand, the 2010 Mexican Census documents that the return migration was 31 per cent for the 994869 Mexicans who moved to the USA during 2005 to 2010; that is, 307783 had returned to Mexico by 2010. Similar figures are obtained from the National Survey of Demographic Dynamics 2006 (ENADID): a return migration rate of 34 per cent in 2006 for those Mexicans who left the country within the previous five years. In the next section, we discuss the challenges associated with measuring return migration.

Although international labour migration tends to be mainly motivated by economic reasons, such as higher wages and better job opportunities, return migration may appear at first glance to be difficult to reconcile with the initial migration drivers. Theories suggest several reasons for returning: target savers, or skill accumulation migrants migrate for a determined period of time so that they can accumulate money or skills before returning. An inherent assumption is that migrants prefer consumption in their home countries. Others argue that return migration is usually unplanned and driven by unexpected events and can be a sign of failure. Section 3 shows that return migration can be consistent with an optimal strategy where migrants maximize their utility over the life cycle.

The evidence on the impact of return migration on the economic development of the home country is relatively understudied, given its importance. Through overseas employment, migrants increase their income, acquire new skills and accumulate savings and assets. When migrants return to their country of origin, they represent an inflow to the country of origin of both financial capital through accumulated overseas savings and human capital through their newly acquired skills and knowledge from working overseas. Furthermore, returnees bring back new ideas and norms that could potentially impact their social, economic and political behaviour. However, the contribution of return migration is far from established and the literature has been far more concerned about who leaves rather than who returns and their contribution to the home country.

This chapter will discuss first the challenges of measuring return migration in Section 2. Then Section 3 will discuss the determinants of return migration, covering both the theoretical literature and the empirical findings. The contribution of return migration to the economic development of the home sending country will be examined in Section 4. Section 5 concludes by summarizing the main findings and the main challenges related to understanding the role played by return migration in development.

2. DATA AND MEASURING RETURN MIGRATION

Return migration is difficult to measure. Statistics on the numbers of return migrants are not well recorded as outflows are not regularly collected by governments and border agencies. Although most countries record immigration inflows, very few do the same for outflows. Another obvious problem is that out-migration does not necessarily mean return migration to the home country. Nonetheless, numbers on return migrants can be accessed from population registers when they exist. Yet population registers too have their constraints, namely, few have systemic procedures in place for de-registering immigrants before they leave.[2] Also, population registries do not capture illegal immigrants, and rarely identify the destination of immigrants leaving the destination country.

Return migration is difficult to measure with the existing data available in most countries. Studies examining return migration have commonly relied on indirect measures in the host country. Many authors use repeated-census data or representative surveys such as labour force surveys where they observe the year of arrival of immigrants in the host country to estimate out-migration rates. Those data sources allow for estimating out-migration rates based on the difference between the initial stock of the cohort and the stock remaining at a later date. For example, Borjas and Bratsberg (1996) apply this method in the case of the USA.

Others have used longitudinal surveys where the initial sample is representative of the foreign-born population and allows for richer analysis of return migration. Among the available longitudinal surveys, the German socioeconomic survey (GSOEP) is one of the most-used panels for analysing return migration. A few countries, such as Australia, Canada, New Zealand and Sweden, also have immigrant-specific longitudinal surveys.[3] However, attrition tends to be a common problem in longitudinal surveys, constituting a challenge for studies on return migration.

The use of administrative data where, for example, population registers and social security databases are linked allows for better measures and analysis of return migration. Although not very common, access to such data sets is increasing. For example, the Longitudinal Immigration Database (IMDB) links immigration and taxation administrative records into a comprehensive source of data on the labour market behaviour of the immigrant population in Canada; see Aydemir and Robinson (2008). Similar administrative data are also available in a handful other countries such as Sweden, Norway, Denmark and the Netherlands.

Return of migrants can also be examined using data from the countries of origin – for example, representative surveys with information on individuals' previous place of residence, or population censuses, which include information on country of residence five years prior to census date, allow for studying returnees. One problem is the relatively small number of returnees in a representative national survey to enable rich analysis. However, population censuses can be useful, although they tend to be limited in their information on the previous destination and the migration experience.

However, there have also been attempts to carry out specialized surveys among migrants in host countries, or among migrant communities in countries of origin, or in some case in both the home country and the host country – for example, the Mexican Migration Project (MMP), which has been running since 1982, based at Princeton University in the USA, and the University of Guadalajara in Mexico, which provides longitudinal data on migration from Mexico to the USA. This is probably the most-used survey on return migrants from the USA, producing a substantial number of studies, for example Constant and Massey (2002) and Munshi (2003).

Although there are a few small surveys on return migrants, a real concern about such surveys is their lack of representativeness of either emigrants or returnees in the country of origin. Such surveys are problematic since generalization of any of their findings would be misleading and might lead to the wrong policy implications. Hence caution is needed in highlighting the limitation of such non-representative surveys and their potentially biased findings.

Overall, although there have been concerted efforts to collect data on international flows, return migration still lags behind. It is clear, though, that there is a need for systematic collection of data on return migration in order to understand this phenomenon.

3. WHY DO MIGRANTS RETURN HOME?

3.1 Theoretical Literature

It is relatively easy to understand why people migrate. As first developed by Harris and Todaro (1970), migration takes place because there is a wage differential between two locations. The crucial assumption of the Harris–Todaro model is that workers base their migration decision on their expected incomes. Hence workers migrate from the low-wage region to the high-wage region because the expected value of their lifetime income, net of costs, is higher in the high-wage region. Using a simple model, as in Dustmann and Weiss (2007), where the immigrant weighs in each period the benefits of remaining a further unit of time abroad against the costs of doing so, the migrant will then decide to return home when the benefits of staying abroad are lower than the costs. Since the reason for migration is higher wages in the host country, this creates additional wealth and allows the migrant to increase lifetime consumption. However, as the marginal utility of wealth decreases, the additional benefit of a unit of time in the host country is lower, the longer the migrant has already stayed abroad (and the more wealth he/she has accumulated). Accordingly, the benefit of migration slowly decreases. This alone does not trigger a return migration, because, whatever the immigrant's wealth, it is always advantageous to remain a further unit of time in a country that pays a higher wage. This, however, implies that the migrant's objective is only to maximize lifetime income and that the migration decision is solely influenced by monetary gains. Thus, in this framework, there is no reason for the migrant to return to their home country.

One way to explain return migration in this setup is to assume that migrants have a preference for consumption in their home country; Djajic and Milbourne (1988) and Galor and Stark (1991) extend this framework to allow the potential migrant to maximize lifetime utility from consumption, given a lifetime budget constraint that depends on the migration decision. If the migrant prefers to consume at home rather than abroad, because of other factors that are complementary to consumption, such as being close to family and friends, living in a familiar environment, enjoying the climate and so on, the migrant's optimal decision may be to migrate only temporarily, although the value of the migrant's stock of human capital is higher abroad. This is because lifetime is finite, so each unit of time spent abroad increases the migrant's lifetime utility by raising their total consumption possibilities, but it reduces their lifetime utility by reducing the time available for consumption at home. Hence preference for home consumption explains why migrants return to their home countries voluntarily.

Another reason put forward by Dustmann and Weiss (2007) is that return migration may be motivated by lifetime utility that includes consumption, and locationally fixed factors complementary to consumption, if there are differences in relative prices between the host and home country. Return migration may be induced by a higher purchasing power of the host-country currency in the home country. Migration is temporary because it allows the migrant to take advantage of high wages abroad and low prices at home. Better conditions at home would also reduce the benefits for migrants from staying overseas.

Within this framework, temporary/return migration is planned and part of an optimal strategy to maximize lifetime utility: due to credit constraints, individuals migrate for a period of time where wages are higher so that they can accumulate savings overseas to use on their return to set up businesses (e.g. Mesnard, 2004). A higher rate of return on entrepreneurial activities in the home country may trigger a return migration.

Alternatively, individuals may migrate temporarily solely due to human capital considerations to acquire skills that are highly rewarded in the source country on their return. Student migration is an example. Another case would be if the returns to human capital acquired in the host country were higher at home, then this might trigger return migration (see Dustmann, 1997). Overseas migration might increase the migrant's productivity only slightly in the host country but may be important and highly valued in the home country.

Another mechanism behind the return decision might be unplanned, when the migrant realizes that their expected value of lifetime income is lower than that in the origin country and returns. In this case the decision arises as a result of failure either due to imperfect information about the host country in terms of labour market prospects or the cost of living, or the inability to fulfil the migration plans in terms of target savings and so on. This kind of return migration is expected to take place relatively soon after immigration, when information is at hand. Borjas and Bratsberg (1996) model return migration in a framework based on the selection model of Roy (1951), in which the composition of migratory flows depends on the relative distribution of incomes between the home and host countries, and average returns on human capital. Within this framework, return migration is explained primarily by an error in evaluating the shape of the income distribution in the host country. Hence both planned and unplanned return within this framework might explain the return decision, given preference for home consumption and maximizing lifetime utility.

3.2 Return Migration and Migration Duration

A small number of papers have examined the determinants of overseas migration duration. Within this literature, the focus is commonly not just on the return decision but also on the length of overseas stay.

If migrants are target savers, one would think that the more income they earn, the faster they will leave. Dustmann (1997) presents a simple life-cycle model where the migrant determines simultaneously consumption and the desired length of stay abroad. The focus of the analysis is to compare decisions under certainty with those under income uncertainty in host and home country. The optimal length of migration and the savings behaviour of migrant workers are examined, where savings and migration durations are jointly determined and where there is uncertainty about income in both the host and home country. Both savings and return decisions depend crucially on future income streams in the home and host country, which are in turn strongly affected by uncertainty. Although the effect of an uncertain future income on the length of the migration period is ambiguous, uncertainty is likely to have a positive effect on the migration duration in situations where the wage differential between home and host country is large and the perceived risk of the home-country labour market is large relative to the host-country labour market. Furthermore, if the optimal migration duration is chosen in conjunction with the optimal after-migration activity, as suggested by Dustmann and Kirchkamp (2002), economic variables will affect the optimal migration duration differently, according to which after-return activity is chosen. Furthermore, an increase in the host-country wage does not necessarily lead to increased migration durations – on the contrary, it may lead to a decrease in migration duration.

An interesting issue that has been understudied is the relationship between the migration duration and migrant's income abroad. Although there is consensus that migration is driven by the wage differential between the host and home country, the effect of changes in wages (or income) on return migration is ambiguous. Migrants would, on the one hand, like to extend their stay overseas as a response to higher wages; on the other hand, the gain from staying longer abroad decreases. As a consequence, higher wages abroad may have a positive or a negative effect on migration duration.

The empirical evidence on the effect of income on a migrant's duration abroad is rather limited due to lack of data and is mixed. Dustmann (2003) analyses optimal migration durations in a model that rationalizes the decision of the migrant to return to the home country, despite persistently higher wages in the host country. Based on a panel of immigrants to Germany over a 14-year period, he shows that if migrations are temporary, the optimal migration duration may decrease if the wages increase. Constant and Massey (2003) find no statistically significant relationship between earnings and migrant returns in Germany, although migrants who are unemployed are more likely to return. Those previous papers relied on longitudinal data that suffer from high attrition rates, lack information on the exact timing of the migration moves and reveal whether the migrant is still in the country only at the interview date. Bijwaard and Wahba (2014) estimate the impact of income earned in the host country on the migration duration of labour migrants. They use a four-state correlated competing risks model to account for the strong dependence of labour market status and income earned, and unique administrative panel data of all recent labour immigrants from LDCs to the Netherlands. The empirical results reveal that return intensities are U-shaped with respect to income, with high intensity for low- and high-income groups and the lowest-income group exhibiting the highest return. Although the intensities of return vary by duration and country of origin, the U-shaped relationship between income and return is consistently found.

3.3 Empirical Evidence on the Determinants of Return

A small but growing empirical literature has focused on the determinants of return migration, attempting to test alternative hypotheses related to the return decision and provides better understanding of why migrants return.

Kırdar (2009), studying Turkish immigrants in Germany, finds evidence in support of the savings accumulation conjecture, in which return is motivated by higher purchasing power of accumulated savings in the home country, but not for the human capital accumulation conjecture. Yang (2006) exploits a unique quasi-experiment to distinguish between the potential explanations for return migration of Philippine migrants. He takes advantage of exchange rate shocks generated by the Asian financial crisis and finds that Philippine migrants are less likely to return home when they experience more positive exchange rate shocks, suggesting that straightforward life-cycle motivations dominate target-earnings explanations for return migration. However, a subset of migrants – those with intermediate levels of foreign earnings – are likely to be target-earners. He argues that these results are consistent with a model where migration helps households accumulate resources for investment in the face of credit constraints and minimum investment levels.

On the other hand, Gibson and McKenzie (2011), using a unique survey that tracks, worldwide, a high proportion of the very top performers in secondary school over the period 1976 to 2004 from three Pacific countries, find the emigration decision to be most strongly associated with preference variables such as risk aversion, patience, and choice of subjects in secondary school, and not strongly linked to either liquidity constraints or the gain in income to be had from migrating. Likewise, the decision to return is strongly linked to family and lifestyle reasons, rather than to the income opportunities in different countries.

A few studies find that labour market shocks are a strong driver for return. A key finding in Kırdar (2009) is a positive impact of unemployment on return migration in Germany, but the direction of the impact of unemployment changes by the period length. Immigrants whose unemployment spells are shorter than three years are more likely to return. On the other hand, older working-age immigrants with longer unemployment periods are more likely to stay. Given the generosity of the German unemployment insurance system in terms of the duration of benefits, it is no surprise that older long-term unemployed immigrants with a small chance of finding employment in either country prefer to stay in Germany, whereas younger short-term unemployed immigrants are more likely to return once they realize that they will not be able to attain their savings accumulation goal due to poor employment prospects.

Similarly, Bijwaard et al. (2014) use administrative data from the Netherlands to estimate the causal effect of unemployment on the return decision and hence the migration duration of recent immigrants. They control for the endogeneity of labour market outcomes and the return migration decision using the 'timing-of-events' method. They find that unemployment periods shorten immigration durations across all immigrant groups.

3.4 The Selectivity of Return Migration: Who Returns?

Probably the most important issue in return migration is who returns. The selectivity of returnees is fundamental for understanding not only return migration but also the performance of the remaining immigrants and their assimilation. Hence there has been a growing interest in the migration literature in the selectivity of returnees. A recent survey by Dustmann and Görlach (2014) is dedicated to the selectivity of out-migrants, highlighting the importance of the issue. The main dimension of selectivity focused on education and/or income. The quest for the Holy Grail has been whether return migrants are positively or negatively selected in respect to the remaining immigrants.

Recently Dustmann and Görlach (2014, pp. 16–17) found

> not only that migrants who leave are unlikely to be randomly drawn from the population of entry cohorts but that the direction of outmigration selection is far from homogeneous across either immigration countries or across different immigrant groups to the same country. This observation in turn suggests that any conclusions drawn for one country about the character of outmigration is unlikely to carry over to another country, and perhaps not even to another group of immigrants in the same country.

Borjas and Bratsberg (1996) early on argued that return migration tends to accentuate the selection that originally characterized the immigrant flow. They show that return migration selection is the reverse of the initial selection process. In other words, if the immigrant flow is positively selected, the out-migrants will be less skilled on average than the remaining immigrants in the host country. Alternatively, if the immigrant flow is negatively selected, the out-migrants will be more skilled than the immigrants who remain in the host country: if the host country attracts relatively unskilled workers, it will be the better skilled among them who are most likely to return.

A number of authors have examined the correlation between return migration and immigrants' overseas earnings. For example, Borjas (1989) finds among the foreign-born in the USA that higher earnings are associated with less return migration. Yet, for Germany, Dustmann (2003) documents, among immigrants in Germany, that higher migrant wages are associated with more return migration (shorter overseas stays), whilst Constant and Massey (2002) find no statistically significant relationship between earnings and migrant returns in the same German data set, although migrants who are unemployed are more likely to return.

Nekby (2006) is one of the few who distinguishes between return migration and onward migration to a third country, using data on registered emigration for Sweden for the period 1991 to 2000. She finds that emigrants up to the age of 35–40 have higher adjusted mean income levels than non-emigrants in general, and that onward emigrants have lower predicted income levels than return emigrants across the age distribution. However, comparison between returnees and onward immigrants from the same origin indicates positive selection of onward immigrants against returnees.

Are highly educated immigrants more likely to return than low-educated ones? The propensity to return at different educational levels has been another important dimension of focus by the empirical studies of return migration. Again the findings are host–source-country specific.

The evidence for the USA shows mixed experiences. Ramos (1992) shows that return migrants to Puerto Rico tend to be more skilled than the Puerto Ricans who remain in the USA. Similarly, Zucker and Darby (2007) find that, in the period 1981–2004, there was a strong tendency of the most highly educated 'star scientists' in several science and technology fields in the USA to return to their country of origin to start up high-tech firms (especially in China, Taiwan and Brazil). However, Zakharenko (2008) finds that the difference between recent immigrants and other immigrants is greater than the difference between men and women, or skilled and unskilled migrants in the out-migration of immigrants to the USA. He concludes that assimilation differentiates immigrants more in their decision to return than education or gender.

Likewise, the evidence from Europe is not conclusive with respect to the role played by education in the return migration rate. For example, Jensen and Pedersen (2007) find that the propensity to return or to on-migrate increases with the level of education among immigrants in Denmark. Similarly, Gundel and Peters (2008), using data on migrants to Germany, show a much higher return rate for the highly educated compared with the less educated.

Focusing on skills rather than education, Dustmann and Weiss (2007) use UK data to show that the tendency of migrants to return to their country of origin is much stronger among workers in highly skilled occupations and that the migrants' return occurs mostly within ten years of their arrival.

An interesting study that provides support to this differing pattern of selectivity being dependent on both the origin and destination is that by Ambrosini et al. (2012), who use a unique combination of census and large survey data that enables them to identify Romanian migrants in three main destination countries (Spain, Austria and the USA) and to match this information with micro-data on non-migrants and returnees in Romania. They find that selection of migrants depends on the country of destination, being positive for the USA and negative for Spain. Returnees are selected in a similar way as migrants to the countries with the highest skill premium (like, e.g., the USA) and hence are positively selected among migrants overall.

These studies show that the selection pattern of out-migration/return migration with respect to education and income depends on both the source and host country. This is consistent with Roy's (1951) theoretical framework, where returnees from a host country with a low variance in the earnings distribution are expected in the main to be the more able (measured by education, skills or income) among the below-average performers in the high-variance origin country who emigrated in the first place.[4] This is because the more able in this group made the smallest relative gain from immigrating to the low-variance host country. The underlying assumption here is that the relative gain from emigration to a country with higher variance in the earnings distribution is positively correlated with the individual's position in the source-country distribution. Similarly, it is assumed that the relative gain from migrating to a country with a lower variance is higher, the lower the individual's relative position was in the source-country earnings distribution. The lower the variance, the higher is the relative gain from immigration for this person than for a better performer. This might explain why there is not one prevailing selection pattern in return migration. Also, as Campos-Vazquez and Lara (2012) show, the degree of selection in observable skills among return migrants can change over time, as happened in the case of Mexican–US immigrants from positive selection in 1990 to negative selection in 2010.

Another important aspect of return migration that is rarely studied due to the lack of data is the differences in the return probability and the intensity of return by migration motive. In almost all studies, immigrants are not distinguished by motive, though we expect immigrants to behave as rational economic individuals as opposed to, for example, tied family immigrants. An exception is Bijwaard (2010), who, using Dutch administrative data where the motive for migration is known, finds that labour immigrants to the Netherlands have the highest return rate and family immigrants the lowest, and, not surprisingly, most students stay in the Netherlands temporarily and then return.[5]

To sum up, the literature has been to a great extent preoccupied with the selectivity of out-migration and has focused perhaps unsurprisingly on the impact of out-migration on the host country.

4. THE IMPACT OF RETURN MIGRATION ON THE SOURCE COUNTRY

Return migration has potentially many effects on the remaining non-migrants. Through overseas employment, migrants increase their income, acquire new skills and accumulate savings and assets. When migrants return to their country of origin they represent an inflow to the country of origin of both financial capital through accumulated overseas savings and human capital through their newly acquired skills and knowledge from working overseas.

More often than not, many view migrants as key agents in development of the source country. Migrants, in particular temporary migrants and those planning to return to their home country, keep strong ties with the home country, and send back remittances while overseas. On return they can potentially contribute to economic development.

Theoretically, Djajic (2014) shows the implications of temporary emigration for the welfare of a source country. The framework of analysis is one of general equilibrium, where the economy's stocks of both capital and labour are endogenously determined by the saving and migration decisions of optimizing agents. Simulations of the model suggest that, for realistic values of the parameters, welfare of non-migrants of the source country is maximized when the migrants are employed abroad for a period in the range of 8–12 years. The ideal duration is found to be an increasing function of the international wage differential, migration costs and the degree to which the rights of migrants are protected in the host country. We review below the literature on the impact of returnees.

Theoretically, there are potentially various gains from temporary/return migration. Yet the main challenge in assessing the impact of return migration is the non-randomness of return migration. Not only are emigrants a select group, but who returns among that group is also selected. Data limitations have been a major constraint in allowing unbiased estimates or quantification of the impact of return migration on the home economy.

4.1 Investment and Entrepreneurship

Many developing countries suffer from high unemployment, and thus small and medium enterprises are seen as a channel to provide jobs and reduce poverty. Hence entrepreneurship is argued to be one of the engines of growth. To the extent that access to credit impedes start-up and development of micro-enterprises, overseas savings provides an opportunity to overcome this constraint. Overseas savings play a crucial role in access to entrepreneurship, given the capital market distortions prevailing in many LDCs, which might not have been possible without migration. This is seen as an important channel through which returnees contribute to investment and development.

Few studies have focused on the occupational choice of returnees and in particular on entrepreneurship among returnees and how international migration provides a channel for accessing credit through overseas savings. Using cross-sectional data from Pakistan, Ilahi (1999) finds that, on return, savings become a significant factor in the choice of self-employment over waged employment. Mesnard (2004) models migration as a way to overcome credit constraints in the presence of capital markets imperfections. She finds that the majority of entrepreneurial projects started by Tunisian returnees were totally financed through overseas savings. Dustmann and Kirchkamp (2002) develop a model where migrants simultaneously decide on the optimal migration duration and their after-return activities. They find that, among Turkish returnees, more than half are economically active and engage in entrepreneurial activities. McCormick and Wahba (2001) add a different insight by showing that savings matter more than human capital acquisition for the probability of entrepreneurship of illiterate Egyptian returnees. However, for the educated returnees, both access to credit, through overseas savings, and human capital accumulation are significant determinants of entrepreneurship on return.

Yet one important question, which is not studied by the early papers, is whether return migrants are more likely than non-migrants to become entrepreneurs (set up businesses). More recent papers address this; for example Piracha and Vadean (2010) examine the occupational choice of returnees in Albania, comparing returnees to non-migrants, and attempt to control for the selection bias associated with return migration.[6] Wahba and Zenou (2012) investigate whether return migrants are more likely to become entrepreneurs than non-migrants. However, they develop a theoretical search model that presents the trade-off faced by returnees, since overseas migration provides an opportunity for human and physical capital accumulation but, at the same time, may lead to a loss of social capital back home. They test the predictions of the model using data from Egypt and find that, even after controlling for the endogeneity of the temporary migration decision, an overseas returnee is more likely to become an entrepreneur than a non-migrant. Although migrants may lose their social capital, they accumulate savings and experience overseas that increase their chances of becoming entrepreneurs.

An important issue regarding the role of return migration in entrepreneurship is the need to differentiate between business set-ups and occupational choice of returnees. It is not the case that all self-employment, for example, should be treated as an entrepreneurial activity, as some self-employment jobs are far from it. Indeed, Kveder and Flahaux (2013) find that Senegalese returnees resort to self-employment as a 'last resort' if they were unable to accumulate capital overseas. Yet there is evidence for many developing and emerging countries that return migration has led to micro-enterprise development.[7]

Woodruff and Zenteno (2007) find that migration networks help overcome capital constraints in Mexico. Using a survey of self-employed workers and small-firm owners in Mexico that have access to remittance flows, they estimate the impact of attachment to migration networks on the level of capital investment, the capital–output ratio, sales, and profits of micro-enterprises. However Woodruff and Zenteno (2007) consider households of migrants receiving remittances rather than return migrants.

Furthermore, there is evidence that entrepreneurs' migration experience significantly improves the chances of survival of their entrepreneurial activities (see Marchetta, 2012). This might be due to having fewer credit constraints, but also the result of utilizing newly acquired skills, ideas and entrepreneurial knowledge throughout their migration experience to start and successfully manage micro-enterprises.

4.2 Human Capital

The return of emigrants is another potential source of growth for the source country through their accumulated knowledge and newly acquired skills (see Docquier and Rapoport, 2012 for a survey on the impact on emigration on the brain drain and brain gain in sending countries). Theoretically, a number of papers, for example Dos Santos and Postel-Vinay (2003), show how return migration can have an expansionary effect on the source developing economy through knowledge diffusion that in turn narrows the technological gap between the host and source economies, resulting in fewer individuals emigrating and more emigrants returning. Furthermore, Mayr and Peri (2009) show how temporary migration opportunities can raise the education level of a sending country through return migration and skill upgrading.

Whether migrants acquire human capital while overseas is an important question for the economic development of the home country since earlier studies on emigration emphasized the resulting brain drain for home developing countries. A few studies have examined the impact of overseas experience on the human capital accumulation of the returnees. One focus has been on measuring what is known as the returns to returning by examining the wage premium of return migrants compared to non-migrants. The evidence on transitional economies is rather mixed. Co, Gang and Yun (2000) find no significant wage premium for returning men, but a positive one for women in Hungary. However, de Coulon and Piracha (2005), who study a slightly different issue, namely the selectivity and performance of

Albanian return migrants, find that return migrants are negatively selected and that if the non-migrants had migrated and returned, they would have earned more than twice the wage of return migrants. On the other hand, contrary to those studies, Ambrosini et al. (2012) find that for a source country, like Romania, relatively high rates of temporary migration have positive long-run effects on average skills and wages.

The evidence for developing countries, however, is more positive. Lacuesta (2010) finds an 11 per cent wage gap between returning migrants and observationally equivalent non-migrants in Mexico, but argues that this premium is the result of pre-migration differences in ability and not human capital gains derived from migration. Reinhold and Thom (2013) also find a wage premium for Mexican returnees from US work experience. The return to a year of occupation-specific migration experience is estimated to be as high as 8.7 per cent for some occupations. Wahba (2007) examines the case of Egypt and finds strong evidence that overseas employment and temporary migration result in a wage premium on return; on average, return migrants earned around 38 per cent more than non-migrants in the 1980s and 1990s. De Vreyer et al. (2010) examine labour market outcomes of returnees in seven capital cities in West Africa and find that experience abroad results in a substantial wage premium for migrants returning from an OECD country but not for other return migrants. Those studies control only for the return migration selection but not for the emigration decision in the first instance.

One potential bias in all the above studies is that they control for temporary migration and labour market participation on return, but do not control for selection into emigration and return migration or for the occupational choice of returnees and non-migrants. Wahba (2014) meets this challenge head on and attempts to control for several selections, namely, the emigration decision, the return choice as well as for the labour market participation decision and the occupational (waged versus entrepreneur) choice. Using unique representative data (ELMPS, 2006) where current and return migrants and non-migrants are observed, she finds that Egyptian return migrants have a positive wage premium compared to stayers because they have acquired new skills overseas that enhance their human capital. Overseas temporary migration leads to a wage premium on return. The estimates show that return migrants earn on average around 16 per cent more than non-migrants if all selection biases are corrected for, rather than a 46 per cent premium when ignoring individual characteristics and selectivity. Although half of the difference in observed wages between returnees and non-migrants is due to observable characteristics, such as age and education, further unobservable characteristics account for another quarter of this wage difference. In fact, controlling only for return migration and ignoring the emigration decision overestimates the impact of return migration, since migrants are positively selected compared to non-migrants while returnees are negatively selected amongst migrants. This emphasizes the significance of selectivity in return migration. The findings also highlight the differential impact of return migration on those returning. Less-educated returnees earn only 10 per cent more than non-migrants compared to university graduate returnees, who earn 24 per cent more. In addition, returns from migration duration peak at six years and lead to a wage premium of about 27 per cent compared with non-migrants.

Another piece of evidence of the skill enhancement of temporary migrants can be measured through their occupational mobility. However, there is barely any evidence. One exception is Carletto and Kilic (2011), who estimate the impact of overseas migration experience on the occupational mobility of return migrants compared to non-migrants in Albania. Controlling for the selection into temporary migration (i.e. emigration and return together), the empirical findings suggest that overseas migration experience increases the likelihood of upward occupational mobility of returnees. However, the impact of host countries is far from homogeneous and the type of work in the host impacts the skill acquisition while overseas and thus the mobility on return. Additionally, the impact of skill acquisition seems to depend on the migrant's educational level. McCormick and Wahba (2001) find that almost 53 per cent of the educated returnees have found the skills they acquired abroad to be beneficial to their current job upon return, compared to 33 per cent of the less educated and 22 per cent of the illiterates. Hence overseas work experience provides an opportunity for human capital enhancement, especially for the educated migrant.

4.3 Norm and Idea Transfers

Another important and yet understudied channel through which return migration influences the economic development of the source country is through the transfer of ideas. Two main outcomes have been examined: political ideas and social norms. Return emigrants could potentially transmit back home political ideas regarding the quality of political institutions, raising awareness and demand for political accountability and increasing direct participation in the political system. In an interesting paper, Spilimbergo (2009), using a comprehensive panel data set on foreign students, which spans 50 years and covers the entire world, finds that foreign-educated individuals bring about democratic change at home if they acquired foreign education in democratic countries. Batista and Pedro (2011) test the hypothesis that international migration experiences promote better institutions at home by boosting demand for political accountability in Cape Verde. They adopt a simple voting experiment to capture demand for better governance at home. Following a survey of perceived corruption in public services, respondents were asked to mail a pre-stamped postcard if they wanted the anonymous results of this survey to be made publicly available in the media. The respondents were told that at least 50 per cent of them would have to return postcards for the information to be released publicly. The results show that international emigration positively affects demand for improved political accountability, with stronger effects for migrants to countries with better governance and for return migrants relative to current migrants, as returnees can directly influence their networks in the home country.

Second, returnees may be influenced by norms in the emigration country and adopt similar behaviour on their return to their home country. Examining the social norm transfer hypothesis, Bertoli and Marchetta (2014) study whether returnees adjust their fertility choices to the norms that prevail in their previous country of destination using Egyptian household-level data where emigration is predominantly towards other Arab countries characterized by a higher fertility rate. They control for the endogeneity of the migration decision and show that return migration has a positive and significant influence on marital childbearing. In that particular case, returnees are likely to have high fertility rates, similar to the norms in their country of destination.

4.4 Return Intentions versus Realized Return

There is also evidence that intentions to return affect migrants' behaviour while overseas. Chabé-Ferret et al. (2014), using a unique French data set, analyse the relationship between return plans and several immigrants' outcomes in the host and origin country, addressing the potential endogeneity between return plans and outcomes. They also investigate the potential trade-off and complementarities between various immigrants' behaviour. They find that return intentions are correlated with higher remitting incidence, more investment in the country of origin and more political participation at home. Thus return intentions, even if they do not materialize, still influence migrants' behaviour positively towards the home country.

4.5 The Challenges of Return Migration

Although return migration provides an opportunity to reverse the brain drain and contribute to the brain gain of the home economy, there are sometimes challenges in benefiting from return migration.

There is a concern that returnees might not be able easily to reintegrate back in the labour market after a period of absence. Return migrants may bring back skills that do not match the demands of the home economy. If returnees acquire specific skills in the host country that are not needed or transferable, this might produce tension for the return and waste of skills (see Lucas, 2008). Furthermore, whether returnees elect to participate or not in the labour market on returning will affect the benefits accrued from return migration. In some countries, returnees tend to return at retirement age. However, there is evidence that they still invest their savings and sometimes even set up businesses even if they have decided to retire from the labour market. For example, Hamdouch and Wahba (2012) find that Moroccan emigrants in Western Europe are likely to return at retirement age, but are still likely to use their savings to invest and start-up businesses.

Another possibility is that the home country experiences a large-scale unplanned return migration. For example, the economy of Kerala experienced a recession in 1991 due to the mass return of migrants from the Gulf States, because of the First Gulf War, and the associated loss in remittances (see Lucas, 2008). Coping with a sudden large-scale return can create problems, at least in the short run, for the home economy.

Finally, though return migration has the potential to foster economic development, quantifying the macroeconomic effect, beyond the impact of remittances, on the macroeconomy tends in most cases to be difficult due to lack of data.

5. CONCLUSION

Return migration is at the heart of the debate on the costs and benefits of international migration, with estimates by the OECD suggesting that on average about two migrants in five will leave the host country within five years after their arrival (OECD, 2008). However, there is a huge variation in return rates by country of destination and country of origin. This chapter has attempted to bring together the scattered and scanty economic evidence on the determinants of return migration and the role played by return migration in the economic development of the home country.

First, the economics literature on why immigrants return put forward and test several economic hypotheses, which at first might seem competing, on what drives voluntary return migration. Yet one important underlying assumption in this literature is that individuals prefer home to foreign consumption. Hence migration is a strategy for individuals to maximize total utility over the whole life cycle. As such individuals migrate temporarily for a period of time where wages are higher, they can acquire skills and accumulate savings and then return. If migrants fail to achieve this, due either to imperfect information about the host country in terms of labour market prospects or the cost of living or the inability to fulfil the migration plans in terms of target savings, they also return. The empirical evidence, not surprisingly, tends to provide support for one of these hypotheses at a time.

Second, the literature shows a positive role of temporary migration on migrants: they accumulate savings that increase their probability of becoming entrepreneurs and setting up businesses. They acquire skills overseas that allow them to gain wage premiums, relative to non-migrants, on return. They also transfer ideas and norms that affect the economic and political outcomes observed in the home country. Hence this suggests that return migration reduces credit constraints faced in developing countries and allows for brain circulation and gains for sending economies.

However, this review also highlights several challenges that limit our understanding of the actual impact of return migration. The biggest obstacle is the lack of data. Given the non-random nature of emigration and return, reliance on non-representative samples of returnees is problematic. Thus there is a need to ensure that census data and representative surveys such as LSMS and LFS collect systematically information on previous location five years ago to capture returnees and also data on members of the household who are overseas at the time.

The second challenge is for policy makers. The right mix of policies is required to maximize the benefits of return migration. Facilitating investment by reducing the red tape and providing information on investment possibilities to migrants and returnees should be promoted. Given that return migrants tend to be willing and more likely to embark on setting up projects/businesses, there is room for encouraging and directing their investment. Also, investors need reassurance about their rights and the enforcement of contracts. Moreover, there is a need to provide information on areas of investment to encourage migrants' investment. Finally, migrants can play an important role in job creation in their home countries through their investment if they are enticed, using the right financial incentives such as tax holidays, to set up businesses and create jobs.

To conclude, return migrants are an important potential resource for developing sending countries that so far has not been fully utilized, and until there is a serious attempt to collect better data on return migrants and their impact, their contributions will not be fully maximized.

NOTES

* Financial support from the Economic and Social Research Council [RES-167-25-0678] is gratefully acknowledged.

1. See Constant et al. (2013) for a survey on circular migration.
2. See OECD (2008) for a discussion on measuring return migration.
3. See OECD (2008) for a discussion on measuring return migration.
4. See Jensen and Pedersen (2007) for a very useful non-technical description.
5. Bijwaard et al. (2014) look at the impact of marital changes such as divorce on the return migration of family immigrants in the Netherlands.
6. Kilic et al. (2009) also looked at Albania, but examined the impact of past migration experience of Albanian households on non-farm business ownership.
7. See, for example, Gubert and Nordman (2011) for the Maghreb; Lindstrom (1996) for Mexico.

REFERENCES

Ambrosini, J.W., K. Mayr, G. Peri and D. Radu (2011), 'The selection of migrants and returnees: evidence from Romania and implications', NBER Working Papers 16912.

Aydemir, A. and C. Robinson (2008), 'Global labour markets, return, and onward migration', *Canadian Journal of Economics*, **41**(4), 1285–311.

Barrett, A. and J. Goggin (2010), 'Returning to the question of a wage premium for returning migrants', *National Institute Economic Review*, **213**, R43–R51.

Batista, C. and C. Pedro (2011), 'Do migrants improve governance at home? Evidence from a voting experiment', *World Bank Economic Review*, **25**(1), 77–104.

Bertoli, S. and F. Marchetta (2014), 'Bringing it all back home: return migration and fertility choices', *World Development*, forthcoming.

Bijwaard, G.E. (2010), 'Immigrant migration dynamics model for The Netherlands', *Journal of Population Economics*, **23**(4), 1213–47.

Bijwaard, G.E. and Stijn van Doeselaar (2014), 'The impact of changes in the marital status on return-migration of family migrants', *Journal of Population Economics*, forthcoming.

Bijwaard, G.E. and J. Wahba (2014), 'Do high-income or low-income immigrants leave faster?', *Journal of Development Economics*, **108**, 54–68.

Bijwaard, G.E., C. Schluter and J. Wahba (2014), 'The impact of labour market dynamics on the return-migration of immigrants', *Review of Economics and Statistics*, **96**(3) 483–94.

Borjas, George J. (1989), 'Immigrant and emigrant earnings: a longitudinal study', *Economic Inquiry*, **27**(1), 21–37.

Borjas, G. and B. Bratsberg (1996), 'Who leaves? The outmigration of the foreign-born', *The Review of Economics and Statistics*, **78**(1), 165–76.

Bratsberg, Bernt, Oddbjørn Raaum and Kjetil Sørlie (2007), 'Foreign-born migration to and from Norway', *International Migration, Economic Development and Policy*, 259–91.

Campos-Vazquez, R.M. and J. Lara (2012), 'Self-selection patterns among return migrants: Mexico 1990–2010', *IZA Journal of Migration*, **1**, 1–8.

Carletto, C. and T. Kilic (2011), 'Moving up the ladder? The impact of migration experience on occupational mobility in Albania', *Journal of Development Studies*, **47**(6), 846–69.

Chabé-Ferret, B., J. Machado and J. Wahba (2014), 'Return intentions and migrants' behaviour', mimeo.

Co, C., I. Gang and M.-S. Yun (2000), 'Returns to returning', *Journal of Population Economics*, **13**, 57–79.

Constant, A. and D.S. Massey (2002), 'Economic opportunity in *Mexico* and *Return Migration* from the United States', *Demography*, **33**(3), 357–4.

Constant, A. and D.S. Massey (2003), 'Self-selection, earnings, and out-migration: a longitudinal study of immigrants to Germany', *Journal of Population Economics*, **16**(4), 631–53.

Constant, A., O. Nottmeyer and K. Zimmermann (2013), 'The economics of circular migration', in A.F. Constant and K.F. Zimmermann (eds), *International Handbook on the Economics of Migration*, Cheltenham, UK, and Northampton, MA, USA: Edward Elgar Publishing, pp. 55–74.

de Coulon, A. and M. Piracha (2005), 'Self-selection and the performance of return migrants: the source country perspective', *Journal of Population Economics*, **18**, 779–807.

de Vreyer, P., F. Gubert and A.-S. Robilliard (2010), 'Are there returns to migration experience? An empirical analysis using data on return migrants and non-migrants in West Africa', *Annals of Economics and Statistic*, **97/98**, 307–28.

Djajic, S. (2014), 'Temporary emigration and welfare: the case of low-skilled labor', *International Economic Review*, forthcoming.

Djajic, S. and R. Milbourne (1988), 'A general equilibrium model of guest-worker migration: a source-country perspective', *Journal of International Economics*, **25**, 335–51.

Docquier, F. and H. Rapoport (2012), 'Globalization, brain drain and development', *Journal of Economic Literature*, **50**(3), 681–730.

Dos Santos, D. and Fabien Postel-Vinay (2003), 'Migration as a source of growth: the perspective of a developing country', *Journal of Population Economics*, **16**(1), 161–75.

Dustmann, Christian (1997), 'Return migration, uncertainty and precautionary savings', *Journal of Development Economics*, **52**(2), 295–316.

Dustmann, C. (2003), 'Return migration, wage differentials, and the optimal migration duration', *European Economic Review*, **47**(2), 353–69.

Dustmann, Christian and Joseph-Simon Görlach (2014), 'Selective outmigration and the estimation of immigrants' earnings profiles', CReAM Discussion Paper Series 1402, Centre for Research and Analysis of Migration (CReAM), Department of Economics, University College London.

Dustmann, C. and O. Kirchkamp (2002), 'The optimal migration duration and activity choice after remigration', *Journal of Development Economics*, **67**(2), 351–72.

Dustmann, C. and Y. Weiss (2007), 'Return migration: theory and empirical evidence from the UK', *British Journal of Industrial Relations*, **45**(2), 236–56.

ELMPS (Egypt Labor Market Panel Survey) (2006), Economic Research Forum, data set, Cairo.

Galor, O. and O. Stark (1991), 'The probability of return migration, migrants' work effort, and migrants' performance', *Journal of Development Economics*, **35**, 399–405.

Gibson, John and David McKenzie (2011), 'The microeconomic determinants of emigration and return migration of the best and brightest: evidence from the Pacific', *Journal of Development Economics*, **95**(1), 18–29.

Gubert, F. and C.J. Nordman (2011), 'Return migration and small enterprise development in the Maghreb', in S. Plaza and D. Ratha (eds), *Diaspora for Development in Africa*, Washington, DC: The World Bank, pp. 103–26.

Gundel, Sebastian and Heiko Peters (2008), 'What determines the duration of stay of immigrants in Germany? Evidence from a longitudinal duration analysis', *International Journal of Social Economics*, **35**(11), 769–82.

Hamdouch, B. and J. Wahba (2012), 'Return migration and entrepreneurship in Morocco', Economic Research Forum no. 666.

Harris, J.R. and M.P. Todaro (1970), 'Migration, unemployment and development: a two-sector analysis', *American Economic Review*, **60**, 126–42.

Ilahi, N. (1999), 'Return migration and occupational change', *Review of Development Economics*, **3**, 170–86.

Jasso, Guillermina and Mark R. Rosenzweig (1982), 'Estimating the emigration rates of legal immigrants using administrative and survey data: the 1971 cohort of immigrants to the United States', *Demography*, **19**(3), 279–90.

Jensen, P. and P.J. Pedersen (2007), 'To stay or not to stay? Out-migration of immigrants from Denmark', *International Migration*, **45**(5), 87–113.

Kilic, T., C. Carletto, B. Davis and A. Zezza (2009), 'Investing back home', *The Economics of Transition*, **17**(3), 587–623.

Kırdar, Murat G. (2009), 'Labor market outcomes, savings accumulation, and return migration', *Labour Economics*, **16**(4), 418–28.

Kveder, C.L.M. and M.-L. Flahaux (2013), 'Returning to Dakar: a mixed methods analysis of the role of migration experience for occupational status', *World Development*, **45**, 223–38.

Lacuesta, A. (2010), 'A revision of the self-selection of migrants using returning migrants' earnings', *Annals of Economics and Statistics*, **97/98**, 235–59.
Lindstrom, D.P. (1996), 'Economic opportunity in Mexico and return migration from the United States', *Demography*, **33**(3), 357–74.
Lucas, R.E.B. (2008), *International Migration and Economic Development: Lessons from Low Income Countries*, Cheltenham, UK and Northampton, MA, USA: Edward Elgar Publishing.
Marchetta, F. (2012), 'Return migration and the survival of entrepreneurial activities in Egypt', *World Development*, **40**(10), 1999–2013.
Mayr, K. and G. Peri (2009), 'Brain drain and brain return: theory and application to Eastern– Western Europe', *B.E. Journal of Economic Analysis and Policy*, **9**(1).
McCormick, B. and J. Wahba (2001), 'Overseas work experience, savings and entrepreneurship amongst returnees to LDCs', *Scottish Journal of Political Economy*, **48**, 164–78.
Mesnard, A. (2004), 'Temporary migration and capital market imperfections', *Oxford Economic Papers*, **56**, 242–62.
Munshi, K. (2003), 'Networks in the modern economy: Mexican migrants in the U.S. labor market', *Quarterly Journal of Economics*, **118**(2), 549–97.
Nekby, L. (2006), 'The emigration of immigrants, return vs onward migration: evidence from Sweden', *Journal of Population Economics*, **19**(2), 197–226.
Organisation for Economic Cooperation and Development (2008), *International Migration Outlook 2008*, Paris: OECD Publishing.
Piracha, M. and F. Vadean (2010), 'Return migration and occupational choice: evidence from Albania', *World Development*, **38**(8), 1141–55.
Ramos, F. (1992), 'Out-migration and return migration of Puerto Ricans', in *Immigration and the Workforce: Economic Consequences for the United States and Source Areas*, USA: University of Chicago Press, pp. 49–66.
Reinhold, S. and K. Thom (2013), 'Migration experience and earnings in the Mexican labor market', *Journal of Human Resources*, **48**(3), 768–820.
Roy, A.D. (1951), 'Some thoughts on the distribution of earnings', *Oxford Economic Papers*, **3**, 135–46.
Shorland, Philippa (2006), 'People on the move: a study of migrant movement patterns to and from New Zealand', New Zealand Department of Labour.
Spilimbergo, A. (2009), 'Foreign students and democracy', *American Economic Review*, **99**(1), 528–43.
Wahba, J. (2007), 'Returns to overseas work experience: the case of Egypt', in Ç. Özden and M. Schiff (eds), *International Migration, Economic Development & Policy*, Washington DC: The World Bank, pp. 235–58.
Wahba, J. (2014), Selection, Selection, Selection: Labour Market Impact of Return, mimeo.
Wahba, J. and Y. Zenou (2012), 'Out of sight, out of mind: migration, entrepreneurship and social capital', *Regional Science and Urban Economics*, **42**(5), 890–903.
Warren, R. and J.M. Peck (1980), 'Foreign-born emigration from the United States: 1960 to 1970', *Demography*, **17**, 71–84.
Woodruff, C. and R. Zenteno (2007), 'Migration networks and microenterprises in Mexico', *Journal of Development Economics*, **82**, 509–28.
Yang, D. (2006), 'Why do migrants return to poor countries? Evidence from Philippine migrants' responses to exchange rate shocks', *Review of Economics and Statistics*, **88**(4), 715–35.
Zakharenko, R. (2008), 'Return migration: an empirical investigation', MPRA Paper 13755, University Library of Munich, Germany.
Zucker, L.G. and M.R. Darby (2007), 'Star scientists, innovation and regional and national immigration', NBER Working Papers 13547, National Bureau of Economic Research, Inc.

13. Growth in forced displacement: cross-country, sub-national and household evidence on potential determinants

Ana María Ibáñez[1]

INTRODUCTION

Forced displacement has shown an increasing trend during the last two decades. While in 1989 the internally displaced population (IDP) totaled 16.5 million, in 2011 this figure reached 26.4 million.[2] The steep growth in IDP contrasts with a declining trend for refugees worldwide. The increased occurrence of civil wars, in contrast to inter-state wars, and tighter border controls that limit the flow of refugees partly explain the rising numbers of IDP. Although both populations are fleeing conflict and violence, the United Nations is legally bound to protect refugees, yet IDP are the sole responsibility of their national governments and thus live in more fragile conditions.

Despite the rising trend and the negative consequences it entails, contributions from the economic literature to understanding forced displacement are fairly recent. Forced displacement was perceived largely as a political problem to which economics had little to contribute (Lucas, 1997; Schmeidl, 1997). The term 'forced migration' reflected the perception of passive victims and not active agents deciding among complex conditions (Birkeland, 2000). However, recent empirical evidence for conflict-ridden countries shows that individuals adopt several strategies to survive and cope with the consequences of violence (Justino, 2011). Migration is among the many strategies households and individuals use. Instead of being forced to relocate, several case studies provide evidence that individuals outweigh the costs and benefits of migration, and choose the lesser of two evils. Although violence plays a determinant role, socioeconomic factors also influence the decision process.

The consequences of forced displacement are manifold.[3] Forced migration is often hasty. Households leave behind assets, and need to seek employment in a new region; access to risk-sharing mechanisms decreases; the settlement process is difficult; and some individuals face the consequences of post-traumatic syndrome due to the violence they have endured. Because forced migration takes place in a context of war, countries often suffer from absence of rule of law, political instability, unprotected property rights and a weak economy. Internally displaced persons frequently face large income shocks, declining labor conditions, post-traumatic stress and immersion in a poverty trap (Ibáñez and Vélez, 2008; Ibáñez and Moya, 2010a, 2010b; Kondylis, 2010; Moya, 2013; Carter and Moya, 2014). In some cases, economic conditions of IDP improve after forced migration. The impact depends largely on the characteristics of IDP, the nature of conflict and interventions from governments or the international community (Kondylis, 2008; Ruiz and Vargas-Silva, 2013). The consequences are not limited to the victims of forced migration. Large and unexpected inflows of IDP exert a strong pressure on labor market and social programs, causing a temporary growth in unemployment, food prices and poverty, as well as worsening health and nutritional outcomes for children (Alix-Garcia and Saah, 2009; Calderón and Ibáñez, 2009; Baez, 2011; Bozzoli et al., 2013). In addition, the expelling areas may face violent redistribution of assets and power, a shortage of goods and a slow-down of economic activity (Morrison and May, 1994).

The objective of this chapter is to review the recent literature on the causes of forced displacement and discuss potential future research.[4] The contribution of the economics literature to research on forced displacement is recent. Thus the chapter also covers literature from political science, anthropology and sociology. The causes of forced displacement are to be understood on three different analytical levels: the onset of war in countries with particular conditions leading to forced displacement; the strategies of armed groups during civil conflict which triggers purposive violence against civilians and subsequent movements of population; and the behavior and decisions of individuals in conflict regions. Sections 2–5 explore each of these analytical levels. Section 6 discusses the return of forcibly displaced persons once the conflict ends or violence ceases. Section 7 examines the potential for future research. Section 1 is a brief overview of worldwide forced displacement.

1. FORCED DISPLACEMENT: WORLDWIDE TRENDS

In 1951, the United Nations approved the Convention Relating to the Status of Refugees. This convention defined the legal status of refugees, their rights and the legal obligations of governments.[5] The convention protected the people forced to flee their country 'owing to well-founded fear of being persecuted for reasons of race, religion, nationality, membership of a particular social group or political opinion', leaving unprotected internally displaced persons in spite of facing similar consequences as refugees. It was not until 1998 that the United Nations issued the 'Guiding Principles on Internal Displacement', which defines internally displaced persons as

> persons or groups of persons who have been forced or obliged to flee or to leave their homes or places of habitual residence, in particular as a result of or in order to avoid the effects of armed conflict, situations of generalized violence, violations of human rights or natural or human-made disasters, and who have not crossed an internationally recognized state border.[6]

The principles guide governments, international humanitarian institutions and development agencies on how to protect and provide assistance to IDP; some governments have incorporated them as national policies and laws, although they are not binding.[7] The protection and assistance of IDP is still the sole responsibility of national governments.

Estimating the precise magnitudes of forced displacement is difficult. First, forced displacement occurs in war-torn countries that rarely keep records of forcibly displaced persons or victims of war. Second, many displacements, in particular those by single families or persons, go undetected. Massive forced displacements are easily detected and are generally accounted for. Third, countries have gradually recognized forced displacement as a legal status. Because some governments caused forced migration in the first place, these countries underreport or hide the real figures of IDP. Lastly, several forced migrations are deemed voluntary because their trigger was not an overt human rights violation.

The United Nations refugee agency (UNHCR) records the number of IDP it protects or assists. Figure 13.1 illustrates the evolution of refugees and IDP trends from 2000 to 2012. These figures are a lower bound of the real magnitude of the IDP population. While the stock of refugees is constant in some years or mildly decreasing, the number of IDP exhibits a steep increase from 2004 onwards. The emergence of new civil wars or the intensification of old ones are the main drivers of the increasing trend of IDP. The sharpest increments are reported in Afghanistan, Colombia, Democratic Republic of Congo, Somalia, Sudan and Syria. All these countries were or are facing civil wars or the violent onset of civil wars. Tightened border controls may force some migrants to stay within countries' borders instead of trespassing frontiers. This contributes further to the reduction in the stock of refugees and the growth of IDP. In addition, the recent legal recognition of IDP in many countries

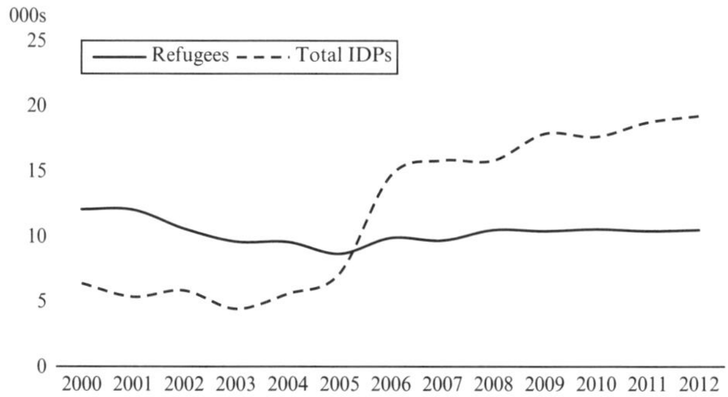

Notes:
Total refugees = refugees and returned refugees.
Total IDP = IDP and returned IDP.

Source: UNHCR.

Figure 13.1 Yearly stock of refugees and IDP protected or assisted by UNHCR

and the refinement of registration records may also partly explain this steep increase.

Table 13.1 reports the ten countries worldwide with the highest stock of IDP in 2012. Colombia has the largest stock of IDP with more than 3.9 million, which is equivalent to 8.3 percent of the country's total population. Although absolute figures for Somalia and Syria are lower in contrast to Colombia's, their percentages, 11.2 percent and 9 percent respectively, are indicative of large humanitarian crises due to a ravaging long war in Somalia and the violent onset of the Syrian civil war. The aggregated figures show Africa and Asia, with 12 and 10 countries respectively suffering forced migration, as the regions with the largest stock of IDP (see Table 13.2). However, the relative figures for IDP are higher for Africa and America, the latter including Colombia with a large population of IDP in absolute and relative terms.

Interestingly, the phenomenon of forced displacement is not limited to countries ridden by conflict. First, forced displacement persists in some countries after the conflict ends. The civil wars in Georgia, Azerbaijan, Bosnia and Herzegovina, Iran and Syria had ended by 2000, yet in 2012 forced displacement persisted. Understanding why forced displacement may linger even after peace is reached is essential. Presumably violence, lack of rule of law, restricted democracy, ethnic clashes and separatist movements, among others, persist after the conflict ends. Little research examines protracted forced displacement in some countries. Second, some

Table 13.1 Stock of IDP in 2002 protected or assisted by UNHCR by country

Country	Stock of IDPs (2012)	Population 2012	IDPs as a percentage of population
Yemen	492 188	23 852 409	2.06
Afghanistan	505 128	29 824 536	1.69
Azerbaijan	600 336	9 297 507	6.46
Pakistan	814 177	179 160 111	0.45
Somali	1 143 151	10 195 134	11.21
Iraq	1 350 610	32 578 209	4.15
Sudan	1 964 854	37 195 349	5.28
Syrian Arab Republic	2 016 500	22 399 254	9.00
Democratic Republic of the Congo	2 973 665	65 705 093	4.53
Colombia	3 943 509	47 704 427	8.27

Source: UNHCR and World Bank

Table 13.2 Stock of IDP protected and assisted by the UNHCR by region

Regions	IDP stock (2012)	IDP/Population countries with IDP	IDP/Total population	Number of countries with IDP
Africa	7 794 143	2.34	0.70	12
America	3 943 509	8.27	0.41	1
Asia	6 856 805	1.36	0.16	10
Europe	621 397	2.22	0.08	3

Source: UNHCR and UNPIN

countries report forced displacement in spite of not confronting a civil war during recent decades. That conflict causes displacement is assumed as tautological. Nonetheless, violence against civilians that is not related to conflict also triggers forced displacement and some countries facing conflicts may not experience forced displacement. Further understanding of this phenomenon is also important.

Table 13.3 examines the overlap between forced displacement and civil wars. Over 13.4 percent of the countries in the world suffered forced displacement during the last two decades. As the table is based on the stock of IDP assisted by UNHCR, this figure constitutes a lower bound. Near 2.6 percent of the countries suffered protracted forced displacement in 2012 although the conflict had ended, 3.6 percent of the countries did not

Table 13.3 Stock of IDP and incidence of civil war

	Positive IDP* stock in 2012 (%)	No IDP stock in 2012 (%)
Civil war between 1990 and 1999 and no civil war after	2.60	11.30
Civil war between 1990 and 2007	7.20	7.70
No civil war between 1990 and 2007	3.60	66.50

Notes: *Stock of IDP assisted by UNHCR.

Source: UNHCR and COW (PRIO)

have a conflict during the last two decades but reported forced displacement, 19 percent had a civil war and did not report forced displacement and 7.2 percent endured a civil war during the first decade of the twenty-first century and faced forced displacement.

Return of forcibly displaced persons when the conflict is still ongoing or after the conflict ends is seldom an option. The UNHCR data on forced displacement show that only 3.2 percent of the IDP stock by 2012 had returned to their home town. Facilitating return of IDP is a usual policy adopted once the conflict ends. However, the evidence suggests that a small percentage of IDP is willing to return. This is another interesting dimension on which research is scarce, yet the results could provide important insights into how to design policies for the return of the displaced population.

Before reviewing the literature on the causes of forced migration, the following figures examine some potential correlations between country characteristics and the magnitude of the IDP population. Figure 13.2a depicts the correlation between the intensity of civil wars, measured by deaths between 1990 and 2007, and the stock of IDP by 2012. The figure suggests that intensity of civil wars and magnitude of IDP are positively correlated. However, a large group of countries faces low-intensity conflicts with a large population of IDP.

Because forced displacement also occurs in countries in which war has ended, Figures 13.2b–13.2d correlate the stocks of IDP with the polity IV indicator as well as an index for political rights and civil liberties respectively, calculated by Freedom House.[8] The polity IV[9] indicator measures the level of democracy in each country. Lower values indicate autocratic countries, whereas higher values are associated with full democracies. Higher values are associated with lower stocks of IDP, suggesting that aggression against civilians is lower in more established democracies.

a)

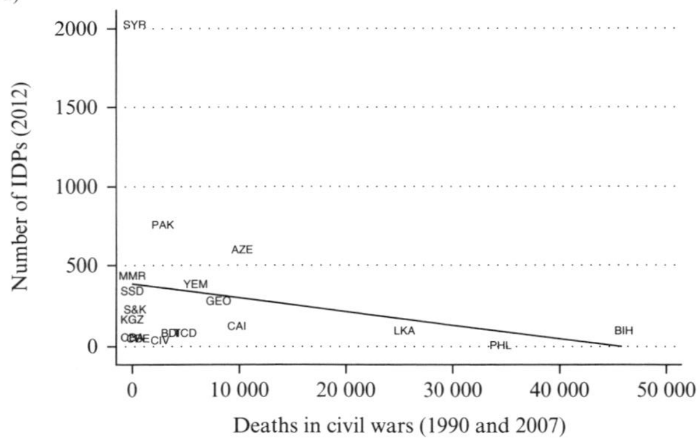

Source: Author's calculations using UNHCR and COW.

b)

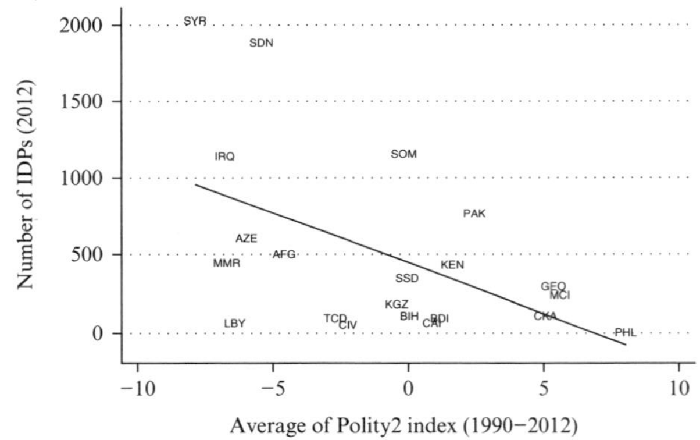

Source: Author's calculations using UNHCR and Polity IV Project.

c)

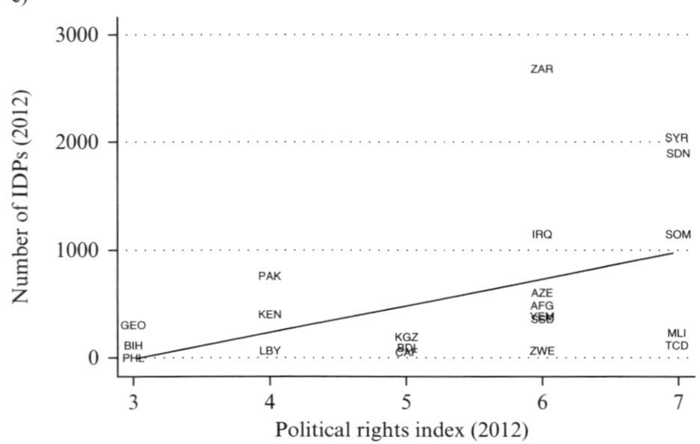

Source: Author's calculations using UNHCR and Freedom House.

d)

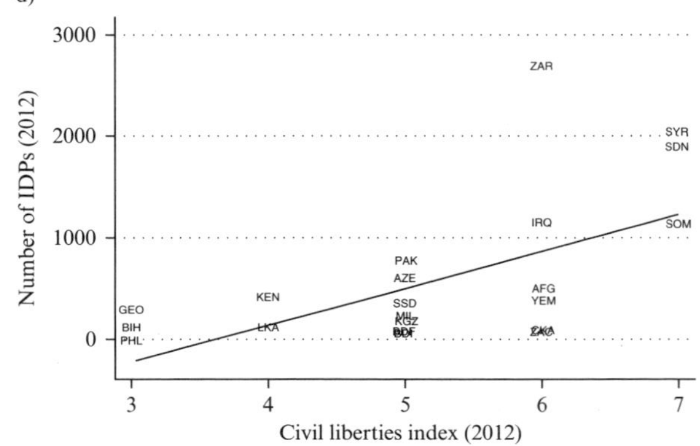

Source: Author's calculations using UNHCR and Freedom House.

Notes: The countries in Figure 13.2(a) with deaths in civil wars near zero and small number of IDPs are the following (listed in order, from greater to lower displacement): MMR, KEN, SSD, S&K, KGZ, LBY, ZWE and CAF. The countries in Figure 13.2(c) with value of political rights equal to 5 are the following (listed in order, from greater to lower displacement): KGC, LKA, BDI, CAF and CIV. The countries in Figure 13.2(d) with a value of civil liberties equal to 5 are the following (listed in order, from greater to lower displacement): PAK, AZE, SSD, MLI, KGZ, BDI, LBY, CAF and CIV.

Key:

AFG	Afghanistan	MLI	Mali
AZE	Azerbaijan	MMR	Myanmar
BDI	Burundi	PAK	Pakistan
BIH	Bosnia and Herzegovina	PHL	Philippines
CAF	Central African Republic	S&K	Serbia (and Kosovo: S/RES/1244 (1999))
CIV	Côte d'Ivoire	SDN	Sudan
COL	Colombia	SOM	Somalia
GEO	Georgia	SSD	South Sudan
IRQ	Iraq	SYR	Syrian Arab Republic
KEN	Kenya	TCD	Chad
KGZ	Kyrgyzstan	YEM	Yemen
LBY	Libya	ZAR	Democratic Republic of the Congo
LKA	Sri Lanka	ZWE	Zimbabwe

Figure 13.2 Correlation between IDP and civil war, political rights and civil liberties

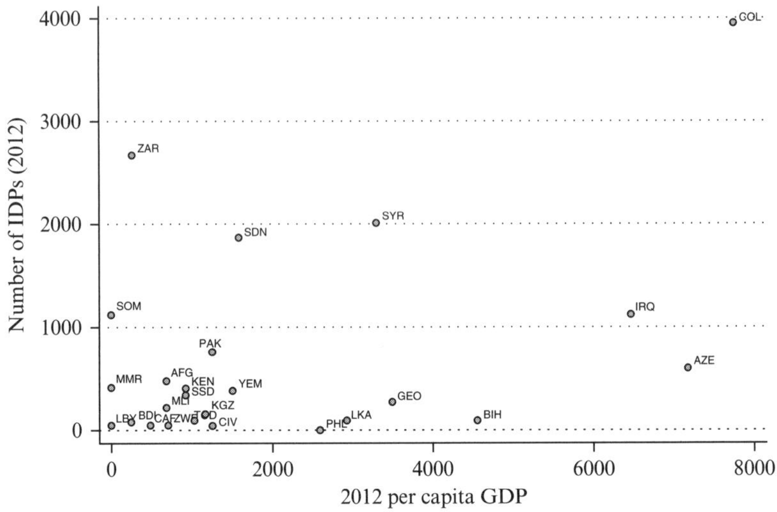

Source: author's calculation using UNHCR and World Bank

Figure 13.3 Correlation between IDP and GDP per capita

Higher numbers in the indexes for political rights and civil liberties indicate the worst situation of political rights and civil liberties. Both indexes have a positive correlation with the stock of IDP. Interestingly, countries that produce IDP, but are not facing a war either because it has ended or never took place, have low rankings for the political rights and civil liberties index. Besides conflict, the limitation of rights, restricted democracies or exclusion of particular groups from political rights may also cause violence among civilians, thereby generating forced migration within the countries.

Figure 13.3 provides a first exploration of the correlation between stock of IDP and GDP per capita. Besides Colombia, which is an outlier, the figure reveals a weak negative correlation between these measures. This negative correlation captures several dimensions, explored in the following sections. On the one hand, economic factors, though not the main determinant of forced migration, also play a role. Forced migration is lower in regions with stronger economic performance, and households with higher incomes are less likely to migrate. On the other hand, countries with higher GPD often have stronger institutions and rule of law, which reduces the probability of conflict and subsequent aggression against civilians.

2. EXPLORING THE CAUSES OF IDP VARIATION ACROSS COUNTRIES

Exploring the Link between Violence and Forced Displacement

Early studies on forced migration emerged on the political science, anthropological and sociology literature. Based on cross-country analysis, these studies' main purpose was to establish whether violence during conflict was the major driver of forced migration.

Violence against civilians is rarely a fortuitous by-product of conflict as it responds mostly to war strategies of armed groups participating in conflict (Kalyvas, 2006). Different types of violence emerge from the dynamics of conflict and the interaction of armed groups. The many dimensions of violence exert a different influence on the decision to migrate and the subsequent costs of forced displacement.

Apodaca (1998), using time series for countries facing conflict, estimates the correlation between human rights abuses and refugee flight for each country. Countries with a medium to high range of human rights abuses experience refugee flight, while those with a good record rarely produce refugees. The refugee exodus occurs mostly after the intensification of human rights abuses.

A more fine-grained definition of violence can be found in Schmeidl (1997). The paper defines different dimensions of political violence and internal conflict: human rights violations, civil conflict, ethnic conflicts and external involvement in conflicts. The pooled time-series estimations cover 109 countries for the period ranging from 1971 to 1990. Civil wars, genocides, ethnic conflict and civil wars with foreign intervention are positively correlated with increased refugee exodus. The strongest correlates are, however, genocides, civil wars, and civil wars with foreign interventions. Genocide is the massive attack of particular groups of the population based on ethnicity, religion or political affiliations, among others, which sometimes may involve the active or passive participation of states. By signaling an increasing risk for particular groups of the population, genocide forces the populations to seek safe areas in other countries (Davenport et al., 2003).

The previous studies focused on refugee migration and ignored internal displacement. Davenport et al. (2003) explore the association between violence and internal displacement. The authors provide a theoretical framework in which people living in conflict regions decide among the plausible location alternatives based on their beliefs about security conditions. Internally displaced persons seek safe pockets controlled by the armed group that offers them protection. Violence is grouped according to the armed actor: state violence, dissident violence, and state–dissident violence. The pooled cross-country estimation for the period between 1964 and 1989 finds that the three types of violence are positively associated with the stock of internally displaced persons.

Different dimensions of violence may also determine the decisions of the population to migrate within or across countries' borders. Moore and Shellman (2006) explore this question using data on refugee and IDP flows by countries and years for the period between 1976 and 1995. In countries with state-sponsored violence, refugee flows are higher in contrast to IDP flows: the population seeks protection outside the country to avoid government targeting. Conversely, people tend to move within their country if confronted with dissident and state violence. Dissidents and the state provide safety in some regions to protect their supporters, thereby reducing the need to flee the country.

Despite the strong focus on violence and political conditions, this research also stresses how other factors such as economic development, the country's institutions and social networks could influence forced migration outflows (Zolberg et al., 1989; Wood, 1994). The estimations show that violence, although important, is not the only cause of refugee flight (Apodaca, 1998).

Schmeidl (1997) finds that economic causes are not correlated with refugee flows. However, the interaction of economic and violence variables is significant, showing that the association between violence and refugee flows is lower in countries with higher levels of economic development. Thus poor economic conditions may act as an accelerator of migration in countries facing violence or conflict.

Social networks in destination locations may facilitate the migration process by reducing the costs and risks of relocation (Schmeidl, 1997; Davenport et al., 2003). The papers use the lagged refugees or IDP from the origin country or region as a proxy for social networks. Davenport et al. (2003) find IDP flows are positively associated with social networks.

The previous studies show forcefully that violence and conflict are correlated with forced migration, either across or within the countries' borders. However, the use of cross-country data imposes several restrictions on the analysis. First, these papers assume that armed groups and the population within countries are homogeneous agents (Kalyvas, 2006; Moore and Shellman, 2006). Nevertheless, armed groups are strategic actors that attack the population according to their war objectives and the constraints they face, and people make choices despite being amid violence and conflict. These papers are not able to explain the variation in migration inflows within countries or the heterogeneity of the individual decision to migrate. Second, the ability to control for other correlates of forced migration is limited by data availability. Third, these studies fail to establish causality between violence and forced migration. Several unobservable variables may cause variation across wars, violence and forced migration. By using cross-country data and not controlling for countries' fixed effects, the authors do not control for a wide array of factors that may determine both processes simultaneously, such as institutional development, dynamics of conflict, geographic and climatic factors and socio-economic conditions (Kalyvas, 2006).

3. VIOLENCE: AN ADDITIONAL DETERMINANT OF SUB-NATIONAL MIGRATION FLOWS

Conflict imposes violence, uncertainty and fear among the population. In spite of facing these extreme conditions, people still make choices and select their location based on the benefits and costs of staying in their region or migrating to other locations. The decision of a large number of people to stay in regions with protracted conflict and high victimization of civilians suggests that additional factors besides violence influence the choices of the population (Birkeland, 2000; Davenport, et al., 2003; Moore and Shellman, 2006; Engel and Ibáñez, 2007).

In order to understand migration flows within countries facing conflict, a strand of the economics literature uses traditional migration models to explain flows of migrants and includes violence as an additional determinant. A simplified version of the model defines migration flows M_{ij} from the origin location i to destination location j based on different pull and push factors in each location: violence in each location (V_i, V_j), traditional migration determinants (E_i, E_j) and unobservable variables (μ_i, μ_j). Migrations flows can be loosely defined by

$$M_{ij} = f(V_i, V_j, E_i, E_j, \mu_i, \mu_j)$$

Violence and Interregional Flows

The theoretical models assume utility-maximizing individuals and incorporate violence in different dimensions of the decision process. Morrison and May (1994) assume that migrants maximize utility instead of income. Violence affects the utility function through a good defined as safety. Gottschang (1987) develops a theoretical model in which disasters, including civil war, reduce the value of expected real income by destroying assets and being a life-threatening event. Similarly, Czaika and Kis-Katos (2009) argue that risk aversion determines the decision to migrate, implying that the risks of threats and direct violence alter the benefits and costs of migration.

Lozano-Gracia et al. (2010) use a gravity model to identify the determinants of interregional flows. The model assumes that violence in each region and among their neighbors affects the utility function of the individual.

The implication of these models is, however, similar: people are willing to trade off income to improve their security conditions. People move to regions with less intense conflict or lower risk of victimization even if their income drops. Thus improvements in security translate into positive population inflows, while the intensification of conflict prompts forced migration (Gottschang, 1987; Morrison and May, 1994; Lozano-Gracia et al., 2010).

Schultz (1971) provides the first empirical evidence on the effect of violence on interregional flows within a country. His paper explores the causes of internal migration in Colombia between 1951 and 1965. The results show a strong correlation between out-migration and politically motivated homicides. The impact is large: one additional death is associated with an out-migration of approximately 18 persons, mostly from the immediate rural area. Other studies for China, Guatemala, Indonesia, Colombia (during the first decade of the twenty-first century) and Spain confirm that out-migration within countries and violence are strongly associated (Gottschang, 1987; Morrison and May, 1994; Czaika and Kis-Katos, 2009; Lozano-Gracia, Piras et al., 2010; Balcells, 2012). A similar study using times series (Stanley, 1987) finds that political violence explains more than half of the variation of the migration from Salvador to the USA during the period between 1979 and 1984.

The choice of the destination location after migration is also related to conflict and security conditions. Migrants seek safer places than their home towns and arrive in regions with better security conditions. Violence in destination locations deters location in certain regions, reducing migration inflows to these regions in Indonesia, Colombia and Guatemala (Morrison and May, 1994; Czaika and Kis-Katos, 2009; Lozano-Gracia et al., 2010).

The effect of violence is not limited to the origin and destination locations. Surrounding locations, by signaling potential intensification of the conflict and spillovers to nearby areas, produce larger population outflows and deter the arrival of immigrants (Lozano-Gracia, Piras et al., 2010).

However, the effect of violence on migration fades with the passage of time. Based on historical data for China (1890–1942), Gottschang (1987) explores the link between internal migrations and the incidence of disasters, including war. The correlation between war in Manchuria and out-migration is strong immediately after conflict, yet the correlation weakens after some time. Thus violence does not explain the persistence of migration decades afterwards. Initial migrations due to conflict create diasporas that in the future may attract additional migration not related to violence or conflict.

The relation between violence and migration flows can be highly non-linear. The impact of violence on migration flows may vary with the intensity of violence in the origin destination. Morrison and May (1994) divide the sample of Guatemalan municipalities between those with low and high levels of violence. While violence has a strong effect on municipalities with high intensity, the effect is not statistically significant for those with low levels. Lozano-Gracia et al. (2010) capture the non-linear effects by interacting violence and the distance between the origin and destination municipalities in Colombia. The estimates suggest that people in municipalities with extremely high levels of violence move as far as possible from their home town. Because distance captures the migration costs, these results indicate that people are willing to incur higher costs to be distant from the violence they have endured. Presumably, these people are traumatized by the intense violence and victimization they suffered before moving out.

Examining variation in migration flows within countries helps to overcome some of the drawbacks of cross-country studies. Estimations at the sub-national level control for institutional and historical contexts particular to each country, reducing the bias caused by unobservable variables. However, these studies also fail to account for the heterogeneity of victimization and risk of violence across the population. Two reasons cause the risk of violence to vary at the individual level. First, armed groups attack particular groups of the population to achieve their war objectives, terrorize and control the population, alienate the population from their rival or separate rebel groups from their support base (Stanley, 1987; Azam and Hoeffler, 2002; Engel and Ibáñez, 2007; Czaika and Kis-Katos, 2009; Steele, 2009). Thereby, characteristics at the household or individual level determine the risk of being the victim of violence (Morrison and May, 1994; Engel and Ibáñez, 2007). Second, some individuals are better able to cope with the risk of violence (Morrison and May, 1994).

Even though these studies acknowledge that armed groups act strategically and the population decides based on a cost–benefit analysis, the empirical strategies are not able to disentangle the different channels causing forced displacement. The coefficient estimates capture both dimensions: the decisions of armed groups and the choices of the civil population. Furthermore, these studies are not able to explain the heterogeneity of individuals in the decision to stay or migrate. In addition, and similarly to the cross-country literature, this research fails to establish a causal relation between violence and forced migration. Nevertheless, the use of panel estimations permits to control for time-invariant unobservable variables, reducing significantly omitted-variable biases.

Traditional Migration Determinants

Traditional migration variables may also play a role in population movements, albeit weaker, during conflict. In addition to seeking refuge, people may decide to migrate to other locations in order to find better opportunities. Other people may decide to stay in violent regions to protect their income and assets. The answer to this question is empirical, and the impact of socioeconomic conditions on migration flows depends largely on the dynamics and intensity of conflict (Czaika and Kis-Katos, 2009). Sub-national studies are better able to control for proxies of traditional migration decisions in contrast to cross-country studies.

The evidence on the influence of traditional economic variables on migration is conclusive. Migration also responds to economic variables even when violence is intense (Schultz, 1971; Gottschang, 1987; Morrison and May, 1994; Czaika and Kis-Katos, 2009; Lozano-Gracia, Piras et al., 2010). Although violence explains a large percentage of the migration flows, economic determinants remain strong, yet in some cases the effect is the opposite from that for voluntary migration.

First, lack of economic opportunities is correlated with larger migration outflows after controlling for violence intensity. Villages in Aceh (Indonesia) with a stronger dependence on agricultural production generated larger out-migration and received smaller population inflows (Czaika and Kis-Katos, 2009). In Guatemala and Colombia, larger tax receipts in destination regions, indicative of more vibrant economic production, attracted higher inflows of migrants (Morrison and May, 1994; Lozano-Gracia et al., 2010).

Second, migration costs, reflected by distance between municipalities and stock of migrants in destination sites, reduce inflows of population. Distance between municipalities, which captures travel, psychological and information costs, has a negative correlation with migration flows (Morrison and May 1994; Lozano-Gracia et al. 2010). However, as indicated earlier, distance interacted with violence has a positive coefficient for Colombia, suggesting the willingness of people to substitute income for improvements in security (Lozano-Gracia, Piras et al., 2010). Migration stocks in destination locations reduce the costs of settlement through the support of family and friends, thereby increasing the inflows of migrants for the Colombian case (Lozano-Gracia et al., 2010).

Lastly, weak presence of institutions and lack of social services are correlated with larger out-migration. Lower supply of health services, lack of police forces in the municipality and the inability of local government to collect taxes is associated with higher population outflows (Czaika and Kis-Katos, 2009; Lozano-Gracia et al., 2010).

Violence may also reverse the influence of traditional migration variables. Lozano-Gracia et al. (2010) find that higher tax collection per capita and higher education levels at the origin favor migrations. The authors interpret this positive correlation as the ability of richer individuals to have a stronger financial leverage for funding migration costs and of better-educated ones to lower migration costs during the settlement process.

However, the previous interpretations largely ignore the dynamics of conflict and the strategies adopted by armed groups. Economic conditions and institutional presence may also influence the dynamics and intensity of conflict. Grievances driven by inequality, limited access to production assets (such as land), declining economic conditions and poverty may create favorable conditions for armed groups to emerge and operate (Stanley, 1987; Collier and Hoeffler, 2004; Miguel et al., 2004; Blattman and Miguel, 2010). Also, wealthier regions with weak state presence and unprotected property rights may favor predation and the presence of armed actors (Hirshleifer, 1989; Grossman, 1991; Skaperdas, 1992; Blattman and Miguel, 2010). Armed groups seeking to achieve territorial control in wealthier regions resort often to attacking civilians in order to achieve this objective, inducing larger population outflows. The positive effect of tax collection may be capturing these dynamics and not the ability of migrants to fund the relocation process.

Herein lies another weakness of this literature. The empirical strategy is not able to disentangle whether these economic and social conditions determine the decision to migrate, or if armed groups seek to establish control in areas with these economic and social characteristics (Steele, 2009). Czaika and Kis-Katos (2009) explore this issue by identifying the correlates of conflict occurrence in the Aceh villages. They find that the incidence of conflict is stronger in villages with a larger dependence on agriculture, weaker governance, and lack of police presence. This reflects armed actors in Aceh (Indonesia) attacking poorer regions and with a weaker state presence. However, the paper does not examine the rationale of armed groups to attack villages with these particular characteristics.

4. FORCED MIGRATION: A DELIBERATE STRATEGY OF ARMED GROUPS

Recent literature, mostly in political science, explores the strategies of armed groups during civil conflicts, and their attacks on civilians. Forced displacement is rarely a fortuitous by-product of civil conflict, but a deliberate war strategy responding to the dynamics of armed groups.

The literature on civil wars and forced displacement often confounds the causes of war with the patterns of violence against civilians during war (Kalyvas, 2006). Moreover, the interactions of armed groups and civilians are largely ignored. However, the evidence shows that armed groups attack civilians with particular characteristics, and civilians decide whether to leave or stay according to these characteristics and the strategies of armed groups (Steele, 2009).

The regional variation of forced displacement is not limited to economic considerations, as the previous literature argues. The dynamics of war play a large role. Thus an understanding of regional variation of forced displacement within a country needs to incorporate the decisions and behavior of armed groups. A spike of violence in a particular region may signal that two or more armed groups are fighting to control territory that is valuable for strategic reasons. Aggression against civilians during this process is in some cases integral to the strategy of armed groups to control the territory (Kalyvas, 2006).

Attacks against civilians seek to debilitate the base of the rival group. During irregular wars, the support of civilians is crucial for providing information, protection and food supplies, among others. Armed groups, which also include the state, need to shape popular support and prevent collaboration with their rival (Kalyvas, 2006). Expelling particular groups of the population is an effective strategy to gain territorial control, weaken the support base of the rival group, augment war booty and engage in illegal activities such as the cultivation of illicit crops (Azam and Hoeffler, 2002; Ibáñez and Vélez, 2008; Balcells and Steele, 2012). By debilitating the rival group's support base, armed groups also gain leverage during post-conflict periods (Azam and Hoeffler, 2002).

Violence Against Civilians: A Military Tactic of the Government

Azam and Hoefler (2002) develop a game-theory model to examine the role of violence against the population as a military tactic. The government and the rebel groups are the two groups making strategic decisions. The model assumes that the effectiveness of the rebel group, defined as the probability of overthrowing the government, increases with increased support from the population. Because the population provides hiding and support to rebel groups, a larger support base reduces the costs of overthrowing the government.

The government displaces population to reduce the probability that the rebel group will overthrow it. Larger displacements of the population by the government reduce the effectiveness of the group. Thus the government uses raiding of civilians as a substitute for fighting.

The fraction of the population displaced depends on the initial endowment of the government and the fighting technology of both groups. First, this fraction is lower when the rebel group is more productive. Second, a higher initial endowment for the government increases the fraction of the population displaced. Third, if the probability of overthrowing the government or the capacity of the rebel group to mobilize the population is higher, the fraction of population displaced is higher. Lastly, a higher efficiency of the government displacing the population increases the fraction of the population displaced.

Azam and Hoefler (2002) test the predictions of the model using cross-country data for Africa. The estimations confirm the results of previous models: refugee stocks are strongly correlated with the occurrence of civil wars. To proxy for the capacity of rebel groups to mobilize the population, the authors use the polity index. The rationale is that mobilizing the population is more difficult in democratic societies. The results show that refugee stocks are indeed lower in more democratic societies. Initial government endowments, measured as overseas development assistance, are associated with larger refugee stocks.

The model concentrates on one responsible group and one driving force: the military tactics of the government. However, rebel groups also expel population to strengthen their ability to win the war. In addition, other goals may also drive aggression against civilians: looting activities, either to finance the armed group or to enrich combatants, and/or to control a particular territory. Also, the model does not account for the decisions of the population, yet civilians interact with government forces and rebel groups and make strategic decisions, seeking to reduce the risk of victimization.

Aggression Against Civilians in a Context of Imperfect Information

Kalyvas (2006) explores the interactions of armed groups and civilians, and the strategic value of aggression against civilians. The model assumes that the main purpose of armed groups is to maximize territorial control. In a context of private and asymmetric information, civilians may provide information that is essential for the armed group to control the territory. Civilians need to decide whether to collaborate with the armed group controlling the territory or with their rival. Individuals prefer to collaborate with the group that provides better protection in the territory, thereby reducing the risk of victimization.

Armed actors resort to selective violence to gain collaboration with the people. However, the use of selective violence depends on the extent of territorial control of the armed actors. If the groups are hegemonic in a territory or do not have control, they do not or cannot resort to selective violence. Conversely, when two or more groups contest a territory, the value of information is high and the benefits from using selective violence are significant. In this case, actors use selective violence, causing an escalation of aggression against civilians.

Balcells and Steele (2012) apply this theoretical model to explain forced displacement. The paper explores why armed groups expel the population that supports their rival in a conventional war (the Spanish Civil War) and an irregular war (Colombia). Armed groups use collective targeting of groups of civilians to generate forced displacement.

Steele (2009) defines collective targeting as attacks against a civilian type, which may signal potential support to the rival. Living in a particular neighborhood, ethnicity or a political affiliation are some of the potential identifiers of the civilian type. Collective targeting is more likely in contested regions. For the incoming groups, collective targeting sends a strong message to civilians: supporting the incumbent group is costly. For the incumbent group, collective targeting serves to punish potential defections (Steele, 2009).

Based on sub-national data for Spain and Colombia, the authors estimate the association between the percentage of supporters of the rival group at the local level and forced displacement. Since both wars had a left–right cleavage, political affiliation identifies potential supporters of the rival groups. Political affiliation is measured as the percentage of support for leftist groups at the local level during the elections. Findings show a strong association between the proportions of leftist votes in a locality and forced migration.

When confronted with the strategic behavior of armed groups, people need to decide whether to stay in their home town or to leave. Steele (2009) explores for Colombia why people decide to stay in a region, notwithstanding the risk they face. The responses of households depend on the type of violence used by armed actors against civilians. If violence is targeted collectively, the likelihood of being targeted is higher for civilians with a profile akin to that of the rival's supporters. Households decide whether to leave or stay in the contested region based on their probability of being targeted collectively. If they leave, civilians select a location based on the probability of being targeted by an armed group.

The qualitative evidence for Urabá (Colombia) illustrates that people decide to stay when associated with the group that can offer them protection. Other households exchange information and defect from the rival group in order to stay in the region. In both cases, the households that decided to stay were signaling a strong willingness to collaborate and were obliged to comply with the dominant group.

After deciding to leave, households select their destination, seeking to minimize the probability of suffering aggression. When they cannot credibly realign or are unwilling to do so, some people move to territorial strongholds of the group they support. Others hide collectively among civilians who also face aggression. If the group reaches a sufficient threshold, the probability for an individual of being targeted decreases. Lastly, some decide to move individually to a place that brings anonymity.

Balcells (2012) uses sub-national data to examine the decisions of civilians during the Spanish Civil War of 1936–39. Leftist violence during the war was deliberately targeted with the purpose of expelling supporters of the rightist rival. The paper estimates regressions for the number of expelled and receiving migrants during the war period. The regressions control for demographic, geographic and political controls. Support for the left before the war (1936) captures the political identities of each locality. Leftist locations received more inflows of IDP, indicating that people select a locality akin to their ideology.

Understanding the behavior and decisions of armed actors is crucial in the analysis of forced displacement. However, this literature ignores the role of economic dimensions. First, armed groups choose strategically the territories to control based on war dynamics, political cleavages, and their economic value, among others (Hirshleifer, 1989; Grossman, 1991; Collier and Hoeffler, 2004; Blattman and Miguel, 2010; Justino, 2011). Second, people decide whether to leave or stay based not only on their risk of violence. The studies reviewed in the previous section suggest that economic considerations are also important. The risk of violence modifies the individuals' decision process, yet they still weigh benefits and costs of different alternatives. In overlooking economic variables, the econometric results are potentially biased.

5. THE MIGRATION DECISION OF HOUSEHOLDS IN A CONTEXT OF CONFLICT

During peaceful times, people deciding whether to migrate or stay in their home town compare the alternatives and choose the location that provides the larger net benefits. Initial models explained the decision to migrate based on wage gaps and later on the expected value of income, determined by the probability of finding a job, wages and relocation costs (Ranis and Fei, 1961; Sjaastad, 1962; Todaro, 1969; Harris and Todaro, 1970; Fields, 1975). Subsequent models explained the heterogeneity of the decision to migrate according to the individuals' characteristics: human capital, contacts at destination locations, access to information, length of the planning horizon, risk aversion, wealth, social networks and relocation costs (Becker, 1975; Maier, 1985; Todaro and Maruszko, 1987; Todaro, 1989; Dustmann, 1997; Rosenzweig and Stark, 1998; Davis and Winters, 2001; Winters et al., 2001). The new economics of migration acknowledged that the decision to migrate is not limited to the realm of the individual. Individuals are members of households that seek not only to maximize income, but also to minimize risk (Stark, 1991). Households use migration of their members to diversify risk and improve access to capital when facing market constraints (Stark and Bloom, 1985; Rosenzweig and Stark,1998).

Violence and conflict modify the migration decision. Nevertheless, people still have agency and decide by evaluating the net benefits of the alternatives, despite facing high levels of violence and personal risk (Birkeland, 2000; Engel and Ibáñez, 2007; Ibáñez and Vélez, 2008; Williams, 2008; Bohra-Mishra and Massey, 2011; Williams, 2013). Thus migration in conflict-ridden countries is not 'truly forced or truly voluntary' (Williams, 2013). Economic and social factors also play a role and partly explain why some people decide to stay in regions with intense violence (Engel and Ibáñez, 2007; Williams, 2008; Czaika and Kis-Katos, 2009; Williams, 2013). The line separating migrants and forcibly displaced persons in conflict periods becomes blurred: forced migration coexists with established patterns of voluntary migration (Birkeland, 2000).

The theoretical framework developed by the traditional migration literature is valid for explaining forced migration. However, violence modifies the migration incentives by reducing the benefits from staying in the region of origin and reversing the role of some of the traditional determinants of migration. In addition, deciding amidst violence and risk imposes high levels of stress, hampering the ability of individuals to make rational decisions and to evaluate accurately the net benefits of each alternative (Engel and Ibáñez, 2007; Ibáñez and Vélez, 2008).

Based on Engel and Ibáñez (2007), the decision to displace can be presented in the following general form. Household i decides to displace if the expected utility from migration to a destination site is larger than staying in their home town:

$$EU_{id} > EU_{in}$$

with $j = d$ denoting the destination site and $j = n$ the home town. The expected utility for household i in site j is defined by

$$EU_{ij} = f(S_{ij}, Y_{ij}, C_i, Z_i) + \varepsilon_{ij}$$

where S_{ij} are the security perceptions in each site, Y_{ij} the economic conditions, C_i represent migration and information costs, Z_i capture the household characteristics that influence preferences and ε_{ij} is a random term.

Incorporating violence and security conditions in the traditional migration model acknowledges that households are willing to trade income for improving security conditions (Engel and Ibáñez, 2007; Lozano-Gracia et al., 2010). Thus forced migration may take place despite negative income differentials, decreases in household wealth and worsening living conditions (Engel and Ibáñez, 2007).

Two features of the model are worth mentioning and will be discussed in the following sections. First, conflict dynamics determine the weight of violence and economic conditions on the displacement decision as well as the willingness to trade income for improvement in security conditions. This is largely an empirical question. Second, the risk of violence for each household is not random. As discussed in previous sections, armed actors target groups of civilians with particular characteristics, and seek to control regions with salient features that have strategic value (Azam and Hoeffler, 2002; Kalyvas, 2006; Steele, 2009; Balcells and Steele, 2012). Furthermore, some households are better able to protect themselves from violence. Wealth, education, political affiliations and other household characteristics may help households reduce the risks of attacks from armed actors (Morrison and May, 1994; Engel and Ibáñez, 2007; Ibáñez and Vélez, 2008; Balcells and Steele, 2012; Adhikari, 2013). This second feature explains why some households decide to stay in regions with intense violence: their likelihood of receiving threats is lower.

Collecting Data on Forced Displacement: The Challenges

Collecting data to examine forced displacement is difficult. Forced displacement occurs in countries raided by war and with intense aggression against civilians. The application of household surveys in the regions producing forced displacement implies a risk for the enumerators and the households surveyed. In addition, because armed actors are often present or control the territory, households are fearful of responding accurately to the questions related to conflict dynamics and their own victimization, which are crucial for examination of household behavior and decisions. Underreports of violence, conflict dynamics and the links between armed actors and households are indeed likely. The bias is presumably systematic and related to household characteristics. Consequently, few studies collect household surveys on forced displacement and all concentrate on three countries: Bosnia and Herzegovina, Colombia and Nepal.

The first group of papers purposively designs household surveys to explain forced displacement dynamics (Engel and Ibáñez, 2007; Ibáñez and Vélez, 2008). The samples include two groups of households: internally displaced persons and people from the same regions that decided to stay. Besides the traditional variables, the survey instruments collect detailed information on conflict dynamics: aggression endured by the household, violence in nearby regions, presence of armed actors and perceptions of risk. The rich information on conflict dynamics comes with a cost: smaller samples collected in particular regions of the country. The results of the case study for Colombia are thus not generalizable and representative of forced migration in the country.

The second group uses household surveys with larger samples, which are collected for other purposes than for studying forced migration (Williams, 2008; Kondylis, 2010; Bohra-Mishra and Massey, 2011; Adhikari, 2013; Williams, 2013). The samples are larger and representative of the Chitwan Province in the country of Nepal, and Bosnia and Herzegovina. However, the surveys do not differentiate between voluntary and forced migration, and do not collect information on conflict dynamics and victimization. In order to overcome the latter, the data are merged with information on incidence of violence at the district level. Conflict dynamics are not accounted for, which may induce bias in the coefficient estimates. For example, victimization of particular households and people is not recorded in these surveys.

Violence and Conflict Dynamics

Violence and the dynamics of conflict cause migration through several channels. First, deliberate attacks against civilians, such as selective homicides, direct threats and forced recruitment, among others, prompt their victims to leave for safer places. Second, the perceived risk of violence and victimization may induce some people to migrate preventively, in spite of not being a direct victim of aggression. Third, besides the risk of violence, conflict has a direct impact on economic and social conditions, deteriorating the livelihoods of households. These worsening conditions are also related to the decision to migrate, after controlling for physical threats (Williams, 2008; Adhikari, 2013; Williams, 2013).

Violence during conflicts is expressed in several ways, and papers use diverse strategies to measure it. Engel and Ibáñez (2007) and Ibáñez and Vélez (2008) elicit directly the violent attacks each household suffered and those suffered by family members, friends, neighbors or people of other neighborhoods. Violent aggression includes selective homicides, threats, forced recruitment, kidnapping and abduction, among others. Adhikari (2013) uses two measures. The first captures actual violence experienced by each individual: physical assault, abduction, physical and mental torture, and sexual violence, among others. The second seeks to capture perceived threats stemming from conflict by asking each individual about their perception of the gravity of threats. Williams (2008, 2013) merges household surveys with incidence of gun battles at the district level. Using a similar strategy, Bohra-Mishra and Massey (2011) rely on district-level data on the incidence of bomb blasts, landmine explosions, and major clashes between government forces and rebel forces. Kondylis (2010) merges the household data with information at the municipal level of war casualties.

All the studies agree: violence is the main driver of forced displacement. After controlling for economic and social conditions and households characteristics, results show that violence is the major driver behind forced displacement in Bosnia and Herzegovina, Colombia and Nepal (Engel and Ibáñez, 2007; Ibáñez and Vélez, 2008; Williams, 2008; Kondylis, 2010; Bohra-Mishra and Massey, 2011; Adhikari, 2013; Williams, 2013). Not only direct victimization is strongly related to the migration decision; perceived threats and violence in neighboring communities are also important correlates (Engel and Ibáñez, 2007; Ibáñez and Vélez, 2008; Bohra-Mishra and Massey, 2011; Adhikari, 2013). Besides migrating after being victims of a direct attack, people migrate preventively to reduce the likelihood of aggression.

The impact of violence is non-linear, however. Low levels of violence are not associated with migration, while after a certain threshold violence triggers forced migration (Morrison and May, 1994; Bohra-Mishra and Massey, 2011). Alvarado and Massey (2010) argue that low levels of violence may prevent migration and limit mobility by inducing people to withdraw to their homes, thereby reducing the risk of victimization. Bohra-Mishra and Massey (2011), in a study for the Chitwan Province in Nepal using a panel of household surveys, find that low intensity of violence reduces out-migration, yet after reaching a certain threshold of violence it increases out-migration. They also explore whether violence has a differentiated effect on the decision to move locally, internally or internationally. Individuals facing higher levels of violence tend to move to more distant destinations such that more violence is correlated with international migration and, as violence decreases, migration is closer to the home town.

Violence and the ability of households to reduce the risk of violence are not random. In Nepal, Maoist and government forces deliberately targeted civilians and forced them to migrate for political purposes (Williams, 2008). Some identifiers that were presumably used to deliberately target civilians were political affiliation, land ownership, insertion in the community and leadership, among others (Engel and Ibáñez, 2007; Ibáñez and Vélez, 2008; Adhikari, 2013). Individuals can also adopt coping strategies to avoid displacement. In Nepal, people resorted to social networks for protection. Community organizations and social networks can provide a sense of security and valuable information to prevent victimization and subsequent forced migration (Adhikari, 2013). Households that decide to stay in conflict regions may thus face a lower risk of violence due to the strategies they adopt or their household characteristics (Engel and Ibáñez, 2007).

In spite of recognizing the purposive and deliberate targeting of armed forces, few studies use empirical strategies to account for this. Engel and Ibáñez (2007) and Ibáñez and Vélez (2008) estimate a reduced form for the displacement decision in which violence is captured by indirect violence. In order to recover the structural parameters, they estimate the household's likelihood of receiving direct threats. The results show that armed groups target landowners and people with stronger community ties. By displacing landowners, armed actors perceive economic gains from the expropriation of land and other assets. Attack on households with strong social ties, measured as years of residence in the community, is an effective strategy to terrorize the population and reduce their willingness to collaborate with rival groups. Younger household heads are also more likely to receive death threats from armed actors.

Safety perceptions of civilians are also related to the dynamic of armed actors. The mere presence of rebel forces or government forces may determine the perceived threat of households (Engel and Ibáñez, 2007; Ibáñez and Vélez, 2008). Results for Colombia show that the likelihood of receiving direct threats increases with the presence of rebel forces and paramilitary groups, whereas the presence of government forces has a contradictory role. Police presence, a government force that is embedded in the community, reduces the likelihood of direct threats. On the other hand, the presence of military forces increases the risk of direct threats. Intensification of threats due to military presence may be the result of attacks by government forces or simply the risk of being caught in the cross-fire (Engel and Ibáñez, 2007; Ibáñez and Vélez, 2008).

Identifying the impact of violence on the decision to migrate is challenging. First, empirical strategies should focus on separating the strategies of armed groups from the ability of certain individuals to reduce the risk of threats. Second, empirical strategies should disentangle deliberate targeting and the influence of household characteristics on the decision to move. For example, wealthy households might face a higher likelihood of targeting or might move more easily as they are less resource constrained. Current studies do not separate properly the causes of aggression against civilians, the ability of individuals to reduce threats and the economic determinants.

Income, Wealth and Assets

Economic determinants play an important role in the displacement decision, albeit violence is the predominant cause. In confronting the risk of losing assets and uncertain labor conditions in destination sites, households weigh the potential costs associated with forced migration. Households with higher opportunity costs from migration may be willing to accept higher levels of risk to protect their income and wealth (Engel and Ibáñez, 2007; Ibáñez and Vélez, 2008; Adhikari, 2013). Also, declining economic conditions as a consequence of conflict and violence may cause forced migration, in spite of low levels of personal risk[10] (Adhikari, 2013; Williams, 2013).

Economic status might also determine the risk of deliberate targeting from armed actors. Armed actors seeking to fund war activities or augmenting their booty may target richer households to seize assets (Azam and Hoeffler, 2002; Collier and Hoeffler, 2004). The final impact of wealth on forced displacement is unknown *a priori*. Wealth may reduce the likelihood of displacement due to higher opportunity costs. Nonetheless, wealthier households may face higher risks of attacks from armed actors or be more able to cover the costs of the migration process, raising the likelihood of displacement (Engel and Ibáñez, 2007).

The impact of assets depends on whether they can be easily moved or sold. Location-specific assets, such as land, deter voluntary migration. However, conflict imposes additional dynamics. First, a deficient rule of law in conflict regions increases the risk of losing land once abandoned. Empirical evidence shows that returned refugees face difficulties recovering land, despite having legal land title (Engel and Ibáñez, 2007; Williams, 2008). Second, although land can be sold and provide fresh capital to start anew after migration, conflict weakens markets, lowering market demand and land prices. Both raise further the opportunity costs from migrating (Engel and Ibáñez, 2007; Williams, 2008). Lastly, armed actors may deliberately target landowners to violently seize land. Weak or unprotected property rights, a feature prevalent in many conflicts, facilitates land seizure (Engel and Ibáñez, 2007; Ibáñez and Vélez, 2008).

The relation between landownership and the decision to displace is determined by conflict dynamics. In the Chitwan Province in Nepal, Bohra-Mishra and Massey (2011) and Williams (2008) find that landownership deters out-migration. However, landownership is positively correlated with international migration, presumably indicating that wealthier households are able to fund more distant migrations (Bohra-Mishra and Massey, 2011). Results for Nepal estimated in Adhikari (2013), with data representative of Nepal, show the opposite effect: landowners have a larger probability of being forcibly displaced. Engel and Ibáñez (2007) separate the impact of landownership on the risk of receiving threats and the likelihood of displacement. They find that landownership raises the probability of receiving threats, yet the standardized size of the land plot reduces the probability of displacement. This signals that wealthier landowners indeed take into account the opportunity cost of abandoning land.

Assets that are easily sold, on the other hand, may prompt displacement by funding the migration process and provide temporary capital to aid the settlement process. Livestock and households goods are associated with a higher likelihood of forced displacement for Nepal and Colombia (Engel and Ibáñez, 2007; Williams, 2008).

The forgone income from wage employment and other income-generating opportunities might also deter displacement. Finding wage employments in destination localities might be difficult. Conflict weakens labor markets, increasing unemployment overall (Williams, 2008). For Colombia, as forcibly displaced persons are originally from rural areas and move to urban areas, their labor experience is not valued in urban jobs and job insertion is slow (Ibáñez and Moya, 2010b). Estimations for Nepal show that people with wage employment are less likely to displace (Williams, 2008; Adhikari, 2013). These results persist after interacting wage employment with violence levels (Williams, 2008, 2013).

Conversely, people who are better able to compete in labor markets might be more inclined to displace. If they can find a new job in the destination location, the opportunity cost of migrating is lower. Kondylis (2010) finds that this is indeed the case for Bosnia and Herzegovina: forcibly displaced persons and refugees were 'more able in labor market terms'.

By limiting income-generating opportunities, destruction of economic opportunities and loss of productive assets in the home town may trigger displacement. Adhikari (2013) measures destruction of income-generating opportunities with dummy variables for industry destroyed, crop/animal loss, land loss and home destroyed. The results for Nepal indicate that forced displacement and these variables have a positive and significant correlation.

All these studies indicate that people self-select for migration. The redistribution of the population as a consequence of conflict is not random. The nature of self-selection is determined by the conflict dynamics. In Nepal, landowners or people with wage employment were less likely to migrate, while in Colombia landowners with strong social networks were more likely to displace.

Provision of State Services: Security and Social Services

Evidence on the influence of state presence and the provision of public goods is scarce. However, state presence, strong institutions and the provision of public goods may deter displacement by raising safety perceptions and providing services such as access to education and health. It is worth noting that in some countries the government is directly responsible for aggression against civilians and forced migration. Also, the emergence of conflict may reflect lack of state presence, weak institutions and unprotected property rights.

Engel and Ibáñez (2007) and Ibáñez and Vélez (2008) find that access to basic services and presence of government forces reduce the likelihood of displacement. Police presence reduces forced displacement through two channels: lower probability of receiving threats and presumably an increased perception of safety. Military presence has a contradictory role by raising the probability of receiving threats and reducing the likelihood of displacement. Nevertheless, the joint contribution of access to social services and presence of government forces to reduce the probability of displacement is not sufficient to compensate for the effect of violence.

Social Networks and Community Organizations

Social networks and community organizations play several roles that may induce or prevent forced displacement. On the one hand, community organizations and social networks may prevent forced migration. Community organizations can provide support to mitigate the economic and social consequences of conflict and to avoid confiscation and destruction of assets (Williams, 2013). On the other hand, these organizations might be instrumental in inducing displacement. Social ties in the home town may assist forcibly displaced persons to look after their properties while they are away (Engel and Ibáñez, 2007), while those in destination locations reduce migration costs by providing information and support (Bohra-Mishra and Massey, 2011). As discussed earlier, leaders and people with strong social networks are more likely to be targeted by armed actors (Engel and Ibáñez, 2007; Ibáñez and Vélez, 2008).

All these potential channels are not exclusive and may act simultaneously. The weight and impact of each on the likelihood of victimization and displacement is context-dependent. The dynamics of conflict, the density of organizations and the institutional context determine the influence of each channel on the migration decision.

Williams (2013) explores how community organizations moderate the impact of conflict on the decision to migrate. She uses panel data from

Nepal for the period ranging from 1997, three years before the outbreak of the conflict, to 2006. The data record the migration history for people in the Chitwan Province during that period and collect individual and community characteristics. Community organizations are measured at the neighborhood level, with a detailed history of key services and organizations such as markets, health centers, farmers' cooperative and mills. The data do not identify whether each respondent had effective access to those services and organizations. The findings show that all community organizations moderate the relationship between violence and migration. However, only some directly reduced the probability of migration.

Employing the same data, Bohra-Mishra and Massey (2011) correlate ties at the destination sites and the decision to migrate locally, internally or internationally. The probability of migration to the three sites is positively correlated with social ties, illustrating that lower migration costs contribute to a larger probability of forced displacement.

Longer years of residence and belonging to community organizations in the home town have a positive impact on the decision to displace in Colombia (Engel and Ibáñez, 2007). The authors do not specify whether this positive impact is driven by higher victimization or by the support that extensive social networks may provide after displacement. Nevertheless, estimations of the probability of receiving threats reveal that the likelihood rises with an additional year of residence. On the other hand, in Nepal, belonging to community organizations reduces the probability of seizure of private property (Adhikari, 2013).

The Interaction of Intensity of Violence and Traditional Migration Determinants

Arguably, economic factors play a lesser role when conflict and the risk of suffering aggression are intense. If violence levels are low or the risk of receiving threats is low, the migration decision is less hasty and may put a higher weight on the traditional migration determinants. Intense violence or suffering direct aggression limits the room for navigating amidst conflict and may trigger immediate migration. Economic considerations in this case might have a much lower influence on the decision to migrate.

Engel and Ibáñez (2007) explore this issue by interacting economic determinants with intensity of violence. Traditional economic determinants indeed play a lesser role for households suffering intense violence. The coefficients for landownership and access to social services, though still significant, are much lower when interacted with intense violence.

Ibáñez and Vélez (2008) differentiate between reactive and preventive displacement. Reactive displacement occurs when people confronted with intense violence or after suffering a direct attack migrate because it is the only option to save their life. Preventive displacement occurs when people decide to leave the region to reduce the risk of suffering an attack, in spite of low levels of violence (Engel and Ibáñez, 2007). In order to identify households that migrated preventively, the survey elicits whether respondents identify fear despite not being threatened as the main reason for fleeing their home town.

The results suggest that traditional migration determinants and violence have a heterogeneous impact on preventive and reactive displacement. Indirect violence exerts a strong influence in both cases, yet the coefficient is higher for reactive displacement. The influence of conflict dynamics indicates that the more risk-averse may self-select into preventive displacement: the coefficient estimates for the presence of rebel and paramilitary groups is much stronger for preventive than for reactive displacement. Traditional migration determinants play a lesser role for reactive displacement. In fact, land size is no longer significant, while land size for preventive displacement is positive, indicating that larger landowners are less likely to displace, presumably because they face higher opportunity costs.

Causality and External Validity

The contribution of the studies reviewed above lies in being the first quantitative research that examines the household and individual determinants of forced displacement. Notwithstanding, the studies have two common weaknesses. First, the studies establish correlations between economic, social and conflict variables, on the one hand, and the likelihood of displacement, on the other. None of the studies reviewed designs a credible empirical strategy to identify causal relations. Thus the econometric estimations do not discover whether the correlations are the result of conflict dynamics or whether people indeed respond to economic and social factors as well. That landowners are more likely to displace may reflect a higher likelihood of being targeted by armed actors, and not more financial resources to fund the migration process, for example.

Second, the difficulty of collecting data on conflict-ridden countries limits the evidence to three countries: Bosnia and Herzegovina, Colombia and Nepal. As discussed earlier, the results appear to be context-dependent and determined to a large extent by the particular dynamics of each country. The external validity of the studies is thus low and is not generalizable across other countries. Some strong and common conclusions emerge from all the studies that are potentially generalizable: violence is the main driver of forced displacement; socioeconomic conditions play a role; and, even amidst violence, fear and conflict, people make decisions.

6. ONCE THE CONFLICT ENDS: RETURN OF FORCIBLY DISPLACED PERSONS

The end of the conflict becomes a critical juncture for forcibly displaced persons. As aggression against civilians eases, returning to their home town becomes a feasible alternative. Thus IDP may decide whether to stay in the destination location, migrate to another region, or return to their home town. Return may offer some advantages. Forcibly displaced persons may recover lost assets and social networks, compete in familiar markets and, if dedicated to rural production, farm in a familiar setting (Kondylis, 2008).

However, return is complex and requires large investments. Land and asset restitution is not always an option. Lack of formal property rights, land seizure despite having formal title, and new land disputes hampered land restitution in many countries (Williams, 2004; Bascom, 2005; Kondylis, 2008; Williams, 2008). The fear of returning and post-traumatic stress imply that many households are not willing to return in spite of the potential economic advantages. This is particularly strong for households that confronted traumatic events and intense violence before displacement (Stefansson, 2004). Resuming income generation is a long process. Conflict in the home town may have deteriorated markets, social networks and local institutions (Arias et al., 2014). In addition, the household needs to start anew and invest to recuperate its production ability. Indeed, evidence for Rwanda suggests that agricultural know-how may have deteriorated as a result of forced displacement (Kondylis, 2008). Thus returnees require large public investments and state support. Lastly, the violence that prompted displacement in the first place may persist despite the end of the conflict, as shown in Section 1.

In spite of being similar to the decision to displace, the decision to return or resettle does not have impending violence as a dominant factor. Households may examine carefully the different alternatives and select the one with the highest net benefits. The decision to return may resemble more closely the decision to migrate, in which economic factors play a dominant role. However, households need to assess the security conditions in their home town and identify whether the original causes of migration have disappeared or are still latent (Arias et al., 2014). In addition, forced displacement and the traumatic events that unfolded before displacement trigger in some people post-traumatic stress (Moya, 2013; Carter and Moya, 2014), presumably reducing the willingness of households to return.

Research on the determinants of return of forcibly displaced population is practically non-existent in the economic literature. Kondylis (2008) evaluates the impact of a resettlement and land redistribution program for returnees in Rwanda. Using a representative household survey for Rwanda, Kondylis identifies returnees after the end of the Rwandan Civil War. Although the author concentrates on the impact of land redistribution programs, she estimates the likelihood of being a returnee. Households with younger heads, in partnership, with fewer children, and with more members born while being refugees are more likely to be returnees.

Arias et al. (2014) explore the correlates of the desire to return of IDP in Colombia. The results of the paper indicate that labor experience abilities, social connections and asset ownership, crucial to reap the benefits from returning, are correlated with a larger desire to return. Agricultural workers, households with dense social networks and families with land access were more willing to return. Household vulnerability and having confronted more distressing events before displacement is correlated with a lower willingness to return. Female-headed households or those with large dependency ratios prefer to stay in the destination location. Families that migrated after being the victim of direct aggression expressed a lower desire to return. It is worth noting that the outcome variable for this paper is the desire to return, and not actual return. Exploring how all these variables influence actual return is important.

7. FUTURE RESEARCH

The economic literature on forced displacement is nascent and provides results that hint of potential future research to pursue. Forced displacement offers an interesting opportunity for explaining the dynamics of violence within conflicts, the rationale for the aggression of armed actors against the civilian population, how armed actors and the civil population interact, and the adaptation strategies people use to prevent aggression and to mitigate the impacts of violence and conflict. The following paragraphs discuss potential future research on two dimensions of forced displacement: (1) the strategic behavior of armed groups and how this interacts with economic and social factors; and (2) the decisions of people and households living in regions with conflict.

Research at the sub-national level permits exploring the strategic behavior of armed groups, and migration flows during conflict. Current research on political science suggests that 'violence' and 'conflict' are not interchangeable. Violence and aggression against civilians are strategies used to achieve war objectives. Understanding in more detail why violence arises in some conflicts but is less frequent or non-existent in others would provide important insights into the decisions and choices of armed actors. The decisions of armed actors to target selectively or collectively and the tactics employed by them to generate forced displacement are also worth exploring. Even though Kalyvas, Steele and Balcells (2006, 2009, 2012 respectively) have contributed important evidence in this respect, additional research on other countries may permit proof of the external validity of their results and developing a richer theory of the behavior of armed groups.

Evidence on the strategies communities use to protect themselves from the aggression of armed groups, adapt to their presence and prevent forced displacement is scarce and restricted to qualitative analysis. However, communities and people are not passive victims, but active agents. In interacting with armed actors, communities also influence the dynamics of conflict, shape a future post-conflict period and generate cleavages that may plant the seeds for future conflicts. Further research on community decisions and interactions with armed actors is essential to explain the consequences of conflict, how the conflict modified the distribution of power and economic opportunities within communities, and design sustainable post-conflict policies.

What happens after conflict ends is important, yet largely underresearched. Evidence for some countries indicates that violence and forced displacement persist after the conflict ceases. Incomplete peace processes in which the structural causes are unresolved and new cleavages are created may explain protracted violence and forced displacement. Evidence on the dynamics of violence in this context, the role of the state to prevent aggression and forced displacement, and policies aimed to reduce violence could identify elements that should be incorporated in negotiating peace processes and designing post-conflict policies.

Dialogue between political science and economics would be fruitful. The political science literature contributes to understanding the decisions of armed groups and the strategies they adopt. The economic literature explores in depth the role of economic factors in the decisions of people and households, and how violence may modify their decisions. If one of these dimensions is ignored, the evidence is incomplete and the econometric estimations suffer from potential bias, which might be indeed large. The design of empirical strategies to identify causal effects and to separate all the potential mechanisms causing forced displacement requires incorporating the economic and political dimensions of the problem. The empirical strategies need to separate the impact of economic and social conditions on the decision to migrate from the decision of armed groups to establish control over a territory.

Several dimensions of the decisions of people and households in conflict-ridden regions are worth researching. First, identifying the causal effect of violence on the decision to migrate is an unresolved and challenging issue. Empirical strategies should focus on disentangling the impact of household characteristics on deliberate targeting of armed actors, the ability of individuals to reduce the risk of threats, and the decision to move.

Second, little is known about different migration strategies adopted by households to minimize the risks of victimization and mitigate the costs of forced migration. The research reviewed assumes that households are unitary decision makers. Nonetheless, households may choose to send some members to other destinations in order to minimize their risk of victimization. For example, younger members who might be forcibly conscripted or highly visible members of the households are more likely to receive threats and their migration may ease the pressure on the household. Other households may decide to leave some members in the home town to continue farming the land, while the bulk of household members migrate. Some others may move to an urban area nearby to periodically farm their land plot.

Third, the risk of migration may modify the economic decisions of households. Households may prefer to invest in movable assets, but with lower returns, or select crops that provide rapid yields but are less profitable (Engel and Ibáñez, 2007). Fertility decisions, school enrollment, and intra-household allocation, among others, may also be pervaded by the risk of migration. These decisions, despite providing households with flexibility if forced to leave the region, may push them to lower income trajectories and trap them in poverty.

Fourth, evidence on the faith of people who decided to stay is scarce. Arguably, these households stayed because their risk of victimization was lower or they had higher opportunity costs from migration. The strategies adopted to navigate amidst conflict, to continue their daily life and to reduce the threat of violence may have profound economic implications.

Lastly, the return of forcibly displaced persons is an alternative once conflict ceases, yet evidence on the decision to return is limited. More research on who decides to return and which policies are needed to ensure welfare-enhancing return would contribute to designing better post-conflict periods. One important policy to explore is asset restitution, a central issue for the return of forcibly displaced persons. Some households may decide to return to recover their assets. However, alternative policies could provide more flexibility by compensating victims and allowing them to decide where to settle (Jaramillo et al., 2012). Another interesting question is the role of social networks, which provide support and protection for returnees. Conflict and violence may severely damage social networks, however. Exploring the experiences of returnees, the obstacles they face after return, and successful resettlement programs would provide evidence on the benefits and costs of returning.

NOTES

1. Mariana Laverde provided excellent research assistance.
2. http://www.internal-displacement.org/, retrieved 20 December 2013.
3. For a review on the consequences of forced displacement, see Ruiz and Vargas-Silva (2013).
4. The chapter covers only forced displacement caused by conflict.
5. http://www.un.org/en/globalissues/briefingpapers/refugees/overviewofforceddisplacement.html, retrieved 20 December 2013.
6. http://www.brookings.edu/~/media/Projects/idp/GPEnglish.*pdf*, retrieved 20 December 2013.
7. http://www.brookings.edu/~/media/Projects/idp/GPEnglish.pdf, retrieved 20 December 2013.
8. Freedom House conducts an annual evaluation for political rights and civil liberties in 195 countries. Data are collected in each country using a survey to measure two indexes of political rights and civil liberties. The index of political rights measures three sub-categories: electoral process, political pluralism and participation, and functioning of government. The index of civil liberties measures four sub-categories: freedom of expression and belief, associational and organizational rights, rule of law, and personal autonomy and individual rights. http://www.freedomhouse.org/report/freedom-world-2013/methodology#.UuhBs037ypq, retrieved 5 December 2013.
9. The POLITY2 index is part of the POLITY IV Project. This indicator captures the level of democracy of all independent countries in the world. The indicator ranges from +10 to −10, where a score of +10 is assigned to a complete democracy and a score of −10 to a complete autocracy.
10. Williams (2013) argues that anecdotal evidence for Nepal illustrated that disruption to farming and trade caused food insecurity, which was the trigger for forced migration.

REFERENCES

Adhikari, P. (2013). 'Conflict-induced displacement: understanding the causes of flight', *American Journal of Political Science*, **57**(1): 82–9.

Alix-Garcia, J. and D. Saah (2009). 'The effect of refugee inflows on host communities: evidence from Tanzania', *The World Bank Economic Review*, **24**(1): 148–70.

Alvarado, S.E. and D.S. Massey (2010). 'In search of peace: structural adjustment, violence and international migration', *The Annals of the American Academy of Political and Social Science*, **630**: 137–61.

Apodaca, C. (1998). 'Human rights abuses: precursors to refugee flight', *Journal of Refugee Studies*, **11**(1): 80–90.

Arias, M.A., A.M. Ibáñez et al. (2014). 'The desire to return during civil war: evidence for internally displaced populations in Colombia', *Peace Economics, Peace Science and Public Policy*, **20**(1): 209–33.

Azam, J.P. and A. Hoeffler (2002). 'Violence against civilians in civil wars: looting or terror?', *Journal of Peace Research*, **39**(4): 461–85.

Baez, J. (2011). 'Civil wars beyond their borders: the human capital and health consequences of hosting refugees', *Journal of Development Economics*, **96**(2): 391–408.

Balcells, L. (2012). 'Violence and displacement in civil war. Evidence from the Spanish War (1936–1939)', HiCN Working Papers **159**.
Balcells, L. and A. Steele (2012). 'Warfare, political identities, and displacement in Spain and Colombia', HiCN Working Papers **124**.
Bascom, J. (2005). 'The long, "last step"? Reintegration of repatriates in Eritrea', *Journal of Refugee Studies*, **18**(2): 165–80.
Becker, G.S. (1975). *Human Capital*. New York: Columbia University Press.
Birkeland, N.M. (2000). 'Forced migration and *deslocados* in the Huambo Province, Angola', *Norsk Geografisk Tiddsskrift*, **54**: 110–15.
Blattman, C. and E. Miguel (2010). 'Civil war', *Journal of Economic Literature*, **48**(1): 3–57.
Bohra-Mishra, P. and D.S. Massey (2011). 'Individual decisions to migrate during civil conflict', *Demography*, **48**(2): 401–24.
Bozzoli, C., T. Bruck et al. (2013). 'Self-employment and conflict in Colombia', *Journal of Peace Research*, **57**: 117–42.
Calderón, V. and A.M. Ibáñez (2009). 'Labor market effects of migration-related supply shocks: evidence from internal refugees in Colombia', HiCN Working Papers 01/2009.
Carter, M. and A. Moya (2014). 'Shocks and helplessness: the formation of expectations among victims of violence in Colombia', Mimeo. http://andresmoya.weebly.com/research.html.
Collier, P. and A. Hoeffler (2004). 'Greed and grievance in civil war', *Oxford Economic Papers*, **56**(4): 563–95.
Czaika, M. and K. Kis-Katos (2009). 'Civil conflict and displacement: village-level determinants of forced migration in Aceh', *Journal of Peace Research*, **46**(3): 399–418.
Davenport, C.A., W.H. Moore et al. (2003). 'Sometimes you just have to leave: domestic threat and forced migration, 1964–1989', *International Interactions*, **29**: 27–55.
Davis, B. and P. Winters (2001). 'Gender, networks, and Mexico–U.S. migration', *Journal of Development Studies*, **38**(2): 1–26.
Dustmann, C. (1997). 'Return migration, uncertainty and precautionary savings', *Journal of Development Economics*, **52**: 295–316.
Engel, S. and A.M. Ibáñez (2007). 'Displacement due to violence in Colombia: a household level analysis', *Economic Development and Cultural Change*, **55**(2): 335–65.
Fields, G.S. (1975). 'Rural–urban migration, urban employment and underemployment, and job search activity in LDCs', *Journal of Development Economics*, **2**(2): 165–88.
Gottschang, T.R. (1987). 'Economic change, natural disasters, and migration: the historical case of Manchuria', *Economic Development and Cultural Change*, **35**(3): 461–90.
Grossman, H.I. (1991). 'A general equilibrium model of insurrections', *American Economic Review*, **81**(4): 912–21.
Harris, J.R. and M.P. Todaro (1970). 'Migration, unemployment and development: a two-sector analysis', *The American Economic Review*, **60**(1): 126–42.
Hirshleifer, J. (1989). 'Conflict and rent-seeking functions: ratio versus difference models of relative success', *Public Choice*, **63**: 101–12.
Ibáñez, A.M. and A. Moya (2010a). 'Do conflicts create poverty traps? Asset losses and recovery for displaced households in Colombia' in R. Di Tella, S. Edwards and E. Schargrodsky (eds), *The Economics of Crime*, Chicago, IL: University of Chicago–NBER.
Ibáñez, A.M. and A. Moya (2010b). 'Vulnerability of victims of civil conflict: empirical evidence for the displaced population in Colombia', *World Development*, **38**(4): 647–63.
Ibáñez, A.M. and C.E. Vélez (2008). 'Civil conflict and forced migration: the micro-determinants and the welfare losses of displacement in Colombia', *World Development*, **36**(4): 659–76.
Jaramillo, P., C. Kayi et al. (2012). 'Asymmetrically fair-rules for an indivisible good problem with a budget constraint', Documento CEDE 2012-05. Department of Economics, Universidad de los Andes, Bogotá, Colombia.
Justino, P. (2011). 'War and poverty', in M.R. Garfinkel and S. Skarpedas (eds), *Oxford Handbook of the Economics of Peace and Security*. Oxford: Oxford University Press, ch. 27.

Kalyvas, S.N. (2006). *The Logic of Violence in Civil War*. New York: Cambridge University Press.
Kondylis, F. (2008). 'Agricultural outputs and conflict displacement: evidence from a policy intervention in Rwanda', *Economic Development and Cultural Change*, **57**(1): 31–66.
Kondylis, F. (2010). 'Conflict displacement and labor market outcomes in post-war Bosnia and Herzegovina', *Journal of Development Economics*, **93**(2): 235–48.
Lozano-Gracia, N., G. Piras et al. (2010). 'The journey to safety: conflict-driven migration flows in Colombia', *International Regional Science Review*, **33**(2): 157–80.
Lucas, R.E. (1997). 'Internal migration in developing countries', in M.R. Rosenzweig and O. Stark (eds), *Handbook of Population and Family Economics*. Amsterdam: Elsevier, pp. 721–96.
Maier, G. (1985). 'Cumulative causation and selectivity in labour market oriented migration caused by imperfect information', *Regional Studies*, **19**(3): 231–41.
Miguel, E., S. Satyanath et al. (2004). 'Economic shocks and civil conflict: an instrumental variables approach', *Journal of Political Economy*, **112**(4): 375–83.
Moore, W.H. and S.M. Shellman (2006). 'Refugee or internally displaced person? To where should one flee?', *Comparative Political Studies*, **39**(5): 599–622.
Morrison, A.R. and R.A. May (1994). 'Escape from terror: violence and migration in post-revolutionary Guatemala', *Latin American Research Review*, **29**(2): 111–32.
Moya, A. (2013). 'Violence, mental trauma, and induced changes in risk attitudes among the internally displaced population in Colombia'. Mimeo. http://andresmoya.weebly.com/research.html.
Ranis, G. and J.C.H. Fei (1961). 'A theory of economic development', *The American Economic Review*, **51**(4): 533–65.
Rosenzweig, M.R. and O. Stark (1998). 'Consumption smoothing, migration and marriage: evidence from rural India', *Journal of Political Economy*, **97**(4): 905–26.
Ruiz, I. and C. Vargas-Silva (2013). 'The economics of forced migration', *Journal of Development Studies*, **49**(6): 772–84.
Schmeidl, S. (1997). 'Exploring the causes of forced migration: a pooled time-series analysis, 1971–1990', *Social Science Quarterly*, **78**(2): 284–308.
Schultz, T.P. (1971). 'Rural–urban migration in Colombia', *Review of Economics and Statistics*, **53**(2): 157–63.
Sjaastad, L.A. (1962). 'The costs and returns of human migration', *Journal of Political Economy*, **70**(5): 80–93.
Skaperdas, S. (1992). 'Cooperation, conflict, and power in the absence of property rights', *American Economic Review*, **82**(4): 720–39.
Stanley, W.D. (1987). 'Economic migrants or refugees from violence? A time-series analysis of Salvadoran migration to the United States', *Latin American Research Review*, **22**(1): 132–54.
Stark, O. (1991). *The Migration of Labor*. Cambridge, MA: Basil Blackwell.
Stark, O. and D.E. Bloom (1985). 'The new economics of labor migration', *The American Economic Review*, **75**(2): 173–8.
Steele, A. (2009). 'Seeking safety: avoiding displacement and choosing destinations in civil wars', *Journal of Peace Research*, **46**(3): 419–30.
Stefansson, A.H. (2004). 'Refugee returns to Sarajevo and their challenge to contemporary narratives of mobility', in L.D. Long and E. Oxfeld (eds), *Coming Home: Refugees, Migrants and Those Who Stayed Behind*. Philadelphia, PA: University of Pennsylvania Press, pp. 170–86.
Todaro, M.P. (1969). 'A model of migration and urban employment in less-developed countries', *The American Economic Review*, **59**(1): 138–48.
Todaro, M.P. (1989). *Economic Development in the Third World*. New York: Longman.
Todaro, M.P. and L. Maruszko (1987). 'Illegal immigration and US immigration reform: a conceptual framework', *Population and Development Review*, **13**(1): 101–14.
Williams, N.E. (2008). 'Betting on life and livelihoods: the role of employment and assets in

the decision to migrate during armed conflict'. Paper presented at the Annual Meeting of the Population Association, Detroit, MI.
Williams, N.E. (2013). 'How community organizations moderate the effect of armed conflict on migration in Nepal', *Population Studies*, **67**(3): 353–69.
Williams, R.C. (2004). 'Post-conflict property restitution and refugee return in Bosnia and Herzegovina: implications for international standard setting and practice', *Journal of International Law and Politics*, **37**: 441.
Winters, P., A.D. Janvry et al. (2001). 'Family and community networks in Mexico–US', *Journal of Human Resources*, **36**(1): 159–84.
Wood, W.B. (1994). 'Forced migration: local conflicts and international dilemmas', *Annals of the Association of American Geographers*, **84**(4): 607–34.
Zolberg, A.R., A. Suhrke et al. (1989). Escape from Violence: Conflict and the Refugee Crisis in the Developing World. New York: Oxford University Press.

14. Economic consequences of conflict and environmental displacement[1]

Florence Kondylis and Valerie Mueller

1. INTRODUCTION

In recent years, conflict and natural disasters have displaced 45.2 million (UNHCR, 2013) and 14.9 million (Yonetani, 2012) people, respectively. The displaced represent those most afflicted by conflict or extreme weather episodes. The link between economic performance and peace or environmental resilience is well documented (Bigombe et al., 2000; Collier, 2003; Deininger, 2003; Miguel et al., 2004; Verwimp, 2005; Schlenker and Roberts, 2009; Hsiang, 2010; Dell et al., 2012). Understanding the consequences of forced displacement is central to designing and targeting policies that can effectively improve economic resilience in areas subject to high levels of civil strife and environmental fragility.

Despite the importance in scope, only a handful of published studies examine the costs associated with environmental or conflict-induced displacement. As Kondylis (2008) outlines, the consequences can span several dimensions, years, and even generations. The disruption in job experience and schooling can have long-term impacts on employment and people's earning potential. The dissolution of households can further exacerbate the economic predicament of the next generation in countries with high returns to schooling. For example, children in displaced households, with fewer able-bodied workers, may face higher opportunity costs of schooling. Lastly, in developing countries dependent on informal economies, the destruction of social networks that facilitate the employment search and offer social protection puts the displaced at risk of economic and welfare losses.

Perhaps the most notable limitation in the current literature is the discrepancy between content provided and demanded. We are not aware of a single study covering refugees from the predominant sources of conflict displacement (e.g. Afghanistan, Iraq, Somalia, Sudan and the Syrian Arab Republic) (UNHCR, 2013). Similarly, the environmental displacement literature focuses on recent disasters in the USA. The paucity of evidence in developing countries is puzzling given the resources designated to relief: $4.6 billion per year is donated for relief efforts, where the USA and Europe account for 33 and 57 percent of those funds respectively (Strömberg, 2007).

In this chapter, we review the existing literature on the economic impact of forced displacement on the displaced population. We highlight two knowledge gaps in the literature, the absence of measured (i) welfare losses associated with displacement, and (ii) knowledge and income spillovers within communities and across generations. Using primary and secondary data, we address the first knowledge gap by documenting differences in asset portfolios across the displaced and stayers in two contexts: the 1992–95 war in Bosnia-Herzegovina, and the 2011 floods in Pakistan. Before our conclusion, we delineate candidate policies for mitigating the employment consequences confirmed by emerging experimental evidence.

2. CONCEPTUAL FRAMEWORK

Documenting the causal impact of forced displacement on economic outcomes of the displaced is a methodological challenge. We examine and discuss conceptual frameworks used in the literature. We first review measurement issues in the empirical study of displacement. We then present central identification issues in measuring the impact of displacement and discuss empirical strategies.

2.1 Defining Displacement

There are significant methodological issues in imputing a displacement status using survey data, whether relying on objective or subjective indicators. We present the options and tradeoffs associated with each.

Time-based definition of migration

The first step in defining displacement in survey data is to determine migration status. Where the researcher has the opportunity to collect primary data and design her own survey instrument, the ideal module would take a full record of migration episodes for all target individuals, with their duration, location and, when relevant, occupational status in that residence (see, e.g., de Brauw and Carletto, 2012). In addition, surveying migrant status (e.g. internally displaced person, refugee, refugee staying in camps etc.) would allow for more granularity of the definition of displacement.

However, the researcher often needs to rely on secondary data, especially when studying countrywide shocks such as civil war. In this case, available surveys are often ill designed to perfectly observe all migration spells. In most cases, only the last migration episode is recorded, and only the date of the most recent move ('When did you move here?') is recorded. The probability of correctly identifying a given episode of forced displacement decreases with the lag between survey and shock year. In addition, the researcher needs to assume the year displacement occurs.

Fortunately, most recent multi-module surveys, such as the Living Standards Measurement Surveys (LSMS), present richer migration modules, especially in settings with high incidence of economic and forced migrations. These modules tend to include the time spent in the previous place of residence. For instance, the 2001–04 Living in Bosnia-Herzegovina (LBiH) panel recorded not only the last migration spell but also the place of residence before the 1992 conflict, and the municipality of birth. The 2001 Rwanda EICV (LSMS equivalent) records similar information on the last migration spell, and occupational status in the previous place of residence; however, it does not record pre-genocide location.

Once migration spells are identified, the researcher can restrict the definition of forced migration as having migrated between certain dates. For instance, Kondylis (2010) uses the LBiH to define conflict-induced migration in the context of the war in BiH; since only the last migration spell is observed, limiting the analysis to 1992–95 would exclude a great many post-conflict resettlement migrations. Indeed, permanent returns of temporarily resettled internally displaced persons (IDP) and refugees spanned years after the conflict ended. Hence conflict displacement in this context is defined as any migration having taken place between 1992 and 2001.

In some instances, surveying migrant status is sufficient to identify forced displacement. Fiala (2013) studies the economic consequences of displacement in Northern Uganda, and focuses specifically on IDP. In such a case, while surveying IDP status is sufficient to inform displacement status, consistency checks should be performed to ascertain the validity of this self-reported measure.

Motivation-based definition of migration

Qualitative information can be used to further establish displacement status. For instance, migration modules will typically record the main reason for moving using predetermined categories. Assuming that such information is available, relying solely on it poses methodological issues. First, the proposed categories are typically non-mutually exclusive, which limits the interpretation of the findings. Second, exploiting self-reported migration reasons can introduce reverse causation. Respondents will tend to rationalize their decision to move *ex post*. For instance, assume that a migrant was pushed to move from her original residence as a result of a flood. The disaster might have acted as an extra 'push', although the migrant may have considered economic migration before the flood took place. Hence she moves to a relatively more economically prosperous location as a result of the floods, and yet reports having moved for economic reasons. In contrast, a migrant moving before the flood for economic reasons may be inclined to declare that the move was driven by a natural disaster if she did not prosper at her new location and could not return to her prior residence because of flood damage. This is merely anecdotal evidence of serious measurement issues that could contaminate estimates of the impact of motivation-based migration.

2.2 Identification

We have established that forced displacement occurs when a person leaves her original place of residence as a result of an idiosyncratic shock, whether man-made or environmental. As displacement is not exogenously assigned, researchers need to exploit natural experiments to draw causal inference. We discuss the main identifying assumptions required to establish the causal impact of displacement. We then review the identifying assumptions used in the literature.

What estimates?
A first step in the search for identification of non-assigned treatments such as forced displacement is to establish a counterfactual and define what measure of the treatment effect will be captured. The ideal experiment would be to randomly assign a shock causing displacement to some localities,[2] and compare the outcomes for individuals from these treated localities with those for individuals from otherwise similar control localities. In that setup, displacement would capture the impact of both exposure to the idiosyncratic shock and the physical move. Unless the shock pushed out entire communities, as, for instance, happened during the Rwandan genocide (Kondylis, 2008), displacement will be endogenous.[3] All individuals in treatment communities will not move, and all individuals in the control group will not stay. Hence the reduced-form estimates from running a simple regression of the outcomes of interest on exposure to the shock would, in a sense, capture an intention-to-treat (ITT) estimate of displacement. In most studies of the economic consequences of conflict or environmental shocks, this is the best estimate available (see References). Assuming that the only channel through which a given shock affects the outcomes of interest is displacement, estimating a local average treatment effect (LATE) (or average treatment on the treated, ATT, where individuals in the control group never move) is now available to the researcher. However, this is true only in our ideal world where the shock

was randomly distributed. The next sub-section presents the robustness checks required to validate the exclusion and independence assumptions in the real world.

Two caveats must be noted when using instrumental-variables (IV) estimation, even when the instrument is assumed to be exogenous to the outcome of interest, uncorrelated with other independent variables in the model, and sufficiently correlated with displacement. First, as noted by Angrist and others,[4] the local average treatment effect (LATE), measured through a two-stage instrument variable procedure, is identified from the 'compliers'. Compliers are individuals who will participate (move) when eligible (pushed out by a shock), and will not participate (move) when not eligible (in the absence of a shock). In contrast, some individuals are 'defiers': some will always move, some will never move, regardless of the occurrence of a shock. This makes interpreting a LATE somewhat perilous, as we do not in effect observe who the compliers are, and that compliance would likely be defined differently with another, equally valid, instrument. Hence the LATE is necessarily instrument-specific and provides an internally valid measure of the treatment effect. This poses a challenge in extrapolating a LATE estimate to a larger population.

Another method to measure the causal impact of displacement is to exploit geographic discontinuities in the placement of strife or environmental events. For instance, Fiala (2013) exploits the geographic placement of conflict events in Northern Uganda to study the fate of IDP who returned to their residence of origin. In this case, compliance is not perfect and the regression discontinuity design (RDD) will be fuzzy, yielding the same estimates as an (instrumental variable) IV estimation at the cutoff. Hence the assumptions required in an RDD setup mirror those required to place any faith in IV estimates, and the estimates obtained are still local. We now present the range of tests required to estimate the consequence of displacement in a LATE framework.

2.3 Robustness

Predicting displacement

The endogeneity in the individual decision to go into displacement can be addressed by using the margin of exposure to the idiosyncratic shock, either in an IV or RDD framework. In both cases, a good first stage is a necessary condition for identifying a causal impact. In working with weak instruments, which are feeble predictors of displacement, the asymptotic bias from an ordinary least squares (OLS) estimation may be preferable to an IV estimator, especially if the instruments are (even) weakly endogenous. Performing thorough checks on the exclusion restriction is therefore warranted to make any inference on the causal impact of displacement.

Exclusion restriction

Since we do not observe the true residuals from the regression of the outcomes on the instrument, we cannot directly check our exclusion restriction. Instead, we must rely on two broad categories of indirect tests to verify that our instrument (exposure to conflict or environmental shock) affects the outcomes only through displacement. We need to establish that, first, the instrument does not systematically predict pre-shock trends, and, second, that our instrument does not pick up post-shock heterogeneity besides displacement.

Establishing pre-shock exogeneity

As in any difference-in-difference framework, the assumption of parallel trends needs to be verified. In the context of developing or conflict-affected countries, pre-shock data may be hard to come by. There, the researcher needs to be creative in finding secondary data sources. In addition, using historical and political studies on the shock of interest can help understand the determinants of the shock, especially in the case of conflict-induced displacement. In the case of environmental disasters, it is helpful to understand whether levels of exposure are systematically higher in the historically higher-risk areas. For instance, in the case of a tsunami, were the low-lying areas more likely to suffer from higher floods? The incidence of floods may not satisfy the exclusion restriction, as living in the low-lying areas may also be systematically associated with higher levels of poverty. In this case, using flood as a local instrument around an altitude cutoff may be a more appropriate source of identification. The effect measured will not be generalizable to the entire population, but may be the most policy-relevant estimate.

An attractive way to check for pre-shock exogeneity is to perform a falsification test, using the instrument to predict migration patterns before the shock (Kondylis, 2010). To validate the assumption of parallel trends, the instrument should not have any predictive power on pre-shock migrations. The intuition is that economic migration patterns are correlated with relative economic performance. For the instrument to be valid, it needs to be orthogonal to pre-shock economic performance. Checking the correlation between pre-shock migration and the instrument is a good way to indirectly test this and ensure that the IV is picking up only forced migration. While it is powerful, such a falsification exercise is available only where multiple migration spells are observed and localities of origin are recorded.

Dealing with post-shock heterogeneity

Civil strife and natural disasters can have lasting economic consequences, such as devastation, changes in the age and ethnic profile of a locality, and reconstruction efforts. Ideally, a study of the impact of displacement would rely on displaced-stayer variations within a labor market or locality, as these socioeconomic consequences will confound the impact of displacement and violate the exclusion restriction of using exposure to the shock as an IV. However, variations in the relocation decision can, in some cases, be exploited to overcome this identification issue. This requires that the displaced population of interest elects to relocate both within their locality of origin and to new areas. Where this is the case, the relocation choice and local labor market conditions can be netted out of the effect of displacement, and the first stage can still be identified with a locality-of-origin-specific instrument. Only under this condition can we control for both push and pull factors. Typically, this is not the case when repatriation is planned, for instance in the case of IDP, or when the displaced unanimously choose to return to their original location.

Finally, exposure to conflict may introduce individual heterogeneity through other channels than displacement. For instance, disruption in schooling for individuals of school age has been documented in some contexts (see Section 3.2). Robustness checks can be carried out, applying adequate sample restrictions to test for parameter constancy to verify the validity of the exclusion restriction.

3. MICRO-LEVEL EVIDENCE ON THE EFFECTS OF DISPLACEMENT

In the conceptual framework section, we describe how natural experiments can be exploited to document the causal effect of forced displacement on economic outcomes. Such an identification strategy requires that the shock at origin be uncorrelated with the outcomes of interest through other channels than displacement. In this section, we first summarize the literature on the channels through which exposure to conflict and natural disaster have long-term effects. One main channel is human capital accumulation at an early age, shown to lead to serious losses in earnings at adulthood (Alderman et al., 2001; Alderman et al., 2006). We then contrast this literature with that which focuses on the impact of environmental or conflict-driven displacement on the labor market outcomes of the adult population. Here, the consequences of exposure are driven largely by an interruption of work experience and the disruption of labor market conditions.

3.1 Exposure to Disasters and Human Capital Accumulation

An emerging body of work links varying exposures to conflict and weather shocks to height at various stages of the life cycle (Bundervoet et al., 2009; Maccini and Yang, 2009; Alderman et al., 2010; Akresh, Bhalotra et al., 2012; Akresh, Lucchetti and Thirumurthy, 2012). While the studies overwhelmingly ascribe the impact of exposure to a reduction in height, there is no consensus on the gender-specific impacts. Maccini and Yang (2009) find that only women exposed to positive rainfall shocks at birth benefit in terms of height. Although rainfall deviations at birth are strongly correlated with nutrition and health markers, the authors impute nutritional deficiencies associated with droughts to the postweaning period of the child (the second year of life). The authors argue the lagged nutritional response to drought exposure is due to a delayed response to crop output, the timing of food insecurity in terms of the number of months following the harvest, and the availability of small-scale storage. Furthermore, household coping responses to a shortfall in production come at the nutritional expense of girls, not boys. In contrast, Akresh, Lucchetti and Thirumurthy (2012) find that boys and girls experience similar nutritional consequences from exposure to war at birth.

Another branch of the literature demonstrates how exposure to war hinders human capital accumulation through reduced schooling (Alderman et al., 2010; Blattman and Annan, 2010; Chamarbagwala and Moran, 2011; Shemyakina, 2011). Chamarbagwala and Moran (2011) exploit the longevity of the civil war in Guatemala to differentiate short-, medium- and long-term impacts on the schooling outcomes of Mayan boys and girls. They divide the exposure of the war into three periods: the initial period (1960–78), the worst period (1979–84) and the final period (1985–96). They find that boys and girls experienced the worst decline in schooling during the final period. Girls were more vulnerable to the exposure in the final period, having completed 30 percent fewer years of schooling than the average woman (compared to a 23 percent loss of years of schooling for men). Boys suffered greater losses of schooling than girls during the initial and worst periods. The authors suggest that the losses were greatest during the final period of the war because of the long-term demise of institutions and infrastructure, declines in parental expectations of the returns to education, and the subsequent impact of having displaced parents exposed to the worst period of the war.

A recent study measures the impact of environmental displacement on the schooling outcomes of student evacuees from hurricanes Katrina and Rita (Sacerdote, 2012). Sacerdote (2012) finds strong long-term gains on the test scores of students who evacuated and remained in Louisiana.

Although changing schools can have negative consequences for student adjustment and performance, the study was motivated by the potential for evacuees to upgrade their school quality when evacuated to another town. Although displacement improved test scores, there was a nominally significant dropout rate in college attendance. One explanation for the discrepancies in test scores and college attendance is that those who experienced the largest gains (students at the lower end of the distribution) were also less likely to attend college at the margin. Similarly, the types of community colleges the evacuees would have enrolled in prior to the move were likely less readily available at their destination.

3.2 Displacement and Labor Market Outcomes

Angrist (1990) provided one of the first motivations for research measuring the effects of displacement on earnings in his study of the long-term losses experienced by conscripts of the Vietnam War. He finds that white conscripts experienced long-term losses of earnings, which are primarily explained by the lack of substitutability in work experience across the military and civilian labor markets. The study also conveys the importance of pre-displacement characteristics on the measure of impacts, as African Americans were more likely to recover following the war.

The spatial mismatch hypothesis brings up the possibility that individuals are suboptimally located in the location of origin, due either to moving costs or other market frictions. An idiosyncratic shock may nudge individuals living in suboptimal locations to areas with more favorable market conditions, leading to positive labor market outcomes (Vigdor, 2007). When comparing the employment and earnings of short-term and long-term evacuees from Hurricane Katrina to those who did not move, Vigdor (2007) finds that short-term evacuees recovered. Long-term evacuees suffered lower employment and earnings. These declines coincided with an increase in income from social protection programs, severance payments and self-employment. Given the favorable employment conditions at destination, either the lack of commitment to the job search or the employer's perceptions that the evacuee might leave could have affected the employment of long-term evacuees.

Groen and Polivka (2008) also find that Hurricane Katrina evacuees who have not yet returned to their origin fare worse than returnees. However, they show that the cause is probably the differential exposure of damages. Thus they interpret the fact that non-returnees' outcomes worsened in the form of higher unemployment as more indicative of the disruption the hurricane had on their lives and their local labor markets rather than poor labor market characteristics.

While displacement appears to affect the long-term employment and earnings of a sub-population of the USA, few studies measure the effects of environmental or conflict displacement on labor outcomes in developing and transition economies. The biggest challenge lies in the lack of data available in conflict areas. Cross-sectional data are more common, and data capturing both pre- and post-conflict or disaster situations are hard to come by. An additional limitation is the need to identify a suitable counterfactual, usually relying on available data on stayers and movers before and after the event in a given locality (Vigdor, 2007; Groen and Polivka, 2008). One concern is that the demographics at the origin change after a major conflict or natural disaster, jeopardizing the stable unit treatment value assumption (SUTVA) (Cameron and Trivedi, 2005). The exodus of workers from the origin affects the labor market outcomes of non-migrants or may generate remittances that promote spillovers in investment and consumption within the community. Groen and Polivka (2010) show that the demographic composition of residents in areas affected by Hurricane Katrina shifted towards having more Hispanics and wealthier and more educated residents. Thus the concentration of refugees may have consequences for the labor market outcomes of stayers, which would probably lead the estimates to understate the (negative) effect of displacement in affected regions.

Kondylis (2010) measures the impact of forced displacement on labor market outcomes, focusing on conflict-driven displacement in post-war Bosnia-Herzegovina. She finds that displacement increases non-employment, generating higher unemployment among men and reducing participation among women. Since there is no additional effect of education on displacement, Kondylis claims that the costs of displacement largely stem from the destruction of labor markets and location-specific capital. These drivers also explain why only the labor participation of women was affected. In what follows, we summarize her empirical strategy to demonstrate the identification challenges prevalent in this literature: selection into conflict migration; the non-random assignment of war or disasters; and the selection of displaced individuals into their destination. We then review other studies that have focused on the displacement effects on labor market outcomes in developing countries.

The main regression model in Kondylis (2010) estimates the relationship between a labor market outcome Y, a vector of time-variant individual characteristics $\mathbf{X}$ and a time-invariant displacement dummy D:

$$Y_{it} = \beta_1'\mathbf{X}_{it} + D_i\gamma + \eta_i + \omega_{iit} \qquad (14.1)$$

The residual comprises two terms to reflect the unobserved individual heterogeneity η_i and unobserved time-variant variables at the individual or communal level ω_{it}. Two issues immediately arise with the estimation of (14.1). First, a fixed-effect model is ruled out by the time invariance of the displacement dummy. Kondylis argues that a random-effect model is probably unsuitable because the unobserved heterogeneity η_i is probably correlated with the parameters in (14.1). Second, the displacement dummy D is endogenous as it reflects the individual decision to move. Opportunities in neighboring locations are likely to pull individuals elsewhere and those with a greater transferability of skills or lower moving costs might be inclined to take advantage of those opportunities.

To address the selection into conflict migration, Kondylis uses an instrumental-variables strategy. In the first stage, she estimates a linear probability model that regresses the displacement dummy D on a function of individual characteristics $\mathbf{Z}$, exposure to conflict at the origin C, economic conditions in the municipality of origin p and the residual, which consists of unobserved individual heterogeneity ν and a random shock u:

$$D_{it} = \beta_2'\mathbf{Z}_{it} + C_o\delta + p_o\Phi + \nu_i + u \qquad (14.2)$$

Kondylis (2010) provides two diagnostics on the validity of the exclusion restriction for her instrument, exposure to conflict at the origin. First, she verifies that the assignment of the wars is orthogonal to pre-war economic performance, using educational attainment and ethnicity as proxies for local economic performance. She further performs a falsification test to check that casualties cannot predict pre-war migrations. Second, she checks that conflict is not correlated with post-war individual heterogeneity. She uses two dependent variables (having suffered from a war disability and having suffered a chronic disease) to regress on her instrument and additional controls and finds no correlation. She employs municipality of destination fixed effects and exploits variations within a labor market to purge her estimates from any bias stemming from non-random return destination and local labor market conditions.

Attrition in the LBiH sample consists of displaced households that migrated abroad and did not return. Kondylis uses data on immigration from the Balkans to Western European countries to check the extent of the selection, and concludes that selection into permanent migration may be negative. Thus the estimates proposed in her study may underestimate the negative impact of displacement.

Blattman and Annan (2010) offer a second study that identifies the impact of displacement driven by conflict. They estimate the impact of displacement on the labor market outcomes of child soldiers in Uganda using a propensity-score-weighted regression to account for the selection of abducted individuals (Hirano et al., 2003). They find that abducted youth are just as likely to be employed as non-abducted youth. However, they are less likely to obtain skilled work and earn one-third lower wages than non-abducted youth. In contrast with Kondylis (2010), these effects are attributed to both losses in human capital as well as work experience.

Blattman and Annan (2010) address the issue of selective attrition and survival of soldiers over the study period (1996 and 2005–06) in obtaining their average treatment effects. First, they use inverse probability weights (Fitzgerald et al., 1998) in their weighted regression to account for the attrition due to war deaths or the non-return of household members. However, the authors recognize that even their regression accounting for attrition weights may be suspect, particularly if attrition is selective among the abductees. For example, the existence of a disproportionate amount of high-ability attritors in the group of abductees might lead to an overestimate of their average treatment effects.

To address the issue of selective attrition, the authors next employ a method proposed by Lee (2005) that bounds the average treatment effect by trimming the distribution of the outcome of the group with less attrition. Comparing the untrimmed average treatment effects with the best-case scenario (dropping the non-abductees with the lowest outcome values) and the worst-case scenario (dropping the non-abductees with the highest outcome values), they find that impacts of abduction remain consistent when accounting for differential attrition across treatment and control groups.

An additional unique feature of the Blattman and Annan (2010) study is their comparison of the displacement effects by age of abduction to observe possible differential effects among adult and child abductees. Interestingly, they find little difference in the outcomes by the age at which the individual was abducted despite the longer duration of abduction among the youth and their tendency to have schooling interrupted. The authors rationalize these findings with evidence that the young abductees are more likely to return to school and reintegrate.

4. ADVANCES IN THE LITERATURE

The aforementioned work measuring the human capital and labor market impacts of displacement has generated renewed interest in the overall welfare implications of displacement. We provide new evidence on the welfare impact of forced displacement from two different contexts: the 1992–95 war in Bosnia-Herzegovina, and the 2011 floods in Pakistan. A second area of interest in this literature is the extent to which displacement generates income and knowledge spillovers within the community. In what follows, we discuss what has been done in these two areas and discuss the knowledge gaps in more detail.

4.1 The Welfare Impact of Displacement

Fiala (2013) utilizes a simple neoclassical framework to conceptualize how displacement affects investment decisions, and therefore welfare. The consumption of the household Y is determined by a Cobb–Douglas production function with constant returns to physical (K) and human (H) capital: $Y = AK^{\alpha}H^{1-\alpha}$, where A represents the total factor productivity of a household and lies between 0 and 1. He assumes the capital stocks depreciate at a constant rate and are restocked through investment. Households choose their level of physical and human capital such that the marginal products of each are equal: $K/H = \alpha/(1 - \alpha)$. Fiala argues that, during a war, human capital is more abundant than physical capital, rendering the $K-H$ ratio less than the ratio of the output elasticities of physical and human capital. Households will shift investments into human capital to accumulate more physical capital until reaching the initial steady-state value. Liquidity-constrained households are probably unable to shift investments towards physical capital. Instead, their lower $K-H$ ratio may lead to a lower steady-state value of consumption.

Following the model's predictions, Fiala (2013) finds that displaced households in Uganda face consumption losses of 28 to 35 percent and a 0.5 standard deviation decrease in the value of assets. The wealthier recover their consumption through a reduction in human capital investment and wealth. In contrast, there is no recovery for the bottom quartile.

Additional studies corroborate consumption and asset losses in different countries. Ibáñez and Vélez (2008) estimate a 37 percent loss in the net present value of rural lifetime aggregate consumption attributable to displacement in Colombia. Verwimp (2012) also measures substantial losses to consumption in Burundi, with a long recovery period for the entire sample (8–10 years).

We use two data sets in Bosnia-Herzegovina and Pakistan to examine the nature of displacement and its consequences for household asset accumulation in two major settings of conflict and natural disasters: the war in Bosnia-Herzegovina in 1992–95 and the 2011 floods in Pakistan. In what follows, we present two case studies based on two data sources: (1) the 2001–04 Living in Bosnia-Herzegovina (LBiH) panel taken from Kondylis (2010); and (2) the 2012 round of the Pakistan Rural Household Panel Survey (PRHPS) collected by the International Food Policy Research Institute. The findings below demonstrate that the duration of the episode as well as the nature of the shock (war versus natural disaster) can have quite diverse effects on the accumulation of assets.

Displacement during the 1992–95 conflict in Bosnia-Herzegovina

The independence of Bosnia-Herzegovina from former Yugoslavia in 1992 was followed by four years of ethnic conflicts (i.e. Bosnian–Croat, Bosnian–Serb and Croat–Serb). Military involvement by the North Atlantic Treaty Organization (NATO) in 1994 was followed by the promulgation of the Dayton Peace Agreement in 1995. The territory was then divided into the Bosnian and Croat-led Federation of Bosnia-Herzegovina (FBH) and the Serb-led Republika Srpska (RS). According to UNHCR reports, 1.3 million people were displaced. Subsequently, 1 million refugees repatriated to their pre-war locations in Bosnia (USCRI, 2003).

As mentioned earlier, Kondylis (2010) concludes that displacement had large and lasting effects on individual labor market outcomes: displaced men and women are less likely to work six to nine years after the conflict ended, with men more likely to be unemployed and women more likely to be inactive. Using the 2001–04 LBiH, we describe the characteristics of Bosnian war migrants and their asset portfolios,[5] focusing on Bosnian heads of households.[6] In Table 14.1, we observe that the sample of war migrants consists of a greater proportion of widowed, women who are less likely to have completed a high-school education or above. Given the dissimilarities in demographics, it comes as no surprise that, on average, war migrants have fewer durable, livestock and farm assets.[7] Although not shown here, the specific assets that were the most valuable and shown to be significantly different across the displaced and stayers were stoves, freezers, TV sets and cars (within the set of durable assets) and dairy cows and tractors (within the set of livestock and farm assets).

Attributing differences in asset values to displacement requires addressing the endogenous nature of the decision to go into displacement. We follow the natural experiment outlined in Kondylis (2010) and employ an instrumental-variables approach using casualties from the war in the individual's municipality of origin as an instrument for displacement.[8] The first-stage regression results from a log-linear specification (Table 14.2) confirm that casualties strongly predict displacement. OLS and two-stage least squares (2SLS) estimates are sensibly similar, and parameter constancy cannot be rejected in any specification. We continue to find a negative effect on durable and farm capital assets, even after accounting for selection into displacement. If anything, the size of the estimated effect of displacement increases in absolute value from OLS to 2SLS on the losses of durable assets, while the loss in farm capital decreases. This suggests a positive selection into displacement on the basis of durable assets, in line

Table 14.1 Descriptive statistics by displacement status of the household head

Variable name	Displaced			Stayers			*T*-test, mean diff.
	N	Mean	SD	N	Mean	SD	
Male	737	0.85	0.36	160	0.68	0.47	0.17**
Married	737	0.82	0.39	160	0.64	0.48	0.17***
Partnership	737	0.01	0.07	160	0.01	0.08	0.00
Widow	737	0.12	0.33	160	0.29	0.45	−0.16***
Age 23–27	737	0.02	0.14	160	0.02	0.14	0.00
Age 28–32	737	0.06	0.24	160	0.12	0.32	−0.06**
Age 33–37	737	0.12	0.33	160	0.14	0.35	−0.01
Age 38–42	737	0.16	0.37	160	0.13	0.34	0.03
Age 43–47	737	0.18	0.38	160	0.15	0.36	0.03
Age 48–52	737	0.17	0.37	160	0.16	0.37	0.00
Age 53–57	737	0.12	0.32	160	0.12	0.32	0.00
Age 58–62	737	0.13	0.34	160	0.11	0.32	0.02
Age 63–64	737	0.04	0.20	160	0.04	0.21	0.00
Complete or incomplete high school	737	0.55	0.50	160	0.45	0.50	0.10**
Above high-school education	737	0.10	0.30	160	0.06	0.24	0.04*
Number of dependants age 0	737	0.04	0.21	160	0.07	0.25	−0.03
Number of dependants ages 1–5	737	0.23	0.49	160	0.31	0.58	−0.07
Number of dependants ages 6–10	737	0.28	0.52	160	0.28	0.53	0.00
Number of dependants ages 11–15	737	0.32	0.56	160	0.31	0.56	0.01
Number of dependants ages 15–16	737	0.13	0.35	160	0.14	0.35	−0.01
Real value of land assets (KM)	736	5836.36	18897.18	160	6485.98	21571.32	−649.62
Real value of durable assets (KM)	736	3025.54	5000.84	160	2244.00	3874.12	781.55**
Real value of livestock assets (KM)	736	323.69	732.99	160	177.11	578.33	146.59***
Real value of farm assets (KM)	736	647.43	4091.90	160	42.52	537.81	604.91***

Note: The sample is restricted to Bosnian households in the 2001 LBiH. * $p < 0.1$, ** $p < .05$, *** $p < 0.01$. KM = Bosnian Convertible Marka.

Source: 2001 Living Standards and Measurement Survey in Bosnia-Herzegovina.

Table 14.2 *Asset–displacement relationship (first- and second-stage regressions)*

	IV	Land		Durable goods		Farm capital		Livestock	
	1st stage	OLS	IV 2nd stage	OLS	IV 2nd stage	OLS	IV 2nd stage	OLS	IV 2nd stage
Displacement		0.101	0.556	−0.221	−0.317**	−0.344***	−0.129*	−0.209	0.227
		(0.376)	(0.522)	(0.140)	(0.139)	(0.065)	(0.070)	(0.268)	(0.223)
Casualties	6.215***								
	(1.420)								
Male	−0.026	0.646	0.673	−0.168		0.248*	0.260**	0.430*	0.456**
	(0.055)	(0.447)	(0.450)	(0.255)	(0.248)	(0.125)	(0.123)	(0.230)	(0.231)
Married	−0.02	1.251*	1.278*	0.956***	0.950***	0.425**	0.437***	1.392***	1.418***
	(0.042)	(0.712)	(0.692)	(0.324)	(0.315)	(0.165)	(0.166)	(0.467)	(0.455)
Partnership	0.103	−0.724	−0.743	1.270***	1.274***	0.168	0.159	−0.2	−0.218
	(0.201)	(0.963)	(0.897)	(0.448)	(0.443)	(0.278)	(0.269)	(0.611)	(0.557)
Widow	0.019	0.522	0.496	0.384**	0.389**	−0.072	−0.085	0.042	0.016
	(0.056)	(0.583)	(0.575)	(0.189)	(0.182)	(0.133)	(0.130)	(0.371)	(0.368)
Age 23–27	−0.518	0.804	1.012	−0.199	−0.243	0.067	0.166	0.925	1.125
	(0.381)	(1.091)	(1.234)	(0.550)	(0.512)	(0.314)	(0.349)	(0.903)	(1.033)
Age 28–32	−0.28	1.167*	1.295*	−0.356	−0.383	−0.268	−0.208	0.722	0.844
	(0.439)	(0.651)	(0.785)	(0.284)	(0.247)	(0.327)	(0.314)	(0.503)	(0.568)
Age 33–37	−0.369	2.631***	2.792**	−0.228	−0.262	0.415	0.491	1.345**	1.499**
	(0.420)	(0.944)	(1.103)	(0.400)	(0.358)	(0.271)	(0.331)	(0.508)	(0.635)
Age 38–42	−0.447	2.514***	2.711***	−0.104	−0.145	0.165	0.258	1.077**	1.266*
	(0.405)	(0.752)	(0.932)	(0.414)	(0.372)	(0.351)	(0.428)	(0.491)	(0.671)
Age 43–47	−0.422	2.932***	3.120***	0.122	0.082	0.783*	0.872*	1.645***	1.825***
	(0.406)	(0.687)	(0.849)	(0.325)	(0.287)	(0.418)	(0.493)	(0.532)	(0.684)
Age 48–52	−0.416	3.033***	3.211***	−0.019	−0.056	0.405	0.489	1.731***	1.901***
	(0.393)	(0.843)	(1.030)	(0.330)	(0.288)	(0.349)	(0.414)	(0.403)	(0.575)
Age 53–57	−0.411	3.672***	3.857***	−0.018	−0.056	0.568	0.656	2.109***	2.287***
	(0.437)	(1.033)	(1.234)	(0.313)	(0.270)	(0.393)	(0.476)	(0.316)	(0.452)

Table 14.2 (continued)

	IV	Land		Durable goods		Farm capital		Livestock	
	1st stage	OLS	IV 2nd stage	OLS	IV 2nd stage	OLS	IV 2nd stage	OLS	IV 2nd stage
Age 58–62	−0.464	3.518***	3.728***	−0.31	−0.354	0.469	0.569	1.623***	1.825***
	(0.408)	(0.713)	(0.923)	(0.365)	(0.330)	(0.321)	(0.396)	(0.475)	(0.578)
Age 63–64	−0.461	3.662***	3.874***	−0.29	−0.335	0.91	1.011	1.418***	1.622***
	(0.410)	(1.114)	(1.305)	(0.413)	(0.372)	(0.591)	(0.661)	(0.442)	(0.568)
No. of dependants age 0	0.008	−0.391	−0.416	−0.14	−0.134	0.446	0.434	−0.096	−0.121
	(0.058)	(0.579)	(0.561)	(0.238)	(0.232)	(0.479)	(0.463)	(0.542)	(0.535)
No. of dependants ages 1-5	0.043	0.047	0.025	0.185	0.189*	0.134	0.123	0.316*	0.295*
	(0.031)	(0.241)	(0.238)	(0.111)	(0.110)	(0.166)	(0.163)	(0.167)	(0.164)
No. of dependants ages 6-10	−0.014	−0.275	−0.269	−0.005	−0.006	0.273***	0.275***	0.134	0.139
	(0.026)	(0.349)	(0.336)	(0.086)	(0.082)	(0.099)	(0.096)	(0.182)	(0.177)
No. of dependants ages 11-15	0.009	−0.124	−0.14	−0.218**	−0.215***	0.086	0.079	0.038	0.022
	(0.020)	(0.221)	(0.220)	(0.085)	(0.082)	(0.059)	(0.059)	(0.184)	(0.182)
No. of dependants ages 16-17	0.021	−0.01	−0.027	−0.222	−0.218	−0.054	−0.062	0.028	0.012
	(0.025)	(0.320)	(0.319)	(0.198)	(0.192)	(0.139)	(0.134)	(0.234)	(0.226)
Incomplete or complete high-school education	−0.034	−0.986***	−0.958***	0.529***	0.523***	−0.474***	−0.461***	−0.878***	−0.851***
	(0.038)	(0.288)	(0.288)	(0.084)	(0.084)	(0.171)	(0.166)	(0.198)	(0.187)
Above high-school education	−0.042	−2.366***	−2.330***	1.155***	1.148***	−0.895***	−0.878***	−2.016***	−1.981***
	(0.041)	(0.442)	(0.432)	(0.154)	(0.150)	(0.300)	(0.290)	(0.357)	(0.347)
Observations	896	896	896	896	896	896	896	896	896
R-squared	0.305	0.203	0.072	0.173	0.107	0.158	0.057	0.268	0.101

Note: The first stage reports the first-stage coefficients of the IV-2SLS regression (linear probability model), where Displacement status is the dependent variable and Casualties (proportion missing/killed in pre-war municipality of residence) is the instrumental variable. The sample is restricted to Bosnian households in the 2001 LBiH. Standard errors clustered at the municipality of origin are in brackets.* $p < 0.1$, ** $p < 0.05$, *** $p < 0.01$.

Source: 2001 Living Standards and Measurement Survey in Bosnia-Herzegovina.

with the findings from Kondylis (2010). That the effect on farm capital decreases once the estimates are purged from the selection into displacement is also intuitive, as displaced households are less likely to engage in agricultural activities than stayers. These findings corroborate the aforementioned results from the conflict literature in Africa: the displaced experience stark welfare losses that persist years after a conflict.

To shed further light on the persistent negative impact of displacement on individual labor market outcomes and household asset value, we look at the characteristics of spouses across displacement status for women age 18–64. We further split the sample by year at first marriage, dividing it into pre-war and post-war marriages (not reported). From Table 14.1, it is clear that displacement did not affect the decision to marry, as differences in marital status are fully explained by a higher incidence of widows. Overall, displacement does not seem to affect patterns of assortative mating, except for ethnic diversity, which is 3 percentage points higher among displaced women (also not reported).[9] Most interestingly, we find that displacement status is concentrated within households: 67 percent of displaced women aged 18–64 who married for the first time after 1995 married a displaced individual; this compares with 9 percent of women stayers in the same demographic group. These matches appear to be made independently of networks in the municipality of origin, as only 48 percent of couples formed after 1995 lived in the same municipality before the war. (Logically, these disparities are higher among individuals who married for the first time before the war, with 1 percent of women stayers and 88 percent of displaced women marrying a displaced man.) Given the large and persistent effect displacement has on asset accumulation at the household level, it is of interest to check whether poor labor market outcomes are concentrated at the household level, exacerbating the cost of displacement.

Finally, we try to bring together the findings on individual labor market outcomes and household-level asset value by looking at joint labor market outcomes of the main spouses. We describe joint labor market outcomes that combine a spouse's unemployment and inactivity (Table 14.3). For brevity, we report only the 2SLS coefficients, as they are remarkably close to the OLS results. The effects are small across the board and imprecisely estimated, which is not surprising as we split the categories into finer intervals. Overall, they suggest that fewer displaced households experience full employment. Alarmingly, we find that displaced households are more likely to experience joint non-employment. This confirms the idea that individual non-employment does not result from specialization within the household but rather from poorer labor market access among the displaced. These findings shed light on the potential channels through

Table 14.3 Joint labor market outcomes by displacement status

		Both spouses inactive	Female inactive, male unemployed	Female inactive, male employed	Female unemployed, male inactive	Both spouses unemployed	Female unemployed, male employed	Female employed, male inactive	Female employed, male unemployed	Both spouses employed
	First stage	2SLS	2SLS	2SLS	2SLS	2SLS	2SLS	2SLS	2SLS	2SLS
Displacement		0.07	0.037	0.083	−0.001	0.054	−0.022	−0.031***	−0.003	−0.187***
		(0.058)	(0.036)	(0.078)	(0.014)	(0.054)	(0.039)	(0.005)	(0.029)	(0.056)
Casualties	7.023***									
	(1.956)									
Observations	3256	3256	3256	3256	3256	3256	3256	3256	3256	3256
Adj. R-squared	0.131	0.381	0.016	0.042	−0.005	0.027	0.066	0.007	0.009	0.097

Note: See Table 14.2. The sample is restricted to Bosnian women age 18–64 who report living with a partner (marriage or partnership).
* $p < 0.10$, ** $p < 0.05$, *** $p < 0.01$.

Source: 2001/04 Living Standards and Measurement Survey in Bosnia-Herzegovina.

which displacement has persistent effects on asset accumulation, seven to ten years after the end of the war. As displaced households are unable to insure themselves through labor allocation, they remain less resilient to future shocks. The low rate of attachment to the labor market is particularly worrisome, especially in the context of an informal economy where labor market outcomes are highly correlated among household members.

Flood-induced displacement in Pakistan

In recent years, Pakistan has been devastated by two severe floods, in 2010 and 2011. The severity of the 2010 flood displaced 14 million people in the short term, of whom 200000 moved to internal displacement camps (Walsh, 2011). The cost of destruction of infrastructure, agriculture and housing was initially approximated at $9.7 billion (Asian Development Bank–World Bank, 2010). Unlike other South Asian countries, Pakistan had faced only two major flood events in the previous 25 years (Dorosh et al., 2010). In addition, the proportion of people displaced in 1985 and 1992 due to flooding was one-third or less of that in 2010 (Dorosh et al., 2010). The 2010 flood was followed by another severe episode in 2011: 2 million people were displaced, while humanitarian aid continued to assist households from the previous flood (Chughtai and Heinrich, 2012).

We use the 2012 round of the PRHPS to examine the nature of displacement in Pakistan primarily from the 2011 flood and its consequences on household assets. The survey covers the economic behavior of 2090 households in the three provinces of Pakistan: Khyber Pakhtunkhwa (KPK) (2 districts), Punjab (12 districts) and Sindh (5 districts). A multistage stratified sampling frame was performed to determine the number of districts selected in each province and ensure a higher probability of selection for rural districts within a province. Rural households are underrepresented in the KPK, due to several challenges in the data collection in that particular province.

A flood module was administered to qualitatively gauge the exposure of the 2010 and 2011 floods and severity of damages experienced by the sample in those years. Markedly, a greater percentage of households reported flood exposure in 2010 compared to 2011 (23 compared to 18 percent). We focus on the 2011 flood's lasting impacts since the survey spans the Rabi 2010–11 and Kharif 2011 seasons. When asked about the extent of destruction caused by the flood, 14 percent of household heads reported having their home damaged, and 8 percent noted that their agricultural fields were inundated in 2011.

Table 14.4. describes the households in our sample by the migrant status of the household head. Seven percent of heads report migrating in the last 12 months, where the motivation for moving is, for an overwhelming

Table 14.4 Descriptive statistics by migration status of the household head

Variable name	With migrant head			Without migrant head			T stat, Mean diff.
	N	Mean	SD	N	Mean	SD	
Household head attributes							
Age	128	39.430	11.622	1962	46.622	13.673	−7.192 ***
No schooling	128	0.484	0.502	1959	0.531	0.499	−0.047
Completed class 1	128	0.070	0.257	1959	0.007	0.081	0.064 ***
Completed class 2	128	0.063	0.243	1959	0.020	0.141	0.042 ***
Completed class 3	128	0.078	0.269	1959	0.023	0.151	0.055 ***
Completed class 4	128	0.023	0.152	1959	0.027	0.161	−0.003
Completed class 5	128	0.164	0.372	1959	0.108	0.310	0.056 **
Completed class 6	128	0.008	0.088	1959	0.021	0.143	−0.013
Completed class 7	128	0.008	0.088	1959	0.022	0.147	−0.014
Completed class 8	128	0.008	0.088	1959	0.074	0.262	−0.066 ***
Reason for migration and remittance behavior							
Employment	125	0.256	0.438				
Natural disaster	125	0.744	0.438				
Head remitted in the last 12 months	128	0.086	0.281				
In-kind and cash remittances received (1000s rupees)	128	5.328	23.308				

Household characteristics							
Number of dependants (3–15 years, >64 years)	128	2.289	1.953	1962	2.463	1.913	−0.174
Value of agricultural assets (1000 rupees)	128	0.570	3.128	1962	34.801	147.163	−34.231 ***
Value of non-agricultural assets (1000 rupees)	128	130.810	268.898	1960	260.330	359.740	−129.520 ***
Asset index	128	−0.421	0.908	1961	−0.045	1.533	−0.376 ***
Latitude	128	26.803	3.642	1959	30.108	2.583	−3.305 ***
Longitude	128	68.817	1.876	1959	71.346	1.805	−2.530 ***
Latitude × Longitude over 100	128	18.511	3.078	1958	21.518	2.264	−3.007 ***
Distance to nearest city (km)	128	11.367	7.157	1962	13.030	8.191	−1.662 **
Elevation over 100 (m)	128	0.772	1.234	1958	1.474	1.061	−0.703 ***
Shock 2011 (Monsoon rainfall 2011 – 30-year average)	128	101.199	52.778	1962	156.553	99.915	−55.355 ***

Note: *** $p < 0.01$, ** $p < 0.05$.

Source: Pakistan Rural Household Panel Survey 2012 and NASA-POWER.

majority, due to a natural disaster (74 percent). A small percentage of households are remitting to the household (9 percent). One possible explanation for the lack of remittances is that household heads are being accompanied by other household members. For example, 78 percent of household heads live in a household that had at least one other household member moving over the same 12-month period.

The differences between the characteristics of the heads and their households suggest that migrants may be negatively selected, which is consistent with characterizations in the displacement literature. Migrant heads are younger, less educated, and hold far fewer assets in value[10] and according to the asset index (constructed from various variables reflecting housing structure and the household's access to services).[11] To address the potential selection of migrant heads in estimating the effect of environmental displacement on assets, we use an instrumental-variables approach. Given the cross-sectional nature of the data, we are limited in our ability to purge the estimates of bias from omitted time-invariant variables. An additional empirical challenge that we cannot address is the selection bias caused by unobserved characteristics that drive decisions to return to the origin. Thus we refer to the empirical estimates as correlations between displacement and asset accumulation due to these two factors.

Due to the suspected influence of excessive rainfall in 2011 on migration, we use the 2011 monsoon (June–September) rainfall deviation from the 30-year annual monsoon average as an instrument for migration. The variable was constructed from data extrapolated from the NASA-POWER data product. As a first step, we examine possible violations of the exclusion restriction. Using information from the 1998 Census, we estimate the correlation between our instrument and pre-existing population and household characteristics of our sample villages conditioning on provinces. Only the village literacy ratio is significantly correlated with the rainfall shock at the 5 percent critical level (Table 14.5). We therefore include the variable as a control in our instrumental-variable regressions.

We present estimates from the migration and asset equations (first and second stage) in Table 14.6. We utilize three proxies for assets: the natural logarithm of the value of the household's agricultural assets plus one; the natural logarithm of the value of the household's non-agricultural assets; and the asset index. The t-statistic on the individual shock parameter in the first stage indicates that the instrument is strongly correlated with the migration of the household head. The F-test corroborates the validity of the instrument as the value is close to 11 in each specification. Environmental migration appears to have a positive, but marginally significant, correlation with household agricultural assets.

We next try to explain the aforementioned findings with household self-

Table 14.5 Correlation between pre-existing population and household characteristics and 2011 rainfall shock

	Parameter shock 2011	Standard error
Population characteristics		
Population	−1.829	4.705
Male population	−0.808	2.396
Female population	−1.021	2.313
Literacy ratio	−0.058**	0.023
Males with primary education	−0.311	0.417
Females with primary education	−0.138	0.19
Males with matric and above	−0.165	0.198
Females with matric and above	−0.094	0.064
Muslims	−2.485	4.584
Individuals 18 years and above	−0.804	2.342
Individuals 21 years and above	−0.821	1.981
Women 15–49 years	−0.414	1.019
Women 15–49 years who are currently married	−0.363	0.711
Housing characteristics		
Have pacca housing structure	−0.517	0.316
Have semi-pacca housing structure	0.153	0.176
Have kacha housing structure	−0.214	0.466
Have potable water	0.0079	0.159
Have electricity	−0.553	0.485
Average household size	0.002	0.002
Number of villages	76	

Note: Province dummy variables are included. ** $p < 0.05$.

Source: 1998 Pakistan Census Survey and NASA-POWER.

reported asset losses (home, livestock and productive assets) attributable to any flood experienced in the last two years. Table 14.7 presents the OLS and second-stage IV results. The results indicate that, although environmental migrants clearly experience losses in their housing infrastructure, there is weak evidence that their livestock assets are less vulnerable to flooding. These findings are consistent with the findings in Table 14.6, where return migrants tended to have a greater total value in agricultural assets. These results suggest that the relative portability of people as well as their assets probably influences the household's ability to buffer against a natural disaster.

The divergent effects of natural disasters and conflicts on assets can be explained by the context in which migration occurs. Often, households

Table 14.6 Asset–environmental migration relationship (first- and second-stage regressions)

Variables	Ln(Agricultural assets + 1)			Ln(Non-agricultural assets)			Asset index		
	OLS	IV 1st stage	IV 2nd stage	OLS	IV 1st stage	IV 2nd stage	OLS	IV 1st stage	IV 2nd stage
Number of dependants	0.033	0.000654	0.030	0.002	0.000680	0.001	0.003	0.000679	0.001
	(0.023)	(0.00242)	(0.023)	(0.017)	(0.00242)	(0.017)	(0.015)	(0.00242)	(0.015)
Age of head	0.013***	−0.000749*	0.015***	0.011***	−0.000755*	0.011***	0.007**	−0.000754*	0.008**
	(0.003)	(0.000397)	(0.003)	(0.003)	(0.000396)	(0.003)	(0.003)	(0.000396)	(0.003)
Latitude	9.346***	−3.332***	15.121***	3.958	−3.337***	5.897	1.573	−3.337***	5.497
	(1.818)	(0.942)	(3.693)	(2.637)	(0.942)	(3.708)	(2.882)	(0.941)	(5.049)
Longitude	3.862***	−1.520***	6.344***	1.449	−1.522***	2.282	0.494	−1.522***	2.181
	(0.807)	(0.424)	(1.563)	(1.111)	(0.424)	(1.582)	(1.229)	(0.424)	(2.180)
Latitude × Longitude over 100	−13.051***	4.741***	−21.097***	−5.511	4.749***	−8.213	−2.277	4.749***	−7.744
	(2.574)	(1.337)	(5.132)	(3.676)	(1.337)	(5.206)	(4.047)	(1.336)	(7.112)
Distance to nearest city	−0.018*	0.00187	−0.024**	−0.009	0.00185	−0.011	−0.007	0.00185	−0.011
	(0.010)	(0.00213)	(0.012)	(0.007)	(0.00213)	(0.008)	(0.009)	(0.00213)	(0.011)
Elevation over 100	−0.169**	0.0107	−0.197**	0.022	0.0108	0.013	0.113	0.0108	0.093
	(0.070)	(0.00980)	(0.086)	(0.060)	(0.00981)	(0.054)	(0.091)	(0.00980)	(0.080)
Literacy ratio	0.004	−0.00245**	0.009	0.024***	−0.00245**	0.026***	0.026***	−0.00244**	0.030***
	(0.007)	(0.00115)	(0.007)	(0.005)	(0.00115)	(0.006)	(0.006)	(0.00115)	(0.008)
Punjab province	0.244	−0.100	0.273	−0.649**	−0.101	−0.639**	−0.779*	−0.101	−0.758*
	(0.323)	(0.0623)	(0.374)	(0.314)	(0.0623)	(0.311)	(0.415)	(0.0623)	(0.407)

Sindh province	0.615	−0.448***	1.576*	−1.286	−0.449***	−0.962	−1.697*	−0.449***	−1.042
	(0.618)	(0.135)	(0.840)	(0.791)	(0.135)	(0.712)	(0.888)	(0.135)	(0.871)
Shock 2011		0.00148***			0.00148***			0.00148***	
		(0.000454)			(0.000455)			(0.000454)	
Has migrant head	0.292		2.515*	0.301		1.049	0.103		1.617
	(0.226)		(1.346)	(0.190)		(1.063)	(0.222)		(1.554)
F-test (Kleibergen–Paap Wald)			10.58			10.61			10.62
Stock Yogo critical values									
10% maximal IV size			16.38			16.38			16.38
15% maximal IV size			8.96			8.96			8.96
Observations	2082	2082	2082	2080	2080	2080	2081	2081	2081
R-squared	0.115	0.367	0.050	0.178	0.368	0.168	0.136	0.368	0.097

Note: Standard errors are clustered at the village level.
*** $p < 0.01$, ** $p < 0.05$, * $p < 0.1$.

Table 14.7 Loss of assets–environmental migration relationship (main equation regressions)

Variables	Ln(Home asset losses)		Ln(Livestock asset losses)		Ln(Productive asset losses)	
	OLS	IV	OLS	IV	OLS	IV
Number of dependants	−0.027	−0.038	0.059	0.062	0.010	0.010
	(0.042)	(0.047)	(0.042)	(0.043)	(0.008)	(0.008)
Age of head	−0.000	0.007	0.001	−0.002	−0.000	−0.000
	(0.005)	(0.008)	(0.004)	(0.004)	(0.001)	(0.001)
Latitude	−4.974	18.512	16.591***	8.999	−0.900	−0.820
	(9.311)	(17.134)	(6.402)	(5.537)	(0.756)	(1.358)
Longitude	−2.775	7.320	6.795**	3.531	−0.429	−0.395
	(4.034)	(7.269)	(2.742)	(2.343)	(0.323)	(0.584)
Latitude × Longitude over 100	7.371	−25.348	−22.758**	−12.181	1.331	1.220
	(13.023)	(23.932)	(8.845)	(7.680)	(1.064)	(1.884)
Distance to nearest city	0.028	0.005	−0.005	0.002	0.001	0.001
	(0.036)	(0.044)	(0.015)	(0.017)	(0.004)	(0.004)
Elevation over 100	−0.147	−0.265	−0.133	−0.095	−0.030	−0.030
	(0.288)	(0.282)	(0.117)	(0.098)	(0.020)	(0.023)
Literacy ratio (1998 Census)	−0.058**	−0.035	−0.014*	−0.021**	−0.005**	−0.005*
	(0.026)	(0.029)	(0.008)	(0.010)	(0.002)	(0.002)
Punjab	−1.293	−1.168	−0.164	−0.204	0.198*	0.199*
	(1.508)	(1.497)	(0.499)	(0.445)	(0.115)	(0.118)
Sindh	2.053	5.972*	5.297***	4.031**	0.282	0.295
	(2.930)	(3.080)	(2.030)	(1.629)	(0.218)	(0.347)
Has migrant head	0.814	9.894*	0.412	−2.521†	−0.198**	−0.167
	(0.964)	(5.521)	(0.482)	(1.612)	(0.093)	(0.569)
Observations	2082	2082	2082	2082	2082	2082
R-squared	0.389	0.227	0.216	0.165	0.013	0.013

Note: Standard errors are clustered at the village level. *** $p < 0.01$, ** $p < 0.05$, * $p < 0.1$, † $p < 0.12$.

move temporarily to a nearby location (such as the home of extended family) to avoid exposure to the natural disaster. These households intend to return to their place of origin. Flooding can have positive effects on the fertility of the soil in the subsequent season. Moreover, existing social protection programs, like the Citizen Damage Compensation Program in Pakistan, streamline rebuilding efforts after the disaster. In the conflict setting, holding on to one's assets is conspicuous and implausible due to the long distances travelled to escape. Humanitarian programs support the transition to the right to return (Weiss Fagen, 2011). However, many displaced people prefer to remain at their destination, which can affect their earning potential (as Kondylis, 2010 has shown) and their ability to accumulate assets (shown here).

4.2 Knowledge and Income Spillovers within Communities and across Generations

A growing literature aims to examine the spillovers from high-skilled emigration on sending countries (Katseli et al., 2006; Gibson and McKenzie, 2010). Gibson and McKenzie (2010) find that the return migration from high-skilled workers in Tonga inspires others to seek higher levels of education, brings remittances and savings to the sending country, and transmits information about education and employment opportunities to those in the sending country. Less is known with respect to whether such spillovers exist in the presence of low-skilled emigration, yet alone in the case of conflict or disaster-induced forced displacement. We review the evidence from this strand of the literature, which sheds light on possible channels through which displacement might affect welfare.

Although not in the context of forced displacement, Hildebrandt and McKenzie (2005) offer one of the first micro-level analyses of how return migration can generate knowledge spillovers within migrant households and their communities in a developing country. Using an instrumental-variables approach, the authors first show that mothers in migrant households are more knowledgeable about health-related issues than mothers in non-migrant households. Although they are unable to account for the selection of specific household members to migrate, they further illustrate that the maternal knowledge in households where the mother migrates exceeds the maternal knowledge in households where the father migrates. Qualitatively, this illustrates that the knowledge transfer comes predominantly from the mother's experience and transmission of information. They also demonstrate the existence of knowledge spillovers from migrants to non-migrants by showing that non-migrant mothers living in communities with a higher concentration of migrants have greater health knowledge.

Kondylis (2008) provides one of the first pieces of analysis of spillovers within communities in a conflict setting. Using the exogenous variation in displacement and the random selection of returnees into resettlement villages in Rwanda, she compares the returns to various inputs and agricultural output among the displaced and the stayers in resettlement and non-resettlement villages. Despite the additional resources provided to the returnees in resettled villages, Kondylis finds that returnees in resettled villages experience lower returns to seeds. This piece of information, combined with the fact that there were positive skill spillovers between stayers and returnees in non-resettlement areas, suggests that randomly allocating returnees to resettlement areas actually reduced knowledge spillovers from stayers to returnees.

A recent study demonstrates how conflict displacement generated negative income spillovers to the children of the displaced. Using information on the displaced Eastern Germans and their children following World War II, Bauer et al. (2013) find that the children of the displaced experienced lower employment and wealth outcomes than similar individuals with native parents. Male second-generation migrants experience an income penalty of 6 percent. Female migrants do not experience an income penalty, but appear to compensate for their shortcomings by increasing their work experience. For example, female second-generation migrants are more likely than their native counterparts to participate in the labor force, have a lower probability of being married, and have a lower probability of having a child.

Parental displacement status and its associated repercussions on the labor market outcomes of second-generation migrants impose additional consequences for intergenerational asset accumulation. Forced post-conflict migrants were behind their native peers in homeownership by 20 percent. The rate of homeownership among their children was also lower by a similar order of magnitude (24 percent for men and 20 percent for women). When reducing the sample of children to those whose parents did not own a house before the war, the displacement effect on child homeownership disappears. This confirms that the displaced parents' inability to transfer wealth to their children largely explains the reduced homeownership rates of their children.

5. POLICY INTERVENTIONS

In both conflict and natural-disaster settings, development interventions and humanitarian programs have primarily focused on the reintegration of refugees in their former places of residence. Qualitative assessments made in other contexts, for example Afghanistan, Bosnia, Burundi and Iraq, suggest that returning refugees to their former residence may be suboptimal (Weiss Fagan, 2011). Given the difficulty of making robust inference about the impact of displacement, rigorous evaluations of policy interventions targeting the displaced have the potential to advance both program impact and analytical understanding of the constraints faced by the displaced. As such, we are unaware of any rigorous evaluations that measure the benefits of post-disaster or conflict resettlement programs, with the exception of two studies. Kondylis (2008) and Isaksson (2013) use quasi-experimental techniques to evaluate the villagization program in Rwanda. These studies corroborate the insights from qualitative work: moving refugees to remote areas, despite an increased provision of land, services and infrastructure may have minimal impact on agricultural and non-agricultural income (Kondylis, 2008; Isaksson, 2013). Ultimately, the disruption in social capital and inferior knowledge of the local soil conditions and markets can impede the overall success of a program. Given the solid evidence on long-term employment effects, we highlight promising employment interventions that have been tested primarily in the setting of natural disasters.

5.1 Migration Policy

In many developing countries, seasonal and permanent migration rates are low despite frequent exposure to shocks (e.g. caused by recurrent civil or weather extremes) and greater expected returns at the destination (de Brauw et al., 2013). At the same time, these shocks can destroy economic opportunities in the refugees' former places of residence. Previous policy efforts concentrate on rebuilding the lives of refugees over the short term at their place of origin (Weiss Fagen, 2011). Designing interventions that make rural–urban migration attractive in climate- or conflict-vulnerable areas by reducing migration barriers and facilitating the job search may be more effective in reducing the number of displaced individuals and their subsequent welfare losses.

A recent study by Falck et al. (2011) evaluates the impact of the 1953 Federal Expellee Law on the occupational statuses of the East Germans who were forced to migrate into West Germany following World War II. The availability of a 1971 Census data set that includes the pre-war information of each respondent as well as his current information renders a unique opportunity to analyze the long-term impact of the integration policy. The Expellee Law provided various services to facilitate the transition and economic assimilation of the refugees. The authors compare the change in occupational outcomes by applying a triple difference-in-difference approach, where both native West Germans and East German migrants who moved before the construction of the Berlin Wall (and therefore were not eligible to participate in the integration program) are used as control groups. Falck et al. (2011) find that the Expellee Law improved the quality of occupations (less unskilled employment) of forced migrants.

While the above evaluation demonstrates the relative success of a historical reintegration policy, for households exposed to frequent (often short-lived) natural disasters governments might consider encouraging seasonal migration. Bryan et al. (2013) run an experiment to test the feasibility of such a policy mechanism in an area of Bangladesh that experiences a severe hunger season every year. Their experiment has three treatments, where the provision of job information, cash incentives and credit incentives is used to induce individuals to migrate for the hunger season. The monetary incentives not only enticed individuals who would not otherwise have migrated, but sustained migration rates three years later. In their setting, a small, monetary stipend relieved the burden of transportation costs, as well as the anticipated losses from unsuccessful migration. At the same time, the initial migration decision allowed individuals to build networks and relationships with employees at the destination to sustain future employment contracts. Using the randomized treatment assignments as instrumental variables, the authors calculated approximately 30 percent returns in the form of consumption to migration. The findings suggest that providing some form of insurance to risk-averse individuals, close to subsistence, may encourage vulnerable populations to migrate. Establishing a precedence of seasonal migration to places with established networks and job opportunities can restore income stability and reduce periodic displacement and its consequences.

5.2 Entrepreneurship Grants

In quite different settings, Blattman and Annan (2010) and Kondylis (2010) both find that the displaced tend to engage in self-employed activities. Although Blattman and Annan (2010) find a strong correlation between wages and education in Uganda, they are unable to detect a significant relationship between the length of a citizen's abduction and their education. In other words, the authors are unable to attribute the deleterious employment outcomes of abductees to interruptions in schooling and work experience.

Kondylis (2010) uses descriptive evidence to offer an alternative explanation for self-employment decisions. The displaced might choose to engage in self-employed occupations out of a lack of informal contacts to facilitate the job search. The success of migrants has been attributed to access to networks to facilitate the job search (Edin et al., 2003; Munshi, 2003; Magruder, 2010; Munshi, 2011; Beaman, 2012). Informal networks are important in these countries due to reliance on the informal sector for employment. In the midst of a conflict, migrants are faced with making a quick relocation decision, where their choice might depend on the availability of camps for internally displaced persons or other humanitarian services. Traveling abroad or even to the closest urban center can mean that the displaced have few contacts in their new place of residence.

Given the preponderance of self-employed activities among the displaced, humanitarian aid could be used to reduce long-term displacement costs by providing grants to boost the enterprises of the displaced. De Mel et al. (2012) test the importance of access to capital in the recovery process by randomizing the availability of grants to micro-enterprises following the 2004 tsunami in Sri Lanka. They find that vulnerable firms benefited the most from having access to capital in terms of increased profits. Retailers experienced the fastest recovery, compared to the manufacturing and services sector. The authors attribute the ability to recover to the extent of the industry's reliance on trading relationships, supply chains and infrastructure that was less likely to be affected by the natural disaster. Offering grants to entrepreneurs in sectors reliant on local value chains and trading relationships is one way to enhance employment of the displaced in countries affected by wars or natural disasters, while also stimulating the demand for local goods.

6. CONCLUSION

Displacement affects the employment prospects of repatriated refugees in the long term. Disruption in work experience, human capital accumulation and social capital is responsible for heightened unemployment and wage losses. Interestingly, in Bosnia, we find that the majority of displaced women marry displaced men. The lack of integration at destinations comes at an additional cost to household welfare. An otherwise sizable fraction of women are leaving the labor force, most likely because of a lack of access to gender-segregated labor markets or informal means of child care. Reducing the number of household income earners most certainly will affect households' ability to accumulate savings. Given the severe effect of these costs on welfare and growth, a concentration of similar research efforts on employment is warranted particularly in places such as Afghanistan, Iraq, Somalia, Sudan and the Syrian Republic.

Displacement-associated losses in assets and consumption are concurrent with the observed employment shifts. Fiala (2013) argues that, during a conflict when physical capital declines, households shift investments in human capital to accumulate more physical capital. Liquidity-constrained households have a harder time making these adjustments, which explains long-term consumption and investment losses in Uganda. Our findings, using available data in Bosnia, are in accord with those observed in Uganda, as well as in Burundi, Colombia and Sudan.

The varying conditions of displacement and the repatriation of migrants in the context of a natural disaster versus a war explain empirical differences in losses to welfare. For example, most rural migrants who move to avoid a flood in Pakistan leave for a brief period and return to their initial residence. Environmental migrants can temporarily transport some major assets (such as livestock) to a safer place, whereas stayers risk losing these assets to the disaster. The assets of war refugees are often left behind. Further, war refugees are reluctant to return to their primary residence, which affects their earnings and asset accumulation. These nuances offer one explanation why we may observe environmental migrants having more assets while conflict migrants have fewer.

New avenues to studying the fate of the displaced probably lie with rigorous impact evaluations. As mentioned ealier, the difficulty of attributing the causal impact of displacement hinders further progress in identifying the main market failures faced after an episode of displacement. Rigorous evaluations of policy interventions targeting the displaced would both increase the effectiveness of these policies and build the knowledge base on the impact of displacement. With the exception of the reintegration policy evaluation in post-war Germany, evidence on which policies effectively ease the transition of the displaced following a war or natural disaster is missing. We see entrepreneurship grants as one of the promising area for researchers and policy makers to evaluate. As many of the displaced are self-employed, offering grants can mitigate employment losses while stimulating the demand for local goods. In areas prone to disasters, earmarking humanitarian funds towards finding proactive solutions to mitigating income shocks can augment household resilience. Another possible avenue for future research in this area is to develop programs that improve workers' versatility and employability outside of their home base. Policies that help insure first-time migrants, for instance by subsidizing moving costs, have led to increases in seasonal migration out of famine-prone areas, welfare improvements, and a strengthening of migrant networks that can secure future income streams (Bryan et al., 2013).

NOTES

1. We would like to thank Hak Lim Lee and Paula Gonzalez for their research assistance, and Madeeha Hameed and Katrina Kosec for feedback on the manuscript.
2. We do not discuss individual assignment, as forced displacement is usually the consequence of a local disaster that affects an area and not just an individual.
3. Similar arguments have been made by Blattman and Annan (2010) to study the consequences of child soldiering in Northern Uganda.
4. See Angrist (1990, 1991, 1998), Angrist and Imbens (1995), Angrist et al. (1996), and Angrist and Krueger (2001).
5. Assets are available only in the 2001 round. The 2004 round is used to determine one's individual ethnicity.
6. Recall that displacement status is classified as any individual who last moved between 1992 and 2001. Kondylis (2010) shows that the analysis is robust to the use of alternative measures of displacement based on self-reported motivations for migration and household residential status.
7. We used the CPI constructed from the household survey to deflate monetary values spatially (BHAS et al., 2002). A convertible mark was equivalent to US$1.9 at the time of the survey (BHAS et al., 2002). The value of land assets includes land that is plowed, has orchards, vineyards, meadows, pastures, forests, water, or their yard, and fallow and uncultivated land. The items included in the value of durable assets are: stoves, washers, dryers, dishwashers, refrigerators, freezers, microwaves, vacuum cleaners, sewing machines, ironing rollers, satellite dishes, TVs, video players, cameras, stereos/radios/CD players, computers, accordions, pianos, bicycles, motorcycles, cars and vans. The animals included in computing the value of livestock assets are: calves, heifers, dairy cows, breeding bulls, oxen, horses, donkeys, pigs, sheep, goats, chickens, other poultry, rabbits and beehives. The value of farm assets includes the following items: moto-cultivators, small and big tractors, plows, harrows, seeders, diggers, fertilizer spreaders, sprayers, mowers, hay tedders and bailers, combine harvesters, threshers, corn crushers, silage equipment, water pumps, irrigation systems, trucks, trailers and milking machines.
8. Casualties are defined as the proportion of the pre-war population that went missing during the conflict. Further description of the identification strategy and several checks on whether the exclusion restriction is satisfied are provided in Kondylis (2010).
9. Non-reported results include literacy and education gap, age gap, and age at first marriage.
10. The following items are included in the agricultural assets variable: large and small tractors, diesel and electric tubewells, hand pumps, sprinkler/drip irrigation, mechanical water pumps, machine-pulled plows or harrows, animal-pulled plows or harrows, combine harvesters, motorized threshers, rice planters, manual corn shelters, mechanical corn shellers, chakkis, fodder choppers, motorized insecticide pumps, hand insecticide pumps, tractor trolleys, animal-driven carts, generator/diesel engines, and other omitted categories. The following items are included in the non-agricultural assets: cooking ranges/stoves, armoires/cabinets, tables/chairs, electric fans, electric irons, radios, audio cassettes/CDs/DVD players, wall clock/watches, televisions, cameras/

video cameras, computers, jewelry, sewing machines, bicycles, rickshaws, vans, bullock carts, push carts, scooters, motorcycles, cars, mobile phones, land phones, saws, hammers, masons' equipment, potters' chakas, blacksmiths' hapors, spades, axes, shovels, guns, refrigerators, water geysers, freezers, microwave ovens, heaters, washing machines, and air conditioners/coolers.

11. The asset index was constructed using the first principal component of the following variables (Filmer and Pritchett, 2001): ownership of house, whether the dwelling is a single house, possession of durable outer walls, roofs and floors, ownership of an indoor flush latrine, possession of a garbage disposal unit, access to drainage, ownership of a tube well, and access to filtered water.

REFERENCES

Akresh, R., S. Bhalotra, M. Leone and U.O. Osili (2012). 'War and stature: growing up during the Nigerian Civil War', *American Economic Review*, **102**(3), 273–7.

Akresh, R., L. Lucchetti and H. Thirumurthy (2012). 'Wars and child health: evidence from the Eritrean–Ethiopian conflict', *Journal of Development* Economics, **99**, 330–40.

Alderman, H., J. Behrman, V. Lavy and R. Menon (2001). 'Child health and school enrollment: a longitudinal analysis', *Journal of Human Resources*, **36**(1), 185–205.

Alderman, H., J. Hoddinott and B. Kinsey (2006). 'Long term consequences of early childhood malnutrition', *Oxford Economic Papers*, **58**(3), 450–74.

Alderman, S., D. Gilligan and K. Lehrer (2010). 'Childhood interrupted: how conflict-induced shocks shape human capital formation in Northern Uganda', Working Paper, Washington, DC: International Food Policy Institute.

Angrist, J. (1990). 'Lifetime earnings and the Vietnam era draft lottery: evidence from Social Security administrative records', *American Economic Review*, **80**(3), 313–36.

Angrist, J. (1991). 'Grouped-data estimation and testing in simple labor-supply models', *Journal of Econometrics*, **47**, 243–66.

Angrist, J. (1998). 'Estimating the labor market impact of voluntary military service using Social Security data on military applicants', *Econometrica*, **66**, 249–88.

Angrist, J. and G. Imbens (1995). 'Two-stage least squares estimates of average causal effects in models with variable treatment intensity', *Journal of the American Statistical Association*, **90**, 431–42.

Angrist, J., G. Imbens and D. Rubin (1996). 'Identification of causal effects using instrumental variables', *Journal of the American Statistical Association*, **91**, 444–55.

Angrist, J. and A. Krueger (2001). 'Instrumental variables and the search for identification: from supply and demand to natural experiments', *Journal of Economic Perspectives*, **15**(4), 69–85.

Asian Development Bank and World Bank (2010). 'ADB–WB assess Pakistan flood damage at $9.7 billion', October 14, 2010. Available online at: http://web.worldbank.org/WBSITE/EXTERNAL/NEWS/0,,contentMDK:22733998~pagePK:34370~piPK:34424~theSitePK:4607,00.html.

Bauer, T., S. Braun and M. Kvasnicka (2013). 'The economic integration of forced migrants: evidence for post-war Germany', *The Economic Journal*, **123**, 998–1024.

Beaman, L. (2012). 'Social networks and the dynamics of labor market outcomes: evidence from refugees resettled in the US', *Review of Economic Studies*, **79**(1), 128–61.

BHAS (State Agency for Statistics), Republika Srpska Institute for Statistics (RSIS), Federation of BiH Institute of Statistics (FIS), and World Bank (WB) (2002). *Welfare in Bosnia and Herzegovina, 2001: Measurement and Findings*. Available online at: http://siteresources.worldbank.org/INTLSMS/Resources/3358986-1181743055198/3877319-1190300029638/BiH_ANNX_poverty10a_updated.pdf.

Bigombe, B., P. Collier and N. Sambanis (2000). 'Policies for building post-conflict peace', *Journal of African Economies*, **9**(3), 323–48.

Blattman, C. and J. Annan (2010). 'The consequences of child soldiering', *The Review of Economics and Statistics*, **92**(4), 882–98.
Bryan, G., S. Chowdhury and A.M. Mobarak (2013). 'Escaping famine through seasonal migration', Working Paper. Available online at: http://faculty.som.yale.edu/mushfiqmobarak/migration.pdf.
Bundervoet, T., P. Verwimp and R. Akresh (2009). 'Health and civil war in rural Burundi', *Journal of Human Resources*, **44**(2), 536–61.
Cameron, C. and P. Trivedi (2005). *Microeconometrics: Methods and Applications*. New York: Cambridge University Press.
Chamarbagwala, R. and H. Moran (2011). 'The human capital consequences of civil war: evidence from Guatemala', *Journal of Development Economics*, **94**, 41–61.
Chughtai, S. and C. Heinrich (2012). *Pakistan Floods Emergency: Lessons from a Continuing Crisis*. Available online at: http://www.oxfam.org/en/policy/pakistan-floods-emergency-lessons. Accessed October 31, 2012.
Collier, P. (2003). *Breaking the Conflict Trap: Civil War and Development Policy*. Oxford: Oxford University Press (for the World Bank).
De Brauw, A. and C. Carletto (2012). *Improving the Measurement and Policy Relevance of Migration Information in Multi-Topic Household Surveys*. Electronically published by the World Bank. Available at: http//go.worldbank.org/4GH8S56F70.
De Brauw, A., V. Mueller and H.L. Lee (2013). 'The role of rural–urban migration in the structural transformation of sub-Saharan Africa', *World Development*. Article in press: http://dx.doi.org/10.1016/j.worlddev.2013.10.013.
De Mel, S., D. McKenzie and C. Woodruff (2012). 'Enterprise recovery following natural disasters', *The Economic Journal*, **122**(559), 64–91.
Deininger, K. (2003). 'Causes and consequences of civil strife: micro-level evidence from Uganda', *Oxford Economic Papers*, **55**(4), 579–606.
Dell, M., B. Jones and B. Olken (2012). 'Temperature shocks and economic growth: evidence from the last half century', *American Economic Journal: Macroeconomics*, **4**(3), 66–95.
Dorosh, P., S. Malik and M. Krausova (2010). 'Rehabilitating agriculture and promoting food security following the 2010 Pakistan floods: insights from South Asian experience', International Food Policy Research Institute Discussion Paper 1028.
Edin, P.-A., P. Fredriksson and O. Aslund (2003). 'Ethnic enclaves and the economic success of immigrants: evidence from a natural experiment', *Quarterly Journal of Economics*, **118**(1), 329–57.
Falck, O., S. Heblich and S. Link (2011). 'The evils of forced migration: do integration policies alleviate migrants' economic situations?', IZA Discussion Paper No. 5829.
Fiala, N. (2013). 'The economic consequences of forced displacement', Working Paper. Available online: http://www.nathanfiala.com/Economic%20Consequences%20of%20Forced%20Displacement.
Filmer, D. and L. Pritchett (2001). 'Estimating wealth effects without expenditure data – or tears: an application to educational enrollments in states of India', *Demography*, **38**(1), 115–32.
Fitzgerald, J., P. Gottschalk and R. Moffitt (1998). 'An analysis of sample attrition in panel data: the Michigan Panel Study of Income Dynamics', *Journal of Human Resources*, **33**(2), 251–99.
Gibson, J. and D. McKenzie (2010). 'How does high-skilled emigration affect small countries? Microeconomic evidence from Tonga', *Annales d'Economie et de Statistique*, **97/98**, 167–85.
Groen, J. and A. Polivka (2008). 'The effect of Hurricane Katrina on the labor market outcomes of evacuees', *American Economic Review*, **98**(2), 43–8.
Groen, J. and A. Polivka (2010). 'Going home after Hurricane Katrina: determinants of return migration and changes in affected areas', *Demography*, **47**(4), 821–44.
Hildebrandt, N. and D. McKenzie (2005). 'The effects of migration on child health in Mexico', World Bank Policy Research Working Paper 3573.
Hirano, K., G. Imbens and G. Ridder (2003). 'Efficient estimation of average treatment effects using the estimated propensity score', *Econometrica*, **71**(4), 1161–89.

Hsiang, S. (2010). 'Temperatures and cyclones strongly associated with economic production in the Caribbean and Central America', *Proceedings of the National Academy of Sciences*, **107**, 15367–72.
Ibáñez, A.M. and C.E. Vélez (2008). 'Civil conflict and forced migration: the micro determinants and welfare losses of displacement in Colombia', *World Development*, **36**(4), 659–76.
Isaksson, A.-S. (2013). 'Manipulating the rural landscape: villagisation and income generation in Rwanda', *Journal of African Economies*, **22**(3), 394–436.
Katseli, L., R.E.B. Lucas and T. Xenogiani (2006). 'Effects of migration on sending countries: what do we know?', OECD Development Centre Working Paper 250.
Kondylis, F. (2008). 'Agricultural outputs and conflict displacement: evidence from a policy intervention in Rwanda', *Economic Development and Cultural Change*, **57**(1), 31–66.
Kondylis, F. (2010). 'Conflict displacement and labor market outcomes in post-war Bosnia and Herzegovina', *Journal of Development Economics*, **93**(2), 235–48.
Lee, D. (2005). 'Training, wages, and sample selection: estimating sharp bounds on treatment effects', NBER Working Paper No. 11721.
Maccini, S. and D. Yang (2009). 'Under the weather: health, schooling, and economic consequences of early-life rainfall', *American Economic Review*, **99**(3), 1006–26.
Magruder, J. (2010). 'Intergenerational networks, unemployment, and persistent inequality in South Africa', *American Economic Journal: Applied Economics*, **2**(1), 62–85.
Miguel, E., S. Satyanath and E. Sergenti (2004). 'Economic shocks and civil conflict: an instrumental variables approach', *Journal of Political Economy*, **112**(4), 725–53.
Munshi, K. (2003). 'Networks in the modern economy: Mexican migrants in the U.S. labor market', *Quarterly Journal of Economics*, **118**(2), 549–97.
Munshi, K. (2011). 'Strength in numbers: networks as a solution to occupational traps', *Review of Economic Studies*, **78**, 1069–101.
Sacerdote, B. (2012). 'When the saints go marching out: long-term outcomes for student evacuees from hurricanes Katrina and Rita', *American Economic Journal: Applied Economics*, **4**(1), 109–35.
Schlenker, W. and M. Roberts (2009). 'Nonlinear temperature effects indicate severe damages to U.S. crop yields under climate change', *Proceedings of the National Academy of Sciences*, **106**(37), 15594–8.
Shemyakina, O. (2011). 'The effect of armed conflict on accumulation of schooling: results from Tajikistan', *Journal of Development Economics*, **95**, 186–200.
Strömberg, D. (2007). 'Natural disasters, economic development, and humanitarian aid', *Journal of Economic Perspectives*, **21**, 199–222.
United Nations High Commissioner for Refugees (UNHCR) (2013). *Displacement: The New 21st Century Challenge. UNHCR Global Trends 2012*. Geneva: UNHCR.
USCRI (2003). U.S. Committee for Refugees World Refugee Survey 2003–Bosnia Herzegovina. Available online at: http://www.refworld.org/docid/3eddc4962.html.
Verwimp, P. (2005). 'An economic profile of peasant perpetrator of genocide: micro-level evidence from Rwanda', *Journal of Development Economics*, **77**, 297–323.
Verwimp, P. (2012). 'Returning home after civil war: the consequences of forced displacement for food security, nutrition, and poverty among Burundese households', Households in Conflict Working Paper 123.
Vigdor, J. (2007). 'The Katrina effect: was there a bright side to the evacuation of Greater New Orleans?', *B.E. Journal of Economic Analysis and Policy: Advances in Economic Analysis and Policy*, **7**(1), 64.
Walsh, D. (2011). 'Pakistan flood crisis as bad as African famines, UN says', *The Guardian*, January 27, 2011. Available online: www.guardian.co.uk/world/2011/jan/27/pakistan-flood-crisis-african-famines. Accessed September 13, 2012.
Weiss Fagen, P. (2011). *Refugees and IDPs after Conflict: Why They Do Not Go Home*. Special Report, Washington, DC: United States Institute of Peace.
Yonetani, Michelle (2012). *Global Estimates 2011. People Displaced by Natural Hazard-induced Disasters*. Geneva: IDMC & NRC.

15. Development, immigration and terrorism

Pınar Derin-Güre

1. INTRODUCTION

Terrorism has been one of the most fundamental global problems in the last decade. Each year we come across at least one major terrorist incident and many other terrorist incidents with casualties. According to the Global Terrorism Database (GTD), there have been 104 689 terrorist incidents in the world between 1970 and 2011. Compared to 1998, in 2011[1] terrorist incidents increased by more than 450 percent. Foreign nationals, who may be either residents or temporary entrants, are responsible for some of these incidents. Nationals perpetrate other incidents. Travel for purposes of contact with overseas terrorist groups may have been involved, whether these people are citizens by birth or naturalized immigrants. Either way, the rising prevalence of terrorist actions has placed security concerns at the very forefront of migration issues for many countries.

In a world with increasing rates of terrorism, many are asking important questions about its causes. Economists and other social scientists have questioned whether economics has anything to do with terrorism. The rather new literature of the economics of terrorism focuses mainly either on the economic consequences of terrorism or its economic roots.

The literature on the economic consequences of terrorism investigates its macroeconomic consequences in the form of poor economic performance. From the perspective of rational-choice theory, terrorists, as rational agents, might aim to increase the cost of terrorist activities to the government and, as a result, the government might be more willing to accept the political goals of the terrorist organizations. Although there are exceptions and the effect might be low compared to a conflict or a civil war, the literature generally agrees that terrorism adversely affects economic conditions such as GDP per capita, tourism, net foreign direct investments, bilateral trade and the stock market. Blomberg et al. (2004), Gupta et al. (2004), and Tavares (2004) found little or no effect of terrorism on growth rate of GDP per capita. However, Abadie and Gardeazabal (2003), Eckstein and Tsiddon (2004) and Araz-Takay et al. (2009) include case studies for Spain, Israel and Turkey respectively, and these authors find a significantly negative impact of terrorism on per capita GDP. Therefore one can argue that, for countries suffering from high and persistent terror, the adverse growth effects of terrorism are higher. Several papers, such as Enders and Sandler (1991), Enders et al. (1992) and Drakos and Kutan (2003), conclude that airline demand tourism significantly decreased or the receipts fell as a result of terrorism in different parts of the world. Enders and Sandler (1991) find that terrorism reduced net foreign direct investment (NFDI) in Spain and Greece. Also, terrorism is found to reduce investments, according to Blomberg and Mody (2005) and Eckstein and Tsiddon (2004). Using a trade gravity model, Nitsch and Schumacher (2004) find that terrorist incidents reduce bilateral trade: if terrorist actions doubled in the world, bilateral trade would decrease by 4 percent. The effect of terrorism on the stock market has been studied as well. Using US data, Chen and Siems (2004) find that military/terrorist attacks affect the stock market adversely, but the effect on the capital markets is short term. Eldor and Melnick (2004) investigate whether the Israeli stock and foreign exchange market reacts to terrorist attacks. They find that suicide attacks and the number of injuries and fatalities had a permanent impact on both the foreign exchange market and the stock market. As we would expect, terrorism is found to increase security and defense spending (Gupta et al., 2004).

A detailed analysis of the economic consequences of terrorism literature can be found in several papers. In 2004, there was a special edition of the *European Journal of Political Economy* on the economic consequences of terror, edited by Tilman Brück and Bengt-Arne Wickström. The editors' introduction gives a summary of the papers in the edition and therefore includes a small literature survey. Also, Sandler and Enders (2004), Llussa and Tavares (2007) and Schneider et al. (2011) include summaries of the literature. Therefore this chapter does not include a further investigation of the literature on the economic consequences of terrorism.

The economic root of terrorism literature asks whether bad economic conditions result in high rates of terrorist activity in the world. The conventional wisdom among policy makers is that poverty creates terrorism; therefore many policy steps have been taken towards the improvement of economic conditions in the highly terrorized regions. However, empirical studies have challenged this view. Krueger and Maleckova (2003), Berrebi (2003), Abadie (2004), Piazza (2006), Feldman and Ruffle (2007), Krueger and Laitin (2007), Kurrild-Klitgaard et al. (2006), Dreher and Gassebner (2008),Testas (2004), and Gassebner and Luechinger (2011) have all found little or no correlation between economic conditions and terrorism. The main purpose and contribution of this chapter is to examine the literature on the economic roots of terrorism and test again whether improvements in the economic conditions will reduce terrorism in the world. The evidence on the economic roots of terrorism will be reassessed. The link between international, domestic and separatist terrorism and economic causes has been investigated by using the MIPT (Memorial Institute for Prevention of Terrorism), a multi-country panel data set. To my knowledge, this is the first study that tests the economic roots of international terrorism as well as domestic terrorism, and categorizes separatist terrorism individually. Cross-country and panel data have been used to estimate the effect of economic conditions on targets and origins of international, domestic and separatist terrorism.

Immigration is another important link between economics and terrorism. Immigration might be seen as an important channel that exports terrorism to the world. Although the literature shows that loopholes in the immigration regulations of the developed world have been used widely by terrorist organizations for international attacks, immigration itself does not seem to be an important contributor to terrorism. This chapter also offers a brief summary of the immigration and terrorism relation set within the economic literature.

This chapter is structured as follows. Section 2 includes a short review of the economic roots of terrorism literature and includes the author's contributions to the literature. Section 2.1 gives the details of the data used and the empirical strategy. This will be followed by the empirical results in Section 2.2. In Section 3, the immigration, economics and terrorism link will be explored using a short summary of the literature. Section 4 concludes with general comments on the link between economics and terrorism.

2. ECONOMIC ROOTS OF TERRORISM

Does economic deprivation lead to terrorism? This question has been asked increasingly in the media and in politics following the September 11, 2001 terrorist attacks. The conventional wisdom among policy makers is that poverty creates terrorism, but several empirical studies have challenged this view. Krueger and Maleckova (2003), Berrebi (2003), Abadie (2004), Piazza (2006), Feldman and Ruffle (2007), Krueger and Laitin (2007), Kurrild-Klitgaard et al. (2006), Dreher and Gassebner (2008), Testas (2004), and Gassebner and Luechinger (2011) have all found little or no correlation between economic conditions and terrorism. Here, I will reassess the evidence on the economic roots of terrorism and question whether international, domestic and separatist terrorism have economic causes by using the MIPT, a multi-country panel data set. International terrorism refers to terrorism committed by foreign nationals. Domestic terrorism is terrorism committed by domestic nationals. Domestic nationals engaged in separatist causes commit separatist terrorism. This study uses cross-country and panel-data analysis to estimate the effect of economic conditions on targets and origins of international, domestic and separatist terrorism.

Several studies have already investigated the economic roots of terrorism. Considering the supply side of terrorism, Berrebi (2003) finds that high standards of living and educational levels are positively associated with participation in Hamas and Palestinian Islamic Jihad (PIJ) terrorist activities in Israel. Krueger and Maleckova (2003) find that the connection between poverty, education and terrorism is indirect, complicated and probably quite weak. Kavanagh (2010) suggests that the likelihood of terrorist group participation is highest for the highly educated, poor members of any population and support this statement using Krueger and Maleckova's (2003) data on participation in Hezbollah. A few studies on international terrorism find that economic development and social welfare policies are important determinants of terrorism (Burgoon, 2006; Li and Schaub, 2004; Li, 2005).[2]

Several cross-country studies have shown that terrorism has no economic roots. Among these studies the most influential ones are Abadie (2004) and Krueger and Laitin (2007). Abadie (2004) shows that terrorist risk is not significantly higher in poor countries when we control for political freedom. The terrorist risk data used by Abadie (2004) include information on the country of occurrence but not on the target countries or on the countries of origin of terrorism. Therefore the data confound different types of terrorism.

Among the cross-country studies that do not include gravity model estimations, Krueger and Laitin (2007) is the only paper that differentiates between country of occurrence, target country and the terrorist's country of origin.[3] The authors use a US State Department data set on international terrorism and find that a country's economic performance is not a statistically significant predictor of international terrorist attacks committed by that country's nationals. On the other hand, it appears that it is mainly wealthy countries that are the targets of international terrorism. While the results in Krueger and Laitin (2007) are indicative, this paper suffers from some potential shortcomings. The US State Department data set used in the paper has many deficiencies, including ambiguity of the definitions used for some variables as well as errors and omissions in the data set, acknowledged by the authors themselves.[4] Moreover, Krueger and Laitin (2007) use only international terrorist incidents. Most of the terrorist incidents, however, are not international but domestic and separatist incidents. The classification of the MIPT data in this chapter suggests that between 1998 and 2006 only 8 percent of all terrorist incidents are international, but 57 percent and 35 percent of all incidents are domestic and separatist in nature, respectively. Therefore it is essential to study the determinants of domestic and separatist terrorism as well.[5] The weaknesses with the data sets used in the previous literature highlight the importance of testing the economic roots of terrorism with an alternative data set.

The most recent data set of terrorism is the Global Terrorism Database (GTD), which includes data from 1970 to 2011. GTD data cannot be used in this study because they give information only on the terrorist organization and do not contain a description of the event. In most incidences, the terrorist organizations responsible for the attacks are not known and therefore in many cases it is not possible to make the international, domestic and separatist categorization. In this chapter, the MIPT database has been used. The MIPT data set has not been used in a study of targets and origins of terrorism until now.[6] The MIPT data set includes information on the country in which the attack occurred and the terrorist organization responsible for the attack, to the extent that it is known. It includes a brief description of the incident, but includes no information on the target country or terrorist's country of origin. I augment the MIPT data by classifying the target country and the terrorist's country of origin for each of 31 662 terrorist incidents listed in MIPT from 1972 to 2006. Each incident is classified as international, domestic or separatist.

The previous literature on the targets and origins of terrorism focuses on cross-country estimations. I replicate the cross-country estimations with the MIPT data. Using the same sample period and the same set of countries as Krueger and Laitin (2007), I find that international terrorism does not originate from poor countries but does target rich countries. I also find the same results using cross-section estimations between 1998 and 2006.[7] The novelty of the chapter is that the larger panel data allows performing longitudinal analysis. Use of panel data also allows controlling for the impact of omitted variables, through the inclusion of country fixed effects. This is important in the analysis of terrorism as we can think of many other variables that can affect terrorism and for which we were not able to control. Panel-data estimations with fixed effects show a substantially different picture. I find that countries that get richer over time export fewer terrorist attacks. At the same time, countries that grow richer over time do not attract more terrorist attacks. This result holds for yearly panel data as well as the panel data that I generate for five-year periods.

Cross-sectional estimations suggest that domestic terrorism does not occur significantly in poor countries. On the other hand, using panel data with country fixed effects, I find that countries that get richer over time produce fewer domestic terrorist attacks. Unlike the previous cross-country literature that considers separatist terrorism as part of domestic terrorism (e.g. the incidents in Turkey and Sri Lanka) or international terrorism (e.g. the incidents in Kashmir and West Bank/Gaza), I consider them separately as the content and motivation might be quite different from international and domestic incidents. Since some countries such as Israel, India, Spain, the UK, Sri Lanka and Turkey have suffered from separatist incidents for many years, these events necessitate individual attention. In order to find if economic well-being has an effect on separatist terrorism, we first need to know the economic conditions in separatist regions in the world and this information is not available directly in any data source. I built a new data set with regional GDP of separatist regions that allows me to look at the determinants of separatist terrorism. I find that separatist terrorists tend to originate from poor areas. In summary, the existing conventional wisdom in economic literature on the lack of economic roots of terrorism may not be as robust as we thought, and some of the data I use suggest that low levels of development do indeed lead to more terrorism.

Another study that is linked to this chapter is Savun and Philips (2009). This study takes a closer look at the relationship between democracy and international terrorism. The authors use the MIPT data set as well, and distinguish between international and domestic incidents. They use negative binomial estimation and they control for income as well, even though this is not the main concern of the study. This present study differs from Savun and Philips (2009) because I perform both cross-country estimations and panel-data estimations, leading to different and interesting results. I also differentiate between country of occurrence, target countries and perpetrator countries. Savun and Philips (2009) concentrate on the country of occurrence only. Similar to the results in the previous studies that perform cross-country estimations, Savun and Philips (2009) do not find any relation between income and terrorist incidents. This result does not contradict cross-country estimation results for international terrorism in this study. In terms of domestic terrorism, the authors find a positive and significant relation between income and domestic terrorist incidents in cross-country estimations. It is important to note that I categorize separatist incidents separately. Therefore the domestic incidents in this chapter are different from the incidents in Savun and Philips (2009). In addition, estimations for domestic terrorist incidents in this study are given for 1998–2006, whereas Savun and Philips (2009) give estimations for 1998–2004.

2.1 Data and the Empirical Strategy

For the empirical investigation, data on terrorism, lagged GDP per capita, population, civil liberties, religion and other control variables have been used for up to 138 countries for the years 1972–2006. More technical information regarding the description of the variables used and the summary statistics is presented in Tables 15.1 and 15.2 respectively. The empirical literature on determinants of terrorism focuses primarily on the number of terrorist incidents.[8]

Similarly, I use the number of significant terrorist incidents as the dependent variable in our estimations. I define significant terrorist incidents as incidents with fatalities. Data on the number of terrorist incidents with fatalities are obtained from the MIPT. Terrorism is defined in the database as violence, or the threat of violence, calculated to create an atmosphere of fear and alarm and intended to coerce or to intimidate governments or societies in the pursuit of goals that are generally political, religious or ideological. Terrorist acts are also intended to produce effects beyond the immediate moment, and they have long-term psychological repercussions on a particular victim audience. They deliberately target or disregard the safety of non-combatants.

The MIPT is a non-profit organization dedicated to prevention of terrorism on US soil. The MIPT Terrorism Knowledge Base has more than 35 years of terrorist incidents data. MIPT integrates several trustworthy databases on terrorism. Between 1968 and 1998 the database includes only international incidents. The 1998–2007 period, on the other hand, includes not only international incidents but also domestic and separatist terrorist incidents.Within the same time period, the MIPT includes more incidents than the US State Department data set. Between 1997 and 2002, the US State Department data set lists 781 significant international incidents. The MIPT database lists 8172 incidents: 831 of them purely international, 3890 of them are separatist, and 3418 of them are categorized as domestic events.

Using the MIPT data set had its own challenges. The data set was not categorized in terms of the target country and terrorist's country of origin. I categorize the target country and the perpetrator's country of origin in each of 31 662 terrorist incidents from the description of each event. The rules for the categorization of terrorist incidents are given in Table 15.3. The country of occurrence is the country/area where the terrorist incident took place and is already given in the data set. Target country is the country/area of origin of the main target of terrorist incidents. In many incidents, even though the attack occurs in the perpetrator's country, if the main intention of the attack is towards a foreign national, the target is

Table 15.1 Description of the variables

Variables	Description
International Incidents Occurred	Total number of international terrorist incidents with fatalities that occurred in the country/area
Domestic Incidents Occurred	Total number of incidents perpetrated by local nationals against a purely domestic target
Separatist Incidents Occurred	Total number of separatist incidents that occurred in the country/area
International Incidents Occurred	Total number of international terrorist incidents that targeted the country/area
International Incidents Made	Total number of international incidents in which the country/area is the country of origin of the perpetrator/terrorist
Separatist Incidents Made	Total number of separatist incidents in which the area is the country of origin of the perpetrator/terrorist
Bilateral International Incidents	Total number of international terrorist incidents with fatalities for a given pair of targeted and perpetrator's country (used in bilateral estimations)
	Source: Author's categorizations and calculations from MIPT data set.
Log GDP per capita	Log of nominal GDP per capita (averaged lagged value)
	(Krueger replicate estimations 1997–2001; cross-section estimations 1998–2005; panel-data estimations lagged value)
Log Relative GDP per capita	Log (target's GDP per capita/perpetrator's GDP per capita) log of population
Log Population Growth	Growth rate of GDP per capita (averaged lagged value)
	(Krueger replicate estimations 1990–2000; cross-section estimations 1990–97; panel-data estimations lagged value)
Gini Index	Gini index on income. Range between 0 and 100. 100 shows perfect inequality.
	Source: UN National Accounts.
Lack of Civil Liberties	Lack of civil liberties shown by an index number between 1 and 7. 7 shows no civil liberties

Lack of Civil Squared	Squared value of lack of civil liberties
	Source: Freedom House.
Muslim	Proportion of Muslim living in the country/area
Buddhist	Proportion of Buddhist living in the country/area
Hindu	Proportion of Hindu living in the country/area
Others	Proportion of people who are not Christian, Muslim, Buddhist or Hindu living in the country/area
	Source: CIA World Factbook.
Ethnic	Ethnic fractionalization
Linguistic	Linguistic fractionalization
Religious	Religious fractionalization
	Index numbers between 0 and 1. Shows the probability of two individuals chosen randomly from same country belonging to a different ethnic/linguistic/religious group
	Source: Alesina et al. (2003).
Distance Common	Bilateral distances between the biggest cities of those countries
Border Common	Dummy variable indicating whether the two countries are contiguous
Language	Dummy variable indicating whether the two countries have a common language
Colony	Dummy variable indicating whether the two countries have ever had a colonial link
	Source: French Research Center in International Economics (CEPII).
Occupied	Dummy variable equals 1 if the country is occupied by any other country in the world
Occupier	Dummy variable equals 1 if the target country occupied by any other country in the world
	Source: Krueger (2007).

Table 15.2 Summary statistics[1]

Variables	Obs.	Mean	Std Dev.	Min.	Max.
Terrorism					
International Attacks Occurred	158	3.22	19.92	0	265
Domestic Attacks Occurred	158	33.94	328.18	0	4574
Separatist Attacks Occurred	158	10.88	60.87	0	700
International Attacks Received	158	3.22	13.12	0	155
International Attacks Made	158	3.22	20.72	0	269
Separatist Attacks Made	32	64.44	146.48	0	704
Civil Liberties					
Lack of Civil Liberties	155	3.51	1.77	1	7
Population (millions)	154	39.2	136	0.003	1280
Economic Variables					
GDP per capita	155	7192	11 140	103	57 019
Growth	156	2.28	4.44	−14.47	14.29
Gini	123	40.00	9.90	24.00	70.70
Fractionalization					
Ethnic	151	0.46	0.25	0	0.93
Linguistic	147	0.39	0.28	0	0.92
Religious	152	0.43	0.24	0	0.86
Religion					
Christian	150	0.55	0.39	0	1
Muslim	151	0.24	0.36	0	1
Buddhist	151	0.05	0.19	0	0.96
Hindu	150	0.03	0.13	0	0.87
Others	151	0.14	0.20	0	1

[1] Summary statistics for variables used in cross-country estimations between 1998 and 2006.
Note: All terrorist incidents show the number of incidents with fatalities.

set as the foreign national. If the main target of the incident is not known, the target country is categorized as the one with the highest number of fatalities. If the main target country is mentioned in the event description, it is set as the target even though that country did not have any fatalities in the incident. The perpetrator's country/area is the terrorist's country of origin. If the perpetrator's origin is not mentioned explicitly in the event description, it is taken as the country of origin of the terrorist group responsible for the attack. In the data set, the nationality of the terrorist is usually given if it is different from the terrorist group base. Unfortunately, in most cases the terrorist group responsible for the attack is not known. If the terrorist group and the perpetrator's origin are not known, the per-

Table 15.3 Data categorization rules

Country of occurrence	Already given in the database
Target country	1) Country that is the main target of the incident (gathered from the incident short summary) 2) If the main target is not known, it is assumed to be the country with the highest number of fatalities 3) If there is ambiguity, the target is set as unknown
Perpetrator's country	1) Country that is the terrorist's country of origin 2) If perpetrator's country is not known, it is assumed to be the terrorist group's base country 3) If the terrorist group responsible for the attack is not known, it is set as the country of occurrence
International incidents	Terrorist attack where the target's country is different from the perpetrator's country of origin Alternative definition: Terrorist attack involving citizens or the territory of more than one country (Alternative definition is used only for the results in Krueger et al. (2007) replicate estimations for comparison purposes)
Domestic incidents	Terrorist incidents where the target's country, perpetrator's country and the country of occurrence are the same (We exclude separatist incidents, even though the official citizenship of the target and the perpetrator are the same in most cases)
Separatist incidents	Terrorist incidents by separatist movements that aspire to autonomy from a dominant political institution

petrator's country is taken as the country of occurrence. There are some complicated cases where the perpetrator's origin is not known for sure; in those instances the perpetrator's country is set as unknown.

The terrorist events are also categorized as international, domestic and separatist. The US State Department data set used by Krueger and Laitin (2007) defines international terrorism as terrorist incidents involving citizens or territory of more than one country. Although this definition helps us to compare the findings in this chapter with the previous literature, it might be misleading and limited. This definition categorizes some domestic and separatist incidents as international if a foreign national is involved, killed or injured in the incident. For example, if an American tourist is killed by chance in a domestic bombing in Algeria, and the main target is not the USA, under this definition the incident is coded as an international incident and not separatist or domestic. Therefore, throughout the chapter, I define international terrorism as the terrorist incidents where the target country is different from the terrorist's country of origin.[9] Terrorist incidents perpetrated by local nationals against a purely domestic target in the local area are coded as domestic terrorist incidents.[10] Separatist incidents are excluded from domestic incidents even though in most cases the official citizenship of the target and perpetrator is the same. I define as separatist incidents any terrorist incidents by separatist movements that aspire to autonomy for a particular group of people from a dominant political institution. Therefore terrorist incidents such as those in the Basque Area, Kashmir, West Bank/Gaza, Southeastern Turkey, South Thailand, Chechnya and so on are coded as separatist incidents. In order to make my categorizations clear, I include some examples of terrorist incidents in Table 15.4.

To measure economic well-being, I use country-level data on GDP per capita from UN national accounts. Population, growth rates and Gini index of the countries/areas are also taken from UN national accounts. Most of the papers in economic literature use economic data from Penn World Tables or data from the World Bank, but these data sets do not include data on conflict regions such as the West Bank and Gaza; therefore I prefer to use UN national accounts instead. To measure the (lack of) civil liberties, I use the civil liberties index taken from Freedom House's data set. The civil liberties index runs between 1 and 7, where 7 shows no civil rights. Religion data are taken from the CIA fact book, and ethnic, linguistic and religious fractionalization is taken from Alesina et al. (2003). Variables of geographical data-distance, common border, common language, and having a colonial link are used in bilateral estimations for international incidents and are taken from CEPII (French Research Center in International Economics).

In all the estimations the number of terrorist incidents with fatalities is used as the dependent variable. The number of terrorist incidents is an event count, which is the realization of a non-negative-integer-valued random variable. Therefore count-data estimation techniques are used. The standard model for count-data analysis is the Poisson regression model. Poisson regression is a special type of non-linear regression that considers the non-negativity and discreteness of the data. One important problem with using Poisson regression models is that the equidispersion assumption may be too restrictive. For example, I find that the number of terrorist incidents in the MIPT data is overdispersed. When there is overdispersion, the Poisson estimates are inefficient, with standard errors biased downwards, and the computed-maximum-likelihood Poisson z-statistics overinflated. In order to solve this problem one can use the Poisson quasi-maximum likelihood (PQML) estimator with corrected standard errors or negative binomial (NB) estimator. Following the previous literature on terrorism, I use NB

Table 15.4 Examples of terrorist incident categorization

Description of the event	Country of occurrence	Target's country	Perpetrator's country/area	Incident type
1) TANZANIA. A suicide car bomb exploded outside the US Embassy in Dar es Salaam. The attack coincided with another suicide attack on the US Embassy in Kenya. The blast killed at least 11 individuals and injured 77 others. No Americans were killed in the attack, and it is unclear how many were injured. Osama Bin Laden's group Al-Qaeda has claimed responsibility for the blast.	Tanzania	USA	Afghanistan	International
2) SPAIN. An ETA bomb was found and defused at the Delfin Park Hotel in Salou. All guests were safely evacuated.	Spain	Spain	Basque Region	Separatist
3) PERU. Explosive devices were detonated in downtown Peru near the National Election Board. Officials attributed the explosion to a leftist guerrilla group, possibly the Shining Path (SL).	Peru	Peru	Peru	Domestic

estimations with cross-country regressions. In NB estimations, we relax the variance assumption of Poisson regression models that the variance is equal to the mean. Instead the following conditional variance will be used:

$$Var(Terror_i|x_i) = \mu_i + \alpha\mu_i^2$$

where $\mu_i = \exp(x_i'\beta)$ still holds and is a scalar parameter showing the degree of overdispersion. We can see from this condition that when $\alpha = 0$, we have the same variance condition as Poisson.

A very important advantage of using longitudinal data over cross-section data is that they allow for more general types of heterogeneity (Cameron and Trivedi, 1998). In the terrorism setting I estimate the impact of economic well-being on the number of significant terrorist incidents in a country, controlling for country-specific propensity to be the target or perpetrator of a terrorist incident. In a cross-section setting these controls can depend only on country-specific characteristics such as civil liberties, but in a panel-data setting I include country-specific fixed effects that might include unobserved country-specific propensity to be involved in a terrorist incident.

Using fixed-effects, PQML estimation performs panel-data estimations. Estimations are done by using the number of terrorist incidents in country i and year t as the dependent variable following the pioneering work of Hausman et al. (1984).

Recent literature has highlighted some problems of using NB estimations in a longitudinal data setting. Allison and Waterman (2002) argue that the NB fixed-effects estimations proposed by Hausman et al. (1984) do not constitute a true fixed-effects model. Authors find that NB fixed-effects estimations do not provide any additional leverage for dealing with overdispersion. Guimaraes (2008) confirms the findings of Allison and Waterman (2002), and shows that the NB fixed-effects model does not necessarily remove the individual fixed effects in count data using a score test. Cameron and Trivedi (1998) show that panel-data estimations for count data are most easily done by Poisson estimations and extensions to the NB do not always work. Panel-data methods already control for individual heterogeneity, and PQML panel-data models with corrected standard errors may be sufficient to treat the overdispersion as we do not include any assumption about conditional variance and conditional mean.

The assumption of Poisson distribution is stronger than necessary for statistical inference. Therefore I use the PQML estimator that maximizes the log-likelihood function but is not necessarily distributed Poisson. This relaxes the equidispersion assumption. The PQML estimator has strong robustness properties for estimating parameters. Wooldridge (1997, 2001) argues that PQML has an advantage over NB in estimating because of its robustness. Except for the conditional mean, the distribution of $Terror_{it}$ given (x_i, α_i) is entirely unrestricted, so that there can be overdispersion as well as underdispersion. Therefore I include only the PQML estimation results for panel-data estimations.

2.2 Empirical Results

International terrorism

In this section, I perform panel-data as well as cross-country estimations for targets and origins of terrorism, controlling for several determinants of international terrorism. First, following the previous literature, I show the cross-country estimation results, and then I present the panel-data estimation results.

As mentioned earlier, the only paper that performs analysis of the targets and origins of international terrorism is Krueger and Laitin (2007). The authors estimate cross-country regressions using US State Department data on the number of significant international terrorist incidents in each country between 1997 and 2002. For comparison purposes I replicate the Krueger and Laitin (2007) estimations using MIPT data for the very same time period, explanatory variables, and the same definition for international terrorism.

Table 15.5 presents a comparison of the Krueger and Laitin (2007) estimation results and my results using the MIPT data set. Generally, the estimation results using MIPT are very similar to Krueger and Laitin (2007). When I use the MIPT data I find that perpetrators come from low-GDP countries, but when I control for civil liberties and religion, the effect of GDP disappears. It appears that, once I control for lack of civil liberties and religion, economic conditions are important only for targets but not for perpetrators. Following Krueger and Laitin (2007), I also find that terrorists originate from countries with low civil liberties. Another finding is that international terrorist incidents not only occur in highly populated countries, but also target and originate from countries with significantly higher population. In terms of religion, in contrast to Krueger and Laitin (2007), I find that international terrorist incidents occur significantly more in Muslim countries.

One advantage of the MIPT data over the US State Department data set is that it is more up to date. Therefore I repeat similar cross-country estimations using MIPT data from 1998 to 2006. The data between 1998 and 2006 are used because MIPT started to collect data in domestic and separatist incidents in 1998. I believe that the data are more reliable after

Table 15.5 *Negative binomial cross-section estimation results for international terrorist incidents, MIPT versus Krueger et al. (2007) results (dependent variable: number of significant international terrorist incidents in each country between 1997 and 2002)*

Explanatory variables	MIPT						Krueger et al. (2007) estimations					
	Occurrence		Target		Perpetrator		Occurrence		Target		Perpetrator	
	(1)	(2)	(3)	(4)	(5)	(6)	(1′)	(2′)	(3′)	(4′)	(5′)	(6′)
Log GDP	−0.13*	0.19*	0.31***	0 5***	−0.3**	0.04	−0.13*	0.12	0 3i***	0 43***	−0.17	0.23
per capita	(0.11)	(0.13)	(0.09)	(0.13)	(0.12)	(0.17)	(0.11)	(0.19)	(0.08)	(0.14)	(0.12)	(0.20)
Log Population	0.54***	0.67***	0.75***	0.75***	0.53***	0.62***	0.64***	0.7**	0.76***	0.73***	0.74***	094***
	(0.13)	(0.11)	(0.10)	(0.12)	(0.13)	(0.12)	(0.12)	(0.14)	(0.08)	(0.10)	(0.16)	(0.17)
GDP Growth		−0.02		−0.06		−0.02		−0.05		−0.44		−0.42
		(0.06)		(0.06)		(0.06)		(0.68)		(0.58)		(0.72)
Lack of Civil		0.42***		0.22		0.46***		0.5**		0.17		0.8**
Liberties		(0.12)		(0.11)		(0.14)		(0.25)		(0.16)		(0.27)
Proportion		1.11		0.72*		0.67		−0.52		−0.45		−0.35
Muslim		(0.46)*		(0.53)		(0.55)		(0.70)		(0.50)		(0.76)
Proportion		0.37		0.69		0.03		1.42		−1.11		−1.25
Buddhist		(0.74)		(0.90)		(0.72)		(1.02)		(0.83)		(1.16)
Proportion		−1.2		0.85		−0.82		0.25		1.34		0.32
Hindu		(1.03)		(0.72)		(0.94)		(1.36)		(0.98)		(1.59)
Proportion of		1.04		1.36*		−1.03		0.87		0.88*		1.52**
Other		(1.19)		(1.14)		(1.83)		(0.90)		(0.67)		(0.91)
Constant	−7.96***	−14.65***	−15.04***	−17.89***	−6.71***	−12.41***	−8.28***	−13.03***	−13.97***	−14.98***	−9.65***	−19.39***
	(2.39)	(2.35)	(1.89)	(2.77)	(2.52)	(2.88)	(2.27)	(3.01)	(1.56)	(2.08)	(2.83)	(3.72)
Sample Size	150	138	150	138	150	138	150	138	150	138	150	138
Pseudo R-squared	0.06	0.11	0.17	0.18	0.07	0.16	0.05	0.07	0.13	0.14	0.05	0.09

Notes:
Standard errors in parentheses
* Significant at 10%, ** significant at 15%; ***significant at 20%

1998 and I can compare the international terrorism results with domestic and separatist terrorism after this year. Table 15.6 shows the NB estimation results for international terrorist incidents between 1998 and 2006. The first three columns show the NB estimation results using the number of significant terrorist incidents that occur in a given country as the dependent variable. Columns (3) and (4) in Table 15.6 show the estimation results using as the dependent variable the number of international incidents that target a given country. The last two columns in Table 15.6 show the estimation results using the number of international terrorist incidents that originate from a given country as the dependent variable.

Following Krueger and Laitin (2007), I use lack of civil liberties and lack of civil liberties squared as independent variables. The same estimations are performed with the lack of political liberties and political liberties squared. As the results do not differ much, I show only the results using lack of civil liberties. Log GDP per capita is used as the independent variable of interest. Following Krueger and Laitin (2007), I also use population, religion and lagged average growth rates from 1990 to 1997 as other controls. Like Abadie (2004), I use ethnic, linguistic and religious fractionalization as other independent variables. Table 15.6 reports that, in line with previous literature, richer countries are the main targets of international terrorist incidents, but international incidents have no economic roots. I also find that the targets of terrorism, just like the perpetrators' countries of origin, are the countries in the middle range of civil liberties, rather than the countries with low or high civil liberties. Abadie (2004) found similar results for political rights.

Another finding is that countries with a higher proportion of Muslims have higher levels of international terrorism within their borders and are targeted significantly more compared to countries with a higher proportion of Christians. Higher ethnic fractionalization seems to impact whether one turns to terrorism or not. There is a negative and significant effect of ethnic fractionalization on the number of international terrorist incidents originating from such a country. If the terrorist comes from an ethnically diverse country, he might have already experienced ethnic differences within his home country and this might reduce the violence against people with different ethnic backgrounds by increasing tolerance towards people. This might result in a decrease in the number of international terrorist incidents that are usually directed at people from a different ethnic background than the terrorist. Alternatively, one can argue that ethnically fragmented countries are busy terrorizing domestic nationals and thus do not consider attacking foreign nationals.

Table 15.6 Negative binomial cross-section estimation results for international terrorist incidents (dependent variable:number of significant[1] international incidents in each country between 1998 and 2006)

Explanatory variables	Country of occurrence		Target's country		Perpetrator's country of origin	
	(1)	(2)	(3)	(4)	(5)	(6)
Log GDP per capita	−0.23		0.35***	0.82***	−0.33	0.31**
	(0.19)	(0.13)	(0.10)	(0.16)	(0.23)	(0.14)
Log Population	0.78***	0.91***	0.70***	079***	0.78***	0.88***
	(0.20)	(0.14)	(0.11)	(0.11)	(0.23)	(0.17)
Growth		0.01		−0.02		0.00
		(0.04)		(0.05)		(0.03)
Lack of Civil Liberties		2.08***		1.13**		290***
		(0.49)		(0.46)		(0.63)
Lack of Civil Squared		−0.15***		−0.10*		−0.23***
		(0.06)		(0.05)		(0.07)
Muslim		1.27**		1.30***		0.76
		(0.59)		(0.50)		(0.64)
Buddhist		−1.33		−0.50		−1.44
		(1.11)		(0.92)		(0.97)

Hindu		−1.99*		1.51		−0.10
		(1.04)		(1.66)		(1.18)
Others		−0.02		−0.26		−1.17
		(1.25)		(1.02)		(1.85)
Ethnic		−1.66**		−0.31		−2.24**
		(0.78)		(0.70)		(0.94)
Linguistic		0.23		0.04		0.14
		(0.69)		(0.67)		(0.80)
Religious		−0.27		0.49		−0.47
		(0.79)		(0.74)		(0.91)
Constant	−10.02***	−22.92***	−13.63***	−21.72***	−9.40**	−22.74***
	(3.11)	(3.37)	(2.03)	(2.89)	(3.92)	(4.08)
Observations	138	138	138	138	138	138
Pseudo R-squared	0.05	0.20	0.12	0.16	0.06	0.22

Notes:
1. Incidents with fatalities
Standard errors in parentheses
* Significant at 10%, ** significant at 5%; *** significant at 1%

As an alternative method of estimation following the relevant international trade literature, I use bilateral estimations for international incidents where the targets of terrorist incidents and their origins are grouped together. Bilateral estimation results for international terrorist incidents between 1998 and 2006 are listed in Table 15.7. Similar estimations using the US State Department data set can be seen in Krueger (2007). Blomberg and Hess (2008) also demonstrate similar bilateral estimations for international terrorism using the ITERATE data set.

The dependent variable used in bilateral estimations is the number of terrorist incidents targeting country i and originating in country j at time t. Using the paired data has its own advantages. I can control for some geographical variables such as countries having a common border, one being the former colony of the other, and the distance between the attacker and the victim of the attack.[11]

In estimation (1) in Table 15.7, it can be seen that terrorists originate from poorer countries and tend to target richer countries, yet once we control for civil liberties the significant relation disappears. I also find that the number of international terrorist incidents falls when the distance between the target and perpetrator increases. As the distance might raise the cost of terrorist activity, this result is quite intuitive. I also find that having a common border and having a colonial link in history increase the number of incidents. The results in Table 15.7 mainly support the previous literature and therefore do not suggest new results.

Following Krueger (2007), when I use the absolute economic conditions of the perpetrator's country of origin and of the target country, I find that terrorist attacks targeting a given country are an increasing function of that country's per capita GDP but are unrelated to the GDP per capita levels of the terrorist's country of origin. Terrorists who engage in international terrorism significantly originate from countries with medium civil liberties. I cannot find any robust effect of the target's civil liberties. Surprisingly, the perpetrator country's lagged GDP growth has a positive and significant effect on the number of terrorist incidents. I find that religion of the perpetrator's country is important as well. Terrorists originating from Muslim countries tend to engage in more international terrorist incidents compared to their Christian counterparts.

As mentioned earlier, one of the contributions of this chapter is that I employ panel-data estimation techniques. PQML fixed-effects estimations have been used because of their robustness properties. It may be argued that terrorism is affected by longer-term changes in GDP levels but not year-to-year changes in GDP levels. I believe that this is a reason-

Table 15.7 Bilateral binomial cross-section estimations for international incidents (dependent variable: Number of significant[1] *international terrorist incidents for a given pair of target's country and perpetrator's country of origin between 1998 and 2006)*

Explanatory variables	(1)	(2)	(3)	(4)
Perpetrator's variables:				
Log GDP per capita	−0.47***	−0.01	−0.05	
	(0.08)	(0.07)	(0.10)	
Growth			0.03	0.06**
			(0.02)	(0.02)
Log Population	0.6***	0.64***	0.66***	0.63***
	(0.07)	(0.07)	(0.08)	(0.09)
Lack of Civil Liberties		0.86***	1.67***	1.30***
		(0.08)	(0.35)	(0.33)
Lack of Civil Squared			−0.11**	−0.07**
			(0.04)	(0.04)
Religion			Yes	Yes
Fractionalization			Yes	Yes
Target's variables:				
Log GDP per capita	0.62***	0.63***	0.51***	0.03*
	(0.09)	(0.10)	(0.09)	(0.02)
Growth			0.03*	0.88***
			(0.02)	(0.12)
Log Population	0.95***	094***	0.89**	−0.76**
	(0.15)	(0.13)	(0.12)	(0.32)
Lack of Civil Liberties		0.05	−0.3	0.08
		(0.07)	(0.33)	(0.04)*
Lack of Civil Squared			0.04	
			(0.04)	
Other Variables				
Log Relative GDP[2]				0.30***
				(0.06)
Distance	−0.33***	−0.29***	−0.21***	−0.21***
	(0.07)	(0.06)	(0.06)	(0.06)
Common Border			1.92***	1.89***
			(0.42)	(0.41)
Common Language			0.37*	0.4*
			(0.28)	(0.28)
Colony			0.92**	0.97**
			(0.40)	(0.41)
Constant	−30.15***	−38.63***	−37.82***	−31.62***
	(3.35)	(3.29)	(3.24)	(2.79)

Table 15.7 (continued)

Explanatory variables	(1)	(2)	(3)	(4)
Number of observations	23104	23104	20976	20976
Pseudo R-squared	0.18	0.24	0.29	0.28

Notes:
1. Incidents with fatalities
2. Relative GDP per capita =GDP per capita of target/GDP per capita of perpetrator

Standard errors in parentheses
* Significant at 10%, ** significant at 5%; ***significant at 1%

able argument for panel-data estimations. Therefore I generate five-year period data for international terrorist incidents between 1972 and 2006 and perform PQML fixed-effects estimations with five-year period data. In contrast to cross-country estimation results and results in previous literature, Table 15.8 shows that poverty is a significant source of international terrorism. I find that citizens are more likely to engage in international terrorism in countries where the economic situation worsens. In contrast to the cross-section estimation results, I find that improvement of economic well-being within a country does not increase the probability of being the target of international terrorist incidents. These results for international terrorism hold for yearly panel-data estimations from 1998 to 2006 as well as from 1972 to 2006. These results can be seen in Tables 15.9 and 15.10, respectively.[12]

Therefore the panel-data fixed-effects estimation results for international terrorist incidents are quite different from the cross-country estimation results. As I mentioned earlier, similar to the previous literature, I do not find any significant relation between economic development and terrorism in cross-section estimations. When I control for country-specific fixed effects, however, I find that countries that become richer over time export less terrorism/fewer terrorists. Additionally, in contrast with the cross-country results, I find that countries that grow richer over time do not attract more terrorist attacks. These differences between cross-section and panel-data results suggest the importance of controlling for country-specific omitted variables by using panel-data fixed-effects estimations in terrorism settings.

Domestic and separatist terrorism

According to the MIPT data set, more than 50 percent of all terrorist incidents between 1998 and 2006 are domestic in nature. Therefore a compre-

Table 15.8 Panel-data Poisson QML FE estimations for international terrorist incidents (five-year; dependent variable: five-year-period number of significant[1] international incidents in each country between 1972 and 2006)

Explanatory variables	(1)	(2)	(3)	(4)	(5)	(6)
Log GDP per capita	−0.88***	−0.84***	0.18	0.12	−0.75**	−0.74***
	(0.23)	(0.23)	(0.26)	(0.24)	(0.30)	(0.27)
Log Population	2.52***	2.56***	0.31	0.15	1.60*	1.60*
	(0.83)	(0.88)	(0.63)	(0.64)	(1.12)	(1.22)
Lack of Civil Liberties		0.31		0.61**		0.86
		(0.38)		(0.28)		(0.50)
Lack of Civil Squared		−0.02		−0.08**		−0.08*
		(0.05)		(0.04)		(0.06)
GDP Growth		0.00		0.00		−0.02
		(0.01)		(0.01)		(0.02)
Year dummies	Yes	Yes	Yes	Yes	Yes	Yes
Observations	778	773	736	726	697	693
Number of countries	116	116	113	112	104	104

Notes:

1. Incidents with fatalities

Standard errors in parentheses

* Significant at 10%, ** significant at 5%; ***significant at 1%

hensive investigation of the nature of terrorism must also include a study of determinants of domestic terrorism. Estimation results for domestic terrorist incidents using cross-country data are similar to the findings of Feldman and Ruffle (2007).

Table 15.11 shows the cross-country estimation results using NB estimations. As the country of occurrence, target country and terrorist's country of origin are the same for domestic incidents, I do not use separate estimations here. Results in the first column show that domestic incidents occur in poorer and crowded countries. Once I control for civil rights, religion and growth, I find that economics does not play a significant role. Domestic terrorism occurs in countries with a medium level of civil liberties. Another economic variable that is important for domestic terrorism is the Gini coefficient and urban population, but I cannot find any link between income inequality and urbanization and domestic terrorism in NB estimations. Surprisingly, PQML estimations suggest a different result. I find a positive and significant link between Gini coefficient and domestic terrorism. This result can be seen in Table 15.11, column (4). Therefore more income inequality might

Table 15.9 Panel-data Poisson QML FE estimations for international terrorist incidents between 1998 and 2006 (dependent variable: number of significant[1] international terrorist incidents in each country each year)

Explanatory variables	Country of occurrence		Target country		Perpetrator's country	
	(1)	(2)	(3)	(4)	(5)	(6)
Log GDP per capita	−1.4*	−1.00	0.15	−0.2	−1.62**	−1.45***
	(0.82)	(0.72)	(1.16)	(0.87)	(0.78)	(0.20)
Log Population	0.48	1.74	1.23	2.1	5.18	5.76*
	(5.98)	(5.95)	(5.03)	(4.66)	(5.55)	(3.01)
Lack of Civil Liberties		−0.1		−0.82		0.65
		(0.88)		(0.75)		(0.38)
Lack of Civil Squared		0.11		0.07		0.04
		(0.10)		(0.09)		(0.04)
GDP Growth		−0.02		0.01		0.03***
		(0.03)		(0.03)		(0.01)
Year dummies	Yes	Yes	Yes	Yes	Yes	Yes
Observations	558	466	630	520	426	426
Number of countries	62	59	70	65	54	54

Notes:
1. Incidents with fatalities
Standard errors in parentheses
* Significant at 10%, ** significant at 5%; ***significant at 1%

suggest a higher incidence of domestic terrorist attacks, depending on the specification.

The PQML fixed-effects estimations for domestic incidents are shown in Table 15.12. I find that the number of domestic terrorist incidents decreases with increases in economic well-being. Just as in the cross-section estimation results, I find that domestic terrorism is highest in countries with medium-level civil liberties. Panel-data estimations in Table 15.12 are performed for domestic terrorism for a shorter period of time (1998–2006) compared to panel-data estimations for international terrorism (1972–2006). Lack of availability of domestic terrorism data for a long period makes it impossible to perform five-year period panel-data estimations. I can perform panel-data estimations using only the number of incidents in each country in each year.[13]

Using NB cross-country estimations, Table 15.13 shows that the countries that suffer from separatist terrorist incidents are significantly richer when I control for ethnic, religious and linguistic fractionalization.

Table 15.10 Panel-data Poisson QML FE results for international terrorist incidents (dependent variable: number of significant[1] international incidents in each country between 1972 and 2006)

Explanatory variables	Country of occurrence		Target country		Perpetrator's country	
	(1)	(2)	(3)	(4)	(5)	(6)
Log GDP per capita	−0.73***	−0.69***	0.26	0.25	−0.65***	−0.6**
	(0.19)	(0.21)	(0.23)	(0.22)	(0.25)	(0.26)
Log Population	2.51***	2.63***	0.32	0.33	1.54	1.69
	(0.81)	(0.85)	(0.61)	(0.61)	(1.13)	(1.23)
Lack of Civil Liberties		0.05		0.38		0.43
		(0.36)		(0.20)		(0.46)
Lack of Civil Squared		0.01		−0.06**		−0.02
		(0.04)		(0.02)		(0.05)
GDP Growth		0.00		0.00		0.00
		0.00		0.00		(0.01)
Year dummies	Yes	Yes	Yes	Yes	Yes	Yes
Observations	3739	3694	3511	3432	3333	3295
Number of countries	116	116	113	111	103	103

Notes:
1. Incidents with fatalities
Standard errors in parentheses
* Significant at 10%, ** significant at 5%; *** significant at 1%

Table 15.11 Cross-section estimation results for domestic terrorist incidents (dependent variable:number of significant[1] domestic terrorist incidents in each country between 1998 and 2006)

Explanatory variables	NB (1)	NB (2)	NB (3)	PQML (4)
Log GDP per capita	−0.55***	0.47	0.52*	−0.41
	(0.12)	(0.31)	(0.31)	(0.61)
Gini	0.04	0.01	0.01	0 14***
	(0.03)	(0.03)	(0.03)	(0.05)
Log Population	0.97***	0.82***	0.82***	1.67***
	(0.17)	(0.15)	(0.15)	(0.36)
Growth		−0.02	−0.03	−0.18**
		(0.04)	(0.04)	(0.08)
Lack of Civil Liberties		3.87***	2.92***	7.42***
		(0.96)	(0.92)	(2.44)
Lack of Civil Squared		−0.43***	0.44***	−0.78***
		(0.10)	(0.10)	(0.26)
Muslim		0.1	0.06	−0.79
		(1.13)	(1.13)	(0.83)
Buddhist		−0.1	−0.15	−0.70
		(0.87)	(0.93)	(0.91)
Hindu		1.57	1.51	−1.51
		(1.11)	(1.19)	(1.54)
Others		−2.57**	−2.63**	−7.83*
		(1.29)	(1.26)	(4.76)
Ethnic		−0.18	−0.15	1.22
		(1.19)	(1.20)	(2.01)
Linguistic		−0.06	−0.06	−0.20
		(0.94)	(0.94)	(1.62)
Religious		−1.38	−1.39	−4.64***
		(1.30)	(1.32)	(1.57)
Urban Population			0.00	−0.04
			(0.02)	(0.03)
Constant	−11.67***	−22.61***	−22 9***	−47.39***
	(3.33)	(4.83)	(4.55)	(12.15)
	109	109	109	109
Pseudo R-squared	0.09	0.15	0.15	0.75

Notes:
1. Incidents with fatalities

Standard errors in parentheses

Significant at 10%, ** significant at 5%; ***significant at 1%

NB are negative binomial estimations; PQML are Poisson quasi maximum likelihood estimations

Table 15.12 Panel-data fixed-effects estimation results for domestic terrorist incidents (dependent variable: number of significant[1] domestic terrorist incidents in each country each year between 1998 and 2006)

Explanatory variables	Country of occurrence	
	(1)	(2)
Log GDP per capita	−0.43***	−1.21***
	(0.16)	(0.24)
Log Population	6.76***	1.46
	(0.78)	(1.95)
Lack of Civil Liberties		1.84***
		(0.50)
Lack of Civil Squared		−0.12**
		(0.06)
GDP Growth		0.03***
		(0.01)
Year dummies	Yes	Yes
Observations	514	514
Number of countries	65	65

Notes:
1. Incidents with fatalities
Standard errors in parentheses
* Significant at 10%, ** significant at 5%; ***significant at 1%

Column (3) in Table 15.13 also indicates that the targets of terrorist incidents are significantly high-population countries with high linguistic fractionalization but low growth rates and medium-level civil liberties. It also shows that religion is significant for separatist incidents. Although the results given in Table 15.13 are interesting, we do not use any information on the economic conditions of separatist regions in these estimations.[14]

In order to find the economic origins of separatist terrorism, we need to know the economic conditions in separatist regions. I generate a new data set with regional GDP of separatist regions, which allows me to look at the determinants of separatist terrorism. It is difficult to come up with precise data for the GDP per capita levels in separatist areas. I tried to overcome these data difficulties as much as I could and come up with approximations on GDP levels by setting some rules. If a specified separatist terrorist group is responsible for the attack, then the area(s) for which the terrorist group demands autonomy is identified as the separatist region. If the terrorist group is not known, the separatist region is identified as the region where most of the terrorist incidents take place. For example, when we look at the separatist incidents in south-eastern Turkey, the terrorist group PKK (Kurdistan Workers' Party) demands independence for certain cities in south-eastern Turkey. These are also the cities that are highly affected by separatist terrorism. These cities include Adıyaman, Bingöl, Bitlis, Diyarbakir, Elazığ, Hakkari, Mardin, Muş, Tunceli, Van, Siirt, Batman and Şırnak. As separatist regions have different cities, I take city-level GDP data for those cities and take an average; this is taken as the GDP level of the separatist region. Data set at the GDP per capita levels for these cities are taken from the Turkish State Institute of Statistics. Likewise, data for other areas in which separatist terrorist incidents take place are gathered from different sources for each separatist area, including Eurostat, UN Human Development Reports, Central Banks and State Institutes of Statistics of relevant countries.

Table 15.14 lists the NB binomial estimation results for the separatist areas. The dependent variable is the number of separatist incidents originating from the separatist area *i* from country *j*. In these estimations the target is the mainland and the terrorist's origin is the separatist region/area. In Turkey, for example, the mainland's GDP stands for the entire GDP of Turkey, and the GDP of the separatist area stands for the GDP level in south-eastern Turkey. The results suggest that separatist terrorism is significantly higher in poor areas. I find that the higher the relative GDP (GDP of the mainland/GDP of the separatist area), the higher the number of separatist incidents in the separatist area. The Gini coefficient also plays an important role here. The higher the income inequality, the higher will be the number of separatist incidents. I also find that the number of separatist incidents in separatist areas increases with the central government's ethnic and linguistic fractionalization. Civil liberties are shown to explain separatist terrorism, but, like international and domestic incidents, they do so in a non-monotonic way. Countries with moderate civil liberties tend to be the targets of separatist incidents.[15]

Unfortunately, it is not possible to come up with panel-data results in separatist terrorism. Although it is possible to generate GDP levels for different years in separatist regions of some countries, such as Turkey, India, Thailand, Israel and Spain, the data are quite limited in other countries. In the future, a case study using yearly data on development in a specific separatist region as well as the number of separatist incidents should be done to gain more insight into separatist terrorism and its economic roots.

Table 15.13 Negative binomial cross-section estimation results for separatist terrorist incidents (dependent variable: number of significant[1] *separatist terrorist incidents in each country between 1998 and 2006)*

Explanatory variables	Country of occurrence/target country		
	(1)	(2)	(3)
Log GDP per capita	0.51	0.66**	2.30***
	(0.37)	(0.32)	(0.53)
Log Population		2.15***	2.48***
	(0.39)	(0.58)	(0.68)
Growth		−0.56***	0.44***
		(0.12)	(0.16)
Lack of Civil Liberties		−0.07	7.00***
		(0.46)	(2.38)
Lack of Civil Squared			−0.86***
			(0.28)
Muslim		0.43	−1.96
		(1.79)	(2.74)
Buddhist		11.92***	8.69***
		(2.25)	(2.94)
Hindu		−1.63	−5.54
		(2.45)	(7.91)
Others		11.62***	1.82
		(2.18)	(2.89)
Ethnic			−9.74
			(7.56)
Linguistic			17.60**
			(7.26)
Religious			0.81
			(4.06)
Constant	−21.90***	−59.30***	−75.64***
	(7.66)	(11.62)	(16.21)
Observations	109	109	109
Pseudo R-squared	0.02	0.10	0.16

Notes:
1. Incidents with fatalities
Standard errors in parentheses
* Significant at 10%, ** significant at 5%; *** significant at 1%

Table 15.14 Bilateral negative binomial cross-section estimation results for separatist terrorist incidents (dependent variable: number of significant[1] separatist terrorist incidents in separatist region between 1998 and 2006)

Explanatory variables	Separatist region (perpetrator's area of origin)			
	(1)	(2)	(3)	(4)
Separatist area's variables				
Log GDP per capita	−1.12***	−0.65**	−0.66**	
	(0.35)	(0.30)	(0.32)	
Log Relative GDP per capita[2]				1.06***
				(0.32)
Buddhist			1.54	−1.85
			(3.17)	(9.47)
Hindu			−0.56	−1.06
			(1.23)	(1.03)
Muslim			3.29***	1.62
			(1.04)	(1.21)
Others			−2.41	−4.42**
			(1.66)	(1.73)
Different religion (From Mainland)				1.38
				(1.01)
Mainland's variables				
Log GDP per capita	0.64	0.15	0.45	
	(0.49)	(0.60)	(0.53)	
Log Population	0.20	−0.09	0.34	1.60***
	(0.35)	(0.36)	(0.32)	(0.46)
Growth			−0.08	0.09
			(0.07)	(0.07)
Lack of Civil Liberties		1.67	−1.38	7.71**
		(1.53)	(1.84)	(3.22)
Lack of Civil Squared		−0.26	0.10	
		(0.19)	(0.24)	(0.54)
Ethnic			3.80	9.54***
			(3.29)	(3.54)
Linguistic			1.12	−14.22**
			(2.86)	(5.56)
Religious			−1.08	8.93**
			(2.20)	(3.70)
Gini Index				0.39***
				−0.12
Constant	3.77	7.00	−1.09	−49.54***
	(8.35)	(8.96)	(10.96)	(14.56)

Table 15.14 (continued)

Explanatory variables	Separatist region (perpetrator's area of origin)			
	(1)	(2)	(3)	(4)
Observations	30	30	29	28
Pseudo R-squared	0.03	0.04	0.11	0.17

Notes:
1. Incidents with fatalities
2. Relative GDP per capita =GDP per capita of mainland/GDP per capita of separatist area

Standard errors in parentheses
* Significant at 10%, ** significant at 5%; ***significant at 1%

Robustness checks

One of the main empirical problems in the economics of terrorism literature is that of endogeneity. Several studies have found that terrorism affects economic outcomes (e.g. Abadie and Gardeazabal, 2003). Abadie (2004) mentions that terrorism is adversely related to economic conditions and ordinary estimates of the effect of poverty on terrorism are biased downwards. All the estimations in this chapter are performed using the lagged values of the economic conditions. Although we can argue that this might treat the problem to some extent, it does not help us get rid of the endogeneity problem altogether. Abadie (2004) uses the instrumental-variables (IV) approach to solve the endogeneity problem and still finds that economic conditions are not related to terrorist risk. Following Abadie (2004), I have performed cross-section IV estimations using being landlocked and latitude as instruments. Assuming that these are good instruments, the findings in the chapter do not change when I use the IV estimations.[16]

In addition to the IV estimations, I have repeated the maximum likelihood estimations in the chapter using generalized method of moments (GMM) estimations. GMM estimations are useful in the presence of explanatory variables that are not strictly exogenous. The main conclusions of the chapter do not change with use of GMM estimations.

Estimations are performed using the number of incidents with fatalities as the dependent variable. The same estimations are also performed using the number of terrorist incidents (with and without fatalities) and number of fatalities as dependent variables. The results are robust when I use different dependent variables for terrorism.[17]

In addition, estimations are repeated using the interaction terms of economic conditions with civil liberties and religion, but the interaction terms do not significantly affect terrorism; therefore I do not show the results with interaction terms. Estimations are also done using first differences, but the results are not robust; I do not find any significant relationship between economic conditions and terrorism with use of first differences.

3. IMMIGRATION AND TERRORISM

The studies that link immigration and terrorism are fairly new and most of the literature includes empirical studies. Among the empirical papers, the fairly early ones use terrorist-level data, which incorporate information on terrorists' backgrounds. These studies are Camarota (2002), Leiken (2004), Kephart (2005), and Leiken and Brooke (2006). Leiken and Brooke (2006) use immigration and biographical data and the authors refute most of the conventional wisdom about the link between immigration and terrorism. Using the biographical data of 373 terrorists in Western Europe and North America, they reveal a close link between immigration and terrorism. They point out that, while 87 percent of the terrorists in the data set are immigrants, most immigrants are not terrorists. Despite media attention, they find no penetration from Mexico to the USA, but mention a high Jihadi presence in Canada. In fact, they emphasize that Jihad ideology is not limited to the Middle East. Most of the sample includes nationals from the West. Likewise, the authors find that there are more French and British terrorists than Middle East nationals. Therefore immigration policy used as a tool of counterterrorism in certain countries may not be as effective as previously thought.

The empirical papers that use cross-country and panel data include Dreher and Gassebner (2010), Dreher et al. (2011) and Fischer (2011). Dreher and Gassebner (2010) and Fischer (2011) concentrate on the effect of immigration on transnational terrorism, whereas Dreher et al. (2011) concentrate on the effect of terrorism immigration. Dreher and Gassebner (2010) empirically investigate whether international terrorism is imported from countries that suffer from terrorism themselves through immigration. Authors find no empirical evidence suggesting that migration increases international terrorist attacks. Several data sources for immigration have been used: World Bank data, which use the whole world sample, as well as the OECD International Migration Database and the international terrorism (ITERATE) and Global Terrorism Database. Authors also use bilateral data to test whether nationals of the emigrating country import international terrorism to the target country using the gravity model for the terrorist incidents. Both the world sample and the OECD data show no significant relationship between immigration and terrorism. Bilateral estimation results show that terrorist attacks are not significantly affected by the properties of the target country. When concentrating on immigrants from Muslim countries, authors find that if more people emigrate from a particular Muslim country, then more terrorist activity will be conducted by this nationality. However, as the authors mention, this does not suggest that immigration from Muslim countries leads to terrorism.

Fischer (2011), following Dreher and Gassebner (2010), investigates whether immigration leads to an increase in international terrorism. The author tests if immigrants are more prone to terror than non-immigrants using the World Values Survey. Survey data support the hypothesis that immigrants show a higher propensity to support terrorism. Fischer (2011) also shows that integration, in the sense of active engagement in social networks and political organizations, reduces support for terrorism. Likewise, the author finds that immigrants in OECD countries from Africa and Asia that are culturally more distanced from OECD countries tend to support terrorism more. But Fischer does not find any support for terrorism from Muslim immigrants. Fischer (2011) also considers whether attitudes signal real-life experiences, thus increasing the number of immigrants that tend to see terrorism as a more acceptable behavior and whether this results in an increase in the number of international terrorist incidents. Fischer uses country panels of international terrorism that target the OECD countries between 1991 and 2004, unlike Dreher and Gassebner (2010). The world data for 1970–2005 use a fairly limited OECD sample: 1990–2005. Fischer's findings (2011) are also different from those of Dreher and Gassebner (2010). Fischer not only finds that support for violence (measured as finding violence justifiable) increases the occurrence of international terrorist attacks, but also that the share of immigrants in the population increases the number of terrorist incidents. It is important to note that a belief in using violence to achieve political goals is different than supporting a terrorist incident that kills innocent people.

Dreher et al. (2011) investigate the relationship between immigration and terrorism from a different perspective. They suggest that immigration to another country might be one of the negative effects of terrorism, as terrorist activity tends to worsen living standards. The willingness and capability to emigrate differs for different skill groups; therefore skilled workers may be keener to emigrate. Authors use data for 152 countries between 1976 and 2000. Taking into account endogeneity, serial correlation and heterogeneity using feasible generalized least squares (FGLS) and system GMM, the authors find that terrorism has a positive effect on skilled immigration whereas middle- and low-income groups seem not to change their immigration status as a result of terror.

As far as I know, the only theoretical paper on immigration policy and terrorism is Bandyopadhyay and Sandler (2011), in which they consider whether limitations on immigration policy might curb international terrorist events. The model includes two countries: a developed country and a developing country that hosts the terrorist organization. There are also unskilled and skilled workers. In a game with two stages, the terrorist group in the developing country finds that skilled and unskilled terrorists perpetrate attacks. The developing country chooses the countermeasures and the developed country chooses the mix of immigration quotas and counterterrorism measures. Assuming that skilled labor does not engage in terrorist activities as much as unskilled labor, authors find that a higher-skilled immigrant quota might reduce the number of terrorist attacks in the host country whereas a higher-unskilled immigrant quota might increase it. The authors also find that the country of origin is better off using proactive measures for international terrorism even though this might increase terrorism at home. When proactive measures and skilled quotas are substitutes, any increase in skilled worker quotas increases terrorism in the host country and shifts the burden to fight against terrorism to the host country.

Immigration might be seen as an important channel that exports terrorism to the world. Although the literature shows that loopholes in the immigration regulations of the developed world have been used widely by the terrorist organizations for international attacks, immigration itself does not seem to be an important contributor to terrorism.

4. CONCLUSION

Economics and terrorism have a two-way relationship. The conventional wisdom suggests that poverty results in an increase in terrorist activity, terrorism has adverse effects on the economy and an increase in the number of immigrants increases terrorism. In an attempt to find out whether the conventional wisdom holds, short summaries of economic consequences of terrorism and the relation between immigration and terrorism have been presented in this chapter.

The main objective of the chapter, on the other hand, is to explain the root causes of terrorism. I question whether changes in economic conditions have a significant effect on international, domestic and separatist terrorism. Empirical results in the previous literature suggest that economic conditions are mostly unrelated to terrorism. I argue that these results may not be as robust as we thought, and some of the data I use suggest that low levels of development do lead to terrorism. Using a panel data set on international terrorism, I find that countries that get richer over time export less international terrorism and do not attract more terrorist attacks from abroad. Similarly, I find that when a country becomes richer over time, the country's nationals commit fewer terrorist attacks at home. I build an entirely new data set with regional GDP of separatist regions and find that the higher the GDP of the separatist region, the fewer will be terrorist attacks committed by native separatists.

Empirical findings in this chapter suggest that policy makers should be more cautious in ruling out the effect of economics on terrorism. Findings show that economic policies can be used to fight terrorism in specific settings. The findings of separatist terrorism suggest that it is important to consider the causes of separatist terrorism as different from those of domestic and international terrorism.

NOTES

1. This is the last year that the GTD is available.
2. These studies focus on country of occurrence but not on the targets or origins of international terrorism. These studies also control for government capacity in the regressions. Krueger and Laitin (2007) mention that government capacity largely affects GDP per capita. Therefore,the sizable positive impact of government capabilities found by the authors is likely to offset the claimed negative effect of economic development on terrorism.
3. Blomberg and Rosendorff (2006) and Li and Sacko (2002) perform gravity model estimations to find the effect of several factors, including interstate disputes and terrorism, on trade. In the gravity model estimations in this chapter, I also differentiate between target country and perpetrator's country in international terrorist incidents.
4. For example, Krueger admits that 'these data [US State Department Data] have serious problems, only some of which, as I detail below, can be addressed' (Krueger, 2007, p. 66).
5. Using the US State Department data, Piazza (2006) also finds that economic well-being is not related to the number of terrorist incidents that occurred in that country.
6. Abadie (2004) performs some robustness checks using the MIPT data but the study does not differentiate between targets and origins of terrorism, and includes no information on international terrorism versus domestic and separatist incidents. Savun and Philips (2009) use the MIPT data but they again do not differentiate between targets and origins of terrorism. Even though the authors distinguish between international and domestic incidents (but not separatist incidents), they include only cross-country estimations but not panel-data estimations. Dreher and Gassebner (2008) use MIPT data but they do not differentiate between different types of terrorism, or between target's country and terrorist's country of origin. Feldman and Ruffle (2007) use the MIPT data, but they focus on the terrorist organizations carrying out attacks.
7. Cross-country estimations are also performed between 1972 and 2006. I report the estimation results between 1998 and 2006 for comparison purposes as domestic and separatist terrorism data are available only between 1998 and 2006. The data set may also be more reliable after 1998.

8. Alternatively, I could use the number of terrorist incidents divided by population in millions (proxy for the number of terrorists per million) as the dependent variable, but this specification is more restrictive than the specification I use. Therefore I use the number of terrorist incidents as the dependent variable and control for population in regressions.
9. However, when I present the replication of the Krueger and Laitin (2007) results using MIPT data, I use the US State Department definition of international terrorism for comparison purposes. Using the alternative definition of international terrorism also performs robustness checks.
10. Domestic terrorist incidents are the incidents where the target's country, perpetrator's country and the country of occurrence are the same.
11. Rather than the regular control variables I used in the previous cross-country estimations, I also control for the target having a different religion from the terrorist's country of origin. I furthermore control for whether the target has ever occupied the terrorist's country of origin before in history, in line with Krueger (2007). The results are found to be similar; therefore I do not list them.
12. MIPT data include the domestic terrorist incidents only between 1998 and 2006. For comparison purposes estimations are performed for 1972–2006 and 1998–2006. It can also be argued that the data are more credible after 1998; therefore it is important to do robustness checks for two periods.
13. It might be argued that changes in economic well-being within countries are important over a longer period than one year. For this reason, yearly panel data might not be as informative as five-year-period data. Therefore the results listed for domestic terrorist incidents may not be as suggestive as those for international terrorist incidents.
14. This result supports the previous literature's findings on international terrorist incidents. Previous literature suggests that targets of terrorism are rich countries.
15. The main problem with these estimations in Table 15.14 is the low degrees of freedom. I specify only 30 areas in the world that are the perpetrator's origin for separatist terrorist incidents.
16. I did not perform IV estimations in the panel-data setting because of the lack of relevant instruments.
17. As mentioned earlier, I also perform robustness checks using an alternative definition of international terrorism and the estimation results do not change significantly.

REFERENCES

Abadie, A. (2004), 'Poverty, political freedom, and the roots of terrorism', NBER Working Paper No. 10859.

Abadie, A. and J. Gardeazabal (2003), 'The economic costs of conflict: a case study of the Basque Country', *American Economic Review*, **93**(1), 113–32.

Alesina, A., A. Devleeschauwer, W. Easterly, S. Kurlatand and R. Wacziarg (2003), 'Fractionalization', *Journal of Economic Growth*, **8**(2), 155–94.

Allison, P.D. and R. Waterman (2002), 'Fixed effects negative binomial regression models', *Sociological Methodology*, **32**, 247–65.

Araz-Takay, B., K.P. Arin and T. Omay (2009), 'The endogenous and non-linear relationship between terrorism and economic performance: Turkish evidence', *Defence and Peace Economics*, **20**(1), 1–10.

Bandyopadhyay, S. and T. Sandler (2011), 'Immigration policy and counterterrorism', Federal Reserve Bank of St. Louis Working Paper 2011-012B, April, revised February 2012.

Berrebi, C. (2003), 'Evidence about the link between education, poverty and terrorism among Palestinians', Princeton University, Department of Economics, Industrial Relations Section, Working Paper 856.

Blomberg, S.B. and G.D. Hess (2008), 'The Lexus and the olive branch', in Philip Keefer and

Norman Loayza (eds), *Terrorism, Economic Development, and Political Openness*, New York: Cambridge University Press, ch. 4.
Blomberg, S.B. and A. Mody (2005), 'How severely does violence deter international investment?' Claremont McKenna College Working Paper.
Blomberg, S.B. and B.P. Rosendorff (2006), 'A gravity model of globalization, democracy and transnational terrorism', USC CLEO Research Paper No. C06-6.
Blomberg, S.B., G.D. Hess and A. Orphanides (2004), 'The macroeconomic consequences of terrorism', *Journal of Monetary Economics*, **51**(5), 1007–32.
Burgoon, B. (2006), 'On welfare and terror: social welfare policies and political economic roots of terrorism', *Journal of Conflict Resolution*, **4**(50), 176–203.
Camarota, S.A. (2002) 'The open door: how militant Islamic terrorists entered and remained in the United States 1993–2001', Washington, DC: Center for Immigration Studies Working Paper.
Cameron, A.C. and P.K. Trivedi (1998), *Regression Analysis of Count Data*, Econometric Society Monograph No. 30, Cambridge: Cambridge University Press.
Chen, A.H. and T.F. Siems (2004), 'The effects of terrorism on global capital markets', *The European Journal of Political Economy*, **20**, 349–66.
Drakos, K. and A.M. Kutan (2003), 'Regional effects of terrorism on tourism in three Mediterranean countries', *Journal of Conflict Resolution*, **47**(5), 621–41.
Dreher, A. and M. Gassebner (2008), 'Does political proximity to the US cause terror?', *Economics Letters*, **99**, 27–9.
Dreher, A. and M. Gassebner (2010), 'Does terror migrate?', University of Göttingen, mimeo.
Dreher, A., T. Krieger and D. Meierrieks (2011), 'Hit and (they will) run: the impact of terrorism on migration', *Economics Letters*, **113**, 42–6.
Eckstein, Z. and D. Tsiddon (2004), 'Macroeconomic consequences of terror: theory and the case of Israel', *Journal of Monetary Economics*, **51**(5), 971–1002.
Eldor, R. and R. Melnick (2004), 'Financial markets and terrorism', *European Journal of Political Economy*, **20**(2), 367–86.
Enders, W. and T. Sandler (1991), 'Causality between transnational terrorism and tourism: the case of Spain', *Terrorism*, **14**(1), 49–58.
Enders, W., T. Sandler and G. Praise (1992), 'An econometric analysis of the impact of terrorism on tourism', *Kyklos*, **45**(4), 531–54.
Feldman, N. and B. Ruffle (2007), 'Religious terrorism: a cross-country analysis', Working Paper Series, Economics of National Security, Samuel Neaman Institute (Technion), No. 8.
Fischer, J.AV. (2011), 'Immigration, integration and terrorism: is there a clash of cultures?', CEIS Research Paper, **182**, Tor Vergata University.
Gassebner, M. and S. Luechinger (2011), 'Lock, stock, and barrel: a comprehensive assessment of the determinants of terror', *Public Choice*, **149**(3), 235–61.
Guimaraes, P. (2008), 'The fixed effects negative binomial model revisited', *Economics Letters*, **99**, 63–6.
Gupta, S., B. Clements, R. Bhattacharya and S. Chakravarti (2004), 'Fiscal consequences of armed conflict and terrorism in low- and middle-income countries', *European Journal of Political Economy*, **20**, 403–21.
Hausman, J., B.H. Hall and Z. Griliches (1984), 'Econometric models for count data with an application to the patents–R&D relationship', *Econometrica*, **52**(4), 909–38.
Kavanagh, J. (2010), 'Selection, availability, and opportunity: the conditional effect of poverty', *Journal of Conflict Resolution*, **57**, 682–708.
Kephart, J. (2005), 'Moving beyond the 9/11 Staff Report on Terrorist Travel', Washington, DC: Center for Immigration Studies Working Paper.
Krueger, A.B. (2007), *What Makes a Terrorist? Economics and Roots of Terrorism*, Princeton, NJ: Princeton University Press.
Krueger, A.B. and D.D. Laitin (2007), 'Kto Kogo?: a cross-country study of the origins and targets of terrorism', in Philip Keefer and Norman Loayza (eds), *Terrorism, Economic Development, and Political Openness*, Cambridge: Cambridge University Press, ch. 5.

Krueger, A.B. and J. Maleckova (2003), 'Education, poverty, political violence and terrorism: is there a causal connection?', *Journal of Economic Perspectives*, **17**(4), 119–44.
Kurrild-Klitgaard, P., M.K. Justesen and P. Klemmensen (2006), 'The political economy of freedom, democracy and transnational terrorism', *Public Choice*, **128**, 289–315.
Leiken, R.S. (2004), 'Europe's immigration problem & ours', *Mediterranean Quarterly*, **15**(4), 203–18.
Leiken, R.S. and S. Brooke (2006), 'The quantitative analysis of terrorism and immigration: an initial exploration', *Terrorism and Political Violence*, **18**(4), 503–21.
Li, Q. (2005), 'Does democracy promote or reduce transnational terrorist incidents?', *Journal of Conflict Resolution*, **49**(2), 278–97.
Li, Quan and David Sacko (2002), 'The (ir)relevance of interstate militarized disputes to international trade', *International Studies Quarterly*, **46**(1), 11–44.
Li, Q. and D. Schaub (2004), 'Economic globalization and transnational terrorism: a pooled time-series analysis', *Journal of Conflict Resolution*, **48**(2), 230–58.
Llussa, F. and J. Tavares (2007), 'The economics of terrorism: a synopsis', *The Economics of Peace and Security Journal*, **2**(1), 62–70.
Nitsch, V. and D. Schumacher (2004), 'Terrorism and international trade: an empirical investigation', *European Journal of Political Economy*, **20**(2), 423–33.
Piazza, J.A. (2006), 'Rooted in poverty?: terrorism, poor economic development and social cleavages', *Terrorism and Political Violence*, **18**(1), 219–37.
Sandler, T. and W. Enders (2004), 'An economic perspective on transnational terrorism', *European Journal of Political Economy*, **20**(2), 301–16.
Savun, B. and B.J. Philips (2009), 'Democracy, foreign policy, and terrorism', *Journal of Conflict Resolution*, **53**(6), 878–904.
Schneider, F., T. Brück and D. Meierrieks (2011), 'The economics of terrorism and counter-terrorism: a survey', CESifo Working Paper No. 3012.
Tavares, J. (2004), 'The open society assesses its enemies: shocks, disasters and terrorist attacks', *Journal of Monetary Economics*, **51**(5), 1039–70.
Testas, A. (2004), 'Determinants of terrorism in the Muslim world: an empirical cross-sectional analysis', *Terrorism and Political Violence*, **16**(2), 253–73.
Wooldridge, J.M. (1997), 'Quasi-likelihood methods for count data', in M.H. Pesaran and P. Schmidt (eds), *Handbook of Applied Econometrics*, Volume 2, Oxford: Blackwell, pp. 352–406.
Wooldridge J.M. (2001), *Econometric Analysis of Cross Section and Panel Data*, Cambridge, MA: MIT Press, ch. 19.

Index